Stone

Stone

THE CONTROVERSIES, EXCESSES, AND EXPLOITS OF A RADICAL FILMMAKER

JAMES RIORDAN

Foreword by
Michael Douglas

HYPERION

New York

LIBRARY OF CONGRESS CATALOGING-IN-PUBLICATION DATA
Riordan, James.
    Stone : the controversies, excesses, and exploits of a radical
filmmaker / by James Riordan ; foreword by Michael Douglas.
      p. cm.
    Includes bibliographical references.
    ISBN 0-7868-6026-X
    1. Stone, Oliver. 2. Motion picture producers and directors—
United States—Biography. I. Title.
PN1998.3.S76R56 1995
791.43'0233'092—dc20   94-5661
                                               CIP

Book design by Beth Tondreau Design
First Edition
10 9 8 7 6 5 4 3 2 1

This book is dedicated to my mother, Nancy Ruth Riordan, who gave me my sense of humor and, hence, the ability to survive in this world.

Contents

Contents
...
viii

Author's Note

In recent years, I have noticed more and more emphasis on the terms "authorized" or "unauthorized" in describing biographies. It seems to me that the true art form of biography has been increasingly obscured by the harsh glare of these categorizations, both of which have become suspect. For most, the term "unauthorized" has come to mean explicit and sensationalistic information, with only a passing relationship to the truth. "Authorized" is generally only a little better, with the tendency to omit anything particularly negative and whitewash the rest. Where is the truth? Without access to the subject, all information is questionable; but if access also means censorship, then it is worthless. I believe that the only valid biography is one in which the author is free to write what he or she wants and still have access to the subject.

Throughout this book, my objective has been to reveal what makes Oliver Stone tick in the precise and somewhat peculiar way in which he does. With that in mind, I approached him about doing a biography—one for which I would have both access and editorial control. In return, I was willing to guarantee that he would not be misquoted. I would allow him to see and edit his own quotes, if he gave me complete access, the right to interview whoever I wanted, and, most importantly, the freedom to write whatever I chose.

To me, this was the only way to approach a serious biography of Stone. It would be ludicrous to try to get people in the film business to talk candidly without Stone's permission. He's simply too powerful for anyone but died-in-the-wool enemies to venture an interview without his okay. My challenge to Stone was not only to instruct his office to tell people they could talk to me, but to encourage them to be candid. The timing was fortunate, as Stone had recently learned that two other books on his life were in the works, and he was concerned about how he would be presented in them. He decided to cooperate with me in the hope that he would at least be able to tell his side. Stone kept our bargain, and at my request, even called a few interview subjects and asked them to tell the truth about some incident they had tried to gloss over or refused to discuss at all.

I have tried to show Stone's faults as well as his strengths. It seems to me that anyone who has seen Stone for more than five minutes, even on television, already knows his faults. He doesn't hide them that well, and they've all received ample press over the years. The real challenge is not exposing flaws or lauding strengths so much as trying to understand how such traits developed, and how Stone functions amid such a sea of extremes. No matter what one thinks of Stone's work or his personality, there is little question that he is a highly complicated and unusual individual.

As an artist of influence, not only must Stone's work be examined, but also his working methods. In an effort to do that, I studied Stone's script notes and accompanied him on several filming locations, including Statesville prison in Joliet, Illinois, and a number of locations in Thailand. I have tried to show the mechanics as well as the inspiration that go into a major Hollywood movie in a way that the lay person can understand.

At the back of the book readers will find a detailed description of Stone's early screenplays (Appendix I), major influences studied in film school (Appendix II), and a complete filmography (Appendix III).

In the three years since I began this project, I have interviewed over eighty subjects, including some of the major forces in Hollywood and nearly all of the stars of Stone's films. Not surprisingly, a few people turned me down. I have also counterbalanced the interviews with information gleaned from an assortment of publications listed in the Bibliography. I have spent considerable time with Oliver Stone in a variety of locations and circumstances, and honestly believe that I've seen him at his best and at his worst.

Though Stone is by nature a cautious man, he is also periodically reckless and ultimately ruled by the artistic manifesto. A few times, he told me something "off the record," only to later agree to include it because it was vital to the project. Until very recently, Stone has abhorred everything related to therapy or objective self-examination. I'm convinced that part of the reason he cooperated so extensively with this project was his own desire to better understand himself. Oliver Stone is so driven by the constant need to achieve, and so much of his past is painful for him to recall, that the only way he can really engage in extensive, serious self-examination is through the artistic process.

Anyone who has had much contact with Stone recognizes that he is a mass of contradictions held together by enormous willpower. That becomes obvious very quickly when one is around him. Stone exemplifies both the best and the worst aspects of the American dream—the grand ideal and the cheap feel, the willingness to fight and, if necessary, die for what one believes, and the foolishness to risk just as much for a good time. The ambition and drive to change the world combined with the capability for self-destruction at any moment. It is fitting that his life spans a time when the classic version of the American dream has died amidst chaos and conspiracy, perhaps to be reborn in a newer, more questioning, more individualistic way.

I would like to thank fellow writer Bill Myers for encouraging me to take on this project, as well as for his friendship and support in the writing of it. I also thank my son Chris Riordan for his help in researching the book, and John Garret for the many hours he put into the project. Also, Doug McIntosh, George Lord, and David Spargur. And my brother Joe for always believing in me, and my agent Julian Bach for his wisdom and honesty. At Hyperion I want to thank Bob Miller for his willingness to endure creative battles. I also extend my gratitude to the following people for their help to me during this project: My daughter Elicia, my son Jeremiah, and my wife Deborah Riordan, Lee and Jan Batchler, Mike Bradecich, Dennis Bettis, Martha Billingsley, Mary Bulliner, Terry Burychette, Martha Cotton, Greg Dix, Dick and Jan Eilders, Jody Eldred, Michael Furl, Bud Gates, Ron Green, William and Delores Griffin, Ron and Barb Guertin, Greg Harris, Dennis Hensley, Jimmy Holmes, Drew and Pat Horn, Bryan Jackson, Phaedra Jensen, Lissa Halls Johnson, Bill Lamie, Briget Linneman, Coleman and Carel Luck, Lynn Marzulli, Greg and Linda Morgan, Peter and Lorraine Pagast, Jerry Prochnicky, Gary Reynolds, Andy Roland, Melissa Rudy, Holt Satterfield, Loren Silver, Vicki Silver, Tom and Debbie Small, Pili Spargur, Tracy Storm, Brenda Tetter, Ed and Maggie Vogt, Byron and Jan Wallace, Marc Wakat, Jim Youell, and Karen Youell.

Foreword

by Michael Douglas

There's no question, Oliver Stone is an exceptional man, but what is truly fascinating about him is not just the magnificent images he has projected on the screen and etched into the collective mind of the moviegoing public, but also the trials and tribulations of his personal life—a life which reads like an epic novel and plays like a thriller. When you know Oliver's story, then you understand why it serves as a hairtrigger for his work. Oliver doesn't create to impress Hollywood, and he certainly doesn't create to make money; he doesn't even create primarily to influence the world, although that's a big part of it. No, I think Oliver Stone creates because he has to—to conquer his own personal demons, survive his own madness, grapple with his outrageous nature.

I've had the opportunity of acting under his direction in *Wall Street*, the film for which I received the Academy Award as Best Actor in 1987, and of being a consistent, if casual, friend throughout the years since that time. Oliver and I don't always see eye to eye either on or off screen, but I respect the man immensely and believe that both his talent and private self have often been misinterpreted and sometimes misjudged. For that reason I have looked forward to this book as a detailed glimpse into one of the film industry's most complex and fascinating individuals.

It's hard to have an impact on the film business these days because the industry has gotten so big that it takes an awful lot to affect it. It's a mega-powerful system, and to make people within this system sit up and take notice, you have to make a lot of money, create income for a lot of people. But to do that you almost invariably have to become part of the system, allow it to absorb you and work within its dictates for success. Consequently, nothing changes the system because everything is developed within the confines of it. Blockbusters come and go; one year the hot thing is science fiction, the next year it's buddy pictures, then action adventures, then erotic thrillers, and so on. Even stars come and go. The system is so big it seems to absorb everything, and about the only thing that has a lasting effect is something that bucks it and yet beats it at its own game.

Oliver Stone is one such individual. When he first broke through, he was a maverick writer whom no one wanted to take a chance on. Finally someone did, with a picture called *Midnight Express*. It was Oliver's first script filmed by a Hollywood studio and it won the Academy Award for Best Adapted Screenplay. But Oliver wanted to direct. When his first effort, *The Hand*, didn't fly, it was four years before he got another chance. And that was *Salvador*, an immensely powerful film. The texture was raw, the performances great, and it was about something, it had a strong message to tell. *Salvador* bucked the system, but it didn't make a lot of money, didn't beat the game. Hollywood was impressed, but not changed.

Then along came a film called *Platoon*, which no one had the courage to make for ten full years, and even then it was done on a shoestring budget and tossed out into the market against a host of big-budget mainstream studio projects, a fledgling baby bird out of the nest. Well, the picture not only flew but won the Oscar for Best Film that year and a Best Director Oscar for Mr. Oliver Stone. Not only that, it was a bona fide blockbuster, taking in over $160 million in America alone. Who says message films can't make money?

And therein was the crack in the armor of the Hollywood system. Oliver Stone was making great movies that had important things to say, bucking the system; but he was also generating hundreds of millions of dollars at the box office doing it—beating the system at its own game. Beyond even this, *Platoon* had a tremendous effect on this country's attitude about Vietnam. It opened the eyes of millions of people to what that war was really like and served as a healing to countless veterans and families still struggling to understand what went wrong over there.

What was the feeling in Hollywood then? People said the film was a fluke. It could never happen again. They said cinematographer Bob Richardson was his eyes, editor Claire Simpson was his timing, that Tom Berenger, Willem Dafoe, and Charlie Sheen were the reasons the film worked. Not to take away from these people, all of whom are immensely talented, but the point is that Hollywood needed an excuse. They couldn't accept someone like Oliver Stone. Not without a fight at least.

Stone's next project was a movie called *Wall Street*. When work on the project began, people thought, "What could possibly be exciting about the world of stocks, bonds, and high finance?" By the time the film was released, there had been insider trading scandals the likes of which we'd never seen, tremendous trading activity and, just before the release, the biggest stock market crash since 1929. Wall Street was in the news. People were saying, "What is it with this guy? Does he have some sort of sixth sense or something? How did he know?" I was in that film, and Oliver and I had several battles during the making of it. No matter how much I gave, he seemed to want more. I don't mind telling you that there were times I hated him during the filming . . . but I forgave him when I won the Oscar.

Then came *Talk Radio*, *Born on the Fourth of July*, and *The Doors*, powerful films all, films that took chances, films that broke rules. *Born* won another Best Director Oscar for Stone, as well as earning $70 million at the box office and imparting a better understanding of another key issue related to Vietnam—the psychology of the soldiers who fought that war and the void left in honoring them. More than that, though, it stands as one of the most powerful films ever made.

Stone has kept an incredible pace, writing and directing nine films since 1985, better than a film a year. Far more than most other directors. And the quality is extraordinary. I wonder sometimes that people take his productivity for granted. I don't know how many hours he sleeps, but not many. Oliver works like a man possessed. No doubt he has his demons, but he has directed them in a positive way. He delivers his best and he's truly inspirational at a time when everybody's playing it safe.

Then there's *JFK*. Like it or not, the film is a technical masterpiece of considerable magnitude and an amazing array of Stone's filmmaking abilities. It is rare for a major director to take this many risks in technique, and yet no one seems as comfortable mixing their images around as Oliver. The fact that three completely different sets of editors have won Academy Awards under his direction should tell you something about his abilities in that department. And all this wizardry, like most of Stone's films, was accomplished under budget and on schedule. Perhaps more important, no one else seems to be as daring in taking on challenging issues. People don't walk out of an Oliver Stone film without feeling something. He's one of the few who remembers why he got into film in the first place—to communicate important ideas in a meaningful and powerful way that would help shape how people think. Even his harshest critics have to agree he has achieved that objective. *JFK*, like *Platoon* before it, had an impact on millions and spawned a movement within this country that shook the rafters all the way to Washington, D.C. Few filmmakers can ever hope to achieve such an effect even once in their lifetime. Stone has already done it at least twice.

To be an artist of such considerable influence in the world today means you have to generate a lot of money. The cost of pictures certainly has increased tremendously. As his films began to get more expensive, Stone has still chosen to deal with real issues despite the increased commercial risk. *Heaven and Earth* was a $33 million film based on the life of a Vietnamese peasant woman. It had no major box-office draws and starred a young Vietnamese girl in her first role. Few directors take chances like that. In the same sense, *Natural Born Killers* combined cutting-edge film technology and centered on one of the most pressing issues in our industry—violence in film and television.

The studios take chances on Stone because his films deliver. They nearly always perform well at the box office and often have blockbuster potential because Stone, for all his desire to impart a message, has never forgotten that people go to the movies to be entertained. In one sense he has proven that you can be an artist and a capitalist at the same time. In another, he's still the maverick, trying to persuade the establishment to let him do his thing. Faced with a choice between his art and making more money, he will choose art every time. Consequently, Oliver Stone has changed the film industry. He has changed it because of his experiments in technique and his adventurous attitude toward how movies can be made. He has changed it because he has shown a rare professionalism that enables him to make numerous quality films without going over budget. And most of all, he's changed it because he's shown all of us that enlightenment can be entertainment if you have the courage to do it right.

The Tearing of the Veil

(1946-1976)

American Dreamer

"A child is just like a flower, his head is floating in the breeze."
Jim Morrison in **THE DOORS**

B orn in New York City on September 15, 1946, Oliver Stone was virtually birthed into controversy—the only child of a mixed marriage between a Jewish American stockbroker and French Roman Catholic girl who met just after V-E Day while Stone's father was serving on Eisenhower's staff in Paris. It was a fitting beginning for such a controversial individual, but the roots of paradox began long before that.

Louis Stone, Oliver Stone's father, was born into considerable wealth in New York City as Louis Silverstein. Lou's father, Joshua Silverstein, was a likable Jewish man who had made a fortune in the dress business and retired early. Lou had two older brothers, Joe and

Henry, and one older sister, Helen, and the children were brought up in luxurious circumstances.

Joshua Silverstein was a kind and lovable man who had a natural playful streak. His wife, Tillie, was gracious, but more strict and both parents expected a lot out of their children. Lou, the youngest, seemed to take this to heart even more than his siblings. "Lou was always aggressive and determined to be successful," brother Henry, now in his eighties, remembers. "At college he was a pretty good athlete and he was fairly well read. He was resolved to achieve in everything he did."

Young Lou decided to change his name from Silverstein to Stone when he registered as an English Lit. major at Yale in September 1927. With the rise of anti-Semitism around the world, Lou thought it made good business sense. The change was not recorded with the courts since Lou was only seventeen at the time, but most of the family later followed suit at one time or another. Joshua Silverstein understood his children's ambition and apparently never held the name change against them.

When the stock market crashed in 1929, Joshua Silverstein was more fortunate than many—he had lost his wealth, but he still had enough to survive. For the family, especially young Lou, it was a major shock. Life would never be the same. Henry Stone, Lou's brother, gives a poignant example: "I had gone up to Harvard, to law school. And Father had given me a check for a thousand dollars for my birthday. After the Crash he wrote me and said, 'Do you still have that thousand dollars, Henry?' Luckily, I had nine hundred of it left, and I sent it right back to him. It was a big change, a much modified existence."

Though doing well at Harvard, Henry transferred the next year to Columbia Law School to cut down on family expenses. Lou finished at Yale, but having such a high achiever mentality, the change in the family's financial status was particularly difficult for him. Oliver Stone believes that this sudden lifestyle change may have been the root of his father's bitterness, which later reared its head in his marriage and his relationship with his son. "Dad had a very perverse relationship to money," Stone says, "probably because his father lost nearly everything in the Crash. My father graduated in 1931 from Yale but couldn't get a job. It was the Depression. He scraped to get a job as a floorwalker in a department store at twenty-five dollars a week and was beset with financial problems from that point on. Until the Crash, he had never given money any thought. From that point on, it seemed he was hounded by it. In a sense, money was his Achilles heel."

Lou Stone also had an artistic side, though his rigid attitude rarely allowed him to show it. He wrote poetry throughout his life, but kept it hidden away, preferring that others not know his innermost feelings. Here is a poem he wrote in 1932, the year after he graduated from Yale:

All things must end. It would be well
If we could but begin where we leave off
For then we could rush on, nor fear to taste
The bottom of the cup.
Ah there I go—my sweet rememberings
Already play my finish at the start
Forgetting order is the rule of art
Forgetting the restraint that's now my part.

I have a tale to tell, of little note
Except it shows a strange philosophy—
The reason for a happiness denied.
The Fates one day were playing at their game
Of carefully dealing almosts and not quites
And mixing things to form a proper broth
Whose bitterness would equal its delights.
They looked down to the Earth this day,
They saw a man who thought he'd found his one desire
A woman who could set his heart on fire.
"This is too beautiful a thing," they cried,
"And Beauty, be it sight or sound or thought,
Was never meant to be a lasting thing.
It must be glimpsed, not stared at or embraced.
We will devise a way of ending it." They did.

Their doctrine is perhaps all wise.
The man is thankful for his glimpse of beauty.
He goes his way, a vision in his eyes.

Stone's mother, Jacqueline Goddet, was born in France. The Goddets were as poor as the Silversteins were rich: "When I was a young girl, we went through four years where we had very little to eat," she recalls in her thick French accent. "And yet, in many ways we were privileged people, my family, because we had cousins who had a farm just outside of Paris. The only thing that was really bad there was the cold. In the winter, in my bedroom, we could not get heat. There was a chimney and we all would undress in the same room and go to bed to try to warm up as best as we could."

Jacqueline was nineteen years old when Lou Stone first saw her. He was thirty-five, already somewhat successful on Wall Street back in the United States, and now a colonel stationed in Paris on General Eisenhower's staff, and she was a beautiful young French girl who rode by him on her bicycle. Most of the girls in Paris rode bicycles because automobiles were hard to come by during the war. Even some of the American officers rode bikes, including Lou Stone. It was shortly after V-E Day in 1945. Like most Americans in Paris, Lou was feeling exhilarated after the victory. Seeing a lovely girl ride by, he gave chase. Stone pedaled hard up the Champs-Elysées and caught her with a final burst of speed, bumping into her and almost knocking her down. Jacqueline spoke very little English and Lou no French, so communication was difficult at best. "I told him to stop following me," Jacqueline Stone says, "and he said he would if I would give him my name and address. Since I was leaving for the South of France the next day, I gave him that address and figured I would never see him again."

Consequently, Jacqueline was surprised when Lou showed up to see her there, especially considering she was visiting her prospective in-laws. She told him she had a fiancé and there was no point in their seeing each other, but Lou Stone wouldn't take no for an answer. Jacqueline began to be attracted to this determined American in spite of herself. A short time later they fell in love and were engaged. They had to have the general's permission to get married, which almost didn't happen when Jacqueline saw Lou playing tennis with another officer and asked in her heavy accent, "Oo is zat fat old man you are playing with?" The man was Lou's superior officer.

As a financial adviser on the staff of Dwight D. Eisenhower, Stone was one of the people in charge of the Occupation funds in Europe, and his duties included printing the money for the U.S. Army. According to Jacqueline, he became embroiled in controversy when he went against a directive and refused to turn over the printing plates to the Russians. Stone was vindicated shortly thereafter when all the facts came out, and he was commended for his actions.

Lou and Jacqueline were married in November 1945, and then came the problem of getting her to America. The Allies were wrapping up in Europe, and Lou was due to ship out soon. He befriended the captain of the troopship *Maritime Victory* and persuaded him to allow Jacqueline to stow away on board. All she had to do was pack.

Jacqueline showed up on the dock with seventeen pieces of luggage just as the boat was leaving the harbor at Le Havre. Stone fired his pistol into the air as a signal for the ship to stop, but on the boat they thought it was just someone saluting them good-bye. Jacqueline was afraid that they would now have to travel on separate ships, or worse, that Lou would take the next troopship and send for her later. But her husband only smiled and said, "I'm not going to leave you behind."

With that, Lou Stone got someone to radio a message and the captain waited just outside the breakwater while Lou persuaded a Navy tugboat to chug out to the ship with the Stones and their seventeen pieces of luggage. A ladder was thrown over the side, and Lou and his French bride climbed aboard. "I was the only woman with one thousand, five hundred GIs on board," Jacqueline Stone recalls. "I climbed up the ladder with a sailor in front and a sailor in back of me. All these GIs were shooting pictures of me arriving on board."

The crossing began on January 6, 1946, and took twelve days. The sea was very rough, and Jacqueline was constantly seasick. She did not realize that she was pregnant. "I was so seasick," she says. "And the only private room on the ship was the mental ward. So they gave me and Lou the mental ward to stay in. Then, when we came into port, the newspaper people were there because we were one of the first three ships coming back to America and everyone kept saying, 'A French woman delayed us three hours because she was late arriving.' We went to the Plaza Hotel, and someone asked me if I wanted a martini. I was not a drinker at all and I had three of them and passed out on the couch. They had to carry me to the room. But coming to America was an experience I'll never forget. There was food all over, you could get anything you wanted. And the room was warm. It was very cold out, but the room was warm."

Good apartments were hard to come by in postwar New York. The Stones wound up spending several months at a hotel until at last they found an apartment on East 86th Street.

Named for Lou's grandfather William and Jacqueline's grandfather Olivier, William Oliver Stone was born at 9:48 on Sunday morning, September 15, 1946. Jacqueline was in labor for twenty-four hours. "It was very hard," she remembers. "And then he had to be taken out with forceps, so when they brought him to me I said, 'That's not my child.' He was all swollen because he'd been pulled with the forceps. But he was a beautiful baby anyway. He was conceived in France, on December 3, and born exactly nine months and fifteen days after marriage, so it was legal, proper and legal. He was a big baby, seven pounds, eight ounces, and he was born at 9:48 A.M. That was the time exactly. It was in the morning on a Sunday."

It was also the onset of the nuclear age. America had dropped the first "big one" in August 1945 and Oliver Stone was born at the beginning of an era: America as a superpower, the onset of the Cold War.

Upon his return to America, Lou Stone had gone back to the world of high finance. Now, his income rose steadily and the Stones' standard of living was very high. For Jacqueline, who grew up in a poor working-class family, it seemed like paradise. They rented a wonderful apartment, and had a nanny, and later a butler. She bought expensive clothes, began entertaining regularly, and traveled often to visit her family in France. In his desire to continue to impress his bride, Lou made increasingly poor financial decisions, renting instead of owning, running up bills, living beyond his income. He gave Jacqueline whatever she wanted, and she began to get used to it.

Oliver Stone's childhood was bicultural, split almost evenly between France and America. He made his first trip to France before he was three, sailing on March 10, 1949. Stone spoke French before he spoke English, and even now he still sometimes thinks in French. As a child, this caused difficulty in school because of his syntax errors. When Jacqueline went to the South of France to visit her friends, Stone stayed in an old hotel that her parents owned in the heart of a run-down section of Paris. The Hôtel Versailles was a magnificent, if somewhat broken down structure, located on rue des Quatre Fils in the fourth arrondissement. It was five stories tall and had no hot water.

Lou Stone had decided to go into business for himself. Though he particularly enjoyed analyzing the market, he was never that fond of the selling aspect of his job and he felt that his expensive lifestyle and his wife's increasing taste for the finer things required him to establish his own enterprise. He chose to go into manufacturing machetes, and bought a factory in Stamford, Connecticut. The Stones moved there when Oliver was two and a half years old, keeping the apartment in New York.

Lou Stone began having to travel a lot, especially to South America and Central America, for his machete business. Jacqueline went on the trips with him, leaving Oliver with the nanny. As Jacqueline began to spend more time away from her son, he started to feel isolated. When he was four he was put in a nursery school on a regular basis, and that summer he was sent away to camp. Being younger than the other children at camp was difficult for Stone, who was forced to compete with bigger kids. "I remember having a hard time at this upstate nursery camp I went to," he recalls. "There was a woman there, a tough old German. She scared the heck out of me. She used to whop us. We had to get out of the cabin in ten minutes or something and I didn't know how to tie my shoelaces so I couldn't get ready in time. Then she'd hit me or make fun of me. I was often embarrassed."

Humiliation at such a young age tends to leave its mark, and Jacqueline, now a gracefully aging but charming woman, still wonders about her decisions back then: "Maybe I put him in camp too early. I did the best I could. He was an only child. It's not good to be with only your parents, you have to be with people your own age. It gave him independence. We were very strict. He had to have good manners at the table. He did not have the right to talk. The American children are just—I am sorry to say—they eat like pigs, sitting in front of the television. Oliver sat at the table when it was dinnertime. Then we had a talking time, where he had conversations with his father and me. He had to keep his room clean. He had to put pants over the hanger, his coat on the hanger. He became very disciplined with himself. If he had work to do, he would do it. He would not go to sleep unless it was done."

By the time Oliver turned four, the machete business had gone bankrupt. The family returned to New York, where Lou rented an apartment on East 81st Street overlooking the East River. Oliver still spent little time with his parents. Jacqueline loved to throw expensive parties and though Lou realized that some of his best clients came to him through his wife's skills as a hostess, the weekly events were becoming more and more costly. Lou had his own loyal friends, but for the most part he was not very social. He preferred his books and an occasional evening with a special friend, and was not all that comfortable acquiring new clients via social means. He was excellent at managing their money once he got them, however, and so he and Jacqueline formed a strange sort of partnership: Lou would allow Jacqueline to have the parties, and she would make an effort to get him new clients.

Lou Stone returned to Wall Street with a vengeance after his business failed, and became a very successful stockbroker. His sense of humor balanced any bitterness he felt over his business failing, but he was far from satisfied. Though he made more money, he never felt it was enough. He didn't mind making others rich off his efforts, but he resented his own financial pressures. He became more angry about the large sums of money he was spending, yet he continued to spend. He saw the world as a cruel place in which one had to be tough to survive. These attitudes would soon have a profound effect on his son.

At age five, Oliver began more formal schooling. He attended Trinity School, an all-boys school in Manhattan, where his closest friends were Lloyd Kaufman and Roger Kirby. "Trinity was a good school," Roger Kirby remembers. "It wasn't snobbish like some of the others, and it had a wide variety of kids from different economic and social groups. Oliver was not a big kid. He looked like a fat little Oriental kid for a long time because he had this short black hair and round fat face. His eyes were dark and kind of went up a bit."

Despite this, Stone was rarely teased, since it often provoked a strong reaction. On the other hand, he was quite good at teasing others. "Whenever Oliver feels socially uncomfortable," Kirby says, "he resorts to teasing. Sometimes he gets very personal in his remarks. In those days he became uncomfortable pretty easily, so he did that a lot; but he hated being teased so no one called him any dreaded nicknames or anything. Actually, the name 'Oliver' was bad enough as a kid."

While Jacqueline Stone was acquiring a reputation as one of the best hostesses in New York among the European jet set, Oliver's life included longer periods of solitude, forcing him to develop and depend upon his own imagination. "I created games when I was about six or seven," Stone recalls. "I collected football cards and created a whole National Football League system and did the same thing with baseball, using cards and dice. I kept statistics. I liked Ping-Pong, but that required a partner. I loved chess; I played with my father. I also had a lot of soldiers and forts. Expensive soldiers were given to me and I had a love of the military early on."

As he reached school age, Stone saw even less of his mother. He began to develop a keen sense of loss, a loneliness and sense of abandonment that would stay with him the rest of his life. "She was like a fairy godmother," Stone says today of his mother. "When she was around, she trailed perfume, laughter, and smiles and beauty. And when she wasn't around, which was for long stretches sometimes, it was very cold. She was the life of the party and the light of my life. It was like she was either an extreme closeup or a longshot. Never just a two-shot."

For Oliver Stone, the withdrawal of his mother's affection created a deep and disturbing fascination with women. They were an illusion to be grasped, but never attained. A dream to enjoy, but not to trust in, for one day, sooner or later, they always changed on you, or went away. "I've been excited by women for as long as I can remember," Stone said in an interview for *Rolling Stone*. "My first memory is of beautiful women in trees in a jungle. Erotic dreams from when I was three or four that have always stayed with me. I had a combination of shame and humiliation for having those sexual thoughts, but at the same time I had this tremendous desire to be around women all the time."

As his life in New York became more regimented, Stone began to look forward more and more to the summers he would spend with his grandparents, Jacques and Adele Goddet, in France. He had a deep affection for them and would write his grandmother often when he was a soldier in Vietnam, a scene that would later be depicted in *Platoon*. "I used to call her Memé," Stone says. "She was very old-fashioned. She didn't believe in banks, so she hid the money in the house."

Stone called his grandfather Pepé. He had been a cook in World War I and had been mustard-gassed in the trenches. "He told me war stories sitting on his knee," Stone recalls. "He had a bad foot and when I slept with him sometimes he would peel off his shoe. His foot was ossified and discolored from having been gangrenous. He'd talk about being in the front lines for the 'Great War.'"

During these times, Stone also grew very close to his cousins, Jean-Pierre and Lucien Goddet, and later to their younger brother, Pascal. In the deep summer the family would go to the house in the country. It was a world out of Chekhov: Taking long bike rides and playing ball amidst the trees in the heat and dodging swarms of bees. And playing "Army" where real battles were once fought. "We'd go out to the old battlefields where the World War I Germans fought and play in the woods," Stone remembers. "Jean-Pierre and I would find old grenades and army helmets, and sometimes mortar shells that had never detonated. We used to find them all the time."

Jean-Pierre remembers how young Stone would create elaborate stories for them to act out while playing "Army." "They were very complicated. In the evening, we would stay in bed and listen to Grandfather night after night. Oliver always liked so much to hear about what was in the past. Then, in the daytime, he would have us act out Grandfather's tales."

At the end of each summer Jacqueline would return and pick Oliver up before she headed back to the United States. One time, when he was nine, she decided to visit a nudist colony and took Oliver with her. The experience was both exciting and frightening to the child, and afterwards he began spying on his nannies in the woods. "I took him to a nudist camp," Jacqueline admits. "I never saw one, so I said, let's go. I was meeting a friend who was a painter. He had a gallery and he, his wife, and his children were nudists. He invited Oliver and me to come for tea and we arrived wearing our bathing suits. And he came out with his wife and children and they were stark naked. Oliver and I were a little bit embarrassed. We never undressed, but he still remembers that experience. That was his first 'excitement.'"

Lou Stone became more successful during this period, and when Oliver was nine the family moved into a five-story town house on East 64th Street, between Park and Lexington. Their butler, Karlo Stojanac, was a fascinating man and a key figure in Stone's childhood. He had spent a grueling time in a Nazi concentration camp where he was imprisoned during the war, possibly because he was a Slav but most likely because he was homosexual. "Karlo was very high-strung, but also very warm and loving," Stone recalls. "He was very fragile, very effeminate. He never got over the terror of the camps. He loved to laugh and gesture flamboyantly, but I always felt that was an effort to forget all the hell he'd been through. It was almost like the *Kiss of the Spider Woman* character where life is so miserable, you dress up and become insane.

We were extraordinarily close. He was my mentor in many ways. He took care of me and he loved me."

The Stones were wealthier than most of the other Trinity kids' families. Virtually all of Stone's friends were aware of the considerable differences between his outgoing, optimistic French mother and his intellectual, serious, and somewhat pessimistic Jewish father. Many of the other children had fathers who were stern and serious most of the time, but few had a mother like Jacqueline. "When Oliver was nine, his mother gave him a dinner party for his birthday," Roger Kirby recalls. "Everybody had to get dressed up for it. There was this sort of red silk wallpaper and the table was set for a formal dinner. But it didn't take very long before Oliver was throwing the food against the walls and we were throwing it at each other. It was an absolute disaster. I remember her screaming at him once in French, but he didn't pay attention. He wasn't being so horrible, just boyishly violent along with everyone else, but I don't think she understood. She actually thought he would enjoy this like an adult would."

Kirby was also a regular overnight guest at the Stones' town house and still laughs about some of his experiences there: "There was a broadcaster from Philadelphia who dressed himself up like a ghoul and called himself Zachary. And he would introduce the original *Dracula*, *Mummy*, and *Frankenstein* movies. Oliver was a great fan of this and so we'd always watch the show and stay up practically all night. But if, during the middle of the night, you had a debate about something like who led the league in batting the previous year, and it so happened that either you were right or refused to admit that Oliver was right, he'd try to throw you out of the house. We were only about nine or ten, so that was a pretty daunting experience."

Though he clearly had a stubborn streak, Stone rarely got in any trouble at school. "Oliver was too smart for that," Kirby says. "He was an angel in the classroom and definitely the sort of kid who appeared to be peaches and cream to the teachers, but was kind of monstrous behind the scenes. He loved the Mummy and he did a great imitation by dragging his foot behind with one hand against his chest and the other hand out. If he could, he would grab one of the kids at school by the throat."

Stone began to develop a stubbornness that went far beyond bossy.

Faced with feelings of abandonment at such an early age, he learned to assert himself much more than most children are able to do.

During the week Karlo helped Stone get ready for school, making sure he was well groomed and wearing his blazer, tie, and gray pants before he shot out the door to meet Roger Kirby and Lloyd Kaufman to ride the bus to Trinity together. Though he saw far less of his parents than he liked and there were a lot of strict disciplines in his ten-year-old life, young Oliver was also lord of the manor in many ways. He was often the leader in games with his friends, and he usually had the best toys and most complete card and comic-book collections in the neighborhood. "Oliver was the first kid to have coffee," Roger Kirby recalls. "And the first to have a charge account at the local drugstore where you could get a sandwich and a milkshake. And Oliver was the only kid in our class who didn't have to go to school all the time. His mother would vouch for him several times each term."

It was at this time that Stone first fell in love with movies. Often his mother would take him to double features at the RKO on 86th Street and then slip him a note to give to the school doctor. He loved many movies, especially action films. Years later, he wrote fondly of *On the Waterfront*: "I remember not wanting to go. It looked like dull black and white with a lot of guys talking, instead of action and spectacle, like Errol Flynn films. But when I saw it, the black and white was wonderful; the New York style, much better than television. I remember the hooks and the crates, Marlon Brando looked so handsome with the bump on his head. Even my father, who thought he mumbled too much, said he was terrific. Years later, when I made *Born on the Fourth of July*, I screened it several times."

Stone was also becoming interested in writing. Since he was seven, he'd been writing weekly essays for his father in order to earn a quarter for a Classic comic book and an ice cream. At eleven, he started work on a book about his family and his life which ran into hundreds of pages before he gave it up. "I felt that writing was an acceptable retreat from reality," Stone says now. "It was as if the world of the imagination was a sanctuary from real life. Movies were another one. I loved being in the dark, and seeing movies. It was a great escape, but writing was rewarded by Dad."

Stone's father expected him to do well in school and was very serious about his grades, so whenever young Oliver got a poor mark he would bring it to his mother. "The good ones would go to Papa," Jacqueline Stone recalls. "His father paid him for the stories, but he was not extravagant with him. His first allowance at age twelve was twenty-five cents a week. I used to buy him things to make up for it."

But when it came to his father, the boy was usually left feeling that nothing he did was ever good enough. If he got a B, Lou wanted to know why it wasn't an A. If it was an A, his father wanted an A⁺. Lou paid him to write the essays, yet rarely praised his work. As a child Stone could recite the names of all the presidents, but whenever he missed one, his father was disappointed. No matter what he did, it could have been better. "I was very self-conscious when I was young," Stone admits. "I'd walk down the street and feel that people were looking at me, judging me. I felt like I didn't belong, no matter where I went, like I was totally irrelevant to the human race."

Still, Stone is quick to defend his father: "My dad was sometimes sarcastic and distant, but he could be very loving at times. He was proud of me. I was the only child and he was afraid I'd get spoiled by my mom, so he would be a little tougher. He wanted me to learn discipline very early. He used to say, 'Every day you should do something that you don't want to do.' He encouraged me to write, he'd give me math problems to do. He was a great writer in my opinion, very intelligent, and had a great sense of humor.

"He had a warm heart, but had difficulty expressing his feelings in the same way a lot of men did in that era," Stone goes on. "He thought expressing your feelings was unseemly."

Though he was building a considerable client list with the assistance of his wife's social skills, Lou Stone's secret joy was writing. "He had a secret side that he never really let loose," Oliver Stone says of his father. "He used to write plays, but then he'd bury them in the desk drawer. He taught me a lot about writing. But he was in conflict with himself."

Lou Stone's brother, Henry, was also a poet, but apparently had less conflicts about his artistic nature. Not only did Henry marry a writer, Babette Stone, but he eventually self-published his own book of poetry. Lou was secretly jealous of this, but could not break out of his conservative mold enough to attempt something similar. Lou Stone seems to have fought any liberal tendencies he possessed, and as a result became more conservative than his brothers. "My father was conservative in an intelligent sense," Stone agrees, "but ultimately he was an apologist—a defender of the Cold War. I grew up really frightened of the Russians; he created them as a nightmare image for me as a child. He did the same thing with liberals. By the age of ten I thought of Roosevelt and John Maynard Keynes as devils."

Because he so enjoyed writing and was very skilled at it, Lou Stone found his niche when he began writing a newsletter for Hayden, Stone & Co. (no relation), the Wall Street brokerage firm where he worked. The newsletter always started off with a literary reference—a quotation from Shakespeare or one of the classics—then discussed economics on a practical level. It quickly became very well respected by the financial community, and Lou Stone's name gained considerable prominence on Wall Street. Though he would change sponsors a few times, *Lou Stone's Investment Letter* would continue to prosper, eventually reaching a circulation of over a hundred thousand copies translated into twenty languages. Stone's outspoken nature and skill as a writer was evident as he cut through complicated financial issues with style and clarity.

Lou Stone enjoyed success with his newsletter, yet he seemed not to have the desire to return to the grindstone with the fierce intensity he once had. The standing joke was that everybody who took Lou Stone's advice became wealthy except Lou Stone. Lou's conservatism and financial training clashed radically with his wife's carefree attitudes and free-spending habits. "My father believed life was hard," Stone says. "The important thing was to make a living. He never quit talking about money. He was always saying he needed to make more. He wanted to save; my mother spent. She was a social climber. She made a lot of contacts that led to a better clientele for him, but the problem was, my mother had no sense of limitations. She always lived flat out, no holds barred, and the debts she ran up made a nervous wreck of my dad."

Inevitably, Lou and Jacqueline began to grow further apart. The decline of his marriage, his continual financial struggles, and the internal frustration of being afraid to reveal his artistic side took their toll on Lou Stone. Oliver was now eleven, Jacqueline only thirty-one, but Lou was forty-seven. Like many men his age, he began to seek solace through an increasing number of affairs. There were several models, but often he preferred high-class call girls. At first he was secretive, but later, as Jacqueline turned her head from the truth, he became more open about it. She knew, of course, but pretended not to. In the early days of their marriage he had often suggested swapping with other couples as a way of livening up their sex life. She agreed at first because she was naive and thought that maybe this was how people were in America. Later, she refused, and despite her love of parties and free-spirited attitudes, she had remained true to him.

Totally oblivious to any of this, young Oliver began to mature. Now, when he went to France in the summers, he would write and put on plays, many about war, for the people in the area with the entire family as the cast. Stone charged the adults to act in the plays, and then used the money to buy comics. Sometimes, Oliver and his cousins would also earn money by picking potatoes in the fields. "We would ship out at five-thirty in the morning on buses from this little village called La Ferte sous Jouarre in eastern France. We'd mostly pick potatoes at that time of year and we'd get paid a bundle by our standards as kids. My other uncle, Jean Brechet, had a huge farm near there with ducks, sheep, cows, and combines. I was always attracted to the country. I think that's part of the reason I went to Vietnam and wanted to be in the infantry— to get out of the cities and get in touch with the country. Be where the land is."

At twelve and thirteen, Stone loved to stay with his grandparents and imagine stories about the people who occupied the hotel's forty rooms. "Thirty or so of them were always rented to the same group of people, like apartments," he recalls. "Each of them had a separate life and everyone was gossiping about everyone else. We had a big dining-room table and when they came into the hotel they picked up their keys in the same room. Each time someone would stop, they'd have a story to tell."

Stone had more of a family life *away* from his parents than with them. Each year his life in New York brought increased discipline and responsibilities. Although he had all the material things he could want in New York, he much preferred his life in France, which was at near-poverty level. "France was still recovering from the war," Stone says. "There was a lot of rationing and lack of material goods. Water was very minimal. We took a bath once a week. We used to go to the butcher shop and only buy a few grams of meat, as it was very expensive. But France always sticks out as a very storytelling kind of place for me. A place where people would stop and talk in the street. You knew what your neighbors were doing. You cared."

Whenever Stone returned to New York, he was aware of the wealth and power of America. "It was modern furniture, supermarkets, fancy cars. The music was cool. The movies were cool. When I was younger I didn't understand the differences between the two places. I was puzzled by it and resented it. As I got older I began to enjoy being amazed and the feeling of being surprised all over again by the differences in the two worlds."

Not all of Stone's memories of France were positive: "I remember very vividly running away from a gang of French boys as they chased me through the streets screaming, *'Amerlo, Amerlo!'* which is a pejorative term for 'American.' I was trying to get back to my cousin, who was a bigger boy than me and my protector."

He had similar experiences in Manhattan when Irish and Puerto Rican gangs would chase him through the park.

Back in New York, Stone and Roger Kirby continued to be friends as they entered the eighth grade. Stone was proving to be a good athlete, playing football, basketball, and baseball. Like everything else, he approached sports with an organized determination. "He had a physical fitness program for himself in an era when this was unheard of," Kirby recalls. "He got hold of a book and taught himself exercises to improve his athletic powers. He was quite competitive, but he always had a theatrical side to him. He'd overdramatize everything. Once I ran into him when we were playing punchball and he fell against the stoop in front of his house. He kept laying there writhing on the ground. I thought he was being theatrical again and I kicked him a little bit, telling him to get up. Then his mother came out and was very disturbed. To me, Oliver was merely acting with the same hideous flair that he brought to many of his activities. But to his mother it was obvious that he was in pain. It turned out he had shattered a bone in his arm."

Though his father was Jewish and his mother Roman Catholic, Stone was raised an Episcopalian. He was often sent to Sunday School on his own, however, and there wasn't much emphasis on spiritual beliefs in his home. The emphasis was on productivity, and Lou often stressed the importance of organized work habits to his son. "Oliver would come home, sit down, and do his homework right away," Roger Kirby says. "He had a lot of things that he memorized and he'd organize them on index cards even as a child. He probably does the same thing as an adult."

He also discussed college with his father. On weekends in the fall, Kirby and some of the other boys would come over and watch Yale football games with the Stones. As an older boy, Stone had begun spending a little more time with his father. "We'd go to the movies and see 'serious' films by directors like Stanley Kubrick and David Lean," Stone recalls. "Dad was always very impressive in his analysis. He'd walk out and inevitably—no matter what movie we'd seen—he'd say, 'We could have done it better, Huckleberry.' Then he'd tell me what was wrong. He'd analyze the plot for loopholes, and of course, movies always have loopholes. He'd say, 'Why didn't so-and-so do such-and-such?' It was quite an education. We saw *Paths of Glory* together, *Dr. Strangelove*, *Lawrence of Arabia*, *One-eyed Jacks*. And Fellini made a big impression. I remember seeing *La Dolce Vita*, and that just blew me away. He seemed to be doing things in black and white that American filmmakers were not doing. He could take an ordinary life and reexamine that life in mythic terms. I loved the theme of that movie."

Stone saw less and less of his mother as her reputation and penchant for parties grew. "She never went to bed before three in the morning," Stone says. "I'd get up for school and I'd miss her in the morning. At night sometimes when I got home from the bus, she'd be getting ready to go out to a party and we'd cross. It was still warm at times, but it wasn't consistent. I can't say she was a cold mother in any sense of the word. It was just that Mom always wanted to live life to the fullest, in a swashbuckling sort of way. She was this kind of Auntie Mame person who loved having a good time."

Lou and Jacqueline shared little in common by now. She had a whole new circle of friends and spent time with them at lunches and small get-togethers. Many of these new friends were European, most of them were great patrons of the arts—and all of them were wealthy. Jacqueline spent much time and money keeping up what she thought was the appearance of a successful Wall Street family. The Stones were well off, but the people Jacqueline entertained were rich. It was nothing for them to have two or three live-in servants. On the other hand, Lou rented everything—the town house, his car, even the furniture. This would later create chaos in the family's finances, and to this day Oliver Stone struggles with having his sense of security connected to owning property. The Stones lived well, but it was a month-to-month wealth.

Lou was not comfortable with this lifestyle. He rented because it was a way of coping on the short term. Often he was disgusted by Jacqueline's need to impress, and chided her for openly lying about their wealth, or connections to royalty and famous people. His occasional escapes with women had grown more frequent and more bold. More than once Jacqueline came home from a luncheon with her friends to find traces of a call girl in the house. Sometimes she would later discover that some of her clothes were missing. The distance between her and Lou was growing intolerable.

Meanwhile, Oliver Stone seems to have developed a personality that was an eclectic combination of his unique mother and father. He was diligent like his father, with a passion to do well academically, work hard, and earn a decent living. He had a gift for business and financial matters, as well as things literary, and a real concern for truth and keeping one's word. But, also like his father, he had an ongoing sense of guilt, whether he'd done anything wrong or not, and was tormented by a fear of failing no matter how much he succeeded. From his mother came a voracious appetite for life that would often get him into trouble and a natural charm that would often get him out again. She also gave him a real love for people and a spontaneous acceptance of the artistic mind. Roger Kirby points out another significant quality that Stone inherited from his mother. "She gave him a sense of unrealistic possibilities, without which he would not have pursued his career," Kirby says. "I think his father would have said you can't go from step A to step E without going A, B, C, D, and then to step E, whereas Oliver's mother would say, 'Of course you can start right off at E. It's not even a question of jumping to step E, you can just start right there.' But I also think Oliver's mother has made it difficult for him emotionally in some respects because she didn't have the same sort of boundaries regarding her child as his father did. She treated Oliver more like a friend than her child. Consequently, Oliver had a much more sophisticated social life at an earlier age than many of us, and he developed a lot of barriers and emotional problems from that."

At thirteen, Oliver had completed eighth grade at Trinity School, but unlike many of his classmates, he was not going back in the fall. His parents felt that it was time for him to move up in the world, and Trinity was not considered an exclusive enough high school. He was told he would be attending the posh Hill School in Pottstown, Pennsylvania. The Hill, as it was called, was an exclusive all-boys' boarding school.

Oliver would be required to live there and come home only on holiday vacations at Thanksgiving, Christmas, and Easter.

Life at Hill was extremely hard for Stone. He had a tough time making friends and was very uncomfortable. It was bad enough to have to go to a school where he didn't know anyone, but coupled with being uprooted from his home, it was almost intolerable. Much of Stone's identity came from his home. It was where he brought the few friends he had, and it was what gave him substance. At school he was just Oliver, but once his friends saw him at home in his huge playroom with all its toys and games, ordering his butler around, drinking coffee like an adult, showing off his beautiful mother and successful father, they had a new respect for him. He felt he needed all that to serve as a proper introduction to who he was, and at Hill he had none of it.

Stone decided to use William, his first name, upon registering at the school, feeling that the name Oliver was simply too easy a target for pitiless upper-classmen. Stone's tendency to isolate himself really kicked in when, turning fourteen on September 15, 1960, he found himself stuck in steel country with four hundred boys. "The Hill was a very tough school," Stone recalls. "A lot of rigidity, orthodoxy, oppression to some degree. It was a cold existence. I missed my mom and dad. I had no friends. I avoided groups and cliques and sort of reconciled myself to being alone. Those four years, '60 to '64, were as rough as it gets."

Also attending Hill at that time was Tobias Wolff, who later became a writer and memoirist (*This Boy's Life, The Pharaoh's Army*). Wolff has much fonder memories of the Hill, but admits it was tough. "You got up at 6:30 A.M. I think, and hit the deck running until you turned in around 9:00 or 9:30 P.M.," he says, "and there wasn't a time when you were not in class, out doing exercises or sports or studying. They kept us on a tight leash. Most of the kids were all right, but some were snobs. A lot of them were on the social register and took expensive vacations to places like Jackson Hole and some of them talked about it too much."

Wolff was much more outgoing; he remembers Stone as quiet and not able to make friends easily. "Back then, he was a very solitary kind of figure," Wolff says. "He was a nice guy, but he basically decided to keep to himself. He was just not at home. There was a seriousness about him, like he had a job to do. I was extremely frivolous when I was that age, but he was a serious guy and there was no frivolity in him. Also, there was a sense of something being held in. I don't know how to put it, but I knew that I certainly was not seeing all of him. There was something being reined in very hard there."

Stone, having felt rejected and abandoned at an early age, tended to look for tangible reasons why people should accept him, as in "People like me because I'm rich," or "People like me because I'm smart." If he couldn't find a reason that made him stand out in a positive way from others around him, he tended to assume they didn't like him.

Stone knew that he was at Hill for one purpose—to get into Yale. With that in mind, he buckled down and worked hard. As he had long been programmed, he thought that the only way out of the place was success. What made it so difficult was that Hill forced him to try to fit in. He had to try to become a person that he could not be. His home environment was very different from most of the other boys', and he simply wasn't like them. Hill was Stone's first brush with a more mundane attitude toward life. At least when he was at Trinity, he came home every night to his own unique lifestyle. But at the Hill, he was always in the midst of people being groomed for the upper management.

"It was a dismal life," Stone says of his years there. "Getting up in the cold dawn. Chapel every morning, then five classes. The teachers were good, but there was a lot of discipline. The smell of locker rooms. Bad food. Boys torturing each other. A lot of athletic rivalry. Four hours of homework a night. It taught me a lot of discipline. I hated it with a passion."

The holidays at home were greatly looked forward to, as they were the opportunity for Stone to see his parents and his friends from Trinity. Unfortunately, life at home, even during a holiday, was not as pleasant as Oliver hoped. He and his father clashed often. Part of this was because Lou wanted his son to accept the responsibility of Hill without complaint, as a necessary step to approaching manhood, and part of it was probably a guilt reaction at having to put the boy through so much hardship. Young Oliver was beginning to rebel against Hill's excessive structure. The bonds were too tight and he was starting to strain at them.

"I always wore suits and ties," Stone recalls. "You never wore T-shirts then unless you were a gangster or a hoodlum. Then, you held your emotions in. I obeyed my father. His philosophy was to blend into the anonymity of life, sort of the worker bee concept. You support the female, who is a bit of the queen bee. He thought a woman should look pretty, wear a dress and be the attention-getter, whereas the man wore a suit and tie. He'd always say, 'Life is no bowl of cherries,' and, 'Nobody gets out of here alive, kiddo.' That was long before Jim Morrison said it. My father was smart, heavy, kind of Eastern European Germanic in his outlook on life, which was dark and pessimistic. Realpolitik governs, the dollar reigns. Capitalism is good, despite its inequalities. Socialism sounded great on paper, as did communism, but they didn't work because people worked for individual initiatives, not for the collective. He drove that into my head. Inequality is a part of life. Faced with another's misfortune, he'd say, 'I'm not going to feel sorry for people from oppressed classes.'"

Oliver grew closer to his mother, who encouraged his rebellion against his father. "If I was going to a nightclub, sometimes I'd take him with me when he was fourteen or fifteen," Jacqueline Stone recalls. "And we received a lot of artists, French actors and writers who stayed at our place on 64th Street. We had three guest rooms and we'd have a big dinner twice a week, mostly for Lou's sake. And Oliver met all those brilliant people at that young age. Pierre Daniels, Major Thompson, Jacques Tati, Denise Darcell. My cousin, Dominique LaPierre, who wrote *Is Paris Burning?* and *City of Joy.* Oliver was always surrounded with talent and well-known people.

"Lou and I were completely opposite. I was the light side of the family. I gave him the light spirit and the fantasy. I liked having fun. I lived, I love to live. Lou loved his work; he was not playful. His father taught him the secrets of Wall Street. How to keep your capital; to be careful in business. Oliver is a good businessman because his father taught him to be. But I showed him the world of the arts."

But when the holidays at home came to an end, he had to go back to school. By the time he was fifteen, Oliver Stone had learn to dread Sundays and, to this day, he tends to get depressed on that day. Sunday was the day he had to board the train to go back to the Hill.

Since athletics were a key to acceptance at school, Stone began to work harder in this area than he ever had before. After considerable effort he made the tennis team, the cross-country team, and junior varsity swimming.

Author Tobias Wolff confirms that Hill was "a very jock school. The wrestlers were the big guys on campus. Hill had a very savage wrestling team that won titles every year and the football team was big. Contact sports were very popular there."

Though Stone was naturally athletic, sports were not always easy for him because he was still somewhat small. "Oliver didn't grow until he was over twenty-one years of age," Roger Kirby says, "which is rare. He must have grown two to three inches and became a large person as an adult. As a kid, he was just average-sized."

With the focus on academics and the importance of athletics, Stone had less time to write for enjoyment, and he came to value those times more and more. "I used to be able to just escape in my head. But as things got worse, the more it became necessary to write as opposed to just fantasizing or thinking."

While Stone did his best to cope at the Hill, his parents were living increasingly separate lives. Lou's sexual meanderings continued, and Jacqueline's crowd was becoming more decadent. It was the dawn of the sixties, and the art crowd was getting into pep pills, poppers, and cocaine. A few were smoking marijuana, but as a whole that group preferred uppers. Their escapes centered on activity, and pot only slowed them down. Jacqueline would often be out dancing all night now, even during the week, while her husband stayed home and read, getting up early every morning to go to Wall Street. More and more, he despised her friends, whom he considered Eurotrash. She in turn considered him a dull man who played around on her.

Their son knew none of this. He had been somewhat isolated from them even when he was living at home and now, continuing to spend his summers in France, he only saw them on holidays during the school year. He assumed that they were living happily together as he thought they always had. In his deep longing to spend more time at home, the family had become something sacred to Oliver. It was the reason he endured the Hill, the only thing in his world that was still good and pure. His family, quirky and abnormal as it was, was his sole basis for trusting in life.

One afternoon in February 1962, all that came to an end. Stone, now a sophomore at Hill, returned from his classes to find a message in his box: He was to see the headmaster immediately. He knew it had to be bad news; Hill students were rarely summoned to the headmaster's office for any other reason. Though he hated his life at Hill, Stone took pride in having near-perfect conduct. It had to be something else. Later that day he got a message from Suzanne LaFrance, his godmother, who had been Lou's French secretary in the war. Stone called and, in her French accent, she told him his parents had separated and were divorcing. Not only that, but his home was gone: his father had closed up the town house and moved to a hotel. Oliver's things were being forwarded there.

Stone's mind was imploding, a dark fog rolling into his psyche with a force he'd never felt before. He stammered and stuttered and finally managed to ask what the reason for the divorce was. LaFrance told him that his parents had both been having affairs. It had been going on for a while. And now they were divorcing. His father would call him from the hotel soon, she was sure of it. His mother had gone back to France, she thought, but no one knew how to reach her.

In shock, Stone hung up the phone. His parents hadn't even called him. His mother never even said good-bye. "I was stunned," Stone recalls. "I went up to my room and was very depressed. Then I put two and two together and figured this was what the headmaster wanted. I couldn't face it. I just wanted to be alone with myself. I tried to call my father, but I couldn't get through to him. My mother was gone to Europe. Just gone. Just like that. I thought about running away to New York and trying to see my father. I didn't know what to do. I was very confused."

The next day the headmaster called Stone in and rebuked him sternly for ignoring his previous message. "I was scared of him and he came down on me hard," Stone recalls. "It was like, 'When I give you a note like this, you come right away. You always obey my orders, understand?' At one point, he took me aside and said, 'I know you're going through a hard thing, but these things happen. You've got to try to do the best you can. Keep working. Keep forging ahead.' I mean, he could have said, 'Take a few days off and go home,' or something, but he didn't. I remember being embarrassed that he had to know about my pain. It was a private matter in my family and I was very upset that he knew about it. I didn't want to express anything; you held it in in those days. I sort of wanted to be a perfect kid. No problems. I wanted to be anonymous. I was proud that I was a good kid and now there was this big dent in my family. Everything was falling apart."

As harsh as it sounds, Tobias Wolff says he's not surprised at the lack of sympathy from the school administration: "That was very much the attitude there. I had a wonderful teacher who took care of me, but

I was lucky. You could really get lost there. You were sent there as a boy to become a young man. If something went wrong, you weren't supposed to complain about it. They didn't have anything like a counselor or a therapist on the staff with four hundred teenage boys there, many of them from broken homes. Hiring a counselor never would have occurred to them, nor, in all fairness, would it have occurred to any other prep school. It was the times. It was only fifteen years after World War II, very much a can-do era, very tough. We had a macho President and it was a time when you just did for yourself and pushed your way through. There was a coldness, a detachment that kind of went beyond the call of duty. It could do a lot of damage."

For the next three days Stone could be found on the pay phone in the lobby of his dormitory trying desperately to reach his father at work or in his room at the Hotel Beverly. But there never was an answer. Finally on the third day, Lou Stone answered the phone.

"He was very apologetic, mumbling and hesitant," Stone recalls. "He said Mom and he had a problem, and he was depressed by what she'd done. She'd had other lovers. I remember him using that term—'other lovers.' And he couldn't stand it any more so he had filed for divorce and she had left for Europe. It was pretty ugly. She'd been crying to him that she loved another man. He had a detective track her to California. He had photographs of my mother and another man at a motel. The New York divorce laws were very tough on adultery. He knew he held the leverage and wanted to sew up the case. The photographs were of her and a man named Dennis. Dennis was someone I knew; in fact, I considered him a good friend. He was a model who wanted to be a photographer and an actor. We used to work out together. He taught me about lifting weights. I liked him. It never had occurred to me that he was her lover. And there were several instances when Mom's eyes were darkened and one time when her lip was bruised. People used to hint about Dennis having a dark, violent side, but I thought he was just a friend of my mother's. I was so naive."

Though Lou Stone was sympathetic with his son on the telephone, he refused to take him out of school. "He kept saying, 'I'll explain it all to you over spring vacation.' He said he'd take me down to Fort Lauderdale or Boca Raton and we'd have a good time. But that was two months away. I said, 'Dad, I don't want to stay here, can I come home? I've got to get out of here.' He said, 'I can't get you out.' It was a very strict curriculum. It was hard to get away even for a few days because the work piled up. He just said to stick it out at school."

This was the turning point in Oliver Stone's life. To this day the shock from this sudden devastation colors nearly all of his decisions. It turned him forever from the innocent expectation and hope of youth and propelled him like a rocket straight for the dark side. Most of those close to him agree that he never recovered. "They should have both come and taken me out of school for a few days," Stone reflects. "I realize they were both going through tremendous conflict and trauma, but nobody even came to tell me in person. That was really hard to take. My mother didn't even want to see me. She was hiding in Europe. You can imagine the way the headmaster tells you these things, 'Buck up, young man, this is not the end of the world.' I felt like shit, like nothing. Everything was metallic. All the adults were dangerous, not to be trusted. I reassessed everything. I had a sense that everything had been stripped away. That there was a mask on everything, and underneath there was a harder truth, a deeper and more negative truth."

It took months before he learned the details, but Stone eventually discovered that, though his father had been having affairs for years, once he found out that Jacqueline had been unfaithful, he immediately divorced her. In fact, according to Jacqueline, she was served with a petition for divorce within twenty-four hours. She then left the country and Lou subleased the town house.

At fifteen, Stone no longer had any illusion of a happy childhood. It had all come to an abrupt end. His boyhood home was gone. His mother was gone, and he had no idea where she was or how to get hold of her. His parents were committing adulteries. He wondered how they had stopped loving each other. "It was a very sudden twist," Stone acknowledges. "The family was over. It just disintegrated. I didn't have a brother or a sister, a second person I could still be family with. The triangle split and we were three people in different places. I'm fifteen, and all of a sudden I'm on my own."

As if this wasn't enough, when Stone accompanied his father to Florida for spring vacation, he received yet another shock. "My father said he was broke," Stone recalls. "He said he was a hundred thousand dollars in debt from my mother's spending and what the divorce would cost. He said, 'I'll give you a college education, and then you're on your own. There's literally no money.' I was shocked. I thought my father was a rich man. I never expected that on top of everything else."

Ironically, Oliver Stone would now have to experience the same kind of loss that had so shaken his father, but at an even younger age. When, while at Yale, Lou learned that his father had lost the family fortune, it was the hardest moment he'd ever faced, and he never fully recovered. Now his son would have to endure the same trial, on top of losing his home and family.

The trauma of seeing his family and home disintegrate so suddenly had a significant impact on Stone's world view, and it also formed strong traits in his character. Faced with such emotional shocks, he had a choice between freezing up or forcing himself ahead. In retrospect, it appears he did both. Much of his personality froze up emotionally, leaving him stunted with the emotional maturity of a somewhat sheltered fifteen-year-old boy. But another part of him took a stand that no longer let others determine his life. While these extremes appear contradictory, those who know Stone well will admit that, though he often reacts childishly to any form of real or imagined rejection, he almost never changes his direction or intentions because of it. Thus, you have a man who is severely wounded by criticism even from sources he deems unworthy, but who has an incredible capacity to push ahead with his goals in the midst of seriously intimidating circumstances. This partly explains his capacity to work long hours with incredible intensity even under extreme pressure, and why obstacles, even sickness and emotional traumas, seem only to further ignite his determination to succeed. It is as if the shocks of 1962 left him resolved never to accept defeat. Each achievement not only reinforces the idea that everything can be achieved, but provides the motivation, in many cases a deep need, to accomplish more. The cycle must continually be completed—more and more difficult tasks have to be attempted so the furnace can be fueled with more accomplishments so that more tasks can be attempted, and so on. Stone is so far beyond a workaholic that the term barely applies. He exists to accomplish and he accomplishes to exist.

Stone had no communication with his mother for well over a month. When she did finally call, she was in the South of France with friends and couldn't come to see him. She invited him there, but he couldn't leave the Hill until the summer.

Now when Stone came home, instead of the five-story townhouse where he had almost two floors to himself, it was to a small hotel suite where he had a tiny room. He would listen to his father complain that he had no money to give him a legacy and that Oliver was going to have to work hard for a living. "Life is tough, kiddo," Lou Stone would say, and his son believed him.

Later, Lou got an apartment. Sometimes Oliver would arrive on a holiday to find a woman there with his father. "Some were call girls," Stone admits, "but others were models or old friends of his. Women would come back to him. It seemed to me that women would come back to him sometimes twenty or thirty years later. They liked to be around him. They found him funny. He loved to tell stories and jokes. Some of the women were very nice and we used to joke about which ones he might marry. He treated women well, but he had very much of a chauvinistic attitude in that he didn't want them around all the time. He seemed to be very ambiguous about my mom. Often he'd say that he never loved her and only married her in order to have me because she was a good mother. So whom did he love? Sometimes he'd mention some name, maybe a girl he met during the war who I didn't know. He'd say that was the girl he loved."

These were increasingly lonely times for Stone. "I felt like a vagrant in my father's apartment. Like I was lucky to have a room. I went through a lot of changes at that point."

Lou Stone was not an unfeeling man. He could see his son was hurting, but he didn't know what to do to comfort him. Perhaps it was better that Oliver faced the hard truths of life at an early age instead of stringing himself along on dreams that never came true. Lou was in his early fifties, alone and struggling financially, but he had started to enjoy life again. And the key to this was that he had finally learned to settle for less. He tried new ways to relate to his son. At fifteen and a half, the boy looked older than his age and sometimes he went to P. J. Clarke's on 55th Street and sat with Lou and his friends. Oliver was sophisticated in many ways, except when it came to women. Going to all-boys' schools had left him somewhat stunted in this area. He confided in his father about this and also about how frustrated he was feeling trying to cope with his burgeoning teenage sexuality. Lou wanted to help, but didn't know how. Then he had an idea. He knew a young call girl whom he felt had a certain gentleness about her. Perhaps he could call her for Oliver.

Oliver Stone had a night to remember. He was shy and caught off guard at first, but once he relaxed, he enjoyed the experience.

There is little doubt now that Lou's gesture, though made with good intentions, helped to cripple his son emotionally for quite some time. Part of a boarding school circle that rarely mingled with the opposite sex until marrying age, Stone was an emotionally underdeveloped teenager, and the experience made a profound impact.

That summer Stone went to France to visit his mother. It was then that he learned of his father's earlier affairs. He had heard and would continue to hear from his father that women could not be trusted and might ruin a man financially and otherwise, but now he heard his mother's side of the story. Instead of taking sides, Stone felt critical and distrustful of both his parents. Jacqueline's new lifestyle gave him another jolt, as well. As long as she was living with Lou, Jacqueline had tempered her wild side; but now, in the South of France with her jet-set crowd, it was "anything goes." Anthony Pompei, an old lover of Jacqueline's, elaborates: "Oliver saw it all there. He was around gays; he was around prostitutes. He saw the seamy side of life, in spite of the fact he was born into a family of means. Jacqueline didn't hide anything from him. And Oliver was like the Shadow. That's how I used to think of him. Standing off to the side, real quiet, watching everything, taking everything in. The Shadow, usually dressed all in black and standing near the corner, watching. It was like he wanted desperately to bust out, but he didn't know how."

Though he'd been to a few of his mother's parties, they were tame compared to this. Drugs. Naked bodies. The bizarre art crowd. Strange-looking people. Group sex. Men hitting on him. Women hitting on his mother. At the end of the summer, Jacqueline got an apartment in New York. Now Oliver had his choice of where to spend his vacations from school. "She was really liberated, going fully into a party scene," Stone says. "They'd stay up all night and party. Lots of heavy sex. But I was distant from it. It was weird to me and I was uncomfortable there because these people really scared me. It was like *Midnight Cowboy* or something. My mother was an example of that sixties thing that happened among adults, who all of a sudden felt so repressed by the fifties that they wanted to explode. And she exploded. There were so many strange people in New York, straight and gay. Some of them were nice, some of them were horrible. But they all came to Mother's apartment."

Roger Kirby recalls being with Oliver when he came to visit his mother at this time. "We came in and she was in bed with somebody. They were half undressed, and Oliver and his mother are just talking like nothing was the matter. I was staring sort of agape and his mother said, 'What's the matter? Haven't you ever seen someone in bed before?' The truth was that I hadn't. Not like that. Oliver's mother had a tendency to be more like a peer than a parent. After his father was gone, she was amazingly candid with him. There was no subject she wouldn't broach. Then, other times, she acted like she wasn't interested."

Feeling betrayed and outraged, and hopelessly isolated, Stone struggled through his last two years at the Hill. In November 1963 President John F. Kennedy was murdered in Dallas. For many, it was the starting gun of the sixties. For Oliver Stone, the event somehow coincided with the steady stream of eye-opening shocks he'd been receiving. The assassination further marked the tearing of the veil that separated repressed childhood fantasy from harsh adult reality. "Kennedy was that breath of fresh air," Stone wrote later. "To see his candle snuffed out so early and viciously was such a shock. I had no faith in my parents' generation after that. I felt I had grown up reading fake history. I was a child of distortions. I thought I was living a happy life, but discovered it was all a lie"

By his senior year, Stone had become good friends with David Leng, the Chinese boy who had been his roommate almost the whole time at the Hill, but Stone was still unhappy. He began to see his life as a treadmill and he started to feel trapped. He'd been accepted at Yale, something he'd worked hard for all his life, but now he no longer cared. He did his senior English Club thesis on three Edward Albee plays: the adaptation of Carson McCullers's *The Ballad of the Sad Café*, *Who's Afraid of Virginia Woolf?*, and *The Zoo Story*. Albee inspired him. He longed to write something epic. But there simply wasn't enough time. Sometimes he wondered if there ever would be. While most seniors at Hill were eagerly awaiting college and spent their free time maneuvering ways to mingle with the opposite sex, Stone became more withdrawn. At the dances arranged with all-girl schools in the area like Shipley and

Baldwin, most of the Hill boys would huddle off in corners with girls, attempting to make out, but Stone shied away. He felt far too traumatized about sexual attraction to deal with women very well.

Roger Kirby comments: "I don't think Oliver ever dated anybody. He had this circle of people whom his mother would make available to him directly or otherwise. But I don't think he could relate to the female equivalent of a Hill person, and those were the kind of people he saw. I think the first real relationship he had was with his first wife several years later."

In June 1964, Stone graduated from the Hill, much changed from the cocky boy who once played punchball in his Manhattan town house. He describes the change as going from "the golden boy to the ugly duckling."

In September, just before his eighteenth birthday, he entered Yale. Stone arrived feeling mentally stale and deeply cynical, only to discover he'd been assigned to room with two boys from the Midwest, both from very conformist backgrounds and who were enrolled on scholarships. He found little in common with them and knew that in their wildest imaginings they could never picture his bizarre background. Roger Kirby describes Stone's room at Yale: "His mother decorated his room in this sort of ultra-French fashion. She brought in leopard skin and all kinds of things, and it wound up looking like somebody's boudoir. It became very clear to me when I saw it that Oliver's conflicts were rooted in the different lifestyles of his parents and the demands they made on him."

Within a week, Stone realized that Yale would be Hill all over again. "I basically cracked up when I went to Yale," he admits. "This was the same crap, and I had to do it for four more years? Now I was competing with boys who were eager and anxious to succeed. I knew I couldn't do what I had done four years ago at the Hill. There was a repetitive boredom to the whole process. I wanted to get out. I was wound so tightly that I exploded. I had a combination of explosion and nervous breakdown."

Stone struggled through the first six months, but his opinions were changing. The tumultuous experiences of the past few years had left him wary of life, distrusting the blind conservatism of his parents, and desperately seeking for answers. He began to find some in literature. Not the classics he had grown up on, but books that described another side of life. "At Yale, I saw myself as a product," Stone wrote, "an East

Coast socioeconomic product, and I wanted to break out of the mold. I felt squeezed, suffocated. I remember reading *Lord Jim* by Joseph Conrad and becoming enchanted by it. Conrad's world was exotic and lush. He was a purveyor of the darker side. He understood that there were various layers of human behavior. *Lord Jim* pulled me, the exotic smell of the Orient pulled me. I had to go to the Orient. I remember I had a Greek final, but I couldn't study because I kept dwelling on the fiction I'd been reading."

Stone wrote away to several organizations about employment abroad. He inquired about teaching positions in the Orient and even about becoming a mercenary and fighting in the Belgian Congo. Before his first year at Yale was up, he had received an answer from the Free Pacific Institute in Taiwan, a church organization which operated a group of schools. One of the schools had a position available for an English teacher if he could pay his own way there.

Stone dropped out, taking a year's leave from Yale. His father was disappointed and somewhat reluctant, but agreed that maybe a sabbatical away from school would be just what the boy needed. The institute's headquarters were in Taiwan, but the school they had assigned Stone to was in another location—Saigon.

"I was fed up with the whole concept of civilization as I learned it from my father," Stone wrote in his notebook at the time. "Refrigerated foods and economic structures that promote health and hygiene. The whole Lewis Mumford urban environment. That's what I rejected. And I went to the heart of Asia. Not even Japan or something more civilized, but the belly of Southeast Asia. Into the tropics."

The Free Pacific Institute was a Catholic school for Chinese students located in Cholon, a Saigon suburb. It was 1965, the year a half million American soldiers landed in Vietnam. Oliver Stone was eighteen years old. "I woke up in Asia and it was everything I hoped it would be," he wrote. "The smell, the heat, the green seas, the blood red sunsets. Saigon was a tremendous thrill. Hookers were everywhere. Bars were everywhere. The 1st Infantry Division was just arriving in Saigon and there were guys walking around with pistols and no curfews. They had shoot-outs in the streets. The place was like Dodge City."

It wasn't long before Stone had his first experience in a whorehouse. "I had always had a penchant for Asian ladies," he says. "I find that they are some of the most interesting women, and they have an amazing sense of restraint. They hold back so much. I've always been attracted to that."

Never having had the opportunity to form real relationships with members of the opposite sex, Stone found himself strongly drawn to prostitutes. "I developed the attitude that prostitutes made public the private, and in so doing dispensed a form of divine grace," Stone says now. "It was a feeling that they didn't care who you were and that they didn't judge you, so there was not a lot of emotional baggage attached to having relations with them. I know now that isn't true for a lot of them, especially most American ones, but I don't have the attitude that they're something to be condemned or that we're better than they are. We don't know their circumstances. I can relate to the classical approach, where the prostitutes were temple maidens who had given themselves over to benefit the gods and the community around them. Sort of like a holy release to satisfy the rage in man."

Once, the attraction proved as dangerous as it was alluring when a couple of Viet Cong soldiers snuck into the outskirts of the city and investigated the brothel for unsuspecting Americans. "The girl hid me," Stone says. "I don't know why she did it. It was all spur of the moment. We heard them routing people out of the rooms in the hall and she told me to go in the closet. The VC came in and said something and she spoke back and forth with them in Vietnamese. They laughed a couple of times, and I was just waiting for them to start pumping rounds into the closet or something. But nothing happened. After a moment they left and I waited until they were long gone before I took off. But I always had the feeling they knew and for some reason just gave me a break."

Stone had successfully escaped civilization at last. Asia soon became a second home for him, something it still represents to this day. He lived a spartan existence in a section of the school, surrounded by lizards, with a Chinese housekeeper, and reading a great deal. He wound up teaching several subjects including English, mathematics, and history. With five classes of fifty or more students, his job was hard, but he enjoyed it and learned from the Chinese, going to their homes and spending time with them. After a while, Stone began to notice some odd similarities in his students. "They all were from rabid anti-Communist families, mostly Chinese kids from Cholon," he recalls. "I remember flunking about twenty percent of the class one term and most of them showed up in the next class at the higher level. Obviously there was some bribe mechanism in place somewhere. I went to the priest who was the head of the school and told him about it and he said, 'Well, it's a tough time for Vietnam. We need the money. Let the kids go.' I couldn't figure out where they got the money, but I think it was connected to their being so anti-Communist somehow."

After the second semester Stone quit, more because he found teaching so repetitive than because of any problems he had with the school. Saigon had fueled his desire to see more of the world, so, going from one adventure to another, he decided to join the Merchant Marine. He'd been fascinated by merchant sailors ever since reading the Conrad novels, and often he would ride his motorbike down to the docks or go to the bars and talk to the sailors, hearing their exciting stories. Since the ships frequently lost crewmen at various ports, the union allowed them to pick up new men abroad, and Stone took a job as a wiper on an American ship.

Though he was living the life of his favorite novels, it wasn't always a glamorous one. "The wiper basically cleans the toilets," Stone says grinning. "I'd clean them all through the ship and then I'd clean the engine room, help out the oilers and the boilerman. One of things I did was called blowing the tubes. The main engines have to be cleaned every night and they would put a wrench around the steampipe to blow it and hot oil would come down. I was always on the bottom so I wore a huge hat, an Australian bush hat, because so much hot oil would come running down. Sometimes I'd get scalded. One night, one of the gaskets blew in the steampipe, which is under a lot of pressure, maybe twelve hundred pounds per square inch, and it came blowing out into my face. It could have really scarred me, but I was lucky."

On one voyage Stone went to Bangkok, a city he would come to visit many times. "The captain on the ship was a lecher," Stone says. "He was a big fat guy, this grotesque three-hundred-pound captain sitting in a rickshaw. I'd been in the city for a long time by then so he'd make me take him to whorehouses in Saigon. I had to try to fix him up with girls that I knew. Then he'd get drunk in his cabin and pass out. He was a real problem. I left that ship and did something else for a while."

Stone tried to get a job as a reporter. He interviewed with UPI as well as ABC News and CBS, but they only offered freelance work. One day he was driving with some French friends to Dalat when they were stopped by a VC unit that controlled the road and collected tolls. Stone had a beard at the time and spoke French, and the VC mistook him for a Frenchman. After the incident, he wrote an article about being an American encountering a VC raiding party. UPI bought the story, but turned it into a third-person article.

After failing to get a job at a French shipping company in Saigon, Stone went back into the Merchant Marine and signed on for a lengthy voyage across the Pacific Ocean, from Saigon to Coos Bay, Oregon. "It took thirty-eight days," Stone recalls, "but we were slow and riding high on the water because we were returning and carrying no cargo. We got stuck off Taiwan. Two or three days in the open ocean, bobbing because our main steampipe went down and we were trying to fix it. Then we hit the northern January typhoons in a storm off Alaska. We were leaning heavy in the water. One night the whole ship almost went over. It was unbelievable. Those were rough waters. There were weird people on the ship. The gay sailors used to come on to me. But, all in all, it was a great experience."

After completing the nightmarish crossing in early 1966, Stone headed down to Mexico. Though life in the Merchant Marine was hard, he'd enjoyed it. But there were other things that he wanted to do. He had been writing while at sea, and now decided to undertake a full-fledged novel. He thought Mexico might be just the place to do it. All this time he had continued to use his first name, Bill. But now, as he began the novel and returned to more artistic pursuits, he once again called himself Oliver.

A Child's Night Dream is a deeply revealing stream-of-consciousness look at the psyche of an intelligent but passionately troubled youth. "I wrote the first four hundred pages in three weeks in a cheap hotel in Guadalajara," Stone recalls. "I wrote it all in longhand. The first burst was an explosion of stuff from my experiences in Asia. It was a wild sort of Hindu time story, where the time period goes back and forth. It started in the present with a boy's suicide note and then went through Asia, the Merchant Marine. Parts were like a poem, without punctuation, rolling, tripping over the tongue. I was very influenced by Joyce and by J.P. Donleavy's *The Ginger Man*. Writing to a beat, to a rhythm. It was so exciting to me, so much fun. I just felt like this is it. I'm so happy doing this. I've found my calling in life."

Thus fortified, Stone returned to his father's apartment to finish the book. He knew he would encounter a wall of negativity from his father, but he felt that he now had the confidence to endure it. "He wanted me to go back to Yale, of course. He believed that you're not supposed to talk about your inner feelings or show them, or be 'an artist displaying himself to the public.' As Flaubert said, art is public prostitution. That's what Dad was saying: art is prostitution, because you're making public your private fantasies."

Roger Kirby recalls that Stone returned to his old, somewhat oddball ways when he got back to New York. "I remember when he came back, he had been taking self-defense lessons from some old Marine whom Oliver really admired tremendously because he was such a tough, crusty kind of person. I guess at the conclusion of one lesson he gave Oliver a knife and said, 'Attack me.' And Oliver said he really couldn't do it, but the guy kept saying, 'Don't worry. Do it!' So Oliver said okay and, as he was approaching, the guy spat at him and kicked him in the groin. Oliver respected him immensely for that. He thought that was just the greatest thing. When he finished the course, he wanted me to walk through Central Park at night with him so he could see if the stuff would work in real life. I still can't believe that we did that."

Holed up in his father's apartment, Stone worked nearly continuously on the manuscript for his book. The recurring theme is the sorrow of youth: "I was ready for death and a lot of my book was about suicide," he says. "Part of it was about the eighteen ways the kid tries to kill himself. Teenage suicide was not that talked about in the sixties. Nobody dealt with it except Salinger in *Catcher in the Rye*. It was like people would scoff at your pain if you were young. This was just before the hippie revolution, before *Time* magazine decided that people under twenty-five mattered. I remember a world where the young were never consulted. It was sort of like, 'What pain can you have?' My dad was responsible for a lot of that frustration in me. He'd say, 'What experience do you have? How can you write? What pain do you really feel?'"

I was conceived by my father, born of my mother, suffered under both, was crucified dead and buried the third day I rose again from the dead and ascended unto heaven and sitteth on the right hand of God the father fiction from whence I shall come to judge both my mother and my father, amen, o wicked, wicked child boy! . . . Father said, it's a rough world kiddo, none of us get out of it alive, he said that and now in my dream when I lay my cheek on the soft Alp and gazed into the mad divinity of the moon, here he was then, through the shit piled empire high on my pinkflesh fraughtfull of feminine odor, sitting at my hushed bedside creaking in a low fast whisper, telling me how very evil that man was who told me it was forespoken that I was to die.

(*A Child's Night Dream*)

Stone had seized upon the thesis of the novel as an alternative to his own suicide, which had loomed large in his mind ever since his parents' divorce. "I extended my first four hundred pages into a mammoth work, fourteen hundred pages," he said. "Ultimately, the person saves himself from suicide by the act of writing. But even then, I played it two ways. I also had him extinguishing himself through the act of writing; he self-destructed at the end of the manuscript. I couldn't decide which way to go."

This double-ending scenario recurs every now and then in Stone's work even today. Sometimes, he will film two endings and then make his decision in the editing room.

As he neared completion of the work, Stone finally gave in to his father and agreed to go back to Yale for the fall term: "I thought I could take five easy courses and finish the novel. But I couldn't. I just continued to write the novel, which was possessing me at this point. I didn't even go to class."

The dean at Yale arranged for him to have a single room in Saybrook College, but Stone chose to work on his novel day and night, skipping classes and ignoring all of his midterms. Eventually, the dean called him in and gave him a choice of making up all his work in the next thirty days or leaving school. Stone chose to leave. "My father was furious," he recalls. "He said, 'You're going to regret this for the rest of your life.' It was the second time I left, and he freaked out because he lost all that tuition. So I went back and finished the novel in New York. It was a tough time for me. I was fighting with him and trying to write. He'd say, 'What are you going to do with your life? You're going to be a bum. You think you're a writer, but you're not.' Stuff that hurt. It was a miserable existence, six, seven months with him. I wanted to commit suicide several times. Many a time I stood looking into the bathroom mirror with the razor out."

Though his father was pressuring him to "make something of himself," Stone persisted in writing the novel under excruciating circumstances. "I was consumed by the book. I was writing ten hours a day, living inside my own world with Joyce, Donleavy, Rimbaud, and Mailer. Those four were really helping me fuel my energy, but also T. S. Eliot, Joyce Carey."

Dear Mother: I was at Chu Lai this week, maybe you heard about it in the papers, it's history now. Many were killed. The marines cornered and slaughtered five hundred viets in a pincer movement that lasted three days. Where I am right now Death seems as thin as air—air all about, air, air, air. In Paris this will only be another piece of news embroidered within the thick columns of your morning newspaper. But it is really more than that, it is military history, imagine five hundred dead, heaps of flesh, it is quite a sight, one that I was both fortunate and unfortunate in seeing. Like the parties you took me to in New York, it is something I must carry about with me for the remainder of my days.

(*A Child's Night Dream*)

Finally, Stone finished. "I thought it was the best thing since Rimbaud," he says, grinning. "I was convinced it would be a missile from the youth. It seemed to me I was saying things no youth up until then had said, speaking right from my heart, saying, 'Here's the state of the youth today. We're into suicide much more than you think. We have our dark side. Here's our sexuality.' I was trying to write about the raw edges of my own experience, from Asia all the way through America. And I was dealing with it honestly, but it was raw. It vomited out. Everything just spewed out."

The monsoon. Head of a mongoose, tail of a mole. Odors in the rain. Things always happen to me in the rain. Can't write about this can I. What do I say. War is hell. People won't understand. Yes, we know, war is hell, why must you tell us? Because.

Like most ambitious first works, *A Child's Night Dream* was doomed to fail. Most publishers thought it was scandalous. One said, "This is either a work of genius or a total mess." Others weren't so kind. "A guy at Simon & Schuster said it was a piece of shit," Stone says. "He sent me a horrible letter. People should remember when they're at the top that it's easy to break a writer's heart. When Simon & Schuster rejected it, I gave up. I said fuck it. I threw half the manuscript in the East River and said, 'My father is right. I'm a bum.' I thought it was over for me."

Stone's father made the rejection even harder by trying to use it as proof that his son should listen to him: "He acted like he was vindicated. Fuck him! I had to get out. I hated him then. I felt the solution was total anonymity. The novel had brought out the ego part of me, the showing-off part, as my father would say, and I wanted to bury that once and for all. I thought, 'I'll never get anything done with my life, with my writing. I'm sick of being special. I'm sick of the act of writing about "self" and therefore I'm going to be anonymous.' I felt I had to atone for the act of individuality somehow. So I decided to join the Army. They'd cut my hair and I'd be a number."

In April 1967, in a desperate and impulsive act, Stone enlisted in the U.S. Army and requested to be assigned to the infantry. "It was a way of announcing to my father that I was a man," he says. "Also, I had a serious dose of patriotism. I believed in our country, believed in the ideals, believed that the Communists were undermining us every-where. To me, the American involvement was correct. My dad was a cold warrior, and I was a Cold War baby. I knew that Vietnam was going to be the war of my generation, and I didn't want to miss it. In that sense, my timing was perfect."

Stone told the recruiting office that his name was William Stone. "I had again given up on Oliver Stone," he says. "They could call me William or Bill or just Stone. I didn't give a shit. I just didn't want to be called Oliver. I was embarrassed by that name again."

He took basic and advanced infantry training at Fort Jackson, South Carolina, and on September 14, 1967, the day before his twenty-first birthday, he took off from Oakland in a transport plane bound for Vietnam. "I wanted to see what I was made of," he says. "Would I be a coward? How would I react, what was bottom line? I really wanted to kill myself, but instead decided I'd just go into combat. I asked for Vietnam and the infantry and they gave it to me. I thought it'd be over in six months and I would either live or die. If I died, then it was meant to be. And if I lived, we'd see what would happen. I was going to put the test up to somebody else." Stone literally never had a twenty-first birthday: "They put me in an airplane on the night of the fourteenth in Oakland, California, going west. On the plane, I smoked a cigarette for the first time in my life. We hit the dateline going over that night and lost a day. The day we lost was my twenty-first birthday. We landed on September 16, 1967."

Oliver Stone landed in Vietnam and became part of an invasion force that had swelled to nearly 500,000 strong. He was a man now, and he would soon have the opportunity to prove it.

CHAPTER TWO

The Purging

"Rejoice, O young man, in thy youth . . ."
Ecclesiastes as quoted in **PLATOON**

Bill Stone, the man who chucked an Ivy League education for a chance to fight in Vietnam, was assigned to the 2nd Platoon of Bravo Company, 3rd Battalion, 25th Infantry, stationed near the Cambodian border. Like his French grandfather in World War I and his American father in World War II, he went off to fight. As he would later depict in *Platoon*, Stone was a rich college boy who, through his own absurd choice, had condemned himself to a hell mostly populated by poor whites and uneducated blacks, about the only people without enough pull to keep themselves out of this, the bottom of the barrel. As Chris Taylor, the lead character in *Platoon*, would say:

"I've found it finally, way down here in the mud. Maybe from down here I can start up again and be something I can be proud of, without having to fake it, maybe I can see something I don't yet see, learn something I don't yet know."

He was a "cherry," someone who had no idea about real war or how to survive in the wild. And he had every chance of getting hurt. It didn't take long for Stone to realize he had made a mistake. "It took about a day," he says. "Hell is the impossibility of reason. I had heard that quote somewhere years ago and I remembered it when I got to Vietnam. It was complete despair. The vets treated the new guys like you were new meat, so you were expendable. The feeling was that someone who'd been over there three months had more reason to live than you did. It was on-the-job training—'Here's your machete, kid, you cut point.' You learn if you can, and if not, you're dead. Nobody was motivated, except to get out. Survival was the key. It wasn't very romantic."

One of men he would meet was Ben Fitzgerald, a large black man from a small town in Tennessee, who was depicted in *Platoon* as King. Fitzgerald hooked up with Stone later in a different unit, but he says the attitude in his platoon was pretty much the same toward new recruits: "These guys just didn't last too long. People didn't like to get close to them because it's very easy to blow a booby trap or make a mistake that can cost you your life. We usually figured if they lasted the first couple of weeks, then they were doing pretty good."

"Man'd be alive if he'd had a few more days to learn something."
Sergeant Elias in **PLATOON**

Unlike the depiction of war in John Wayne movies, there wasn't that much loyalty in the front-line troops because they never had much time to get to know each other. The platoon was divided into layers. One group would be leaving within a month, while others were three, six, or nine months away. The men just arriving had, of course, been though training in the States, but received little instruction after they arrived. "Sometimes somebody took pity on you and showed you something, but it's not like they went out of their way," Stone says. "Nobody taught me anything. You learned it as you went. The 25th was a fairly demoralized unit."

The Purging

43

Part of the way the men in his platoon initially reacted to Stone had to do with his vastly dissimilar background. They didn't have to know where he was from or what kind of life he'd had. All they had to do was look at him. He was cerebral, a boy who lived in the abstract. They were living in a very focused world where reality was six inches in front of their faces. They were ready to kill and ready to die.

Life was cheap here. Oliver Stone was about to find out how cheap. His second week there, his platoon embarked on a night ambush. "I was put on point my first day in the field," he recalls. "It was tough. I was about to pass out with fifty pounds of equipment on my back. We didn't see any action until we were out about a week. That night I had second watch. The mosquitoes were driving me crazy and I fell asleep. I passed out. I let my people down. Then I awoke and the Viet Cong were there. These guys just appeared. I was numb, scared shitless. All my training went out the window. Thank God the guy in the next position saw them and opened up. The firefight was very messy. I was wounded in the back of the neck—an inch to the right and I'd have been dead—and the guy next to me had his arm blown off. I really froze up. I felt pretty shitty afterward and, in a way, it was good I got wounded, because I wouldn't have been able to take the derision from the other guys."

"Out here, assholes, you keep your shit wired tight at all times . . . and that goes for you, shit for brains. You don't sleep on no fuckin' ambush. Next sonofabitch I catch coppin' Z's in the bush I'm personally going to take an interest in seeing him suffer—I shit you not."

Sergeant Barnes in **PLATOON**

Out of action only briefly with a flesh wound, Stone was soon back in combat, but he was changing. "I got better after that first one. The first time, you don't know if the fire's coming in or going out. You don't know where anybody is. There's a lot of confusion and you get killed a lot from your own side. It takes a while to get a sense of it, but each time I got a little better."

If this wasn't the "bottom" Oliver Stone had been searching for, it was certainly close. And it was here that many changes began. One of them had to do with his political outlook. He'd come from a family of conservative Republicans and, as a student at Yale, had even rooted for

Barry Goldwater in the '64 election. He was patriotic, loved war movies—especially those starring John Wayne—and had adopted his father's politics right down the line.

In Vietnam, Stone discovered that the poor were doing all the fighting. He knew all the rationales behind such injustice. He'd heard them since he was ten. The well-to-do were either busy at home keeping the country running or becoming officers to administer the war from behind the lines. They were better educated and better suited for those jobs. It all makes sense in a textbook kind of way. But knowing such things are true and actually living them are two different things. Seeing the lives of poor whites and uneducated blacks being forfeited while the rich and favored stayed home seemed more like bribery than philosophy to Stone. Watching teenagers who had not finished high school get shot to pieces because their fathers didn't know who to call or have any favors they could trade seemed less "for the benefit of the whole" than it had sounded back at Yale. "All of a sudden I was with black guys, poor white guys," Stone says. "Poor people see through that upper-class bullshit. They know the score."

"Sheeit, gotta be rich in the first place to think like that. Everybody knows the poor always being fucked by the rich. Always have, always will."

King in **PLATOON**

He began to relate more to the guys in his platoon. He was an odd one to them. No matter how quiet he was or how much of his personality the new "anonymous" Oliver Stone held in, it was evident that he wasn't like them. "He was never a regular GI Joe," recalls Crutcher Patterson, a former member of Stone's platoon. "He was pretty green, a loner and moody, always writing things. Whenever we got a break, he would stop and write a little descriptive story about it."

Larry Robinson, a friend of Stone's, remembers that Stone liked classical music. "No one else did. He listened to a lot of different music. He listened to The Doors, of course, and the current music as well. But he was fairly quiet. I mean, you wouldn't notice him from any other soldier until you got to know him a bit."

Stone insists he wasn't the odd man out in the platoon. "I did my job and didn't fuck with anybody," he says. "I did carry some books in the field at the beginning. And I tried to take notes and, of course, they all got wet and soaked. So after this happened a few times, I decided I'd better abandon the literary aspect of my life for a while."

As he later showed in *Platoon*, Stone's fellow soldiers more or less fell into one of two camps. "On one side were the lifers, the juicers, and the moron white element," Stone wrote. "On the other side was a progressive, hippie, dope-smoking group—some blacks, some urban whites, Indians, random characters from odd places. This group was out to survive the war with some integrity and a sense of humor. I fell in with them."

Crutcher Patterson turned him on to pot, but they would only smoke it at base camp or when they were sure they weren't going out in the field. None of the guys smoked it in the field because it slowed the senses and quite often, your senses were the thing that kept you alive. "And that stuff," Stone says, "the Vietnamese weed, was so fucking narcotic."

Oliver Stone was becoming more progressive. "The guys I liked best had been around drugs for ages, and I started doing acid and marijuana with them. I also got into the music. I had never heard Motown before then. Or Jefferson Airplane. Or The Doors. It was all part of the Zeitgeist. I was a Yale boy who heard soul music and smoked dope for the first time in his life. I think my soul got out of Vietnam intact because of the blacks and the potheads who turned me on to these things. The times in the field deadened me, but hanging out with them in the bunkers, doing dope and listening to that kind of music, restored me."

Stone may have been primed for rebellion all his life, a teenage time bomb long due to go off, but it was Vietnam, drugs, and rock 'n' roll that at last triggered the timer.

Robinson recalls Stone coming into his own: "I remember he would go along the road and tell stories, entertaining the other guys. He'd tell them what it was like in South America, in Paris, in some of the places he'd been. He was the only one of us that'd been to those kind of places then, and he told really good stories."

Although he grew closer to some of the men, there were others to whom Stone could never relate. Some were juicers and considered him a pothead. Others were so ignorant that they hated his intellect. And some merely hated. But always, waiting a half step outside, was death, the great equalizer. Part of what made Vietnam so insane was that the threat of death came from all sides, even your own. "That's something that is not talked about very much," Stone says, "but it's been estimated that twenty percent, maybe even thirty-five percent of our total casualties in Vietnam were as a result of accidents or people killed by our own side. I tried to show it in *Platoon* in the scenes where artillery was landing on our own troops. I think that first wound in my neck was caused by an American sergeant who threw a grenade. It just gets so confusing."

The longer Stone was in Vietnam, the more futile the war effort began to seem. The soldiers in the front lines realized there was no moral objective and no victory in sight. They would take a hill at great sacrifice of human life and then leave it, only to return two weeks later to take it again. They were risking their lives for nothing. Stone claims this pervasive feeling of hopelessness was the source of the tension that led to so many unnecessary killings, including the fraggings—the killing of American soldiers by men on their own side—which he says were far more widespread than was acknowledged by the government. "It was probably six to ten times more than the official count. The officer corps—not just the officers but especially the top sergeants—were pretty much hated, most of them. I came to hate them because so many of them were fat cats, sitting there getting rich off the PX deals, but very rarely risking their lives. I heard about fraggings while I was there. But some people have suggested that if I really participated in some of the scenes in *Platoon*, I should be tried for war crimes. A pamphlet was sent around UCLA saying that I was a war criminal. So I'm not going to be any more specific. I'll just say that if you kill somebody during a battle, you put your M-16 on somebody and you just do him, nobody's going to see it. Types like General Westmoreland don't want to admit how widespread it was."

As his time in the service wore on, Stone occasionally got R&R, short holidays where servicemen could catch a ride with an outbound transport or supply plane to the nearest ports of civilization, ostensibly for rest and recuperation. Of course, for most of the men, this meant serious partying. Though he'd been exposed at a young age to all sorts of sexual adventure and was well familiar with Saigon whorehouses, Stone was still rather shy about participating in these visits to Asian brothels or weekend flings with girls whose name no one bothered to ask. "I fell in love with this waitress at the Whiskey À Go-Go in Sydney," he recounts. "I went to Sydney a couple of times. She was beautiful in my eyes and she liked me. I couldn't believe anyone would like me. She picked me up and was nice to me. We had an affair for a few days in a hotel. It was my first experience with a woman for more than a few hours. That was great. And then she wrote to me in the States and told me she was pregnant. I sent her some money, eight hundred dollars to get an abortion. I never found out if it was true or not."

Back in the field, things continued to heat up. On the evening of January 1, 1968, Stone was involved in a horrible battle at Firebase Burt. Captain Robert Hemphill, company commander of Bravo, had four platoons under his command, including 2nd Platoon, Stone's outfit. He describes the strength of the firebase that night: "The perimeter was made up by two battalions. We were three kilometers south of the Cambodian border and a dirt road divided the two battalions with us on the east side and the mechanized, infantry unit on the west side. In addition, we brought in three batteries of 105mm artillery and one battery of 155mm. So we had four batteries with twenty pieces of artillery inside the firebase."

A truce had been negotiated at the highest levels of command covering Christmas, New Year's, and Tet, the Lunar New Year, which the Vietnamese celebrate on January 30. "That year we got hit on all three of them," says Hemphill. "The truce for January 1 was from six o'clock at night on December 31 until six at night on January 1. We got word during the day that it was extended for twelve hours until 6:00 A.M. on the 2nd. Afterwards we always said it was only extended so they could hit us."

The firebase was attacked by two full regiments, between 2,000 and 2,500 Viet Cong troops. The initial probe came in from the west but backed off after running up against the mechanized unit's 50-caliber machine guns. This was followed by a two-prong attack from the south. Captain Hemphill describes the situation: "I had 1st Platoon out on an ambush along the road north of the perimeter, and 2nd and 4th were inside the perimeter in reserve. The mortar started coming in somewhere before midnight, around eleven-thirty or so. That was the beginning of it, and then the ground attack started about 1:00 A.M. At about two or two-thirty, Alpha Company collapsed. We got the word to counterattack and restore their perimeter. Stone was in that force to counterattack."

Oliver Stone will never forget that night. "What made it worse was that we were somewhat stoned from getting high the night before," he says. "The stuff was pretty strong, and sometimes you'd be wound so tight that it would hit you even harder because it enabled you to really relax for a change. It was New Year's Eve and there was a cease-fire for the holiday so we figured, what the hell, nobody would hit us then."

The next problem came with 1st Platoon out on ambush to the north. "That's where most of my casualties came from," says Hemphill. "They got surrounded for most of the night."

Larry Robinson was in 1st Platoon, and he remembers the battle well: "It was a big battle. 3rd Platoon was down in their foxholes on the perimeter and they were completely overrun. There was hand-to-hand fighting going on and the Viet Cong took over the bunkers. There was a good depiction in the movie [*Platoon*] of what was happening back in the perimeter. I could hear it from about 350 yards down the road. There were a lot of guys about forty feet in front of us who'd been hit, a lot of dead and dying guys. We were pinned down on all sides, isolated and scared to death. Then Oliver was sent down with another guy, Mike Blotchet, to try to get some of the guys out. You have to understand that a lot of what's going on out there is just self-preservation. There is an awful lot of wishing you were a chameleon so you could change colors and blend in. You get low and keep your head down. Oliver coming up there, knowing full well he was going to encounter fire, took a lot of guts. His odds of dying were pretty good and it meant a lot to us for him to be able to bring some of the guys back alive."

Altogether Firebase Burt only had seven hundred men defending, since several men in each company were on medivac or operating in the rear. Captain Hemphill reports what happened next. "Around this time Charlie Company's portion of the perimeter collapsed," he says. "The mech units were facing outward on the other side so they weren't any help. We were being overrun fast. Then, our reconnaissance platoon was sent by battalion headquarters to counter attack in Charlie's area."

Throughout the night, battalion had been sending in airpower, and this latest attack was accompanied by an extensive air strike. Oliver Stone remembers: "They laid bombs right on top of us. For all I know we could have been bait. You put a small group into a firebase and you bring out the enemy. And then you bomb the shit out of them. Our command was always trying to get them to expose themselves. It would make sense. It was quite a battle though. We took about 25 dead and

175 wounded, and we killed about 500 of them. We buried them in a huge pit, pushing the bodies in with a bulldozer."

Captain Hemphill would not have been privy to any high command strategy, but he doubts that the firebase was used as bait. He does believe the North Vietnamese knew their positions, however. "When it was over we took a sketch map off one of the bodies that showed the plan of attack," Hemphill says. "They had planned to come in on our side away from the mechs. They'd conducted a reconnaissance on us and knew basically where the opposition was."

Stone had his second near-death encounter that night. After coming up to help Robinson's platoon, he was running across an open field when a beehive round went off in his vicinity. Though he wasn't wounded, the force of the explosion carried him a full thirty feet across the field. "I remember being picked up and whooshed through the air," Stone says. "I woke up fifteen to twenty minutes later, totally out of it. Then I stumbled back to the perimeter and I saw firsthand the results of this battle."

The conflict, called the Battle of Firebase Burt, lasted until after daylight. "When it was over, we buried over five hundred bodies," Hemphill confirms.

"Death? What do you all know about Death?"

Sergeant Barnes in **PLATOON**

As time wore on, Stone began to conquer a worse enemy than fear—the ongoing grind, the wear on the psyche caused by the constant battles with heat, jungle rot, insects, and fatigue. According to some vets, this is what did most guys in. They couldn't take it, and they'd get careless. Then they'd die. "It was very rough in the field," Stone confirms. "People would look for excuses to get out of combat all the time. A lot of guys used to spray mosquito repellent on their feet to make them sore so they couldn't walk. The hospitals had a very tough attitude about everything, too. It was get them in and get them out as quick as possible. My time in Vietnam, the way I remember it, is one of really not sleeping for almost a year. It's an amazing fucking thing . . . you sleep on the edge of your nerves. You have to be able to wake up right away and so you don't relax. You become very attuned; you develop your own sort of radar. They're in front of you, they're behind you—you're into action and reaction. That's the key."

Captain Hemphill describes the startling contrasts that made up much of the Vietnam experience. "Combat can be the dullest thing in the world, suddenly punctuated by incredibly intense pressure," he says. "You can go a month or two without finding anything and then, all of a sudden, two regiments attack you."

This time there wasn't much waiting. Bravo Company got hit again hard on January 15, 1968, just two weeks after the battle at Firebase Burt. The company was patrolling in the jungle in the early afternoon about seven kilometers away from the firebase. Third Platoon was on point, scouting out the area about 300 meters in front of the rest of the company, when they walked into a large Viet Cong bunker complex and came under intense fire. Two men were killed, several were wounded, and the rest were pinned down. The VC were firing RPGs into the area and Hemphill ordered 1st Platoon up to help the 3rd.

As so often occurs in the confusion of combat, 1st Platoon made a key error in judgment when they moved in at the wrong angle. Instead of coming around to the side, they cut in front of the bunkers, where they too came under heavy fire. The platoon leader, the platoon sergeant, and one of the squad leaders were killed, and several others were badly wounded. Hemphill then moved 4th Platoon up to form a small perimeter behind the men who were pinned down, while 2nd Platoon went up to evacuate the other two platoons and help the wounded.

Larry Robinson of 1st Platoon remembers what happened next. "Oliver saved my life," he says. "All hell broke loose. Our platoon was pinned down and most of the guys were dead or wounded. Out of twenty-four guys, I would say at least twenty were down. I was hit, hiding behind an anthill. For about two hours we just listened to the Viet Cong jabbering, plotting and scheming, and we kept wondering when they were going to jump out of their foxholes and finish us off. Then Oliver came running up. They'd been close by in the jungle, but it was so thick they couldn't find us. We couldn't talk to them on the radio because all the officers and sergeants had been killed, so there wasn't anyone with a radio. One of our guys said, 'Shoot your rifle, Robinson, and they'll hear it.' My rifle had been hit by a bullet and part of the mechanism was exposed, but I shot it anyway and it went off, and up came Oliver with about seven other guys. I said, 'Be careful,' and they said, 'Oh, we'll go get 'em,' and they jumped over the anthill I was hiding behind. They weren't very careful and they ran right into a tripwire the VC had rigged. Three of them were wounded, including Oliver."

According to Stone, this battle was also the basis for a scene in *Platoon*. "It was a jungle ambush, like the one that gets Elias," he says. "We took about thirty casualties and I don't think we got one of them."

"All I know is Stone saved me," Robinson says. "That took the heat off us. They tried to help us and they ended up getting pretty messed up themselves and wound up crawling back until someone else came for them. But Oliver would do things like that if called upon, things like that to help others out. He was a good soldier."

This time Stone was wounded with shrapnel in his leg and behind. "The guy next to me popped a satchel charge, a wire," he recalls. "We felt it go and I knew the amount of time we had and I ran like hell. Then something weird happened. It was like the hand of Fate or something. I think I could have hit the ground and probably not gotten wounded. I'm a pretty good athlete and I think I could have avoided that hit, but for some reason, I just stood up. It was like somewhere in the back of my head, I knew we were in for it. And I took the hit and was swept off the ground. I remember lying there and the first thing I did was reach for my testicles. Then, once I knew that they were still there, I suddenly felt happy. It was weird, almost like I was happy to get wounded. They morphined me and put me in the helicopter. It was like the end of *Platoon*. And fifteen days later the Tet Offensive hit while I was in the hospital. The 25th Infantry was really slaughtered in that fight and a lot of guys in my platoon were hurt. By the time I returned there was hardly anybody there I recognized."

The Tet Offensive, the North Vietnamese surprise attack on January 30, 1968, inflicted the worst American casualties of the war. Having received his second wound, Stone was transferred out of the field to an MP Auxiliary Battalion whose main function was guarding the installations in Saigon. By that point, he was a veteran who knew his way around the jungle and had seen combat. He had also become something of a rebellious, defiant kid and he hated being in the rear, spit-polishing his boots. He found guarding the barracks "the most boring job in the world" and he couldn't stand the attitude of the lifers, the rear guard. His notions of romanticism and patriotism were vastly diminished and, like so many others, his objective became counting the days until he could get back to the real world. "I started smoking a lot of pot because it blurs the consciousness and I didn't want to know what was going on any more," Stone says. "Then I got into a fight with this lifer sergeant and he wanted to court-martial me for insubordination—article 15— and I said, 'Let's make a deal.' They might have extended my time in 'Nam and I wanted to get out, so I said, 'Let me go back to the combat zone and you drop the charges.' And he did it."

Around this time, Stone went on another R&R excursion where he met with his father who, naturally, had been very worried about his son ever since he enlisted. "Oliver's father really loved him deeply," Roger Kirby remembers. "When Oliver was in the military, his father went off to someplace in Hong Kong just to basically visit with Oliver. He was very fearful that Oliver might not come back from Vietnam."

In fact, Lou Stone used his connections in the military and government to try to get his son transferred out of combat action. Yet, seeing the way Oliver had already changed since he'd gone off to war, he was not terribly surprised when his son said he did not want to be excused from combat. On the contrary, he wanted back in. A letter to Lou Stone from the Treasury Department of the American Consulate in Hong Kong dated June 6, 1968, states that after being contacted by the CIA with an offer of noncombat duty, Oliver Stone was "looking forward to his transfer to the 1st Cavalry Division to complete his tour of duty in combat."

"The truth was, I missed combat," Stone admits. "I missed the adrenaline rush. But, more than that, I just wanted to see if I could do a better job of it than I had done the first two times."

Stone got his wish. He was transferred to 1st Cavalry and assigned to a Long Range Reconnaissance Platoon (LURP) in April 1968. "The LURP units are highly trained specialized units," Stone says. "They drop small groups of four or five guys deep into enemy territory and you recon with binoculars. Then you get the fuck out. You don't fight, you recon."

It was here that Stone met Juan Angel Elias, the basis for the character of Elias in *Platoon*. "He was about twenty-three, part Spanish and part Apache," Stone recalls. "He was handsome, electric. Everything we were later going to recognize in Jim Morrison, Elias had. He was like a rock star in the body of a soldier. Real danger turned him on."

Elias was a sergeant and a man of compassion who believed in inspiring his men rather than terrifying them. "Everybody seemed to love him except for the lifers and the juicers," Stone wrote in his notes for *Platoon*. "Especially the guys making profits from rear-echelon deals on beer and PX supplies, screwing over the grunts who were doing the actual fighting. These guys were the trash of Vietnam as far as I was concerned. They were the cancer on the balls with which we tried to fight."

Stone clashed repeatedly with the rear-echelon mentality, and to this day admits he tends to be a bit prejudiced toward those who served in that capacity. The soldiers who went to war and didn't fight are far worse to him than the protesters who stayed home and refused to fight. "I know not everyone in the rear participated," Stone says, "but so many were selling contraband from the PX and partying with tax-free booze . . . some of these guys lived like kings off our rations. People like Elias pissed them off a whole lot more because he smoked dope and didn't care if they knew. And in 1968, they all thought pot was for faggots, hippies, and Black Panthers. They hated him."

But it was Elias's compassion which inspired Stone to believe that a person could be a good soldier and a decent human being, that one didn't have to totally throw away one's moral standards in order to survive. That there could be dignity on the battlefield as well as valor.

"Fucking guy's got three years in and he thinks he's Jesus Fucking Christ or something."

Corporal O'Neill, speaking of Elias in **PLATOON**

It was Elias who taught Stone to be a better soldier. The key for Stone was submerging his intellect and learning to trust his senses. "You have to live off your senses," he wrote. "You listen, you smell, and you see. You feel, you taste. That's how you survive. You don't survive by being a cerebral person as an infantry man. That's the art of war. The House of Mars requires alert radar, skill, cunning. A sixth sense about things."

It was also in 1st Cavalry that Stone met Ben Fitzgerald, who is depicted in *Platoon* as King. "Oliver was actually in 1st Cav. when I arrived," Fitzgerald says. "We got a lot of action. Our mission was usually to go out and find the enemy and then pull back, but finding them was never a problem and I don't remember a time when we got to pull back."

Fitzgerald recalls another of the platoon's regular activities—mine sweeps. "We'd clear the roads and make sure there were no mines. Sometimes we'd use a magnet to find them and sometimes we'd just do it by sight because after a while you learn to tell where it's been dug. Conditions were usually real miserable. Just terrible. There was a picture of the group of us together in *People* magazine and it showed it pretty well. The picture was taken right after we had come off the hill and had spent a week up there." (See photo section)

Fitzgerald says that Elias's platoon usually encountered small numbers of North Vietnamese Army (NVA) soldiers and occasionally ran into a few Viet Cong out on patrol. But in August 1968, at South China Beach, the platoon was caught off guard by a major force of NVA troops. "It was somewhat of a surprise," Fitzgerald recalls, "because it was after a cease-fire had been called. When we went out, they told us that there were about seven or eight NVAs in the area. Then we got in and found out there were hundreds of them."

Facing a force that later proved to be composed of well over six hundred North Vietnamese troops, the platoon radioed for backup. "We called in and tried to pull back, but we had to wait," Fitzgerald remembers. "We couldn't get out. They were everywhere."

The platoon took cover, only to find that an NVA soldier with an automatic weapon was hiding in a foxhole in their midst. He fired a few rounds at them, trying to trick them into a crossfire as they couldn't shoot back without endangering their own men on the other side of the foxhole. Suddenly Stone sprang to action and charged the foxhole. "I flipped out," he says. "I took off running and lobbed a grenade toward it while on the run. The truth is that was foolish, as there was a very slim chance it would actually land in the hole, but it did and people started calling me a hero. I just lost it, that's all. It was very close to the way I felt when I couldn't react during my first firefight, only this time I reacted. But it wasn't conscious either time, just a freezing up and no reaction one time, and a reaction the other time. I think fear and courage are different facets of the same emotion."

In any event, Stone's action may have saved the lives of several men, and he was later awarded a Bronze Star for combat gallantry. "Oliver was real good under fire," Ben Fitzgerald says. "He was calm and took care of himself and tried to take care of others. He was a good soldier."

Stone's action bought the platoon a little more time, during which help arrived. Fitzgerald elaborates: "Operations called in some more troops and they were able to get Marines and Navy people because it was right near the beach. So the Marines came up, the Navy was out, and we kind of surrounded the area. They had nowhere to go. The battle lasted three days, I think. In the end they had something like two hundred and eighty killed and three hundred captured."

Stone had accomplished his goal. Though he'd been wounded twice in battle before, the real test was keeping his head under fire. Maybe even more than that, it was honing his senses down to a fine art, developing an animal-like instinct: "I don't think I was a particularly strong soldier at the beginning," Stone says. "I was like Charlie Sheen in *Platoon*. I did learn, though. I was a better soldier after I went back into the 1st Cavalry. I wasn't great, but I was better, more attuned to the jungle. I got into it heavy. The smell, the look, the feel. Once, when I was on point with a full pack, carrying sixty pounds, with a machete, I walked right up on a deer without him knowing I was there until I was very close. I'd become like part of the jungle."

The things Ben Fitzgerald remembers most about Oliver Stone had to do with the quiet times the platoon would spend together back in camp. "We just about had to get along since we were so close together," Fitzgerald says, "and didn't ever know who would be there the next day. We sat around and talked and smoked quite a bit of marijuana."

Though he was a seasoned soldier by now, Stone still had his oddities. "I remember his poetry," Fitzgerald says. "He wrote one particular poem that started off from the time when he was in the 25th Infantry and went up to when he was in the 1st Cavalry. It was really interesting. I liked the way he described everything. I wish he'd kept that, I'd like to have a copy."

As they'd come to know Stone, the others in the platoon would discover his background and the fact that he had volunteered and requested the infantry in Vietnam in order to experience another side of life. "Yeah, we all thought that was a little strange," Fitzgerald says. "But everyone liked him anyway."

Well, not everyone. Stone continued to have problems with some of the lifers: "I got busted again by another lifer sergeant for my attitude and they transferred me out of the Recon unit. I'd seen a lot more combat than most of the LURP guys and I guess I just didn't fit the mold they wanted for a LURP. They sent me across the road to a motorized infantry 1st Cav unit, driving Jeeps, APCs, and a lot of helicopter work."

It was here that Stone met Platoon Sergeant Barnes. Immortalized by Tom Berenger's riveting performance as the scarred and ruthless killer in *Platoon*, few people realize that the man really existed. "Barnes had this cold stare that used to really terrify me," Stone wrote in his script notes for *Platoon*. "He was an incredible soldier. He'd been wounded some six or seven times, yet he always survived. I was his radio guy for a while so I was right behind him. We used to hunt 'gooks' at dawn. One time Barns smelled something cooking and we snuck up on two guys having their breakfast and he killed them before the fishheads hit their lips. They died surprised."

Much of the terror Barnes inspired came from a large sickle-shaped scar that ran down the whole left side of his face. "He once was shot right above the left eye," Stone wrote. "The bullet somehow lodged in his head and after a year in a hospital in Japan, he had this huge scar, all layered with grafted skin from above his eye to his lower jaw. I used to think anything so massive had to have caused considerable damage to his brain. Especially, since when he got out of the hospital he came back to the Nam by his own choice. I think he wanted to get even— either with the gooks or, if they weren't around, with us. When Barnes looked you in the eye, you felt it all the way down to your balls."

But according to Stone's notes, Barnes wasn't completely repulsive. In fact he had a strangely alluring quality to him. "He was kind of fascinating in a way. I mean, he was usually very quiet, he never talked about his wounds or anything. I found out he was married to a Japanese girl he'd met in the hospital, but he never talked about that either. He'd get drunk at poker and occasionally crack a country smile, but he'd never let you in. His only vulnerability was the scar."

"You smoke this shit so's you can escape from reality? . . . Me I don't need that shit. I am reality."

Sergeant Barnes in **PLATOON**

Barnes was a survivor, and those who clung to him seemed to survive as well. If Elias had taught Stone how to use his instincts, Barnes taught him how to hone them into a well-oiled machine. "In Vietnam I had to come to terms with the negative aspects of being a cerebral person. I had to learn to set aside any doubts. The kid in *Platoon* writes these letters in the beginning, but as the movie goes on, his voice-over drops off, because as a soldier surviving in the field you don't think or write down that much. It's easier to survive in the Barnes mode. The machine. You are part of a machine and the machine works."

As Stone steeled himself more and more into controlled reflex and perfected instinct, he discovered that he began to almost enjoy combat, especially the high associated with such intense bursts of activity. "It's probably the greatest high mankind knows," he wrote in his notes. "There's something about it . . . the adrenaline goes and time just shortens . . . every second becomes heightened like a Hitchcock movie in slow motion. It becomes very vivid and intense. It's still with me. You never forget those moments. They're burned into my head forever."

Hand in hand with this insanity, and born out of the same frustrations, came increasing incidents of inhumanity. Stone had arrived a sensitive onlooker, but to survive he had to become cold and unfeeling. In hamlets near the Cambodian border, he repeatedly witnessed sudden outbursts of rage against innocent villagers who happened to be in the wrong place at the wrong time, victims of the futility that the continual heat, mosquitoes, lack of sleep, and constant threat of death provoked.

Though initially outraged, as the war wore on, Stone's own sense of right and wrong began to erode. "We burned the villages, we did a lot of damage," he admits. "Not on the My Lai scale, but we did it on a steady basis. It was random. We'd be pissed off on certain days. We'd walk up to a village and an old gook lady would be going down the trail. One of the guys would be pissed off and he'd say, 'Hey, gook, come here.' She wouldn't hear or else wouldn't turn around because she was scared and just kept walking for a few more steps. The guy wouldn't even ask her a second time. He'd just raise the fucking '16—*boom, boom, boom*—dead. No questions asked. Just because she hadn't come when he told her to."

Much of this kind of random violence sprang out of racist attitudes. "A lot of the guys had the attitude that 'The only good gook is a dead gook,'" Stone says, "and that meant women and kids, too."

Many of the scenes Stone witnessed were later shown in *Platoon*. The man that the Bunny character (played by Kevin Dillon) was modeled after really killed a woman. "He hit her with the butt of his M-16 and burned her hooch down," says Stone. "But it was in an isolated part of the village. Nobody saw it. He clubbed this old lady to death and then he kind of boasted about it. We killed innocents. It was never planned, nothing preordained or ordered, but it happened."

"The village, which had stood for maybe a thousand years, didn't know we were coming that day. If they had they would have run. . . . Barnes was at the eye of our rage—and through him, our Captain Ahab—we would set things right again. That day we loved him."

Chris Taylor
Narration from **PLATOON**

Stone's worst personal experience with this kind of violence, the time he lost control in a village, was also portrayed in the film: "The bunkers used to make us all nervous because you never knew what the fuck was down there. You'd yell, 'Get the fuck out! Get out!' And you'd find weapons and arms and rice stores for the Viet Cong in there. Anything could happen. That was where I lost it and began firing at this old man's feet. I hated this guy. I told him to get out of the hole. He wouldn't get out and he wouldn't stop smiling. I just got pissed off and lost it. I made him dance. I just wanted to scare him to the verge of dying. Actually, I wanted to kill him, but I couldn't quite cross that barrier. I almost blew him away. I could have gotten away with it. I could have killed him and nobody would have busted me. I'm so glad I didn't, now. I felt sorry for the civilians because I could see they were getting pressure from the other side. They were just into survival, like we were."

There was a down side to the Barnes method of survival: as time wore on, Stone felt his sensitivities begin to fade. He wasn't afraid of death, but he no longer cared about life. He was closing off the world and focusing inward, not caring whom he hurt or what he destroyed. While he was aware that his humanity was slipping away, Stone seemed unable to stop the process. The turning point came one day when he came upon a village girl being raped by two American soldiers. "I think they would've killed her," Stone says now. "Something in me snapped and I went over and broke it up. They weren't too happy about it, but when I saw them and saw how afraid she was, I had to do something about it, so I made them let her go."

This step toward rationality and basic human decency soon led to others. Stone realized that the price of his insensitivity was the diminishing of his creative passion. He might have had to ignore this part of himself to survive in Vietnam, but he had gone beyond that. He was choking it to death. There, amid the madness of chaos and sudden death, he resolved that he would never let this part of him come so close to dying again, no matter how much pain it might cost him.

Fittingly, as he became more convinced of the need for sensitivity in his life, Stone began to notice the beauty of Vietnam. He began to cultivate an appreciation of the world around him in an effort to stave off the eradication of his human qualities. He even bought a 35-millimeter Pentax and began shooting some of the scenes around him. "I was just starting to use my eyes, my visual sense," Stone says. "There were so many images. Being on the 'Street without Joy' [the rue sans Joie] with all those cathedrals and Buddhist temples, the old ruins just there in the jungle. Chasing the enemy there, the pit vipers, the bamboo, the villagers. They were seminal images for me. I'd never been into photography, but I got some great shots the last three months I was there. Those months were fairly calm in the 1st Cavalry Division. We were up in the Ashau Valley, we worked Hué, we worked the beaches, we were at Camp Evans. So it was a time of many pictures, rolls and rolls. When they didn't get wet, they came out beautiful. I started to tell stories through pictures more than writing. I'd always been a writer before, but I started to visualize the Vietnam War."

This proved to be a key development in Stone's decision to become a film director. "Photography was the bridge," he says now. "You couldn't write in Vietnam because you couldn't keep the paper from getting damaged, so I turned to photography and that triggered something. There is an interior process to writing that you don't get in directing. The director takes all the various internal processes and somehow unites them and makes them exterior."

Stone completed his tour of duty and was discharged in late November 1968. After fifteen months he left Vietnam with a Purple Heart with Oak Leaf Cluster, signifying the multiple awards of the medal for the two times he was wounded; a Bronze Star for combat gallantry; and lots of painful memories that wouldn't go away. Just before shipping out, he received a final blow. Juan Angel Elias had been killed. "They said one of our grenades went off and killed him," Stone recalls. "He died on a hill in the Ashau. It never seemed right to me. Elias was too smart to go like that. Maybe one of the guys that hated him did him in. I never found out, but it broke my heart when I heard he was gone."

For all the horrors of his season in Hell, Stone had somehow gotten what he came for. He had shattered the aristocratic business life laid out for him by his father. His parents would no longer be able to shape him, for he had broken the mold. "I saw combat at the ground level," Stone wrote in his notes of that period. "I saw people die. I killed. I almost was killed. Almost immediately I realized that combat is totally random. Life is a matter of luck or destiny, take your pick. Two soldiers are standing two feet apart: one gets killed, the other lives. I was never a religious person, but I became spiritual in Vietnam. Organized religion is for people who fear Hell, but true spirituality is for people who've been to Hell. Possibly, I was saved for a reason. To do something. To write about the experience, maybe. To make a movie about it."

"The war is over for me now, but it will always be there the rest of my days. As I am sure Elias will be—fighting with Barnes for what Rhah called possession of my soul. There are times since I have felt like the child born of those two fathers."

Chris Taylor in **PLATOON**

CHAPTER THREE

The Fire Inside

"Pain makes me feel more alive. Pain is meant to wake us up. People try to hide their pain, but they're wrong—your feelings are a part of you. If you feel ashamed of them, you're letting society destroy your reality. We've got to fully experience *all* our feelings. . . ."

Jim Morrison in **THE DOORS**

Stone returned to the United States in late November 1968, part of the legions of walking wounded now regularly being exchanged for malleable fresh-faced recruits. But Vietnam, for all its embittering savagery and frustrating ambiguity, had proven that there was something beyond money and women and power in life. He had glimpsed it, hovering at the edge of death countless times—a sense of purpose, a reason to live beyond life itself. He'd found it once, when he was writing his novel. Now he knew he needed to find it again.

The Oliver Stone who stepped off the boat at the Army release station in Fort Lewis, Washington, was alienated and angry. He was smoking marijuana and doing acid whenever he could get it. He decided to use the name Oliver again, burying Bill Stone in Vietnam with a lot of memories he sought to leave behind. Still, he wasn't yet ready for America. The thought of returning to his disjointed family in New York was too much for him. Instead, in a strange reenactment of the journey he'd taken when he returned to the United States from Vietnam via the Merchant Marine, Stone meandered down the coast, stopping in San Francisco, Santa Cruz, Los Angeles, San Diego, and Tijuana, without even bothering to call and tell his parents he was back. He was restless, and getting high off the marijuana he'd smuggled out of Vietnam was not helping much. A few days in Mexico were enough, and he decided to go back to the States. He should've left the grass behind.

Busted at the border with two ounces of Vietnamese pot, Stone was tossed into a San Diego jail on a federal charge of smuggling, which carried a five-to twenty-year sentence. He was not even allowed to make a phonecall. "That San Diego jail was a shithole," he recalls. "It seemed so immense. It seemed like there were twelve thousand inmates and beds for only five thousand. Most of us slept on the floor. Inmates in every fucking nook and cranny. Chicanos, blacks, white kids. There was little time for due process, and the Legal Aid guy would never show up."

The experience seemed to confirm the disillusionment Stone was feeling about America. He was a vet just returned from combat in Vietnam who'd been thrown in jail, and America didn't seem to care. There was no fanfare or ticker-tape parade for these vets, no sense of victory. It wasn't even considered a real war. "It was Amerika with a 'k,'" Stone says. "I thought, 'So that's the way they treat the vets?' It took some guys a long time, but I got the picture right away. I hated America at that point, I would have joined the Black Panthers if they'd asked me. I was a radical, ready to kill."

It was here, in a San Diego jail, that Stone first came to know the side of his generation that didn't go to war. In some ways, this experience was as significant as his time in Vietnam. In jail, as in 'Nam, the pot smokers tended to hang together. Many of them were intelligent; some were radicals, out to change society. Others were hippies who just wanted to be left alone. Most of them were poor. They told him about the war at home. And they also told him his chances of getting out were not as good as he thought. "The word was that if you went up on a Tuesday or Thursday, you'd get the lenient judge, and he'd give you a suspended sentence," Stone recalls. "But if you went up the other three days, you'd get the hard-case judge and he'd give you five years minimum."

After nearly two weeks in jail, Stone was becoming desperate. It was clear the public defender was never going to get around to seeing him. He had slipped several notes to the guards pleading to be allowed to make a phonecall, to no avail. Finally, they came for him and took him to a phone. "They could've and probably would've kept me in six months," he says. "So I called my father and he said, 'Where have you been?'"

Stone had been out of Vietnam now for almost three weeks and his father was truly worried. Their conversation went something like this. "'Dad . . . I have to tell you something. I'm out of Vietnam, but I'm in jail facing five to twenty years on a federal charge for smuggling marijuana.' The reaction was a long pause followed by 'Shit! I knew something like this would happen.'"

Stone's father contacted the public defender, who showed up that very afternoon. "He was beaming, rolling his hands," Stone remembers. "He loved me. I showed that scene in *Midnight Express*—the lawyer who's really happy because he suddenly realizes I'm somebody who has money. And he did get me out, thank God. It became a non-event. The charges were dismissed in the interest of justice and there was no record."

The public defender billed Stone's father $2,500, a sizable sum for the time. He put Stone in a San Diego hotel and told him to "stay clean" for a week while he got the files eradicated. Afterwards, Stone was put on a plane for New York. Though he was relieved to get out of jail, Stone was faced with the bleak prospect of returning home to his father's apartment. "It was a pretty embarrassing compromise. I had sort of gotten my independence by going to Vietnam and then, for the second time, I had to come back to this country and be reduced to being a child again."

As expected, Stone and his father clashed almost immediately: "He was horrified. I was dirty. I was speaking black talk; 'Hey man, what's happening?' and 'Cool.' I was smoking grass and he hated that I looked like a bum. My hair was long. I didn't have a college education. I was coming back from the war and had just been in jail. What could I do? I had no skills."

Though he wouldn't have admitted it at the time, Stone had hoped his war experience would meet with his father's approval, that this man who had talked so much about his time in the big war under Eisenhower might now be better able to accept his son's independence and coming of age as a man. Such was not the case. Stone had returned damaged and shocked from the war, but his father's attitude was one of casual dismissal, as if to say, "Well, that wasn't even a war. That was just a police action. I was in the real war."

Things were not much better at his mother's, as Stone's old friend, Roger Kirby, recalls: "When Oliver came back, he wanted only to talk about Vietnam. He had some tapes of conversations with one of the guys who later was a character in *Platoon*. Oliver's mother arranged a little dinner party for him with all these elegant, well-dressed friends of hers, and my impression was they expected more than Oliver was capable of socially at that time. The idea was certainly laudable, but it put some pressure on him. He was definitely not in that sort of world."

Indeed, Stone was having trouble letting go of Vietnam. Much of his difficulty in readjusting was caused by the culture shock of returning to an America where the war was simply not a life or death issue. "It was an enormous shock," he admits. "Nobody was fighting the war. The problem wasn't the hippies or the protesters. They were a very small group. It was the mass indifference. Nobody cared. That was what hurt. People were going about the business of making money. The whole problem with Vietnam was that Johnson never made it a war. Either you go to war or you don't go to war. You just don't send poor kids and draftees and let the college kids stay in college. That divides the country."

By now the country was beginning to get tired of hearing about Vietnam. Unless they were directly affected, most people had seen enough of the war to last them a lifetime. It covered their newspapers and bombarded their living rooms on a regular basis. It was at his father's apartment that this attitude was the most painful, as part of the ongoing battle between father and son. But the real issue was authority. At the heart of their bitter arguments was whether youth had the right to question their elders—in the streets of Berkeley, Chicago, or Washington, or in Lou Stone's apartment on 55th Street. "Dad and I had tremendous battles," Oliver Stone recalls. "I just wanted to destroy him. It culminated one night when I gave him LSD. I wanted to shake his head up and I put it in his drink. After a while he said he felt strange, 'like something was in me.' And then I laughed. There were eleven or twelve of us at that dinner and I said, 'Someone must have slipped you something . . . it sounds like acid, somebody must have put it in your drink.' He said, 'You did. You're the Judas.' And later on he was hanging on to a tree in the garden for dear life. He drank milk and ate cookies to calm down. The next day he told me most of his fantasies were about African women and drums.

"But he was cool about it," Stone hurries to add. "He didn't take it out on me. He found it interesting. Years later he would still refer to it. He had a good sense of humor, Dad did. He was a very bright man, with emotional problems like we all have, and the limitations of his era. I think he was really a liberal trying to get out of a conservative skin. He struggled with that dichotomy."

Unsure of what he wanted to do, Stone found himself living day by day. He didn't want to go back to writing, as the rejection of his first effort was still painful, but he wasn't sure he was ready for anything else. So he began keeping a journal with great diligence, writing about the day's activities and his impressions of life each night. The diary soon became a significant discipline in his life and something he has done on and off ever since for over twenty-five years. Eventually, Stone moved out of his father's place and into an apartment in the East Village, between Avenues A and B. He continued doing drugs, especially smoking pot, essentially remaining so stoned that he didn't mind living in the broken-down tenement.

"I was doing grass on a daily basis, getting really high," Stone admits. "I would do acid just about anywhere, in the subway, in restaurants. I didn't care if it was in a soothing environment. I'd do it just for the rush. I had some volatile trips, bad ones, but I kept doing it. I didn't know any vets around New York. My vet friends all went back to small towns. They'd write about being unemployed and on drugs and alcohol. It was depressing. I didn't have a network to fall back on." Stone was nearly destitute at the time, and these were austere and impoverished surroundings, but they were his and he answered to no one.

Anthony Pompei was living with Jacqueline Stone when Oliver came back from Vietnam. Pompei describes the changes in Stone: "Before Vietnam, he was an ethereal, very soft-spoken young man. Perfectly mannered. He sounded the way he does today sometimes when he makes speeches. After he came back, he was harsher. He was still an observer, though. We went to see Timothy Leary at the Fillmore East after he got back and Oliver was intently watching it, taking everything in . . . looking at the audience, watching their reactions. After he came back, he started to get more serious. He had been this half man, half boy, and then all of a sudden he became all man. I realized he was coming into his own."

But Stone's independence had cost him. No longer did he have the comfort or security of his father's apartment. "I was robbed three times," he says. "The first time I had a knife stuck in my gut in the hallway. I wanted to kill him. Fucking guy sticks a knife in my stomach and says, 'Gimme your money.' I got frightened because I knew either he'd die or I'd die, but because I was a vet I knew the meaning of death and he didn't. I glared at him and he saw the look in my eyes and figured I was pretty screwed up, and he got a little scared. I just backed away, eyeing him. He never followed me. But then I got robbed a couple of other times when some one broke into my windows. It was nerveracking."

"Sometimes you know I think people . . . they know you're back from Vietnam, their face changes . . . the eyes, the voice . . . the way they look at you."
Ron Kovic in **BORN ON THE FOURTH OF JULY**

It was around this time that Stone realized he would have no peace until he wrote about his experience in Vietnam. One day he returned to his apartment and painted his room blood red from floor to ceiling. He started wearing all black and listening incessantly to Jim Morrison; dropping acid, playing "The End" over and over, thinking about Vietnam. His recent fascination with visual images and his earlier rejection by the book world led him to attempt a new medium, the screenplay. "One of the first things I did when I got back to the States was borrow a Super 8 camera and start making home movies. I found I really liked telling stories through film and also thinking about screenplays, and trying to marry the two. I wrote *Break*, my first screenplay, in the first month or two I was back—fresh from the heat of war, wanting to get this surrealistic vision down. The hero falls in love with this lady from the forest who's like Dionysius or something out of *Hair*. She's leading the tribe against the American soldiers, and he comes under her sway and deserts to join her group. Then he dies and goes to the Egyptian underworld where Osiris judges him. He ends up in prison, back in the States where I ended up, and where he's dreaming all this. He wakes up in prison and then goes back into the dream and has a sort of homosexual liaison with the Elias character, who is also in prison. Then he escapes in the dream, a sort of massive breakout from our society."

At first look this story may sound like a far cry from Stone's Vietnam experience, but he claims it's there in symbols and imagery. With the painful memories so fresh in his mind, the only way Stone could process the experience artistically was through surrealism. By creating a new world in which to play out his war scenarios, Stone diluted some of the pain the writing would have caused. "I couldn't yet deal with Vietnam," Stone says now. "I had to maintain my life apart from the writing somehow, otherwise I'd crash and die. There was just too much chaos. Even with *Platoon*, which I wrote seven years later, I was struggling with the chaos of the event."

Break is ripe with fascinating imagery and contains the roots of many projects that Stone would create later, especially *Platoon*. The script is filled with the characters who would form the heart of *Platoon*— Rhah, King, Bunny, Lehner, Barnes, and Elias—and many have the same names (with the exception of Elias and Barnes, here called Isaac and Lee, perhaps because of the acute pain their memories summoned within Oliver Stone in 1969). At one point, when Anthony, the lead character, is in prison, he has a strange interlude with another prisoner who reminds him of Isaac (Elias). Though nothing overtly sexual happens here, there are clear homosexual overtones in the way the man comforts Anthony. More than anything, the scene reflects Stone's own confusion over his genuine love for Elias, a man who saved his life by the knowledge he passed on to him and his soul by the sharing of his heart in a place where there was no heart. It appears that Stone wants to admit his love for Elias as being more than the macho bond of buddies in combat, but he is thwarted in that attempt by his confusing memories of the endless stream of homosexuals who passed through his mother's villa. His macho side is revolted at the sexual connotations, but his poetic side seeks something more than the unfulfilling male friendships he has experienced all his life. It is as if he was seeking the vulnerability of unaffected, sincere male kinship, but because his adolescent experiences both stifled and intensified his sexuality, he was not able clearly to separate the two. To a degree, these attitudes still affect Stone today—he gets along great with men, but finds it difficult to trust them for very long, and many of his friendships end abruptly before they become threatening.

Break contains many other biographical touches, such as when Anthony throws his poems into the river before departing for the Eastern wars, much as Stone tossed the manuscript of his novel into the Hudson before he went to Vietnam (other examples can be found in Appendix I). Many involve bizarre images that center on Anthony's parents—his withdrawn father, whose apartment seems to be a haven for seductive women, and his disinterested mother, whom he pictures as a harlot one moment and a virgin the next. Such images appear to be scars from Stone's subconscious, the residue of viewing his heritage as changing from wealthy and honorable to fearful and degenerate. Anthony Darnell is a product of Stone's childhood, suspicious and wary, and always afraid that behind each door is a new family secret more decadent than the last.

Not only did the script call for the music of The Doors through much of the film, but Stone's choice for the lead role was none other than Jim Morrison himself. He made several attempts to get *Break* to Morrison, but had no way of knowing if the rock star ever saw it. Stone also circulated the screenplay among his mother's friends and connections; though it generated some excitement from the hipper New York crowd, the film was never financed. "I feel it could have been a breakthrough movie, especially in 1968," Stone says now. "It contained *Apocalypse Now*-type surrealism. But *Break* sort of had its own life. Once I took the surrealistic path, it reached its own end."

Ultimately, the script's melodramatic symbolism takes away from the natural impact of the story. *Break*, though bizarre, is not nearly as powerful as *Platoon* would later be.

After completing *Break*, Stone moved to a slightly better apartment on Houston Street, right below Canal and near Little Italy. He was out of junkie city, but still so impoverished that he couldn't afford to fix the broken windows in his new apartment and at times the snow would drift into his bedroom.

What *Break* did more than anything else was lead Stone to apply to New York University's Film School. While waiting to start classes on the G.I. Bill, he wrote a second screenplay, entitled *Dominique: The Loves of a Woman*. "It was based on my mother and her trip in New York," Stone says. "I had really loved [Fellini's] *Juliet of the Spirits*, and I was trying to get that exuberance."

Dominique captures Jacqueline Stone's relentless gaiety as well as her persistent sorrows. The screenplay accurately depicts the madness of the New York art crowd in the mid-sixties. Here are up-close portraits of people who view life as a deep void that must be filled to the brim daily, and who will go to almost any extreme to do it. They have sacrificed love for sex, purpose for parties, and reality for escape. They are at the same time charming and horrifying. They have more friends than anyone, but they are the loneliest people in the world.

Dominique gives evidence of Stone's increased skills as a writer, especially in the area of character development. Most of Stone's works have elements of comic relief to soften the tension, and his comedic talent begins to surface in this script (see Appendix I).

Dominique, like all Stone's work, reveals much about himself. It accurately depicts the candid relationship he shared with his mother after his parents' divorce. There is also a scene which hints at the kind of sexual activity Stone might have been exposed to as a child. While attending a party at the house where she and her husband used to live, Dominique and a woman who is about to become her lesbian lover search for privacy and enter a room where a little boy, the host couple's son, sits in his pajamas. The boy complains that his model car is missing a wheel and asks the women to help him. The other woman becomes impatient, but Dominique helps him find the wheel and then hugs him, whereupon the script reads: "CAMERA CLOSE on DOMINIQUE hugging the little BOY close to her, as if it were her own child." She then leaves to make love with the lesbian.

Through his screenplays, Stone was finding a renewed interest in life. Entering the NYU Film School allowed him a somewhat unstructured way to rejoin society. Learning how to channel artistic passion into the functional craft of making movies gave him a much-needed release. He began with only a few classes in April 1969, as that was all the structure he could handle at the time. Gradually he took on more, and by September, Stone was a full-time film school student. "At that time, nobody really believed you could study films," Stone recalls. "To be able to study movies in college was any movie lover's dream. Films were exotic pleasures from Hollywood, and I was from the East Coast and didn't know anyone in the film business."

As he submerged himself in this new obsession, the agonizing memories of the Cambodian frontier began to fade, but he still had to be careful to avoid politics on campus. "I didn't like the protesters because of the baby-killing image they stuck the vets with," Stone says. "When they took over NYU after Cambodia was invaded, and all the kids trashed the place, I thought they were nuts. I said, 'If you want to protest, let's go to Washington and do it right. Let's form a guerrilla unit like the Viet Cong, put snipers on rooftops and really go after the system. I'll get a sniperscope and do Nixon.' I mean, part of me wanted to kill. If the right people had said the right things to me, I might have gone after him. I believed in Morrison's incantation, 'Break on through. Kill the pigs. Destroy. Loot. Fuck your mother.' All that shit. Anything goes. I would've tried anything in that state of mind. I mean, let's take over the fucking country, but don't give me this jerk-off-parading-down-Wall-Street-making-films kind of crap and expect to change the system."

Ironically, years later, the film school student who was most successful at influencing the system through films would be Oliver Stone. Yet this man so associated with the extolling of the sixties really didn't get to experience much of it. "Yeah, I missed out on the sixties," Stone admits. "I thought they were horrible. I was doing as much dope and acid as the hippies, but *The Big Chill* is like a foreign movie to me. *Platoon* was my *Big Chill*. I'm not angry about it, but I am saddened that I missed it—especially the healthy male/female relationships. I never had a coeducational existence. The sixties had this enormous sense of sexual liberation. Women started to come out of the closet and fucking was *in*. It was stylish, fashionable. I missed all that, and the honest, open man/woman communication that came with it."

When he started attending NYU, Stone moved over to 9th Street, between Second and Third avenues. "It was a small village apartment," he says. "There was a girl with a sewing machine in the front who had a little shop and I had an apartment in the back. It looked like a little prison, a birdcage, when the light would stream in from the back."

At NYU, the first professor Stone encountered was Martin Scorsese. On his way to establishing himself as a major force in the film world, Scorsese was charismatic, energetic, and insightful. He inspired Stone. "Scorsese helped tremendously. His energy, his devotion to film, helped me feel focused. He was very good with auto-criticism. He knew a lot about movies. I remember him having long, long hair and always being exhausted from having stayed up to watch the late late show. He'd talk about the movie he'd seen at 3:00 A.M. that morning in loving and intimate detail. He was like a mad scientist, someone on an equal wave of nuttiness. And he helped channel the rage in me."

As a film student, Stone initially did short essays, 60- and 90-second films. "They were terrible," he recalls. "Crude and really screwed up. But they enabled us to learn the essence of screen direction, lenses, shooting and editing your own film. Later, I helped shoot a film called *Street Scenes '71*, a documentary on the riots that occurred in New York City over the war in Cambodia. I was one of the cameramen in the streets who shot footage for it. I learned a lot about camera work and editing there."

At NYU, Stone also studied the history and theory of film, including the great innovators of the medium. Many of these would later influence his work, but the four who had the greatest impact were Orson Welles and three New Wave filmmakers, Jean-Luc Godard, Alain Resnais, and Luis Buñuel. (For a more detailed discussion of these filmmakers and how they influenced Stone, see Appendix II.)

While at NYU, Stone also made three short films in black and white, 16 millimeter. The first was *Last Year in Vietnam*, which was eight minutes long and concerned a vet wandering the New York streets. *Madman of Martinique* ran twenty minutes, and was an ambitious black and white effort in which Stone's father portrayed a man killed in the subway. The third film was entitled *Michael & Marie*. "They were arty, kind of abstract poems," Stone recalls, "with a touch of Orson Welles, Godard, Resnais, and Buñuel. I was trying to get away from a normal narrative line."

Stone was starting to discover that his war experience had had some positive effects. Not only had it successfully challenged his conservative upbringing, it also helped form a new consciousness that was in touch with the man on the street. Somehow, the ordeal of surviving the madness had given him a new and deeper sensibility and something worthwhile to communicate. "I thought he was a real filmmaker," Martin Scorsese says today. "He'd been through a lot more than other students and had something to say. Some of it was a little excessive, but I think that excess is what's kept him going."

Despite his hardworking attitude and passion for the subject, Stone did not fit in at NYU, even in the somewhat renegade film school. "He was a couple of years older than the other students and he'd been in Vietnam," recalls Stanley Weiser, one of Stone's classmates. "He was more mature in a way, but he was also very intense, and arrogant, even cocky. He kept to himself, the archetypal embittered loner. Very alienated, very suspicious, very sarcastic. We both worked on different films in the editing room late at night, and I became his only friend by default. Even then he was extremely distant, brooding. A real macho man who carried the torture of Vietnam with him but never talked about it. He had a lot of mystery about him. But he definitely showed talent right away."

Weiser was impressed with *Last Year in Vietnam*, which he describes as an Alain Resnais mock-up of *The Heart of Darkness*: "The thing I remember most about Oliver was that he was a fan of Céline [*Journey to the End of Night*], which showed me that he had a very dark side. I remember thinking he would succeed because I saw how diligent he was. There were all sorts of students with vision and people imitating Godard and Sam Peckinpah, but they never read. And Oliver actually had worked on a novel, he read, and he was obsessive about his work. I could see that he really had talent, but there was always this dark side pulling him down. I remember feeling that he was just wired and could detonate, go off at any time. He really had a dark, dangerous edge to him."

Stone could have been headed for disaster. Fortunately, shortly after he entered film school, Stone met Najwa Sarkis. Najwa was from a well-to-do Lebanese family and had come to America in 1961. By the time she met Oliver Stone she was an attaché in charge of protocol at the Moroccan Mission to the United Nations. Raised in traditional Old World circumstances, Najwa was instantly attracted to Stone. "It was really the first time I was attracted to a man with no thought of his station in life," she recalls. "Oliver looked older than he was; I thought he was my age. He's four years younger than I am, and I was a very late bloomer. We came from two different backgrounds."

Despite their differences or maybe partly because of them, Stone and Sarkis began to see each other. They grew closer and in March 1971 Stone left his modest lodgings and moved in with Najwa in her one-bedroom apartment in the East 50's. Najwa was enamored with Stone's writing and was convinced he would become a great success someday. While he was in film school she insisted that he work on his screenplays and consider that his job, while she supported the two of them. "Oliver worked very hard," she says today. "And I always had an admiration for his talent. He's a very deep thinker. And he's a wonderful human being, not like they paint him to be sometimes in the press."

The dining room was converted into Stone's work area, and he began to write screenplay after screenplay. For the first time since becoming interested in film, he was free to work without having to struggle with finances or endure the oppressive influence of his family. "The third screenplay I wrote was *The Wolves*," Stone recalls, "which was a contemporary Greek tragedy on an island like Scorpios. It was my version of the Onassis-type families in Greece, and was based on the Orestes Greek tragedy by Euripides. The son comes home to find the lie at the heart of the family. He discovers the secret. It was very hard to write."

The Wolves was significant in Stone's development as a writer in that it was not written in a surrealistic form like *Break* or with a direct autobiographical correlation like *Dominique*. *The Wolves* is good old-fashioned storytelling and contains Stone's most elaborate plot up to this time.

By May, the relationship between Stone and Najwa Sarkis had become more serious. "We had a wonderful time," Najwa recalls. "We went out and walked from one club to the next. We really lived. We were young and carefree. I used to go out until four or five in the morning and come home and change and go to the office."

On May 16, 1971, they were married. "We went to the Club Med at Martinique for our honeymoon," Najwa says. "I had a 102-degree temperature, but couldn't stay sick. Oliver wouldn't let me. He threw me in the water."

Back in New York though, Stone became engrossed in his work, something which Najwa had grown to accept. "His work came before anything else. That was very hard for me at first. But remember, when I was married to Oliver, we were both very young. I was raised in a very secluded, family-oriented environment . . . I was too nice as far as my Americans friends think, but I wanted to provide for my husband. I adored him. I used to work all day and then type his scripts, and I didn't mind. We lived well. We traveled. My parents were helping. Lebanon then was at its peak. And it was a very lovely life. We didn't lack for anything."

"We traveled to Lebanon just before the civil war began," Stone recalls. "We went to her hometown of Kusba, which was in the north, near Tripoli. In a wonderful symbolic gesture her father gave me an olive grove . . . not for real, but symbolically, like a dedication. It was very beautiful."

In September 1971, after working hard and finishing in just over two years, Stone graduated from film school. For his next script, he returned to the issue that was still burning in him—Vietnam. "I think *Once Too Much* has sort of an eerie parallel to Ron Kovic's *Born on the Fourth of July*," Stone says. "For me, it was a different version of *Break* in a way. It was a more realistic story about a kid who comes back from Vietnam, goes to jail, and eventually gets killed in Mexico with a hooker."

The script was Stone's best yet. The lead character, Eric Welles, is compelling, and though simple, the plot holds one's interest. It is also significant because for the first time Stone seems to have mastered blending the surreal with the real. Eric's somewhat strange lapses into the past and fantasies about the future are neatly interwoven, adding excitement and just the right degree of eccentricity without overwhelming the narrative. The rapid juxtapositions of illusion and reality here work as quick flashes of insight and inspiration. Stone seems to be honing his gift for the visual, developing a penchant for powerful images that come out of left field to enhance the story, something that would later become a hallmark of his work.

Neither *Once Too Much* nor *The Wolves* met with success. Like *Break* and *Dominique* before them, Stone showed the scripts to the people he knew. A few of them promised to get them to someone who might be able to help, but nothing tangible materialized. The few agents he managed to reach were not even interested in reading his work. Producers were looking for scripts from proven writers. Stone was in a classic Catch-22: The only way to sell a screenplay was to have sold one already.

Not that some progress wasn't being made. Najwa knew some influential people, and she was very adept at getting to those she didn't. But progress wasn't what Oliver Stone wanted—he wanted success. Never one to cope well with rejection, Stone grew even more restless, and problems began to develop between him and Najwa. "I was less liberal than he wanted me to be with my lifestyle," she admits. "I just didn't understand the whole drug thing. I only smoked marijuana to please Oliver and our friends. I bought it for them. It was always at the table for anyone who wanted it. But I only smoked it two or three times. I'd get a headache. Coke was also available at every party we went to in those days. Everybody was doing it. People lost fortunes. The people I knew in New York were very well off and could afford anything they wanted, but I had a responsibility. I had to go to the office every day, so I couldn't stay up all night drinking and taking drugs. Because I was from a different culture, I didn't understand that Oliver had to find himself. He was experimenting with everything."

Stone worked several different jobs at this time, taking just about anything that would still enable him to write. He was a Xerox boy for a typing pool, then took a temp job as a messenger. Next, he began driving a cab at night, working two, sometimes four nights a week. "The cab driving was tough," Stone recalls. "I used to smoke joints all the time and try to drive at night. I remember taking fares up to weird places, driving out to the boroughs and not getting paid, being scared in Harlem. Doing the night shift. I'd make thirty, thirty-five bucks and get out at four in the morning. Cold, cold winters. I'd be freezing and there'd be no way to get home that time of night. I'd walk from the garage on 11th Avenue to 51st Street. Hands in the pockets of my green fatigue jacket, walking to the apartment I had with Najwa at four-thirty in the morning through Times Square. New York winters were pretty dreary."

It was during his tenure as a cab driver that Stone's future publicist, Marianne Billings, says she first saw him. Billings took a cab one day when she was handling the publicity for Martin Scorsese's film, *Mean Streets*, and claims Stone was the driver. She recalls he was very talkative and at one point he asked her what she did for a living. When she told him, he said, "I'm a writer, but I'm going to direct films some day." Naturally, Billings was amused. But her amusement turned to shocked surprise fourteen years later when she went to meet the director of *Platoon*, after having been told he had requested she handle the film. It was the cocky cab driver, Oliver Stone.

Around this time Stone had a terrifying nightmare in which he and Najwa were living in an old mansion. They were visited by three maniacs—a bloodthirsty dwarf, a hideous-looking strongman, and a beautiful but heinous woman—who proceeded to murder the weekend guests. In the dream, Stone had a son whom he wound up betraying in order to save himself. Stone and a friend named Ed Mann wrote a script based on this dream and called it *Seizure*. "I wrote it down exactly as it happened in this vivid dream," Stone says. "The structure, the maniacs, betraying my son, everything. In the film, the father wakes up and realizes it's all a dream. And then he dies."

After working for his childhood friend Lloyd Kaufman as a production assistant on a soft-core sex film called *Sugar Cookies*, Stone became convinced he could produce *Seizure* as a low-budget horror film on his own. Not only had he learned a lot on the film, but he got along very well with the other two production assistants, Jeff Kapelman and Garrard Glenn. Both were from wealthy families and agreed to back Stone. The three of them formed Euro-American Pictures, and with Najwa's help they set out to raise the funds necessary to produce *Seizure*. But Stone's personal finances were at an all-time low. A new ambassador had been appointed to the Moroccan Mission, with the result that Najwa was not receiving the bonuses she had grown accustomed to. In November 1971, Stone borrowed $125 from his friend Roger Kirby, and in December he borrowed $100 from his father. But this still wasn't enough. In January 1972, he was suspended from driving his cab for a week for driving with the meter off and pocketing the fares. "I didn't cheat a lot," Stone says, "but I did then to get extra money, and I got caught."

Stone still had to turn to his father for money occasionally. Lou Stone was not having it easy himself. In early 1971, Hayden, Stone & Co. went through a major financial crisis. Though not a partner in the company, Lou had been investing in the firm for years and lost most of his savings. The company was reorganized under the name Cogan, Berlind, Weill & Levitt, four brokers who had a smaller but growing firm. Disgruntled, Lou Stone left to join another company. It was an unfortunate move, as Sandy Weill would build Stone's former employer into one of the largest on Wall Street. Had he stayed and invested in it, Lou would have made a fortune. Whenever Stone borrowed from his father, he had to give a full accounting of his financial standing. In an effort to look good, at times he padded his assets a bit. The following letter, dated February 18, 1972, is as amusing as it is revealing:

Dear Dad:

I am writing you because it seems the intertwined fortunes of Najwa and I have reached a new nadir. However, I find hope even in this believing that, as in the stock market, the sun will suddenly set through the storm on our lives. Here is the gloomy picture.

OLIVER STONE

LIABILITIES			ASSETS	
Feb. Rent (apartment, due Feb. 1)	$325		Cash	$50
March rent (due Mar. 1)	325		EAP [Euro-American Pictures] 4000	
Loan from R. Kirby (outstanding since Nov. due Mar. 1)	125		(20% of issued and outstanding shares)	
TOTAL	**$775.00**		**TOTAL**	**$4050.00**

As you see, I am ahead on paper and $725.00 behind on cash. I have no doubt that soon my balance sheet will reflect a more realistic cash flow.

The $100.00 you gave me on February 3, as you know, went into the EAP petty cash fund. Of the $300 you gave me on January 24, $80.00 went to electric and gas and telephone: $125.00 to Najwa for payment of debts (see below) and the remaining $95 for a total of 4 weeks' living expenses. As you know I am driving at least twice a week (more if I have the evenings free; all my other evenings go to social occasions that may benefit EAP) and making $30 per driving night. However, as you know I was suspended for one week and could not drive. The profits from this job go to living expenses and, in one form or other, to small EAP expenses which all the partners have agreed to pick up till the first picture is totally financed, which I expect will be soon.

As for Najwa's situation, I must first say that she is sensitive about it and I would not like her to know that you know the details. However, it is up to you. . . . We expect her consolidation debt to be entirely paid off by April 22—two months from now. . . .

In conclusion, by liquidating my cash debts on March 1, I will have 30 days therefrom to earn the rent for April 1 without previously owing anything. . . .

I have set forth our problems as clearly as I can and hope you can understand them. I ask that you contribute $725.00 to our cause at this crucial juncture of our lives in the understanding that now is sometimes more important to the morale and the need for hope than later.

Sincerely Yours,

Your son Oliver

P.S. I am also enclosing some just-received deposit slips.

"It's yourself you've got to be proud of, Huckleberry, how much ya need?"

Carl Fox in WALL STREET

The summer of 1972 was filled with election news as George McGovern campaigned on unconditional withdrawal from Vietnam. Stone focused on raising money for *Seizure*, and by November, as President Nixon won by 18 million votes despite rumors about Watergate, he was close. "Raising the money for the film was a real mess," Stone recalls. "Najwa had a few friends with some dough. My partners put up some money. We raised about fifty grand and made a deal with a Toronto company for the other half."

Plans were made to film in Canada, and Stone recruited Jonathan Frid of the horror soap *Dark Shadows* to star, along with Martine Beswick, Christina Pickles, Joe Sirola, Mary Woronov, Troy Donahue (well after *Surfside Six*) and Hervé Villechaize (well before *Fantasy Island*). If raising the money was difficult, making the film was more so. Stone got his first harsh lesson about film financing as soon as he arrived in Canada: "We got there and found the Canadian company was bankrupt. They had issued fake stock and had fake diplomas on the walls with 'London School of Economics' on them. So we had no money, and we were stuck in Canada. We made a quick deal with

Harold Greenburg, a big-shot Canadian. He agreed to finish the film as long as he owned it. He basically took it over, and that was that.

"Oh, we tried our hardest to make the best of the movie, but we had money problems all the way through. The crew didn't get paid, the crew struck, the crew even tied up the producers and put them in a rowboat and rowed them out into the middle of the lake as if to drown them. And little Hervé Villechaize was threatening to kill us all. He would glare at me, shake his tiny fist, and growl, 'I kill you, Stone. You no pay me, I kill you! I take a knife and stick it into your heart! You die! Fuck off!' My Canadian director of photography went nuts, totally crazy, and quit ten times, vowing to take his equipment with him. He had a deal where we had to edit at his place in Montreal and, when we had no money left, he seized the movie. *Seizure* was seized. Well, actually he just locked the editing room on me and kept the film. I couldn't edit my precious movie. The producers and I got a court order and seized it back from him. We came in at dawn with an actual Mountie and raided his office and his house looking for the materials. Still, he somehow managed to hide sixty-five rolls of sound negative. So we had to redub a lot in the movie. It was an awful learning experience."

Najwa remembers that at one point Villechaize, who played the murderous dwarf in the film, locked himself in the closet with the huge knife he carried for the movie and demanded to speak to her because he felt she was the only one who understood him.

Today, Stone laughs in spite of himself at the painful memory of making *Seizure*. "It was several weeks of madness. At one point a crew member on the set did try to kill me with a machete. He was fucking one of the actresses, and he came after me with a machete because he saw me coming on to her. After the film was over I had an affair with the actress, which was quite interesting. She was a beautiful, sensuous Jamaican. She was a cult horror film figure. But I got unmasked and Najwa got really upset. Always squealers . . . there are always squealers in the woodwork."

Najwa also remembers those days with a smile. "You know I'm very honest," she says now. "I say what's in my heart. If I knew then what I know today . . . I was young. To make scenes about such things— not scenes, really. Sometimes I was jealous, upset. He used to say to me, 'You always say patience, patience, I'm sick of your patience.' All these years were rough on him, because none of his scripts sold, the rejection after rejection."

After moving from Montreal to Toronto to complete the editing, Stone decided to call the film *Seizure* although he had been planning on titling it *Queen of Evil*. It was eventually released in a very limited run on 42nd Street in 1974. "I had to steal the answer print in Canada and drive it myself across the border," Stone says, laughing. "And then we got turned down by the distributors. Finally, it was distributed in the United States by Cinerama Releasing, which had done all those classy Hammer horror films. But we were not classy enough for them. They saw it as lower grade, and only released it on 42nd Street as part of a double bill. But I was proud of it anyway. I went with my mother, took some friends and drank champagne. And I loved it. The black guys on 42nd Street would come up to me and say, 'Hey, man, that's cool, that's really cool.' I loved that little fucking dwarf."

Seizure never had a chance to find an audience. The failure of the film to make even a slight dent in the big time or to alert people to Stone's talent made a lasting impact on him. "After he did *Seizure*, he seemed like a different person," says Stanley Weiser. "He was beaten down in a way. I think he kind of had his mind blown by experience. He seemed so much humbler and softer. Much softer. It was such a complete transformation of character that I couldn't quite get it. I thought he had a loose screw at the time."

It was then that Weiser showed Stone the first screenplay he had written. "He gave me a lot of help and encouragement. He was generous with his time. He's loyal to his friends and he really is honorable. The thing about Oliver is that he always comes through, and there are very few people who are like that."

Seizure had to be an eye-opener for Stone in many ways. It was his first clash with the reality of the filmmaking process. Theory is marvelous and art is grand, but such things are sometimes far removed from the business of making films. As a first-time director, many of Stone's decisions, such as having the cast actually live in the spooky old mansion to get a feel for the film, must have seemed hopelessly romantic. He was young and inexperienced and they all knew it. In the future, he would be wiser. But, to his credit, instead of compromising these ideals as most young artists do, Stone would strive to develop the business savvy necessary to make them work within the film process and, eventually, the clout to make others go along with them. "Everything was hard on that movie," he says now. "*Seizure* was the best training I could have for movies because it laid in me a deep seed of paranoia and fear of betrayal, and the truth is you practically do get betrayed by everyone by the time you finish making a movie. Of course it hurt my career at the time. As a result of that picture, I didn't direct for a long time."

The failure of *Seizure* further alienated Stone and his father. Against his better judgment Lou Stone had ended up investing $15,000 in the film. It wasn't so much that he lost his investment, although the money was certainly an issue, but more importantly it heightened his fears about the future of his son. Why couldn't he take up a sensible profession?

Looking for a way to recover from this experience, Stone spent several months in 1974 writing a comedy about the making of a horror movie. Indeed, the entire nightmare of *Seizure* is there in the script to *Horror Movie:* the angry dwarf threatening to cut off the director's balls, the mad makeup man bedding down the lead actress and stalking the director with a machete, the crew getting wilder each night until they trash and rob the mansion rented for the film, the financing collapsing and checks bouncing before the end of the shoot, and the director of photography confiscating the sound negative. It is a testimony to Stone's sense of humor that he was able not only to laugh at his own misfortune but actually write about it. The script has many genuine comedic moments, but unless you know the circumstances behind it, it's too confusing to make a viable film. It is a case of the truth not fitting the Hollywood formula. By now, Stone was capable enough to alter the script to make a more digestible film, but he chose not to do so, probably because by sticking to the truth he was best able to cleanse the entire incident from his mind. "Sometimes," he muses, "the flawed work is just as interesting. The script doesn't work, but it was an attempt to put down a truly mad experience. I actually spent four or five months writing that in 1974 so I guess it was pretty important to me at the time."

On August 9, 1974, after nearly two years of investigation, cover-ups, denials, and deceit, President Richard Nixon resigned as the truth about Watergate threatened to emerge. For Oliver Stone, the Watergate scandal confirmed his worst fears. "It was a turning point," he says. "Watergate hammered the point home that the government was a lie.

They lied to us about Ho Chi Minh, they lied about the Vietnam War, and now they were lying about Watergate."

Stone forged on, writing a western for Charles Bronson, his idol at the time, called *The Ungodly*. The Sergio Leone "Dollars" trilogy of westerns starring Clint Eastwood had proven very popular in the sixties, and *The Ungodly* seems to be Stone's attempt to write something more accessible to Hollywood. Stone thought that once he wrote something commercially successful, he would have the power to reach the masses and could return to more inspired work. He particularly liked Leone's *Once Upon a Time in the West* (1968), with Charles Bronson as the hero and Henry Fonda as one of the coldest and most vicious hired killers in screen history. *The Ungodly* is patterned along similar lines.

The script falters near the end, amid a bloody Indian massacre and betrayals from most of the principal characters, but redeems itself with a strong conclusion and a solid message about the effect of greed. Stone was now creating characters far more interesting than the standard action hero and was able to come up with powerful vignettes that communicated this to an audience. However, *The Ungodly* would only lead to more frustration, as no one was interested in producing the film.

Stone finished *The Ungodly* while he was working at a sporting films company called W & W Films, a job he obtained through one of Najwa's connections on Madison Avenue. Since he had directed a feature film, he was hired to sell the company's production skills to advertising agencies. W & W Films was successful at making baseball and football films and paid Stone very well, but he was a terrible salesman. He hated trotting the company's reel around Madison Avenue, but couldn't afford to quit. Eventually, it turned into a con job. "I went in every day and just worked on *The Ungodly*," Stone admits. "I'd tell them I was on the phone trying to make sales all the time. I finished *The Ungodly* while I was there and then I wrote with Geoffrey Holder, an extended treatment, of a mythological sort of Cocteau/Orpheus movie about Trinidad. I was at the company for about a year, but the boss got more and more concerned as time went by and no business was coming. All that time and I still wasn't out on the street. They let me go, but I got away with it for a while."

On April 30, 1975, General Duong van Minh surrendered Saigon as the North Vietnamese closed in. All told, the war cost the United

States $141 billion and took the lives of 56,000 Americans and 1.3 million Vietnamese. The end of the Vietnam War gave Oliver Stone little peace, for very few Americans still had any idea of what really happened there.

Ever since he filmed *Seizure*, things had grown worse between Stone and Najwa. He was more restless than ever and became convinced that he needed to be on the West Coast to break through as a screenwriter, but Najwa wasn't ready to make the move. Her job was important to her; besides, it was still their primary source of income. Troubled and starting to feel trapped, Stone buckled down and began an eighth screenplay, *The Cover-Up*.

This was the first of Stone's scripts to involve a government agency in a conspiracy. Though centering on a fictional FBI plot, the screenplay suggested the possibility of a government conspiracy in the Patty Hearst kidnapping. Stone again tried to reach some producers and agents, but nothing developed. Then, early in 1975, an Australian friend said she would try to get the script to the producer Fernando Ghia. Within a few weeks, the friend called and said that Ghia had liked the script, and passed it on to screenwriter Robert Bolt (*Lawrence of Arabia, Dr. Zhivago, Man for All Seasons*). Bolt wanted to meet the writer. It was Stone's first real break: "At the time I considered Bolt the best screenwriter in the world."

Bolt, Ghia, and Franco Christaldi optioned *The Cover-Up* for their company and paid Stone a $15,000 advance until the work could be sold to a studio. It was an excellent deal for that time and a tremendous validation of Stone's instincts. Almost overnight he was flying to Los Angeles to work with Robert Bolt. He couldn't help but feel he had been right about his talent. He was going to make it. "From when I was twenty-one, I just felt like I had a call," Stone says now. "Living up to that call was the hardest part. I knew I had a lot of work to do on myself and on my craft, but I knew I was supposed to make films. I've had periods of doubt and lack of confidence. I wasn't prepared for all the shit that's thrown on people by others. In the beginning I thought it would be a celebration of joy to do good work. I didn't realize that doing good work is often not enough, that there's a lot . . . a lot of jealousy as well as a fashion to the times, and there's such a thing as luck."

Stone began going back and forth to L.A. on a regular basis to work with Bolt, and it wasn't long before he was talking more about moving to L.A. Najwa was against it, but he wouldn't relent. At Stone's insistence, she came to L.A. with him several times. But while he responded instantly to the hip and loose West Coast scene, Najwa was repelled by the permissive attitudes toward sex and drugs. "It was the lifestyle there I didn't like," she recalls. "He wanted to go to California and live. He said, that's where the action is. Well, you know, for me it was very difficult. We didn't have any capital. I had spent a lot of the capital I had because we were making movies. I couldn't leave my job and go out there and live . . . he said, 'Well, if you loved me, you would come and you'd work as a waitress.' I said, 'No, Oliver, I don't even know how to drive a car. How could I live in L.A.?' "

In L.A., Stone began running with a fast-paced crowd of struggling artists. "There were about ten of us staying in this house," he says. "Actors, musicians, comedians . . . I was having an affair with a girl who was a stand-up comedian. We'd go to the clubs all the time. Another comedian friend was a guy named Sosimo Hernandez. He was about five foot three and had the saddest face you ever saw. We'd go to these second-rate clubs in L.A. and I was his only audience half the time. I would encourage him and then we'd go to these clubs and nobody would laugh. I'd be in the audience trying to direct him and tell him what went wrong. And he'd always bomb. The few times he was funny, there was nobody there to see it."

After a while Stone began spending most of his time in L.A. and got his own apartment there. Sometimes Najwa came out to see him, but the visits grew further and further apart. They hadn't broken up yet, but both feared it was coming. On the strength of *The Cover-Up* and his relationship with Robert Bolt, Stone was signed to the William Morris Agency, at that time under the direction of Stan Kamen, who many considered the most powerful person in the film business. In New York, Stone was represented by Owen Laster, the head of Morris's literary department. Laster introduced him to his first screenplay agent, Ron Mardigian. Throughout that summer Stone and Bolt rewrote *The Cover-Up*, with Mardigian waiting in the wings to hustle it to the studios for them. Though the film was a long way from being made, Stone was already walking in a dream.

"Robert helped me enormously on *The Cover-Up*," he says now. "He stripped down my original screenplay, pointed out what was amateurish and shallow, then made me rethink every scene with him in the room with a tape recorder going. He talked eloquently, describing the scene and the motivations, and sharpening the characters. I was intimidated. Here was this great screenwriter spending all this time with me— a nobody. But he liked my original idea, and he agreed with my political convictions. I loved working with Bolt. It was a wonderful break for me, like a huge gust of wind in my sails that helped me go on. I suddenly felt I could get somewhere."

By November 1975, the script was finished. Mardigian and Stan Kamen began to shop it, with Ghia and Bolt as producers and Stone as the director and writer. This proved difficult as none of the studios wanted to risk such a controversial script with an unknown director, so the agency began pushing it to other directors as well.

Stone had high hopes as 1976 dawned, but they soon began to crash. Stan Kamen was not having his usual luck with the studios. "Nobody wanted to make *The Cover-Up*," Stone says. "It was just too extreme for Hollywood, I guess."

By March it was all over. Kamen tried to encourage Stone, reminding him that *The Cover-Up* was still a great script and a great introduction to Hollywood. He needed to start circulating a little bit. Meet some more people, pitch some new ideas. But Stone hadn't heard much of what Kamen said after he told him the script wasn't going to get made. His old fears were kicking into high gear, and the voice reverberating in his head was his father's.

Stone knew he'd have to return to New York. He didn't have the money to stay in L.A., and felt his identity was in New York. All he'd been in L.A. was "the guy who was writing a screenplay with Robert Bolt," and now he was afraid he'd be no one.

He also decided that now was the time to break with Najwa. "I realized that, though I loved Najwa, we really didn't belong together," Stone says. "I had been so sheltered in some ways because of the all-boy world I grew up in that I'd married someone who had a lot of similarities to my mother's values. Najwa was a very socially conscious person. She always wanted to do the proper thing. I had to break away. On my way back to New York, I decided this charade could go on no longer. Najwa didn't even know I was coming, but I went straight to the apartment and told her I was going to leave. We both knew it was over, I think, but she didn't want to accept it. It was very difficult for me, but I knew it was what we had to do.

"So, I left that very night and moved in with my friend, Kenny Roberts, a Welsh art director on Madison Avenue and a film aficionado. He lived on 52nd, right off Second Avenue, on the second floor, with no air conditioning. I started reading, at Ken's urging, a lot of Henry Miller and Orwell while living there and being very influenced by them, especially Henry Miller's Paris writings of opinions and essays. And Orwell's *Down and Out in Paris and London* was fabulous. These books said it was okay to be poor and down and out. This is the place to learn. And I learned and learned."

Around this time, Ed Mann, Stone's co-writer on *Seizure*, got him hired to write a screenplay based on a Robin Moore book entitled *Barkoon*. The story dealt with Green Berets in Thailand and Vietnam, but the film was never made because it was so expensive. Stone and Kenny Roberts then wrote *The Rascals* along with another friend, Robin Harvey. *Rascals* is a celebration of young and impoverished artists trying to make a go of it in mid-seventies New York.

"'The Rascals,' Stone wrote in his remembrances of this period,

came out of the wild period when I lived in this hole-in-the-wall . . . totally storm-tossed by the chaos all around me; being alone again and being a bachelor. So many girls were in that apartment, it was like Henry Miller time. I'd had no youth. I came from Vietnam, got married and was trying to be a film student and a serious person, and integrate into society. It was great in the first flush of a separation to live that turmoil. I tried to put that chaos of people dropping into your apartment, having many friends, going to group parties, wild sex, two girls at a time, drifting around New York with no money but a lot of dreams.

I got into a drug called phencyclodine ethylamine—it was like the ultimate high/low combination. It was a powder. We were selling these small bottles out of the apartment, but the stuff was so good that people would stay high for long periods of time and not need to buy any more. All these interesting and strange people used to come over. Emmet Grogan, the writer [*Ringolevio*], came over one night with a buddy and he cleaned us out. He went to the bathroom and found our stash and took it. He died not long afterwards on the subway.

Kenny Roberts had several wealthy contacts, and he and Stone decided to produce the film themselves. "So we'd go to all these Mafia clubs and talk to people," Stone recalls. "We saw a lot of people—weird doctors with money, strange people in Chinatown, Jewish princesses, people in Queens, Park Avenue druggies. We were really canvassing New York, trying to raise the money. We would go from Canal Street to Queens. It was just like the screenplay. We came pretty close to financing it, but the deal didn't close."

In the meantime, Stone and Roberts worked on another screenplay called *Brazil Run*. This was an action adventure about an ex-CIA man who gets involved with a former Nazi leader hiding out in Brazil. Stone wanted Lee Marvin for the role, but he turned the part down. Elliot Kasner, a producer, almost optioned it, but never did. "Kasner almost optioned it about fourteen times," Stone says. "He had it for three years and never paid me one fucking cent. And this is when he had millions of dollars and I was fucking starving. He just kept stringing me along. But that's part of the way this business is done."

Stone also wrote a film treatment on the killing of George Jackson during this time, entitled *The Life and Times of Deacon Davis*. He had met a young woman at a party who told him about the Symbionese Liberation Front and her feelings about the FBI. She convinced him that the government really was capable of organizing things to discredit leftist groups.

Though he'd gained a great deal of experience, Stone began to question whether he was really getting anywhere. He'd written eleven scripts in six years and was still scrounging around New York. He wondered if he should quit. But something happened that summer that filled him with a new sense of conviction. His grandmother died, the one he called Memé, to whom he wrote so often from Vietnam. Stone went to France for her funeral. As is the custom there, he found her laid out on the bed in her apartment. "I talked to her," he says. "I was almost thirty, and I felt that I was still a bum. I hadn't achieved anything. Her dying at this time made me rededicate myself to being serious. I felt I should live up to something for her."

By now it was mid-1976. *The Rascals* still wasn't financed, and Stone was starting to believe that Stan Kamen was right: he needed to move to the West Coast. But he just wasn't ready yet.

On the Fourth of July, while the rest of America celebrated the Bicentennial, Oliver Stone walked down to the harbor. He would be thirty in a few months. More important, despite the breakup of his marriage and his continued financial woes, he had readjusted to life in America after Vietnam. He was starting to be comfortable again. He could almost let go of the burden of his Vietnam experience. To Stone, this kind of thinking meant only one thing: It was now or never. As the Tall Ships rode into the harbor for the Bicentennial celebration, Oliver Stone made a decision. He would write *Platoon*. "I realized I had forgotten a lot in eight years. I thought, 'If I don't do it now, I'm gonna forget.' It's part of our history nobody understands—what it was like over there, how everyday American boys from little towns in Ohio who grew up by the 7-Eleven store with the souped-up cars and the girls on Friday night turned into these monster killers."

Stone returned to his apartment that day and resolved to write the story the way it had happened, as close to the truth as possible. He would make only slight adjustments, combine a few characters, change a few names, and take dramatic license solely to assure that the story had the same kind of impact as his memories. His goal was to write the truth as he remembered it.

"It took me eight years to get to that screenplay, because I couldn't deal with it before," he says. "I needed the distance. Essentially what I wanted to say was, 'Remember what that war was. Remember what war is.' I felt Vietnam was being omitted from the history books, like one battle I fought in: a lot of people got hurt that day, and it wasn't even listed as a battle by the army, as if they didn't want to admit the casualties we suffered."

Stone worked quickly, banging away on the same cheap typewriter he had been using for years. "I wanted to hone in on those characters without the symbolism and Cocteau drama of my previous Vietnam scripts," he recalls. "All those guys existed in one platoon or another. I mixed them, mixed archetypes. Barnes and Elias were never in the same unit, but I felt there was an inevitable clash of thought processes that would occur, and did occur in Vietnam on a daily basis. The Hawks and the Doves who were splitting the country. The heads and the juicers. America was becoming a civil war."

To go back to a project is hard enough, but when the subject is a painful one, it becomes even more difficult to examine it objectively, ferret out the flaws, and approach the piece in a new way. Nonetheless, this is exactly what Stone did in reworking the themes of *Break* into *Platoon*. Reexamining the material and the experience, he realized that the real story revolved not so much around the lead character as around the two people who most strongly influenced that character. As a narrative, *Platoon* fits the classic Greek warrior myths in that a young and somewhat innocent man goes off to war and through the experience learns a great lesson. But the essential conflict that grows out of these roots is between Elias and Barnes. "Two gods," Stone later wrote in an essay for *American Film* (January 1987).

> Two different views of the war. The angry Achilles versus the conscience-stricken Hector fighting for a lost cause on the dusty plains of Troy. It mirrored the very civil war that I'd witnessed in all the units I was in. On the one hand, the lifers, the juicers, and the moron white element—part Southern and part rural. And against them, the hippie, dope smoking, black, and progressive white element (although there were exceptions in all categories and some lifers smoked more dope than I ever dreamed). Right vs. Left. And I would act as Ishmael, the observer. At first a watcher. Then *forced* to act to take responsibility and a moral stand. And in the process, grow to a manhood I'd never dreamed I'd have to grow to. To a place where in order to go on existing, I'd have to shed the innocence and accept the evil the Homeric gods had thrown out into the world. To be both good and evil. To move from this East Coast social product to a more visceral manhood, where I finally felt the war not in my head, but in my gut and my soul.

Within a few weeks, Stone had finished the script. "In a sense, I wrote it as straight as I could remember it," he says now. "In some ways it's probably the least writing I've ever done, more like a newspaper report. The hardest thing was getting the right tone and the character of Elias. I loved this guy. He was a free spirit, a Jim Morrison in the bush. Handsome . . . he was our god. How do you capture that spirit of someone who was mythic when you were young? I think we got some of that spirit, but it was hard. But I always felt that Elias needed to be seen as a definite minority, an endangered species."

The nightmare of Vietnam comes to life in Stone's script. It depicts a world of fear and loathing, where the ultimate purpose was not to win the war, but to get out alive. It was a bizarre world. A place of countless terrors—snipers, boobytraps, firefights, napalm, horrible wounds and hideous deaths. Even during those brief moments when the fighting stops, Stone's Vietnam is loathsome—torrential rains, acres of mud, rot, mosquitoes and snakes.

The script is so close to Stone's actual experience that at times it reads like his Vietnam diary, with the dialogue fleshed out and the characters more well rounded. His memories come to life in *Platoon*: The night the NVA attacked while Stone, choked with fear, was unable to make a sound. The day the men went on a sadistic rampage in a Vietnamese village and the normally detached Stone joined in, firing rounds at the old villager's feet to make him dance. And the time the platoon was pinned down and Stone went berserk, lobbing grenades at an impossible target, only to connect and be decorated as a hero for his effort.

The people of Stone's Vietnam are there as well: the weirdly mystical Rhah, the easygoing King, and the somewhat deranged Bunny. But dominating throughout is Stone's vision of the two sergeants—the horribly scarred and psychopathic Sergeant Barnes, a virtual killing machine, whom the smart guys stayed close to because they knew he would survive, and the sweet-spirited Sergeant Elias, whose uncanny Indian ways and ingenious approach to combat were only exceeded by his humanitarian philosophy and concern for his men. These two men—diametrically opposed in beliefs, but strangely linked in purpose by the paradox of war—are the men the narrator refers to when he says he is "a son of two fathers."

When Elias comes upon Barnes and his men, out of control and wreaking horrible havoc in the village, it is his amazing ability to remain a rational and decent man amid chaos and savagery that restores sanity to the situation. And it is his unswerving commitment to these values that pushes him to confront Barnes and challenge his authority in front of the men, when he knows that such an act to a man like Barnes is tantamount to a personal declaration of war. Later, amid the fray of battle, when Barnes tracks down Elias and catches him alone, Elias smiles and lowers his gun. As Barnes shoots Elias, it becomes evident that in Oliver Stone's Vietnam, good is ultimately no match for evil. In the end it was Elias's trusting nature, his guileless desire to believe in good, that did him in. His astute battle sense, his inherent Indian cunning and years of shrewd jungle war experience, could not save him.

When Chris Taylor ultimately avenges Elias by killing Barnes, it is not the naive and innocent Chris, the idealistic son of Elias who does the killing, but the hardened vet who has come to accept the ruthless Barnes as his father as well. The last line in the script is Chris's narration as he leaves Vietnam: "Those of us who make it have an obligation to build again, to teach to others what we know and to try with what's left of our lives to find a goodness and meaning to this life."

But the real theme of *Platoon* is best illustrated when Chris exchanges his childlike sense of decency for fierce and brutal justice by killing Barnes. It is then that the theme and true madness of war is driven painfully home: the first casualty of war is innocence.

Although *Platoon* strongly impressed Stan Kamen, Stone had little hopes of a quick sell. He'd been down that road already. On September 15, 1976, Oliver Stone turned thirty. His only film credit was a grade-B horror movie. He realized he would have to go to where the film business was. So, with little clout and even less money, Stone headed West. Even now, remembering his days in New York triggers a strange image for Stone:

"The pirate thing has always been an image in my life, in my youth . . . the idea that we have islands in our lives as opposed to cities as we go port to port. When I first got back from Vietnam, I was with two friends that I was very close to, a girl and a boy. And the three of us took this acid trip and it was very powerful . . . I had this image that my life would be a series of islands that I would visit. And I thought of Ulysses, the Greek sailor, who goes from island to island and has this series of adventures and challenges. I remember thinking at that time that I would lose track of these two people that I loved so much that day, that I would never see them again. And that this would be the most intense moment of our relationship. I loved these two people, but I knew I would lose them . . . because I would have to sail on. It seems to be part of who I am. And that happened. I never saw them again."

Breaking Through

(1976-1992)

CHAPTER FOUR

Midnight Express

"What is the crime? And what is the punishment? The answer seems to vary from place to place and from time to time. What's legal today is suddenly illegal tomorrow 'cause some society says so; and what's illegal yesterday all of a sudden gets legal today because everybody's doing it and you can't throw everybody in jail. Well I'm not saying this is right or wrong. It's just the way things are. . . ."

Billy Hayes in **MIDNIGHT EXPRESS**

As soon as Oliver Stone settled in Los Angeles, he began to feel better about himself and his career. It wasn't until some time later that he realized that by leaving New York, he had escaped countless painful memories that leaped up at him from every street corner. The simple truth was that there were less things in L.A. to remind him of his frustrated childhood. In California, Stone moved into a cheap hotel, with enough money to last him a month. He was convinced he'd end up having to wait tables, but almost as soon as he was settled, Stan Kamen called and said that producer Marty Bregman (*Serpico*, *Dog Day Afternoon*) loved his script for *Platoon*. "Kamen flew me right back to New York," Stone recalls. "He put me in an apartment and all of a sudden I was in another world. I met with Al Pacino, who said he liked my writing a lot, and was encouraging. Bregman and I also talked to Sidney Lumet, who didn't want to direct my script, but it was great for me to meet him."

At Bregman's request, Stone rewrote the script, tightening it and polishing it even more. Yet even Bregman couldn't get the film financed. "For two years in the late seventies I banged on every door in California to get it done," Bregman says, "but at that time Vietnam was still a no-no."

Still, Stone was making considerable headway. *Platoon* began drawing attention to him as a writer of unusual force. Although it usually drew favorable comment, the script was always rejected. "It was turned down at least a hundred times," Stone says. "It became sort of a joke because everybody ranted at some point or other and said, 'Are you seriously considering making that movie?' Nobody thought it would be made. It was the bugaboo about Vietnam. All the studio guys said Vietnam wouldn't make a dime, and that was all they cared about. The indifference of the studio system to that war was equivalent to the indifference of the civilian population when we first came back."

Though they weren't interested in making *Platoon*, Columbia Pictures recognized the power and passion of the writing. They were looking for just this kind of writer to adapt a book called *Midnight Express*, the true story of a young American named Billy Hayes who was brutalized in Turkish prisons after being arrested for smuggling hashish. The film was budgeted at around $3 million and was to be produced by the English producer David Puttnam and directed by another Englishman, Alan Parker. Columbia made Stone an offer to write the screenplay. "I had a few contacts there," Stone recalls. "Peter Guber knew me vaguely. His right-hand man just loved *Platoon*. Guber was very supportive. They sort of forced me on Puttnam and Parker, who were skeptical. I think they figured that, out of courtesy to Guber, they'd bring me over to London and run through a quick draft, and then get rid of me. I believe that's probably what was going on, although I didn't know it at the time."

Stone drew upon his own jail experience for motivation and burned through the screenplay. His script not only utilized the dramatic force of such classic prison movies as *Cool Hand Luke*, *The Great Escape*, and *Papillon* but took on a somewhat surrealist effect as Stone drew upon his own peculiar sense of the bizarre—little explosive surprises and bits of distinctively shocking violence to assure that the audience could never relax. In the script, Stone used violence as a painter employs color, splashing it here and there at seemingly random intervals. Just when the viewer thinks it's safe, suddenly there is a blast of ferocious brutality that shocks the senses and festers right beneath the level of conscious thought until the next explosion.

After finishing the *Midnight Express* screenplay, Stone returned to California to exciting news. Though he couldn't get *Platoon* financed, Marty Bregman was interested in producing another Vietnam movie and wanted Stone to write it. First, Stone had to meet the person on whose life it was based, the former Vietnam veteran and anti-war activist Ron Kovic. Bregman gave Stone Kovic's book, *Born on the Fourth of July*, which he had optioned, and told him that Al Pacino was interested and William Friedkin, one of Stone's idols at NYU Film School, was going to direct. Kovic had several friends with him the day he and Stone met at the Borg sidewalk café in Venice, including a man named Richard Boyle. Ironically, it was the Fourth of July, 1978. "I had hidden Vietnam away," Stone recalls, "and with Ron, I really was exposed to the raw nerves. I didn't realize that there were brothers out there who were suffering, but not so silently. It helped me in a lot of ways to come into contact with them."

Kovic was impressed with Stone. "There was something about Oliver," he says. "I really felt he was going to be somebody. I told him that I thought he was going to win an Oscar someday."

Meanwhile, *Midnight Express* was being shot in Malta. Although he was not invited to the set, "I must say that Parker, though he was cold to me the whole time, maintained the integrity of the script," Stone says. "Alan and David Puttnam were put under a great deal of pressure to tone the film down, but they held out. They fought to shoot my screenplay.

"I tried to show the Turks as a little crazy, not super-sadistic torturers. Cruelty is a part of life, but so is humor. I had some scenes with the Billy Hayes character being tortured, and then the camera would pan over to one of the Turks watching TV or bringing hookers in. It had a carnival feel to a degree. There was no uniformity in those jails and that was comical to me. But that wasn't in the movie. I also did a second version of the ending at Alan's suggestion that ended abruptly in prison. They didn't have the money or the time to shoot the exit across Turkey to Greece the way I'd written it and the way Billy had lived it."

Even so, things were not entirely amiable between Stone and Puttnam and Parker. "Not only did they not invite me to the set, they didn't invite me to the Cannes Film Festival, which was a very big opening," Stone says. "My feelings were hurt. I think they had a problem with American involvement in the film. They wanted to make their movie without the Americans, whether it be the writer or the financial backer. I was very supportive and tried to be a member of the team. They claimed to be very pleased with the script and went off to Malta and then I never heard from them. I was writing *Born on the Fourth of July* while they were shooting. I kept moving on—I tried not to dwell on it."

Puttnam and Parker may have had other reasons for keeping Stone at a distance. Stanley Weiser elaborates: "Oliver has this Hunter Thompson side, where he says or does outrageous stuff just off the top of his head. He had a meeting with a story editor around that time and she was thrilled that she was going to get to give him her criticisms. It was her first meeting with a big-time screenwriter. So Oliver comes in and looks through these notes and mumbles something to her. She says, 'Excuse me?' And he mumbles the same thing again. She still doesn't understand him so she says, 'What?' And he does it again until she says, 'What? What are you saying?' And then he says, 'I'm dying to fuck you.' Well, she was pretty shocked. But I mentioned that incident to him recently and he didn't remember it at all. He didn't deny it. He just doesn't remember it."

Despite its power, Hollywood is a small town, and small towns like their gossip. In the mid-seventies, a good portion of that gossip was about a new screenwriter named Oliver Stone. He was a wild man, they said; a heavy drug user—acid, coke, just about anything. And women? One female friend says, "Oliver had a million women in his life then— I don't think he missed too many."

One wonders how Stone, if he was so wild, could have possibly been able to navigate the extremely complex political waters of Hollywood. According to Stone, he knew when to rein it in. Ron Mardigian, his agent at William Morris in those days, maintains Stone was not one of his more difficult clients. "Oliver wasn't hard to deal with," Mardigian says. "He trusted that you were doing the best you could. He made it clear that he wanted to work, though. His object was to make money, and he worried about not having enough. I think he has a fear of being broke. He wasn't greedy, but it was important for him to have a nest egg and a place he either owned or where he could be secure. But he had his own opinions about his writing and what projects to do and he wouldn't rely heavily on anyone else's ideas. He would ask for advice a lot, but he would seldom take it. He had very strong creative ideas and the courage of his convictions. Few people really do. Also, he was immensely fun and never dull."

Stone soon acquired a reputation notable even by Hollywood standards. Although studio heads and film producers might be thought to prefer to hire more timid writers who are reliable and take orders well, it seems as if Stone's reputation may have actually helped his career at the time. By the mid-seventies, even people in the big business end of the arts were starting to appreciate the maverick mind-set. And having a reputation that preceded him made Stone stand out from the rest of the pack which, at that stage in his career, was what mattered. His spec script (what a writer offers to demonstrate his talents) was the powerful *Platoon*, and his sole serious credit, the soon to be released *Midnight Express*, was generating quite a buzz around town. Clearly, he was someone to be reckoned with.

Edward R. Pressman was looking for just such a writer to develop a script around *Conan the Barbarian*, the Robert E. Howard comic-book hero. Ron Mardigian showed Pressman *Platoon*, and he was very taken with it. "Oliver was living up above Sunset." Pressman recalls, "We met in his apartment and started working on *Conan* together. He was a very vivacious character and we were both bachelors, so we hung out a lot. It was always evident that he wanted to direct, and at one point I tried approaching *Conan* with him as the director. We were actually going to do it as a co-directing thing with Joe Alves, who had done second direction on *Jaws* directing the action sequences. That was a pretty crazy idea and we didn't get anywhere with it, but we tried."

After spending considerable time and money in legal fees, Pressman obtained the screen rights to the *Conan* books, but was unable to sell the deal with Stone attached as the director. Dino de Laurentiis did give the go-ahead for Stone to write the script, however. "My original draft was a $40 million movie," Stone recalls. "It dealt with the takeover of the planet and the forces of life being threatened by the forces of darkness.

The mutant armies were taking over, and Conan was the lonely pagan—as opposed to Christian—hero; he was Roland at the pass, he was Tarzan, he was a *mythic* figure. I loved that he had been enslaved and suffered, and that he *rose*. What was great about the Howard books was Conan's progression from a peasant to a king. At the end of the movie, in my draft, he is the king, and it means something that he came from these roots. Then he forgoes the kingdom and tells the princess, 'I can't be a king this way, as your husband. I can't inherit the throne. I will earn my throne.' Then he went riding off to the second adventure, which was supposed to be the follow-up sequel. If they'd done it my way, they would have had a Bond-type series, several pictures, which is what I had wanted to do."

Stone's version of *Conan* reads like a medieval Armageddon, complete with an enormous demonic army composed of hideously deformed mutants, half-beasts, and other marvelous creatures. Within the Satanic ruled city is a Boschian vision of Hell—slimy green snakes writhe through the eyesockets of skulls stacked in great heaps, huge insect-headed mutants boil vats of old people, a birdlike man nails the tongue of a old woman with red hot spikes, while another forces hot coals down a man's mouth. Reigning over everything is the demon incarnate, Thulsa Doom, a terrifying creature who has been called back from Hell to lead the forces of darkness. All in all, Stone's screenplay is a powerful spectacle, the likes of which has still never been seen on the screen.

Many writers claim that screenwriting is the least satisfying form of writing possible. Only a very small percentage of scripts that are written ever make it to the screen, and those that do are often radically changed without the writer's input. Oliver Stone has two such horror stories, the first of which was *Conan the Barbarian*. In this case, a change of directors precipitated the script changes. Since the studio wouldn't accept Stone as director, Pressman approached Ridley Scott. Scott was enthusiastic, and Stone wrote the project with him in mind. Though he liked Stone's first draft, Scott then became interested in doing another film instead.

"Ridley Scott pulled out at the last second," Stone elaborates. "I begged him not to. I went down on my knees to him. This was after he made *The Duelists*. *Alien* was finished, but we hadn't seen it yet. He said yes, and then he said no. It broke our hearts when he decided to do *Blade Runner* instead. After Ridley's turndown, we turned it over to John Milius and Dino [de Laurentiis]. Although I have come to like John very much as a human being, at that time he didn't want to collaborate with me. My *Conan* was closer to Robert E. Howard's book. John put that whole snake-cult stuff in, which I didn't care for."

What the world eventually saw as *Conan the Barbarian* barely encompassed the first and weaker half of Stone's epic. While budget considerations must have been a factor, Stone claims that this was never discussed and there was virtually no collaboration with John Milius. "I never really got a second pass at the script," Stone says. "John rewrote it and I gave him my notes on his rewrite and basically, he tore up the notes and we never talked about the movie again. It was like he had a stone wall about him, and since I had less credits at the time, he didn't care about my input. He went more with the bodybuilding aspect of Schwarzenegger, whereas I thought Arnold had a more romantic side. They shot in Spain because it was cheaper there, but I wanted to shoot it in Germany or Russia—and to get the whole Russian Army, thousands of people in the green, fertile fields of Russia. The picture should have been green; John made it rocky desert yellow, like a Sergio Leone western. He had to cut back on the extras and I still think because of de Laurentiis's influence, the rocks looked like cardboard boulders. Since that time, oddly, I have grown closer and closer to John. I truly respect him and like him for his stubborn independence. I think he's a great raconteur. He reminds me of the John Wayne character in *The Searchers*."

Milius, the writer of *Apocalypse Now* and director of *Red Dawn* (among many other films), has also come to respect Oliver Stone over the years. He describes the time Stone came over to his office at Warner Brothers: "I had a Claymore mine on my desk and it was facing so it would explode toward the door. I used to click the trigger all the time when I had to meet with agents and studio execs and they had no idea what it was. But Oliver just went right over to the desk and said, 'Hey! You got a Claymore! Wow, I was nearly killed by one of these.'"

Milius had never read the Conan books until Stone told him about the script he wrote for Dino de Laurentiis, claiming that Milius should consider directing it. "I said I didn't know anything about Conan, and Oliver said, 'Well, you were born to make the movie,'" Milius recalls. "He didn't give me the script, he gave me these comic books and the

Franzetti paintings and stuff like that. Well, I like that kind of stuff and I had always wanted to do a Viking story and this was in the same realm. And I already had a deal with Dino."

However, once Milius did see Stone's script, he thought it was too bizarre to shoot the way it was written. "I got excited and then he gave me the script and it was useless. You couldn't shoot a thing, it didn't make any sense. It was a total drug fever dream, but it was inspirational to read. It had nothing to do with the story or what we did, but he deserved every bit of credit he got, because he totally inspired me to do it. He was around all the time I was writing, and he'd look it over and give me ideas and stuff. His script had some wonderful passages and I tried to get the flavor of it. He had the thing in there which came from the original story of the father telling the son that he could trust steel. Oliver understood that it should be barbarian as opposed to sword and sorcerer stuff."

Just as Stone was getting discouraged over the direction *Conan* was taking, *Midnight Express* was released. From that point on, nothing would ever be the same for him. *Midnight Express* not only fulfilled a dream, it validated the quest. If he'd had doubts about his talents or chances for success, it eradicated them. Released in October 1978, *Midnight Express* was an immediate success. It generated big grosses at the box office, and was a critical favorite as well. Since the film had not been a big-budget affair or heavily hyped before its release, it was viewed by the Hollywood establishment as a dark horse made good, a little film with a message that proved all over again that such films could still succeed on their own merit.

The success of *Midnight Express* changed the attitude of Stone's family, as well. Jim Stone, Oliver's cousin, remembers: "I think there was a residue of skepticism until we opened the paper and saw that *Midnight Express* was actually being advertised. Before that there was always the possibility that it would be a grade-D movie or something that wasn't even going to get shot. When it turned out to be a serious picture, our feelings changed. Right after *Midnight Express* came out, his father said something about being wrong, something like, 'I thought Oliver was just being self-indulgent, but this proves that he can actually succeed in that field.' And, since his father was a writer, the idea that Oliver could make money writing was thrilling to him. Now that he knew Oliver wasn't going to be ruined by it, of all the things he could hope for his son to have, success as a writer would be first. It was a complete 180-degree turnaround."

Fittingly, since it was Oliver Stone's first success, *Midnight Express* also proved to be extremely controversial. The success of the film brought a hailstorm of criticism from people who believed that it unfairly depicted the Turks, including charges of being "racist." "I think the Turks had a point," Stone says now. "It's extreme. I think the humor in the screenplay might have softened it some if it would have made it into the movie, but it didn't. So, the Turks were right. It was rabid, but I was young."

Ironically, *Midnight Express* was a great antidrug film because it so dramatically brought home the dangers of fooling around with drugs in foreign countries. Over the years, countless people have expressed their gratitude to Stone, and said the film deterred them from taking chances with drug smuggling and probably kept them out of serious trouble. "I saw *Midnight Express* as a story about justice," Stone comments. "It wasn't about drugs. He could have been busted for carrying a pistol as far as I was concerned. The charge didn't really interest me; it was the miscarriage of justice."

Other charges were leveled at the film. Some claimed that it didn't deal properly with prison homosexuality, avoiding the issue or presenting a negative slant on it. Others merely argued that Stone had deviated too much from Billy Hayes's book. But *Midnight Express* was a sleeper hit. It not only packed the theaters, it created quite a stir in Hollywood. For every voice that charged "needless violence," there were many more who cried "courageous filmmaking." Oliver Stone didn't mind the heat. He knew something important was happening. He had always felt that nonfiction was by nature more important than fiction, but he loved the artistry and power of good prose. Nonfiction was the truth, and the truth needed to be told; but it was fiction that had the power to move people to tears and, equally important, to action. He must have sensed that *Midnight Express* proved his instincts were right about *Platoon*, *Born on the Fourth of July*, and the other films he wanted to do. Without fully realizing it, Stone had demonstrated that the perfect vehicle for his particular talents was taking a passionate true story and making it into a riveting film. He became the hottest screenwriter in town.

In December 1978, *The Deer Hunter* was released. Though he had been hearing about the film for months while it was being made, Stone had no idea that director Michael Cimino's movie about Vietnam and its impact on the lives of a group of friends would be so powerful or successful. The film did well at the box office and the critics raved over it. Naturally, since Stone had been trying to make a film that told the truth about Vietnam for nearly ten years, it frustrated him when Cimino's film, which used the war as more of a backdrop, became accepted by Hollywood. Stone envisioned *Platoon*'s message as a truth which he felt couldn't be compromised or told in allegorical terms. *The Deer Hunter* was a powerhouse of a film. Stone respected its technique, and admired Cimino for exploring the disturbing psyche of the Vietnam vets and how the war changed them forever. On the other hand, little of the actual Vietnam war experience was shown in the film, and Stone knew that the most powerful of those scenes, where American prisoners are forced by the Viet Cong to play Russian roulette, was not based on fact. Now a longtime friend of Cimino's, who was co-writer on *Year of the Dragon*, Stone calls *The Deer Hunter* a "visual feast." "It is a very powerful movie," Stone says, "expertly made. Michael at the top of his powers. But it's a sensory experience that is in many ways unrealistic . . . all the kids from the same town staying together, that's unrealistic, so the whole premise of the movie is based on an impossibility. And the Russian roulette scenes may have happened somewhere, but no one has documented it."

The Deer Hunter is more about the effects of Vietnam than Vietnam itself. This was even more true of another film released earlier that same year, *Coming Home*, starring Jon Voight as a paraplegic vet and Jane Fonda as the woman who falls in love with him while her own husband (Bruce Dern) is overseas. The movie showed no combat scenes, but deserved praise for attempting to understand the Vietnam veteran's parallel wounds of mind, body, and spirit. For Stone, this film was particularly frustrating because it severely hampered the chances of *Born on the Fourth of July* getting made. *Coming Home* did poorly at the box office despite receiving Oscar nominations, and the studios promptly backed off *Born on the Fourth of July* as being too similar. Both stories dealt with a man returning from the Vietnam War as an embittered paraplegic. Further, Ron Kovic had served as an adviser for *Coming Home*. Although Stone's concept for *Born on the Fourth of July* differed in that it also explored other themes, such as how men are conditioned for battle by society from birth, by Hollywood's standards the two pictures were too similar.

Marty Bregman had been having problems getting backing for *Born on the Fourth of July*, and it looked now as if it would be even more difficult. "It was almost an impossible film to make," Bregman says. "We couldn't get a studio, we couldn't get a director, and I approached everyone in town."

Both *The Deer Hunter* and *Coming Home* drew rave reviews, and despite the protests of many vets, Hollywood was already patting itself on the back for dealing with Vietnam. For Stone, this idea in particular was a slow knife inching its way into his psyche. To him, Hollywood was evading some of the harder issues, and this was worse than not dealing with them at all.

For some time now it had been clear to Oliver and Najwa that their marriage was over. Though they continued to communicate and speak highly of each other—something they do to this day—the legal papers were finally served and processed. "He called me and said, 'Sarkis, your divorce is final,'" Najwa remembers. "He said, 'Do you want to have a glass of champagne on it?' and I said, 'Why not?' He said, 'I'm coming to New York tomorrow,' and we had dinner."

When the Academy Award nominations were announced *The Deer Hunter* led the pack with nine; it was followed by *Coming Home* with eight. Nominated for Best Screenplay Adapted from Another Medium was Oliver Stone. Though thrilled by the recognition, more than anything else Stone saw his Oscar nomination as an opportunity to get the films he so desperately wanted to make financed. And, for a while, things seem to fall into place. Marty Bregman finessed a deal to get money for *Born on the Fourth of July* through some European sources, and Al Pacino was pleased with Stone's screenplay. Though it was Kovic's story rather than his own, it looked as if Oliver Stone was about to have his say on Vietnam.

Elated, Stone began moving forward on several other projects as well. One of them was based on *Baby Boy*, a book by Jess Gregg about two men in prison. It was while doing the research for this project that Stone met Richard Rutowski, who has been his friend and associate ever since (Rutowski later co-wrote *Natural Born Killers* with Stone and David Veloz). "He was going to go to prisons to do research for *Baby Boy*," Rutowski recalls, "and I knew a few guys who had been in prison. Also, I knew Bill Clinton's people then, and figured I could get us into some prisons in Arkansas. So we went to Cummings Prison in Arkansas, then to Parchman in Mississippi and Angola in Louisiana. Oliver was a tough guy at that point, very angry, very cynical. He hurt people. He had an ability to see a weakness in you and touch you there. My first impression was that he was very corrupt and very perverse. He was dangerous, definitely an outsider. He was threatened by Hollywood, I think, and Hollywood was threatened by him. He was very intellectual, and there was a certain sixties attitude that he embraced which the Hollywood elite rejected, so he was considered an outsider. He couldn't relate to that whole game aspect of Hollywood. When I was with him at parties, he used to offend people all the time."

As Rutowski and Stone traveled together, they realized they had a great deal in common. It turned out that Rutowski had been very well acquainted with one of Stone's idols, Jim Morrison ("He used to stay at my house a lot when he was trying to hide out and clean up"). Rutowski was discovering another side of Stone as well: "As I spent some time with him going to these prisons, I realized he had incredible compassion for people. I saw him with guys who were former soldiers in Vietnam. Guys who would never get out. And I saw this incredible, compassionate and interesting kinship that he had with these men. He really felt for these guys. Some of them were artists. They had written out reams of music on lined paper and told their life stories and were desperate for someone to listen to them. And Oliver really gave them time. He has the ability to penetrate to a deeper story, not the story that everyone tells, their own mythology so to speak, but to what the real thing was. What motivated people."

Rutowski also discovered that Stone was not easily intimidated, either by prisoners or the law. "We interviewed a lot of killers for this movie, very intense guys. Multiple murderers with chained ankles and arms, living in stifling old prison rooms. Some of the cells were made of rock, some had bars, one had steel straps. It was like a cage that had been wrapped like a Christmas present. Some were guys who had done a lot of killing, and were very powerful in the prison system because of it. But it didn't bother Oliver. He'd talk to them like anybody else. In those days, we were both doing drugs. We took coke in and snorted it in every prison we went to. We snorted coke in the electric chair at one prison. Once you say you're in the movies, they walk you in. It was walking the edge, kind of insane if you think about it. They frisk people all the time, so we were taking a chance. But they never bothered us at all.

"Oliver would do things that other people just wouldn't do. Most people live by the rules, but for Oliver the rules are a guideline. It's not that he disrespects the laws—not the laws of nature, the laws of God, or the laws of the state—but he has a curiosity about breaking the law. It's like an exploration, a spiritual exploration in a way, and I think he's suffered from it a lot. He's done a lot of things he's regretted. But it's one of the things that makes him such a unique artist."

While in Baton Rouge, Stone decided they should interview some strippers. "We went to a black whorehouse and interviewed strippers," Rutowski remembers. "It wasn't like you might think. I mean, it's not like—he doesn't go crazy or anything. It seems pretty innocent in a way. He has this love for hookers and strippers and . . . women who are on the outside. He seems to feel a kinship to them."

While touring the prisons, Rutowski says that he and Stone encountered a lot of corruption. "In some of the places where the guards and trustees had more control, the prisoners were like slaves. They had these outshacks on the edge of the prison and all kinds of stuff would go on there. The prisoners had to agree to weird sexual favors, provide their wives for the guards sometimes. Some of these prisoners were totally into their dark side and cultivated their darkest impulses—rape, torture, and murder were what got them off. They didn't believe there was any redemption possible for them. They were not coming out, and they were trying to spit in the face of God. But the impulse killers were very moral and religious. Most killed only once, and it was out of passion."

A key element in Stone and Rutowski's relationship became the spiritual quest. Closer to Aldous Huxley, Carlos Castaneda, and sixties acid trips than religious orthodoxy, the quest centered on expanding the mind to understand the spirit. The goal, as with all such quests, was to discover the purpose in life; why things happen the way they do. "We were trying to unravel all of this shit that happened to us," Rutowski says. "While Oliver was in Vietnam, my wife died very young of cancer and I had a lot of near-death experiences. We wanted to know what the point was of all this; how we were supposed to assimilate it and grow."

Shortly after this time, the financing for *Born on the Fourth of July* fell through once again, and Al Pacino walked out of the deal. Stone was angry then, and when he thinks of it now, fifteen years later, he is still angry. "We were three days from shooting," he says vehemently. "I had spent a year on the screenplay, working with Ron Kovic, who had written a terrific book, poetic, a wonderful piece. I saw the whole movie in rehearsals. We changed what we had to change. Pacino was white heat. William Friedkin, the director, had dropped out before, which was a real shame, but he had been very ably replaced by Dan Petrie. But then the money fell out three days before shooting. It was one of those crazy half-German, half-U.S. deals. Pacino wouldn't wait. He was pissed off and he went to do *And Justice For All*, because it was a paying deal and it was a set time. It broke my spirit. I didn't realize then there was a larger purpose at work."

Stanley Weiser was down on the boardwalk in Venice when Stone broke the news to Ron Kovic. "I'll never forget this," Weiser says. "Kovic was chasing Oliver down the boardwalk and punching him, screaming at him. And here's Oliver—he's got a nut in a wheelchair trailing after him. Chasing him, screaming at him. And Oliver can't do anything. Kovic was pretty crazy back then."

Stone smiles at the memory, but his voice reveals a sadness in recalling it: "Yeah, Ron was pissed off. He took it very hard. He was on the verge of committing suicide. He was pissed at me and I was pissed at him. He'd been acting crazy anyway, acting like a movie star because Pacino was playing his life story. That night I said, 'You know you've become sick. That Hollywood shit has gotten into your head.' And then he chased me down the dock in his wheelchair. He was angry and hurt. I understood. Al had pulled out and the financing wasn't there."

Resolutely, Stone set *Born* aside and it joined *Platoon* on the shelf. He began to wonder if he was kidding himself about projects like these ever getting made. Here he was, nominated for an Oscar, and still he couldn't get things done. "It was very upsetting to me. I went to Poland and I got drunk. I vanished. I went to a place where nobody knew me. Jane Fonda had approached me to do something on the world of high finance, but I didn't feel I could deal with that at the time. [Fonda's idea later became the movie *Rollover*.] I just wanted to be in a total oblivion. So I went to Poland and Czechoslovakia. It was like being in a Kafka dream. I didn't know anybody and nobody knew me. I got lost in both countries and I'd end up walking for hours trying to find my way around these circular streets with weird names."

Stone also visited Amsterdam around this time. One evening he snorted heroin and became so disoriented he almost fell into a canal. Back in America, Stone had attended the Golden Globe Awards in January 1979 as a nominee for writing *Midnight Express*, where he forged another key link in Hollywood's image of him as a rebel. "That night I was stoned out of my head on quaaludes and coke," Stone recalls. "So was practically everybody else at my table. I was hurt about Puttnam and Parker not inviting me to Cannes. That was such a petty thing. I think they were surprised that I got all this recognition, the Acadamy Award nomination, a Golden Globe nomination. Well, I won the Golden Globe and I made this long, obfuscated speech attacking the drug laws. I was saying, 'Don't just look at Turkey, look at America.' I also attacked the television people, and since the program was being televised, that probably wasn't too wise. I said, 'You guys on TV promote all this simplistic bullshit and don't present the truth the way it is. You make these small-time drug dealers look like demons instead of focusing on the real issues.' I was being hissed and booed off the stage. So Chevy Chase and Richard Harris, not exactly angels themselves, came up and dragged me off the fucking stage, like they're the models of sobriety. And David [Puttnam] comes over to me, and he's like, 'You fucking blew it! You'll never get an Academy Award!' And Alan Parker was glaring at me, all pissed off."

"You need people like me so you can point your fucking fingers and say that's the bad guy."

Tony Montana in **SCARFACE**

So much for Stone's chance to fit in with the Hollywood establishment. "I knew I'd crossed the line," he admits. "I mean, my balls aren't all brass, you know, and I knew these people could hurt me. But the drug laws are screwed up. Not just in Turkey, but in this country as well. All these people were hypocritical as far as I was concerned. Like it was okay to talk about Turkey, but don't mention it's going on in America."

The Academy Awards were held in Los Angeles on April 9, 1979.

As Stone arrived, he saw two groups of protesters outside the hall, demonstrating against the Best Picture nominee, *The Deer Hunter*. The members of Vietnam Veterans Against the War were distributing statements that said: "Many of us were part of the antiwar movement ten years ago. Tonight we are opposing another war, one that never happened, except in the mind of Michael Cimino." The vets claimed the movie was racist, reactionary, and Fascist. The other group, the "Hell No, We Won't Go Committee," waved placards that read: "No Oscars for Racism." Both groups were angry over the POW scenes, particularly the Russian roulette sequence in *The Deer Hunter*. The film had already won the Directors Guild Award for Best Picture, usually a strong indicator of which film will take home the Oscar. Before the night was over the demonstrations became violent, and thirteen people were arrested by police for inciting a riot. To Oliver Stone, it was yet another painful reminder that the real story of Vietnam had not yet been told and a challenge that perhaps he had not yet done all he could to tell it.

The Oscars that year were, as always, a bizarre combination of glitz, chutzpah, style, and grace. The television broadcast began with a disco number and the cameras zoomed in tight on the entrance to the theater, neatly avoiding the protesters in the process. Johnny Carson joked that the evening would be two hours of sparkling entertainment spread over a four-hour show. The 51st Academy Awards were on their way.

Early in the evening Dyan Cannon announced the Best Supporting Actor Award, which went to Christopher Walken for his compelling portrayal of the deranged Vietnam veteran who couldn't face going home in *The Deer Hunter*. Also playing a Vietnam vet and nominated in the same category was Bruce Dern in *Coming Home*.

Later in the show, Raquel Welch and Dean Martin introduced the Scoring Awards. Welch wore a tight, low-cut, blue-sequined jumpsuit, and Martin cracked to the audience, "I'll lay eight to five that only two of you are looking at me." Moments later Giorgio Moroder was proclaimed the winner for his score for *Midnight Express*. It was the film's first award, and Stone's heart skipped a quick beat. It was possible he would win. Though he has stated he doesn't approve of anything that implies or inspires competition between artists because he believes that art should stand on its own, Stone knew what the Oscar would mean to his career. Besides the glory and the higher writing fees, it would increase his chances of getting *Platoon* and *Born on the Fourth of July* made. Beyond that even, it would enable him to direct again.

On stage, eighty-three-year-old George Burns and thirteen-year-old Brooke Shields had just presented the Best Supporting Actress Award to Maggie Smith for *California Suite*, and now Lauren Bacall and Jon Voight came out to introduce the writing awards. There are two writing categories: Original Screenplay and Adapted Screenplay. The Original Screenplay Award came first, and Voight and Bacall read off the nominees—the writers of *The Deer Hunter*, *Interiors*, *Unmarried Woman*, and *Coming Home*. The winners were Robert Salt, Nancy Dowd, and Robert C. Jones for *Coming Home*, which naturally pleased Voight, who was the film's star. Despite the way *Coming Home* had hurt his chances for *Born on the Fourth of July*, Stone liked Jon Voight, especially when he learned that Voight had Ron Kovic accompany him to the Oscars. Before she left the podium, Nancy Dowd reminded everyone that she had written her screenplay in 1973. Because the script dealt with Vietnam, it had taken five years to get it made. In the audience, Oliver Stone smiled to himself.

Now Voight and Bacall turned their attention to the Best Adapted Screenplay awards, and Stone tensed. The nominees were *Bloodbrothers*, by Walter Newman; *California Suite*, by Neil Simon; *Heaven Can Wait*, by Elaine May and Warren Beatty; *Same Time Next Year*, by Bernard Slade; and *Midnight Express*, by Oliver Stone. Neil Simon, Warren Beatty . . . these were big names, but still *Midnight Express* had done well. It could even be called the darkhorse, the underdog favorite . . . Such thoughts raced through Stone's mind as he watched Voight open the envelope. Voight smiled. "The winner for Best Adapted Screenplay is Oliver Stone for *Midnight Express*."

"Life all comes down to a few moments, and this is one of 'em."

Bud Fox in **WALL STREET**

Stone strode to the stage in a half-daze, going over what he would say. His speech was short, but expressed his hope that the award and the recognition of the film would lead to "some consideration for all the men and women who are still in prison tonight."

The Best Director Award went to Michael Cimino; Jane Fonda, who twice visited Hanoi to protest the U.S. war effort in Vietnam, won the Oscar for Best Actress in *Coming Home*; and Jon Voight took the Best Actor Award. John Wayne announced the Best Picture Award: *The Deer Hunter*. It was certainly the night Hollywood saluted the Vietnam War.

Though few in the television audience knew it at the time, another Vietnam veteran had also been honored that night. Today, Stone recalls the moment as a genuine thrill. "It was like a fairy tale," he says. "A magic night. A lot of the old Hollywood stars were there. I was backstage with Cary Grant, Laurence Olivier, and John Wayne. All of a sudden, I was thirty-two years old and the golden boy for a few minutes. But I really wasn't ready for it."

Jacqueline Stone and Najwa attended an Oscar party in New York, where they watched the awards on television. Ironically, Lou Stone, who had been looking forward to watching the program, fell asleep in front of the TV in his apartment before the screenwriting awards were announced, only to be awakened by phone calls congratulating him on his son's success. Roger Kirby remembers how proud Lou Stone was of the award: "Oliver's father talked about the Oscar quite a bit among his friends. So, thereafter, among those gentlemen, Oliver ceased to be Oliver. They'd ask, 'How's Oscar?'"

Stone says that the sudden success that came with the Oscar stunned him: "All of a sudden I went from being nobody for ten years—total reject—to being wanted by everybody. I wasn't quite ready for it. I was very much an artist in my mind, and I didn't understand that the movie business is a collaboration between art and money. It was like being on a magic carpet. In a two-year period, I lived intensely all the fantasies I'd had of Hollywood. I had the Oscar and a bachelor apartment in West Hollywood and I was living pretty wild, lots of parties and wild escapades, a lot of girls—and everybody I knew was sorta crazy, either alienated from cocaine or tripping on acid or ecstasy. I remember wild mushrooms were heavy in those days as well as mixing stuff, ups and downs."

John Milius remembers an evening when he and his wife went out to dinner with Stone around this time: "Oliver brought this blond actress. She was very good looking, very friendly, but she didn't seem all that taken with Oliver. I think he was too intense for her. So at one point, she went to the bathroom, and Oliver looks at us and he pulls out a Quaalude and puts it in her wine. We couldn't stop laughing. So she comes back and she sees this glass of wine that looks like an Orange Julius. She didn't know quite what to do and we didn't know whether to warn her or what. She just sort of gave him a dirty look and didn't drink it. I called him the next day and he said that he didn't do very well with her."

One of the people Stone frequently partied with was Sergio Premoli. Premoli, an Italian painter, sculptor, and entrepreneur, had been introduced to Stone by the French film director Roger Vadim. "We clicked because Oliver is one of the few people who has a real love for and grasp of history," Premoli says. "He has a tremendous sensitivity. Most people when they open a conversation, try to jump the other person. Oliver will listen to see if the person has something exciting to say. At the time, he was very handsome and he had long hair and wore leather pants, very tight, like Jim Morrison. He would tease or harass everybody, man or woman. He was very aggressive and extremely demanding. It didn't matter if it was a little executive from Paramount or a well-known director from Europe. Oliver, he was in charge of his destiny, and he knew it. We were at one party and he was saying hello to everyone, when he saw this woman. So he went over and gave her a joint and she was digging him very much. Then I said, 'I'm going upstairs,' and Oliver stayed with the woman. A few moments later, I came back down the steps and . . . Zow! Oliver was banging the woman against the wall . . . right there."

Stone doesn't remember the incident, but he doesn't deny it either, since there are a lot of things from those days which he no longer remembers: "From 1976 until 1980, I had a ball. I partied hard and did the Hollywood scene. I'd try everything. Before I met my second wife, I was sexually wild too. But I always kept a sober side. No matter how hard the night was, I would always write in the day."

Stanley Weiser remembers Oliver well in this period, and says, "There's a thousand strange stories from those days. After he won the Academy Award he was doing a lot of drugs and every time he'd go somewhere, there'd be trouble. Like at one party he had invited this studio head's girlfriend to go with him to the Caribbean. He was saying, 'How can you be with this asshole, this crypto-Fascist?' And on and on . . . and I was thinking, 'My God, he is taking his life into his hands.' And I remember another party where this Brazilian model was the hostess . . . I was talking, and all of a sudden I heard pounding and smashing noises and kicking. And it clicks in my mind, 'It's Oliver.' And then I saw some big bodybuilder guys kicking the bathroom door from the outside and somebody else was kicking it from the inside. Then, the whole door explodes, wood and splinters flying. The hostess is saying, 'Who is this idiot who goes to my party and is destroying my door?' and Oliver came out of the bathroom and there was sawdust all over his head. He'd been locked in the bathroom and was so stoned he couldn't open the door. He'd broken down the door. And she said, 'Who is this maniac? I'm going to call the police.' And I said that's Oliver Stone and she said, 'Oh, didn't he just win the Academy Award?' So she came over to him and started helping him, brushing the sawdust off, asking, 'Do you need medical assistance?' She was trying to take care of him, and still he said, 'What kind of dump is this, don't you have a door that works?' "

According to Weiser, Stone used to go to parties and systematically annihilate the egos of the guests: "He'd do it all the time. One time we went to this party and the hostess was sucking up to him the whole night. And they kept laughing and giggling for a long time and then he said, 'Don't worry, I'm not laughing with you, I'm laughing at you.' It was like, *bang!* She was shocked. She had thought she was on his wavelength. By the end of the party, the hostess had left, another guy there had a migraine, another person was in the corner completely depressed, and Oliver was starting in on these hippies, saying, 'But what is your relationship to the land?' " He was just ripping everyone apart. Everybody except this one girl who was sitting on his lap, stoned. He offended a lot of people in those days. I remember whenever people would worry about being perceived by the industry as crazy or a troublemaker, someone would say, 'Well, look at Oliver. They don't care how crazy you are. They'll let you work as long as they need you.' He was like the most extreme example that anyone knew about."

Ron Mardigian recalls what it was like to represent Stone at this time: "Oliver would offend the wrong people, especially in his worst drug days. For Oliver, the shortest distance is always a straight line, and he had no patience for tennis or any of that kind of political bullshit. But he was smart. If he felt it was important to be obsequious or polite, if his goals were going to be achieved by doing that, he would do it. But if it was just a matter of routine, like let's just be nice because that's the way it's supposed to be, he wouldn't do it. Sometimes he would want to pull out of a deal. He'd get fed up dealing with the people and decide he wasn't the right person for the project. That would happen a lot. Sometimes I'd have to glue the deal back. Tell him that he had to go through with it. The thing that had the most impact, as I recall, was that while he didn't mind having a reputation for being difficult, he didn't want a reputation for being unprofessional. In other words, he didn't care if you thought he was an asshole, as long as you thought he was a talented asshole. So I would do this a lot with him, I'd say, 'If you drop out of this thing, they are not going to hire you again.' Professionalism was very important to him, and I would have to dwell on that to get him to see the logic in a situation."

One time Stone even returned $250,000 because he decided he didn't want to write the project (a P.D. James mystery, entitled *Innocent Blood*). Still he was wild. According to Mardigian, part of Stone's problem was the fast-paced crowd he hung out with. "Hollywood is weird, and the movie crowd in those days was about the weirdest it ever got. Oliver ran with the cutting-edge crowd; you had to be using the drug of choice, the language of choice, and the activity of choice. Once in a while I would say, 'I think you're going out with fucked-up people,' and that was as much as I'd get into it. That was about all I could say."

In those days, whenever film industry people were present, especially studio executives, Stone tended to act even more obnoxious, as if he had an irresistible urge to bite the hand that was feeding him. Since he had to submit to these powers in his work, he had to rebel in other ways, just to prove that Hollywood hadn't yet knotted the noose he felt tightening around his neck. He had a particular disgust for Hollywood's tendency to pretend that it was more concerned with celebrating art and furthering humanity than making money. Stone hated this kind of pseudo-liberal posturizing more than he hated outright rejection. If the film industry was more about art than playing politics, then his work could never be rejected because of something like being rude at a party, and this became another enticement he couldn't resist. He loved flirting with disaster, testing the boundaries—seeing what he could get away with.

Many of Stone's antics derived from his sense of humor. He liked to tease, put people on and do the unexpected. Stanley Weiser recounts another anecdote from this period: "Some guy from film school came out to L.A. and kept trying to get with Oliver, hoping that maybe he could work with him. He kept leaving messages, and so one day Oliver finally called him up. The guy's wife answered the phone and said, 'Here, it's Oliver,' but then she kept on talking and says, 'Wait. He says he wants to talk to me. He wants me to have lunch with him.' And her husband exclaims, 'What about me?' She gets back on the phone and then says, 'He says it's just platonic.' Well, she never went, and he and Oliver never got together.

"So the guy told me this story. But the funny thing was that about four years later, he was divorced and he had another girlfriend. Out of the blue, Oliver called up and invited *her* out for dinner. This girl actually went, and then for some reason she stopped seeing the guy. I told this to Oliver recently and he didn't remember it at all. We laughed and then he asked if the guy had gotten remarried and I said yeah. And he said, 'Maybe I should call his new wife.'"

The prank may have been on impulse, but Weiser says it still had a definite point. "The thing was, Oliver turned it around on the guy. They weren't good friends. The guy was obviously trying to get something from him, and Oliver was aware of that, so he turned it around to where he was trying to get something from the guy. Most people's minds run on one or two tracks, but Oliver's mind is running down twenty or thirty tracks all the time. He's clicking back and forth like a railroad car switching. When you work with him, the hard part is following his train of thought. Especially since he's doing so many different things. He thrives on chaos. He has to have a lot of energy where things happen in swirling undercurrents. Wherever you go with Oliver, something interesting is going to happen; something strange, something unexpected. That's been consistent throughout the years I've known him, whether he was famous or not. It used to be more outrageous. It used to be that wherever you'd go with him, you were going to have trouble. He was very bitter in those days and doing a lot of drugs. Oliver's got about twenty-eight or twenty-nine different moods and, back then, like about twenty-seven of them were bad."

"You know what you need, buddy—an optorectomy. That's when they cut the nerve that runs from your brain to your rectum—to change that shitty attitude of yours."

Marv in **WALL STREET**

Having Najwa in his life provided Stone with a firm foundation. In many ways this was even more true for his second wife. Though his career was already in high gear, Stone's personal life was in a mad spin when he attended the party in West Hollywood where he first saw Elizabeth Cox.

Elizabeth was raised in Texas. Her father was in Army Intelligence and was killed during the Korean War when she was only one and a half. Her mother remarried, and Elizabeth, as the second oldest, had to help her raise seven children. Having a somewhat restricted childhood, it wasn't until Elizabeth studied psychology at the University of Texas that she really felt she came into her own. Right after graduation she drove her Fiat to California with the idea of making it as an actress, but by her own admission was too shy to act. So, she worked various jobs and did some commercial modeling here and there.

"I was sort of a jack of all trades and master of none," she says. "I could dance, I could act, I could type, teach school. I was a scrapper. I paid the rent. I worked in the censoring department at CBS, as a paralegal, an executive secretary, schoolteacher, but I never 'found myself.' I was never a professional person, but I was happy. I was twenty-nine when I met Oliver, I had dated a lot, had a few relationships, had never been married, and was very content with the idea that I was going to be a single woman."

Even more than her Texas good looks, Elizabeth's down-to-earth attitude makes her stand out from the crowd. She doesn't put on airs and she doesn't try to be what she's not. But the night she met Oliver Stone in May 1979, there were other factors that caused her to stand out as well. "I'd gone for a roller-skating commercial and just broken my ankle roller-skating at Venice Beach," Elizabeth says. "I had a cast on up to my hip. I was living in a house with five Texas girls—my roommate and three of my sisters—in West Hollywood. We decided to have a big open-house party one night, and Oliver walked in the door. I was sitting on the couch with my leg stuck in front of me with this cast on. I saw him come in and our eyes just locked and really, it was love at first sight. After a few weeks we were together from then on until now. It was very emotional on both our parts I think. It was an instant attraction."

He saw a tall, blond, blue-eyed California woman whom he soon found out was from Texas. She saw a tall, dark-haired Hollywood screenwriter with "irresistible Mongolian eyes." Though she was sure a real bond was formed between them that night, Elizabeth didn't hear from Stone for two weeks. "Then finally he called," she says, "and I asked him where he had been. He said he was severing all his relationships so that we could start with a clean slate. Oliver is unequivocal."

They moved in together almost immediately. "Because of my family I was used to taking care of people, so I just naturally started taking care of Oliver too. I remember when I met him, he only wore black. Even to the beach, he would wear a black coat and pants and shoes. His mother had convinced him that if he wore a white shirt he'd look like a waiter, so he wore black. Of course, now I know that part of this was because he was in a very black phase, having just come out of writing *Midnight Express*."

Elizabeth began to type Stone's scripts. "He likes people to be functional and I felt that, after all, he was the one who was the breadwinner. But he did sort of need me to have a purpose, a reason for being that somehow related to work, not just to having a good time. So, since I typed ninety words a minute, he used me as his assistant and script typist. That way I was functional. This goes back to his childhood. He resents the fact that his mother was all decoration and not a functional person. She didn't work at the hospital for charities or write a book or do any kind of work outside the home. All she did was give parties and do a few housewife-type things. He's always resented the fact that society—royalty and celebrity—is so important to her. They have an incredible love/hate relationship. This is partly why he was attracted to me—because I'm a functional, down-to-earth person, not impressed by royalty or celebrity, or into the social scene."

For a while in those early days of the relationship, Stone introduced her to his friends by saying, "This is my girlfriend, Elizabeth. She can type ninety words a minute."

Though he was in love, Stone was far from happy. In August 1979, *Apocalypse Now* was released. By far the most eagerly anticipated Vietnam War epic, Francis Ford Coppola's dark and troubling work was surreal and symbolic. "Like *The Deer Hunter*, *Apocalypse Now* was an extravagant, rich-looking, well-done picture" says Stone. "But *Apocalypse* never showed the Vietnamese. The Brando character is extraordinary, but it's more Conrad than Vietnam."

Apocalypse Now was the third major film in two years to deal with the war, but Stone soon discovered that making a film that told the Vietnamese perspective from the average grunt's point of view was now even more impossible. "I pretty much gave up for a while," he admits. "After *Apocalypse Now* and *The Deer Hunter* came out, there was a kind of lull. I thought it was over. I had met with Ron Kovic and tried to see the war through his eyes. I was writing *Born on the Fourth of July*, which was my fourth Vietnam script, but nobody wanted to make that either. I was frustrated because none of the four had been produced and I was beginning to wonder if the truth about that war would *ever* come out. So I got the message: America didn't really care. Watergate was over, Carter lost, Iran had taken the hostages, liberalism was dead. The truth was dead. I got harder and more cynical. So I buried the screenplay. *Platoon* was dead."

Obviously, being an Oscar-winning screenwriter did not give Stone enough power to make the kinds of films he wanted to make. He'd always known he wanted to direct—now he knew he would have to. He felt that his best chance to make films that mattered was to first establish himself as a director by doing whatever kinds of projects he could get made. He knew he had enough clout to get a horror picture made and he decided to write and direct *The Hand*. It seemed like a good idea at the time.

"For now that I control you, I must consider how you can best serve me."

from Jan Lansdale's comic strip in **THE HAND**

Scarface

"This country ... first you gotta get the money, then you get the power and when you got the power, then you get the women—and then, chico, you got the world by the balls."

Tony Montana in **SCARFACE**

Shortly after Oliver Stone returned from Poland, he had agreed to write and direct what was initially designed to be a psychological horror film based on Marc Brandel's book, *The Lizard's Tail*. The *Born on the Fourth of July* deal falling apart and Hollywood's continued rejection of *Platoon* had left Stone bitter, believing it was impossible for him to make the kind of films he wanted to make.

After the success of *Midnight Express*, Orion had offered Stone the opportunity to direct a film within a certain budget range. Stone suggested that Ed Pressman, whom he'd worked with on *Conan the Barbarian*, be brought in to produce whatever this film might be. Stone's first choice was *Baby Boy*, and Pressman joined Stone and Richard Rutowski in visiting some of the prisons. But after seeing the reality of prison life, Stone felt the movie they were planning was unrealistic and the book less compelling than he had first thought. So, when Ron Mardigian gave him a copy of *The Lizard's Tail*, he chose that instead, adapting it into a screenplay called *The Hand*.

Stone admits that because of his desire to become established as a director as quickly as possible, he didn't listen to his instincts. He felt he'd be on safer ground with *The Hand*, but this would prove to be a mistake. It was one of the last times he would play it safe.

The plot of *The Lizard's Tail* focused on a cartoonist who loses his hand in an automobile accident and then discovers that his dismembered limb has gone on a murderous rampage, propelled by years of suppressed rage. "I liked the idea of *The Hand*," Stone recalls, "but I didn't feel passionate about it. I was in a very dark frame of mind and it was a film about the disintegration of an individual. I wrote it as a psychological horror story with special effects. It was less an actual hand and more psychological in its origin."

When it came time to cast the film, Stone's first choice for the lead was Jon Voight. "He turned me down," Stone says. "Then Mike Medavoy had me talk to Dustin Hoffman. I was totally intimidated. I made arrangements to have breakfast with him at 7:00 A.M. at the Westwood Marquis and I woke up at like three-thirty in the morning and started going over what I would say. I made a complete fool of myself. I was a babbling idiot."

Christopher Walken also turned Stone down at the time. Fortunately, Michael Caine was interested in doing a horror film because he had never done one; he wanted to see what the experience was like, and also was impressed with Oliver Stone. "I found him fascinating," Caine says. "We were both ex-infantrymen, and gradually our conversations became based on these experiences. He used to talk about how a proper film of Vietnam had never been made and how he was going to do it one day. The other topic we discussed often was the assassination of President Kennedy. I agreed with his theory that Oswald could not have possibly shot Kennedy from where he was with the rifle and ammunition that he carried."

The Hand was shot at Laird International Studios in the spring of 1980. It was a poor Hollywood directorial debut. Part of the problem was that the studio refused to trust Stone. Though he'd directed *Seizure*, it was such a bomb that he now had to deal with the studio second-guessing his every move. He may have won an Oscar as a writer, but there was big money at stake, and Orion wanted to make sure they'd get a return on their investment. "They kept wanting more horror, more hand," Stone recalls. "We spent close to a million dollars on forty or fifty of these hands. You had to be a mechanic to make this movie. It would've been better to work with a shark or a gorilla, because you have more space to put the gear in. But a hand?"

Ed Pressman describes the pressure from Orion: "They pushed it in the wrong direction and made it tough on Oliver. He was very frenzied in those days. Our offices adjoined each other and we had an argument about something. It was pretty petty as I recall, but the next thing I knew Oliver had put up a blockade so I couldn't cut through his office any more. It was like a war zone for a while. But he also had a kind of big brother attitude at times. During production he introduced me to my wife. She was playing one of Michael Caine's students, and when the film was over, Oliver invited us to dinner. He had a lot to do with us getting together."

Another problem Stone had on *The Hand* was his use of cocaine, which he was occasionally freebasing. Despite all this, Stone says he got along well with Michael Caine. "It was hard to get him to take direction sometimes," he says, "but I was an inexperienced director and he knew that. So, he'd do it his way. I'd say, 'Michael, can you do more of this?' and he'd say, 'Oh, I did that. You'll see it in the rushes, Oliver.'"

Stone laughs now at the memory. "Sometimes it was there, sometimes it wasn't," he says. "Overall, Michael was patient. He would try to listen to me. I learned a lot from Michael. And I think he gave a good performance."

The Hand also included a cameo by Stone as a frighteningly grungy bum. Stone autographed a still of the shot, in which he looked truly disgusting—"To the lucky girl that's got me"—and gave it to Elizabeth as a joke. Elizabeth worked on the film as Stone's assistant, but it was also the first time she did some set photography and hence the beginning of what would prove to be a successful career.

Stone shot the film as closely as possible to the way he originally envisioned it, but the studio's contract gave them final edit. "I fought them, but I lost. It was a good lesson. They cut my legs away because they had control over the editing process. I wanted the picture to succeed, so I bowed. I had Jon Peters in my face. He's a strong man. The studio made me shoot more horror. I did re-shoots to make them happier. More horror, more hand shots."

"Why they make all these fuckin' stupid movies. . . . I tell ya out there in Hollywood somebody's a taco short of a combo plate."

Mickey Knox in **NATURAL BORN KILLERS**

The picture was released in April 1981. It was mass-distributed across the country in May, but was a critical and box-office disaster. *New York* magazine's David Denby wrote, "Oliver Stone has some talent as a director (he has none as a writer) . . . he takes considerable risk in making his hero a bastard . . . but it's all so damned unpleasant. . . . Stone depends far too much on conventional, hack director's 'boos' . . . the grim purposefulness of 'The Hand' is a drag."

A number of critics complained about the lack of psychological suspense and noted that many of the horror scenes were unintentionally funny because of the limited form of the villain (a disembodied hand).

Caine, as the stricken artist haunted by his dismemberment, does a fine job, but the film is inconsistent and more or less stumbles along. Though still considered a hot writer, Stone was now unbankable as a director—worse, an outright bad risk.

"I'd been hot and all of a sudden I was cold," Stone says. "People who had wanted me a year before didn't even want to talk to me. I felt like a pariah. It was the opposite of any success *Midnight Express* had brought me. I went from the top to the bottom right away. I was called everything: a hack, a bum, a hype artist. You can't say much worse than what was said about me . . . it was like the same thing that happened to me in Vietnam happened to me in Hollywood: I got wounded, blown up right away. As a result, I was unemployable as a director."

The Lizard's Tail is a frightening book, but it works as a psychological thriller and should have been filmed more in the Alfred Hitchcock style. By giving in to the studio's desire for more special effects, Stone thought he was increasing his chances for commercial success, when in fact he was diminishing them.

After a limited run, the box office was so poor that Orion pulled back its support. Stone, however, refused to give up, and using his own money went to Chicago to campaign for the movie.

"Both *The Hand* and *Seizure* were about artists who self-destruct," Stone says now. "In a lot of ways when I did *The Hand*, I was sort of redoing *Seizure*. So why did I get in this karmic cycle of recommitting the same mistake?"

Stone questions every failure repeatedly, even those rendered obsolete by success. No matter how much money or power he has, he cannot silence these voices.

On June 7, 1981, Oliver Stone and Elizabeth Cox were married. Elizabeth describes his proposal: "I was thirty-one and Oliver was thirty-four. We had this sort of volatile relationship. A lot of tempers, a lot of travel, a lot of hashing it out. After we'd been living together for about a year and a half we were on our way back from Peru—we went to Machu Picchu. I was standing upstairs and he was downstairs and out of the blue he yells 'June 6th.' And I yell down, 'What's June 6th?' And he says, 'We'll get married June 6th.' I said, 'Okay.' We never had discussed it really. We'd discussed attitudes on children and this and that. Then all of a sudden I heard, 'No, June 7th.' I said, 'Oh, why?' And he said, ' 'Cause June 6th is a Saturday and you have to get married on a Sunday.' I said, 'Okay.' So that was how he proposed and I accepted. We were married on June 7."

Though he often offends people out of his brashness, Stone rigidly adheres to his own curious sense of what's proper, and his formal breeding attaches an odd importance to protocol whenever a significant event in his life is about to take place. So it was to be expected that before announcing his engagement to Elizabeth, Stone decided to tell Najwa in person. "He came to me when he decided to marry Liz and asked what he should do," Najwa recalls. "I said he should marry her, of course. I will love him until the day I die. But it's a different kind of love now."

Stone's family knew they had no say in his choice of a wife, but nonetheless his mother felt he should know she disapproved of a nonsociety person like Elizabeth. "Oliver's mother lives out every single thing in her life as an event," says Elizabeth. "It's a big drama. She has a great *joie de vivre*, a great love of life. She is Madame Duvan with the sweeping rings and the hats and the scarves and the bows. She doesn't walk into the room, she makes an entrance. Her life and Oliver's life when he was with her was like a big stage play. His mother hated me because of my 'mediocre country background' and my 'retarded education' and 'no social skills.' She demanded that he not marry me, but of course he didn't listen to her. Over these past fourteen years, though, she and I have learned to love each other. She's a different person now. She's an old lady who loves to be with her grandchildren."

The Stones had a most un-Hollywood wedding in Texas, in Elizabeth's grandparents' backyard. Ed Pressman was Stone's best man, but few other film people were invited. Jacqueline Stone had wanted to hire a plane to bring down her New York society friends and when he couldn't talk her out of it, Stone forbade her to come unless she came alone or with his father. She came by herself. After the wedding, the couple went to Tahiti for their honeymoon and, true to form, Stone soon became bored with relaxing on the beach and wound up sitting in a dark hotel room all day typing. "Each day I would put on my bathing suit and little sarong and drive a bike by myself all around the island," Elizabeth recalls. "I'd come back in the late afternoon and we'd take a quick dip and hit the winelight, as he calls it—the twilight of the day. He spent part of each day in the room writing."

Stone often makes conflicting demands on those close to him. After they were married, Elizabeth soon found herself in the middle of such incongruities, including whether she should have her own career or be a full-time wife. "I decided to try writing," she says, "because I was conscious of the fact that Oliver believes women should be functional and not just doing shopping or something equally 'decadent.' The 'LWL,' he says; the Ladies Who Lunch. Anyway, I tried to adapt a book called *A Princess in Berlin*, and a funny thing happened. I'd be upstairs madly typing away every day, and Oliver would be in the basement in his office, madly typing away. And he'd yell, 'I need coffee,' or whatever, and I would be typing and I'd yell back, 'What do you want? I'm right in the middle of a thought.' And so then it got to the point where he said, 'All right, you don't have to write any more. Some people are just meant to be loving and good people and help their mates.' By then, though, I'd already realized I really didn't know how to write a script anyway."

"Elizabeth was wonderful for Oliver," says Sergio Premoli. "He was very vulnerable and romantic—living the creative young writer/artist from the East Coast life. He wanted to be at everything that was happening, he wanted to be immortal as a director. He was giving big parties and Elizabeth was cooking for everybody. She'd say, 'How many people are you bringing tonight?' And Oliver would say, 'Four,' and then there would show up twenty-five people. Elizabeth would be so completely fucked up because there were all these people, but she was so supportive of his ego, she'd make it work. He can never deny the fact that she was there when he was very breakable . . . when he could be destroyed by others."

Like it or not, Stone was starting to adjust to a home life. Elizabeth was an excellent homemaker and provided an increasing sense of security in his life; they even got a golden retriever. But life was far from idyllic. By now, most of Hollywood viewed Oliver Stone as a frustrated rebel, and Stone himself saw his lone attempt to play along with the powers-that-be as a disillusioned commercial sellout. He was far better off financially than in his days in New York, but he was still not making the kinds of projects he had set out to do, and he was growing increasingly dispirited about his own stagnation. He returned to writing screenplays, but it wasn't long before he was forced to deal with an increasing problem—his drug use. For the last year it had gotten to the point where Stone even stopped keeping his diary. This, he knew, was a sign that he was losing control. Soon, an even clearer sign developed: It began to affect his writing.

Stone was approached by producer Michael Phillips to do an adaptation of *Wilderness*, a novel by Robert B. Parker. While working on the script, he realized he might have a problem. "I was snorting coke and heroin in the form of speedballs," he says. "I liked going both ways, loved the up/down combination. It was like being on a tightrope. I'd been doing drugs off and on for several years, but not all the time. *Conan* was written on cocaine and downers. The drug period was from *Conan* through *The Hand* and into my research for *Scarface*. But when I was writing the adaptation for *Wilderness*, it started to get to me. I was living in Marina del Rey by the ocean, and I remember closing the shades, doing drugs, and trying to work. I felt like my mind was going soft. My *Wilderness* adaptation wasn't awful, but it wasn't great. I knew something was wrong."

Around this time, Stone saw *Reds*, Warren Beatty's powerful film on the life of the journalist John Reed. He was moved by its vision and courage. "I thought, 'Goddammit, that man [Beatty] is right.' I don't care how much money he spent, he went out and did something that he believed in. You have to make films as an idealist. Renoir, I think, said, 'If it's not to the greater glory of man, don't make it.' Then, even if you fail, even if the film doesn't work, you don't have to be ashamed, because you tried. But if you try something that's small and negative and you fail, then you're really in deep shit. I was trying to show the horror and disintegration of a man in *The Hand*, but ultimately you don't win with that kind of movie."

Stone knew that before he could do the kinds of films he wanted to do, he would have to get off drugs. Once again, fate seemed to lend a hand. He was asked to write *Scarface*. Originally, it was Sidney Lumet's idea to redo the 1932 Howard Hawks/Paul Muni classic as a modern-day rise and fall story of Cuban coke dealers in Miami. Martin Bregman was producing, and no matter how many drugs he was doing, Oliver Stone seemed like the perfect choice to write the screenplay. He researched it in the homicide-ridden city of Miami. "In 1980, you could draw a parallel between Miami, El Salvador, and Nicaragua," Stone says. "In each place, it heated up. There was more killing, more violence, an orgy of blood. I didn't understand it at first, but years later the threads came together because of the connection between coke and the contra trade. It was fascinating."

Stone also traveled to South America, where he hung out with both police and the drug dealers to do research for the film. During one such expedition, he got a little more than he bargained for: "I heard about these drug dealers that hung around this hotel in Bimini, so I went down there with Liz. We checked into this beautiful old hotel, right on the ocean. It looked like it was right out of an Edward G. Robinson movie. It reeked seediness. There were all these Colombian guys waiting around all day for the night to come. I started snorting coke with them and they invited me back to their digs. So I went with them and I told them I was a screenwriter from Hollywood doing research for a movie.

"Well, after a lot of tooting, these guys started to get paranoid, and then I made a real mistake. I dropped the name of a guy I knew who was a defense lawyer, but it turned out he used to be a prosecutor who nailed one of these guys at one time. The guy went white. He thought I was setting him up to get busted again. The whole fucking conversation shifted gears and he and this other dangerous-looking character went into the john to talk it over. I figured this was it; they were going to come out and blow me away. The next three minutes were tense. Well, they came out and said there would be no more talking about drugs. I figured they planned on getting me later in my room. So I made my utmost effort to convince them I really was a screenwriter and talked my way out of trouble. But it was very scary for a while. It reminded me what real fear was. I'd kind of forgotten that. Later, I tried to put that into the chainsaw scene I wrote for the movie."

"Talk about what, what's there to talk about? I ain't killed anybody lately."

Tony Montana in **SCARFACE**

Stone's research into the insidious evil of the coke trade confirmed what he already feared about himself. "I got excited by the subject," he says. "I got a fire in my belly. This was something I really wanted to do; but I knew my writing wasn't going to be there unless I stopped doing coke. I felt like I was ceasing to use my brain. I could feel a staleness in all my thought processes. I was losing my third dimension. In conversations I'd use concept-image retention and not care about detail. The drug was flattening out my existence. I was becoming more one-dimensional, fueled by the need for the drug. Coke is only into one track which has too much to do with powder and not enough to do with all the other things that are going on. I knew I was in trouble."

But, as most former coke addicts will tell you, recognizing you have a problem and quitting are two different things. Stone drew upon the discipline of his childhood. "I went back to the Hill. I said, 'Remember, you were there. You had another life in all these layers of life you've had. Go back now to your youth and reassume those positions, think about that innocence and think about that discipline.' I did it very strictly within myself and it helped me get through that period."

Stone also decided that a complete change of scenery would help him break the habit, so he relocated to France to write the script. In December 1981, he and Elizabeth flew to Paris and both of them quit cold turkey that day. They rented an apartment, and for the next six months Stone worked on *Scarface*, his swan song to cocaine. Elizabeth describes those days: "We'd both been into the Hollywood drug scene, which is why we had so many fights, I think. Coke makes for such a volatile relationship. We got this beautiful apartment next to the Bois de Boulogne, which had a great skylight. Oliver put heavy purple drapes across the skylight and made it a dark place. Every morning he'd close the drapes and turn on the light on his desk. He always uses a portable electric typewriter because he likes to pound. He likes to take the paper and cram it in or rip it out. He'd turn on this sort of Edith Piaf–sounding warbling French singer and the minute this started I'd know that it was time to leave the apartment because he would play it all day long. He's compulsive/obsessive when he writes. It's sort of a tunnel vision, he gets fixated. He goes into this world in his head. He has to write in a closed, dark place. He goes into the womb."

The script Stone wrote in that Paris apartment is among his best work. "I wrote *Scarface* basically as an adieu to cocaine," he says. "It had beaten the hell out of me, but I got my revenge by writing about it. What better farewell than a guy falling into a ton of cocaine and, when he looks up at the camera, there is all this white powder on his nose."

When the first drafts were finished, the Stones moved back to America; they bought a house in Sagaponac on Long Island, and rented a small apartment in New York City. Stone continued working on *Scarface*. Although it is often criticized for its excessive violence, Stone says the picture was conceived as a comic opera. "Tony Montana was a composite of about four or five gangsters that I had heard about," he says. "He's a gangster, but he's also funny. Some of my friends called the film *Scarfucci*. It's the rise and fall of a petty hood. The guy comes to the shores with nothing and within a year he's making millions. Of course, he has to be corrupt to do it, but there's no question that great wealth in America is accumulated in this fashion. That was also the idea for the Paul Muni version, how the rackets became sort of an immigrant business. It was the same thing with cocaine for the Latins. That was Lumet's idea for the picture."

As Stone did the polishes for *Scarface*, he began another project, *Defiance*, which was about dissidents living in Russia. He decided he needed to go to the Soviet Union to prepare for the writing. Once again, his tenacity in reseaching a project got him into trouble. "I contacted an organization in Paris called 'The Committee of Thirteen.' They were in touch with the human rights movement in Russia. Liz and I took as much stuff into Russia as we could get away with—clothes, batteries, radios, anything we could. I had a list of some twenty dissidents in eleven or twelve cities in the Soviet Union."

The Stones visited several places from Baku up to Leningrad and down to Georgia. "Ukraine is tough," Stone recalls. "I'd track these people down and we'd meet in obscure places like on park benches at midnight or on the subway and then walk to their houses. Some of them had been in jail for years or in Siberia. Some were medically tortured or put through shock treatments. These people were naturally very paranoid. They were always looking for bugs and being followed. It was a bad time with Brezhnev, and a reporter from the *L.A. Times* had been arrested there. I felt like I could be arrested at any time."

Finally, Stone did get picked up by the Russian police. "We were called in when we were in Tbilisi in Georgia. They assign guides, and I would have to shake the guide. One of them became suspicious and reported me. Next thing I knew, we were being hauled into this huge office with no lights and there's one guy sitting behind a desk in the middle of this cavernous room. He was wearing these green glasses and he said, 'You've been saying things about our country we don't appreciate.' I didn't know what his information was or anything. It was like a James Bond movie to me, like something out of *From Russia With Love*. He kept us there for two hours and said, 'If I went to your country, I wouldn't say bad things about your country.' I said, 'I don't know what you're talking about.' He said, 'We're going to be watching you. We can revoke your papers and ask you to leave. Please, I'm telling you for the last time. A warning.'

"I didn't know if he knew I was meeting with all these people or not. From then on I was looking over my shoulder all the time. The last place I went, this woman said to meet her at midnight in this park on this bench. I figured, great, it'd be dark, easier to hide. Then I find out that in Leningrad the sun is still up at midnight. So we're meeting in broad daylight at midnight in a Leningrad park. She looked like she'd been through a mental asylum and I think she was being followed. I was trying to get the story out to the American people and the script was based on my interviews with all these dissidents. It was never made."

Meanwhile, big changes were happening with the *Scarface* project. After he saw the script, director Sidney Lumet pulled out. With Al Pacino lined up to star, Brian De Palma was quickly brought in. "Sidney Lumet just didn't like it," Stone says, "and De Palma came in, shooting it very much as I had written it, but some of the script had to be cut. I was very pleased with the movie. It was a great experience for me. We went way over budget, but I learned a great deal."

Stone moved back to L.A. to be on the set during the filming, and he worked closely with De Palma. He and Elizabeth moved to a house in Brentwood and Stone began to study aikido, which he felt helped him in many ways. Things went very well until he saw the first cut of the film. "I had major problems with the first cut and I stated them openly to Marty Bregman and Brian De Palma," Stone recalls. "I also told Al Pacino. Marty and Brian got really upset because I told Al this stuff. They were afraid he would go crazy on them."

Twenty years later, Stone still takes the writer's point of view: "I still think the writer is right up there with the director as a creative source. He is as important. Especially considering I had spent six months on the set with these people. I was part of the creative family, and I was suddenly being relegated—like my *Midnight Express* days—to janitor duties. I was being told to stay out of it, and that of course triggered my defiance. I wrote a long letter to Marty Bregman and some of the points were dealt with. Marty and I have since made up, but he went ape-shit because I copied Al on the letter. Al, of course, has his own demons, and they were worried I'd upset him. But you have to deal with the actors on the cut. You can't run away from them. They figured the less said, the better. I think the truth is they thought Al was a lot nuttier than he is. He has his idiosyncrasies, as we all do, but he's much more reasonable than they thought."

Ron Mardigian says the incident was indicative of Stone's passion about his work: "Oliver's always invested more of himself in these things than an ordinary writer. He really loves his work. That whole thing with him writing letters to Pacino was really sticking his nose where it didn't belong, but that's how he is. He had a point to make and he was not shy about doing that. They might ignore him once or twice, but he was going to be heard."

After the uproar settled, Stone decided he was not getting the opportunities he needed to direct, and he left William Morris to sign with Jeff Berg at ICM. Although Ron Mardigian felt wronged over this, he took it quietly as a matter of course in the film business. Stan Kamen, however, hit the roof. "Stan had a temper," Mardigian recalls, "and if he thought you crossed him, he'd rip your heart out. He went into a huge tirade directed at Oliver and I think it genuinely shook Oliver up."

"I'd never had anyone that powerful that mad at me," Stone admits. "Ron had been a wonderful literary agent, very genuine in his affections to me, but I didn't feel he was taking me enough into directing. I didn't think Stan Kamen would react that way. Stan was one of, if not the most powerful person in the film business then, and he was really pissed. He was screaming at me right there in the office."

But Stone survived. It seemed the more errors in Hollywood politics he made, the more his reputation as a gutsy artist was solidified. The more outrageous his work, the more he seemed destined for outrageous success. Nowhere was this more apparent than upon the release of *Scarface*. Few films have inspired as much hatred, and *Scarface* was attacked by critics for being excessive on all counts: relentless profanity in the film (Pacino uses the word "fuck" as a habit of speech, the way some people say "you know"); extreme violence (critics particularly singled out the chainsaw scene for exorbitant bloodshed); and extravagant drug use (Pacino falling face down into a mountain of coke was often cited). "Scarface is a long, druggy spectacle," wrote Pauline Kael in *The New Yorker*, and many others echoed her sentiments.

Stone still defends the movie heartily. "The degree of excess I wrote about was true," he says. "I knew I was going to be in hot water over that one, but I did it because I really wanted to show that fascinating South Florida scene. One year they had something like two hundred drug-related homicides, including two Colombians who were killed by chainsaws and carved up worse than in the movie. But there's also a fascinating theme there of immigrant growth: a kid with two cents in his pocket arrives on the shores of Florida and inside of two years is a kingpin making a hundred or two hundred million a year. Where else in the world could that happen? People criticized it on the basis that we were espousing the point of view of the characters in the film. To suggest that is to not see the film for what it is. *Scarface* got trashed beyond belief. It was a very big setback for me emotionally. Critics thought the movie was indulgent and violent. I wrote about a hundred 'fucks' and Pacino added about two hundred, so by the time the final movie comes out, he's got about three hundred 'fucks' in there."

Actually, according to a fan who stopped Stone once in New York City and claimed to have meticulously counted them all, the word "fuck" is spoken 142 times in *Scarface*. Despite that fact, the dialogue is some of Stone's best. "A lot of young businessmen quote me the dialogue," he says, "and when I ask them why they remember it, they say, 'It's exactly like my business.' Apparently, the gangster ethic hit on some of the business ethics going on in this country. *Scarface* has probably got me more free champagne than any film I've ever worked on. I've bumped into Spanish and Jamaican gangsters throughout the Caribbean and South America and gay gangsters in Paris, who bought me champagne all night long. I've even read reports in newspapers where gangsters have modeled themselves on Tony Montana."

Scarface cost about $23 million to make and ran for nearly three hours. While it was not the box-office smash that Stone and De Palma had hoped for, it was not a failure either. Al Pacino still says it's his all-time favorite role. "In *Scarface*, the bad guy is a hero, and people don't like that," Stone comments. "Brian got burned on *Scarface*, so he learned his lesson—*The Untouchables* is the one the critics loved. But *Scarface* wasn't exactly lame—it did forty to fifty million dollars. People still love that movie."

Scarface was widely hailed in Europe and has become a cult classic here. Its repugnant excesses solved the problem of describing a gangster's life without making him seem a hero. More than anything it is about hubris—the Greek idea that a man who thinks he can challenge the gods is doomed to fall. Tony Montana refuses to recognize that he has limits. In the end, he opts for warring with a Columbian drug king who has him hopelessly outnumbered, shaking his fist at fate in much the same way he did when he arrived as a peasant in chains on the Miami docks. In one of the best scenes in the film, Montana rages at the posh patrons of a Miami nightclub that they need people like him to be "the bad guy." Creating a huge scene, he shouts, "None of you got the guts to be what you want to be." This is a recurring theme with Stone. Glimpses of the nonconformist battling the conformists can be found in much of his work, from the quirky Jim Garrison mouthing southern witticisms as he methodically warns people against accepting official history in *JFK* to the wild Jim Morrison bellowing to another Miami audience that they are "all a bunch of slaves" in *The Doors*.

Stone was paid $300,000 for writing *Scarface*. That made him one of the highest paid writers in Hollywood, but he was still not a director. If anything, *Scarface* further alienated the critics who had embraced him on *Midnight Express*. Both *The Hand* and *Scarface* seemed to indicate that those who had attacked him as excessive and needlessly violent were correct. Words like "vile" and "sensationalistic" were becoming attached to his name, and *New York* magazine film critic David Denby called him "the dread Oliver Stone." Oddly enough, he was being labeled right-wing. The racial overtones of *Midnight Express* and *Scarface*, coupled with the violence in these pictures and in *Conan*, created an image for Stone that was far from his actual liberal attitudes. "I was always hurt by the right-wing categorizations," Stone says now. "I grew up fairly internationally. I'm half-immigrant. I've always felt that urge to rise, that driven thing that Tony Montana has, coming to a new country. Making my mark—I've always had that hunger. Just doing provincial American subjects is really boring. I'm interested in alternative points of view. Ultimately the problems of the planet are universal. Nationalism is a very destructive force."

After *Scarface*, Stone and a director/producer named Floyd Mutrix began trying to develop a film based on the Hillside strangler murders in the Los Angeles area. It was at this time that Stone first met LAPD detective Stanley White, who would wind up working in one capacity or another on several Oliver Stone films.

In May 1984, Elizabeth Stone discovered she was pregnant. She and Oliver were excited but somewhat anxious, since their first pregnancy had ended in a miscarriage.

Though he worked hard at developing it, Stone was unable to get much interest in a film based on the Hillside strangler, even though he had a huge amount of documentation at his disposal. Searching desperately for a project he could direct, he optioned a book entitled *8 Million Ways to Die* by Lawrence Block, with the intention of developing it. A producer named Steve Roth became interested, and Stone made a deal with him on condition that he would be allowed to write and direct the film once the financing came through. But that was not the way it worked out; they had a hard time getting the money and Stone was dropped as the director of the project. Hal Ashby eventually directed a mutation of this script.

Though he was developing a lot of projects, nothing was coming through. One night Stone had a curious dream: "I was sixteen years out of Vietnam, but in the dream, they had shipped me back. Somehow, they found me at the age of thirty-eight and sent me back. I woke up in a sweat, in total terror." The subconscious connotations of Stone's dream are obvious. He could give up on the film industry ever making *Platoon*. He could tell himself that *Born on the Fourth of July* was doomed to waste away on the shelf. He could play the Hollywood game, earn big money, and try to find enough exotic things to buy. But for Oliver Stone, Vietnam wasn't going to go away.

Stone began exploring the idea of raising money to do his own project. When *Scarface* came out in December 1983, he and Elizabeth had moved back to New York once more. "I'd spent nearly two years of my life involved with that film," he says. "I went back to New York and became massively depressed. I really felt like getting out of the business. Nothing I was doing was working."

Then Michael Cimino contacted him with an interesting idea. Cimino, the director of the hugely successful *Deer Hunter* and the infamous failure, *Heaven's Gate*, had read the *Platoon* script years before. Now he believed he had a way to get the film made. Cimino was going to direct a version of Robert Daley's book, *Year of the Dragon*, for Dino de Laurentiis, and wanted Stone to co-write the film with him. He thought that if Stone would agree to write the script at a much lower fee than he usually charged, then de Laurentiis might finance *Platoon*. "I told him, 'Nobody cares about Vietnam any more,'" Stone recalls, "and Cimino said, 'Vietnam is going to come back and be big. I'm serious, man.' It was Michael who convinced me that the climate was right for it. So I pulled down the script of *Platoon* and read it. It was a little dated, but it was still great stuff. I started getting excited about it again."

"How can anybody care too much?"

Stanley White in **YEAR OF THE DRAGON**

Stone met with de Laurentiis and after a bit of gambling, wining, and dining in Cap d' Antibes in the south of France, the Italian mogul did indeed promise him that he'd make *Platoon* if Stone wrote *Year of the Dragon*. Stone and Cimino undertook a lot of research, interviewing as many people as would talk to them about gangs and heroin dealing in New York's Chinatown. Unfortunately, getting good information proved to be difficult. "For *Scarface*, it was easy to get the Latins to talk, but we couldn't get the Chinese to talk about gangsters," Stone admits. "We went to a dozen banquets in Chinatown, where we had to gorge on ten-course meals, trying to get friendly with these guys who wouldn't tell us the time of day. We both gained like fifteen pounds.

We got information finally from a dissident gangster group. These were guys who were on the outs and very unhappy. They took us to Atlantic City and showed us the inner workings of the gambling world, and also showed us their side of what was going on in Chinatown."

The link to these gangs had been provided by a young Chinese line producer named Alex Ho, who had been working with de Laurentiis for the past two years. "I knew the gangs and the policemen, because I worked down there for years," Ho says. "We'd hang out with the gangs at the gambling houses in Chinatown. One time Oliver and Michael wanted to see this gambling house where only Chinese people are allowed to enter. So this policeman who was really nice to us busted one of the gambling joints that night so we could see what it was like. I was totally embarrassed. Another night Michael wanted to see what happens when someone is shot with a shotgun, so we spent the whole night sitting in an ambulance."

Eventually, Alex Ho would become a significant part of Stone's team, going on to produce or co-produce seven films that Stone directed, from *Platoon* through *Heaven and Earth*.

Ho reports that the villains in *Year of the Dragon* were based on real gang members: "Before he went to jail, one man talked about having a bullet inside him and how his girlfriend's brother was trying to kill him. Another guy, whom the John Lone character was partly based on, had a big black bodyguard who followed five steps behind him and carried two guns, one in a shoulder holster and one in an ankle holster. The Chinese guy, Eddie Chan, used to be a sergeant in the Hong Kong police force. He was very corrupt, and then he came to the States and became the head of this gang."

For the hero of *Year of the Dragon*, Stone suggested changing the name of the lead character in Daley's book to that of his police detective friend, Stanley White. "I introduced Stanley to Michael and said this guy could be a great character for us. Stanley gave us permission to use his name and we used a lot of Stanley's eccentricities."

In some ways *Year of the Dragon* was perfect for Stone's peculiar talents. Stanley White, the beleaguered police detective at the heart of the movie, is a raging antihero, someone who scathingly denounces hypocrisy but is so empowered by raw passion that he is blind to his own injustices. As White, Mickey Rourke lets his personal passions dominate to the detriment of all those around him, but still somehow retains enough childlike naïveté to ask, "How can anybody care too much?" It is a line that could be taken as an anthem for many of Stone's characters.

Although he likes Cimino, Stone does not consider their collaboration a success: "I had a very good relationship with Michael. He wrote the screenplay with me; he was there all the time. He *breathed* me. With Michael, it's a twenty-four-hour day. He doesn't really sleep. You get into his skin, he gets into yours. He's truly an obsessive personality. He's the most Napoleonic director I ever worked with.

"Also, Dino got his paws into it. The original ending of the movie was brilliant. The Mickey Rourke character had two women in his life. The Chinese Mafia character, John Lone, was also supposed to have two women in his life—a Hong Kong wife and a New York wife, a relationship which a lot of richer Chinese enjoy. In a moment of sentimentality, he brings the Chinese wife to the States, and the Mickey Rourke character finds out about it. So, after he can't get him legally with a bust or wiretap, he busts him for bigamy. He wants to insult him and take away his 'face,' and that forces the issues to a head."

This is not the way the movie was shot, however. It ended instead with a more conventional *French Connection*–type shoot-out. "That's because Dino had a very fifties mentality," Stone says. "He was indignant. He wanted to know how could the hero of the movie be an adulterer? How could he be married to one woman and fuck another? We said, 'Dino, you're living in one of your *Helen of Troy* epics.' Michael won that argument, but in the process we lost the battle for the ending, which was probably more important."

Casting also proved difficult. "We went to several people, but they didn't want the part," Stone says. "In some cases, it was because of Michael's reputation after *Heaven's Gate*, but also most actors didn't care for the character. He's a right-winger. He's a racist. That is the way the character was conceived and written. He's a sexist on top of it. You had to have a big pair of balls to play that part. I think Mickey was marvelous casting by Michael. He wasn't even a star at that point. For de Laurentiis and Cimino to bank twenty million on him was a big step."

It was at this time that Stone first met Janet Yang, who, years later, would become vice president of production at Ixtlan, his production company. "My boyfriend at the time, Justin, met Oliver and Michael

Cimino because he had made a number of documentaries in Thailand and they were thinking of shooting *Year of the Dragon* there," Yang says. "Oliver asked them to go out to dinner in SoHo in New York. I went to meet Justin there, and when I walked into the restaurant, this man comes running over to me, saying, 'You're the one, you're the one!' I'm thinking, 'What are you talking about and who *are* you?' and it turned out to be Oliver. They were looking for a Chinese American woman to play the female lead in *Year of the Dragon* and he said, 'You've got to come over and do a screen test.' So that was my introduction to Oliver Stone."

The film was shot on location in North Carolina; nearly all the New York settings (including Mott Street) were recreated there. According to Alex Ho, there were many of the kind of budget excesses that Cimino was known for at the time: "Michael and I had an argument—a simple thirteen-million-dollar dispute. Dino said he'd do the picture for eleven million dollars, but then I did the budget and it was between twenty-three and twenty-four million dollars. Michael went ape-shit but he would never compromise. Like there were two Mercedes that were to be in crashes. There was a 380 and a 450, and I said, 'Could I buy a 380 and then just change the number to 450 for the crash scene?' and Michael said, 'No.' That was like ten or fifteen thousand dollars. You have to make certain compromises. And Dino and Michael had this great swordsmanship game. Dino would say, let's have the meeting at six, and Michael would say five, and they'd meet at five-thirty in the morning and I'd have to get a double espresso just so I could go to this fucking meeting. It was all game playing between the two of them. The truth is, Michael doesn't care about the money. He would tell anybody anything so he could just do it his way and then later, it's your problem."

The conflict between Ho and Cimino almost resulted in a split between the young producer and Stone before their first picture together. Alex Ho elaborates. "Michael wouldn't talk to me and I said that's fine. I didn't want to do the picture then anyway. So Dino said he wanted me to start working on *Platoon*. Then I talked to Oliver and he said, 'You and Michael didn't get along and so you fucked him.' I told him, 'I didn't, it's a twenty-three-million-dollar film.' Oliver said, 'No it isn't, but I think you can do a good job so we'll do this together [*Platoon*].' He never cared what the other side of the story was really. Today, he still doesn't care. It just depends on what he needs to get done. I think he's just always like that. He's always for the creative side of things."

As shot by Cimino, the 136-minute movie centers on a New York City cop battling corruption in Chinatown. What makes it different is that the cop is a vet whose psyche is still fighting his own private Vietnam. In some ways *Year of the Dragon* is a companion piece to *The Deer Hunter*, but its heart is overwhelmed by excess and takes itself so seriously that it becomes almost one-dimensional. There are certainly some mesmerizing moments, and the Stanley White character is a fascinating one. Unfortunately, his complexity and mass of contradictions wind up coming across on film as a sort of continual ranting and raving. When one thinks back, the images that remain are crowds of innocent bystanders being machine-gunned down at regular intervals, and Mickey Rourke yelling at the top of his voice directly into the camera every five minutes or so. When one actually views it, however, one realizes that *Year of the Dragon* could have been a great film—a few different choices in the editing room and one or two small scenes would have made a world of difference.

John Lone's performance as the Chinese crime lord is compelling, and the brutal clash at the end when hero and villain literally run full speed toward each other, guns blazing, comes off powerfully. It's as though both men were so sick of the brutal struggle between them that all that mattered was ending it, even if they had to die to do it.

Once released, the movie fared modestly at the box office, and only stood out for the many attacks on it as racist, slurring the Chinese people. Stone feels differently. "It's hyped up a bit, but the movie is essentially honest about the Golden Triangle [the area that borders Laos, Burma, and Thailand, where the opium poppy grows most prolifically], and how young gangs are exploited like little surface fishes to do the dirty work while the whales stay deep down and control this enormous dope shipping. The thing critics never realized is that the Chinese were at that time the biggest importers of heroin in this country. They outdid the Mafia, but nobody knew about it because they did it quietly. People only recently started to accept this."

One of the leaders in attacking the film was the Chinese director Wayne Wang, who often spoke out against it in the press at that time. Janet Yang recalls those days: "I managed a company that imported films from Asia and I shared an office with Wayne Wang. Wayne and all these people knew that I was friends with Oliver, and they erroneously assumed that I was sleeping with him, which I never had and I'm sure never will—just to get that straight. Oliver was very outspoken about the gang activity in Chinatown. And Wayne Wang, being the most successful Chinese American film director, was a spokesperson. His attitude was, 'How dare someone present such a negative image of the Chinese.' Of course, a week later there would be a huge article in the newspaper about the gangs in Chinatown. And Wayne certainly wouldn't deny that there's a serious gang problem now, but at the time there was this kind of polarization."

Stone's response at the time was: "If Wayne Wang is to be believed, then the Chinese are some of the most boring people in the world."

Over the years, however, Stone and Wang patched things up, and Wang later directed the film version of Amy Tan's best-selling novel *The Joy Luck Club* for Stone's Ixtlan production company. "It shouldn't be about pointing your finger at others, but about creating solutions," Janet Yang says today. "Some people make conscious efforts to appease the community and end up with washed-out films. You can't work out of fear. You have to work out of conviction, love and truth. That's what Oliver does."

As Stanley White remarks in *Year of the Dragon*, "I give a shit, and I'm gonna make you people give a shit."

As for the Stanley White character being a racist and a sexist, Stone hedges on whether or not the movie ultimately endorses such attitudes. "I condemn vigilantism, which is basically the attitude that Stanley White adopts in the end. But there's also a part of me that hates the bureaucracy that prevents things from getting done. The truth is, nobody in that Chinatown precinct wanted to do anything about the drugs, and this guy was a mover and shaker who rocked the boat. That made him an interesting protagonist. I don't like the way he did it, his excesses, the unrelenting humorlessness of his character."

Scarface and *Year of the Dragon* were both hard-hitting stories, solidifying Stone's reputation as a serious writer of outrageous, action-filled movies. He had worked with two of the most controversial figures in modern cinema—Brian De Palma and Michael Cimino. Both films were roundly attacked by the critics and met with mediocre box-office results, but there was no denying the unique power of the screenplays.

Stone's scripts were invariably controversial and ambitious, yet they were also fascinating. People began seeing him as a wild man with a testimony. Here was an upper-class white man who often set his stories in nonwhite, lower-class cultures. Four of his scripts—*Midnight Express*, *Scarface*, *8 Million Ways to Die*, and *Year of the Dragon*—were set within the world of the drug trade. His protagonists were a gallery of raging anti-heroes, denouncing conformism in every scene and sacrificing their all in the battle against hypocrisy. Stone had established himself as a force to be reckoned with.

After *Year of the Dragon* was finished, Stone's mind was on the long-awaited filming of *Platoon*. His diary, which he had diligently returned to once again, reflects a fresh excitement about the project. In the summer of 1984, he cast it and went to the Philippines to scout locations. But it was not to be. Dino de Laurentiis pulled the plug. He was willing to put up the $5 or $6 million to make the film, but no distributor would partner with him, even though all they had to risk was the $3 million necessary (by 1985 standards) to give the movie a commercial release. He told Stone he was dropping the project.

"My heart really broke," Stone says. "Why, I wondered, was the film resurrected, only to be killed once again? I couldn't understand why this happened. I went into a major depression. This marked the fifth time I'd had that script thrown back at me. I was really in the dumps. I knew then what my father must have felt like in 1963 when he lost his wife, and his money. I, too, felt like a total failure."

Stone's response reflects his belief that everything has a purpose and fits together in some sort of natural order. What frustrates him is that he thinks he should be able to figure it all out. He tends to ponder over the undecipherable, looking for a pattern, a link, a key to understanding why the universe functions in the way it does.

Alex Ho recalls de Laurentiis's decision to drop *Platoon*. "We were in Dino's office when he told us. Oliver was fully depressed. He was just totally destroyed standing there. He just felt his career was over. That's the thing about him. I love Oliver's passion. His movies are made with passion and a lot of people are missing that in what they do. And without it, why do a movie about anything if the director, the central driving force doesn't even care about it. If he's just doing it for money or fame or whatever. Oliver makes films because he really has passion. And I thought anybody with this kind of passion is going to succeed.

So I said, 'Oliver, in a year you're going to be the hottest director in the world. Don't worry about it.' Later, he reminded me of that, after *Platoon* was finished."

Today Stone looks back on the *Year of the Dragon* episode with more understanding. He has found a place for it in his cosmic puzzle. "Actually, I would have left *Platoon* buried if it hadn't been for Michael Cimino. When Dino passed on it, I was really heartbroken. But it was alive as an idea again."

It may have been alive as an idea, but it was an idea now controlled by Dino de Laurentiis. Stone soon discovered that he no longer held the rights to his own screenplay. "Not only had Dino reneged on his promise, but he wanted me to pay him back the scouting money for our trip to the Philippines," Stone says. "Until I did, he refused to give me back *Platoon*."

To make things even worse, Stone discovered that Hal Ashby, who had been attached to direct *8 Million Ways to Die*, had ordered a rewrite on Stone's script without even telling him. "He gave it to Robert Towne behind my back," Stone says. "Robert later called me and was very nice about it, but it wasn't his fault. Hal wanted it totally changed. He was on a completely different wavelength than I was. I remember going over to their set in Malibu and seeing this L.A. crew driving up in Porsches, eating shrimp barbecue. It was just rich and decadent. They were way over budget. Hal and Jeff Bridges would sit in the trailers for hours and talk about the script. And Hal and the producers were fighting like dogs and cats. They were going to take the movie away from him. That's part of the reason I work in overdrive when I direct. I have this nightmare image of that set."

Stone was more desperate than ever. The anticipation and preparation to make *Platoon* had revitalized his belief in the project and in his talents as a director. The betrayal—for there was no doubt in Stone's mind that that was what it was—had convinced him that taking the traditional route in Hollywood was just not going to work for him. Trying to ease his way in inch by inch, compromising as much as his artistic and personal integrity would allow in order to do what *they* wanted in the hopes that they would then give him a chance to do what *he* wanted, was just not working. Either he simply couldn't make himself compromise enough to satisfy the Hollywood chieftains, or else it really didn't matter how much he compromised—in any case, working the

Hollywood system was not paying off. He was making money all right, but he hadn't moved any closer to achieving his true artistic vision in the six years since he won the Oscar than the day he got out of film school. He'd had money before. Oliver Stone already knew that there was a void in him that money was never going to fill.

"That's all I am, a deal? This is my life you're talking about."

Barry Champlain in **TALK RADIO**

On December 29, 1984, at 4:00 P.M., Elizabeth gave birth to a baby boy, named Sean Christopher Stone. Oliver had always liked the name Sean, and Christopher was his favorite name—he'd named the lead character of *Platoon* Chris Taylor. "Sean was the only good thing that happened that year," Stone says. "When he was born, something happened. Another burst of wind came my way. I got re-energized. I felt everything was going to work out."

Babies bring good luck, they say, and shortly after Sean was born, an investigative reporter named Richard Boyle paid Stone a visit. What happened next could only be described as fate. Stone remembers: "I was still reeling from the *Platoon* deal falling through and Richard showed up. He didn't have a dime to his name, but he had a sense of humor and adventure. Out of that we created the story that became *Salvador*, and before long we were making a movie."

Salvador

"In the name of human decency, something we Americans are supposed to believe in, ya gotta at least try to make something of a just society here."

Richard Boyle in **SALVADOR**

Richard Boyle had been covering wars for twenty years when he went to El Salvador. His skills as an investigative reporter were only exceeded by his reputation as an outrageous and flamboyant personality. In 1969, he was expelled from Vietnam by Nguyen Van Thieu for joining a pacifist Vietnamese student demonstration. He secretly returned in 1971 and broke the story of the mutiny at Firebase Pace, in which a company of American troops surrounded by North Vietnamese on the Cambodian border signed a petition to Congress calling for an end to the war.

In 1975, as foreign editor of the Pacific News Service, Boyle was one of the last American journalists to leave Cambodia after the Khmer

Rouge occupied Phnom Penh. He was held captive, along with Sidney Schanberg and others, for three weeks at the French Embassy. In 1979, he was covering the Nicaraguan civil war when he was arrested and then released by the Guardia Nacional in Estali. The next year, Boyle returned to El Salvador to cover that war for NBC News and the Cable News Network (CNN). There he filed the first report on the death of Jean Donovan, one of the four American churchwomen murdered in El Salvador, that made headlines around the world.

Stone had known Boyle since the late seventies, when Ron Kovic introduced them while Stone was writing *Born on the Fourth of July*. "Richard and I were old friends," Stone relates. "I'd even bailed him out of jail once. He'd been talking to me since early 1980 about the situation in El Salvador, and I'd sort of half paid attention because I was so involved with other things. In December of '84, I was in despair, going nowhere in my life creatively, and I decided to make a break from Hollywood. I went up to San Francisco to see Richard, and he was a breath of fresh air for me.

"When he was taking me back to the airport, I found this stack of pages in the back seat of his car, all oil-stained and under a bunch of stuff. I dug it out and he said it was some notes from his trips to El Salvador. It was pretty fractured, but I started to read it, and right away my mind clicked. 'This is it,' I said. 'I'm going to make *Salvador*.' It's cheap. It's close. I knew we were going to make this somehow with whatever money we could scrape together—and given the subject, I knew we weren't going to get any help from the standard sources."

Alex Ho had been trying to sell *Platoon* with Stone in L.A. They developed budgets ranging from $4 to $6 million, but though everyone seemed to like the script, no one came through with the funding. "I finally ran out of money and had to go back to New York," Ho recalls. "I had to pay my rent. I'd turned down a lot of projects that were more lucrative, but I really believed in *Platoon*. So one night Oliver was in New York and we were really depressed, running around, going from one bar to another, drinking, talking about how miserable things were. Then we went back to my loft and we were having another drink and Oliver said, 'I have this book in the car from Richard Boyle.' And he started telling me the story. He said, 'Do you think we could do it real cheap?' And I said, 'Yeah, probably. Salvador's pretty inexpensive. We're talking about a million, a million and a half dollars.' He said, 'Great, well, let's do that next.' So then he went back to L.A. and he sent me these pages and it was great, absolutely wonderful."

Boyle's manuscript detailed his experiences in El Salvador as a radio reporter for NBC and a field producer for CNN. In 1980, after his wife took their child and left and he was evicted from his apartment, Boyle realized he was drinking too much and, worse, he was out of money again. So he headed back to El Salvador, where he'd always been able to make a few bucks getting combat shots and generally operating on the fringes of establishment journalism. Also, he wanted to see a young peasant girl there with whom he'd had an affair. Once Boyle walked into the madness of the death squads of 1980 El Salvador, he was pushed into a deeper knowledge of where liberation lay, not only for a country but for himself.

"I loved the idea," Stone recalls. "We got a story structure, went to Salvador, and wrote a screenplay from January through March. That's three months, including traveling to Honduras, Costa Rica, Belize, Mexico. We were just floating; I was financing the whole thing myself. I said, 'We're going to make this picture starring you, Richard.'"

The script revolved around the events of the early 1980s in El Salvador, including murders committed by the right-wing death squads, the killing of the four churchwomen, and the assassination of Archbishop Oscar Arnulfo Romero—all from the point of view of a man who'd seen Vietnam and feared that the same thing might happen if the United States intervened in Central America. According to Stone, he and Boyle made one key modification in the true-life events for the good of the script. "Dr. Rock, Boyle's companion in the film, was a real guy, but he never went to Salvador," Stone comments. "Boyle said he asked Rock to come and Rock would say, 'I want to go,' but he'd always cop out because he was scared of going there with somebody as crazy as Boyle. So I said, 'Well, let's take him to Salvador then and see what happens.' Take this character who's freaked out by anything, who hates any kind of nonurban experience, and put him there. And that became a key to making the movie work."

This decision is a good example of how Stone makes a deadly serious and somewhat offensive subject more palatable and entertaining for the screen. Most fervent, impassioned films about true-life events fail, quite simply, because they are not very much fun to watch. The bottom line in Hollywood always has to do with entertainment. People don't go to the movies to get depressed about how badly off the world is—they can get that from the news or their own lives. They go to be entertained, and Stone entertains them, whether through high action and the occasional gruesome effect or by weaving in entertaining sequences or characters like Dr. Rock.

One question Stone's detractors often raise is, does the adding of such characters or the slight altering of the sequence of events change the factual authenticity of the film? The answer is yes, but perhaps a better question is, Does it change what needs to be communicated to the audience through such a film? In the case of *Salvador*, Dr. Rock, trapped in a mad world with a madman, not only provides some comic relief but also gives us, the audience, someone more or less normal with whom we can identify. Does this fictional addition falsely sway our opinions about the situation that existed in El Salvador? Not likely. Dr. Rock only reacts to the madness; he is not particularly victimized by it, and he certainly doesn't cause it. He only makes it more palatable for us to observe. The choice to include this character does not affect the film's message, but it surely affects the amount of people who hear, or rather see, that message. It is Stone's ability to entertain which enables him to reach millions with his messages.

To help prepare for the film, Stone also read *Weakness and Deceit* by Ray Bonner. "It's such a huge story," Stone says, "and nobody in America really knew about it; 30,000 to 50,000 people killed by death squads. Another 500,000 split the country. That's approximately fifteen to twenty percent of the population dead or gone, because of this right-wing repression, essentially a military mafia supported by the U.S. It's very clear cut to the people there, it's not ambiguous."

Salvador crystallized the changes Stone had gone through since leaving Vietnam. While the rest of America drifted to the right politically during the seventies and eighties, Stone, who had once supported Barry Goldwater, was becoming a liberal. His experiences in Vietnam and in the aftermath of the war were a large reason for his shift, but people like Ron Kovic and Richard Boyle were also catalysts. "What I did was to give him an education," says Boyle. For all of the hard realities in the script, Richard Boyle was adamant about one thing. "This was not an indictment of El Salvador," he says. "El Salvador is a great place with great people and I love it. Before the war, La Libertad used to be a great surfer hangout. They'd come from all over the world. Good beer, beautiful women, cheap rent. What more do you want in life?''

As soon as the script was finished, the two men went back to El Salvador and set up the whole production, getting the cooperation and involvement of the Salvadorean government and the military. In fact, the filmmakers even had the go ahead to use the Salvadorean armed forces and equipment. They met with the advisers of Robert d'Abuisson, the right-wing leader whom many held responsible for the death squads. "They liked Oliver because they loved *Scarface*," Boyle says.

Drinking tequila with death-squad hitmen was indeed a risk for Stone and Boyle, but one they considered necessary. "These guys were carrying weapons on their hips and slapping us on the back," Stone recalls, "drinking toasts to Tony Montana. They kept talking about their favorite scenes and acting out the killings. They'd go, 'Tony Montanta, *mucho coliandes* [lots of balls]! Ratta-tat-tat! Kill the fucking Communists!' I was 'macho,' they kept saying. But it got us a lot of mileage there. We penetrated to the highest command. They were ready to give us their helicopter support system. We were going to pull off an *Apocalypse Now* there with no money, using U.S. military machines on loan from the Salvadorean government.''

There was only one hitch: It was all a con. Stone and Boyle planned to trick the Salvadoreans by showing them a fake script and shooting the battles and nonpartisan scenes at the government's expense, then slip off to Mexico to shoot scenes that actually portrayed the rebels as the film's good guys.

Risky, to say the least. But for a while it worked. The government of El Salvador assigned Colonel Ricardo Cienfuegos to act as an adviser to Stone and Boyle, and the three met on a regular basis. Stone put up the money for these trips, as well as for the scouting of other areas throughout the region. In the end, he felt so strongly about *Salvador* that he even borrowed money against his home to make it. Elizabeth Stone recalls those days: "Right after Sean was born, he put our house in New York on the block to get the money to shoot it. He got out a mini-camera, put Richard Boyle and Dr. Rock in a rented convertible, and drove them around Brentwood rehearsing.''

In the midst of all this, the Stones were trying to cope with parent-hood. For Oliver, having a baby around the house required a good deal of adjustment. "It was hard for Oliver to understand why I did so many things with the baby that his mother never did with him," Elizabeth says of those first few months with the baby at home. "He kept asking me why I didn't let the nanny do this or that, because it was the nanny who did all the motherly caretaking-type things for him. All of a sudden it was, 'Hey, you're not there for me any more. All you care about is Sean.' It was hard on him at first. But parenthood was a real learning experience for both of us. It takes a lot of compromise."

To make things worse, the Stones were now contending with the somewhat disruptive presence of Richard Boyle. "Richard was staying at my house," Stone recalls. "He'd extended his stay on behalf of the script into a major sojourn of several months. Elizabeth was going nuts and wanted me to get him out of the house. One morning we woke up and he had passed out in front of the TV. He was rocking back and forth in the chair in the middle of the living room at dawn and there were beer bottles all around. And Elizabeth, who wakes up earlier than I do, went to the kitchen and opened the refrigerator and everything was gone, everything had been drunk, even the baby's formula was missing. And she went back and looked at him and he was holding the baby's formula. He'd drunk the whole fucking thing. He must've been blind drunk and just grabbed whatever was in a can."

Stone was soon deeply immersed in *Salvador*. The idea had evolved into making a very low budget, almost *cinéma vérité* type of film, with Boyle and Rock playing themselves. This plan went askew in March 1985, when Colonel Cienfuegos, the military attaché who by now had become a friend of Stone and Boyle, was shot in the head on the tennis court. "They draped the FMLN flag [leftist rebel forces] over his body," Stone says. "Of course it could have actually been a right-wing coup, I don't know. The government then pulled back their support for the film. All of a sudden they changed their attitude to 'It's not good for El Salvador, it will hurt our tourist economy.' What tourist economy? I wondered, but I think if we'd have gone ahead and filmed there, we would have gotten into a lot of trouble with the military. They were still extremely right-wing and still linked to the death squads."

"Come this far. . . . Greased by a fucking tic-tac monster in Salvoland, they won't believe this one . . . aw who'll give a shit anyway!"

Richard Boyle in **SALVADOR**

In the meantime, Stone had shopped the script around Hollywood, although he knew too much now to expect the studios to get behind it. "I knew what the reaction would be. I had a reputation around town as a 'cause freak' because of *Platoon, Born on the Fourth of July*, and *Defiance*. I figured *Salvador* would be too controversial for the American money people. Also, the track record on Central American films was real poor. *Missing* didn't do any business in this country, even though it got Academy Award nominations, and *Under Fire* was a total disaster in terms of receipts. But when I tried to sell *Salvador*, the script was not just turned down—it was *hated*. Anti-Americanism, I heard, was a factor in why some of the studios turned it down."

In March 1985, Lou Stone was hospitalized. "I remember taking Sean, who was very tiny then, back with us to the hospital in New York," Stone says. "I was at my father's deathbed going through a lawsuit with Dino, yelling at my attorney because Dino would not give me back *Platoon*. I just remember being in that hospital and being massively depressed."

Within a few days, Lou Stone died. "He was seventy-five when he died," says Elizabeth Stone, "but considering how hard he lived, that was a pretty good age. He was a smoker, a drinker, lots of women, lots of booze—a meat and potatoes kind of guy even to the end. I kept trying to get him to eat vegetables and he'd say, 'I'm going to go anyway— let me have my martini.'"

Stone was able to reconcile with his father. "We had a sort of conversation before he died," Stone recalls. "It was awkward but we expressed our love. Then he said, 'You'll do all right. There'll always be a demand for great stories and great storytellers.' In the end he accepted that I'd made the right choice. In a sense I wanted it to be like the scene I wrote later in *Wall Street* [between Charlie and Martin Sheen], but it never really happened that way. It was more about his pain and his anger. And ultimately, I felt useless and unprepared for his death. To this day I regret that I was not able to be more supportive to my father and I think about him often."

Lou Stone didn't live to see that he had passed on his work ethic and a solid business sense to his son, and that it would be these qualities, just as much as the artistic ones, which would enable Oliver Stone to tell the kinds of stories he wanted to tell on such a grand scale. In the end, after all the battles, Lou had set aside insurance money for Jacqueline, but had only been able to leave his son $19,000, which Oliver Stone put into a trust for Sean, but his head for business and love of art was Lou Stone's real legacy.

Meanwhile Stone had decided to fight de Laurentiis for *Platoon*. The first step in this battle was separating from his lawyer, Tom Pollock. Pollock was one of the top lawyers in the business, but he also represented de Laurentiis, and Stone believed the only way to move forward was to eliminate this conflict of interest. "Steve Pines, my business manager, introduced me to a lawyer named Bob Marshall," Stone recalls. "Marshall had a reputation as a guy who didn't mind fighting. He'd go to court if he needed to. He was a hammer, a litigator."

Marshall, who has been Stone's attorney ever since, comments: "It's always been interesting to me that *Platoon*, this incredible war movie, was birthed out of so many battles. In this case I filed a lawsuit against Dino de Laurentiis's company arguing that the value they paid Oliver for writing *Year of the Dragon* was far lower than what the market price was for his work at the time. And, of course, Dino had promised to finance *Platoon* and wasn't doing it."

Essentially, the lawsuit argued that Stone should now reacquire his rights to *Year of the Dragon* since de Laurentiis had not honored his end of the agreement. Marshall knew that until the case was settled, there was a distinct possibility that the release of *Year of the Dragon* would be held up. "Bob sued with a massive document," Stone recalls. "And since Dino had a finished film that was about to be released, he didn't want anything to hold it up, so he gave me *Platoon* back within a week and swallowed the scouting costs."

Platoon now belonged to its rightful owner, and Stone was even a notch up on the project—he'd already scouted the locations. Fittingly, it was around this time that Hemdale, a small independent production house, began to express interest in Stone's work. One of the people he had given the *Salvador* script to was producer Gerald Green, who sent it over to John Daly at Hemdale. Both men loved the project and wanted to do it with Stone as the director. Today, Stone still shakes his head when recalling this sudden turn of events. "In John Daly I found somebody who would back me. He said he liked *Salvador* and *Platoon* and would do whichever one I wanted to do first."

Later Stone wrote in an article for *American Film* (January 1987):

I got there at the right time which is the key. Luck comes from persistence and talent. If you're talented your luck will eventually come. Somehow life has a way of taking care of you when you relax, when you don't want something so bad. *Salvador* became the most joyful picture I ever made. Producer John Daly, who comes from the poor streets of London, was loose and wild enough to defy (with the critical help of Gerald Green) the "No's" of the American conglomerates who would never in a million years soil themselves on something as radical and ugly as *Salvador*. It was all done in six months from script to shooting. It was like a fairy tale. If you persist, I guess, the worm does turn, though without rhyme or reason.

John Daly recalls his first meeting with Oliver Stone well. "I sort of immediately took to him because there was this sense of humility about him," Daly says. "He covers it up by being provocative with his questions and chipping away at you a little bit, but there's something about him that is endearing in a way. I felt I was talking to a man who really had an incredible passion about making his project. I loved the idea for the movie."

John Daly had formed Hemdale as a management company with the British actor David Hemmings in the mid-sixties, and got into films in 1971. They arranged financing for movies, and Daly, along with head of production Derek Gibson, took executive producer credit. At the time, one out of four of their films was picked up by a major distributor. Hemdale brought both scripts, *Salvador* and *Platoon*, to Orion. Orion wanted to do *Platoon* first. "I told them I'd rather do *Salvador* first," Stone recalls. "I'd been beaten down too many times with *Platoon* and *Salvador* was ready to go. Gerald Green had some kind of weird tax deal in Holland where if he could make the movies in Mexico, he could get them financed. Gerald had this Arnold Schwarzenegger project called 'Outpost,' and Schwarzenegger could not for various reasons fulfill his obligation, so all during shooting we were called 'Outpost' because we had that slot. Arnold Kopelson was also instrumental in making the film happen. He got the foreign interest going, which we really needed. We shot it the way it looks—hand-held, urgent—I love that movie. It was an ugly duckling. It went after American policy in Central America and it said some things Americans didn't want to hear."

Arnold Kopelson actually became involved through his interest in

Platoon. He and Gerald Green both had offices in the same building in L.A. and Green knew that Kopelson, besides being a lawyer, had produced several movies and was very adept at raising money through presales of foreign licenses to distributors. When Green mentioned he had an Oliver Stone script about Vietnam, Kopelson said he would like to see it. "My kids had been asking me questions about the Vietnam War," Kopelson recalls. "There was nothing in the high school history books about it, even though we were coming up to the tenth anniversary of the withdrawal. Also, independent distributors around the world were asking for war films. I felt compelled to stop whatever I was doing and start reading the script. I read fifty pages, though I knew after ten that it was special. Then I called Gerald and asked for Oliver's number, and I called him and said I wanted to do this movie. I told him that I had been in the Army and though I never saw any action, I was walking through the jungle when I was reading that script. I have a visual sense when I'm reading and I was in the jungle and really very terrified. Oliver writes like no one I've ever experienced in all my years.

"So we agreed to talk. That night, when I went to bed, my wife Anne was reading a magazine and I read the script. I started with page one again and when I finished, I was crying. Anne said to me, 'What's wrong?' I said, 'I just read the greatest screenplay I have ever read. It's Academy Award time—we'll never get closer.' I remember those exact words, and Anne said to me (she's my partner as well as my wife), 'Will it make money?' I said, 'I really don't know, but I have to do this. I'm compelled to do this.' And she said, 'Follow your instincts.'"

Kopelson, today one of the most powerful producers in Hollywood, whose works include *The Fugitive* and *Falling Down*, maintains that this was a key point in his career. "From the moment I read that script, I knew this was the turning point in my life. I'd been a lawyer, put together some money, was in foreign sales and made a lot of money making movies. You get this surge of power that you can do anything. You don't think you can fuck up. Well, I fucked up really badly. I invested in a bank and a gold mine and dropped considerable money. I hate to admit failure, but I had failed. So I went back into the movie production business full time, and the very first call I got was from Gerald Green. So it was like the skies opened up and God said, 'Give this kid a break, he's been suffering quite a bit.' And Oliver was not easy at all. He'd been screwed over by every con man and every major studio had turned him down. He was very disenchanted with the studio system."

Stone and Kopelson made an agreement for *Platoon* whereby if Kopelson raised the finances within a certain period of time, he would produce the film and Stone would direct. "We were each taking a $350,000 fee and a $150,000 deferment if and when it was earned," Kopelson says. "Then John Daly asked me to look at a script of *Salvador*. He said he hadn't made any disposition on the foreign rights and wanted me to look at it and see if it had any value. I read the script and I really liked it a lot. So I agreed to help with the foreign sales and I wound up being involved in both films."

Stone began to assemble a film crew. *Salvador* marked his first association with several key people who would go on to make many films with him, including Robert Richardson. Prior to *Salvador*, Richardson had never shot a feature film, but he had done reshoots for *Repo Man* and several documentaries, including *Crossfire* for the BBC, which was shot in El Salvador. He heard about the opening for a DP and though he'd already made up his mind to take the job, he was shocked when he actually met Stone.

"I thought he was a bit of a lunatic," Richardson says. "His behavior was manic. My first impression was that he was possibly doing coke because he was moving at a hundred miles per hour. He was in this tiny little office, eight feet by eight feet, sitting on his desk. His hands were constantly moving and he was talking very rapidly. And beyond that he's sweating up a storm, constantly patting at his head. He looks at me and he says, 'I only have one question for you. Can you cut a long lens with a wide-angle lens?' I thought, 'Are you kidding? Of course you can. No problem.' I mean why not? That was sort of my initiation to him. If I didn't care whether a long lens was intercut with a wide-angle shot, then clearly I wouldn't be a problem on the set."

Stone, who had quit coke in 1982, says he was sweating out a cold when he met Richardson. With the establishment of a budget, albeit still small for a feature film, the production became somewhat larger and the decision was made to cast real actors in the roles. Richardson claims that Stone had really liked the idea of casting Boyle to play himself and only reluctantly let it go. Stone agrees, laughing over the memory. "I did a test with Richard and Rock in the car. It was hilarious because Richard's face would turn different colors every day. He'd been drinking a bit and he'd be green one minute and blue the next and red and orange the next. Bob Richardson was saying, 'Oliver, you've got to be fucking crazy,' and he was right about it. It wouldn't have worked at all."

With the entrance of Green and Daly, Alex Ho bowed out of the project. "When Gerald Green got involved with this thing in Mexico, the budget went up to $2.7 million," Ho says. "I said I didn't think we should do it for that kind of money. I figured we were going to get killed. Besides, I wasn't getting paid and had really run out of money, but I promised Oliver I would come back and do *Platoon*." Other key members of what was to become Oliver Stone's team were being assembled, however, including production designer Bruno Rubeo, editor Claire Simpson, and music supervisor Bud Carr. At this time Stone also began his association with Paula Wagner of Creative Artists Agency, who represented him until July 1992, when she left CAA to form C & W Productions with another CAA client, Tom Cruise.

"Someone had given me a copy of the *Platoon* script," Wagner remembers, "and when I read it, I was truly moved. It brought forth a lot of personal experiences because I grew up with boys who went and didn't come back. I was completely devastated emotionally and I remember thinking this is one of those rare and special moments. I thought, this movie has to made, and I tracked down Oliver Stone. He didn't know me, and I said, 'I just read your script and I want to help you any way I can.'"

When Stone told Wagner that *Platoon* and *Salvador* were being made by Hemdale, she asked to see the *Salvador* script. Finding that another powerful work, she then helped bring James Woods, who was also represented by CAA, into the project. Woods describes meeting with Stone to discuss the film. "He originally approached me to play Dr. Rock," Woods recalls. "But when I read the screenplay, I got excited about the idea of playing the lead because it was such a great role. So when we met, I asked who he had in mind for the lead and he said Marty Sheen. Now, I think Marty's a great actor, you know, but hell, I'm up for a role here so I'm going to cut his legs out from under him if I can, do what I have to do to get it. So I said, 'Martin Sheen, huh? Oh, he's great, great actor. He's kind of religious, isn't he?' And Oliver goes, 'Well, yeah, a bit.' And I go, 'Gee, I'm surprised he didn't have a problem with some of the language here. It's pretty strong.' And Oliver says, 'Well, he did have a few things that bothered him.' So then I say,

'Oh . . . I see. I thought you were going to do this thing for real . . . go all out? I mean, if you're just going to do another bullshit Hollywood picture . . . ' And Oliver starts assuring me that he wants to do the thing for real, so then he decided to cast me for the lead. The point being that this was all a dog and pony show which every actor goes through to get a part, but this time it worked."

Before *Salvador*, James Woods had appeared in a variety of films, but he was probably best known for his portrayal of a violent killer in *The Onion Field*, for which he was nominated for a Golden Globe. It was the reality of the film that particularly attracted him to *Salvador*: "It doesn't sugarcoat the situation," Woods says. "I found it interesting that this man with all his shortcomings and vices would be ultimately interested in finding the truth. He goes back to El Salvador, even though he's on Major Max's death list, just to make some money. But then he gets swept up in it on a personal level and becomes truly interested in finding the truth. That's what the script is finally all about, his search for the truth."

Portraying Richard Boyle with the real Richard Boyle on the set every day did not prove a daunting experience to Woods. "Usually the person is not able to give you much of a clue about themselves. That might sound preposterous, but take their mannerisms, for example. They may or may not be ones I could do very effectively. A character's psychology to me is more interesting than his behavior. So I try to find equivalent things that are counterpoised against each other the way his character traits are counterpoised against each other, and then bring that to the role, more than just do an imitation of him."

It was a gutsy choice for Woods. After all, he was going off to Mexico on a shoestring budget with a director that many people had warned him was a madman. "It was a lot of the same people who now say, 'Oh, Oliver, you're so wonderful,'" Woods says. "I mean, let's face it. This town is full of a lot of limp-dick assholes who make sucking up a way of life. I could name names, but I won't. They'd say, 'You're going to work with Oliver Stone? Isn't he like a junkie or something? He's a jerk. He wrote *Conan the Barbarian* and directed *The Hand*.' And I'd say, 'He also wrote *Midnight Express*' and they'd go, 'Oh, yeah.' People said he was a drug addict, a drunk, violent, a liar . . . everything. They were really vitriolic about him, and I thought, 'I wonder why?' I'd met him once and he seemed like a nice guy. 'Why does he affect people this way? There must be something different about him.'"

For the role of Dr. Rock—the unsuspecting out-of-work disc jockey from San Francisco who accompanies Boyle to El Salvador in search of a good time—Stone cast Jim Belushi. Belushi was also a CAA client, represented by Mike Menchel. Menchel would soon join Paula Wagner in handling Oliver Stone. "To this day, *Salvador* is the best screenplay I ever read in my life," Menchel says now. "I asked my associates what was up with this movie? Who was cast in it? Then I found out nobody was doing anything with it. So I just figured I would help. It came out of a love for the material. I didn't even know we were going to represent Oliver. I told Oliver he should hire Jim Belushi, and he got very excited because he liked Jim's 'white man's rap' skit on *Saturday Night Live*. I called Jimmy and said, 'Jimmy, I just read your next film. Deal's done.' And Jimmy said, 'If that's the way you feel about it, I'll do it.' And then Jimmy read it and realized what I saw in it."

Like Woods's, Belushi's character was based on a real person; but since the real Rock never went to El Salvador, Belushi decided to take his own track with the role. "To me, it was like creating a totally fictional character," he says. "He was ignorant of Central American issues like most of the American general public, so I feel like I was a touchstone for the audience at the beginning of the movie. My character discovers El Salvador as the audience does."

John Savage played the only major character who is not a real-life person, although his role as John Cassady was based on the photojournalist John Hoagland. Savage describes the role: "I had a line about capturing the nobility of human suffering and death in these tragic situations. That's what Cassady's trying to do, as opposed to the effort of a war photographer to capture as much action or tedium as possible. Cassady wants to make people aware."

The supporting actors—Michael Murphy, Cynthia Gibb, and Eldepla Carrillo—also had a wide range of experience. Once the funding was committed, the crew assembled, and the actors hired, the next step was to scout out locations. "When I showed up in Acapulco, Oliver was sick," Bob Richardson recalls. "He had a 104-degree temperature and the outside temperature was matching it. And this man had on a black leather jacket zipped up to his chin and he was reeking of sweat. I was thinking, 'What am I in for here?' It's like a deranged Hunter Thompson mixed with Count Dracula. And his hours—not human. He would get up at 6:00 A.M. and we'd start scouting. The whole time he would constantly be saying we're not moving fast enough. He'd be barking out orders and everybody was being torn apart inside the van. Whoever was closest to Oliver would always be the one to get beaten up. So the longer we rode, the further and further away I'd move. I mean, I think Bruno Rubeo who production-designed the film must have a permanent soul scar. Eventually, the seat next to Oliver remained empty."

But the real action was at night, according to Richardson. "Oliver would take me out on these night surveillances. He would say he had to do location and background research. Well, what he calls location research was scanning whorehouses and the background was when we would go to these villages, little tiny towns in the middle of nowhere. And he'd walk along and we'd be kidding with each other and he'd go, 'Do you think that's a man or a woman?' He'd put his arm around me and say, 'Let's go meet her.' And he would hit on every single one of these women or men. Didn't matter what they were, he'd just hit on them.

"With the guys, he would just ask them stuff," Richardson continues. "Like, how much? What are you looking for? Typical things. That was his research. We went out for like three nights in a row and we'd get back no earlier than two in the morning. And I would end up sitting on these benches waiting for him. I didn't speak a word of Spanish. Oliver would disappear for forty-five minutes to an hour, come back out, and take me in a taxi to another place. For me it was uncomfortable. At the time I think I was twenty-eight years old. Really a novice in world affairs. And this guy was stretching what he called my 'living experiences,' and somehow still expecting me to get up in the morning and to be rather intelligent regarding work. Oliver is a night vampire; he can survive on two or three hours of sleep and function with maximum performance. Amazing energy. I, on the other hand, am an old hag. I need my eight hours."

Early versions of the *Salvador* script contained several whorehouse scenes, and real hookers were used in a few of the filmed sequences. "Oliver was doing research on transvestites, hookers, everything, because he said it was for the script," Richardson says. "He had this affair with a hooker. The assistant director, Ramon Menendez, also had an affair with this hooker. Well, eight years later when we're scouting locations in Bangkok for *Heaven and Earth*, I told Oliver that Ramon had an affair with this same hooker and he just laughed. Then I said, 'Oliver, you know what she said? She said Ramon's dick is bigger than yours.' So what does he do? He gets on the phone and calls Ramon and asks if he told me that. Ramon says, 'No, man, that's a total lie. I didn't have anything to do with it. Richardson is full of it. I don't know what he's talking about.' So then Ramon calls me and says, 'What the fuck are you telling him this stuff for? Don't tell him that!' Well, Ramon is prone to provocative exaggeration, so who knows where the truth lies."

Salvador began filming on location in Mexico in the states of Guerrero and Morelos and in Mexico City. Working on a severely limited budget made things tough enough, but Stone's demanding nature no doubt added to the difficulties. "I had to do the movie fast because I never knew when the money would dry up," he recalls. "I worked cheap and I worked fast, which is redundant. *Salvador* took fifty days, and about four and a half million dollars."

"It was the toughest movie I've made in my life," producer Gerald Green agrees. "I really mean it, and I've done pictures far bigger than this one. We were the co-production company for *Dune*, and that movie was easy compared to *Salvador*. *Dune* was a year and three months, but we would shoot maybe a third of a page a day. Everybody used to arrive in the morning at the same time, shoot, and at the wrap time— the normal wrap time—you'd leave; and we didn't work on Saturdays. It was great."

Part of what made *Salvador* so difficult was the logistics of it all— the schedule, the locations, the number of actors. *Salvador* has ninety-three speaking roles and well over a thousand extras, not to mention horses, tanks, airplanes, and helicopters, all accommodated in a film which had only seven weeks to shoot. That would be difficult enough if everything went according to plan, and that of course rarely happened. "The Battle of Santa Ana sequence," Green recalls, "was originally going to take place around a bridge that exists in Salvador, but it was blown up. We found a bridge which had collapsed in Acapulco. That bridge was quite similar and we were going to film the battle in the countryside—a column of tanks would come in, and they'd ambush them. Two pages of the script. No big deal. We arranged to shoot there, and then when we arrived, we discovered that they'd started to rebuild the bridge, so we had to come up with something different. I think the scene that we wound up with is actually much better—and bigger. It was spectacular."

Stone spared little in the way of authenticity. "We took over this entire town for a week to shoot the Battle of Santa Ana," he remembers. "The mayor was great. He loved movies. We redesigned his office and used it as a whorehouse set (with real prostitutes). He liked the decor so much he kept it that way, red walls and all. Later, he said, 'Go ahead, blow up the whole fucking City Hall,' and we blew it to pieces."

The crucial battle of Santa Ana was staged in the tiny village of Tlayacapan, with its cobblestoned streets and a church built in 1572. Production designer Bruno Rubeo and his team came in early and added second stories to many of the stores and homes. They also put up fronts of new buildings to blow up and changed billboards and other set dressings to create the Salvadorean town. The Mexican Army brought in 175 soldiers each day to portray the government troops and provided the tanks, trucks, jeeps, rifles, and other hardware. The 150 rebels and civilians were played by members of the village.

The sequence took over a week to film and the force of the special effects explosions was so great that, at one point, the windows of a passing car were blown out, and another time, a blast actually dented one of the army tanks. The special effects creators, Gordon Smith and Ginny Stolee, had to show up on the set at 4:00 A.M., four hours before the crew's regular call time, in order to do their work on the battle's victims.

"What happened in the real Battle of Santa Ana in 1981," recalls Boyle, "is that the government troops ran out of ammunition, and by their own admission, they would have lost the war within a week if it wasn't for the resumption of U.S. military aid. We show that. Planes and tanks run out of gas. So much of this movie is real. I'm real; Dr. Rock's real; Maria, my girlfriend, is real; Major Max is real—we changed his name, but he's real."

Much of the tension captured in the film was also real. In *Salvador*, Stone was learning to wind the cinematic mechanism until it coiled with productive tension, both on the screen and on the set. Initially, much of this came from Woods and Belushi. "I like Jimmy and all," Belushi says, "but he always had to have the last word in a scene. He would improvise things to call attention to himself. There was this scene in the car where I was explaining some things I felt were pretty important about my character, and right in the middle of my fucking speech, Jimmy suddenly pulls out a switchblade and clicks it open right into the camera. So naturally, they have to cut over to him for a closeup during my speech. So when the scene was over, I told Jimmy, 'If you pull that knife out again in one of my scenes, I'm going to open the goddamn glove compartment and pull out a gun and start waving it around.'"

According to Belushi, Woods, now totally into character as the wild and unpredictable Richard Boyle, was incorrigible. "There's a scene where we come out of this tanklike thing, an armored personnel carrier, when we're going to that town where all the students are laying down on the ground. And they make us get out and get into the back of an open truck. So Oliver says, 'Jim Belushi, you come out first and walk in front with your hands over your head and get into the truck, and then Jimmy Woods, you come walking right behind him.' So we get out and start to walk toward the truck, and Jimmy literally knocks my arm out of the way, and sort of elbows his way in front of me, and we get in the truck and I'm pissed and Jimmy just won't shut up. He's like improvising all these lines because he knows that as long as he's talking, the camera has to stay on him. And I finally said, 'Will you *shut up*!' And Oliver left it in the movie because it fits, but it's really just me telling Woods to shut the fuck up!"

Woods laughs at the memory. "Belushi and I would always tease each other. And the same thing with Savage. I remember when the three of us would be in the same scene, Oliver would say, 'This will be a struggle to see who's going to steal the scene.' But of course that kind of situation is what makes for great movie making."

Things came to a head between Belushi and Woods over a joke Belushi tells in the film. At a fancy outdoor party where Boyle hopes to talk to the American ambassador, Belushi as a stumbling, drunken Dr. Rock comes on to an uptight blond American newswoman. When he asks her what her sign is, she looks disgusted and replies, "Stop." He snaps back, "Oh, I thought it was 'Slippery when wet.'" Belushi tells how the scene went: "I had put that joke in with Oliver, and it's where I'm sitting on the ground at this table and I put acid in that girl's drink. Jimmy had a big speech there where he tells her she's an asshole. Well, I finally caught on to Jimmy's tricks and every time we'd get near the spot where the joke was supposed to go, Jimmy kept closing the cue on me. There were a lot of set-ups with that scene, so by the time it would get to me, there was no space for the line, and Jimmy would overlap it. When you overlap someone, you have to loop it, and that meant they would probably lose my line. I knew this shit already, so I was fighting to keep my space. I kept asking, 'Hey, Jimmy, you're gonna keep that open for me, right?' And he'd say, 'Oh, yeah, yeah, sure.' But he kept fucking with me. At a certain point I said, 'Fuck you! I know what the fuck you're trying to do, fuck you!'"

But Belushi says he got his revenge. "As a supporting player, I'm giving the lead actor power. And I'd been doing it. I supported that motherfucker. Helped make him look good. All I asked for was this fucking space for my joke, but he wouldn't give it to me. So I pulled my support out. Now, no one knows how supporting another player is until he's not there. And it was weird. He could not get through the lines. He would stop in the middle of a fucking take. So we got in a big fight and we walked off the set. I was so pissed off. Jimmy was pissed off. Now, where was Mr. Stone through all this? He was sitting back and letting the two boys fight.

"After about forty-five minutes, Oliver came over and said, 'Okay now, let's be professionals.' We were like a couple of kids. So we said okay. Jimmy let me have my joke and then he knew I was with him and he shot right through the scene. But what's interesting about Oliver is that he allows that to happen. He let it get crazy, hell, even made it crazier, because lots of times he'd say little things to me like, 'Woods is all over you, man. You better push harder on some of those lines.' And I figure now he was probably saying something to get Jimmy going at me. But part of what makes Oliver great is he's able to feed off that energy, that tension, and he gets it down on film."

Though Woods and Belushi reached an understanding, there was no question that, as the film progressed, tensions were increasing between Woods and Stone. Woods was not a huge star at the time, but he was a star, and though Stone had won an Oscar as a writer, both of them and most of the crew knew that Stone still had to prove himself as a director. *Salvador* was his moment of truth. "Working with Stone was like being caught in a Cuisinart with a madman," James Woods says. "And he felt the same about me. It was two Tasmanian devils wrestling under a blanket. Still, he was a sharp director. He starts with a great idea, delegates authority well, scraps like a street fighter, then takes the best of what comes out of the fracas."

Woods recalls some of the more difficult moments between him and Stone: "Oliver and I are great friends now and were then, but there was a lot of tension between us during the making of the film. At one point we were rolling in the mud, pushing and shoving each other, and people had to pull us apart. Another time I was strapped down to the street with all these wires [tied to explosive squibs] running up my legs because I was supposed to get shot, and this Mexican pilot who didn't speak any English was about to fly this old single-engine plane real low right over me. Well, there were all these low powerlines hanging right over me, and just before the scene starts, Oliver's looking over the scene, and I hear him say, 'God, I miss combat.' So I think, 'You get down here and be wired to the damn street with this screwy plane flying over you, then.' But all the tension worked wonders on the screen."

Bob Richardson agrees. "I think that Jimmy would raise the stakes of each scene intentionally because when he amps up to a high level, his performance is outstanding, and when he didn't crank himself as high, he wasn't quite as good. At least I think this is what he thought. As a result, he clearly made a decision to go at Oliver, deliberately push him, whether subconsciously or consciously. He pushed Oliver hard, and Oliver ended up pushing back. The two of them just came to that end, ego against ego. As a result, his performance is what it is, and I believe that's one of the reasons it's so fine."

Stone acknowledges the battles between him and Woods. "With Jimmy, the thing is that he tends to direct himself," he says, "which is not good because he overplays a lot. I've seen that in lots of his performances. It's as if the director could not control him or criticize or challenge him—I have a feeling that Jimmy is so bright with his high IQ that he's intimidating. You know he has a very eccentric genius, no question about it, and I was lucky enough to tap into it. But in order to do so I had to get in the way of his reflection."

Richardson says it went a lot farther than that. "One time we were setting up to shoot a bar sequence and all of a sudden there was this screaming from another room. Then we heard this sort of movement. So we opened the door and it was Oliver just beating Jimmy's head against the ground. They were taking swings at each other. They came to blows a number of times. They would just pound each other."

Stone shrugs and a malicious grin comes over his face. "Jimmy's like the guy you want to punch out in school. He's a whiner. He complained so much he drove everyone crazy. The crew, me, his fellow actors. Everyone wanted to kill him because we had no money and we really had to depend on his mercy. He was, at that time, the biggest single star in the whole thing, so it was like we were all amateurs and he was the professional always telling us what to do. When someone is always reminding you of that, it becomes tiresome. I don't believe in confronting everyone, but I think confronting Jimmy helped. He wasn't used to being confronted and I think he gave the best performance I've seen him do. Because I drove him nuts. On certain days, I tried to work on his insecurity a bit. To use the anguish. By the time we got to that, he was ready to pop. But that was a little long into the shoot when we started to get under each other's skin."

Woods recalls the time he became the most frustrated. "That was the day of the famous five-kilometer walk," he says. "I'd got so pissed off with Oliver, I walked off the set. But I was in Mexico. Where was I going to walk? So I walked down this road for about five kilometers in the middle of fucking nowhere. I was waiting for a car or a bus to come by. They come by about once every half hour. But nobody was coming by. Nothing. Well, I get back, and then I find out later that Oliver had people set up a roadblock and they were stopping cars on the road and saying there was a crazy gringo with a gun up ahead, don't pick him up at any cost."

One of the greatest scenes in the movie, and the one most referred to when Woods's Oscar-nominated performance is discussed, is where Boyle goes to confession for the first time in thirty-two years. "I remember the day we were shooting the Romero assassination scene at the church and Oliver said maybe you should do a confession," Woods recalls. "And I said, 'Oh really? First of all, let me tell you something, Oliver. You don't go to confession on the morning before the Mass. And he says, 'Well, they won't know the difference.' Right. There's like eighty million Catholics in the United States but they probably won't notice. Sure. And the irony is, they didn't. He was right. That's what's so aggravating about him! So I asked him for the lines, but he said, 'I don't want to give you the lines. I want you to just look into that dark murky soul of yours, into that weasel soul of yours, and come up with whatever you want.' And I said, okay, fair enough, but I don't want you around.

"So Oliver didn't say anything, but he did listen while we improvised the scene. We didn't even do a rehearsal; what you saw was the first time it came out of my mouth, just total improvisation. I just used the whole thing to get back at Oliver. Just about everything I said was getting back at him for stuff that happened during the film. At one point he'd actually called me a weasel and a rat, so I mentioned that in the confession and so on. In the film they cut back to some extra, but it was actually Ramon Menendez, the AD [assistant director], off camera, asking me questions. There was a sequence where Ramon says, 'Have you had carnal knowledge?' And I said, 'Well yeah, I'm not a saint or anything, but I'm not bad. It's not like I've been out fucking quadrupeds.' 'And he says, you had sex with a quadriplegic?' And I said, 'No, with a quadruped, like a goat or a Shetland pony or something.' And when I got done, Oliver says, 'It's frightening the shit that you think of,' and I said, 'You'll use it, believe me.' And he did."

Although not unheard of in a business as unpredictable as the film industry, the financial problems encountered during the shooting of *Salvador* were extreme. "They didn't have any money," Richardson recalls. "The crew was union and if you didn't pay them on time each week, they wouldn't work. And so, invariably, when Saturday came we weren't working for hours until the money appeared on the set. I remember once we were in the middle of the battle scene, and when Saturday came along, we had to close down because there was no money. The sad part was I never knew if we were going to get through the whole film. There was a feeling that each day would be our last. Perhaps Oliver drew inspiration from the uncertainty."

"We're not firing you, Richard, we're putting you on hold without a retainer."

Cesar in **SALVADOR**

Arnold Kopelson recalls visiting the set and observing the financial chaos. "I remember Gerald Green was sitting in a bunker, in the low light, with spreadsheets all over the place, and he looked half crazy. I said, 'What's wrong?' And he said, 'I'm looking for money. I don't know where I'm going to get the money.' But on the set I saw greatness, dailies with texture that just blew my mind. I'd heard people in the industry say they didn't trust Oliver's ability to direct, but after I saw him work, I remember coming back and telling John Daly and the Orion people, 'Not only is this guy good, he's great.'"

Jim Belushi says the conditions on the *Salvador* set formed a strong bond between cast and crew. "Even though we don't hang out, I have a connection with Oliver and Jimmy that lasts. We were all practically starving down there. Fucking no trailers. We finally got a couple of trailers toward the end of the shoot, and the Mexican crew kept thinking my trailer was the portable john. So like everyone shits in my trailer. I got sunstroke on the shoot. They wouldn't spend a hundred and fifty bucks to fix the muffler on the Mustang until we were like dying of asphyxiation, and then we're out in the middle of Mexico, miles and miles out, and six Mexican guys are trying to fix the muffler with a Coke can while everything stops. It took us two hours and all they would've had to do was spend the one fifty. It was wild."

Woods says he almost quit because he found out he wasn't being paid. "One time I got a phonecall through to my agent and he said, 'You haven't been getting paid for two weeks so get a fucking plane and come home.' And I said, 'I'm not gonna do that to Oliver. Tomorrow is our biggest day. Half the budget is on the battle scene.' And he said they were going to fuck me so I should just split. So I said, 'You call Daly and tell him I'm not working until he pays you. Then you call the set. There's only one phone line so I'll never be able to call you, but just leave a message. Don't say I haven't been paid because they won't give me the message or they'll lie to me. So if you say Todd Smith called, I'll know I haven't been paid, but if you say Jose Smith, then I'll know I've been paid.'

"So the next day we're on the set with the fucking armored personnel carriers, the troops and these tanks and everything, and they're ready to go, and I say, 'Oliver, I'm really sorry about this but I haven't been fucking paid and I'm not gonna work unless something happens real soon.' And I give Oliver credit for this. He said, 'Jimmy, I understand and you're right, it's not fair. I'm as pissed off as you are.' He wasn't mad at me. We sat there for three hours and then one of the crew came up and gave me a message, 'A man called for you and said his name was Jose Smith,' and I said, 'Okay, let's go to work.'"

Once work on the battle scene began, more money problems were encountered. It was here, Jim Belushi says, that he realized just how committed Stone was to the project. "Oliver is more committed than anybody," Belushi maintains, "and to me that's what a leader is. We were shooting the battle, and Oliver got the idea of having these rebel troops riding in on horseback and charging the tanks. There wasn't any money in the budget, but Oliver wanted that fucking horse cavalry charging over that bridge. So Gerald Green's saying, 'No, we don't have the money. We can't do it.' And Oliver says, 'Then take my salary. I've got twenty-five thousand dollars coming, take that twenty-five thousand dollars and get those fucking horses.' He didn't care about the money. Didn't care at all."

"We ran out of money a lot," Stone admits, "since the money was coming in increments and the financing was so shaky that we never knew when it would end. We had tremendous problems, completion company fights, sitdown strikes, calls almost shutting down the picture all the time. For a while it drove me nuts and then I just stopped caring. I couldn't give a shit any more, I was so tired. They said, 'We're on strike,' and I walked over and got into this old beat-up car and just went to sleep in the back seat. They woke me up three hours later and said, 'We're back.' You had to have a laissez-faire attitude about it, because you never knew how long anything would last. We were living near the edge and there's a desperation humor to it—it's laugh or die. They closed us down the forty-second day, which was sad because my heart was really in it. I wanted to finish the picture so bad, it hurt. But there was no more money. We had to get out of Mexico. The unions, creditors, everyone was on our tail."

Today, Stone confesses that he intentionally misrepresented the budget to Hemdale at the outset. "I told them I could make the film for two million dollars and I couldn't. It was really a three- to four-million-dollar movie. I knew I couldn't do it for that, but figured I just had to do it. I was desperate. I just barged in and took my chances."

How did the movie get finished? "I called Daly," Stone recalls, "and told him I hadn't shot the beginning or the end, just the middle. It starts and ends in the United States. He says, in his British accent, 'Oh fuck. Well, can't you just cut the beginning?' I said, 'Are you crazy? You loved the beginning, remember? Let me finish it. I can do it in seven days. I'll go to San Francisco and the desert outside Las Vegas. Just give me three or four hundred thousand.' He finally agreed. Then, years later, I heard the whole tax scheme fell apart and the guy who issued the original letter of credit went to jail, partly because of this case. It kinda shows you that movies are houses built on cards."

"Oliver was always thinking," Richardson says. "One time he told me that, whenever you're working with a producer, you should have certain sequences and scenes that you know you can get rid of built into the budget. So, if you fall behind, you can specifically pull out this or that sequence. If you don't fall behind, then you can keep shooting anything you want."

Once Daly relented, Stone shot the opening scenes in San Francisco and then finished the film in the Las Vegas area as he had promised. James Woods describes the last scenes: "After John Savage's character gets shot he gives Boyle the film before he dies, and then Boyle gets grabbed at the border and fucked up by these guys in the bus. Oliver had it that they find all the film and open it up and ruin it, and I kept saying he has to at least get a roll of film through. And Oliver was saying, 'No, I don't want a Hollywood ending.' I said, 'It's not a Hollywood ending. It's redemption. The movie is called *Salvador*, it means 'saviour.' The guy has got to bring one piece of film through . . . he has to have something. He winds up losing his girl, he loses his credibility. But he gets the film through, so that means something.'

"But Oliver kept saying no, so I admit I did sort of fuck him over on that. I went to the wardrobe and prop guys and asked them to make a hollow heel in my boot. We actually had only one take we could do. We had no light left and could do one shot of me sitting at the table with those guys who beat me up on the bus, but who were now acting like my pals because they got the word not to kill me from the ambassador. So we're drinking and Oliver's filming the shot, and all of a sudden I pull my boot off and I say, 'I'll show you old American trick.' And I slide open the hollow heel of the boot and take out the roll of film. And I hold it up and go, 'Look what I got,' and they all laugh. So we finish the scene and Oliver charges over and starts yelling at me, 'What the fuck?' And I said, 'I didn't hear you say cut!' And he's screaming, 'You know I can't do another take because there's no light left!' And I said, 'I guess you're just going to have to let him get the film through then, aren't you?' He said, 'You are such an asshole.' But if he'd really wanted to change it, he'd have found a way. He liked it."

Fittingly for such a wild and turbulent shoot, the very last scene was shot under the worst conditions. "I had a production manager who'd quit that day," Stone recalls "He ransomed the negative because he wanted to make sure he got paid. The receipts were everywhere and they'd sent a post production supervisor down to try to sort out the mess. The assistant cameraman was sick, lying in bed with a 105-degree fever, and I was trying to get him to work. I was saying, 'Look, I went through worse than this in Vietnam. You've got to take a Foreign Legionnaire's attitude. I want you to get up and go out into the desert.'

"I'd had no money to scout the last scene. So we all headed off into the desert. I was riding in the front car leading thirty to forty vehicles out of Las Vegas into the desert and I had no idea where we were going to shoot. So I said, 'Keep driving,' and then I saw a spot and said, 'There! Pull over!' And we all piled out and shot the last scene where the cops come and grab Maria off the bus inside the United States. The very last shot is Jimmy Woods watching Maria go off into the sunset with the cops."

James Woods describes the moment after the last shot: "Oliver just sat down on the curb. The film was over and he had this kind of stunned look, amazed that he actually managed to finish the picture. I sat down beside him. We had just fought so much. The thing is, we always fought about the right stuff. Not about credit, billing, perks, trailers, or that kind of bullshit, but about things that mattered for the film. All of a sudden we got this really close feeling. We sat on the curb and I said, 'I guess all we ever did was fight.' He said, 'Yeah.' I said. 'You know what? You're not going to believe this, but I really love you and I think you made a great film. And all this stuff I fought about with you was because I really wanted this film to be like no other. I wanted this to be the one they put on our gravestones. The one that we're most proud of.' And he said, 'Yeah, I think you're right. Everything we did made it better.' I never expected we'd be friends, but because of that one moment when we both let our guards down, I've felt this brotherhood with him ever since."

When Stone came back to the States he discovered that *8 Million Ways to Die* had been completed while he was shooting in Mexico. "I hated it," Stone says. "It had already been credited or I would have taken my name off. I wrote a script that took place in New York and Hal Ashby changed it to L.A., but that was minor compared to everything else he changed. He changed the feel."

As it came time to edit *Salvador*, Stone became concerned about how Daly would react to the footage. The truth was that the budget wasn't the only thing Stone had misrepresented. "John had always loved the idea of there being a comedy element to the movie," Stone says. "He had wanted a comedy, and I sold him on the idea of this being sort of a road movie . . . a bit like *Abbott & Costello Go to Salvador*, along with some social realism. Hemdale saw the sense of irony about it. They saw these two scuzzbags [the Boyle and Dr. Rock characters] as funny, almost in Monty Pythonesque terms. There is some comedy in it, but that's not really the focus . . . I sort of exaggerated it. I was desperate to make a film the way I wanted to make it, without compromises. I did a lot of wacky things toward that end. Going off to El Salvador with Boyle was crazy in the first place, to say nothing of trying to deceive the government there into helping support a film that was going to announce their atrocities to the world." After a moment Stone grins. "I told you I was desperate."

There is in fact an Abbott & Costello feel to the beginning of the film. Stone elaborates: "I wanted the movie to start that way and then twist. Like *Dr. Strangelove*, going from extreme absurdity to extreme seriousness. Or *Viva Zapata* because of the liberating pulse beating through it. The movie that most influenced me as a filmmaker, to be a filmmaker, was Godard's *Breathless* because it was fast, anarchic. I'm into anarchy. *Salvador* was a total explosion without any marination. It was raw, it was crude, it was what it was supposed to be."

Stone, who even today shoots a tremendous amount of film, knew that the editing of *Salvador* would be difficult because many scenes would have to be cut for length, and that left open the possibility of compromise on the material. After going the extra mile on the budget, John Daly was determined that the film succeed, and much of that hinged on getting Orion's full cooperation for distribution. The editing room is often where the worst arguments on a film take place, especially between producer and director. It's unlikely the producer will hold back the release of a film because so much has already been committed to the project and his or her desire is to edit the movie to appeal to the largest audience. The director, on the other hand, has reached the zenith of his or her artistic vision for the film by the time final editing begins, and becomes more rigid, seeing each compromise as marring that vision, disfiguring the work.

"We had tremendous battles in the editing room," Stone admits. "John and I fought on everything. There were moments that were really bristly where I felt like he was going to throw me out. But I provoked him a lot. I took it to the edge. Before I started the project, I promised myself that I would do it right. I said, 'I've worked on scripts, but I'm no closer to where I set out to be than when I left film school. This is not working.' Either you give up directing, just write or find another occupation, or you do it a hundred percent right. I undertook it with that spirit—that I would go down on this one. It was a principle movie, as they all have been since then. But I haven't been as tested as I was on *Salvador*. I felt I would do it or die. I wouldn't sell out the vision. I came close because of the financial crunch, but I never sold out the inherent vision of the film. I kept to it. John respected that. He fought with me, disagreed on a lot of stuff, but he respected my vision."

John Daly also recalls the editing room battles: "He thought I was very British in my attitude, but I felt that certain scenes, more graphic ones, were not necessary because the acting was so powerful that you didn't need to show the end result. So we had a couple of clashes. But basically I think Oliver can sit back and watch the film and he doesn't miss the things we clashed over."

"Gore became an issue with John because there were a lot of bloody heads," Stone says. "I was into showing war realistically. Some of his suggestions were good. I can't say they weren't. But it was like a Peckinpah battle where the producers are scared of it."

Arnold Kopelson tells a humorous story on the gore issue. "One of the scenes was an execution of four or five soldiers by a female rebel officer who was shooting them in the back of the head. And Oliver showed one guy's face being blown off. It was so wild. His face exploding. Well, I went to Milan to attend MIFED, the independent film festival, to engage in sales activity for *Salvador*, which involved screening a portion of the film for foreign distributors. And I'm waiting and waiting for ten minutes of footage to show. It finally arrives about twenty minutes before I have to show it and I have two hundred people in the screening room. I put it on and it's brilliant, but it includes this scene where she blows this guy's face off. At that point there were screams in the audience and one woman fainted. And people were saying it's too violent. They were also saying it's great, mind you, but too violent. I get back to the

States and I tell Oliver, 'Listen, I think the scene where you blow this guy's head off is just too violent.' He says, 'I've been shot in the head. This film is not violent at all.' "

Still, Kopelson sold $2.5 million worth of foreign contracts on the film. "I predicated it off of *Midnight Express*. That's how I sold it," he says. "I touted him as the great Academy Award-winning writer who was about to do something very great. And they bought it. And actually, it was true."

Not surprisingly, since *Salvador* was not only an attempt to relate Richard Boyle's experiences but also to show the major events that occurred there in the early eighties, length was a problem. Stone had been working from a 150-page screenplay, and knew many scenes would have to be cut. "I wound up pulling a lot of the violence out, and that weakened the story. The picture was two hours long and it really should've been two and a half hours. But I knew we couldn't get that version played, so I cut ruthlessly. The final version has been criticized for being choppy, and it is. There are scenes that are abruptly cut: the scene where the Colonel saves Boyle's ass, and they all go back into the whorehouse together—in my script that scene develops into an orgy, a [Jorge Luis] Borges-type scene. I wanted it to go from darkness to light. I shot this tremendous scene: Dr. Rock is getting a blowjob under a table, Boyle is fucking a girl while trying to pry information from the Colonel, and the Colonel is so drunk out of his mind that he pulls out this bag of ears and throws the ears on a table and says—'Left-wing ears, right-wing ears, who gives a fuck?' He throws an ear into a champagne glass, proposes a toast to El Salvador, and drinks the champagne with the ear in it."

Oliver Stone's critics have always claimed that his films are excessive, but Stone insists that, like Tony Montana gorging himself on cocaine in *Scarface*, this was a place where excess was required. "That's the way it was down there. There's a scene at the end that captures that madness: These guys are ready to kill Boyle, when they get the word from the Colonel that he's an important hombre, so they let him go. In the next scene, they're having beers together and slapping each other on the back. That's how it is there. You can go from light to dark so fast. South American audiences would've understood the whorehouse scene and liked it, but when we screened it for North American audiences, nobody knew how to take it because it was too early in the movie and it confused them. Is this supposed to be a comedy or is this a serious political movie? Very much an Anglo frame of mind. Why do we have to have that kind of specific intention? Can't we just drift with the movie and see where it takes us? The previewer, an expert on this sort of problem, advised us to take it out. I also had scenes with Belushi as Dr. Rock in the whorehouse that were deemed too much, a funny scene when he is making it with Wilma, that shocked audiences. It was too lurid. But to me it captured the exact flavor of Central American whorehouses."

The incident so soured Stone on the film-testing process that he now has a special clause in his contract allowing him to veto any test screenings. "The testing process destroys so much originality," he claims, "because whenever people see something that's new or interesting, they are always disturbed by it, whether it's good or bad. Any kind of disturbance goes against the whole testing principle. Previews should be calm and ordered because they want to control the emotion. They want to lead, seduce, manipulate. They never want the audience to have a genuine spontaneous emotional disturbance. That's not to say I won't test if I feel like I need to. I'm very confident in my films and I don't feel that a test is always in the best interest of the movie, so I have a hold-out position. The tests are usually stupid anyway. It's like they give you a huge questionnaire to find out if you want to see a movie based on the life of Jesus Christ and Mickey Mouse and who would win if they met on the Cross. It's ridiculous. Pretty soon they'll want penis meters. Wire you up to see if the penis rises or shrinks when you see a scene."

Finally, when the smoke had cleared, Stone and Daly had something they agreed upon. It may not have been either man's exact vision, but it was a powerful film in which both took pride. Stone dedicated the film to his father who, though he probably would have been appalled by its politics, would have recognized and appreciated a great story and the courage it took to tell it.

The executives at Orion were called in for the all-important screening. It was these men, chairman and CEO Mike Medavoy in particular, who would determine how many people got a chance to see the fruit of their labor. Oliver Stone remembers: "That was our worst moment . . . when we showed it to Orion in a late-cut form and Mike Medavoy turned it off and walked out of the room at the halfway point. It still rankles me. They just said it's too bloody, it's exploitative gore. Orion turned it down even though they had a sweetheart deal with Daly as distributors. They didn't have to spend a lot of money."

More than nine years have passed for Oliver Stone since that moment in the screening room when the projector was shut off. Nine years that have seen him awarded two Best Director Oscars and immeasurable acclaim. Yet, as he recalls that moment, the hurt is still there and the anger still colors his voice. "To this day I think Orion's management was cowardly. They should've released that movie. It was a great movie, but they didn't see it. And they didn't see me as a director."

"No doubts, just learning a few unpleasant lessons about the way things are."
Jim Garrison in JFK

Orion, which had the right to a first look, saw the more lurid version of *Salvador* with the ears on the table and the whorehouse scene. They may also have been influenced in their decision by the fact that they had previously distributed the unsuccessful *Under Fire* (also about journalists covering combat in Latin America). Hemdale was now faced with the option of shopping a film around Hollywood that had already been thoroughly rejected in the script stage or attempting to release the film themselves. Knowing full well that most major distributors were even less courageous than Orion, they decided to make the film the first release of their new distribution arm.

John Daly recalls that decision: "Oliver puts a thousand percent of himself into a film. It all goes up on the screen. For *Salvador*, he waived his salary, he waived his expenses. I think he would have given up his house. For him, it's the film. And that is why, whether he gets things right or wrong, there is an intensity up on the screen that could only come from a man with absolute passion. I don't think Oliver goes and directs a film. I think he *lives* the film. It's a rare quality. When you have a filmmaker like that and he's made a picture like *Salvador*, the studio has to do whatever they can to get it to the public."

Salvador had its world premiere at the Santa Barbara International Film Festival on February 28, 1986, and was released commercially on March 7 at the New Carnegie and the Waverly theaters in New York. Hemdale counted heavily on getting good reviews in New York to launch the film. Shortly before the opening there, Stone had to leave for the Philippines to begin shooting *Platoon*, so he asked Elizabeth to call him and let him know how the film was received. Arthur Manson, an independent distribution consultant working with Hemdale at the time, describes what happened: "Unfortunately, *Salvador* got a very negative review in *The New York Times*. It was more of a political review than a critic's assessment. Elizabeth, our publicist Marian Billings, and I went to the theater on 57th Street in Manhattan. And it was a disastrous opening. Hardly anyone was there, maybe only fifty people in the whole theater. Elizabeth turned to me and said, 'I have to call Oliver in the Philippines and tell him . . . I can't do it. Will you do it?' And I said I would, but I thought, 'What can I say?' He's over there trying to prep *Platoon*, in the midst of the revolution. How do you tell a man who has put so much time into making a film like *Salvador* that it's already failed?

"It was one of the most difficult things I had to do. I wanted something encouraging to say, so I went to the theater in the Village where it was playing, hoping things would be different. And there was a pretty good crowd. People were really into the movie. So when I called Oliver, I was able to soften the blow somewhat by telling him that even though the review was bad, there was a very gutsy response at one of the theaters. Of course he knew that without the review, we were dead. But to me the real strength of Oliver Stone is that he was able to face that defeat and go on to make the film that won the Academy Award for Best Picture the following year. To me, the lesson is that you fight back and never quit. That's Oliver's great strength."

Salvador opened in six additional eastern cities and in Los Angeles in mid-April, and was also shown at the San Francisco Film Festival. Left to its own resources and limited finances, Hemdale was not able to do much in terms of promotion, muscle, or manpower, however, and *Salvador* died rather quickly in the theaters.

Released at a time when most Americans didn't have the knowledge or desire to decipher the pat phrases of the nightly news to determine what was happening in Central America, *Salvador* dramatically revealed the effects of what Stone saw as U.S. complicity. To him, this was not just about crazed groups of Latins fighting over power, but about the slaughtering of a nation—masses of innocent men, women, and children being tortured and killed on a daily basis. Those who had seen *Salvador* could no longer ignore the violence in Central America. Now it was real.

Salvador was not for the squeamish, but it was more than just a bloody look at a Latin American civil war. The character of Richard Boyle is the classic "ugly American": out only for his own gain and determined not to be affected by the problems of what he considers an inferior people. That this hardboiled character can change suggests that not only were the injustices which occurred in El Salvador severe beyond even what a jaded journalist had seen, but also that there was hope that the American consciousness might be roused. In this sense, salvation really is the theme of *Salvador*.

"The word *Salvador* means 'to save,'" says Stone. "It's not just about saving El Salvador but also about saving Richard Boyle, and how really hard it is to find salvation in this world. Richard tries to con Maria into marrying him, he becomes a better man and even goes to church; but it's not so easy—the Archbishop gets shot. Then, when he finally gets her out of the country, she gets arrested and sent back. Always, Richard is being disappointed, defeated. It isn't *easy*. That's the point of the movie. The country is damned."

"I can't even go to Communion without fucking it up. The one time in thirty years I go to Church, they kill the Archbishop on me, can you believe my luck?"

Richard Boyle in **SALVADOR**

Many believe James Woods's performance stands as the greatest of his career and one of the greatest captured on film. Part of what makes it so remarkable is the character arc, or range of change, his role requires. He begins the film as an opportunistic cad, with a very loose sense of morals and no sense of commitment. As the picture develops and he becomes involved with Maria and others he meets in Salvador, he changes, finding himself drawn to their plight and for the first time in a long while truly concerned with someone other than himself.

By the end of the film, Boyle's character has evolved to the point where he actually puts his life on the line to save someone else. What makes it all work is that Woods is very convincing as the sleazeball in the beginning. He's not playing a basically nice guy with a mean streak— he's playing a scumbag who has virtually no hope of redemption. When the turn of events creates the possibility of that redemption, the character seizes it, despite the risk involved, as if he knows it's his last chance for salvation. Traditionally, Hollywood leading men tend to soften the negative aspects of characters they portray because they don't want to alienate their audience. Woods, on the other hand, seems to go full tilt the opposite way, intentionally playing the character as sleazily as possible in order to make the change more dramatic. Critics and film enthusiasts generally have praised him for this aspect of his performance in *Salvador*.

In the era of the blockbuster, few films are able to find their audience during the limited time allowed for theatrical release. Fortunately, *Salvador* was saved by video. Like so many inexpensive but quality films of today, *Salvador* was unable to compete with the big-budgeted, heavily marketed movies that were its competition during theatrical release, but found its audience later. "The only reason the picture survived was, thank God, the video revolution," Stone says, "which we all assume had always been here, but it wasn't. *Salvador* did very well on video. People started talking about it and it got nominated for two Oscars, for Screenplay and for Acting. That wouldn't have happened if it hadn't been for video."

Ironically, it wasn't until *Salvador* came out on video that it made an impact on the critics. Six months after the film's release, *The New Yorker*'s Pauline Kael said that Stone "writes and directs as if someone had put a gun to the back of his neck and yelled 'Go!' and didn't take it away until he'd finished." *New York* magazine's David Denby called *Salvador* "an electrifying tour of hell in Central America," and said that the movie "combined Stone's talent for hard-driving, sometimes trashy excitement with a new moral and dramatic seriousness." The *Los Angeles Times* said it was "a film that sings and screams . . . it's alive, it broils."

Many critics started calling it one of the best films of the year and *Salvador* appeared on most Top 10 lists at the end of 1986. The movie was a milestone in that it marked the moment when Stone's reputation with the critics began to change. Many of them loved the film for the way it harnessed his fierce energy to serious issues.

Prior to *Salvador*, the important critics had relegated Stone to the right-wing quarter of film politics. Now he surprised many by speaking out as a liberal. "Central America has a right to be what it wants to be," Stone was quoted as saying at the time. "If a Russian nuclear sub can be 15 miles off the coast of New York harbor, what difference does it make if the Russians are in Nicaragua? If they are. It's not a question of Capitalism or Communism when your kid dies of dysentery or diarrhea; it's really a question of health, education, and welfare. And they're not getting it. American government officials don't seem to realize that revolution is a response to social and economic conditions, not a Cold War game. It's a North/South conflict, not an East/West one."

"You in Washington are so rich. Why are you so blind?"

Archbishop Romero in **SALVADOR**

The more publicity, the more outrageous Stone became in his interviews. By the following year he was extremely candid about the issue. Witness this excerpt from an interview with Alexander Cockburn in the December 1987 issue of *American Film:*

I'm so depressed by the power of a few ignorant assholes to determine the course of a political debate on Central America—Jesse Helms, Robert Dole, Reagan, Bush—this whole Mafia of cold warriors that has existed since my birth. I'm beginning to think that the only solution is a war that involves Americans, because it's the only way this country is going to wake up to what is really going on down there. I think America has to bleed. I think the corpses have to pile up. I think American boys have to die again. Let the mothers weep and mourn. Let the mothers fucking wake up to what's going on. Because they don't give a shit about the 100,000 Guatemalans that got killed because of our technology, but when an American kid dies in Honduras, they're going to get upset. I tell you, I'm never going to let my kid go. I'll break the law, go to Canada. I'll take him out of the country. The only problem would be if he decided he wanted to go.

So, while it failed to perform at the box office, *Salvador* gave Oliver Stone a forum from which to speak. And people listened; not many perhaps, but enough for Stone to know that this too was part of the role he had to play in life. Equally significant, *Salvador* made such a strong impression on film critics that it ultimately caused the movie industry to take notice. "We had limited financial ability and could only give the film a certain amount of money," John Daly comments. "But I don't think in his wildest dreams Oliver believes he could have improved upon that film. Jimmy Woods deserved an Oscar without a question. They gave it to Paul Newman [*The Color of Money*] out of sentimentality for his great performances in the past. But I'm sure he probably had first-class expenditures all the way through. Probably had a lovely, heated dressing room, putting on his camel-hair coat and stepping out onto a large budget. But *Salvador* was Jimmy Woods in a Third World country living among the pigs, the grime, the rubbish, the poverty, and carving out a performance under Oliver's direction that stands out yet today. It was a great performance. Oliver deserves to be lauded because he went for a very honest ending, in which the girl gets caught and has to go back. It's not the happy ending Hollywood likes. *Salvador* is a great film, and had it come out after *Platoon*, it would have had a completely different reception."

Unfortunately, Stone and Richard Boyle began having their differences almost as soon as *Salvador* was released. "I paid him about twenty-five grand out of my own pocket," Stone says. "There had been a significant amount of expenses on his behalf, and it was well worth it, but I didn't get that money back from Hemdale for a long time. Well, the moment the film was done, he warned me that he was broke. I didn't feel like it was my responsibility to carry him, and he blew the WGA [Writers Guild of America] whistle on my ass because I'd signed a contract with him before Hemdale. That really pissed me off. I felt like he'd betrayed our friendship. He said I owed him the money and I said, 'Richard, I haven't been fucking paid!' So then I got a little money on some small fees for *Platoon* and he wanted me to give him that and I didn't feel I could. Besides, that was another issue. He ended up getting his WGA minimum and I got paid some money back, and got my fee as a director and writer. But that was a year, maybe even closer to two. Richard threw the WGA at me and that really hurt me. If he was smart, he'd have stayed in with me because I would have used him again. We would have continued the series or, if not that, there would have been something else. He thought that because I had more money than he did, I was ripping him off. That was basically it. Richard lives an angry socialism, sort of an Irish revolutionary. He sues everybody. But it's stupid to sue your friends."

Stone and Boyle may have parted ways, but not before their idea had been captured on celluloid. The film that grew out of their relationship stands and will stand for some time to come.

And in 1986, for Oliver Stone, the dream of directing was at last a reality. For once his vision had been fully and uncompromisingly articulated. He would stand by his film's success or failure proudly. Now it was time to tell the tale he had become a filmmaker to tell. It was time for *Platoon*.

Platoon

"I think now, looking back, we did not fight the enemy,
we fought ourselves—and the enemy was in us."

Chris Taylor in **PLATOON**

With the release of *Salvador*, Oliver Stone began a pattern of behavior that followed for the next several films: whenever possible, as soon as a major work was finished, he immediately submerged himself in the next project. Partly, this was because he's happiest when he's working, but mostly it was because it diverted him from any anguish over how the previous work would be accepted.

So in February 1986, just two weeks before *Salvador* was released, Oliver Stone embarked for the Philippines to film his beloved *Platoon*. After editing *Salvador*, he had rewritten the *Platoon* script one last time, then spent the next few months casting and assembling the crew. "We made them back to back," Stone says of the two films. "No breaks. I wanted to do it before there was a problem with the money. *Platoon* took fifty-four days and about six and a half million. I sort of expected John to cop out on making it because *Salvador* was such a monster to edit. But he was true to his word."

John Daly recalls that meeting: "He was very cynical in the way that Oliver is. The cynicism really trying to get the answer he wants. 'I don't suppose you're going to back me now in my next picture, are you?' he said. And I said, 'Yes.' He seemed surprised. 'You are? You're going to put the money up? And you're going to let me direct it?' I said, 'Yes.' And then all he said was, 'Oh.' I don't think he expected it."

The same team—Daly, Green, Gibson, and Kopelson—who had financed *Salvador* put together enough European money to make *Platoon*, but, Arnold Kopelson tells a different version of the financing. According to him, Stone's fears were well grounded. "No one knows this story," Kopelson says now. "Not even Oliver knows it, and it's very significant. At that time I was told by John Daly that he was not about to finance *Platoon* because he did not believe Oliver would make the cuts in *Salvador* that Hemdale wanted. I told Daly to tell me which cuts he wanted Oliver to make and I'd get Oliver to sign off on them. I then said to Daly, 'I want a document, I don't just want to hear it from you.' And I sat with him and Derek [Gibson] and worked out eight or nine cuts that they wanted, and they signed over to me in writing something that read, like, 'If you can get these cuts, we will put together the financing of *Platoon*.' I called Oliver and said, 'You're going to have to do some cutting or John is not going ahead with *Platoon*.' He said, 'What are they?' and I went on to list them, and he said no problem, and he did it. And that got *Platoon* launched. I legally locked Daly in on that document. He had to go ahead, but Oliver never knew about that part."

Hemdale of course hadn't yet made a profit on *Salvador*, and since Orion had backed out, they knew the odds were against them ever making back their investment. When the trades asked John Daly why he agreed to back *Platoon* after his previous project with Oliver Stone failed at the box office, he quipped, "We felt we couldn't do any worse than we did with *Salvador*." Later Daly said, "We respect Oliver's passions. Besides, he's spending only $6 million on *Platoon*—about half the budget of a typical Hollywood film."

With the help of Pierre David, who worked for Kopelson, an initial commitment was obtained from Orion Pictures to handle U.S. distribution for the film and put up a third of the money. "The whole budget was 5.9 million going in and Orion came up with a million or $750,000 for the foreign rights," Kopelson recalls. "Barbara Boyle at Orion was very much in favor of Oliver Stone. She urged the company to do it. There was a video deal with Vestron, and then John through Hemdale borrowed the balance. Orion took the domestic rights without putting up a minimum guaranty, but Orion was financing half of the print and advertising costs and the other half was to come from John Daly's company. Daly subsequently defaulted on this commitment, but Orion took Daly's share out of the first receipts from distribution."

Industry people are well aware that there is no love lost between Kopelson and Daly, whom Kopelson later sued, claiming he was cheated out of much of his income from *Platoon*. (Kopelson won $14 million in the lawsuit.) The bottom line in October 1985 was that *Platoon* was financed at last. The movie was going to be made.

Though he was pleased when the funding came through, Stone couldn't help attempting to find meaning for all he had endured. "The ironies of life continue to amaze and educate me," he later wrote in his notes on the film. "How could I know that what was solely history in 1976 would wait until now to become a possible antidote to the reborn militarism of Grenada, Libya, Nicaragua? Perhaps, after all, there was a reason all along."

"The best bowl of rice is the one for which you worked the hardest, is it not?"

Monk in **HEAVEN AND EARTH**

As soon as he got the go-ahead, Stone set about meeting the strict nine-week shooting schedule and made several key decisions. The first was to retain much of the same crew who had shot *Salvador*, including director of photography Bob Richardson, production designer Bruno Rubeo, editor Claire Simpson, Gordon Smith for prosthetics, and special effects man Yves de Bono. Another very significant move was to bring in Alex Ho as producer. Ho had already done important groundwork on the project and, like Richardson, would now become an essential part of the Oliver Stone team.

Hiring the retired Marine Corps captain and Vietnam vet Dale Dye as technical adviser was another crucial decision. This was to be the beginning of a long and prosperous relationship for the two men. Dale

Dye remembers: "I wanted to form a full-service military/technical advisory service to the film and television industry. What I had seen Hollywood do in regards to the military and especially Vietnam was just terrible. It was an insult to the veterans. I formed a company called Warriors Incorporated, but I was getting nowhere. Hollywood's attitude was 'We've done this without you before, so why do we need you now?' Then I saw a piece in Army Archerd's column in *Daily Variety* that said, 'Novice director/writer Oliver Stone has gotten the green light for a war picture based on his own experiences in Vietnam.' The antenna went up and I went out of my way to find Oliver Stone. I knew if I went the agent route, I'd be another pile of papers on his desk, so I noodled around and bought lunch for people with money I didn't have. Eventually, I got Oliver's home phone number and I called him one Sunday morning and said, 'Look, you don't know me but if you're going to do this, you need me.' And I think Oliver kind of liked that approach."

The cast of twenty-five black, white, and Hispanic actors came from all across the United States, many of them teenagers who were fascinated by the history of the war. None were really "stars" at this point in their careers, but the best known among them were Tom Berenger, Willem Dafoe, and Charlie Sheen. Stone's casting of Berenger as the vicious, amoral Sergeant Barnes and Dafoe as the almost saintly Sergeant Elias was definitely against type and a very bold stroke at the time. "Berenger had sort of been like a pretty boy," Stone recalls. "I liked his acting in *The Big Chill* a lot, but I saw where he was used inside a framework that wasn't working for him. I felt like there was a redneck side to Tom, an ugly side that could really be seething, and I used it. With Dafoe, I felt the opposite. He'd been playing ugly roles and I thought there was something spiritually heightened because of the ugliness. So I went the other way."

Stone believed that both men had been generally underestimated as actors. By the time he did *Platoon* at age thirty-five, Berenger had played a variety of parts in nine films. He was intrigued by the dark Sergeant Barnes and came on hard for the role. "He went after it," agrees Stone, "like Jimmy Woods in *Salvador*, he just took the part. He said, 'You gotta use me, I was born to do it.'"

Willem Dafoe has always had a flair for the unusual. In high school, he was booted out senior year when a teacher got hold of a videotape he was making about a pot dealer, a streaker, and a witch enthroned on a toilet in a transparent gown. In 1977 he moved to New York and joined the Wooster Group, one of New York City's most celebrated avant-garde theater ensembles. He had appeared in *The Loveless*, *Streets of Fire*, and *To Live and Die in L.A.* before *Platoon*.

As Sergeant Elias, Dafoe is the conscience of his troops and a reluctant role model for Charlie Sheen's virginal grunt. "I met Oliver one of the times he was trying to get *Platoon* together," Dafoe recalls, "but it never happened. And then he called me up at five o'clock in the morning one day. 'Hi, remember me? Oliver Stone.' And at that point he was considered a writer with some respectability, but also pretty outrageous. But he was a guy I was attracted to because he seemed real driven. There was an intensity about him and he didn't remind me of anyone I'd encountered in the movie business. What he did was set me up as a backup in case he couldn't make a deal with John Savage for *Salvador*. I called my manager and she said, 'Oh, honey, that part went to John Savage.' Then, every time Oliver saw me, he said he wanted me to be in *Platoon*, but he couldn't figure out what role. I seem to remember there was some talk about playing Rhah, some talk about playing Barnes, and some discussion about playing Elias. Then one day, he saw a trailer for *To Live and Die* on TV—I was on for just a few seconds, but in that time he decided I was Elias. But back then, Elias was written very much as an Indian. Jet black hair and all."

Caught between Barnes and Elias is Chris Taylor, played by Charlie Sheen, the third child of actor Martin Sheen. He grew up an archetypal Malibu kid—a good enough baseball player at Santa Monica High to get a scholarship to the University of Kansas, but skipping so much school that he failed to graduate.

The acting success of his older brother Emilio Estevez intimidated him at first, so when Emilio chose to use his father's real name, Charlie decided to use Sheen. He had appeared in several films, including *Red Dawn*, *Ferris Bueller's Day Off*, and *The Wraith*. Charlie had auditioned for the role of Chris back in 1983 when he was just eighteen. "At the time, Oliver wasn't interested in me at all," he remembers. "He felt I was gawky and underweight. He offered the role to Emilio [Michael Pare was going to be Barnes; Elias was never cast], but then the financing fell through. By the time the project got restarted, I had a couple of films under my belt. When I went back in to read, Oliver just looked at me and said, 'I'll see you on Monday.' And I thought, 'Right.' But that's exactly what happened. He wanted me for the part. I knew it was the chance of a lifetime. Not only was it a great part, but it gave me the chance to work with someone I'd always admired. I'm a big fan of *Midnight Express* and *Scarface*, and I thought it would be cool to play the man on the screen and be directed by him at the same time."

Stone describes the change in Sheen the second time he read for the part: "The first time around, Charlie was a kid. But this time I knew in ten minutes he was right. It was like fate. The eyes, the look, the mood, the feeling, the face—it was just right. There was a rightness about him. It flowed. When Charlie walked in, it flowed."

Sheen prepared for the role by talking with his father, who starred as the tormented Army captain in *Apocalypse Now*, Francis Ford Coppola's surreal Vietnam epic. Shadowing his father's most significant role felt rather strange. "If you compare the two," Charlie Sheen says, "*Apocalypse* and *Platoon*, Martin Sheen and Charlie Sheen, both of us the lead characters, both narrating, both films shot in the Philippines, you'd think you'd win the lottery before that would happen."

Charlie had visited his father on the set of *Apocalypse Now* when he was ten. "My dad was there working on it for sixteen months. We were there three months at the start, when he replaced Harvey Keitel. He also replaced Harvey Keitel in *Death of a Salesman* on Broadway, so when he finally got back from the Philippines, we had a big sign at the airport that said: 'Welcome Back, Harvey,' with 'Harvey' crossed out and 'Martin' written underneath it. I was also there for a couple of months later on, and then for another three months when he had the heart attack that almost killed him. Having witnessed that whole Coppola experience, I decided I never wanted to be an actor, but later I changed my mind."

Although Sheen had only one week between finishing *The Wraith* and starting on *Platoon*, it proved to be an anxious few days. "Someone from *The Wraith* called Oliver and said some not-so-kind things about me," Sheen recalls. "Oliver was urged not to hire me and it was suggested that I drank while I worked, which just isn't true. For a while it looked really bad. And, as a result, Oliver made me agree to only one beer a day while we were in the Philippines. But by the end of the fourth week, he was so pleased with my work he was buying me drinks at the bar."

With the casting decided, Stone prepared to fly the crew and twenty-five actors to the Philippines, where the jungles, bugs and heat could stand in for Vietnam. Unfortunately, a revolution got in the way. The actors had been scheduled to arrive shortly after the presidential election in February 1986, but the shoot had to be put on hold when the fraud-riddled proceedings touched off a score of deaths, a revolution, and the possibility of civil war. The actors were told to hang loose and see how the revolution went. It went just fine: President Ferdinand Marcos fled on February 25 and Corazon Aquino took office. Most of the platoon flew in nine days later.

While the rest of the cast was awaiting news of the revolution at home, Willem Dafoe decided he'd join Bob Richardson on a trip to the Philippines to get settled in. After twenty-four hours in transit, the actor went to sleep in a Manila hotel, only to wake up a short time later to the sound of tanks in the streets. "I turned on the news, and the shit was going down, but still, I didn't know what it meant," Dafoe remembers. "I went out on the streets to get dinner and all I see are people with guns. And they said, 'Go back where you came from. You don't want to be out on the streets.' So I mostly hung out at the hotel, but it was kind of exciting because things were uncertain and you felt like you were in a historical time."

Trapped in the throes of revolution, Dafoe and Richardson were able to witness first hand the protest at Camp Aguinaldo, where thousands of Filipinos formed a human barricade to protect rebel officers seeking Marcos's overthrow. In the next few days, the People Power revolution was victorious and Manila became a massive carnival of celebration as Corazon Aquino took power. On that day, Stone was very relieved. If a full-scale civil war had broken out, it would probably have meant shifting the production to Thailand, and that would have meant more delays, more money, the probability of losing a few actors, and perhaps a pullout of the financing. "Considering how many times I'd come close to making the picture," Stone says, "just the thought of it happening one more time . . ." He winces.

Admitting to the trades at the time that "the elections put us a little back," Stone also said, "We can't pull out now," despite the concern of many that the situation in the Philippines was still volatile and could make for a problematic shoot. The locations were to consist almost entirely of jungle areas within two hours of Manila, and only one day of shooting had been scheduled for the capital. Still, the revolution meant cutting an entirely new set of under-the-table deals with the new cadre of generals, sergeants, and mechanics for the use of their choppers, jet fighters, tanks, and infantry battalions. The American bases and their men were closed to the team because the U.S. Defense Department had deemed the *Platoon* script "totally unrealistic."

"What we got here is a crusader."

King in **PLATOON**

For Charlie Sheen, returning to the Philippines triggered some old memories: "The first thing that hit me was the smell. I stepped off the plane and . . . *wham!* I got hit in the face with that odor—this weird and powerful smell like burning rubber, just malaria and poverty and rot—and it was instantly like I was ten years old again. All the memories I had of being there as a little kid and watching my father. It was like walking back into this bad dream all over again."

Although the revolution was supposed to be over, the tension was still heavy, and it left many of the actors uneasy. "Some of us had experiences that kept us on edge," Sheen remembers. "One night, for example, I was driving back to the hotel at around 2:00 A.M. and I was stopped at a military roadblock. They didn't know who I was and they could have done anything. One of the running jokes on location was, 'Well, we all have weapons so at least we *look* dangerous if anyone ambushes us.' "

For Stone, the chaos was "exhilarating." The extras were hastily assembled from drifters, bar crowds, and school kids—even a group of Nigerian tribesmen studying in the Philippines were called in to double as black soldiers. The massive crew of 250 was mostly Filipino, but also American, Italian, Irish, Canadian, and English—a group even Stone referred to as "highly mixed and inflammable."

Privately, Stone was concerned. After a decade of rejection, several near misses on financing, and almost getting caught in the middle of a revolution on location, he proceeded ahead with a sort of emotional detachment. "I'd written and revised *Platoon* so much that by the time I came to shoot it, it was dated in my head," he says. "I came in and I did it detached and emotionless as a workmanlike director trying to just keep a steady course."

In filming a project as deeply personal as *Platoon* with all its true-life experiences, the lapse of ten years since writing the original version and eighteen years in which to distance himself from the actual experience may have also been an asset to the directing process. "If it had happened in the beginning, I don't think I could've done it the same way," Stone agrees. "Also I don't think I had the skill as a director and the experience which came from working on *Midnight Express*, *The Hand*, working with De Palma on *Scarface*, being influenced by Cimino—all these people left an imprint on me that influenced the way I thought and directed. Still, even though I knew that a dream was coming true for me, I started to worry that I wasn't up to it. What if I screwed it up? I remember getting letters from all these Vietnam vets offering to work on the film for free and imploring that I tell the truth in the movie. I really started feeling the burden of that responsibility. I was worried that I'd be stale since I'd done the film so many times in my head. Michael Cimino warned me not to leave the game in the locker room—he meant not to get so excited about preproduction that I'd peak before I started shooting. Movies come down to catching moments you never anticipated. I was afraid I might miss some of them."

Stone turned to a familiar outlet to cope with the anxieties of preproduction. "He did the same kind of thing on *Platoon* that he did on *Salvador*," Bob Richardson recalls. "Almost every night, myself, Bruno Rubeo, and Alex Ho would basically pull straws to see who had to spend the night going to bars, whorehouses, dance halls, dark streets, apartments with weird people. And Oliver would go every goddamn night when we were in preproduction. Not when we were shooting, but on weekends and on preproduction. I'm telling you, man, I was with him all the time. In the beginning when I was first working with him, it was kind of a test for me. But, by *Platoon*, it was just too exhausting. I gave up trying to hang with him."

Alex Ho and the production team began firming up deals with the new Philippine government for military hardware and equipment. Most people in the film industry agree that *Platoon* looks as if it cost twice the money that it did, and much of this was due to Ho's production skills. He describes some of his financial maneuvering: "I cut a lot of corners. I didn't hire a production manager, I didn't hire a wardrobe designer, basically packaged the thing in a different way and made it sort of like a business. I killed myself on that movie. It came out great, but it was rough, a lot of bleeding on that movie."

Meanwhile, Captain Dale Dye began his task of training the ensemble of young actors, putting them through a fourteen-day boot camp to prepare them for their roles and basically drilling and harassing them until they acquired the grunt's-eye view of combat that Stone felt was necessary. "Oliver said, 'I want you to take them to the bush, beat them up, make them understand what it was like for you and me in Vietnam.' So I designed it to be the closest thing you can get to combat. The kids were warned. I wrote a letter to every kid and said, 'Look, this is what you're in for. If you have any problems with it, it's just like an induction notice, now is the time to let us know.' "

The first night, Dye held a briefing on the training schedule. Assisting him in giving the actors the talk, walk, and look of the guys who did the fighting would be Stan White, Stone's police lieutenant friend who inspired so much of *Year of the Dragon* and an ex-Marine himself, and three young "ringers"—Marine reservists Robert Galotti and Mark Ebenhoch, and a former reconnaissance Marine, Drew Clark, a tough, bawdy kid whom the actors soon affectionately nicknamed "Recon." The ringers were classic Marines—they stuck together, drank a bit, and kidded and cussed each other without mercy. Clark was particularly ferocious at first glance.

Dye, who served twenty-one years in the Marines, laid out the training camp ground rules. The actors were told that for the next two weeks their home would be Camp Castaneda, a Philippine Constabulary training camp located in an overgrown, tropical area some sixty miles south of Manila. They would be in the bush all the time and there'd be no beds, no bathrooms, no hotel time, no hot showers, no Cokes, no calls home to mothers, wives, girlfriends, or even agents. Their field-training schedule called for them to sleep in two-man fighting foxholes, live off two packets of cold Army rations for each day, set night ambushes, man LPs (listening posts), and learn of such things as klicks (kilometers), bloopers (M-79 grenade launchers), Claymore mines, M-60 machine guns, M-16 rifles, and "rock-and-roll" (firing on full automatic). They'd rappel down a fifty-foot tower. And go on patrols, known as "humps," with full gear and weapons. With luck, they'd get four or five hours of sleep a night.

As if this wasn't enough, Dye informed them that there would be plenty of stinging red ants, mosquitoes, bats, blisters, and the possibility of close proximity to artillery fire at any time. At first the actors were somewhat indifferent, determined not to be shaken by Dye's drill sergeant discourse, yet not wanting to appear aloof. Perhaps it wouldn't really be that tough.

Wrong. By noon the next day in Camp Castaneda the cast was starting to believe the training was for real. "The first thing I did," Dye recalls, "was make them break out the shovels and dig themselves the holes they'd sleep in for a couple of weeks. I said, 'This is an entrenching tool. This is all you need to make your home. Commence digging fighting holes.' Half these kids had never had a shovel in their hands in their life, and they were all blistered and raw and bleeding."

Charlie Sheen remembers talking with his father before leaving about what to expect, but this trip was not the same. "We were given these seventy-pound packs and were broken up into three companies," Sheen recalls. "I'd expected barracks, showers, telephones. There was nothing. This was a cram course in an infantryman's life. And it was rough."

Willem Dafoe recounts the actors' first night of training: "We were outfitted with all the standard military gear, and it was getting dark, and Dale Dye said, 'Sergeant Elias, take your men over there and dig in.' We couldn't believe it. We knew it was going to happen, but we couldn't quite believe it when it actually started happening. And you get these pathetic little shovels, the collapsible kind, and you're digging very hard ground—your hands are bleeding. I mean, it's extreme. And then, just to scare the shit out of us, they simulated a mortar attack. So you'd have to stop work, get in your hole, as deep as it was, and then the second it cooled out, you'd have to resume digging. It was essentially fireworks, but it felt pretty serious, even if the stakes weren't actual."

Dale Dye had asked the special effects people to stage the mortar "attack" at dusk and they had buried a bunch of charges on the hill. The actors had no idea it was going to happen and by this time were thoroughly exhausted. When the explosives started going off, there was a mad scramble. "The charges were close and I intended them to be," Dye says. "I started screaming at them to return fire and they didn't even know how to load their weapons at that point. I was jumping in holes and locking magazines in and cranking rounds out. It was utter chaos and they were shaking by the time it was dark."

According to Francesco Quinn, the twenty-three-year-old son of the renowned actor Anthony Quinn, the actors took the explosions pretty seriously. "Bombs and mortar rounds started going off," he recalls, "and I couldn't even hear what they were shouting. I was looking for pieces of my M-16, but they were scattered all over the place and it was dark. Charlie Sheen had been out on LP—listening post—and he came back a wreck. He was so pale, he was glowing in the dark."

"We were really injected with a seriousness about it," Dafoe maintains, "because this guy, Captain Dale Dye, who was a three-year Vietnam vet and pretty much professional soldier, was *dead* serious about it. We had to follow his lead or I don't know what would have happened. There was a lot of pressure. I think when we found ourselves out in the jungle, everybody was taken aback. Everybody kind of went, ah fuck, what have I done?"

By the second day many of the young actors had their doubts about continuing, according to Charlie Sheen. "I think it was Day Two when me, Kevin Dillon, and Francesco Quinn got together and said, 'We're actors, not infantry. Let's just walk.'"

But they stuck it out. During the next two weeks the actors lugged fifty-pound packs on ten-mile hikes, dug more foxholes, cleaned M-16s, had target practice with real weapons, and learned the lingo of war. They weren't allowed to use their real names, and had to refer to each other by their character in the script. Real sleep in a two-man foxhole is impossible. The idea is for one guy to sleep while the other keeps watch in two-hour shifts, but the reality is that no one really sleeps at all. Each morning wakeup call was at 5:30 A.M. After that there were two hours of calisthenics, followed by military exercises and the grueling humps. They had a chain of command similar to a real platoon, with orders from Stone passed down the line to the grunts through Captain Dye. "Oliver was the regional commander, he was the colonel," Dye says. "I even got him a bird for his hat. I was company commander, so I was responding directly to him. I had a lieutenant who was my presenting commander, Mark Moses. I had a platoon sergeant, Tom Berenger was Sergeant Barnes, and we had individual squad leaders. Willem Dafoe was Sergeant Elias and he led one squad. John C. McGinley [as Corporal O'Neil] led another squad, and the third was Tony Todd."

Charlie Sheen adds: "It was a hundred percent military. We were told if we disobeyed an order, we'd be off the film."

According to Dafoe, his squad got the worst duties: "Everything was set up to kind of mirror what went on in the film, so my squad got all the shit. We were run ragged, we were doing everything. Tom Berenger worked real hard but he was in the CP, the Command Post, so he also had better surroundings sometimes than us. And the other two squads, particularly McGinley, who was the goldbrick in *Platoon*, had it easy. They got to sleep, they didn't have to do a lot of stuff . . . they were barely on patrol."

At night, after a long day's training, the actors would gather in small groups around the Coleman lanterns. They were an incongruous lot in their dirty, sweat-stained Army fatigues, packing M-16 rifles and grenade launchers while trying to read through their scripts. Every evening before they began night activities, they would have something called a "stand down" where the actors could ask questions about being a soldier or their role in the film. Dye, who was awarded three Purple Hearts during the war in Vietnam, had also been assigned the task of helping the actors get a realistic approach on their lines. He became a sort of combat Stanislavsky, combining infantry training with scene studies and character analysis. "I'd tell them things like, 'Never say, "Over and out" because it's Hollywood, and it drives me nuts,'" he says.

Although the first week was tough, the kinds of tension evoked were exactly the kinds that happen in a real infantry platoon. As feet got sore and muscles strained, a few arguments almost became fights and black-white relations grew tense; but eventually, as Stone and Dye had hoped, a spirit of camaraderie began to develop between the cast members. Berenger remembers misreading a line during one of the campfire rehearsal sessions only to have another actor threaten him. "Hey, that's my freakin' line," the actor said. "You take my freakin' line and I'll frag you!"

Each day of toil and each night of simulated combat brought the men closer. And not only closer to each other, but closer to the Vietnam experience they were about to emulate on film. As time wore on, the sessions around the campfire became more intense as well, and Dale Dye began spending a good deal of time talking about the war. "Contrary to what you see in the movies," Dye told his troops, "death on the battlefield is not a dramatic thing. Mortally wounded men die in two ways, one of which is 'give-up-itis,' where he turns white from his cheeks up and sort of fades out. The other way, the man who fights death will die quickly."

Dye coached those who would be wounded in the movie about how it felt to receive morphine. "When you get hit and you get morphine," he spoke from the voice of experience, "it hits you like a wet dream."

Some of the actors, especially Berenger and Dafoe, had by now acquired the mannerisms of the men they played. Berenger, normally an easygoing guy, had begun to look every bit the experienced field soldier, his voice occasionally taking on a hard edge. Dafoe, a naturally intense person, had evolved into Elias; he was now speaking slowly, thoughtfully, and gradually taking on the persona of a decent, rational man trapped in the most irrational of circumstances.

Still, Dafoe maintains there was no animosity between him and Berenger. "Well, we're both the kind of actors who are activated by the camera," Dafoe says. "We were trying to learn what we were supposed to do as far as a 'soldier.' But I can honestly say we helped each other out, I think. We had to just get through this exercise, and that was the main thing. I don't have to create any animosity. That's jive, at least it is for me. I can do this business of pretending well enough that I don't have to make things miserable twenty-four hours a day."

Kevin Dillon studied for his role as "Bunny," the cocky baby-faced soldier who likes to kill, by reading *Run Between the Raindrops*, a novel by Dale Dye. "I see Bunny as a lost kid who doesn't know wrong from right," Dillon says. "I figured he came from a bad family, from a bad neighborhood, and maybe had no mother and a drunken father."

As the training continued, the actors were becoming soldiers not just physically but emotionally. By day they did their grueling exercises and by night they listened to war stories. The result was that they took on warrior personas. Quinn, for example, grew comfortable slinging his bayonet over his shoulder, a look that came to identify his philosophical, dope-smoking character, Rhah. "You forgot who you were after a while," he says. "You were just someone walking with a weapon in your hands."

By now the training was even more rigorous. Each morning at dawn Stan White led the men in calisthenics, including something he called "the Stomp," a brutally fast run in place. This was followed by two-man wrestling matches and another favorite drill called "the Punch," where the actors briskly pummeled each other in the gut, in many cases causing quarter-sized bruises around the midsection. But no one complained or gave in to the obvious whine, "but I'm an actor . . ." In fact, the strongest comment heard was, "This is the last time I do a nonunion picture."

The full-gear hikes—"humps," as the actors called them in military fashion—gradually increased in length, building up to a twelve-klick, uphill-downhill monster. On one such march, ex-Marine Drew Clark, the one the actors called "Recon," slipped and fell into some large rocks. He was taken to Manila where his knee was examined by the nearest doctor. Fortunately, it was only a bad sprain, and after it was bandaged, he was driven back to camp. As he limped in, Clark was greeted by loud cheers which turned to laughter when he announced, truthfully, that his knee had been examined by a gynecologist—the nearest doctor available.

By the last day of training Dale Dye could see a marked difference in the actors. "They were becoming a rifle platoon," he says. "They were getting mean and hard and dirty, treating each other with a certain lack of human respect. The slackards had developed and the good guys had developed, as always happens in a rifle platoon. So . . . I took them to a rappel tower and we put them up in the air, sixty-five feet, with a Swiss seat-harness on. I had them right on the edge of the tower backing out backwards and rappeling with two bounds to the ground on a single rope, and I'm telling you there were some wide-eyed scared people. As their rappel master, I talked very quietly in their ear saying, 'Remember what you've been through. Think of how far you've gone now. Just put it out and stretch it a little bit more. Courage. Courage. Courage.' I popped them all off, all thirty-two of them. I knew then that these kids were beyond themselves, beyond what they were ever going to be."

> "If you want a challenge, if you want to try something difficult, try to achieve the impossible—thirteen weeks of hell at Paris Island South Carolina and find out if you got what it takes."
>
> Marine Sergeant in **BORN ON THE FOURTH OF JULY**

Sitting backstage at the Wooster Group Theater in New York in the spring of 1993, Dafoe admitted he was still somewhat affected by the training for *Platoon*. "I get a little self-conscious talking about it because actors tend to glorify their preparations and celebrate their machoism. But this was difficult and it was challenging. I think it's only because the film was small enough and down and dirty enough that we could do it the way we did. On a bigger film the studio would never allow us to prepare the way that we prepared. We were lucky we didn't get hurt, to tell you the truth. No one got hurt bad."

The training concluded with a night exercise directed entirely by the platoon leaders. First observed by Dye and then repeated for Stone, it included an ambush highlighted by a maneuver called a "Daisy-chain" mine blast. The strategy was well executed and clearly displayed a newly mastered competence among the troops. The following dawn there was a graduation ceremony with awards for best and worst in various categories, and that night there was a beer bust. Afterwards, Dale Dye admitted he initially thought Hollywood actors were a bunch of wimps who needed to be coddled by their agents, but as the training camp wore on, his impression changed. "These are tough youngsters, who like a challenge and who are professional enough to understand that the more they suffer before they go into that role, the more they will bring to their character. It restored my faith in everything. Not a wimp among them."

That no one quit during the training was due to a combination of reasons: personal pride, the challenge, peer pressure, and, of course, the desire to be a part of such a film. But it was also due in large part to Dale Dye and his assistants, who knew how to take their little brigade right to the edge, but not over it, and to use humor as a release. Stone wrote about it at the time: "Dale Dye is the type of man you find in 'The Right Stuff,' brave and laconic, and true. He imparted the samurai ethic to the actors, although at times he drove the liberal contingent of the crew nuts with his fervent anti-communism. But, as someone once said about John Wayne, 'His politics aside, you do love the man.'"

Stone saw the grueling training as absolutely necessary. "The idea was to fuck with their heads so we could get that dog-tired attitude, the anger, the irritation, the casual way of brutality, the casual approach to death. These are all the assets and liabilities of infantrymen. What I remember most about Vietnam and what a lot of guys remember is the tiredness . . . being so damned tired that I wished Charlie [the Viet Cong] would come up and shoot me, get this thing over with. We wanted to immerse the cast in the Vietnam infantryman's life, his way of thinking, talking, and moving. Then, once the cameras roll, subconsciously what will slip out is the tired, don't-give-a-damn attitude. The only thing that could not be taught to the actors was the reality of instant, violent death—that's something that no one can describe for them except their imaginations."

At the time, it was still uncertain whether *Platoon* would be accepted by audiences as a pro-war or an anti-war film, but the actors certainly got the message. "I'd probably be in Canada if there was another Vietnam," Charlie Sheen said. "My respect for the guys who served in Vietnam escalated seven hundred percent. We were just scraping the surface because it was not a life and death situation for us. If it was real—a different ball game, man, a very different ball game. It was the longest two weeks of my life. But also some of my most valuable days."

Tom Berenger agrees. "The training gave me a sense of how awful the war must have been. The jungle is an ass-kicker . . . after this, one guy said, it would be hard to go back to making Twinkies commercials. It was kind of like playing 'Army,' but when it was over we were all cranky, blistered, hollow-eyed—and ready to start filming."

And that was exactly how it went. What Dye had not told the actors until the last day of training was that they were to go directly from the camp to the camera with filming commencing before they even had a chance to take a shower or sleep in a real bed. "They picked us up at dawn in the bush the morning we began to shoot," Dale Dye says. "They were just flat exhausted and that was exactly the look that Oliver wanted. I humped that platoon in a staggered column down the road and Oliver looked at it and just grinned that grin of his and I knew I had it right."

Elizabeth Stone, on location with her son Sean, recalls seeing the actors arrive: "They'd been sleeping in the trenches, had mortar fights, been eaten alive by bugs . . . they had leeches. The lights and cameras were all set up along the river, and these guys came marching over the bridge. They came in from the jungle and I looked at their faces. They wouldn't look at us. They were so down and dirty and ravaged and pissed. I couldn't look at them. It wasn't like, 'Hi, guys, how'd it go?' 'Oh, swell.' They were like they had blinders on. They were just with each other, they were looking down, they weren't looking left or right. They were totally transformed people in those two weeks. That's when they started shooting, and that put the realism in it."

Platoon wasn't filmed on location as much as it was filmed in Oliver Stone's theater of operations. For fourteen days Dale Dye had trained the cast, teaching them first to be soldiers and then to be bush rats, and when that was over, he and Stone pushed them for another fifty-four days. Even after filming began and the cast moved into hotels in Manila, the effects of the training lingered on. Stone also found ways of keeping the men off guard. Tom Berenger says that shortly before shooting, Stone told him he was worried about his playing the role. "Sergeant Barnes is an unusual character," Berenger says. "I've never met anyone like that, and even Oliver was in a quandary about it. He was really worried that I wouldn't be able to do the part. He was a little worried about Willem, but he was really worried about me. I said, 'Don't you fucking worry about it. I'll be fine.' "

On the set, Stone showed a discipline and organization that belied his "wild man" reputation. *Platoon* was shot on a tight nine-week schedule and Bob Richardson says there was more unity and cooperation throughout the shoot than on *Salvador:* "For one thing, *Platoon* was a lot closer to Oliver in terms of experiences he'd actually gone through, so it was easy for him to get a grip on the development. Also, he was much more secure as a director than he had been on *Salvador.* And he had a much better relationship with everybody. Part of that was due to Dale Dye. The training he put those guys through out in the wilderness really formed a tight unit. And Dale pretty much commanded them. The shooting was extremely laborious and consuming, physically demanding on all those guys. But Dale could get them to do whatever he wanted because that was the way he established it. It was a military unit, and they called him 'Captain.' And Oliver was 'Colonel.' "

Not that there weren't difficult moments. *Platoon* required a lot of night shooting and a lot of explosions, and there was very little money. While the actors had been training, the construction crew and locals hired on to help had built a three-mile dirt road into the jungle. As shooting began on one set, they tackled two other projects—damming a stream to create a river and digging a series of tunnels. During the tunnel digging there was an accident and a Filipino worker died in a cave-in. Before continuing, a special ritual was held in the jungle to "exorcise his spirit." Later, a ruined French church had to be constructed, as well as the base camp for the 25th Infantry.

Four or five production people were fired during the shoot, and there were the usual fights, a few broken limbs, a near-fatal viper bite, hordes of insects, early monsoon rains, and many scary moments in helicopters. "We were shooting a sequence where they were evacuating soldiers that had been wounded in an ambush," Bob Richardson remembers. "We were filming a chopper coming down and using a wide-angle lens and Oliver's calling it in. I'm shooting it drifting slowly down toward the lens. It was getting pretty large in my frame when I realized I was looking through a wide lens which distorts distance so that everything appears smaller and further away. I turned around and realized my camera assistant was ducked down as the helicopter rotor is moving perhaps a foot and a half over our heads. And I was like holy . . . and I leaped off the camera and, as I hit the ground, I saw Oliver laughing in the background, like, 'This is really funny, Bob.' I'm thinking, 'Oliver almost killed me and he finds it very funny.' He's over there just retching with laughter, quite a distance away from the helicopter, I might add, and I'm on the ground shaking with fear.

"Well, four or five days later we had another helicopter sequence, air to air, where we're in one civilian chopper filming two military choppers. I'm shooting out the side panel and we're falling further and further behind. So I tell the pilot that we've got to go faster. This is much too slow. Oliver's the only other person with me and suddenly the chopper starts to shake violently. It's wiggling like crazy. And Oliver is on the floor screaming, 'You've got to slow down! We've got to stop it!' And I'm, like, 'Faster, we've got to get the shot.' And Oliver's literally pissing in his pants, he's so scared. He thought he was going to die. And out of spite, I just took it further and further because at that point I didn't care if we crashed. We heard over the radio, 'You better slow down. Your chopper's about to go down, you're out of control.' As far as I was concerned, this guy deserved everything he was getting. For me it was great. Oliver needs to be tested. He did it to me throughout these films."

Told of Richardson's story about the helicopter, Stone responds, "Yeah, that's his version. I've seen a lot of death in helicopters and it's a hard thing for me to get into a helicopter and shoot. We came very close to exploding. One scene where we were evacuating the dead . . . I don't remember if Bob was there or if it was the second camera operator, I'm not sure. But there were just too many people in that chopper. Dale Dye was there, and I looked up at Dale and I knew we were headed right for that ravine, I could see the fucking thing. I said, 'This is it. We're going down. It's going to hit that ravine ahead.' We scraped it by that much. We were so low, and these Filipino pilots are good, but they're crazy. They didn't do the maintenance on the chopper—there was a major accident about a year later with Chuck Norris's crew or something where about ten or twelve people died.

"We talk about looking death in the face. Well, I looked it in the face again that day, and I'll never forget it because I had a baby boy just born and I really wanted to see him again. It gives you that tug to live. But Dale looked at me and he was white too, and whatever he says now, he knew we were close. We had so many crazy calls on *Platoon*. There were about six or seven major risks. And that day with Bob, that was pretty spooky, man. I was terrified."

Later Stone wrote: "Dale Dye and I both know how close we are to buying it, having seen choppers go down in 'Nam, but we have no choice: Money is tight, chopper time limited, so we go for broke, flying out of the jungle canyons in wild wind currents, shooting film as fast as we can. It's the worst week of fear I've had since Vietnam, yet I feel younger than ever, the years dropping off me now with the terror."

According to Richardson, the firefight scenes were nearly as dangerous as the helicopter shots. "Oliver would be saying, 'We've got to get things going faster,' and he'd tell special effects to 'Just go out and bury a bunch of firebombs. Put them out there and we'll all just run right through them. Just before we shoot, be sure and tell me where they are.' Well, I mean these are bags of gasoline that explode. I don't know how much they put in them, but certainly it can do serious damage. We did the night battle scenes where we had no idea exactly where the bombs were. We just roughly knew that they were somewhere around here or there. In Oliver's mind we were relatively safe, but it was an odd, odd way to handle special effects."

Surprisingly, Richardson thinks taking these kinds of risks was good for the picture. "I think the madness is good. Oliver has a death wish and I relate to it to a certain extent. To create that kind of uncertainty raised the level for all of the actors, too. Imagine not knowing where these damn bombs were and no one seems to know. I mean, they would explode a few feet away from us. We literally lit entire scenes by gasoline explosions. That forces more upon the actors than putting on some sound effects in the background. The environment became real."

Fortunately, Stone was able to connect with the actors. Charlie Sheen remembers him as being "brutally honest. Which is why we clicked. After a scene he'd say, 'You sucked,' or, 'You nailed it.' That's just my style."

There were a few clashes, of course, and Sheen recalls the most heated one. "During one scene, in which I was to help unload a helicopter,

I wanted to keep my T-shirt on to protect my back from the rocks and debris kicked up by the chopper. Stone wanted me to take the shirt off. I told him no and he turned on me and said, 'What? Are you a pussy? Are you a little pussy from Malibu? Played too much volleyball all your life?' I got so pissed off that I ripped the shirt off, did the scene, and had scars on my back for weeks."

Which of course was exactly the kind of intensity Stone had wanted. It wasn't the first and it certainly wouldn't be the last time that the director would resort to verbally taunting or in other ways manipulating his actors to get the desired effect. "When he arrived for filming, Charlie was still a nerd," maintains Stone. "Then each week there was a perceptible change as he became a soldier. I was always satisfied that Charlie had the right spacey quality, which is what I had at the time. He looks like he's sort of floating, and early on, he has a completely lost look. Then week by week as we shot, another layer of hardness would come on."

"I was more or less under the microscope," Sheen acknowledges, "because my character was the guy standing twenty feet behind the camera. Yet he gave me enough freedom to bring in my own elements."

For Stone, Sheen's performance provided something of an inner revelation: "Through Charlie, I saw myself as a young man," Stone wrote in his notes. "And I could step back without any self-consciousness and see myself for the first time through that mirror of time. And it was sad. To see what I'd become in Vietnam through him. I mean, certainly part of me was stupid, ignorant, evil, and I didn't have any realization of that at the time. . . . That's where the bottom line is. You find out if there is an intrinsic goodness or not. That's what the film's about. I'm not unique. I was one of 4 or 5 million guys who were there. I'm just in a position to do something about it."

Though wary at first of this "Malibu kid," the other actors also grew to respect Sheen over time. "Charlie does have a taste for the 'finer things,'" says Dafoe. "We expected this little creep. He got pampered a little. He was younger. A rich kid from Malibu. His mother packed him eight hundred boxes of things. You imagined he'd really cry foul when things got down dirty, but he really got his nose in there."

Dafoe has no stories comparable to Sheen's or to the violent disagreements on the set in *Salvador*. "I don't know what to say about Oliver except that he really thrives in the face of adversity. He was like a little kid—he flashes that gap-toothed smile. He's fun. He's got a lot of conflicts in himself. That's what really charges him, and that's what makes him an interesting guy. As a director he deals with everybody differently, but I think one of his greatest strengths is he creates a charged atmosphere. The thing you want from any director is to create a certain kind of excitement and a way to articulate the world that you're supposed to be living in. And I think he does that very well. With some people he definitely fucks with them. He's a manipulator sometimes. Lots of directors are, but he is a little bit of a mind fucker because he believes that if he turns up the heat on someone, they'll be tested in a way that they may surprise themselves. He's pretty wise at dealing with different people in different ways, but he can be very perverse. I will dish him in this respect, though, if you turn the tables on him and give something back to him, all of a sudden he gets this hurt puppy dog look like you fucking hit him with a low blow."

Dafoe says Stone teased him throughout the shoot to keep Elias's narcissistic streak vivid: "He'd say, 'You look like a drowned dog. Elias is beautiful. Hair, let's dry his hair. Give me some of that Burt Lancaster smile.'"

Tom Berenger also had the benefit of hearing Stone describe the person on whom his role was based. "Oliver told me one time they were in the bush, humping along the Cambodian border for days, marching up and down jungle trails. Never saw nothing. And all of a sudden, Barnes puts his hands up, the silent signal for the platoon to stop. And he signals for one side of the platoon to go to the right and the other side to go to the left. All silent signals. And they come upon three NVA guys with their weapons laying on the ground. They got no campfire, eating cold rice and fish with chopsticks. Barnes gives the signal and they open up. Like thirty fucking guys opening up on three guys with their weapons on the ground. Rice and fish flying all over the place. The fucking guys are annihilated. So when Oliver told me the story, I said, 'How did he know they were there?' He said that Barnes smelled the fish. Now that's the kind of fucking guy you want to be with in 'Nam."

Berenger is reluctant to accept criticism that his cold-blooded character taints the majority of good, decent men who fought in Vietnam: "I met a guy who was a platoon sergeant with the 101st Airborne and

I asked him if he was as mean as I was in the film. He said, 'At times. Otherwise, your men will die.'"

With *Platoon* Stone brought the portrayal of the Vietnam War to new levels, some of which were sure to whip up controversy. One such scene, and one of the more difficult to shoot, featured Kevin Dillon, who as Bunny, a young, ignorant southern white soldier, is a seething powderkeg waiting to go off. When the platoon enters a Vietnamese village they suspect aided in the killing of one of their men, Bunny explodes, savagely beating a peasant with the butt of his rifle. Kevin Dillon describes the shooting of the scene: "When I did that scene, I was flipping out because the poor guy I was doing it to was a Filipino they had picked up somewhere. He was deaf and blind in one eye and missing a leg. I felt bad for the guy because he was a nervous wreck the whole time, and I wasn't sure if he knew we were just filming a movie. That scene was so intense that my mom couldn't bear to watch it."

Once again it seems as though Stone, as the director, had found a way to give the actor a needed edge, a real tension to add to his performance. In playing Bunny, Dillon thought up one of his character's more memorable bits in which he casually takes a bite out of a beer can. "I learned it two years ago from a friend who was a Marine. But I wouldn't recommend that anyone try it because if you're not careful you can get hurt."

Bunny is also modeled on a real person and the village scene is based on real events. And like Chris in the film, Stone both took part in the brutality and took action to stop it. When the old man frustrated him during the search of a Viet Cong pit, Stone made him dance by firing bullets at his feet, but later, becoming horrified by his own actions, he also stepped in and stopped the rape of a village girl.

"Ain't no need or time for a courtroom out here."

Sergeant Barnes in **PLATOON**

Platoon, like its maker, is a startling mass of contradictions held together by the power of its convictions. After the harsh brutality of the village scene, the soldiers march away from the hamlet they have just torched and, in classic G.I. Joe big brother fashion, carry Vietnamese children on their shoulders. The scene is panoramic and one of many that are amazing feats considering the small budget of the movie. Arnold Kopelson gives some insight into how it was done: "Naturally, we couldn't afford an electronic press kit, which was beginning to be used by the industry. Whenever I would call the studio, they would say, 'Look, there's no money! You can't have any promotional material.' So somewhere around the second week, I went to Hong Kong for the weekend and I bought a video camera and started filming the movie being made. Of course, Oliver had total disdain for this. He would say, 'What the fuck are you doing? What is that piece of shit you're playing with?' And I'd say, 'Listen, I'm just playing. Leave me alone, let me play.'

"So one day he was shooting the village scene. We couldn't get any equipment, so he had the crew make their own crane or boom to get high enough when they blew up the village. So, he's up there on that and I'm on a twenty- or thirty-foot ladder, taping video. Then for the first time, he says, 'Let me see that.' So I ran it back to him and of course he wouldn't say, 'Very good,' or, 'Jesus, that's fantastic,' but every so often after that he would ask to look into the camera to see what the shot looked like."

Among other things, *Platoon* had no official stunt coordinator, so for the fight that breaks out between Barnes and Elias in the village scene, Stone turned to Tom Berenger. "I asked Oliver, 'What do you want to do for this fight between Elias and me?' And he goes, 'You've done this shit before, right?' I said, 'What do you mean—movie fights? Yeah, I've done a few.' So he says, 'You do it.' I thought, 'Boy, that's confidence.' I loved it. I was used to having to hammer the director to get to do anything. But he had Dale doing all kinds of things and we helped out whenever we could."

With conflict and tension an integral part of the script, it's not surprising that there were off-camera battles during the filming. Many of these involved the Filipino crew. "One time I came on to the set rather early and everyone was standing around," Arnold Kopelson recalls. "They were separated into two camps, the Americans and the Filipinos, and nobody was doing anything. I found out that Oliver had gotten pissed off at the head of the Filipino crew over something and he'd kicked him in the ass in front of the entire Filipino crew. The man was really upset. I understand that he was carrying a gun and was seriously contemplating shooting Oliver, and no one was going to work until this was straightened out. Finally, Oliver agreed that in a gesture to show his apology, he would let the man slap him in front of his crew. And that's what he did. It was like something out of an old Tarzan movie or something . . . winning the cooperation of the tribe."

Another battle ensued when the Filipinos discovered they were not being paid the correct per diem. This one was settled by Tom Berenger. "Some of the people involved were part of my platoon," Berenger explains. "I mean, I was the platoon leader, right? I take care of my boys. So I went to Alex Ho and I said, 'You either give these young Filipino kids their per diem or I'm going to tell Oliver and he'll be all over your ass.' Alex sort of shook it off. Well, after thirty-six hours, nothing had happened, and I went to him again and I said, 'Okay, it's gone up.' I told him that now I expected him to pay them more. I said, 'The platoon is behind me and you know it because your first AD told you. If you don't come through by midnight and they don't get the money, that's it. At eight o'clock tomorrow morning there will be a slowdown and I'll tell Oliver, "I told Alex Ho about this three days ago."' At that point he conceded, and Oliver never knew anything about it. Alex was like a Chinese warlord, but I had the whole platoon behind me on that one."

Naturally, the tensions on the set were only heightened by the startling reality of the film. Berenger says that sometimes the scenes were a little too close to home for war veterans Stone and Dale Dye: "One was when we came into the village and had to check to see if anyone was hiding in the hole. And I grab a willypete [white phosphorus grenade] off of Forest Whitaker and I go, 'Get him up, get out of there, you motherfucker.' And I'm yelling at him in Vietnamese, and a few women and children come out, but the rest of them stay in, and I throw the willypete in. And Oliver and Dale had a weird reaction. Oliver just said, 'Cut, print,' and he and Dale just turned and walked away. I think it was the screaming in Vietnamese, the high-pitched language, and the fact it was so right on. They were, like, 'Yeah, let's just print it and move on to the next scene.' Obviously they didn't want to talk about it."

Berenger got a different reaction over a scene with Mark Moses, who plays Lieutenant Wolfe. "There was a scene where I come up and hit Lieutenant Wolfe over the head with the radio handset because he called in the wrong coordinates, and I knocked his helmet off and he put it on backwards. Oliver and Dale just hit the ground, laughing hysterically. They said for me to do it like that every take because the American helmet turned backwards looks like an Italian Army helmet, like Mussolini."

Perhaps the most dramatic scene in the movie is the death of Sergeant Elias. Here, Stone moves away from his own experience, although he does feel the scene is symbolically in line with the death of the real Elias. In the film, during the confusion of an ambush, Barnes tracks down Elias and shoots him. Moments later, several members of the platoon, including Barnes and Chris, are rescued by a chopper and they look down to see Elias, somehow still alive, running madly, being chased by a horde of Viet Cong who are riddling him with bullets. After stumbling several times, Elias is finally overcome and sinks in slow motion to his knees. He spreads his arms Christ-like above him while still more shots are fired, then falls forward as the rescue helicopter banks away into the sky.

To shoot this scene required two cameras on the ground and one in a chopper, the coordination of several extras, and an especially difficult long run for Dafoe. When all the divergent elements finally came together for a great take, another problem almost spoiled the scene. "My body hits didn't go off," recalls Dafoe, referring to the tiny explosives strapped to his body that were designed to detonate spurts of blood. "I'm supposed to be gushing blood and guts. I'm pressing this little button and it's not happening. My body's jerking and taking the hits, but no blood." Despite the lack of sufficient gore, Stone left the scene in the movie as filmed, correctly believing it to be chillingly convincing even without the blood.

"We got hit by an ambush just like the one that gets Elias," Stone says of his experience. "We took about thirty casualties, and I don't think we got one of them. You know, films like *Rambo* make it look real easy, but I remember the NVAs as being terrific fighters. They were always nailing us."

One of Berenger's best scenes follows shortly after Elias's death, when Barnes confronts Chris and the others who sided with Elias in their bunker. Though Stone opted otherwise, Berenger suggested that he be framed with an ironic halo of Christmas lights for this scene, during which he challenges the "potheads" with one of the most quoted line in the film: "I *am* reality."

Berenger comments: "That speech may not just be Barnes's truth, but the absolute truth. Certainly war is always gonna be here. Perhaps from movies like this people will think twice. When the legislators or the President send people into combat zones in Central America, which is also jungle, you better make sure you're ready for a five-year war."

Near the end of the film, the platoon is pinned down when Chris suddenly charges toward the machine-gun fire and heroically wipes out a nest of North Vietnamese. This scene is also based on Stone's experience, for which he was awarded a Bronze Star.

In the film's final scenes, the platoon fights an apocalyptic battle with a large enemy force and is about to be wiped out when, in desperation, their captain (played by Dale Dye) orders an air strike on their position. Stone does a brief cameo here as an Army major who is blown to bits when a booby-trapped Viet Cong soldier dives into his bunker. Taking advantage of the confusion of the battle, Barnes is about to silence Chris forever when the air strike hits and the entire area is engulfed in flames. Chris survives, to discover a severely wounded Barnes. At last confronting his nemesis, Chris raises his rifle, but then hesitates until Barnes angrily barks, "Do it." And he does.

"The thing about that scene," Tom Berenger says, "is that Oliver and I had talked about that early. The end was going to be me screaming at Charlie Sheen and Charlie just blowing me away with an AK-47. I said, 'From what we know about Barnes, doesn't he want to die? I mean, isn't he ready to fucking go, especially after being shot up again? It seems to me he'd just say, "Do it."' Oliver went 'Hmmm, uh-huh,' and just walked away. He'd act like he wasn't listening, but he would always listen. Nine times out of ten he'd do exactly what I asked him to do. He must have a fucking photographic memory. It was eight or nine weeks later when we did that shot and that's what he went with."

Just as Chris's experiences parallel Stone's, the choice he must make is the choice Stone faced repeatedly. Would he abandon moral codes under intense fire, or would he attempt to maintain his humanity? "The Charlie Sheen character is an endangered species," Stone says. "Basically, he's a down-to-earth, decent, cleancut kid who wants to live up to his responsibility. He has innate values, but the war seems to chastise him for that. In the end, when he kills his sergeant, there's an element of irony: on the one hand, he is meting out righteous justice and 'doing the right thing'; on the other, he's emptying an M-16 rifle into a man whose crime is that he emptied an M-16 rifle into another man. The audience may feel satisfied that justice has triumphed, but they also have to wonder if Chris has become as barbaric as Sergeant Barnes. Does the end justify the means? Will Chris carry over this new set of values to civilian life when he goes home? It *isn't* a happy ending. Ultimately, he forgives himself and lives the best life he can from then on. He decides he has done a duty. He tries to draw redemption from chastened blood. This was how I felt. I never killed my sergeant, but like all soldiers, I had to work through an acceptance of my part in the war."

The film ends with the wounded Chris being airlifted from the bloody scene, knowing that though he survived the war, his life will be forever changed. Though not as flamboyant as Berenger's Barnes or Dafoe's Elias, Charlie Sheen's role as Chris Taylor was equally difficult to play. The part called for response more than stimulation, and required a talent for understatement. Stone's overall approach with Sheen was more one of communicating his experiences than specific acting techniques. "I tried to convey the way I felt in 'Nam," Stone explains. "The fear I felt in the jungles for the first time. I was a kid from New York and it was suddenly like everything I'd read in Homer was coming true. I was with real warriors. To me, Barnes and Elias were like Achilles and Hector, and I was with them in another world. Most of all I wanted to convey to him how my sense of innocence changed over time. For me, that's the key to the movie."

"It's the way the whole thing works. People like Elias get wasted and people like Barnes just go on making up rules any way they want and what do we do, we just sit around in the middle and suck on it. We just don't add up to dry shit."

Chris Taylor in **PLATOON**

Just as Chris develops as a soldier, *Platoon* also provides a good metaphor for Stone's development as a director. "In the movie, the main character began by writing letters that were very literary and cerebral, but as the film progressed, his thoughts went into a minor key and his instincts and senses started to prevail," Stone says now. "Similarly, I may have originally approached filmmaking in a cerebral way, but as time passed I became more instinctive and sense-oriented. As a filmmaker, I want to move in the environment of the film, but I don't want anyone to sense I'm there. The good point man doesn't draw attention to himself or his platoon; likewise, the good director doesn't draw attention to himself or his crew within the context of the film."

Despite all the preparation and hard work, the film almost wasn't finished in time. The night shooting had proved extremely difficult, and the budget was dwindling at a faster rate than the pages of the script left to shoot. Knowing the rainy season was about to start any day, Stone compromised on the last few shots in order to make the deadline. Elizabeth Stone remembers: "They finished on the last day before the rainy season started. I'd gone back to the hotel at about two in the morning. And Oliver dragged in at about 6:00 A.M. with this smile on his face and said, 'We got it. It's raining.' At dawn as the sun was coming up they'd gotten the last reel in the can, and then the rains fell."

Willem Dafoe found playing Elias a rewarding experience. Too young for Vietnam, before *Platoon* he considered the soldiers of that war "uneducated yahoos who went over to kick butts," but working on the film changed his mind. "*Platoon*," he says, "presses the question, 'Is there any morality in war?' What kind of a guy do you want leading you in war, Barnes or Elias? What's decent if you're dead?" Dafoe says the actors stayed almost obsessively in touch afterwards, like people who'd really been to war.

Berenger also went through some heavy changes. As shooting neared its end, he had a day off and was reading about a battle in the American Revolution. "All of a sudden I just started crying," he says. "It wasn't the book. It was the state I was in at the end of this traumatic filmmaking, and all the thoughts of guys who have to go to any war—their despair, loneliness, and fear. That's what affected me."

Berenger maintains that early on he knew they were filming "something special, that it might be the greatest war movie ever made." He also felt unusually attached to the *Platoon* cast. "I started missing guys as they would get 'killed' or 'shipped out,'" he says. "But we've stayed in touch. We've even had mini-reunions. I remember telling them, 'This may be the best experience you'll ever have in filmmaking.'"

Oliver Stone described finishing *Platoon* in his *American Film* article:

I compromise on some shots, and we finish on the fifty-fourth day, at five o'clock on a May morning. Alex Ho, the Chinese production manager with me since Dino, now beaten to a pulp by cast and crew, comes over and says, not without some irony, "Congratulations, Ollie, it's been a long two years." ". . . No, a long twenty," I murmur, sad because I know that although I finished the film, a part of it will never be there, any more than the faces of the gawky boys we left behind in the dust. As close as I came to Charlie Sheen, he would never be me and *Platoon* would never be what I saw in my mind when I wrote it and which was just a fragment, really, of what happened years ago. That, too, is gone. And we move on. I don't want to party with the cast and crew—they're having too good a time and I don't want to bring my director's consciousness to bear on them—so I ride home alone with the driver as the light comes up over the paddies and the water buffalo, and the peasants come out as they always do to work the fields in that first pink light of an Asia dawn. It is just another late spring day in the World (as we called it in Vietnam) and nobody cares that we just finished this little "thing in the jungle." Why should they? Yet as I press my face against the window of the silently moving car, in my soul there is a moment there and I know that it will last me forever—because it is the sweetest moment I've had since the day I left Vietnam.

Wall Street

"You're on a roll, kiddo. Enjoy it while it lasts—'cause it never does."

Lou Mannheim in **WALL STREET**

Once the shooting was over, Stone faced the task of editing. Though it had much of the realism of *Salvador*, *Platoon* was more pulled back stylistically and required a whole different mind-set in the editing room. "It's more period, more 1967," Stone agrees. "We didn't shoot right on top of you. Although we still did a lot of hand-held, there's more dolly work, and more crane work. We also had a little more time."

Platoon has less of a herky-jerky style than *Salvador* and is more assured, lyrical at moments, even in its grotesque images of battle and death. These images are powerful, and it is for capturing the essence of the war on film that Stone has been most praised. "Those images you don't forget that easily," Stone says. "That war never went away. I got good technical advisers to help me with details, but the actual feeling of combat stayed with me."

"You all, take a good look at this lump o' shit . . . Remember what it looks like. You fuck up in a firefight and I goddamn-guarantee you a trip out of the bush . . . in a body bag."

Sergeant Barnes in **PLATOON**

There is no question that *Platoon* is a violent movie. But according to Charlie Sheen, some of the more violent scenes were eliminated in the editing room. "There was one shot," Sheen recalls, "where I look down in the mud and see a human eye. That was cut . . . I guess they felt audiences might start walking out at that point if they left it in."

Stone responds: "There's a good-taste factor that comes into play. You don't want a head blowing apart because it turns off a certain segment of the audience. I wanted women and children to see the movie. So you pull back and show the violence in a reserved fashion. It's not like Arabal's *Viva La Muerte*. In *Platoon*, the power of suggestion is strong and I think it does the work for you."

There were other scenes cut from *Platoon*, including something Bob Richardson says is filmed in almost every Oliver Stone movie. "We nearly always shoot a ghost shot." Richardson smiles. "Like in *Platoon*, there was a shot where all the guys who were dead more or less appeared to Charlie. They're just sitting there like in a group portrait. We shot the sequence for it, but Oliver cut it later. In almost every film he puts in a ghost scene. They rarely last through the editing because they generally don't fit, but he shoots them anyway."

Assembling *Platoon* was not nearly the battle that *Salvador* had been. "There were no fights over the editing of *Platoon*," Stone recalls. "From the get-go it was just accepted and loved in the first cut. My first cut was almost the last cut. I just showed it and they said release it."

But releasing it meant getting Orion's cooperation as well. Still bitter over their spurning of *Salvador*, Stone feels that Orion initially held back on *Platoon*: "They got cold feet. And John Daly and Arnold Kopelson and Gerald Green really took it to the mat. They made it very attractive to Orion. Their risk was limited, but even then, when they released it they were very cautious."

Orion's initial plan was to release *Platoon* in New York and Los Angeles in December 1986 and then go into a slow-building release pattern in January and February 1987. After some enthusiastic word of mouth at a November 18, 1986, screening for Motion Picture Academy members and industry executives, Toronto was added. Despite the industry "buzz" over the quality of the film and depth of the performances, Hollywood still pretty much regarded the picture with indifference—it might be well made, it might even be great, but it would never do big box office.

On December 19, *Platoon* quietly opened in six theaters in New York, Los Angeles, and Toronto. Arthur Manson, who still worked for Hemdale at the time as an independent consultant and has since been a consultant to Oliver Stone on a regular basis, says that having two theaters in New York was an important strategy. "We always felt the movie could succeed on both levels. That you had on one side a film that had an important statement to make about war, that might get critical acclaim, but also an action film that might appeal to the people who go to 42nd Street. I'll never forget the opening, eleven-thirty in the morning, they were lined up around the block on Broadway! And uptown on the East Side they were in line there as well as a result of the reviews. I called the manager on Broadway and he described the reaction . . . people were in tears. It was very emotional for them."

After that weekend, everything changed. Hollywood's analysis of the Christmas season box office received a slow but deeply reverberating shock wave. Orion, realizing it was about to be caught with its pants down, scrambled to make amends, and Oliver Stone would never be ignored again. In New York, the reaction was nothing short of amazing. Though it was showing on just two area screens, the film took in $93,693, giving it a $46,846 per screen average, the highest in the city. Nationally, the story was nearly as impressive. *The Golden Child* was number one in total box office for the week, grossing $7,887,899 on 1,667 screens for an average of $4,732. *Star Trek IV* was second, with $5,809,960 on 1,886 screens for an average of $3,081. *Platoon* (sixteenth in total gross) took in $241,080 on only six screens for an astonishing average of $40,180.

Orion just wasn't ready for this kind of momentum. Arthur Manson elaborates: "They weren't prepared to move it quickly enough, especially because it opened at Christmas. Exhibitors were calling on the first weekend anxious to book *Platoon*. Garth Drabinski, who founded Cineplex Odeon, called me at home saying, 'I got to get this movie next week.' He booked it for New Year's in Chicago and San Francisco. It started picking up its pace because of him but it went very slowly. The attendance of women in the audience didn't become significant until about the third week in the run. I remember a theater in Canada calling and saying, 'Guess what, tell Oliver, we're getting women!' It just kept gaining momentum, all the way to the Academy Awards."

Oliver Stone recalls the change in attitude at Orion: "It took off and then they tried to get as many theaters as they could as quickly as they could. Orion would make somewhat offbeat movies, but they would never distribute them with any confidence. *Platoon*, thank God, went through the roof. People were swept up in it. It was almost a universal phenomenon. Across the world, people just loved it."

The critics were more than impressed; they were impassioned. *New York* magazine's David Denby wrote that "the realistic details, soberly gathered, culminate in the explosion of surreal horror that Francis Coppola labored for in 'Apocalypse Now' . . . the kind of Vietnam movie that many of us have longed for . . . one comes out excited, yet shaken and close to tears. With this movie, Oliver Stone completes his amazing transformation from bum to hero."

That summed it up. What with the outright thrashing of *The Hand* and the attacks on so many of his scripts as being too graphic and violent, Stone had surely done time in critics' hell. Though he would just as surely come into their sights time and time again, after the release of *Platoon*, he was their "darling." Richard Corliss of *Time* stated: " 'Platoon' matters . . . Stone's film is a document written in blood which after almost twenty years, refuses to dry." Vincent Canby of *The New York Times* wrote: "The tension builds and never lets up . . . a major piece of work, as full of passion as it is of redeeming, scary irony. . . . A singular achievement." And Sheila Benson of the *Los Angeles Times* said: "This is movie making with a zealot's fervor. War movies of the past, even the greatest ones, seem like crane shots by comparison. 'Platoon' is at ground zero. . . . Stone has summoned up, like a Goya with a camera, the impact of cruelty on the faces and souls of its perpetrators."

Soon, block-long lines were forming outside the theaters, not only during the evening on weekends but at lunchtime on weekdays, in the bite of a January wind in New York and after midnight in early-to-bed Hollywood. Orion quickly moved the film into about sixty theaters in thirteen major cities and made moves to add another hundred the following week. An unanticipated benefit that came out of the movie's slow release pattern was that theater owners were now bidding against each other. Orion got higher film rentals than it would have if the movie had been sold before its box-office potential was recognized.

Platoon was originally sold as "Oliver Stone's story." The ads consisted of three or four Polaroid snapshots of Stone in uniform, and the copy described his being wounded twice, winning the Bronze Star, then making a movie about "men he knew and fought with in the country they could not win."

Naturally, this kind of a marketing approach required Stone to do a great deal of interviewing with the press. Consequently, he hosted screenings, though he can barely sit still to watch one of his own films ("I keep seeing all the things I did wrong or could have done better," he says), and spent endless hours talking with reporters about his Vietnam experience. Stone admitted that he included deliberately gruesome and shocking events in *Platoon* to display the horror of combat and counteract the usual Hollywood-style evasion of war's physical and moral destructiveness. "I hope they see real violence as opposed to that obscene TV violence where somebody just raises a gun and goes, '*pop, pop*' and the other person dies without blood. That's worse to me than realistic violence. The point is that violence ruins you in some sense forever. It takes a piece of your soul."

The character of Chris Taylor is so interwoven with Oliver Stone's real-life experiences that Stone sometimes answered questions by referring to the screenplay. "Why did you volunteer for the draft?" someone asked him, and Stone picked up the script and read: "CHRIS VOICE-OVER: I guess I have always been sheltered and special, I just want to be anonymous. Like everybody else. Do my share for my country. Live up to what Grandpa did in the First War and Dad in the Second. I know this is going to be the war of my generation."

Meanwhile Stone moved quickly to set up another project. Stanley Weiser, Stone's friend from film school, was now a screenwriter in Los Angeles. He describes the chain of events: "I called Oliver and we went to dinner and I said I'd love to work with him on a script. He talked about an idea he had to do a story about quiz-show scandals in the fifties. So I spent the entire weekend in the library doing research and coming up with a story because we were going to meet with Ed Pressman.

"We met at some German restaurant on Western Avenue and I told them my idea and Oliver's listening, but he's checking his watch because, like usual, he's got twenty other things on his mind. Then he said, 'What about this idea? *Crime and Punishment* on Wall Street. Two guys abusing each other on Wall Street.' And I thought, 'He doesn't like my idea.' But I had to admit the Wall Street idea sounded interesting. So then he said, 'Make a deal, Ed. I've got to go to New York.' Just like that. All he'd said was a couple of things, like, 'Two guys using each other in a relationship . . . I don't know what happens, something to do with this drab prosecutor coming after them, like the one in *Crime and Punishment*.' Then he said to me, 'Read *Crime and Punishment* over the weekend and call me Monday.' This was like on Friday night. And he stood up to go and said, 'I have to go. Make a deal, Ed. Don't waste time.' And he left."

Having been through many a Hollywood meeting where nothing but talk ever got accomplished, Weiser expected the worst. "I figured this is just bullshit. But sure enough Ed made a deal. I got the Cliff Notes to *Crime and Punishment* and Monday I called Oliver and told him why the schematic he had in mind wouldn't work. He said, 'Okay, read *Gatsby* tonight and see what you find there.' So, I rented the *Gatsby* video and then told him why that didn't work, and he told me another book to read. 'Read Dreiser's *The Financier* . . . and don't be lazy.' Each night he would give me a different reading assignment."

For Stone, the essence of *Wall Street* had been germinating for a long time. "It started for me back in 1981," he remembers. "I had a friend in New York who was my age—mid-thirties—and he was making millions. He had a tremendous beach house in Bridgehampton, and as if that was not enough, an even larger house a few miles down the road. It was very Gatsbyesque. He was working sixteen-, eighteen-hour days. He was on the phone to Hong Kong, Europe, all over. This guy was the New York version of what was going down in Miami, where people were hyperconsuming. Wall Street is the equivalent of the cocaine trade in some ways. Anyway, my friend got more and more money until inevitably he reached a point where it just blew up in his face. It was like a cocaine high. He started to make mistakes and one of those mistakes cost him everything. He was forced to reassess everything in life: his friendships, the value of objects, the value of life.

"That story frames what happens in my movie, which is basically a *Pilgrim's Progress* of a boy who is seduced and corrupted by the allure of easy money. And in the third act, he sets out to redeem himself. He goes back to an essential decency that he rediscovers in himself—very much like some of us do in life. For me it was when I gave up using drugs and wrote *Scarface* cold turkey."

By the weekend of January 9, 1987, *Platoon* was in seventy-four theaters and averaged more than $22,000, the highest per-screen take of any film during the period. By January 20, it was number four in the country in total grosses, even though it was still not in wide release. Such statistics sent shock waves through Hollywood because it was a well-proven axiom that a film's per-screen average dropped dramatically when more theaters were added, but *Platoon* had only dropped $1,000 per screen after adding a hundred theaters. *Critical Condition*, the number-one movie in the nation, averaged only $4,256 per screen but was on 1,343 screens for a total gross of $5.7 million. *Platoon* was doing far and away better business than any of its main competitors, with a total so far of $11.1 million.

By the beginning of February the industry trades were reporting that *Platoon*, a movie no studio had wanted to make, was the top-grossing film in the country for the week, selling $8.3 million worth of tickets even though it was appearing at less than six hundred theaters, a still amazing average of more than $14,000 a theater.

Interviewers and talk-show hosts around the country began taking their cues from the Orion campaign, which touted Stone's combat experience and gravitated toward *Platoon* as *the* human interest hook of the moment. It was the perfect occasion for inviting Vietnam vets to let loose with their feelings about the war—on camera, of course. CBS's "The Morning Program" flew three of Stone's former Army buddies to New York and taped their reunion. Ben Fitzgerald was now a die cast operator living in Humboldt, Tennessee; Crutcher Patterson co-owned a used car parts yard in Pulaski, Tennessee; and Jim Pappert, a third member of the same platoon, was a production mechanic in St. Louis. The session was aired as a four-part series the week of the Academy Award nominations. While primarily a promotional gimmick for the film, the televised reunion did allow people to see the easy banter of friendships born in war—as when Stone kidded Patterson about turning him on to pot. By now *Platoon* was generating a good deal of controversy and much of it centered on the more violent aspects of the film, particularly the scene where the soldiers go on a rampage in a Vietnamese village. Although Stone was willing to discuss such incidents on the show, none of the three with whom he served wanted to dwell on it.

That night, the reunited Army buddies adjourned to the Lion's Head, a Greenwich Village pub where, later on, Tom Cruise stopped by to meet Stone. "We talked about *Wall Street*," Cruise says. "I told him that I wanted to do it, but he had already committed to Charlie Sheen. Charlie had dropped out at one point, but then changed his mind, but Oliver still honored his commitment. And I respect him for that. In fact, I was impressed by his stand. Oliver keeps his commitments."

There's no question that Cruise was a bigger star than Sheen even then, but Stone already knew that his reputation as a filmmaker wasn't hinging on working with stars. He was impressed with Cruise, however, and the two discussed working together on some future project, although Stone says he didn't mention *Born on the Fourth of July* specifically at that time.

In New York and Indianapolis, local television stations invited Vietnam veterans to a screening of the movie, then interviewed them for their reactions. There was also the anti-war angle; many pacifist groups were promoting the film to their rank and file. "We want to use the movie to educate people," Ross Yosnow, a member of Veterans for Peace, said at the time. "You see clowns like Rambo and kids think if you wear an American uniform you can't be hurt."

Jane Fonda seemed to agree about the film. Fonda, who sparked worldwide controversy when she visited Hanoi as a protester against the war, said, "I had to sit down and cry after I saw it. It was so real."

Stone's fellow directors also laid on their benedictions. Steven Spielberg said, "It is more than a movie, it's like being in Vietnam. *Platoon* makes you feel you've been there and never want to go back."

Brian De Palma, who filmed *Scarface*, saw Stone achieving a new maturity in *Platoon:* "He has now channeled his feeling and energy into a cohesive dramatic work. He's an auteur making a movie about what he experienced and understands. Seeing 'Platoon' get through the system makes the soul feel good."

Martin Scorsese, the director who taught Stone at NYU, said, "He's got power and force. It's good to see our country can still produce directors like him. He has a unique style and he's become a real personal filmmaker. No one else is doing the things he's doing. He's out there by himself."

Had *Platoon* been made and released a decade before, when the script was first completed, it would almost certainly have failed at the box office. The ten years' delay provided flawless timing. By December 1986, America had started viewing Vietnam in a different light. The film was neither pro- nor anti-war in most people's minds. It was simply the truth, and it provided both relief and accommodation. Though Stone insisted it was more "scar tissue than a healing of the wound," there was no question that a healing process was triggered in many of those who saw it.

Vietnam left wounds on the national psyche that demanded satisfaction. America not only had to deal with a lost war, but also with a loss of faith. One of the functions of myths has always been righting wrongs, resolving contradictions, smoothing over the scars of reality. And this is what Hollywood did with a series of "fantasy" Vietnam movies. Movies where the outcome was changed and the wrongs were righted, from Gene Hackman assembling a group of vets to invade Laos and search for his son in *Uncommon Valor* (1983) to Sly Stallone conducting his own rescue on a much grander scale in *Rambo* (1985). But, by 1986, Americans were tired of superhero fantasies and there was a need for real sustenance after the junk-food gorging on *Rambo*. Vietnam was an issue that was still unresolved. Most Americans, even the conservative right, knew that something had gone wrong there and they had a real longing to know what happened over there. They'd glimpsed the madness of it (*Apocalyse Now*), seen it as a backdrop (*The Deer Hunter*), and seen its effects (*Coming Home*), but none of this really enlightened them. Enough time had passed. The pain had stopped and there was a need to dress the wound. There was a need to know.

When *Platoon* was first released, it was not considered an anti-war film. America was still reeling from the protest movement of the sixties and the intensity of these efforts made *Platoon*'s relatively straightforward portrayal of the conditions of the war seem unobtrusive. It was a simple story, one man's tale of what happened to him in Vietnam. And it was the answer America had been looking for. In many ways *Platoon* is a basic and honest effort to honor the Americans who fought in

Vietnam. Instead of using the inhumanity and bizarre contradictions of the war to criticize the troops, Stone uses these elements to solicit our understanding of what the soldiers had to endure.

The theme is loss of innocence. It shows what it was like to be an American and a source of horror, to learn from war at too great a loss, to become a warrior and pay the price. *Platoon* argues that in times of extreme stress, our morals can explode under us like land mines. The scene where the overwrought soldiers, interrogating villagers about a weapons stash, commit senseless murder is indescribably nerve-wracking. By plunging us into this madness the film captures the fear, disorientation, and crazed high of battle; we are suddenly able to understand what is possible when we've seen people we know cut to pieces and have no idea where the next bullet is coming from. *Platoon* reverses the lie at the heart of *The Deer Hunter*: it's not what they did to us that haunts the American soul, it's what we did to them.

Jean-Luc Godard, the French filmmaker, once said that the only time a good film becomes a popular film is through a misunderstanding. To a certain extent, *Platoon* was misunderstood into a blockbuster. The Rambomaniacs loved the film because it gave a good bang for the buck. The anti-war left accepted it as the prime example of war's callous futility. The establishment rightly saw it as a tribute to our fighting men, and there was enough symbolism and philosophical perspective to keep the intelligentsia happy. And perhaps best of all, the average moviegoer, too young to recall Vietnam even as the war that aired nightly in our living rooms, finally understood why Dad came home so changed or didn't come home at all.

On February 11, 1987, *Platoon* was nominated for eight Oscars, and Oliver Stone was nominated for three. The nominations included Best Picture, Best Director (Stone), Best Screenplay (Stone), Best Cinematography (Bob Richardson), Best Editing, Best Sound, and two nominations for Best Supporting Actor (Berenger and Dafoe). Besides his nominations for *Platoon*, Stone was also nominated along with Richard Boyle for Best Screenplay for *Salvador*, thus giving him the rare opportunity of competing against himself for the Oscar. Also from *Salvador*, James Woods was nominated for his riveting portrayal of Richard Boyle. The two *Salvador* nominations and the attention that movie drew from *Platoon*'s success completed *Salvador*'s transition from box-office failure to one of the most respected films of the 1980s.

The only real surprise was the omission of Charlie Sheen, who was splendid in the understated lead role of Chris Taylor. Perhaps the Academy considered him too understated or maybe even too young or too privileged to deserve an award. Oscars are sometimes awarded or denied for reasons far less substantial than these. Stone says that Sheen submerged his natural bad-boy quality for the role. Elizabeth Stone comments, "We had dinner one night at this trendy restaurant. There were about five or six of us at the table and Charlie walked in with this scarf around his neck. And then, at one point during the dinner, I noticed the scarf moved and I realized it was a snake. It was his pet boa. When the waiter realized what was around Charlie's neck, he couldn't move he was so scared. We all started laughing and the concierge came over and said, 'Sorry, sir, but no pets are allowed in the restaurant.' Charlie said, 'Hey, it's not going to bug anybody, it's just sitting here,' and the man said, 'I'm sorry, sir, but you're going to have to take it outside.' So he went out to put him in the car. When he came back, I looked at him and he tapped his pocket and smiled. He's such a bad boy, Charlie."

Sheen's likable nature was not only prevalent during the filming, but also during the promotion efforts for *Platoon*. Years before, much to his father's chagrin, he had a dragon's head tattooed on his right shoulder; on the *Platoon* press junket to Toronto, Stone goaded him into having eyeglasses put on the dragon. Oscar nomination or not, there was no question that *Platoon* had launched Sheen into the big time. Because he was the lead, his career perhaps benefited the most among the actors. After all, his is the first image we see—a fresh-faced recruit in a peaked fatigue hat brushing grit from his eye as he leaves the transport plane, caught in the yellow haze of an airstrip, amid body bags and malarial hollow-eyed combat vets. It's also the last shot we see in the film's reprise during the credits as the principal actors roll by in still shots. Sheen once asked Stone why he gave him the last card and Stone said, "I just thought it said it all, like saying, 'Remember, that's the way he was.'"

Because of *Platoon*'s popularity, a host of Vietnam-related projects received more attention, including *We Can Keep You Forever*, a BBC documentary about the mystery surrounding MIAs. The groundwork was laid for television shows like "Tour of Duty" and later "China Beach." In addition, at least four Vietnam war films that were in the works benefited when *Platoon*'s high grosses piqued studio interest and turned them from somewhat questionable to easily marketable films: Stanley Kubrick's *Full Metal Jacket*, Patrick Duncan's *84 Charlie Mopic*, Lionel Chetwynd's *Hanoi Hilton*, and John Irvin's *Hamburger Hill*.

One sure sign of success in Hollywood is backlash. With all the hoopla over *Platoon*, it was no surprise that its detractors began to gain a following of their own. The heart of the criticism leveled at *Platoon* was not that it wasn't a great movie about the Vietnam War, but that it wasn't *the* movie about the Vietnam War. Many people resented the public's mass acceptance of *Platoon* as the bible on what actually happened in Vietnam. Though he admitted that he didn't think any of the movies previously made about Vietnam had done it justice, Stone never maintained that he had made the ultimate Vietnam movie. "I'm not going to be so pretentious as to say this is *the* Vietnam War movie," he stated in interviews at the time. "I think there are many more that can be done. There are a thousand stories. A million stories."

Some of the criticism came from the vets themselves. Most of them agreed that *Platoon* looked and felt so much like the war that it brought back the sensory experience of it in an almost overpowering way, yet they resented the way it portrayed how soldiers handled the horrors they encountered. The simple truth is that each veteran has his own view of the war. Dale Dye elaborates: "Oliver took me along on the publicity jogs for *Platoon* and I fielded hundreds of questions from people who had a problem with something in the film because they didn't experience anything like it. I would ask them questions like 'What year were you in?' or 'Where were you? Chi-Wy? Okay, you were not in a drafted infantry outfit. You were in a Marine outfit. That is entirely different than Cu Chi in the 25th Infantry Division, and you've got to understand that.' Their problem was that they were worried people would think that *Platoon* was the way it was for all of us."

Despite its great popularity, *Platoon* remains controversial to this day. For Stone, Vietnam was always far more personal than it was political. He is mesmerized by exotic cultures and by the possibilities of America as reflected in its melting-pot civilization, and this enchantment crops up regularly in the settings and concerns of his movies. It is interesting to note that, after *Platoon*, he actually thought he had gotten Vietnam out of his system. Nothing could have been further from the truth. Like the allure of Joseph Conrad's *Lord Jim*, which first drew him to Vietnam, Stone became obsessed with this small Asian country. It is a place which encompasses the same contradictions that plague Stone's soul—the beautiful and the ugly, the sensitive and the brutal, the pure and the carnal. In many ways, Vietnam and Oliver Stone will always be inseparable.

> "I'm gonna remind you of this war for the rest of my life so what happened there never happens again."
>
> Ron Kovic in **BORN ON THE FOURTH OF JULY**

By mid-February, after winning the Golden Globe awards for Best Drama, Best Director, and Best Supporting Actor (Tom Berenger), *Platoon* was clearly the front runner for the Oscars and Hollywood was jovially patting itself on the back for making a big bold message movie. Now, when Stone read the Hollywood trades, he would see his movies competing with each other in the ads for the attention of Oscar voters. Despite the more personal nature of *Platoon*, Stone said at the time that he couldn't root for it over *Salvador*. "I've got as much of me invested in one as the other," he said. "They are both like my children. 'Platoon' is just a child that's been with me longer."

The Academy Awards were held on March 30, 1987. *Platoon* was up against some strong contenders for Best Picture—*A Room with a View*, *Hannah and Her Sisters*, *Children of a Lesser God*, and *The Mission*—but it won. The film also won for Editing (Claire Simpson) and Sound, and Stone won the Best Director Award. Many were surprised when neither Berenger nor Dafoe won for Best Supporting Actor. The award went to Michael Caine for his work in Woody Allen's *Hannah and Her Sisters*. Perhaps most disheartening for Stone was James Woods losing out to Paul Newman (*Color of Money*) for the Best Actor Award for *Salvador*. All in all, *Platoon* won four Oscars. The film everyone had refused to make for over ten years was the Best Picture. And Oliver Stone, who just a little over a year earlier was the man no one in Hollywood would let direct, was not only the Best Director, but the originator of a phenomenon. *Platoon* won the Best Picture Oscar, grossed $160 million, and helped millions of Americans understand for the first time what had gone wrong in Vietnam. Though he would be both loved and hated throughout his career, Oliver Stone had clearly shown himself as someone who risked everything to put what he believed on the screen.

Stone also won the Directors Guild of America Award and the British Academy Award for his direction of *Platoon*, and he immediately began marshaling this success into more projects. Besides moving *Wall Street* into production, Stone began rethinking *Born on the Fourth of July*, and was considering directing a script he had written based on Clifford Irving's novel, *Tom Mix and Pancho Villa*.

The Stones purchased a large home in Santa Monica, and many friends noticed moments of relative tranquility. Yet Stone was still wary; he didn't trust his success. Elizabeth says that every time they went out for a drive, he would make detours to pass by theaters where *Platoon* was playing, reassuring himself that the crowds were still there. "He'd stand outside the theater and listen to remarks," she says. "He was amazed that people liked it so much. He was kind of cute. He'd get mad at me when I didn't do it and say, 'Aren't you driving around?'"

Stone was forty and Elizabeth thirty-seven at the time, and he was still paying her $125 a week to type his screenplays. Sean was only two and Oliver adored him, playing with him constantly whenever he was home—but not changing him. "Oliver changed one diaper in two years," Elizabeth says. "It was an hour-long ordeal that ended with a bathroom full of used towels. It was the event of the afternoon, and they both had to tell me about it. The classic Oliver story is him making his own instant coffee. He put a pan full of water in the oven to boil."

Although the Stones now had a maid, Elizabeth still did most of the cooking and all the child rearing. She also kept a cheerful attitude through Stone's frequent mood swings. She was used to his anger and depression and knew that even the worst moods would soon pass. Elizabeth was also his front-line defense against the kind of isolation and doubt that had gotten him into heavy drug use. "I wouldn't go back to those excesses," he said at the time. "Life does not suffer fools gladly—twice. I'm more able to cope with the pressures. Now, I know to concentrate on the matters at hand. If you do good work, the rest follows. For me, that means keeping my head down, concentrating on the next project."

But this was only another way to escape the rising anxiety Stone felt whenever he slowed down long enough to listen to the sounds in his head. There was no question that he had triumphed over his personal demons, but they hadn't vacated the premises by any means. The glow of victory was always good for pushing the fears and the loneliness back down. The problem was that as soon as things got quiet, they came back.

Although Stone loved his child desperately, he was increasingly bothered by the fact that he received less attention from Elizabeth. "I told myself it didn't matter," he says, "but ever since Sean, I didn't feel she was enamored of me. It was like the child was what she really wanted and now that she had it, she wasn't as interested in me. I felt we weren't a team any more."

"You know the only thing that kills the Demon? . . . Love."
Mickey Knox in **NATURAL BORN KILLERS**

The majority of conflicts that began to divide Oliver and Elizabeth were rooted in a growing clash over how their child should be raised. Stone had been brought up with the concept of fatherly discipline deeply ingrained. Elizabeth, on the other hand, lost her father at an early age and had a difficult relationship with her stepfather, which left her feeling that such discipline had to be carefully monitored. The Stones had also changed as individuals since their marriage. When Oliver met Elizabeth, she was something of a radical. A former Socialist Party worker in San Francisco, she had even been investigated by the FBI. He saw her as rather a dangerous, freethinking figure, but now, after nearly six years of marriage, she was clearly the more conservative of the two. Though his own success had in a sense also made him more of a part of the establishment, Stone saw it as a liberation, the freedom to become more radical, to break away from the constraints of society rather than embrace them. They were growing apart.

Meanwhile, things were moving ahead with *Wall Street*. Stone and Weiser had gone to New York and researched the world of hot stocks, junk bonds, and corporate takeovers. "He was outrageous," Weiser recalls. "I remember being on the trading floor when one of the brokers was talking and Oliver said to me right in front of him, 'Watch this guy. He has a tic in his eye. Write that down.' And then we went to see Carl Icahn. We had a meeting at eight o'clock in the morning and I was about two minutes late and Oliver was frantic. He said, 'Where were you? I've been waiting.' And he was wearing a black jacket with a pink tie. He looked like a gangster, and he says, 'God, we're meeting a really important guy and you're not even wearing a tie? Jesus Christ, I can't go to meetings with you!'"

Besides Icahn, Stone and Weiser met with such Wall Street powers as John Gutfreund, Alan "Ace" Greenberg, Michael Milken, Asher Edelman, and SEC enforcement head Gary Lynch. "It was quite a world—lots of drugs, sex, parties," Stone said. "Guys like Icahn and Edelman are fascinating buccaneers. Half of me likes what they do because they shake up entrenched management bureaucracies. I'm generally on the side of the noncorporate types. I didn't want to make the raider character in the film a big ugly cat."

After returning from New York, Stone and Weiser began moving ahead on the script. "It went pretty fast," Weiser recalls. "I talked out my idea of the story and he told me things that he wanted. It was very free form. He gave me a lot of space in the first draft."

Weiser worked up the first draft and then Stone wrote another draft and they did changes back and forth. The script was initially called *Greed*, and in Stone's original draft, the lead character was a young Jewish broker named Freddie Goldsmith; but Stone decided to drop the Jewish angle and change the name to Bud Fox because he didn't want to add to the mistaken idea that Wall Street is controlled by Jews. He also had Charlie Sheen in mind for the role and knew Sheen's laid-back manner would prevent him from being convincing as a nervy, excitable Jew. There were many minor changes as well, but gradually the script began to take shape. Weiser says Stone was easy to work with: "Oliver was very accommodating. A lot of directors like to change lines just for the sake of changing them. That happens all the time; but Oliver doesn't do that. If it's good, he leaves it in. While I was writing it, Ivan Boesky was busted. I remember I had a scene where they were transferring money in an attaché case and Oliver said, 'That's so corny, get that out of the script.' And then he read the newspaper account of Boesky making a payoff with an attaché case full of money and he said, 'Put that back in the script.' So there were a lot of things where reality started to imitate the script."

Weiser was a worthy collaborator. He could plug into Stone's vision and ride out the storms of his passions. "I was doing my third film in three years so I had less time to write," Stone says, "and by working back and forth I think we developed the script more quickly. But no matter how busy I get, I never want to get away from writing. I write in my diary every day. My father used to say, 'Writing is ass plus seat.' It's very hard work. Screenwriters are always looked down upon, which is bullshit. Capra knew that he owed Robert Riskin, and Ford knew he owed Dudley Nichols. Hitchcock always had good writers, like Ernest Lehman. A mediocre director can make a good movie out of a good script, but a great director with a bad script cannot make a good movie. I always fret before I write a screenplay, get very nervous, very insecure. Writing is extremely anti-social. I used to get into a very depressed mode."

Stone has said that the Hal Holbrook character, a somewhat antiquated stockbroker who believed that honesty really was the best policy, was based on his father. While Weiser studied speeches of famed Wall Street powerhouses like Ivan Boesky, Sir James Goldsmith, and T. Boone Pickens, he says that some of millionaire corporate raider Gordon Gekko's lines were inspired by the business side of Oliver Stone. "When I was writing some of the dialogue," Weiser says, "I would listen to Oliver on the phone and sometimes he talks very rapid-fire, the way Gordon Gekko does. He'd leave messages on my machine, like, 'Where are you? Having a gourmet breakfast? Ten o'clock and you're not working. What are you doing? Playing with kids in the park?' And one time he said, 'The one thing you never do is everything I tell you to do' . . . and then he told me to do twenty different things.

"It was like working with a Marine general. I kept forgetting to bring these files he wanted over and one time he said, 'The next time you come here, write a note and pin it to your fucking head to bring those files over.' So I came over the next day and I had this note glued to my forehead that said, 'Bring SCC Files,' and I sat down and Oliver came over and looked at me and said, 'I bet you still forgot.' But the great thing about Oliver is that he doesn't mask his emotions. He's very honest about how he feels. It's all right there on his face. He's very sensitive and very vulnerable and he's not afraid to show that, and this is in Hollywood where practically everybody puts on a mask."

True to his method of working, Stone insists that, as the script developed, the Wall Street environment became less important: "It became more about the boy. He could have been a cop, he could have been in Vietnam, he could have been a soldier. Wall Street became background. I start with an individual and a moral equation."

Stone took the *Wall Street* script to John Daly to see if he wanted to be involved, but Daly declined, believing, according to Stone, that audiences wouldn't go for a movie about people who were making millions of dollars. The big budget was also a factor. Since Stone needed to shoot in New York, *Wall Street* would require a budget in excess of $15 million, which would have been a huge risk for Hemdale. Stone and producer Ed Pressman then took the project to 20th Century Fox, which loved the idea. For Fox, it was a medium-budget film.

As Stone completed his script, 20th Century-Fox began working the many merchandising angles afforded by a film like *Wall Street*. One scene, for example, had the main character taking a magazine from his pocket and referring to it as "the bible." *Forbes* magazine offered to run two full-page ads for the movie for free if the magazine used was their own (an equivalent value of $83,000 at the time). Later in the script, Wall Street honcho Gordon Gekko buys a magazine at a newsstand. *Fortune* magazine offered two free full-page ads ($103,000 value) to be used in the scene. While this kind of trade can be lucrative, it can also lead to problems, as Stone describes: "Actually, Malcolm Forbes wanted Gekko to be on the cover of *Forbes* in one scene in the film, but I wanted it to be *Fortune*, so I nixed the *Forbes* deal. Malcolm Forbes was furious and in the next few weeks ran the most awful story on Ed Pressman. Ed was trying to go public and *Forbes* went after his offer and destroyed his chances. Forbes was a very petty man."

There were other tie-ins as well. A liquor distributor of upscale brands, Carillon, offered to supply all the liquor needed as props for the film as well as the refreshments for the wrap party, any premieres, and special events involving the film. Peugeot offered one car for Bud Fox to drive on screen and another to give away in a national sweepstakes promoting the film. Godiva Chocolates suggested creating a *Wall Street* chocolate bar backed by elaborate point of purchase displays in all their retail outlets. Evian water offered to fit its bottles with special collars featuring the title treatment of the film in exchange for screen exposure. Bufferin/Advil proposed paying $50,000 as a production subsidy if Bud Fox would take their product when a client gives him a headache. And Motorola offered to provide their new "8000-X" mobile cellular phones for any scenes, as well as two free units for promotional use or any purpose Stone wanted.

Stone responded positively to some of these offers, but not all, taking care to avoid anything that might overhype or trivialize the film. The headache remedy made sense, as did the cellular phones and a few other ideas, but he nixed other proposals, including a *Wall Street* chocolate bar. One thing was clear, however; an Oliver Stone film now meant big-time business.

"Bought my way into this club and now every one of these ivy league schmucks is sucking my kneecaps. . . ."

Gordon Gekko in **WALL STREET**

In May 1987, filming began. Charlie Sheen was again cast in the lead—this time as ambitious stockbroker Bud Fox. Sheen, probably the hottest young actor in Hollywood after *Platoon* took Best Picture honors, passed on dozens of scripts to work with Stone again. Also starring this time was Michael Douglas as the powerbroker, corporate raider Gordon Gekko.

Douglas describes his initial reaction to the script: "When I read *Wall Street*, I thought it was a great part. It was a long script, and there were some incredibly long and intense monologues to open with. I'd never seen a screenplay where there were two or three pages of single-spaced type for a monologue. I thought, whoa! I mean, it was unbelievable. So I assumed this was like an early draft and we'd be cutting this and that. My producer side would have suggested some structural changes, but I was trying to take off my producer's hat and get into the joy of acting and just look at the part. Moneywise, they weren't offering a lot, but I'd done several pictures with Fox, I had a long history there. And everyone had high hopes. Oliver was just coming off of *Platoon* and I was very appreciative that an Academy Award-winning director was considering me for one of the leads in his next movie."

Douglas's decision to take the role was also influenced by a desire to move his acting career in another direction: "At that time I was looking for darker parts than *Romancing the Stone* or all those sensitive young man roles I used to play. I was looking for parts with an edge. They are genuinely more fun to play. That was really the year. I went back to New York to get more credibility as an actor by doing more theater work and it turned out to be the year I did both *Fatal Attraction* and *Wall Street*."

The rest of the cast included Daryl Hannah, Martin Sheen, Terence Stamp, Sean Young, Hal Holbrook, James Spader, Saul Rubinek, Sylvia Miles, and John C. McGinley. It was a big Hollywood cast and Stone was wary—already dodging comparisons to Michael Cimino, who after winning the Oscar for *The Deer Hunter* followed with *Heaven's Gate*, the most costly cinematic blunder of all time. "Sure, I have those fears of a 'Heaven's Gate,'" Stone said at the time. "I'd rather now be doing a smaller movie, but I'm doing this. It's a medium-sized movie for New York, under $20 million. Same number of shooting days as 'Platoon.' It will require a lot of discipline to bring it in."

Actually, *Wall Street* was budgeted at $17,680,000, with Michael Douglas receiving $1 million, Charlie Sheen $650,000, Daryl Hannah $500,000, and Martin Sheen $500,000. Oliver Stone was paid $685,000 as director and another $45,000 as writer. The writing fee was practically the Guild minimum as Stone gave most of the screenplay money to Stanley Weiser, who received $135,000.

Though he wasn't in the million dollar a picture club yet, Stone had far exceeded his salary for *Platoon* and *Salvador*. He was, however, about to make considerable money from his points in *Platoon*. Though the film had grossed over $160 million, Stone had so far received less than $300,000. While his contract with Hemdale called for him to receive a small percentage of the profits, Hollywood is notorious for getting around these payments, and it is almost standard practice on a big hit to use creative bookkeeping to obscure profits and inflate expenses. Legal means are often necessary to collect, usually resulting in great delay while a court-ordered team of accountants goes over the books. Stone had neither the time nor patience for such things and so, before any payments were due, he arranged a buyout agreement with Hemdale, under which he would receive a flat rate based on certain monies received. Although it meant paying up sooner, John Daly knew that he would save a great deal of money in the long run, so he agreed.

Of course, after *Platoon* went through the roof, Stone received an enormous amount of offers to write and direct. "I was the golden boy, the flavor of the month," he admits. "I couldn't deal with it. I just kept my head down and focused on *Wall Street*. My attitude was, plunge on, do the next film. I knew it would never do the same box office, get the same great reviews. It was inevitable that *Platoon* would be the one against which the others would be measured. The only way to top that is like Spielberg did, go from a *Jaws* to a *Raiders*, to an *E.T.* then to *Schindler's List* and *Jurassic Park*."

"We're all just one trade away from humility."

Marvin in **WALL STREET**

Though Stone now could have probably made $750,000 as a screenwriter and at least a million to direct, he wouldn't hire out. He wanted to do his own projects, even if it meant he'd be doing them for less money.

Next to the script, casting is all-important to a film's success. Helping with this task for *Wall Street* were Risa Bramon García and Billy Hopkins. The film marked Stone's first association with the casting team he would use through his next seven films. "We got a call to go and meet him the week that *Platoon* opened," Bramon García recalls now. "It was at his hotel room and Elizabeth was there and this strange Oriental man with dark glasses who sort of scared me. I later found out that was Alex Ho. Oliver was a little adversarial, and I felt like we were being challenged and tested. I remember walking out thinking this guy is really intense."

One of Stone's early casting decisions was Michael Douglas, which proved to be an excellent choice. Douglas was not the person 20th Century Fox initially wanted for the role. They wanted Warren Beatty, who wasn't all that interested in the part. Stone approached Richard Gere, but Gere passed. Then Stone settled on Douglas and fought for him with the studio.

Not all his casting choices for the film were as good, and Stone readily admits he made a few blunders, most notable of which was Daryl Hannah as Sheen's girlfriend, Darien Taylor. Hannah, though a fine actress in the right part, was miscast for *Wall Street*. "If I'd known Oliver better, I would have never let him cast Daryl Hannah for that part," Bramon García says. "But it was my first movie with him and I had to be careful. We had Mary Stuart Masterson and Mary Elizabeth Mastrantonio and a bunch of other people standing by to replace her. But it was that whole shiksa goddess thing. He sort of saw her running on the beach and he couldn't get it out of his head. Bob Richardson kept saying to me, 'Get rid of her.' I ended up coaching her and she got better during rehearsals. She was scared of it. I remember saying to her, 'Daryl, my God, you can play a fish.' She said, 'Yeah but I understood that.' Also at that time, she was going through an abusive relationship with Jackson Browne and was flying back to L.A. every week to see him. She wanted off the movie but she didn't know how to ask for it and no one knew what to do. I remember driving around the Hamptons with Alex Ho saying, 'We gotta get rid of her, we gotta get rid of her.' Now, I would fight Oliver on a choice like that."

Stone and Hannah had problems throughout the film, and she criticized him in the press. He has never responded to that criticism publicly until now. Stone admits that as soon as rehearsals began, he recognized a problem with Hannah but, coming off his Oscar for Best Director, he was too proud to admit he'd made a mistake. "The rehearsal process is very intense and very revealing," Stone says. "It's always hard for the director. After auditioning actors, meeting with actors, there finally comes a day when you all interact, and then, if something doesn't work, that's a very tough problem. Daryl Hannah was not happy doing the role and I should have let her go. All my crew wanted to get rid of her after one day of shooting. My pride was such that I kept saying I was going to make it work. To let her go would have hurt Daryl's feelings. I worked very hard to make that work, and I think she accepted it passively. Her reviews were negative, but I think she did all right. She resented me for having her in the film and said negative things about me to the press which astounded me. I think she's an unhappy woman and probably we were both wrong. She should have left it at that."

"We had rehearsals for like a week or ten days in New York," Michael Douglas says. "And we all went through the script a number of times. The girls were uncomfortable. I used to joke about how the director always takes aside the leading actress and talks to her and sort of coddles her while the leading man just stands around and waits until they get back. There is a power element involved. A lot of directors are patriarchs, like father figures. Actors are like children that have to show their insecurities in front of a camera. They need this figure to kind of bolster them. Oliver's not like that. He is not afraid to be your adversary. He is not afraid to let you hang out there in the wind and feel insecure so you will work to overcome it. He will not patronize you, and some ladies particularly have a problem with the male comradely thing. Of course Oliver has some baggage he carries from the war, his mother, and movies he's made before. He's not going to dote on you whether you're a man or a woman. The two female characters were never that developed, either. My wife's part was sort of just there, and Daryl's part was really not well developed. I think it was miscast. Daryl was uncomfortable being a high-paid energetic New York interior decorator and she never overcame it."

Hannah, who prides herself on being natural, had problems relating to her character, who was supposed to be an artificial, materialistic person. She retained a voice coach to try to turn her mixed Southern California/Chicago accent into a nasal, affected, New York upper-class inflection, but it remained another stumbling block. Stone admits he was tough on her occasionally, because he was so displeased with her "wanness and passiveness." "She needs a very strong director," he said at the time. "I'm not sure I succeeded."

Had this been the only problem, the press during the shooting of the film wouldn't have been so bad and Oliver Stone might have never acquired a reputation for having difficulties dealing with actresses. Unfortunately for Stone, Sean Young was also very verbal in the press. "Actually the problems with Sean grew out of the mistake I made in casting Daryl," Stone says, speaking out on this too for the first time. "As soon as Sean got on the set the first day, she made no bones about it and said I should fire Daryl and give her the part. 'I should be playing that role,' she said, and then she moved her stuff into Daryl's trailer. Daryl let her. Daryl was intimidated by her. Sean was quite aggressive about it, which irritated me at the time, and irritated the crew. But she was dead right. In her Cassandra-like madness she had made the point clearly that I should have switched her to the larger role and made Daryl the wife of Michael Douglas. It would have been much better then. I clashed with Sean because of her stubbornness, headstrongness and ruthlessness, but this is a rude business. You have to get to the point fast. You only have a certain amount of days."

Weiser remembers Young causing trouble on the set and agrees with Stone that switching her role with Hannah's might've worked. "The first time I ever saw Sean Young, I was talking to Oliver. All of a sudden Sean is walking backwards toward us with a Polaroid camera. She falls right on top of him and then takes a perfect photograph of her sitting on his lap. She was like that. She had all these gimmicks."

Most people in the crew felt the same way. One member, who asked to remain anonymous, described a scene between Young and Charlie Sheen: "There was a scene with Charlie Sheen where she's supposed to join him in the shot and she sat down so hard and moved right over and knocked him half out of the frame. She just took over the frame."

The worst episode with Young was actually the fault of Sheen who, after days of putting up with her antics, taped a sign on her back that read: *"Biggest Cunt in the World."* When Young failed to notice the sign for a considerable amount of time, Sheen had his revenge in the continued laughter of crew and cast. Naturally, once Young discovered it, there was hell to pay. She launched into a tirade lambasting Sheen and Stone, since the director is the person in authority on the set who in her mind should have stopped the joke as soon as it began. Stone, who says he never saw the sign until Young discovered it, wishes the incident never happened, but admits he would be reluctant to interfere if such a thing happened again. "It wasn't just Charlie being upset with her. The problem was that I think Charlie reflected the entire crew's feelings, male and female, about Sean's behavior, which was highly unprofessional. Things like not being there on time, being unprepared for rehearsals, not knowing her lines, making other actors stand around while she asked dumb questions."

Naturally, all of these hassles affected Stone during the shooting. Under the pressure of such situations, he tends not to handle the press well and his real feelings often escape, sometimes making him sound silly. He was quoted at this time as saying, "I love to be around women, they're very pretty. Except some of the actresses are too neurotic, some of them are driving me nuts."

The problems with Young continued, according to Stone, and came to a head when Young complained that one of her lines had been given to Hannah. She said she didn't want to shoot the scene if she didn't get to say the line. "I told her to forget it then and leave," Stone says. "There were several incidents, but that was the last. She didn't want to rehearse and she wasn't prepared, so I told her to leave."

Despite all this, Stone feels he doesn't have problems working with actresses in general. "That was the only unprofessional relationship I've had with an actress," he says now. "I've had failures with actresses, but not these kinds of problems. I think I've succeed with actors about eighty percent of the time. Oftentimes the twenty percent in which I fail is not seen because it's cut out of the movie. But that's with men or women. It's not a gender problem. Some of the actresses are high-strung but so are some of the actors. Some females may be used to a more flowery approach than the way I direct, but that's just how I direct. It's the same with males or females. I treat both the same."

(Both Sean Young and Daryl Hannah refused to be interviewed for this book, although they were offered quote approval and the option to read what was being said about them before they commented.)

With six more years and six more movies under his belt, Stone like he has this strange part of him which feels good that you cared enough to attack him.

"I think he was trying to toughen me up for the role," Douglas continues, "with his own sick and devious way of getting me to dig down deeper. And also by not being afraid of being disliked if it meant that he was making a better movie. As a director, he's not afraid to have you focus your anger at him. Hell, part of him probably likes it. He wanted a little more of an edge, and that was his way of getting it. Both on and off camera I was developing that Gekko mystique—'If you want to go eyeball to eyeball, that's fine with me'—that kind of thing, and the anger I was feeling toward him played right into that. That toughening-up process was helpful. Then I began to draw on my producing background as well. It all worked together."

In the end, Douglas felt that working with Stone was one of the high points of his career. "He takes more chances than anybody," Douglas says. "He really puts faith in the actors and the people around him. He really treats people like big boys and girls. He allows you the opportunity and demands the results. Nobody I've ever worked with will allow actors as much opportunity as he does. He's not the kind of man you can tell very easily that you really like him, but I do. I always have. Ever since the last day of shooting."

Douglas's wardrobe in the film is an essential ingredient of the powerful persona he creates as Gordon Gekko. Costume designer Ellen Mirojnick studied the wardrobes of dozens of real-life Wall Street figures such as Ivan Boesky, T. Boone Pickens, Carl Icahn, Asher Edelman, and Donald Trump. "Gekko was a composite of how the superrich looked then," Mirojnick says. "Actually, no two of them looked alike. When you get to that kind of position of power, you create your own style."

Mirojnick went to Manhattan tailor Alan Flusser for Gekko's clothes because of Flusser's reputation for mastering the power look. By the time Mirojnick and Flusser were finished, Douglas's wardrobe cost $28,000, about 17 percent of the film's $165,000 wardrobe budget. It consisted primarily of eleven suits ($975 to $1,500 each) made of English and Italian worsteds, twenty-four Swiss and English cotton shirts ($250 each), and assorted handmade silk ties, all of which were given to Michael Douglas when shooting was finished.

Douglas says the wardrobe and overall look given to his character really helped his performance: "It was another key for me to Gekko—

today is convinced that the problems with Sean Young on the set could have been averted with better casting. "When she took the role, *No Way Out* was still being edited. I thought I was helping her career by giving her a small role in *Wall Street*, but little did I know that she already had done a bigger thing with *No Way Out*. She was probably resentful about playing the smaller role; but in that case, she shouldn't have taken it."

Bob Richardson agrees that *Wall Street* was somewhat miscast, but cities other problems as well: "Very early on Oliver had an attitude, which was I think partially a result of the success of *Platoon*. See, what Oliver does is he bounces. Immediately after a film is finished, he wants to be working on another one. And in *Wall Street*, I don't believe the script was at the level it needed to be. He was vacationing at the time in Hawaii, and I know he'd get calls from Alex [Ho] and whoever else, and his response was, 'Well, I'll work on it later.'"

In spite of the controversy, or maybe in part because of the energy he draws from such things, Stone pulled the divergent elements together and created a powerful film which did a good box office. "There is no question that *Wall Street* was successful, and Oliver made it happen," Richardson adds. "See, what happens with all of his moments of insanity is that they're always followed by a moment of sanity. So even if he becomes super-indulgent, he has a real intuitive sense of finding a place of sanity inside the insanity. He worked very well with Michael Douglas."

Stone's work with Douglas is the stuff Hollywood legends are made of. Stone had been warned by a studio executive that since Douglas was also a producer, he would spend too much time in his trailer reading scripts and being on the phone to Los Angeles. But nothing was farther from the truth. Douglas knew from the beginning that this could be a big role for him and was always on time and ready to shoot. He admits he was nervous right from the start and a bit shocked when Stone gave him three pages of monologue the first day. "I was edgy," Douglas acknowledges. "I was having a hard time trying to find out how much of myself to bring to this part. Early on, I made a big mistake because I kept waiting for him to cut these long monologues. I was doing them during rehearsal, but kinda waiting for him to cut. And he never cut. We kept getting closer to the shooting schedule, so I kind of made a suggestion at one point like, 'Say, are you thinking about cutting this down?' And he said, 'No, do you need me to cut it down?' I said, 'No him and it shocked him, too. No director had ever told him that he looked like he couldn't act. But, in fact, it was terrible. He hadn't really learned the lines or ingested them. We had to do fifteen, twenty takes Day One and Two with everything he did."

Stone acknowledges that Douglas's role was a tough one right from the start, but still believes he did the right thing. "I think the criticism helped because he did get better. When he found it, he locked in and he went. He was excellent. By the time he saw the dailies, he was doing so great I didn't want to screw it up by arguing with him over the first couple of days. He was a little mad for a while, but along with his father, he thanked me at the Oscars."

Once he clicked into the role, Douglas was superb, but throughout the shoot he had to continually work on memorizing the lengthy monologues. Often, Stone would make some last-minute change and throw him a new curve. Douglas recalls, "I begged them to please resolve things like the names of companies, because of the size of Gordon Gekko's speeches. And in the eleventh hour, all of a sudden Cromwell Papers was now called Teldar [due to legal requirements]. And I'd go, 'No, no.' I'd have this whole rhythm going—just throwing these names off the tip of my tongue—and now in the back of my mind, all I'm doing is trying to remember the name changes. Oliver was pretty much word perfect as far as the writing. I had gotten into some sloppy habits like putting handles on things and he'd correct me whenever I went off."

Once their initial clashes were over, Stone and Douglas settled into a working pattern. But there were things that kept Douglas smoldering. "He would never say anything complimentary," Douglas says. "His style was, 'Let me see whether you can cut it.' He's brutally honest. I tried not to clash with him. I didn't say he was a prick. I mean, I didn't know what his exact motives were. I've got a lot of respect for him, and I kept reminding myself, 'Hey, he offered you this part and it's a great part.' But I did get upset when we did the 'greed is good' speech."

This lengthy speech has become a classic among film enthusiasts— one of the best-written and best-delivered monologues in modern film. "By then I had it down," Douglas recalls today. "I worked and I worked and when it came to that scene I was ready. I got it in one take. Every fucking camera angle. I had that motherfucker nailed. Closeups? Okay, do your closeups. And we did the closeups. One take. So, as I was doing it, I started watching Oliver. He was right next to the camera. And he's

not even looking at me. He has a script over there and he's reading it, making sure that every word is correct. Every single 'but' and 'the.' He looks at the script through the whole thing. Doesn't even look at me or the camera. Then, after I nail it, he just says, 'Okay, fine, let's move on.' So I pulled him aside and we had it out. 'Hey,' I said, 'I been busting my ass here. I mean, it's a fucking six-page monologue. I do one take, and you're not even looking at me. You got a problem?' There's a mean streak in Oliver. There is nothing wrong with having a healthy strong ego as a writer and director, and maybe the piece called for some of that kind of tension, but I thought that that was beyond the call. And, to this day, I think he struggles between writing great parts and the fear of having someone deliver them too well—to the point of things getting out of balance for him."

"I'll never forget how angry Michael Douglas got at Oliver that day," Risa Bramon García recalls. "Oliver wouldn't look at him and all he would say to him after each take was something like, 'Okay, on the third line, you didn't say this word.' Douglas was seething, and I went up to Oliver and said, 'Hey, Michael is really getting pissed off,' and he said, 'Good!' It didn't hurt him, it didn't hurt Michael. Michael had to be so focused on the words and so focused on holding back his feelings that you saw incredible concentration and power in that scene."

Stone claims he always wants the best performance he can get from an actor, and that if he wasn't watching Douglas all the time it was because he was concentrating on hearing the lines. "I did look up at him sometimes. He just didn't see it. If you look at the scene, you'll notice that Michael's eyes are moving all the time so he couldn't have been watching me. I don't worry about each word in the script. I'm more concerned with the spirit of the scene being what I originally intended."

Douglas believes a lot of power can be generated by feeding off one's anger in this kind of situation and, in retrospect, is philosophical about Stone's methods. "I use anger a lot," Douglas says. "I use it as a form of energy. Oliver and I kept our respective distances. What happened was he allowed me to use my anger toward him in the role. I had never done it before, but a lot of times, I was acting to him. I loved to turn right to him when we were filming and look him right in the eyes and talk to him. Say the lines right to him. I think he probably loved that. I mean, if you give it back to him a little bit, man, he loves it. It's the hair, cufflinks, suspenders, immediately gave me a costume. Gordon was what you might call a counterpuncher; he'd always give the jab while the other guy was winding up, so he was always in your face one beat before. A city guy, very clean. Just like a white shark, you know, swimming and eating, swimming and eating. Anything that's in the way, just go right through it."

The shark motif was designed by Stone to be a deliberate undercurrent in the film, even to the point of camera movement. "We did enormous amounts of moving camera in this film," Stone says, "because we are making a movie about sharks, about feeding frenzies. Bob and I wanted the camera to become a predator. There is no letup until you get to the fixed world of Charlie's father, where the stationary camera gives you a sense of immutable values."

Since he internalizes the essence of each of his films, during *Wall Street* Stone found his escape from the pressure by living the high life of a wealthy New York power trader—expensive suits, fancy restaurants, exotic nightclubs, and lots of parties. One of the people he often went out with was Chuck Pfeiffer, a Vietnam vet turned writer and actor whom Stone had met shortly before filming began. "I interviewed him for *Interview* magazine," Pfeiffer recalls, "and we related pretty well. Then, I heard through a scenic designer that he was going to cast me in the film. He cast me as this aging hustler, kind of a lost, cartoonlike figure. I wasn't in the movie that much, but because I am a writer, he let me play with it a bit. Right in the beginning of the picture, Charlie says, 'Hey Chucky, how's the ladykiller?' I respond, 'I'm still looking for the right eighteen-year-old wife.' And Charlie comes back, 'How do I get to be like you?' And I say, 'Genetics, a Yale education, and the right tailor.'"

Pfeiffer and Stone went out regularly during the shooting and were often joined by Douglas, Sheen, and Willem Dafoe. "Oliver wanted to party," Pfeiffer says. "He has great magnetism, a certain Brando quality. People can't put their finger on it, but it draws them. He makes people do what he wants done in the manner in which they want to do it. Which is a great technique. He doesn't inhibit people. When he gets irritable, he has this bratty side, but he's very strong. He takes chances with himself, with his work, with his life. And Oliver won't ask anybody to do anything that he wouldn't do himself."

Willem Dafoe agrees up to a point: "Oliver's struggling with demons. He's conflicted. It gives everything he does a certain kind of drama, a certain passion. He's not at peace."

This was becoming more evident in Stone's personal life. Though he'd seen a few women here and there, during the filming of *Salvador* and *Platoon*, for example, it wasn't until now that he regularly began to have affairs. He had been unhappy in his marriage for a while and wasn't sure what to do about it. The cracks in his relationship with Elizabeth widened when the success of *Platoon* required him to spend more time away from home. And no matter how hard he worked, the hotel bed always looked empty. Women were coming on to him all the time. It was easy. All he had to do was stop resisting.

Charlie Sheen was also having his difficulties. Younger and not as experienced in balancing wild partying with such a demanding workload as the others, he had problems with the aftereffects. "Charlie would show up on the set screwed up from the night before a lot," Stone says. "He was only getting a couple hours of sleep. I think it affected him. He was good in the role, but he might've been better. He let me down a bit, but I like Charlie. He's gotten himself together since then."

Stone took pains for authenticity on *Wall Street*, hiring a former deputy mayor of New York, Ken Lipper, as a consultant to bridge the gap with the wary people in the financial district who felt they'd already had enough bad publicity. Lipper, the managing director of Salomon Brothers, helped Stone persuade the city's traders that the film would be objective and show both sides of the Street. After Stone shot a scene in which Lou Mannheim, the honest, hardworking, but somewhat old-fashioned broker (based on Stone's father) succumbs to insider trading because he "needs the money," Lipper warned that audiences might then assume that every broker was dishonest. On his advice Stone cut the scene. "I wanted to show the ambiguity of everything," Stone says. "Even my father took tips. But it would have left the wrong impression."

Lipper also suggested that Stone modify the ruthlessness of Gordon Gekko, but Stone flatly refused. Besides helping with details on the set—how brokers talk to clients, write out tickets, and even hold a telephone—Lipper also got the actors into Salomon Brothers, the 21 Club, Le Cirque, and the New York Stock Exchange, the first time a film crew was ever allowed there. "We actually shot on the floor while they were trading," Stone says. "A lot of the older traders were upset because they were trying to make money and we were creating a disturbance, but there were many more Vietnam veterans on the floor than I had imagined, and they had seen *Platoon*."

Stone even had Lipper do a cameo in the film as he did with another noted Wall Streeter, Jeff Beck of Drexel Burnham Lambert. (Later, the *Wall Street Journal* would reveal that Beck had been lying to Stone about being a Vietnam vet and other things, triggering a scandal in the New York financial press.)

Before building and furnishing a huge $500,000 trading room in a vacant office space near Wall Street, Stone's crews spent days photographing layouts and observing the mood and rhythm of trading rooms at Salomon Brothers and other firms. Stephen Hendrickson's production design retained authenticity while adding excitement, turning Gordon Gekko's ultramodern office, for example, into a financial war room that implies awesome power.

For his role, Charlie Sheen met frequently with David Brown, a broker convicted of insider trading who served as an adviser on the film. "The main feeling I got from Brown," Stone said, "was one of extreme isolation. He was an ex-convict, and it showed in a lot of his actions. I tried to get that feeling of loneliness and isolation in Charlie's character. Charlie responded very emotionally to his meetings with David and he got very emotional over playing a character who gets arrested. The idea of playing an informer was tough for him, but all those Wall Street guys made deals after they were arrested."

The effort to capture Brown's isolation in Sheen's character may have been what led many to criticize the actor's performance in the film as being too one-dimensional. Several top critics argued that Sheen was bland, playing the same emotion throughout the role. Of course, with Douglas typifying the perfect Machiavellian businessman, Sheen was expected to be understated. This is the same kind of portrayal that he was praised for in *Platoon*, and the reason Stone thought he would work so well in *Wall Street*.

Sheen, who invested $20,000 in the market during the filming in order to intensify his feelings for the part, admitted having trouble with a few scenes, particularly the love scenes with Daryl Hannah. "She carried those scenes. She had to set the tempo for me. I was like losing my mind. There were too many witnesses, I guess. It felt weird. I had trouble with romantic sexual scenes in those days. I was more comfortable killing somebody."

The worst scene for Sheen occurred late one day when he was rushed script changes for a monologue he was to do while sitting at his desk watching the Quotron, the computer brokers use to scan stock quotations. "They gave me, I swear, a whole half page of dialogue, handwritten," Sheen says. "I blew it. I taped my lines to the Quotron off camera and I'm reading the lines. I can't memorize print like that. You got five ADs, producers tapping their feet, Oliver scratching his head. And it's down to me. We did it and it's in the film and it sucks in the film. I knew it sucked when I did it. I was really pissed. To walk away from a scene without getting another shot—people will see the absence of performance."

Stone claims he got what he wanted in that scene, but Sheen was quite upset at the time, and after it was over he was seething in a room off the set when he noticed a baseball on the floor. Before he thought much about it the young actor fired his best fastball at the wall. The ball not only smashed right through the plywood wall, but nearly beaned a crew member on the other side. "I threw it as hard as I could," Sheen admits. "It's outrageous to vent that kind of total frustration. That's what I had to overcome in those days—moving from acting to reality without losing it."

For Sheen, some of the best moments occurred after his father arrived. "Working with Dad was amazing. He's so centered and focused, and he's one of the greatest performers of our time. He arrived the last two weeks of the shoot when we were starting to drag a bit. He was like a white knight. His energy picked us up. The hospital scene was the last day. It was heavy, what with the sadness of the good-byes to everybody and the scene itself. I improvised the ending, the kiss on his forehead. I think in five minutes, my pop and me, we showed a closeness most guys don't have with their dads in a lifetime. We never really loved each other more as friends than we did right there."

Shooting in New York was a nightmare as crowds of passers-by continually hindered filming. Since he didn't have the right to stop people from passing through, Stone hired two hundred extras to fill the sidewalk and thereby discourage people from lingering in the vicinity. He also tried to hire some real derelicts, but New York law dictated that the first 125 extras in a scene had to be union. This meant he'd have to use 125 actors in every scene to get one real bum, so Stone tried to hire union extras as bums, but ended up cutting all the bum shots because they looked fake.

Stanley Weiser visted the set a few times. Unlike so many other experiences he's had as a Hollywood screenwriter, he was treated very well. "Oliver was great," Weiser says. "He told me what he was doing and the moves he was making, and I must say that was a very different experience than I was used to on the movies. Also, there was very little improvisation from the script. It was pretty much shot the way we wrote it, and that is also pretty rare."

Weiser reports that Stone was still given to crazy impulses during the shooting: "One time we were driving around and he was reading some other script when suddenly, the script went flying out the window. He just threw it out the window. He said it sucked. The pages were flying all over the street."

Elizabeth Stone also visited the set and took some photographs. "For *Salvador* and *Platoon* I was credited as assistant to Oliver Stone. Of course, I've always taken photos, but I couldn't be credited for that then because of the union. Oliver wanted to give me credit for something on the set. Then we took a trip to Japan, and while we were there we discovered that some women have an official title which is called *naijo no ko*. And it translates as 'success from inside help.' It's a term they use in official language to refer to wives of politicians, businessmen, celebrities, or whomever to imply that because of the wife's help that person has become a success. So, from *Wall Street* on, if you look through the credits after the assistants, around the secretary/assistants stage you'll see '*Naijo No Ko*—Elizabeth Stone.' It was his idea to do it, and I've always liked it."

But all was not well and Elizabeth soon discovered that Stone was occasionally seeing other women. After she returned to Los Angeles, she called and threatened to divorce him. The clash came near the end of filming, and Stone had no other choice but to push on.

Besides the usual pressures of film directing and the anxiety that his marriage might be over, Stone found himself in a race against the clock to finish shooting before a strike was called by the Directors Guild. The Guild had never before called a strike in its fifty-one-year history, but negotiations with movie and television producers over issues like royaties on pay-per-view and videocassette sales had come down to the wire, and a strike call was expected at any time during the last week of shooting. Stone responded to the threat by working the company night and day. He came in seven days ahead of schedule and close to $2 million under budget. *Wall Street* was shot in fifty-three days, one day less than *Platoon*.

Shooting wrapped on July 4, 1987. Though it had been a much bigger-budgeted project, loaded with experienced professionals and shot entirely on American soil, the problems with the cast had made *Wall Street* in many ways harder than *Platoon*.

Shortly after Stone returned to L.A., he and Elizabeth made up and divorce plans were called off. In the end, Elizabeth decided to give her husband the benefit of the doubt. Stone also wanted to believe that their relationship could return to what it once was, but deep down he knew it was unlikely.

"You must treat the things that you love with irony. There's more of a chance then that they'll survive."

Dmitri Shostakovich in **DEFIANCE**

Editing *Wall Street* was easier than the battles Stone encountered during *Salvador*, but not as charmed as the *Platoon* sessions. As is always the case with Stone's films, a number of the problems came from overwriting the script. Many scenes that had been written and shot would now have to be cut in order to make the film flow and come in at an acceptable length. About twenty of the eighty speaking parts were eliminated in the process.

While he was editing, it was announced that Stone had been awarded the ACLU Foundation Torch of Liberty Award. A few months later he attended the award ceremonies in Los Angeles. His acceptance speech on September 17 concluded with the following lines:

Our own country has become a military-industrial monolith dedicated to the Cold War, in many ways as rigid and as corrupt at the top as our rivals, the Soviets. We have become the enemy—with a security state now second to none. Today we have come to live in total hatred, fear, and the desire to destroy. Bravo. Fear and conformity have triumphed. . . . Where does a man or woman turn? How do we fight this? What do we do? How can we possibly win against the overwhelming force of this government of the future, this Darth Vaderian empire? . . . I don't know. I am lost . . . but somewhere on the back burner of a bewildered mind, I feel I gotta go back to those movies I believed in as a kid . . . where my hero is facing certain extinction surrounded on all sides by enemy swordsmen, but, by some shining light of inner force and greater love, turns the tables of fate and triumphs over all odds.

On August 19, Stone finally received the first installment of the *Platoon* buyout deal. He had made a flat rate deal with John Daly for around $9 million, and this first check was for $4,129,673. Astronomical as that sounds, the percentage points on the film, if he'd been able to collect them, would have been much greater. But Stone didn't have time to waste on lawyers and lawsuits. He still had a lot he wanted to do. He needed complete financial security, and now he had it.

"I'm talking rich pal, rich enough to fly in your own jet, rich enough not to waste time."

Gordon Gekko in **WALL STREET**

But Stone also knew that more than money was needed to accomplish his goals. Equally important was having a team of people he could trust. With that in mind, Stone did something very rare in the film industry—he gave money away. Bob Marshall, Stone's attorney, discusses something that Stone has never made public: "He gave participation to some of the people who made significant contributions on the film [*Platoon*]. And the interesting thing was that he gave these points away when he knew the film was going to be a big success. It wasn't like giving a piece of nothing, like points in a film in the beginning stages when no knows what's going to happen. This was at a point in time when he knew the film was going to make big money. Also, these participations weren't part of the contractual relationships, it was just a show of generosity and gratitude. Oliver's style is to push people to the edge to perform in ways beyond what they would normally do. Now, some people don't like that. To work with Oliver, you have to be willing to be put in an uncomfortable position. The people who do stick with him and give their best become his allies, and he has a tremendous amount of loyalty. When you're close to him, he appreciates the kind of work that you put in. Basically, he gave away about a million dollars split among five or six key people."

Wall Street was released in December 1987, to much hoopla. For the first time, the release of an Oliver Stone film was a major Hollywood event. Much of the publicity focused on the timeliness of the film. Indeed, just as *Platoon* had touched off a sociological phenomenon of sorts, *Wall Street* seemed to have been lifted directly from the headlines. Stone had started the project before Ivan Boesky got caught with his hand in the portfolio. While he and Weiser were creating their imaginary world, corporate raiders in the real world were buying and gutting businesses and stockbrokers were being arrested for insider trading, sometimes even being led away from their offices in handcuffs like Bud Fox in the film. As Ken Auletta pointed out in *Vanity Fair:* "Fox starts to put together an insider ring. . . . Like Boesky's accomplice Boyd Jeffries, he whispers code words into the phone and a network of arbitrageurs put companies into play. Like Martin Siegal (also part of Boesky's ring), he tells fellow brokers of sure things."

The film's opening came in the wake of the worst stock market crash in recent history. When Bloody Monday hit in October 1987, the whole country began to focus on what was wrong with Wall Street and reevaluate the get-rich-quick big-money mentality that had so marked the eighties. Stone's film had finished shooting in July. Few major Hollywood movies have hit the screens when their subject was still a headliner (ironically, this distinction also belongs to another film starring Michael Douglas, *The China Syndrome*). The effects of the insider trading scandals and the changing attitudes that resulted from them and the October crash were so significant that Stone decided to superimpose a title card that read "1985" near the beginning of the film because the events depicted in it couldn't have happened in the paranoid environment that was Wall Street in December of 1987.

It was almost as if the very things Stone warned against in the film had come to pass. The quick deal and fast buck mentality burned by the heat of its own fire and, just as Lou Mannheim predicted in the film, "only the steady players survived the bear market."

"The pressure was enormous on these young guys to produce," Stone says. "I think they were perverted right off the bat. Why would someone who is making a hundred million dollars have to make another twenty million dollars? Because he has to stay ahead of the next guy.

Money is a way of keeping score. A line in the script says it all: 'How many yachts can you water-ski behind?' Ultimately, it's not about money, it's about power. There is something patently unhealthy about using money just to make money rather than to create value. You hear about these kids who are making a million, two million bucks a year—it demoralizes the person making forty thousand dollars a year. All of a sudden everybody needs a Porsche or a VCR or a fishing boat. And this is what fuels America, more and more greed."

Although, like most Oliver Stone movies, *Wall Street* divided audiences and critics alike, it gave the yuppies their ultimate hero in Douglas's Gordon Gekko, who simultaneously romanticized and villainized the greed of the eighties. Douglas is amazing as Gekko. Scary when he threatens to rip a rival's throat out, he retreats into high-gloss appeal and jocular charm a split second before we realize that such threats are merely corporate hardball. The result is that Gekko seems like a real predator, not just a financial one.

There is no question that his Oscar-winning performance in *Wall Street*, along with *Fatal Attraction*, which he did the same year, marked a significant change in Michael Douglas as an actor. Before these films, one sometimes got the feeling that he didn't really like himself on screen. In *Wall Street*, Douglas acts with tremendous gusto, making Gekko one of the screen's great characters—a vicious man who loves shocking people almost as much as he loves boasting about it. Someone who forces people to accept him on his own terms, as a true bastard, because he's too proud of himself to pretend to be anything else.

One critic acclaimed Douglas as "the best shark seen in the movies since 'Jaws.'" Much of the credit has to go to Weiser and Stone, who supplied the actor with some wonderfully fast-paced dialogue that was rich with warfare metaphors and often vicious and funny at the same time. When buying out a rival's company Gekko says, "This turkey's totally brain dead. . . . Well Christmas is over and business is business. . . . Dilute the sonofabitch . . . I want every orifice in his body flowing red." Gekko's best segment comes when he addresses a stockholders' meeting of a company he is trying to buy out and closes with the following lines:

> The point is, ladies and gentlemen, greed is good. Greed works, greed is right. Greed clarifies, cuts through, and captures the essence of the

evolutionary spirit. Greed in all its forms, greed for life, money, love, knowledge, has marked the upward surge of mankind—and greed, mark my words, will save not only Teldar Paper but that other malfunctioning corporation called the USA . . . Thank you.

The "greed is good" speech was inspired by a commencement address given by corporate raider Ivan Boesky.

It's not surprising that when Douglas is off screen, there is a lull in the energy. Many critics cited this as a weakness, and blamed the writing or Sheen's performance. As Roger Ebert pointed out in *The New York Post*, Bud Fox "never seems quite relentless enough to move in Gekko's circle." Of course, Fox's gains are not based on personal charisma or even smarts, but on the deceptive practices that Gekko teaches him. After all, a fox is sly and crafty, not powerful. Sometimes it is difficult even to see Bud as sly because he is so hopelessly naive compared to a kingpin like Gekko. Gekko continually plays Bud like a textbook example from Machiavelli 101—alternately baiting and rewarding him, building him up and tearing him down, keeping him spinning with reverse psychology and the promise of a big tomorrow. There's no question that Douglas carries the film, but he does it with such flair that the audience is taken for the same ride that Bud Fox is on, with even less of a choice in the matter. Rather than have Bud be a true hustler out to get Gekko, Stone plays him as a nice kid, in over his head and hopelessly outclassed. This works splendidly in the beginning of the film, but Sheen comes across so perfectly powerless with Gekko there that it's hard to accept him fighting his master so effectively in the end.

Whatever problems there are with Sheen's performance, they are nothing compared with Daryl Hannah's. Best as an ethereal, nonconformist mountain girl or mermaid, Hannah is hopelessly miscast as a hardboiled urban opportunist. Stone was going for the same kind of against-type casting in a supporting role that had worked so well in *Platoon* with Willem Dafoe and Tom Berenger, but it failed here. Hannah is wooden and stiff, never comfortable as a money-hungry and tasteless interior designer.

Sean Young is better as the mother surrounded by nannies and still complaining how much "kids take it out of you," or the perfect entertaining wife whose conversation centers around, "Can I get you a drink?" An interesting side note is that the role of Gekko's son Rudy was portrayed by Sean Stone, now three and appearing in his second film (his first role was that of Richard Boyle's baby in *Salvador*). As Rudy Gekko he continually clamors for attention and is continually put aside for business purposes. "The relationship between Gekko and his three-year-old son is based on observations I've made," Stone said at the time. "These powerful men love their kids. Sure they do. Or they think they do. But they basically think of their children as possessions, and they polish them and make them shine."

Whatever errors Stone made in casting Hannah and Young were more than made up for by the master stroke of having Bud Fox's working-class father played by Charlie Sheen's real father, Martin. The chemistry between real-life father and son is the most energetic thing in the movie besides Gekko. When the two men meet in a Queens bar, the depth of their conflicts and loyalties flows easily through the scene. Fathers and sons can relate to the way young Bud wants to help his father by outsucceeding him, or outsucceed him by helping him. Later, when Carl Fox walks out of a meeting Bud set up with Gekko, the intensity of their confrontation in the elevator is only heightened by their real-life relationship. When Charlie tells Martin that he has already exceeded his father's success, it's as if the younger Sheen has broken out of the script and is talking about his acting career, which at that time was receiving more media attention than his father's ever had. This conflict is at least equaled by the genuine love shown in the almost wordless hospital scene. Just as Stone's *Platoon* had drawn an eerie parallel for Charlie to Martin's role in *Apocalypse Now*, *Wall Street* proved to be another milestone for the two actors.

The rest of the principal cast delivered as well. Terence Stamp is distant and cool as Gekko's rival, James Spader is deliciously sneaky as Bud's lawyer friend, and former *Platoon* cast member John McGinley manages to be irritating and likable as Sheen's co-worker. Another star is the film's soundtrack. Put together by Stewart Copeland, drummer for The Police at the time, it is a clever mixture of Manhattan-romantic pop songs and stimulating electronic high-tech by David Byrne and Brian Eno.

Many critics found the film highly entertaining, with a strong message. Others were brutally negative. The headline of Sheila Benson's review in the *L.A. Times* was " 'Wall Street' Lays An Egg." Some complained about melodramatic scenes such as the one in which Sheen, after gaining power through his unholy alliance with Gekko, peers out over his balcony and asks the night, "Who am I?" Bud's scheme to outwit Gekko and save the company was also frequently attacked as being too juvenile. A more valid criticism was that, while the message conveyed in the script was "slow and sure is the best route to success," the techniques used in the film screamed "pillage and plunder your way to the top." The energy in the Gekko scenes is so alluring that one walks away from the theater wishing for a taste of power instead of being more wary of it.

"Money's the sex of the 80's."

Bud Fox in **WALL STREET**

Of course, the real target in this Faustian financial fable isn't the high-finance criminals who break the rules, but the value system that places money and the deal above everything else. The market collapse that occurred a few months before the film's release was a symptom of an even deeper malady—the almost pathological greed that Gordon Gekko so perfectly typifies. As Ken Auletta remarked in *Vanity Fair*, it was ironic that "at a moment in our culture when Harvard and other business schools are vexed about whether ethics can be taught, Stone has cut through the whole silly debate. Of course ethics can be taught." Even in movies.

Once again, Stone had taken a powerful issue, condensed it into its most salient points, and woven together a fast-moving story that everyone could follow and a message that all could understand. The critics complained that he was preaching, but the film was so entertaining that most people never noticed. He had made the issue so enthralling that no one minded being confronted with an actual point of view. In a sense, as Roger Ebert said in his review for *The New York Post* at the time, Stone had "earned the right to preach to us." And as long as the films were enjoyable to watch, he would keep it.

Wall Street did well at the box office, taking in $44 million domestically and over $100 million worldwide, but as a follow-up to *Platoon*, it was disappointing. Stone has always felt that 20th Century-Fox worked harder to launch James Brooks's *Broadcast News* at the time because they saw it as having more commercial potential than *Wall Street*, though in the end the movies fared about the same. When the grosses came in from abroad, however, Stone was appalled at the studio's accounting practices and he made references in the press about movie studios being "cocksucker vampires," which served to alienate him from the Hollywood establishment that had only recently accepted him.

"I knew that *Wall Street* had been successful for the studio," he says now. "It had done especially well in foreign markets, but the accounting statement registered about fifty percent of the value it accrued abroad. The Foreign Division at Fox at that time, under Barry Diller and prior, was a highly suspect organization, and Bob Marshall [Stone's attorney] and [business manager] Steve Pines went crazy."

As he'd done with *Salvador*, Stone dedicated *Wall Street* to his father. Stone says, "*Wall Street* is a fantasy about the life I might have led if I hadn't dropped out of Yale to go to Vietnam. It's really about a son's relationship with his father."

Bob Richardson thinks that contending with his father's memory may have been one of the problems Stone had to deal with in *Wall Street:* "I think he tried to elaborate on his respect for his dad and I don't think he completely found it. Perhaps he was getting ahead of himself. I don't think he was capable of jacking into his dad. He couldn't and wouldn't just hop onto the typewriter and start writing about his dad. He is much too private a person to reveal his demons so overtly. He had a great deal of respect for his father, and he's still trying to find a way of describing what his early childhood was like. Even now, he talks about wanting to make a film about kids. It's for that reason. He needs to find a way to understand the early part of his life."

Perhaps this is the reason *Wall Street* always seems to be the film people forget Oliver Stone made. Most everyone remembers the movie, yet few associate it with Stone. It is perhaps the one script which another director could have shot and made work.

"*Wall Street* is a little cooler emotionally than the other films," Richardson says. "The passion level isn't as strong. The dilemma was that the madness wasn't as large a part in that project. Madness has always been a part of every other film [by Stone]. Oliver applies his own insanity, and *Wall Street* doesn't have as much. You don't feel the same kind of stamp at the same level. I think when he plugs into his dad, he drives away from the creative part of his madness. The shadows of his life are yet to be revealed."

It was from his father that Oliver Stone got his strong work ethic.

Lou Stone represents the cool, calculating, logical side, the part that can effectively wheel and deal through the corporate maze. But trying to tap into that mind-set from an artistic point of view is another matter entirely. Although his father was creative, he is also the symbol of discipline and responsibility in Stone's mind, whereas he equates his mother with freedom and recklessness. Consequently, for Stone to try to be artistically creative and identify with his father at the same time (as he attempted in *Wall Street*) means that the warring sides of his personality have to merge—the "father" and the "mother" have to be yoked together to work in harmony. If attainable at all, this usually results in a renewed breaking of the bonds, a bitter divorce, where clashing factions go their separate ways and the ongoing paradoxes that make up Stone's mental state suddenly have to be resolved in one direction or the other. In the case of *Wall Street*, it appears that the father won.

"Man looks in the abyss. There's nothing staring back at him. At that moment, man finds his character. And that is what keeps him out of the abyss."

Lou Mannheim in WALL STREET

Talk Radio

"Know what my greatest fear is? Being boring."
Barry Champlain in **TALK RADIO**

While finishing *Wall Street*, Stone decided his next project would be *Born on the Fourth of July*. Like *Platoon*, it was a long-deferred dream, but now that he had the clout, it was time to do it. And he was sure he had found the right young actor to play Ron Kovic: Tom Cruise. It would be a challenging role for Cruise, but Stone believed he could do it. The only problem was that in order to get him, Stone would have to wait nine months for Cruise to finish shooting *Rain Man*. That sounded fine at the time, but the closer *Wall Street* came to completion, the more anxious Stone became about starting something else soon.

Then something funny happened. In keeping with his internalization of the film, Stone had invested heavily on a stock tip—and lost. Ed Pressman was there the day Stone found out the deal had gone bad, and he was smart enough to take advantage of the situation. "It was one of those sure-thing companies," Stone says. "A can't-miss stock. This sophisticate from Wall Street conned me into the deal. I blew quite a bit, and Ed was there at the right moment and said he'd give me the money back right away if I came in as a producer on *Talk Radio*. He'd made a deal for the play with Eric Bogosian, and if I came in on it, he could get it financed. So the little weasel gave me the money the next day and I became co-producer with him."

Eric Bogosian had met Ed Pressman when the New York producer Joseph Papp had brought him by to see Bogosian in *Drinking in America*. Before that, Bogosian had done more than twenty performance pieces and also appeared on television several times, including starring in *The Caine Mutiny Court Martial*, directed by Robert Altman.

Talk Radio was originally created by Bogosian and artist Tad Savinar as a play, with Savinar's rear-projected images providing a visual counterpoint to Bogosian's rapid-fire monologues. In May 1987, an expanded and more elaborately staged version debuted in New York. Directed by Fred Zollo, the play dealt with an obnoxious radio talk-show host named Barry Champlain and the night he finally came to terms with the self-loathing that powered his entertaining but hate-riddled program. It takes place on Champlain's last night on the air before going national with the show, and chiefly concerns Barry's abusive relationship with his co-workers and the legions of lost souls that called in nightly. By the end of this program, however, Barry has tapped into some of his own problems, eventually growling into the mike: "I despise each and every one of you . . . The only thing you believe in is me."

Ed Pressman, in New York for the production of *Wall Street*, became interested in *Talk Radio* as a film project. He figured it could be done for $2 million with Bogosian playing the lead, and began bringing directors, including Adrian Lyne, William Friedkin, and Alan Parker, to see the play. The project stalled at that point because, while Pressman and Bogosian agreed that they didn't want to just film the play as a performance piece, no one was sure what direction to take with it. Pressman suggested Bogosian go ahead and write the screenplay and then they would have a better chance of interesting a director. Eric Bogosian recalls what happened next. "Somewhere around that point Ed said, 'Would you mind if Oliver Stone sort of acts as your big brother on the screenplay and kind of watches over it?' Looking back with hindsight, I assume that Ed knew what this was all leading to, but I didn't. One of the things I really don't like about Hollywood is the pecking-order idea—anybody who's higher up, you just bend over and grease your asshole for them. But I'd really liked *Platoon*, so I thought, 'This will be good. I'll work with this guy.'"

Bogosian still recalls his first impressions of Stone, and the images have as much to do with physical presence and personal power as they do with intellect and Hollywood clout. In this age of the pseudo-refined modern man, such things often go unnoticed, but Bogosian claims they are as much a key to Stone's success as his other talents. "Just think for a moment," Bogosian says. "His last name is Stone. Like a rock. He's over six feet tall. He looks like a fucking bear. He's good-looking in a really great, sexy way, and he's extremely intelligent. He has a great captivating way of dealing with people—it's sort of aggression mixed with nonchalance, an 'aw shucks, I was just joking' attitude. He's found a perfect blend, which is very important in Hollywood because at the level at which Oliver is operating it's very political. I don't know anybody at his level who hasn't perfected some gorgeous spin on dealing with people."

Despite a rough beginning, Stone and Bogosian hit it off once they started relating on an artist-to-artist basis. During the time since Bogosian had done the play, the book *Talked to Death, The Life and Murder of Alan Berg*, by Stephen Sinclair, had been published. It concerned the Denver talk-show host who was assassinated in 1984 by members of an extremist right-wing organization. "Oliver and I wanted to be able to use Alan Berg's story," Bogosian says. "Ed got the book and it came with all the rights to Alan Berg's life, so we could use whatever we wanted. The thing I wanted was his relationship with his wife. I thought it was amazing. Oliver wanted the shooting death. I said that I believed the story arc had to be completed before the guy got killed. And it should be like the way John Lennon died, in that your celebrity is what causes you to be killed. I couldn't let it be like a punishment for what he had done. He had to come to a realization where he understands that he's been wrong, but by then he has sowed so many seeds that he must die. It's more like a Greek classic. And Oliver understands all that stuff."

Even so, when it came to writing the script, Stone's advice was blunt and to the point. Bogosian describes what happened: "Finally one day, I said, 'So, Oliver, what's the secret of these screenplays? What do I do, now that you're working with me on this thing?' And he said, 'Well, it's your problem. Go write it.' So that's what I did."

While Stone finished editing *Wall Street* and prepared for its release, Bogosian worked on his first draft of the screenplay for *Talk Radio*. He finished it in December 1987, around the time *Wall Street* was released. "We were going to visit my wife's relatives in Australia for Christmas," Bogosian remembers. "I shipped off the screenplay to Oliver and figured I'd get notes back from him in a month. Well, we're getting ready to leave and we're having a party at our apartment, and the phone rings. It's Oliver Stone. 'Eric, it's Oliver. Listen, I'm in Florida waiting to catch a plane to Cuba. Your screenplay, man. I have some notes here. Where are my notes? I can't find my notes. Screenplay sucks, man. What's wrong with you? What have you been doing for the past two months up in your place up in New Jersey? Chopping wood? Come on. Get on the stick, man.'

"I said, 'What? What's wrong with it? Is there anything . . . ?' and he goes, 'No, there's nothing good in it. It's a piece of shit. What's your problem?' I go, 'I don't know. What am I supposed to do?' He goes, 'Well, do this to the first act. Do this to the second act. And get rid of that thing out there and do this over here.' I go, 'That's all you have to say? I've been working on this for months and that's all your notes?' He says, 'Those are the things you have to do, man. It's your problem. Fix it.' And that was it."

Bogosian figured his only option was to rewrite the screenplay while in Australia. Taking the computer wasn't practical, so he went out and bought a thermal typewriter. "I have thirty days in Australia, so I figure I'll write five pages a day while I'm there," he says. "Every morning for two hours I'd lock myself in the bedroom. Remember, this is all family; kids running around in the hallway. 'Shh, shh, Uncle Eric is writing.' The babies are crying and all that stuff. My kid is nine months old and it's my first kid. I got the typewriter on the bed and I'm sitting in a chair next to the bed. It's ridiculous. The first thing I did was write a letter to Ed and Oliver saying I was outraged that I'd get this kind of treatment on something I had worked so hard on. I spent a whole day writing this letter. Then I put it aside and thought about the notes Oliver had given me. And I realized, he was right. He was right about every single thing.

I said, fuck it. I threw the letter away. On going with Oliver I realized that there's no substitute for experience. After a while you know this has to happen and this is shit."

Around this time Stone was also considering another film. "My next movie is called 'Contra,'" he said in the press, "because the word symbolizes 'against.' It's not just about contras. It's about America being against everything that's progressive. But I decided to approach it in a completely opposite way than 'Salvador.' This time I'm going to go in from the right, and my two protagonists will be CIA guys. The older one has been around and involved in a lot of shadow schemes going back to Vietnam. Paul Newman is interested in playing him. I want to make these guys likable. I hope Americans will see themselves in these two guys, and by watching what our 'heroes' do, they'll feel the full force of what America is doing."

Later the *Contra* title was changed to *Company Man*. According to Stone, the script had a few problems, but the project was eventually shelved primarily because of the difficulty of arranging to film in Nicaragua.

For Eric Bogosian, knowing that Stone's suggestions for the *Talk Radio* screenplay were correct was one thing, but being able to incorporate them into the script was another. However, he persisted with his work schedule and was about halfway through the script and two weeks into his "vacation" when he got a call from Ed Pressman. "Ed says, 'Congratulations,'" Bogosian recalls. "I said, 'Why?' He goes, 'Oliver's going to direct the movie.' I said, 'What? I haven't finished it. He told me the draft he got sucks. How can he direct it?' Ed goes, 'He wants to do it.' So I call Oliver and I go, 'Hey, all right.' And he goes, 'What?' I said, 'I heard you're directing the movie.' He says, 'Who said that? We'll see when you get back. Have you finished the script yet?' I said, 'No.' He says, 'Well, stop in California on the way back.' I hung up and went back to writing."

Stone had indeed agreed to direct *Talk Radio*, but felt it was better to keep Bogosian in the dark until he finished the script. Just as Ed Pressman had figured, getting Stone involved as a producer had hooked him into the project. "Ed sucked me in," Stone says. "*Wall Street* was criticized a lot. I was a little down and wanted to work right away. At the same time, I was able to break into Dallas. I wanted to shoot *Born* there, and I wanted to get set up and build a stage in Dallas."

Part of what gave Stone such a need to throw himself into a project was that Elizabeth had suffered a miscarriage that January. She'd had them before, and would have several more later, but this time the pregnancy had lasted six months and both she and Stone were very distraught over it. They had gotten their hopes up for a second child, and the miscarriage was a real tragedy that would mark their lives for some time to come. As usual, Stone said little about this personal loss to his associates and instead focused even more intently on his work.

Ed Pressman recalls Stone's decision to direct *Talk Radio*. "We were in Hawaii and I showed Oliver the book on Alan Berg. He began taking the film more seriously from that point. One day he said, 'You know, I want to direct this with a low budget. Get back to my roots. I don't want to do a big-budget movie after *Wall Street*. I want to go against the grain.' It seemed to us then that doing it that way gave us freedom, gave us the ability to just say, 'Hey, we're going to do the movie.' We could practically finance it ourselves."

But due to circumstances that soon developed, it proved more profitable to bring in some partners, and this was another factor in Stone's decision. *Talk Radio* was a chance for Stone to make some really big money. "That was a big part of it," Stone admits. "Garth Drabinski came into my life. He was a Canadian promoter who owned Cineplex Odeon. Drabinski wanted a movie from me, so I sold him the picture for ten million dollars. Ed Pressman and I figured we could make it for 2.5 and then we'd split up the profits. It ended up costing four, so basically there was a profit of six million dollars before we even released it. That was the biggest deal I ever made."

Pressman and Stone had been primarily interested in making a presale deal to help finance the cost of the film, but Garth Drabinski had no way of knowing that. Drabinski pushed for the meeting because he had a small distribution company of his own and wanted to land a major film to guarantee presales. He felt that having Oliver Stone's next film would be the best possible move he could make at the time. Since he knew Arthur Manson, who had by now become Stone's producer representative, he asked him to arrange a meeting. "I remember Garth arrived first at the meeting," Manson says, "and he looked around the room and told me, 'I'm not letting him [Stone] out of this room until we have a deal.' Ed Pressman had all the numbers, but Oliver wanted to make sure that Cineplex Distributing could do the job. It wasn't just about the money with him. He wanted to know if they could distribute. And I said, 'Well, they own theaters. They'll get it distributed.' And that was it. Drabinski said, 'I'm going to make you an offer you can't refuse.' And he did.''

In late January 1988, Bogosian flew to L.A. with a finished script in his hands, and was surprised to find Stone's team in full preproduction. "I did it. Fucking finished it in thirty days, and he had already begun moving his vast crew, Alex Ho and everybody, toward making *Talk Radio*. But it was like Project X or something in that he wasn't telling anyone what he was doing. He was mobilizing them toward Dallas where they were going to do *Born on the Fourth of July*. He had Bruno Rubeo already designing a set for *Talk Radio*. They were all doing their jobs, but no one had seen the script because I hadn't finished it. What he wanted to do was basically pop off a movie while he was prepping *Born on the Fourth of July*. It was un-fucking-believable."

It wasn't the first time that Stone had created an insanely pressured situation. Working at a feverish pace, Stone did a rewrite of Bogosian's script, and the two did final polishes literally at the same time sets were being built and actors being cast. "We disagreed about a couple of things," Bogosian says. "One was a monologue he wanted in there about legalizing drugs, and the other was he wanted me to really hammer Barry's wife at a certain point. And I go, 'Why? It's like misogyny to just stick that into the story,' and he goes, 'No, I want it.' I said, 'I don't see the motivation for this. How about he overhears her talking on the phone just innocently saying to her husband, "Yeah, things are really okay down here, he's a real basket case as usual." Then he gets incredibly offensive and insane over this casual remark he overhears, and he saves it in his head and when he gets her on the air, he just pommels her.' Oliver said, 'Okay,' and that's the way it ended up in the picture.''

The process of transforming Bogosian's play into a screenplay required adding an entire new act and a new major character: Ellen, Barry Champlain's ex-wife. New callers were also added, including a neo-Nazi and a rapist. Some of this material was based on events in Alan Berg's life. In addition to drawing from the Sinclair book, Stone and Bogosian used personal recollections by people who were close to Berg, including his widow and his producer. One scene taken from Berg's life has to do with Barry responding to an elderly woman calling about her Social Security problems by asking her off-the-wall questions like,

"Do you have any views on lesbian priests?" And one of the most arresting scenes in the movie, when Barry is booed at the basketball stadium while trying to introduce the new coach, is based on a true-life incident.

All of these changes were a result of the Stone/Bogosian collaboration on the screenplay. Actually, it is surprising how well the two collaborated, considering that they had somewhat different views of the script's direction. "We were working on two movies at the same time," Bogosian recalls. "I was working on the inner man, which was the part that I found most interesting. A guy who is basically addicted to his fame, and it destroys him. Oliver was working on the idea of the voice of the people who was constantly criticizing the status quo, and untimately eats lead for his efforts. I'd say to him, 'You know, this movie's about you.' And he wouldn't answer. I said, 'Look, you're a guy that is now carried on the shoulder of the public, and what you say is suddenly so much more important than it used to be, and it can really get to you and drive you crazy.' But he never responded to that. I really thought we were making a movie about Oliver Stone."

By March 1988, final preparations were being made, but one thing still wasn't ready—Bogosian's contract. With only three weeks left before shooting, the deal still wasn't set. "That required some yelling between me and Oliver and Ed," Bogosian says now.

The agreement made, *Talk Radio* began shooting in Dallas in April. In addition to Bogosian, it starred Ellen Green, who played Audrey in *Little Shop of Horrors* both Off Broadway and on film; *Platoon* and *Wall Street* veteran John C. McGinley; as well as Alec Baldwin, Leslie Hope, John Pankow, and Michael Wincott. The crew was virtually the same as the *Wall Street* team. Once again, Alex Ho co-produced, Bob Richardson served as director of photography, Ellen Mirojnick designed costumes, David Brenner edited (with co-editor Joe Hutshing), and Stewart Copeland did the music. The chief exception was production designer Bruno Rubeo, who returned to Stone's team after leaving to do Alex Cox's *Walker* (Bob Richardson was also approached by Cox at the time but elected to do *Wall Street* instead).

In his quest for authenticity, Stone hired Anath White, Alan Berg's former producer, and Bill Abbott, a fourteen-year radio veteran, as technical advisers. Abbott created the sound of the fictional KGAB radio station by supervising the recording of station ID's, promos, commercials, and a newscast. KGAB was patterned after an actual Dallas talk radio station, KLIF, and during the production the entire cast visited the station and spoke with their real-life counterparts. The only real breach of authenticity was that, in order to prevent the film from becoming too static, Stone had Barry wear a headset occasionally so he could stand up and walk around while doing his show.

Though similar to Alan Berg in some ways, everyone involved with *Talk Radio* agreed that Bogosian's Barry Champlain had his own unique style and personality. "Barry Champlain is a completely different person," said Anath White. "But some of his more interesting characteristics—his ability to be outrageous, his playfulness and facility with words—remind me of Alan."

The shooting schedule was intense. "Oliver moved right in at about ninety miles an hour," Bogosian recalls. "It was one year after we were casting the play and we're shooting the movie already. It was insane. We shot the movie in twenty-five days. We shouldn't have done that. On the set, everything was so rushed. I have all kinds of things that I am very particular about. For example, my hair drives me crazy and we never figured out what to do with it. It ended up in a stupid haircut. Too short. And, as soon as we started shooting, I realized that there was an element of humor in the play that was now being moved away from, toward a much more intensely dramatic, darker insane kind of thing. I liked how the play seduced the audience into liking this guy and then made him into the biggest asshole in the world. At any rate, we shot for about three days, which is about the time it takes for the film to come back from the lab and look at the rushes. Now these are twelve-hour days with just me. Oliver came up on the third day of shooting and said, 'I saw the rushes last night. They're no good.' I'm in the middle of a shot, I'm on my third take or something. I thought, 'I know what this is about,' because I'm friends with John McGinley, who had been in *Platoon*, and I knew that Oliver could be a hammer on the set. I don't know why he shoves like that, but in my case it just meant that I had to try harder. But I didn't know what to do to try harder."

Stone admits to pushing Bogosian, but claims he wasn't deceiving him about the first three days of filming. Six years after the filming of *Talk Radio*, Bogosian agrees. "I've asked him since if he was trying to do some kind of psychology on me then, and I don't think he was. He just says what's on his mind, but because he's a very bright guy, he realizes it's a great way to get a reaction—to throw people off. There's no question he pushes and pressures people. Look at Bob Richardson. He's in his thirties and he was gray when I met him and now he's pure white. He says it's some kind of genetic thing or something, but I don't know. There are so many people running around Hollywood, going crazy, being hysterical about the smallest thing, that they lose perspective. Oliver has perspective. He knows that if he chews out a costume designer about some petty thing, it can result in better costumes. The end result is a better picture and the feelings at the moment aren't really that important. These people are being paid a shitload of money and if they can't stand the heat, they should get out of the kitchen. If you want to make tough movies like the movies that he makes, then everybody has to pull their weight."

Manipulated or not, Bogosian's performance did change after that third day of shooting, and he is the first to admit that he was a little slow off the mark. But since the scenes shot during that time were all of Bogosian in the studio doing his radio show, Stone was able to cut around him in editing so that he's heard, but not seen, a device that serves to build the tension. "You see everybody reacting, but you don't see the guy," Bogosian says. "You see my character from behind. Oliver was right. We tossed those first few days and it made a more dramatic beginning for the picture. When you do see the guy, it's from the fourth day of shooting and I'm finally up to speed. I started getting better as the picture actually began. The first cut did not have the toughness."

Stone says that Bogosian was excellent in the role: "He had some hard moments because he hadn't done that many movies and I think sometimes he had an image of what a star is, but he was very adaptive. He learned very fast. He had to master a lot of complicated moves and staging. We put him on the dolly tracks and made him do weird things. He had to walk, talk, remember forty-five lines and hit camera marks that were very complicated. He did what he had to do. I took him to the desert and stoned him."

Bogosian refers to that incident as "The Great Walk into the Desert," which he says began because Stone caught a cold and couldn't get rid of it. "That's why we were going out there, because he's got this flu. One day he goes, 'Tomorrow, man, we go out to the desert,' so the next day we all get in the car. Our baby is ten months old and Sean, Oliver's son, is about four years old and our wives are with us. So we head out on this highway and go, go, go, until we get to this reptile museum, and Oliver says, 'The women can go around the museum while we walk into the desert.' So I go up to Jo Anne, my wife, and say, 'We're all going to go out into the desert, but me and Oliver might end up going off by ourselves, okay?' And she goes yeah, sure. So the women both get walkers for the kids, these little stroller things, and we just walk out the back door of this reptile museum right out into the desert. It's like a path. Oliver and I are walking together with our wives walking ten feet behind us pushing their strollers through the sand. We continue with this absurdity for about five hundred yards or something and we come to this rocky hill and Oliver says, 'Sean, climb up that hill.' So Sean climbs up. He makes him climb to the top and back down again. Basically that was Sean's exercise for the day. He'd done his work. Elizabeth then says, 'We're getting tired of pushing these strollers around. Why don't you guys go ahead we're going to go back.' So they took off and Oliver and I kept walking. Now we're getting really deep in and I'd never been in the desert in my life. I don't know what the hell we are in the middle of. We go by a sign that says, 'No water past this point.' It's like a warning, with a skull and crossbones. And we keep walking, and I say, 'How far does this path go?' and he goes, 'I don't know, probably two hundred, three hundred miles through the desert.'

"So we get to this dry gulf, everything is very dry, very hot. We sit in this dry riverbed on some stones. He's not saying anything and he hasn't said anything. We're spending a lot of time with each other and he's not talking about himself or about his life or nothing. He sat down on the rock, I sat down on the rock. The sun was beating down on us. I think I'm sort of getting what this guy is about. He's got to test you. I know what he wants. He wants me to cry. He wants me to whine. He wants me to say I'm scared. I knew about *Platoon* and how he hammered the guys. I wouldn't have wanted to have gone through that. He wants me to say something like, 'What are we doing?' So I figure if he's not going to say anything, I'm not going to say anything. We sat there for fifteen minutes, boiling, to what end, I don't know. I'm still not sure what we were doing exactly. And then he said, 'Okay.' And then we walked off. And that was it. We bonded in the desert. It was like walking with Jesus or something."

After *Wall Street*, a key question for Stone was how well he could get along with the actresses in the film—Ellen Green and Leslie Hope.

Stone and Hope worked well together, but though he never had an open clash with Green, there were a few difficult moments. Green, known for her perfectionism, can be picky over a scene and not want to give the director final say, but it's in a nonconfrontational way. The actress can be so nice that it's hard to be tough with her—a particularly difficult situation for a confrontational person like Stone. According to one crew member, Green's desire to keep redoing a relatively minor scene got Stone so upset one day that he was almost in tears, but he kept his cool.

Bogosian and Green clashed frequently. The worst confrontation was on an elevator which, unknown to them, was wired into the microphone system. What started out as a simple discussion turned into a heated argument which the entire crew and everyone else visiting the set that day heard in explicit detail. When the two got off the elevator everyone just stared at them, except for Stone, who couldn't stop laughing.

The scenes that would later be most often criticized in the film are the flashback sequences. Through them Barry is seen as he was before success; though he was a loudmouth even then, he also seemed to have genuine affection for his wife and an attitude of hope toward life. The flashbacks show how eight years of hosting a talk radio show have changed Barry Champlain. Eric Bogosian defends these scenes enthusiastically. "I wanted to understand the psychology of this man," he says. "Take the scene where me and McGinley are in the house fucking around and the wife comes home. To me, that's a very meaningful scene because the guy just doesn't want to be with his wife, he doesn't know how to be with her. For me, the piece has always been a warning about a possible route I can take in my life. I can throw away the best things in my life. The Ellen Green character was something that he basically blew and, by the end of the movie, he understands he's blown it. He goes looking for her and he's horrible to everyone around him."

As Stone was shooting *Talk Radio*, he was getting ready for *Born on the Fourth of July*. It would be wrong to imply that he didn't focus on *Talk Radio*, because he did, but after his ten-year struggle to bring *Born* to the screen there was no question which was the more important project. Eric Bogosian says that it was never a problem for him, but one incident does stick in his mind. "One day we were shooting the basketball game scene, and while that basketball game is going on, Tom Cruise is upstairs doing makeup tests for *Born on the Fourth of July*. At one point, they brought him out in a wheelchair and said, 'This is a guy we want you to meet.' I didn't know who he was, and I said, 'Oh hi, how are you doing?' and then everybody started laughing. It's Tom Cruise! Ha ha! That's about the only time it bugged me."

Producer Clayton Townsend (*JFK*, *Heaven and Earth*, *Natural Born Killers*) was production manager on *Talk Radio*. He describes some of the ways in which that production helped prepare for *Born*: "The biggest advantage was really being able to test out the environment in Dallas. We had a chance to work with the local crew there and get a big jump on preproduction, as well as save some dough on overlapping costs."

Bogosian is in virtually every scene in *Talk Radio*, which meant that for him, the filming was a marathon run. Though the filming was intense, Bogosian says Stone was well mannered during the shoot and limited his wild side to experimentation rather than reckless behavior. "All I saw was a workaholic; a man who put in amazingly long hours, and then would go to the editing room at the end of the shooting day for a few hours. Then he would write and then get up early and do it again. He was on some kind of intense burn all the time. I just don't see him as a tough guy. I see him as a very hardworking, very smart guy, who has been inserted into the body of a football player and kind of gets all of the perks that come with that. The ability to drink large amounts of alcohol and intimidate people frequently. I grew up with some tough guys, and there is a look in the eyes of a guy like a Hell's Angel who is going to clock you before you know what's going on. Oliver's not like that. There are some truly mad people in Hollywood and, while Oliver likes to bluff and gruffle like one of the bad guys, the vulnerability that gets expressed through his work and his sheer complete commitment to the effort show that he's a mensch underneath it all. He's afraid of being a mensch, I think, and he will do everything he can not to be thought of that way. But the world kind of divides into people you want to be in the trenches with and people you wouldn't want to be in the trenches with. And you can be safe in the trenches with Oliver. He understands what's important at the end of the day."

"You're not the bad guy you think you are."

Laura Johnston in **TALK RADIO**

It was true that shooting *Talk Radio* and getting ready for *Born* put Stone under even more intense pressure than usual, but it is also his nature to work these kinds of hours on a shoot. All in all, the filming of *Talk Radio* went pretty well. Shooting finished on schedule after just twenty-five days, and as Stone began to edit, he and Pressman prepared the marketing campaign. Stone works on every aspect of the filmmaking process both before and after the actual shooting, including the financing, editing, distribution, marketing, and publicity. "People think every director does that, but they don't," Bogosian says. "And as other directors let go of those things, those things get fucked up. Oliver's there on everything. There's a number of things I disagreed with him about in these stages. I didn't like the poster design, for instance. I felt it was too artsy, too theoretical. I thought they should just have a guy talking into the microphone. I felt like they didn't want to have my face on the thing, like the less of my face you see, the more it's an Oliver Stone movie. But there's always disagreements on poster designs. There were a lot of ways this movie could've been presented to the public. It could've been as Oliver Stone discovers Eric Bogosian or presents Eric Bogosian to the public, but it wasn't. It was always presented as an Oliver Stone picture and I was sort of the guy who was in an Oliver Stone picture."

Nonetheless, Bogosian was extremely pleased with the final cut. "I'm very proud of it," he says, "and I'm very, very happy that Oliver worked on this with me. I learned a shitload from Oliver. If my performance is very strong in the picture, I credit that to him, because Oliver always knows what he wants. He doesn't always know how to get there, but he isn't going to stop until he gets there. He'll pound you until he gets what he wants. He doesn't have any respect for people who aren't going to put in the effort. He likes people who aren't going to whine. I'm a whiner, so he doesn't like that. I didn't think I was a whiner, but his attitude is that you shouldn't complain at all."

Talk Radio is an intense glimpse into the seedy underbelly of life. Bogosian is entirely convincing as Barry Champlain, a talented but paranoid control freak torn between his disgust for mankind and his disgust for himself. The hopeless desperation in the voices of those who call in to the show is matched by Barry's inner turmoil. His insulting yet witty banter has an edge of madness to it, but also the ring of truth. When a major company expresses interest in syndicating Barry's show, he is unable to change gears and accept his own good fortune. Instead, he intentionally alienates everyone around him, snaring his ex-wife, co-workers, and volatile audience into a darkly comic venture to the edge.

Barry's ratings may be high enough to have the syndicators buzzing, but it becomes evident that the phone-ins are finally getting to him as he sabotages his career and his life. Barry has made a career out of being angry so long that he has forgotten what he was angry about. The issues he and his callers discuss—war, crime, racism, poverty, sex, fear—are real, but they have become overshadowed by the entertainment machine. Like today's "reality programs" or even news shows during rating sweeps, the truth is shaped and bent to serve the audience's continual need for more sensationalism. It's not about reality or news or issues any more; it's about ratings.

"Barry really does care," says Bogosian about his creation. "If he didn't, he wouldn't have become a star. But he has put this genuine concern on the auction block and made it a product. And as he sells it again and again, it just becomes rote, the yelling and screaming become just an act. He's dealing in a currency that has become debased, but the audience demands it and keeps wanting more, they want blood."

Barry's disgust has left him with only the hope that by continually challenging the airwaves to prove him wrong, he may at last find something worth believing in. But there are mostly just dull and hateful minds on the other end, little to halt Barry's downward spiral but neo-Nazis and lovable loonies. Their solutions, like their problems, are based on ignorance and fear, and only serve to convince Barry that he's right.

For the sensitive viewer, the film may come across as a barrage of verbal abuse, sarcasm, and human pathos, but the relationship between Barry's sick callers and his slick persona is far more than one of sufferer and opportunist. On the surface, Barry Champlain is the last angry man, driven mad by the endless stream of dreary souls who vent their frustration with the world on his radio show. But beneath it all, Barry understands his callers far more than he lets on and he feels for them in an almost cathartic way. The desire to find meaning in their hopeless lives is the hidden power behind his anger. Like a dying man searching for a cure, Barry desperately needs to know if there is anything out there worth living for.

Unfortunately, the conclusion he comes to seems to be a negative one. When Barry is killed in the parking lot after the show, the feeling is partly one of relief that such a tormented soul has been put out of his misery. The murder is not based on Alan Berg's story; Berg was killed by a deliberate and carefully executed plot, while Barry seems to have been killed by a random nut, looking to make his mark on society. In the end, Barry Champlain dies by the sword by which he lived.

Talk Radio was released in December 1988 and well promoted, but died quickly at the box office. Stone feels that a big part of the problem was the way Garth Drabinski's organization marketed the movie. Naturally, they played off *Talk Radio* being an "Oliver Stone Film," but they saw it as a big Christmas film rather than a character piece. Coming at Christmastime, it was up against major releases from most studios. As a result, the film never had the time it needed to find its audience which a slower release pattern relying on good word of mouth might have accomplished.

Bogosian is candid: "What happened was, the majors all came out with very heavy dramas, the kind of things you expect to see in September or October. *Rain Man* came out, *Torch Song Trilogy* and *Dangerous Liaisons* came out. Suddenly there were all these dramas out at the same time as *Talk Radio*. In the motion picture business, almost doesn't count, because if your average film goer goes to a movie once a week and you are third on their list, by the time they get around to you, the owner of the theater has replaced you with another movie. We were replaced by *The 'burbs*. There was a tremendeous response to *Talk Radio* when people saw it; but if you have a choice of seeing a drama with Dustin Hoffman in it, or a drama with Eric Bogosian in it, you will go see the Dustin Hoffman drama first. I would."

Bogosian's performance did not go unnoticed. He drew many rave critical reviews and was awarded the coveted Golden Bear at the Berlin Film Festival. Many thought he deserved an Oscar nomination for the demanding role, but nominations generally go to pictures that do better at the box office.

Stone looks back on the *Talk Radio* experience fondly. "Of all the films I've done, *Talk Radio* is the furthest from me. It's hard to sympathize with the character. I wanted to try some things and I learned a lot about film. I look at it more in terms of technique. We did a lot of work with voice as a theatrical device. Also, how to make him claustrophobic. That was also very important for *Born*. A wheelchair is also claustrophobic, and I needed to understand that. I wanted to study claustrophobia

Above: **Lou and Jacqueline Stone with their newborn son, Oliver William.** (Stone family photo)

Left: **Oliver at age 6.** (Stone family photo)

Below: **Oliver and his mother, Jacqueline, when he was 11.** (Stone family photo)

Stone's platoon in Vietnam.
(Oliver Stone Collection)

Oliver Stone in Vietnam.
(Oliver Stone Collection)

Above: **Oliver and his first wife, Najwa Sarkis.**
(Oliver Stone Collection)

Below: **Stone directing *The Hand,* starring Michael Caine.**

Above: **Oliver, Elizabeth, and Sean during the filming of *Salvador*.** (© *John Daly, Hemdale Films*)

Below: **James Woods and Stone during *Salvador*.** (© *John Daly, Hemdale Films*)

Top left and right: **Stone directs Tom Cruise in *Born on the Fourth of July.*** *(© Elizabeth Stone)*

Center: **Director of Photography Robert Richardson, behind the camera, and Stone filming *Born on the Fourth of July.*** *(© Elizabeth Stone)*

Right: **Alex Ho and Oliver Stone in the Philippines for *Born on the Fourth of July.*** *(© Elizabeth Stone)*

 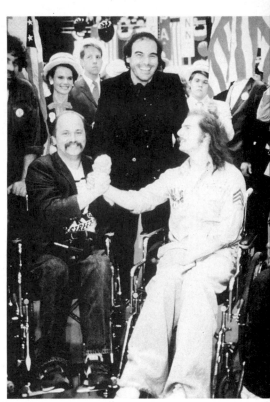

Above left: **Tom Cruise and Oliver Stone preparing to film the Vietnam sequences of *Born on the Fourth of July*.** *(© Elizabeth Stone) Above right:* **Ron Kovic, Oliver Stone, and Tom Cruise at the end of filming.** *(Copyright © Universal City Studios, Inc. Courtesy of MCA Publishing Rights, a Division of MCA Inc.)*

Below: **Oliver Stone after receiving the Oscar for Best Director for *Born on the Fourth of July*.** *(© Elizabeth Stone)*

Elizabeth, Oliver, and Sean Stone.

(Copyright © 1989 Matthew Rolston)

Oliver Stone in the entryway of his Santa Monica home as he prepares to film *The Doors*.
(© Elizabeth Stone)

A light moment with Val Kilmer on the set of *The Doors*.
(© Elizabeth Stone)

Directing Kyle MacLachlan in Malibu during *The Doors*.
(© Elizabeth Stone)

Preparing for a concert sequence with Val Kilmer in *The Doors*.
(© Elizabeth Stone)

Above: **A portrait.**
*(Copyright © Lee Crum
Photography, Inc.)*

Left: **Writing *JFK* at
his Santa Barbara
home.**
(© Elizabeth Stone)

Left: **Directing Kevin Costner and Sissy Spacek in** *JFK.* *(© 1991 Warner Bros. Inc., Regency Enterprises V.O.F. and Le Studio Canal +. All Rights Reserved)*

Left: **Clowning with Jack Lemmon and Edward Asner during** *JFK.* *(© 1991 Warner Bros. Inc., Regency Enterprises V.O.F. and Le Studio Canal +. All Rights Reserved)*

Left: **Showing Gary Oldman how to die like Lee Harvey Oswald in** *JFK.* *(© 1991 Warner Bros. Inc., Regency Enterprises V.O.F. and Le Studio Canal +. All Rights Reserved)*

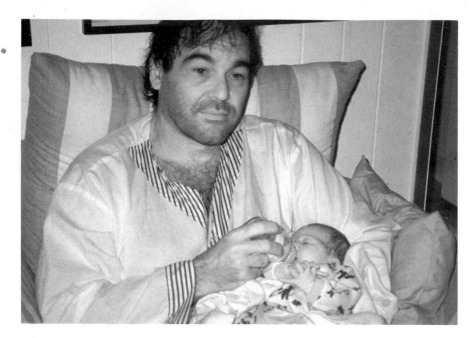

Above: **Feeding baby Mikey.** *(© Elizabeth Stone)*

Below: **Directing Dr. Haing Ngor and Hiep Thi Le in *Heaven & Earth*.** *(© Janet Yang)*

Above: **With Sean in Stone's office at the Santa Monica home.** *(© Elizabeth Stone)*

Below: **With Juliette Lewis and friend during Natural Born Killers.** *(© Richard Rutowski)*

Oliver Stone and Richard Rutowski in Nepal. *(© Janet Yang)*

Riding his horse in Hawaii. *(© Elizabeth Stone)*

and those emotions. In some way, I don't know how, but instinctually, it was necessary for me to make *Talk Radio* in order to make *Born on the Fourth of July*. I think it was an interesting movie, and I made a lot of money. It's a ruthless picture, but I'm proud of its technique."

Bogosian has his own ideas on what makes Oliver Stone such a successful filmmaker. "He finds a way to take the most moving and intense experience and make it into entertainment. Serious shit has always been entertainment for the intellectual crowd, but something about *The Bridge Over the River Kwai* feels different since *Platoon*. I don't think people who go to movies understand this, but there are film devices used in Oliver's pictures that create a tremendeous sense of excitement that is larger than the events you're looking at. The montage in *JFK* is so intense that it's closer to MTV than most movies. You can make a distinct parallel, I believe, between *Platoon* and the movie *Aliens*—the unseen monsters coming through the darkness. Who are they? We don't know what they look like. Are they everywhere? We're shooting everywhere. The finale of *Platoon* and the finale of *Aliens* are very similar. I think there can be a sexuality, a sensuality in filmmaking. The sensuality of the filmmaking seems to be very great in *JFK*, considering the somber subject matter. That's a lot of the commerciality of the picture. Audiences are very jaded and they need a lot to get excited."

Bogosian feels that Stone is misunderstood as a filmmaker, not only by his critics but even by his fans. "There are certain things that I feel akin to with Oliver. One is that you really wrench right up out of your guts and throw everything you can into the thing. There will be some very sincere moments when you make that kind of effort. It's like throwing punches. He also likes to stop the movie and say something right at you. It's almost like Marxist filmmaking or something where he just says to you what it is. But I love that. I don't like the seductive kind of movie that hypnotizes you into thinking it's real, because it's not real. If we are going to talk about JFK or Vietnam or something, then I need to understand that I am watching a picture, watching somebody's point of view, and Oliver does that. He says, 'This is me saying this.' I think that he's carrying the mantle of the academic film scene that grew out of the New Wave cinema in France and Italy, to the academics here like Scorsese and Coppola who studied movie making. Everybody wants to believe that he's a John Huston kind of moviemaker, but he's not. He's too careful. He's too analytical. It has a feeling of freedom, but it's only because he's thought everything through. There's a very big brain working there."

Talk Radio was far from a failure. It has a strong cult following and is one of the films most often cited by Stone's fans as a favorite. One of them came up to him on the street in Chicago not long ago and said *Talk Radio* was the most prophetic American film of the late twentieth century. Considering today's television talk shows and their utter obsession with perversity, he may have been right.

Both *Wall Street* and *Talk Radio* were important films for Stone, even though they are not usually regarded as his best. *Wall Street* proved that *Platoon* was no fluke, and that he could direct contemporary drama with passion and power even without the benefit of gunfire and explosions—and still do big box office and get Academy recognition. *Talk Radio* showed that Stone was not afraid to push the boundaries of film technique even as he dealt with dangerous subject matter. Though it was far from a hit, *Talk Radio* eventually made enough money on video to turn a profit. It also demonstrated that Oliver Stone the artist was Oliver Stone the businessman. He came out of it a rich man. Most directors who achieve huge success with a film invariably go overboard with the next one. They become caught up in their art and lose sight of the Hollywood business ethic. But Stone's projects were right on budget and made money.

Perhaps this was because Stone was neither motivated nor confused by money. He saw it as a tool, one that demanded lots of respect and careful attention, but a tool just the same. "Some people enter Hollywood simply to scam the large amount of easy money, but you couldn't say that the way Oliver makes his money is easy," Bogosian comments. "He works very hard for it and doesn't even enjoy it that much. He buys houses and he knows the good places to eat, but this guy is not a relaxed guy. He doesn't make films for the money. He does it because it's a tremendously challenging arena that uses all of his skills. Even most people in show business never give their all—they just find a safe niche that is well below their ultimate effort. Look at television. And in this business when you fail, you fail publicly. You make your ultimate effort and then you get criticized for it. And so, being the kind of person he is, Oliver puts himself in a tremendously vulnerable spot in the public eye. It's kind of a kamikaze thing. He doesn't go about it like somebody who knows that they are going to win. He does it with complete passion and commitment, almost like he's daring fate to smash him down."

"I'm glad you take it all so seriously. But you gotta know when to stop or it's gonna kill you."

Dan Starbles in TALK RADIO

For Oliver Stone, greater dares were still to come. Though he was proud of *Wall Street* and *Talk Radio*, neither project was as dear to him as *Platoon*. They were good films, but they were not a mission that had to be completed, a dream that had to be fulfilled. Now he was about to embark on such a project. The second dream, *Born on the Fourth of July*, was about to become reality.

CHAPTER TEN

Born on the Fourth of July

"There are people sacrificing and getting killed every day over there and nobody back here seems to care."

Ron Kovic in **BORN ON THE FOURTH OF JULY**

Like Oliver Stone, Ron Kovic seems to have always had a sense of destiny. His life was an odyssey, a journey through the American dream to the nightmare of Vietnam and back home to the punctured delusion that his divided country had become. Kovic enlisted in the Marine Corps because he loved America. When he left, they were waving the flag in the streets. When he returned home from Vietnam, paralyzed from the mid-chest down, they were burning it. Kovic still loved his country, but it no longer loved him. Kovic's saga, the story of what it took to bring him full circle to become a leader of a powerful anti-war movement, forms the heart of *Born on the Fourth of July*. The film has the same title as Kovic's best-selling book, which he pecked out with two fingers on his $40 Sears, Roebuck manual typewriter, purging himself of emotional baggage and often pounding so hard that the periods left holes in the paper. Kovic says "the words poured out like a scream."

Later, much to Kovic's surprise, the world actually heard that scream. He was asked to give a prime-time speech during the 1976 Democratic Convention, and a month later his book was reviewed on the front page of the *New York Times* book review section.

Kovic had a real reason for wanting to see his story done as a film. "I wanted to undo those romantic images presented in films like *Guadalcanal Diary* and *Sands of Iwo Jima*, the John Wayne mentality that led me to war," he says. "For years, I felt there was nothing worthwhile about the tragedy that had befallen me. Making a movie would enable me to give something back to others instead of merely being a victim. Life isn't about avoiding conflict and pain, but shaping it into something beneficial."

Oliver Stone wanted to bring Kovic's story to the screen, and it had been exceedingly painful to both him and Kovic when the effort went down in flames in 1979 only a few days before filming was to commence. But afterwards, Stone put it out of his mind. He did not think seriously about the project again until his agent, Paula Wagner, suggested it to him in 1987. She was also representing Tom Cruise, and said that she thought Cruise might take the Kovic role, and that with Tom Pollock as the new head of Universal, they might make the film. "Suddenly it seemed relatively easy," Stone says. "I reread the script, and I got excited about it all over again. I'd forgotten, but I had killed myself writing it back in '78."

Wagner remembers the incident well: "One of the greatest screen characters I've ever read was Ron Kovic in *Born on the Fourth of July*. I remember pulling that script at Universal and reading it. I had the same kind of cathartic reaction to it that I'd had when I read *Platoon*. I thought, 'Oh, my God, how often do you have a character that goes on a journey like that?' That's what good characters should be about, but so very few ever have that scope. I called Oliver right away."

At the time, Stone had been considering rewriting *Once Too Much*, the screenplay he had written in 1971 that was loosely based on his own experiences as a returning Vietnam veteran. "I started another script called *Second Life* about those same experiences, but I hadn't finished it. I reread that one and then I reread *Once Too Much*, and I put them both aside in favor of doing *Born on the Fourth of July*. My story was frankly esoteric, coming from a wealthier background. Ron's story is a broader story, but I could relate to much of it on a very personal basis. And what a privilege it was to go back for the second time in my lifetime and do an old script that I really loved."

Stone then called Ron Kovic. Kovic had taken the 1978 disappointment pretty hard, and Stone's call came totally out of the blue: "When things fell apart back then, Oliver had said to me, 'If I ever get the opportunity to direct, if I ever break through, I'll come back for you.' And he never forgot that promise. When *Platoon* came out, he could have done any film he wanted, but he came back. He called and he said just three words, 'Ronnie, I'm ready.'"

Stone and Kovic then got together and made some changes in the script. "We changed the Georgia scene where he confesses to the parents of the man he accidentally shot, and also the ending." Stone says. "We ended with the Democratic Convention where he spoke, and I think the original script ended with the 1972 Republican Convention where he's thrown out. Also, the structure was changed around after he returned from Vietnam a bit, but most of those elements were kept in some form or another."

Tom Pollock was indeed interested in making *Born on the Fourth of July*. "I realized that it was one of the great unmade screenplays of the past fifteen years," Pollock says. "I told Stone we'd be interested if he could do it real cheap."

"Cheap" meant $14 million with a major star attached. Stone felt in his gut that Tom Cruise was destined to play the role, but he considered Sean Penn, Charlie Sheen, Nicolas Cage—all of whom he believes the studio would have accepted. In the end, though, he went with Cruise.

Stone's feelings were confirmed when he met with Cruise to discuss the role: "I sensed that Tom could do the part because I'd met him a few times before and I knew there was a darkness in him. Tom had a hard childhood, and there were emotional problems there. I felt that Ron and I could tap into that and help him bring it out."

It was the right time for Cruise. Coming off of hits like *Cocktail*, *The Color of Money*, and the blockbuster *Top Gun*, and about to embark upon the prestigious *Rain Man* project, he was primed to make the turn from big box-office attraction to genuine star. "I was looking for a progression," Cruise acknowledges. "Something that was going to challenge me. I look for that in every film, but I knew that this was going to be one of the most important films I'd ever do and certainly the most complex, physically and emotionally."

There were several interesting similarities between Cruise and Kovic, not least of which is their birthdays—Kovic really was born on the Fourth of July, while Cruise was born on July 3. Both were raised as Catholics from working-class families with a strong drive to succeed. Cruise's parents were divorced, and he attended nine grade schools and struggled with dyslexia. He was an outsider. "I grew up with 'no's' and 'can'ts,' but I learned to look ahead," Cruise says, "always pushing myself forward so I wouldn't be overcome by the situation."

Kovic was initially skeptical of Cruise, but once he met him, he changed his mind. When Stone and Cruise arrived at Kovic's childhood home in Massapequa, Long Island, the actor rushed out of the car and gave Kovic a hug. "I felt an instant rapport with him that I never experienced with Pacino," Kovic says. "They descended upon my house, going through my books, playing old home movies on the VCR. We talked for hours in the kitchen and then I began to cry. Oliver asked if I was okay. All I could say was, 'Tom understands, he really understands.' I felt like a burden was lifted and that I was passing all this on to Tom. I also knew what he was about to go through. He was going to the dark side, in his own way. He was going to Vietnam . . . and worse."

Stone had known that the only way Cruise could do the role was if he waited until after *Rain Man*. But even before he began filming that project, Cruise was visiting VA hospitals and rehabilitation centers, learning as many details as he could about the effects of paralysis and life as a disabled man.

Although Stone says he didn't cast Cruise because of the actor's bankability at the box office, he admits he did play off Cruise's image. "I figured people saw him as this kid who had everything because he was so young and such a big star, and I thought that would work for the film," Stone says. "This kid in the prime of life, what if tragedy strikes, cuts him down, and one thing after another unravels in his life like in Ron's?"

The casting of other key roles in the film also gave Stone a lot of satisfaction. For Kovic's parents, Stone chose Raymond J. Barry and Caroline Kava, both of whom had been in *Year of the Dragon*, Kava as Mickey Rourke's wife and Ray Barry as his superior officer. "I cast them before I barely looked at anybody," Stone says. "I just knew that I wanted them. Also, Josh Evans was great as the brother. I thought Kyra Sedgwick was so sweet and impeccable as the girl he loves, but can't make love to . . . I love that scene where he meets her again and you know it's really over. He sees it in her eyes right away."

It was a large cast, 160 speaking roles and 1,200 extras. The vast numbers needed for the film's Fourth of July parades, student demonstrations, and presidential conventions were recruited from local Dallas organizations such as the American Legion, Campfire Girls, and the National Paralysis Foundation. There were several actors from the *Platoon* cast, including both Willem Dafoe and Tom Berenger. Also cast as one of the vets in wheelchairs that Kovic meets in a bar in Mexico was Tom Sizemore, who would later work with Stone in *Natural Born Killers*. Many of the handicapped roles went to people who really were in wheelchairs. Kevin McGuire, who appears in the Republican Convention at Miami scene, had been in a wheelchair since 1968, the victim of a drunk driver. He was working as an assistant district attorney in the Bronx when he wrote Oliver Stone a letter. Two months later he was called and told he had gotten a part.

As word spread through Hollywood about the project, people began to think that Stone was going too far. Paula Wagner remembers: "It was like, 'Oh no, another Vietnam movie?' Oliver put himself way out there with that picture. A lot of people out here were expecting, almost wanting it to fail. Oliver deals with primal emotions and big sweeping philosophical concepts. And yet he's an emotional filmmaker. He takes an intellectual idea and turns it into emotional stakes that lunge at you on screen. Popular filmmaking just isn't an intellectual medium. Ideas have to be translated into the visual. In films you have to walk out having experienced something, and that has to be done through the visual. Oliver has an ability to pull emotions from the audience. He's a director that knows how to zap you. He decides what he wants you to experience and you experience it. I think one day his movies will be viewed to understand what the world was like in the middle of the twentieth century."

> "Do you hear me? Can I break through your complacency? Can I have an inch . . . a moment of compassion for the human beings who are suffering in this war?"
>
> Ron Kovic in **BORN ON THE FOURTH OF JULY**

According to Wagner, *Born* was a very difficult film for Stone to make because he wanted to do an epic-scale film, but only had a modest budget. "But he wouldn't compromise his production values, the technical aspects of the film," Wagner says. "He's a great technician and his demand for quality, his values, are extraordinary."

Though Stone nearly always resents battles over money because he says they siphon off his creative energy, he was pleased with the compromise he made with Universal. He and Cruise agreed to forego their usual salaries and take a percentage of the profits instead. If the film did well, they would make out, but if not they would walk away with zip. Still, Stone has praise for Tom Pollock. "Pollock is the only executive I know who would have made the film at all in those days," Stone says, "and he deserves credit for that. Of course, when it came to numbers, it was like pulling teeth. Naturally, he was concerned about the commerciality of the piece, and that's part of his job."

Stone was facing a Herculean task. He was attempting to cover twenty years of a man's life, taking place in locations as diverse as a New York small town, coastal Vietnam, college campuses, a VA hospital, and the Mexican desert. This meant more demand than ever on Stone's production team, including Alex Ho. "By the time we did *Born*, Oliver had learned a lot about the realities of production," says Ho. "But I still had to present these kinds of problems to him in the right way because, naturally, being so creative, he tends to always be for the creative side. I don't work like other people. I don't go in and say, 'Well, you have to do this.' I'm not going to argue with him. You don't argue with the director. He's the creative center, so what are you going to do? You give him choices—this is the course and this is the end result. One of my favorite lines with him is, 'This is Plan A, Plan B, or Plan C.' We always say that now. Each plan is just a different way of cutting the cake. These are the downsides, these are the upsides. I present it and he asks what I recommend, and then he makes his choices."

Ho frequently had to be the bearer of bad news. It was his job to hold down the costs and keep within the budget. Stone was known at this time for never having gone over budget, a real rarity among Hollywood directors. Besides that, he'd never been late with a film. "Oliver has learned that you can do it a certain way if you want, but it will cost more," Ho says. "He's learned how to work with that. Sometimes we clash. On *Born on the Fourth of July*, we went through a gigantic argument—we were scouting locations and the art director wanted to build a bank building at the end of the town that was like four blocks away. The building was going to cost fifty thousand dollars. I said, 'You'll never see that in print.' Oliver said, 'Yes, you will.' I said, 'It's your decision.' He told them to build it. Fifty thousand dollars and you never saw the goddamn bank building in the movie. Well, actually you saw a corner of it on a pan that goes from bottom up."

"That's Alex's favorite story," says production manager Clayton Townsend. "He loves to tell that one. Hell, Oliver only shot the corner of the building just so he didn't have to hear Alex complain about it.

"The production demands for *Born* were incredible," Townsend goes on. "We had a lot of materials to cover and not a lot of money. We saved a little by having done *Talk Radio* in Dallas, but still the demands of duplicating Massapequa, Long Island, in Dallas were extensive."

Production designer Bruno Rubeo gave several blocks of houses on Oak Cliff Street new faces and landscaping in an effort to recreate Massapequa as it was in 1957 for the film's opening sequence and the section on Kovic's high school years.

Also under intensive preparation at this time was Dale Dye, who besides being a technical adviser did a joint cameo with Oliver Stone in the film when he played a colonel being interviewed by Stone as a TV reporter. "*Born* was easier for me than *Platoon*," Dye says, "because I had a smaller unit of men to work with and they were supposed to be Marines. We had to split the training period though, a week in the States and a week in the Philippines. Tom Cruise was out with us, and I treated him no differently than I treated anybody else. We were less concentrated on the Vietnam experience and more focused on a preproduction mode. A big part of it was, of course, helping Tom Cruise get the mentality he needed for the film. Naturally, I had to draw a lot on Ron Kovic. Ron and I have different views about a lot of things, especially about the Marine Corps, but regardless of that it was important for me to be in his mind and see how he felt so that I could help Cruise in what he had to learn."

"It was very important that Tom knew what it was like to be a Marine," Stone confirms. "In the 1960s, for kids like Ron, to be a Marine was to be the best. With Dale, we tried to instill in Tom that essence, which, given Tom's nature, wasn't as difficult as it might have been."

"Marines are all volunteer," Dye adds. "We have different motivations, we talk and act differently than drafted soldiers."

Dye returned to Camp Castaneda in the Philippines where the training had been done for *Platoon*, but he also trained a week near Houston, Texas: "Oliver is very smart about assembling his team. He's aware of everything on the set, unlike some directors. He knows if the grips or the gaffers are screwing up and he keeps using the same people, the ones who care about making good films. When I'm training, he always comes out and stays a night and runs a night ambush just to see if we got our bush feet. How many other guys in his position will do that? He wants to see what's going on. I welcome that. I love to show off what I'm able to do. I'll say, 'Hey, Colonel, look.' And he's usually very impressed."

Cruise and the other actors had to dig their own foxholes and live in them, learn how to handle weapons such as grenades, mines, rifles, and pistols, and study the basic aspects of combat, tactical maneuvers, setting up a base camp and chain of command.

Cruise's training also included extensive time in a wheelchair and learning other significant aspects of being handicapped. "I've learned that people react to you [in a wheelchair] one of two ways," Cruise says. "They're either uncomfortable and they come across as if they're angry, like the clerk in the store, or else they take the back of the wheelchair and try to help you when you don't need help. Either way it's very frustrating."

Stone has a penchant for bringing in advisers to ensure that everything is accurate in his films; in addition to Dale Dye, specialists were called in on parades, high school wrestling, political conventions, life as a paraplegic, and sixties fashions.

Besides Ron Kovic, Stone consulted with several sixties activists, including Jeff Nightbird and the legendary Yippie co-leader, Abbie Hoffman, who was brought in to help everyone understand the feelings and dynamics of the peace movement. The late Hoffman even played a small part in the film, as a speaker at an anti-war demonstration.

Other preparations included locating over 350 vehicles to coincide with the time periods covered in the film. The cars ranged from the late forties through the mid-seventies, but there were also quite a few odd requirements, such as a 1956 bulldozer.

As filming was about to commence, Stone and Kovic held a press conference and told the local Dallas newspapers what they wanted to accomplish with the film. "I want to tell the truth to the American people," Kovic said. "I want them to know what really happened in Vietnam and what happened when we came home. This film also is about not giving up. It's about people fighting against adversity, about overcoming adversity—about never giving up, and making something good and decent out of life."

Stone said simply, "We want to show America through Ron's story that they need to redefine their concept of heroism."

Around this time Stone got sick. He'd been having a lot of congestion, headaches, and fatigue ever since he got to Dallas, but had ignored the symptoms until they started interfering with his work. He went to Baylor Hospital, where they suggested some tests and gave him some medicine, but his condition worsened. Now, fearing that filming might have to be delayed, Stone began to agonize until his psychological state was as bad as his physical. He views illness the same way he views any other obstacle, as something to be overcome. In fact, because of his tendency to dramatize, even something as simple as the flu can lead to questioning the cosmos. As things worsened, Leeane Stonebreaker, the production coordinator for the film, called a local Dallas physician who had treated a few people in the production office. Dr. Chris Renna, who has since become Stone's personal physician and good friend, recognized the symptoms as an allergic reaction to a particular type of pollen that is common in the Dallas area during that time of the year and treated Stone effectively.

Filming began on schedule in October 1988, with a residential section of southeast Dallas that had been transformed into the Massapequa, Long Island, neighborhood in which Kovic grew up. "We built Long Island in Texas, which was an amazing achievement by Bruno Rubeo and our staff," Stone says of the opening scenes. "I wanted the big sky look of Long Island before the trees came in. We tried to show the quintessential American experience. The parade was tough because it was a big parade to stage in the downtown area we were using."

For the parade scenes, the film company suggested that two schools in the area find people who would volunteer as extras, and donate their acting fees to the schools. It proved to be a large fundraiser for both schools.

The opening scenes of boys playing "Army" in the woods lead into the classic Fourth of July parade of the fifties—flag waving, marching veterans. Young Ronnie Kovic, atop his father's shoulders, strains to take it all in. In the early scenes, Sean Stone, age four, appears as Ron Kovic's younger brother Jimmy. It was his third film appearance.

After the 1957 scenes were shot, the crew returned to update the town for the parade scenes that would take place in 1969. The Dallas suburb of Pleasant Grove was used as the Kovics' neighborhood in 1965. The film picks up with Kovic in high school, part of the wrestling team, where he learns the importance of "sacrificing" and "never giving up no matter what the pain."

> "If you wanna win, you gotta SUFFER . . . you gotta pay the price for Victory. The price is SACRIFICE. SACRIFICE, people!"
>
> Wrestling Coach in **BORN ON THE FOURTH OF JULY**

Young Ronnie works after school in the A&P store his dad manages, dreams of Donna (Kyra Sedgwick), and is deeply impressed with the Marine sergeant who addresses the school (Tom Berenger), looking for a few men good enough to be Marines. Cruise is very believable as a boy of sixteen who wants nothing more in the world than to win the state wrestling championship. We watch him evolve into a young adult, contemplating his future and hating himself for lacking the courage to ask Donna to the Senior Prom. Probably the best scene in the opening third of the film is the night of the prom when Kovic, frustrated at home, at last summons up the courage and races through the rain in his flannel shirt, jeans, and stocking feet right into the Senior Prom where he finally embraces Donna for the last dance of the night and, tragically, what will turn out to be the only dance of his life.

Stone shot the prom scene with a sweeping 360-degree tracking shot that made the moment as romantic as some others in the film are painful. "I consider the camera another actor," Stone says. "I hate the type of direction that makes the camera a slave. I always respect the camera. I walk on the set and I see a triangle between the actor, the camera, and myself. Even though the camera is inanimate, it is as much a human participant to me as I am. Often the camera will speak to me on the day, and say, 'Not this, that.' I might make notes for days on what I want to do, but then the camera suggests a better way of doing it."

Stone prefers to shoot sequentially whenever possible because he believes this helps everyone involved with the film develop the right mind-set as it progresses. Actors especially like shooting that way because it helps them follow the appropriate character arc. Unfortunately, budgetary considerations often make shooting in sequence impossible, as changing locations more than necessary can be very expensive. According to Tom Cruise, Stone shot *Born* in sequence except where it proved to be unfeasible. "It was pretty much in sequence except that the stuff in Mexico and Vietnam was shot last," Cruise says. "Those scenes were shot in the Philippines, at the end of the shoot. In the beginning of the shoot, I was able to start as a young man, thank God. We shot the wrestling scenes first and it went on from there."

Early on in the filming, local Dallas papers were carefully following the movements of Tom Cruise. They dutifully reported everywhere the star had been seen, including a late night appearance at Dallas Stadium where Cruise and others from the production rented out the stadium after that Sunday's Cowboys game and played touch football until 2:00 A.M.

The biggest transition for Cruise was going from the high school sequences to the scenes that followed. Since the Vietnam section was being filmed at the end of the shooting schedule in the Philippines, the next sequence was the VA hospital where the wounded Ron Kovic first had to face life as a paraplegic. The Old Parkland Hospital, as it was called, in Dallas had been a minimum security prison for many years before the sheriff's department turned it into a training facility. That made it a fitting location for the grim hospital ward scenes. Bruno Rubeo and his crew took over an entire floor and recreated dozens of antiquated hospital rooms.

One of the most difficult periods in Ron Kovic's life was the time he spent at the Bronx Veterans' Administration Hospital in New York, where the conditions were abominable. For Tom Cruise, these scenes would be the greatest challenge he would face in the film, and quite possibly for his entire career as an actor.

Besides the huge physical change, Kovic's emotional state had also undergone a drastic transformation. One of the things that made his tragedy so particularly frustrating was that it was not only the issue of whether or not the entire Vietnam War was even necessary, but also the fact that his paralysis could have easily been avoided. On that day on the shores of a beach in Vietnam, Kovic was shot first in the foot. With most of his heel blasted away, all he had to do was stay down and wait for the medics; but filled with the images of heroism he had taken in all throughout his youth and the Marine dogma he so heartily believed, Ron stood on one leg and began firing, charging the enemy in a mad burst of heroics. In return, Ron Kovic was blasted to bits with a barrage of machine-gun fire that tore into him and shattered his spinal cord, rendering him paralyzed from the waist down.

Shipped back to the States, Kovic tried to accept his injury. After all, he had known the risk when he signed up—he had put his life on the line for his country. There had been virtually no anti-war movement in Massapequa before Ron went to Vietnam. For the most part the protests had begun across the country while he was over there, and now, sentenced to a wheelchair for life, he was about to encounter a huge segment of society that believed he had done it for nothing. Even worse, that he was wrong in going to war in the first place. Instead of the hero the flags waved for on his birthday, the Fourth of July, he was considered by many the murderer of innocent villagers, a baby killer.

This was Kovic's darkest fear come to life to torment him until the end of his days. And the horrendous conditions he encountered at the Bronx VA Hospital, due to the fact that Vietnam was an undeclared war and VA hospitals lacked funding more than in previous wars, only seemed to validate this horrible realization. Ron Kovic was not being rewarded for sacrificing himself for his country, he was being punished for having been a fool.

"Vietnam's a white man's war, a rich man's war . . . if you ain't part of the solution, then you's part of the problem. . . ."

William, a ward attendant in **BORN ON THE FOURTH OF JULY**

This was the panorama that Tom Cruise was now expected to portray. These were the scenes that had always worried Stone. He knew Cruise was good, but he also knew this role was the most demanding one he had ever written and these were the most difficult scenes of all. "Tom was a bit cocky," Stone says now. "He was sure he could handle everything, but I wasn't so sure. I knew he'd bitten off a lot—more than he'd thought. He was shaky at first, but we shot in continuity as much as possible, and step by step, he began to understand."

Cruise acknowledges that the hospital scenes were the hardest. "I'm gonna tell you, it was pretty brutal sitting in that hospital," he says. "It's hard to say which stuff was the hardest because you've got days where you're physically exhausted. Then some of it is emotionally hard. It was very difficult, I remember it was very hard for me to go and see people in wheelchairs and stuff. But the hospital . . . there's a scene where I'm in the hospital after my leg was broken and I'm in a full body cast. I remember that day was a very tough day. To be honest, every day was kind of that way. But that day, it was interesting because Ron Kovic was smiling the whole time. I was surprised by that and later I was talking to Oliver about it and then I asked Ron, and he . . . I mean, can you imagine your whole life being played out before you? He was exorcising all of this, the pain, the demons of the anguishing memory that had been gnawing at him all these years, it was very cathartic for him. He was great, very supportive, but I remember that day he was smiling because he said that's the way it was, that's the way it happened."

Kovic recognizes the cathartic process. "It was extraordinary," he says. "It became a very healing experience. I felt like I had been through a lot of injustices, and every time a scene was completed, every time an injustice was portrayed the way it had happened, I felt a release from that injustice."

Part of what made Kovic's hospital experience such an ordeal was that he had to lie strapped to a bed for four months in a desperate bid to save his leg from amputation. For these scenes Cruise was strapped down to the bed, helpless and immobilized in much the same way Kovic had been. "He was stuck in that bed for four months," Cruise exclaims. "Four months! We were only in that hospital for a week and a half, and when the shooting was over, I could get up and walk away. To know how he believed that he was doing the right thing by going to Vietnam, to have put your life on the line for your country, and then to be treated that way. It was easy for me to find the rage after that. It was so real looking. You'd show up on the set and it was so disgusting. It was degrading being on those tables while they're cleaning your bowels out and all of that. I'm thinking, 'My God, think what it was like for these men. How they were treated at these hospitals.' It was an emotionally difficult thing. People at the VA hospital were fired because they allowed us in to look around there. These were people who were risking their lives for their country so you would think that they'd have decent health care."

> "I fought for my country . . . I fucking deserve to be treated . . . decent . . . decent! I earned that right, you fuck!"
>
> Ron Kovic in **BORN ON THE FOURTH OF JULY**

Stone insisted on reproducing the conditions as accurately as possible. This included vomit and human feces left uncleaned for long periods of time, just as it was in some of the real VA hospitals. "I think we were all shocked and horrified to see that stuff," Stone says. "The enema scene was probably the worst. I remember I insisted that there would be real shit all over the place, so they brought in animal waste and that was tough. And seeing the body parts so twisted and exposed and the paraplegics left helpless like squirming dolls. The grittiness, the oppression, the emotional intensity. It was just hard. And I was pushing Tom. He was getting tired. It was really hard on him."

What was Stone pushing for? Cruise was already feeling so bad for Kovic that he could hardly continue. What did Stone expect? Then it happened. Cruise stopped feeling sorry for Kovic and began feeling the pain in his own psyche. This was the crucial moment Stone had been agonizing over. Could Cruise handle this kind of torment and still deliver? Would he come apart or retreat back into some kind of formula performance, simply delivering lines and putting on emotions? Or would he break through, drawing inwardly upon Kovic's pain to empower his performance with heart? Was he a good-looking guy who could memorize his lines and hit his marks, or was he a great actor?

Cruise remembers the moment: "Suddenly, I stopped thinking about the pain or the humiliation there would be in that situation and I began to crumple inside as I realized a sense of the loss of manhood. The loss of the ability to create on a physical level. Not just not being able to feel a woman, to be inside her, but to never be able to create a family. To procreate is a very important aspect of life. It was something I'd never thought about before and suddenly I was feeling it."

Ron Kovic also recalls the moment when he knew that Cruise was giving the performance of his life. "I was watching the dailies and one of the crew leaned over to me and whispered, 'He's going to do it, he's going to do it.' Something special was happening and Tom Cruise was at the heart of it. He went to the edge."

"At that moment a part of Tom passed from youth to middle age," Stone says. "Just as *Platoon* sucked something out of Charlie Sheen, it will be hard for Tom Cruise to go back to being innocent again. He'll always carry around Ron Kovic inside."

Cruise admits it was difficult for him, even to the point of acknowledging that he couldn't have handled such a role not long before. Fortunately, in the last few years Cruise had worked with Martin Scorsese and Paul Newman in *The Color of Money* and with Barry Levinson and Dustin Hoffman in *Rain Man*. "I would have had to be an idiot not to walk away with something from that. Charlie, my character in *Rain Man*, was spiritually autistic, so I didn't play the emotion. Ron holds nothing back, so I had to put everything out. It was my most challenging role ever. I made it work one day at a time. If I looked at the mountain, it was just too high."

While Stone tends to rattle the cages of his actors to keep them on their toes, he doesn't always take the same approach. The idea is to make them better and perhaps bring out something that they didn't even know they had. Sometimes this can be done through encouragement instead of getting them where it hurts. This was the case with Tom Cruise. "Cruise was a horse, an iron horse," Stone says. "We had a few icy moments because I was pushing him too hard and he said to me once or twice, 'I put enough pressure on myself, I don't need you to put pressure on me.' He was right. Tom is kind of macho and he wants the best. Perfection is his goal, and if he doesn't achieve it, his frustration is high. He was usually very polite under very tough circumstances, but he has a temper, he's not a saint, but anyone who's healthy does. And I did put pressure on him. But I think it helped because the Kovic role needed the pressure—the guy was living on the edge."

Cruise felt that he and Stone got along exceptionally well. "We didn't have many conflicts," he says. "It's important that the actor and the director work together as a team. There are times that he was actually kind of laid back on me. I worked so hard on it that I didn't need to be pushed much, and he helped me more by just saying, 'Hey, try it this way,' and then I would go in that direction."

Elizabeth Stone was on the set taking photographs. By now she had noticed a pattern in her husband's relationships with actors: "He likes to rile his actors to make them better. He does that on one level or another with every actor and actress in his films. But he's also very good at encouraging their input. When he hears lines, when he rehearses, which he's very religious about doing, he respects the actors enough to where, if it comes out a different way, he'll just sit and rewrite it. He'll say, 'Yup, you're saying it right,' and then he'll change it."

Since she had been his assistant on *The Hand*, this was Elizabeth's sixth Oliver Stone film, and being a naturally encouraging person, she was always popular with the cast and crew. More than once, in fact, she wound up playing the role of "set shrink." "I'm often the mediator," she acknowledges. "I guess it's because I'm very accessible—anybody can talk to me—and it's a roundabout way of communicating a problem to Oliver. He's usually working and can't be interrupted, so I get a lot of the kind of petty grievances, gripes, hurt feelings or whatever, and they know that it will eventually get to Oliver."

The Stones' son, Sean, is also well liked on the set, partly because of the effect he tends to have on his father. "Oliver loves having Sean on the set because he's comic relief for him," Elizabeth says. "He says there's nothing takes the tension off a set more than to see a kid run in. And Bob Richardson has always had a funny thing with Sean where he'll pick him up and put him into a wastebasket, put him in a punch bowl or put him into the cake. That's been a running motif from film to film—where is Bob going to put Sean next? Oliver's face will lighten up when he sees his son come running around the corner. That's one reason it's always been important for me to be there. Not so much me; I mean, he likes to know that I'm there backing him up, but no matter how angry or upset he is over something, there's been very few times that Sean has not been able to make Oliver smile."

Born on the Fourth of July was unfolding as Stone had hoped. He began to relax a little. Clayton Townsend recalls one evening around this time when the carousing got a little out of hand. "We went out to dinner after shooting another one of those all day into the night things. It was Oliver, Bob Richardson, Alex, me, and a few other people. Well, we partied pretty good that night, and we were walking back from the hotel after about forty tequilas or whatever, and Bob and I, for some reason, decided to tackle Oliver in the lawn across from the Crescent Court shopping center. So we had a quick wrestling match on the ground at about two in the morning and suddenly Oliver starts yelling . . . 'Ahh my thumb, my thumb!' So we stopped and he said his thumb was hurting, but he was so drunk he forgot all about it by the time we got back to the hotel. We went to the hotel bar then, and after a while Steve and Billy Baldwin, two of the actors in the movie, showed up and started fucking around with Oliver, sort of jabbing and sparring with him a little bit. Well, the next morning Oliver woke up in real pain because his thumb was hurting, so he went to the hospital and had it X-rayed and it was broken. So he came back from the hospital and asked Bob and I if we knew how it happened because he didn't remember anything. So we said it was fucking Billy and Stevie Baldwin who did it. And to this day he still doesn't know it was us. Well, not until he reads this book anyway."

The next scenes had to do with Ron Kovic's return to his Massapequa home—paralyzed, wheelchair-bound. The scene where his mother watches through a window from inside the house as Ron is helped from the car into his wheelchair is very moving. She had hoped to conceal her pain by watching from a distance, but runs from the house to embrace him and, at his touch, is overwhelmed and begins weeping.

For Ron Kovic, these scenes were the most difficult. "The house that I had grown up in had been completely recreated inside of a warehouse," Kovic says. "I went up a ramp into my house, and all of a sudden I was sitting next to someone in a wheelchair. I didn't know that it was Tom at first—I hadn't seen him in a wheelchair with his long hair and mustache. All of a sudden I turned, facing Tom, and Tom turned, facing me. With his hair and mustache, he looked just like me, and he was deeply in character. I mean, he was fucking serious and made me feel very uncomfortable, because he was a mirror of myself twelve years before, and it bothered me, it upset me inside."

After a while Kovic couldn't take it and finally had to let it out: "I looked over at Tom and I said, 'Fuck you. You're making me depressed.' And Tom's yelling, 'You're making me depressed.' It was a crazy scene. We were laughing and cursing and shouting and screaming. And it was great."

This aspect of sharing the burden in Kovic and Cruise's relationship became very apparent during the filming of another painful scene. Kovic comes home drunk and, having lost his faith, tells his staunchly religious mother that "There's no God and there's no country . . . it's just me and this wheelchair forever . . . for nothing . . . me and this dead penis." So that Cruise could grasp the feelings of Kovic's mother (something which added to the pain Kovic was feeling at the time), Stone had Cruise take the role of the mother while Kovic read his own part in rehearsals.

"Don't say penis in this house."

Mom in **BORN ON THE FOURTH OF JULY**

After four readings, Kovic was drained. He began to doubt if doing the film was worth the pain he was having to experience, and when the set wrapped for the day, he headed toward the airport planning to hop a plane back home to Redondo Beach. "I felt so alone," he says. "Like I was running point on the biggest adventure of my life. I wondered if I had it inside me to get through this. Then a Jeep pulled up next to me, and it was Cruise. I rolled down the window and he yelled, 'Why does your life have to be so difficult, so challenging? This is very depressing for me.' We shouted and laughed back and forth, all the frustration came out. I began to realize that I wasn't alone, that Tom was paying a price for this film, too. He was agonizing through this part, and he didn't know if he could go on, either. All of a sudden, I realized that Cruise understood. I had a brother, I had a friend. We were in this till the end, no matter what. That night, I slept well. The film has helped me let go of the anger, the regret and the pain, and search for the better person inside myself."

"You know, Mom . . . I never made love to a girl. . . ."

Ron Kovic in **BORN ON THE FOURTH OF JULY**

Stone remembers these as the hardest scenes of the entire shoot: "Those were grueling fucking scenes. Four days in that house. We built it to match Ron's home in Massapequa which was a small house, and I had them keep it that way because I wanted it to feel cramped. And the emotions of the scene are at a hysterical point. I didn't want it to fall into a stereotype, and scenes like that can, so we sort of took it in waves. Like the colostomy bag part, that was very hard."

"Why did it happen this way . . . I prayed for you over there, Ronnie, you didn't know how much I prayed . . . you were always the best, the brightest little boy . . . that little smile. . . . I loved you most of all."

Mom in **BORN ON THE FOURTH OF JULY**

Though few in the crew would have been able to tell, Kovic and Cruise weren't the only ones feeling the trauma. A few days later, Stone got sick again. It came on when he was shooting outside on a cold night in the rain. It was the scene where Kovic is drunk out of his mind playing pool and his buddies carry him outside the bar and put him in the car. By the time they wrapped, Stone felt horrible and thought of closing the film down for a day, but he didn't want to have any insurance claims so he pushed on, feeling worse and worse as the week continued. The production had that Saturday off, but Stone was booked to do a press junket for *Talk Radio*. He had forty-five interviews scheduled, but after number twenty-seven he nearly collapsed. The next day he was taken to a nearby hospital where Chris Renna examined him and discovered he had a high fever and serious viral infection. Nonetheless, shooting resumed on time the following day.

It was here that Renna began to notice a curious phenomenon. Stone was taking on the identity of the protagonist of his film; part of him was becoming Ron Kovic. "Not having known him before, I didn't know if this was his natural personality or if it was because of the film," Renna says. "But there were certain characteristics, even peculiar ones, that were right in line with those of Ron Kovic. It was the sense of intermittent hope and despair, of idealism and disappointment, and it permeated the set. It wasn't conscious, but the longer I began to know Oliver, the more sure I became that he was sharing his life with the life of Ron Kovic and seeing that through the face and body of Tom Cruise. It was part Oliver, part Ron, and part Tom."

How did Stone respond to Chris Renna's theories at the time? Renna smiles, remembering the incident. "Oliver put me in the film . . . as a psychologist."

Paula Wagner agrees with Renna's theory. She visited the set a few times and describes it as being "electric": "There's always electricity on an Oliver Stone set, but this was a movie that everyone brought passion to, and it was incredible. Oliver draws in every single person that's involved in the shot into that moment with him. It's more like theater sometimes than film. He put everything on the line with that film—his health, his reputation, his sanity. He took some real risks."

The scene where Kovic visits the only girl he'd gotten close to, his almost high school sweetheart Donna, are especially tender, and also essential as it is through Donna that Kovic is able to understand the protest movement. Her kindness and concern enable him to transcend the pain of accepting that he sacrificed so much in vain.

"I mean I gave three-quarters of my body for that war and if you give three-quarters of your body for something you'd better believe it, man, you'd better fucking believe it. . . ."

Ron Kovic in **BORN ON THE FOURTH OF JULY**

The college campus scenes where Kovic and Donna observe an anti-war student demonstration led by radical Abbie Hoffman being violently squelched by police were shot at Dallas's Southern Methodist University, and they are essential to Kovic's shift in political persuasion. Emotionally, they are also important because not only does Kovic start to question his beliefs, but he also has to come to terms with the fact that Donna still cares about him as a friend, but could never have a relationship with him now that he is in a wheelchair.

Breaking sequence again, Stone next shot the scene in which Kovic tracks down the parents of an American soldier he feels he may have accidentally shot while in Vietnam. Though telling the man's family that it was he who may have shot their son instead of the enemy makes the man's death seem even more pointless, it also may save their grandson from a similar fate.

Before breaking for the Christmas holidays, Stone shot both the 1972 Miami Republican Convention and the 1976 Atlanta Democratic Convention Scenes at the Dallas Convention Center. It was at the Republican Convention that Kovic and other Vietnam Veterans Against the War were brutally ejected by security people. "That was a night shoot," Stone recalls. "The planning for the scene where the vets take on the police in the park was exhausting because so much was involved—large groups of people, gas bombs, and all that stuff."

Stone's friend Chuck Pfeiffer appeared as one of the security guards who rough up Kovic in the scene in which he was ejected.

The 1976 Democratic Convention was the complete opposite for Kovic, as he was invited to speak from the podium. These scenes were shot back to back, but Cruise was able to rise to the occasion. As filming wrapped for the Christmas holidays and the crew began to prepare for the move to the Philippines, it was evident that Cruise and Stone had really clicked in. "We really worked as a team," Cruise says. "He was very trusting—he'd let me go with my ideas quite a lot. I call him the 'Van Gogh filmmaker' because his films are intense, vibrant, explosive, unrelenting . . . just like he is. His films are very personal. The imagery is what he sees."

During the holiday break, Stone watched the dailies repeatedly and even edited several sections of the film. In fact, from this project forward he would make a point of editing on a regular basis during the shooting phase of his films. But this time he had a purpose in mind. Stone had never gone over budget. It was an achievement he was proud of. But now that he had shot so much, his vision for *Born on the Fourth of July* had grown. And he knew that it would take more money to fulfill it. He could finish the film on what he had, but not the way he wanted to finish it. There was only one thing to do.

"I went back to Tom Pollock and told him I needed more money," Stone says. "The film was shot in widescreen format to free the viewers more, get them out of the chair, and this added to the cost. I needed $3.8 million to do what I wanted to do. That would take it to $17.8 million. Tom was reluctant at first, so I put some sections of the film together and took it to him. He loosened up when he saw what we'd done and gave us more support. He also let me go ten minutes over the two-hour-and-fifteen-minute limit that was delineated in my contract. He didn't have to do that."

Having been a top entertainment lawyer for years and a studio executive who greenlighted many controversial films, Pollock knows how to balance creativity and the bottom line: "You have to reconcile what you think is good with what you think is profitable. That's what we do all day. In the end, we sprung for changes and let Oliver reshoot some scenes. We got an epic film at a very reasonable cost. There's no one else who could have made it with the emotional impact Oliver did. I'd work with him again in a minute."

As he headed to the Philippines to finish the shoot, Stone knew that he had made it better than halfway. There was no question that many of the hardest scenes were out of the way, but still remaining were the scenes in Mexico where Kovic comes to accept his destiny, and the moments which dictated it in Vietnam. What made the pressure of these next days even greater was that *Talk Radio* was dying at the box office. Arthur Manson, who'd called Stone in the Philippines when he was shooting *Platoon* to tell him that *Salvador* was dying at the box office, once again had the unpleasant task of calling him there to inform him that his previous film was failing. The failure of *Talk Radio* did not cause Stone the magnitude of personal loss he experienced when *Salvador* failed. Still, it bothered him greatly.

The Vietnam scenes were to be shot next. All were hard physically and emotionally. In one, Kovic's platoon is ordered to open fire on a village believed to be harboring Viet Cong. After they decimate the area, they enter to find only old men, women, and children. "That was a killer," Stone says. "Filming the deaths of all these innocents, showing the killing of babies . . . it was difficult."

One of the most technically difficult scenes to shoot was the one in which Kovic accidentally kills one of his own men when he sees someone running toward him during a battle, but then is blinded by the sun. Unsure what to do, he fires, only to discover it was one of the younger recruits. "We had to film with the sun in a certain place in order for that to work, and that was also hard," Stone says.

These scenes and the section where Kovic was wounded were shot in sweltering heat on a Philippine beach. "We were shooting for twelve hours a day in temperatures around 100 degrees," Stone says. "There was no shade on the beach. It was horrible. A lot of people fainted, it was so bad. Tom got this Siamese sinus thing. He was allergic to the dust and it had got in his face and he was out for three days. But I kept on shooting. I couldn't close down, so I kept shooting what I could."

Cruise had carried on throughout with great intensity and commitment. As the picture progressed, he was also gaining increased respect for Stone. "Oliver's a leader," Cruise says. "A big part of the director's job is you gotta move that whole crew. There are so many people you have to move forward. The thing about Oliver is that he makes a decision and if that decision's wrong, he can change, and quickly. Most people who are as creative and open as he is tend to waffle and have a hard time making a decision. Oliver's very sensitive, but he can still lead. He's creative as hell. An incredible writer, an incredible storyteller, but I think that vision is his other greatest strength. He has a powerful vision and he has the ability to bring that vision to pass. That's a rare combination."

Sometimes, after an intense day of shooting, there was some intense partying as well. Clayton Townsend describes one such incident. "It started when I asked Alex Ho for an associate producer credit on the picture back before we started filming," Townsend recalls. "He said, sure, but it would have to cost me a sizable cut in pay, so I said forget it. Then, near the end of the shoot, we were all out one night and we were drinking pretty good. We started talking about the Super Bowl and I knew Oliver was a big 49ers fan so I told him I'd bet him five hundred dollars against an associate producer credit that the Bengals would beat the 49ers in the game. But then Alex spoke up and said five hundred wasn't enough and that it should be ten thousand instead. Well, I was pretty loaded by then, so I said okay. Well, the Bengals lost and I lost the bet. And Oliver said to just forget it, but I paid him anyway. Then later, he decided to give me the credit."

The last sequence to be shot was the Mexican scenes. This section chronicles Kovic's descent into despair, as he attempts to trade his pain for a sea of booze, dope, and decadence in Villa Dulce, a Tijuana-like border town. It is here that Willem Dafoe gives an incredible supporting performance as Charlie, one of the wheelchair-bound Vietnam vets Kovic encounters in Mexico. Charlie is a paraplegic who has some of the same qualities as Elias in *Platoon*, but they are buried beneath his own hard-edged bitterness and pain. In fact, it's easy to imagine that Elias might have wound up like Charlie had he had a different fate—perhaps if the chopper carrying Chris Taylor had been able to rescue him before the last barrage did him in.

"It was nice to return in that kind of role, because there was a logical progression to it," Dafoe says. "Of course, the conditions were quite a bit different. By *Born*, Oliver had a lot of success, while on *Platoon* he was still a scrapper trying to show people something. *Born* was great for me because I went to the Philippines again, but I was at the end of the shoot, the last two weeks, and it felt like the end of the movie. In this case I enjoyed it because I was preparing for another movie [*Triumph of the Spirit*] and the day we wrapped I left for Poland to shoot four months in Auschwitz. So that was very much on my mind and somehow I think that may have been a liberating thing. It was nice to come from the outside with everybody kind of tuckered out and me having all this fresh energy. They were excited but really were beat, and I came in fresh as a daisy. It let me have fun with what is a small but very showy down and dirty role."

Most of the Vietnam vets who'd made it down to this seventh circle of Hell were pretty bitter. Suddenly Kovic was not around people who would enable him to wallow in the self-pity that was slowly destroying him. These men had as much to feel bad about as he did. It is Charlie who first reaches out to Kovic and makes him a part of the group: "Hey, you guys, say hello to Ron Kovic. Just got in from the States."

"Just what we need, another limp dick," responds another vet.

Though the drunken and disabled vets are a sad sight, it is through his relationship with them that Kovic begins to find himself. It is also here that he comes to terms with the source of his greatest pain—not being able to have sex. It is Dafoe's character who by example convinces Kovic that he doesn't have to give up on sex because he no longer has use of his penis. In the scene that follows, a sexually impotent Kovic is straddled by a Mexican prostitute. As he does throughout this film, Cruise, an actor whose natural athleticism and grace is often a key ingredient in his roles, must convey emotion solely through facial expression.

"This scene was another tough one," Stone says. "Tom is by nature a bit shy, but the girl who played the hooker was very free with her body in that Latin sort of way. We kept trying it and it got easier as we went. Then we came to the place where Tom cries. On that take, something happened inside him. As the character he's playing, Ron, he was thinking about everything he'd miss, but the tears . . . those tears come from someplace in Tom."

"That scene was hard for me," Cruise admits. "I went to Oliver and said, 'I'm just not getting it. I'm not there.' I had a lot of anxiety about it, I think, and Oliver picked up on that. I kept going, 'Why do I feel this way . . . all this anxiety?' And he said, 'Just don't think about it. Just do it, man, just do it.' And then we started shooting again, and it started working and I just started crying. I just let go, and pretty soon I was crying and laughing a little bit, too."

Stone describes the Mexican scenes: "We created Mexico in the Philippines, which was a complicated task. We had some various fundamental Spanish architecture we found there and we worked with it. Bruno Rubeo and his art director, Victor Kempster, worked on it, and they had several good art people that really made it come alive. Then, in that little village, we had to deal with all these issues—the vets in the wheelchairs and their anger. Tom Sizemore was great in that small role. And Dafoe gave us a big lift late in the movie because he was so professional. He came in fresh and really nailed it. That wheelchair fight is a classic."

The fight occurs after Cruise and Dafoe are left stranded on a country road in the desert sun by a taxi driver whom they have accused of ripping them off. Helpless in their wheelchairs, left for dead miles away from civilization, the depth of their inner despair surfaces as they begin to argue with each other rather than look for a way to survive. But it is the subject of their argument—who committed the most atrocities in Vietnam—which best reveals the heart of their problem: a deep self-loathing, reinforced by their injuries and confirmed by their inability to cope with them.

"Maybe I killed more babies than you did, you fuck, maybe I killed a whole buncha babies but I don't talk about it! I don't have to talk about it."

Ron Kovic in BORN ON THE FOURTH OF JULY

After the verbal argument reaches its peak, the fight becomes physical. How do desperate men in wheelchairs fight? Like desperate men everywhere—any way they can. After spitting in each other's faces, they begin punching and slamming into each other until eventually they topple out of their wheelchairs and tumble down a hill away from the road.

Lying helpless in the sand at the bottom of the hill, unable to crawl or even to move below the waist, Ron Kovic begins to realize that he has been hiding something behind the facade of playing the hero—he has been hiding himself.

"Why not, Kovic? Why the fuck not? What are you hiding? What are you—better than anybody else? You a hero? Is that what you are?" Charlie says.

It is through this scene that Kovic's pain and rage, as well as his helplessness, can best be grasped. The internal struggle is effectively externalized by the wheelchair fight, which is one of the most powerful scenes in this or any film. From this point Ron Kovic rises to accept his handicap and his mistakes and can at last turn toward his true destiny.

Tom Cruise remembers: "It was literally the last shot, and to me, this day is really what Oliver Stone is all about. We were losing the light and had a minute to get the shot and I realized that I was totally out of gas. I thought, 'What am I going to do? This is a major scene. It's the epiphany of the character, when he confronts what happened to him, it's the beginning of his realization toward accepting his change. And I don't have anything, Jesus, I don't have anything left.' We're on these sand dunes so we're sprinting up the dune to get the last piece of light. Running up the hill and trying to set up and shoot before the light fades further. And everybody's freaking out, 'Goddamn it, just put the camera down—let's go.' And I'm saying, 'I don't have anything left . . . I just can't. . . . ' And Oliver's saying, 'Just do it! Go! Do it.' And we did. And it worked. We got it. Now to me that says, here's a guy who can get things done. Nothing's going to stop him. You hear about all these people, talented people, some of whom have made great films in the past, and then for years they can't get a film made. That'll never happen to Oliver. If he wants to make a movie he just gets the job done."

The sixty-five-day shoot was a tough one, the toughest yet for Oliver Stone. "We pushed and pushed and pushed," Stone admits. "As the sun was going down, I said, 'Let's move them up,' because they were on the ground at that point and we could shoot closeups of them. So we kept moving them up the hill on the sand dune chasing the sun. We finished the last shot as the sun went down."

For Tom Cruise, it was the end of a memorable experience. "I'm so proud I had the opportunity to make that movie. It's one of the things that when I look back on my career, I'm so glad that I played that character. It means a lot to me. The nomination [for Best Actor] meant a lot to me. It's nice to be recognized like that. But just the fact that we did it. We actually did that movie. I'll always treasure that."

Cruise had given his all for the film. And Stone had taken everything he was willing to give and then some. After the shoot was finished, Stone advised Cruise that he should slow down and enjoy life. "Actually, it was touching," Cruise says. "I remember we were sitting in this hotel that [Ferdinand] Marcos built for his daughter's wedding, and we were going to be leaving. Oliver gave me a hug and said, 'Take time to enjoy your life. Have fun while you're young.' It was from his heart."

The gentler side of Stone often surfaces at such times. In the quiet moments after a particularly intense period, he often displays an affectionate kindness. It's as if his madness has been vented, leaving him vulnerable and concerned about the things that endure—love, friendship, truth. But these brief respites never last long. Soon the dragon is at the gate. Richard Rutowski, who had worked with Stone on the *Baby Boy* prison project and was about to come back into his life, comments: "All of his movies seem to have an instant beginning. You enter the process with the character and, as it unfolds, there's pain and disillusionment, and then you're faced with dilemmas that are impossible to resolve. You either rise to it and survive, face the fucking demon, pull up your loincloth and go to battle, or you die. You may come out wounded, but like in *Born on the Fourth of July*, you might survive to discover another aspect of yourself. Of course, that doesn't mean that there isn't another demon waiting out there."

It may sound quixotic and even strange, but in many ways this is how Oliver Stone approaches his life.

At the other extreme is business, and by now, Stone was an enterprise. His offices were humming with secretaries and assistants who kept things going while he was away. Whenever he returns from a shoot, the business mode shifts into gear and he's ready to make deals and decisions. *Born on the Fourth of July* was being prepared for editing. One of Stone's first tasks when he returned was to hire a new assistant, since Elisabeth Seldes, who had worked with him since *Wall Street*, was leaving and she had lined up possible replacements. The person they hired was Kristina Hare, who was living in Washington, D.C., in order to help with fund-raising on the Dukakis campaign. She'd gone to Shipley, an all-girls' school which used to have dances with the Hill School, and studied in France and at Tufts University in Boston, but Stone picked her more for her sense of idealism than anything else. Hare wasn't jaded, like most of the people working in the film business in Los Angeles. She'd work long hours without complaining, and she still believed that film could change the world. When he hired her, Stone said they would have to play it by ear; it all depended on whether or not she could learn to read his mind.

As editing began, it became evident that *Born on the Fourth of July* was going to be something very special. But there were two areas that still concerned Stone. The first was the music. Stone felt the score needed more heart and he wanted to bring in the acknowledged master of film scoring, John Williams, to do it. Second, he wasn't happy with the ending. As shot in Dallas, the ending was Ron Kovic's speech at the 1976 Democratic Convention. Cruise had given a good rendition of Kovic's words, but Stone had doubts about the scene. "The overall look bothered me. The style of it wasn't right, we rushed it and there weren't enough extras. It didn't have the impact we wanted."

At the urging of both Cruise and Tom Pollock, Stone was considering reshooting the scene when another issue surfaced. Pollock wanted to push up the release of the film to Veterans Day instead of the Christmas season. Stone and his producer's rep, Arthur Manson, didn't think that was wise. Pollock was insistent, however. With the reshooting and release issues still undecided, Stone and Pollock clashed hard over additional money for scoring. "I felt we were a little light on the music budget for the film anyway," Stone says, "and when I went to Tom Pollock because I needed a couple of hundred thousand to pay John Williams, he said no. I went ballistic. I thought we had done a sufficiently grade-A film for him to do that, and by stalling on it I was afraid we were going to lose Williams. So it became an issue."

Stone also felt strongly about not moving up the release date of the film, so he went to Mike Ovitz, the head of Creative Artists Agency (CAA), and got him involved. Stone, Ovitz, and Paula Wagner then met with Pollock to discuss all three issues. "There was some give and take," Stone says of the meeting. "I agreed with them to shoot an alternate ending because I felt it was needed. Tom finally caved on the release date and the John Williams thing, but only after an enormous amount of pressure, and it left a lot of bad blood. I didn't continue to work with Universal."

It was decided to reshoot the ending at Olympic Auditorium in Santa Monica. This time, instead of reenacting Kovic's speech, they would end the scene with him being wheeled into the cheering convention. Although principal photography had ended two months before, Cruise was brought back and wheeled into the auditorium by John C. McGinley who, though it was brief, was making his fourth appearance in an Oliver Stone film. "I felt it gave a more dramatic exit to the movie," Stone says. "He doesn't do the speech. He comes down the corridor and then we pull out as he's being cheered. That cheering, that acceptance, *was* the victory."

With this final scene in the can, editing continued. As the last touches were being put together, it became apparent that Stone's willingness to fight for a score by John Williams was yet another master stroke. In many ways the music carries the film from scene to scene.

According to Paula Wagner, the battles over the music were another example of Stone's commitment. "He wanted to have an extraordinary score and bring John Williams in. It was like, 'What do I have to sacrifice, what do I have to do to make this happen?' And he was that way throughout the film. It was the same with the production values and the length of the film—'What do I have to do to make this happen?' He will cut off his arm if that's what he has to sacrifice to put his vision on the screen. That's what's extraordinary about him. But he's also a businessman, he's not a fool. He has a sense of commerce as well as art, and to make a movie you have to be in touch with both. Oliver is tough and he's very smart. I don't think that Oliver is motivated by money, but he knows how to play the game. *Born on the Fourth of July* was another breakthrough film for him. It looks like a forty-million-dollar movie."

As Stone's agent, Wagner has had to deal with him in a variety of situations and not all of them were easy: "I've always spoken my mind to Oliver and we didn't always agree. Because he's so candid, if he spots fear or insecurity in you, he can be frightening, but you just have to hold your ground and be who you are. He's fully candid and expects the same from you. You can spar with him and he responds to that kind of thing. You can give it back to him. He's called and said, 'How could you do such-and-such? What kind of agent are you?' And I would say, 'A good one, Oliver. What kind of a director are you?' People were always surprised to learn that I was his agent because they don't think he can work with women. I'd hear them talking and I'd say, 'Ex-cuse me, but I'm a woman and I'm Oliver's agent.' He deals with me as straight on as you can get, and that's fine with me."

Around this time Stone began a key business relationship with Janet Yang, who had been a production executive at Universal before she agreed to head up Stone's Ixtlan Productions. "He hired me the way he does most things," Yang says. "He went by his gut. I dare say I think I'm a good match for Oliver because I like to ride with his iconoclasm and spontaneity. Many people couldn't handle the lack of structure here. We never had a meeting about my job duties per se. I just followed my nose and sniffed out what seemed appropriate. In the beginning I couldn't even have told you what kind of movies we were looking for. I just knew I had to feel something in the gut when I read a script. Then I'd give it to Oliver and he had to feel something in the gut."

Yang's main job, as vice president of production, is to find and develop material for Stone to produce through Ixtlan. "I get stacks and stacks of scripts and I pick out things that I think might be interesting to him. I send him memos regularly and everything we do has his approval. It's amazing how thorough and responsive he is—even for the woman from Ohio who claims her dog should be in the movies. He may actually respond to her. He doesn't shirk anything off."

Yang says that, like its founder, Ixtlan does things a little differently from most production companies. "Oliver is very lean and mean. He doesn't believe in going out and schmoozing and doing these long lunches and finding out what everybody else is doing. By the same token, he doesn't want people to know what we're doing."

Of course, working with anyone as mercurial as Oliver Stone has its ups and downs. "There was one night not long after I first started when Oliver had been out with Sergio [Premoli] and Sergio goes, 'Oh, Oliver, you're working too hard, you should take more time off.' Sergio wants Oliver to do things like go to Paris and party with women, take drugs and you know, be Jim Morrison or whatever. One day, Oliver came in and said, 'I think I'll take a year off and close up shop.' I just about died. But then the next day, he came in and said, 'We should produce ten to twelve films a year.' I've learned to wait a beat before I get too worked up about anything."

Born on the Fourth of July was released in December 1989, and was almost immediately steeped in controversy. Although many of the top critics called the film an incredible masterpiece ("Best movie of the year, if not the decade"—David Sheehan of NBC-TV), others attacked it for its message and claimed that it was grossly inaccurate. One trivial but popular criticism concerned the college demonstration scene; critics pointed out that Abbie Hoffman wasn't at Syracuse for a war protest. "I just used him for a cameo in the scene," Stone says. "I thought it was a nice touch. I fucked up because Syracuse wasn't the college Ron visited. But there were something like fifty protests on that day, so I think people were missing the point."

Stone felt that such criticisms were focusing on minor story details in order to avoid the painful truth at the film's center. He says the theme of the movie is the theme of Kovic's life: "It's a boy running into his destiny, being betrayed by it, and, through having the courage to face and accept that betrayal, discovering another destiny. All Ronnie's life he wanted to be a hero and he wound up in a wheelchair. But in so doing, he became another kind of hero."

A more significant criticism centered on the fact that one of the key scenes, where Kovic visits the parents of the man he accidentally shot, never actually happened. "I consider that dramatic license, and my justification for it was that Ron did confess to killing his own man in his book," Stone says. "I felt I could show him writing the book, but I'd rather show him going to Georgia and finding those people because he thought about it repeatedly. He had dreams about it, and even located where they were. I thought that Ron in a sense had acted this out by writing about it, which is a significant confession, so I took the liberty of actually having him go down there in the film. In the movie it becomes a key scene because after the fight with Willem Dafoe, it allows him to come back to the States and deal with the reality of what he did. That frees him up to become a public persona who is ready to go out into the world and become a spokesman. You can't go public like that until you conquer it within your private self."

Pauline Kael and a few other top film critics argued that Stone's style was too pushy and made too naked an appeal to the audience's emotions. "They said the same thing about Van Gogh," Stone said at the time. "His work was rude, loud, vulgar, emotionally direct and raw, but it stood well the test of time because it had one thing all his detractors never had—it had life. I love emotion. I love the scene when Tom Cruise comes home from Vietnam and sees his mom. I've gotten a lump in my throat every time I've seen it and I've seen it 150 times. I told John Williams that I wanted the most romantic moment in the score to come at that exact moment when she's running down the ramp to see her son come home from the war. And I wanted the whole thing framed by trees and the Long Island sky, with the neighbors coming in from all sides and the music to mark it as a shining moment.

"That's old-fashioned, but it works. Maybe it's bullying the audience. It does if you're watching that movie from some place where you're trying to hedge as opposed to sharing the experience—sharing the feeling of Ron when he came home. It's a huge moment. He was living loud. When you see your home and your mom the first time after that war— my God, your heart is going to burst. I was making that scene from inside the character's head."

Stone also took heat for the intensity, being accused of making a film so painful to watch that it was almost unbearable for many in the audience. "I wasn't forcing anyone to go see the movie," Stone says. "I'm not destined to be Spielberg or Lucas and I don't expect to get the broadest possible audience, but I made a commitment to a story that I believe has to be told this way. Ron's experience was worse than I showed. We lost a lot of business from young males and I wondered why, and I found out that in some theaters a lot of them walked out just after they found out he lost the use of his penis. I believe that yes, you have to shock and you even have to repulse, but hopefully people will understand there's a wisdom behind it. There's a reason for the madness because it takes you through to the light. That's what I try to do, and if people trust me and they trust my films, they should know that there is a reason. I really want to try to find the light through the darkness."

Stone admits that he may sometimes work too hard at getting his message across, but claims it has more to do with reaching the lowest common denominator than it does with overkill. "I think it's better to be wrong on the side of clarification than of obscurity. That's the thing my father used to drill into me. Concerning my earlier writing, he'd say, 'That's too obscure.' And all my English teachers would drive me nuts with that. Something I'd broken my heart writing that was so clear to me and nobody understood it. My novel was mostly obscure. I just want to be clear. Because I feel I come from a background of obscurity and confusion."

Stone took some of the attacks very personally, especially Pauline Kael's: "Pauline Kael, I gather, didn't like the flag-waving patriotism of *Born*. As if she felt macho American heroism was almost embarrassing. She made a reference in a review to Ron's character not having a sense of humor. Something like, 'Why was he so gung-ho in the first place? Is he for real? Didn't he ever read *Mad* magazine as a kid?' It was mean to Ron. I read *Mad* magazine and I went to war. I was still a believer. Maybe I wasn't exactly a rocket scientist, but I wasn't stupid either. Sometimes it doesn't matter what you read. If you feel this way, you do your duty. You think your country needs you and you do it. There are still people who play football and break their limbs because they think it's a noble thing to do. I guess that's hard for some people to understand. They didn't grow up in that world so they don't relate, especially to a kid from a working-class family."

The attacks in the press took on a new intensity after Ron Kovic announced that he was considering running against Robert Dornan for Congress in Southern California. "That politicized everything," Stone says. "It became instant news. Dornan was terrified of Ron, he hated him. He immediately attacked the movie everywhere he could, on public radio, in the newspaper. Then all the conservatives attacked it. George Will wrote about it, Patrick Buchanan, William Buckley went after it, and that hurt the movie a lot. People all of a sudden started seeing Ron as an overachiever instead of as an underdog, which is unfair. The whole idea is for people who have been wounded and hurt to start to be achievers. How else are we going to improve things?"

Tom Cruise gave several interviews at the time of the film's release. Cruise, known for being careful with the press, primarily stayed away from the controversial issues but made it clear that he stood by the work. Most of the heat was directed at Stone, who is a much easier target because of his outspoken nature. "I don't think it matters whether you're careful with the press or not," Stone comments. "You're not going to be able to control it anyway. They'll find something to make you look bad if they want to. You get dumped on anyway, so you might as well be who you are. Fuck it. If I were the sweetest guy in the world they'd still be saying I'm a monster, so what the hell? I'll revel in being a monster when I want to be a monster and I'll be a good guy when I want to be a good guy. I'll just be what I am."

There may have been controversy in the press, but not at the box office, where *Born on the Fourth of July* grossed $70 million in the United States alone, and more than that abroad. For Ron Kovic, it was a long-awaited victory. "When Oliver called me up and told me that we were going to do this film again, it was like being given a second life," Kovic says now. "I could never quite reconcile being in this wheelchair after Vietnam. I could never quite understand how my sacrifice could have any kind of meaning at all. Working on the script with Oliver was the first time that I began to understand that my sacrifice, my paralysis, the difficulties, the frustrations, the impossibilities of each and every day would now be for something very valuable, something that would help protect the young people of this country from having to go through what I went through. It took a long time, but it happened."

"I am the resurrection and the life, saith the Lord; he that believeth in me, though he were dead, yet shall he live, and whosoever . . . liveth and believeth in me, shall never die."

Priest in **BORN ON THE FOURTH OF JULY**

CHAPTER ELEVEN

The Doors

"The program for this evening is not new
You've seen this entertainment
Through and through
You've seen your birth, your life and death
You might recall all the rest
Did you have a good world when you died?
Enough to base a movie on?"

Jim Morrison in **THE DOORS**

T he Doors were the quintessential Los Angeles band. They captured the dichotomy of that city even in their first album (*The
Doors*, 1967) with "The End," the ultimate dark musical venture
to the fringes of sanity. And "Light My Fire" was the single song most
identifiable with the Summer of Love. By their last album, *L.A. Woman*,
only four years later, they had captured the growing alienation of an
entire generation and would forever be enshrined as the band that best
embodied the dark side of the sixties.

For Stone, the attraction to the Morrison story began in a bunker
in Vietnam when he first heard the music of The Doors. It grew far
more significant when he wrote his first script, *Break*, inspired in part

by Morrison's lyrics. Hollywood had been chasing the Morrison story for longer than The Doors were around as a band. Over the years, the story had been pursued by eight directors: Brian De Palma, Martin Scorsese, William Friedkin, Walter Hill, Paul Schrader, Ron Howard, Barry Levinson, and Francis Ford Coppola; six producers: Allan Carr, Jerry Weintraub, Aaron Russo, Irving Azoff, Menahem Golan, and Yoram Globus; and twelve actors: John Travolta, Jason Patric, Keanu Reeves, Michael O'Keefe, Gregory Harrison, Charlie Sheen, Michael Ontkean, Steven Bauer, Christopher Lambert, Timothy Bottoms, Richard Gere, and Tom Cruise. Even the lead singers from INXS (Michael Hutchence) and U2 (Bono) had looked into being in a film of Morrison's life. Yet none of them were involved in the eventual film.

By 1985, after a series of convoluted negotiations, producer Sasha Harari, rock promoter Bill Graham, ex-agents Tony Krantz and Tony Ludwig, and Columbia Pictures wound up with rights from The Doors and the Morrison estate to do a film. Harari's first choice for the script was Oliver Stone; he called Stone's agent, but never heard back. Stone claims he never got the message. Two scripts later, Imagine Films had replaced Columbia; Harari was still unhappy with the writing, so he contacted Stone again. This time Stone met with The Doors, who had approval over the director as part of their deal, but when Stone mentioned he'd like to keep a scene from one of the early drafts (a particularly wild one), the group was offended and rejected him. After another draft and more options, big spenders Mario Kassar and Andy Vajna at Carolco got into the fray, and in August 1989, Vajna called Harari with some great news. He knew the perfect person to direct the movie—Oliver Stone. The Doors, having been strongly impressed by *Platoon*, were now much more receptive to Stone. Stone agreed to shoot the movie as soon as he finished the project he had been planning to direct next, *Evita*.

Stone had been working on developing *Evita*, the Andrew Lloyd Webber/Tim Rice hit musical about Eva Perón, off and on for two and a half years. It was to be his first film with a female lead, and initially he was attracted to it partially as a tribute to his mother, whose flamboyant but endearing personality is similar to that of Eva, wife of the Argentine dictator Juan Perón.

Stone initially envisioned Madonna in the title role, but this didn't last long. "We had a meeting and she wasn't crazy about doing it at first," Stone says, "but she didn't know much about *Evita* except that she was a Fascist and she didn't want to play a Fascist. I told her, to me the idea was that Eva Perón was the most loved and hated woman of her time. After more discussion, she got excited about it. So I took her up to Andrew Lloyd Webber's apartment in Trump Tower to meet with him and some of the other key people involved. She's brassy. She said that, as much as she wanted to do it, she was a composer in her own right and really wanted to work on the music first. Change some of the songs a bit. Webber sat there, not really believing it."

But telling the most successful composer of modern times that she wanted to rewrite his songs wasn't all Madonna had to say. She also demanded that Stone give her script approval. "I said to her, 'Look, you have script approval in an informal way,'" Stone recalls. "'I'm directing, you're acting in it. I'm not gonna force you to do something you don't want to do. You read the script and we discuss it, but don't start demanding a formal script approval in your contract because it's meaningless and it's an insult to me.'

"It blew the deal. She didn't understand the film business. I thought she could be a good actress, but at that time she had no humility. It was just one of these bogus, fucking bullshit Hollywood demands, like, I have to be treated special, or something like that. It was stupid. I just said, 'Well, we have nothing to talk about, do we?' She left and I got a call from Sam Cohn, who loved the idea of his client, Meryl Streep, being in the movie. I met with Meryl and decided to sail with her. She has a beautiful voice and she was hungry to do it. This was before the comedy she was doing [*Postcards From the Edge*]. And then Madonna said a bunch of bad things about me in the press. That I was a chauvinist pig, etc. And then she went after Meryl Streep. Actually, for a movie that never got made, I took a lot of shit in the press over it."

With Meryl Streep as Evita, Stone was considering Mandy Patinkin as Che Guevara, the male lead. Stone then scouted locales in Argentina, Spain, and Italy. Robert Stigwood was producing the project, and had been trying to put the movie together for twelve years. "Stigwood, Rice, and Webber were very committed and cooperative," Stone says. "But the budget was always problematic. It's a big production. Basically, you're shooting two movies and there's choreography involved. I had Paula Abdul working with me. I felt I had a plan of attack, but Stigwood had a deal with Jerry Weintraub, who then went bankrupt. They had no money and Stigwood couldn't get financing anywhere else. I could've gotten it financed at Carolco, but then Meryl bowed out."

Meryl Streep dropped out of the project in October 1989. Publicly she said she'd withdrawn "because of exhaustion from filming *Postcards From the Edge*," but she had also decided she should be paid more and upped her salary demands for the role. "She was upset about men getting bigger salaries," Stone says, "and she wanted to make an issue of it. I understand how she felt, but it was the wrong film to make an issue over that because we just didn't have any more money. I already wasn't very happy about my deal. It was a giant risk and we were all doing it because we wanted to try something radically new in our lives. But the plane weighed too much to get off the ground, and I didn't want to make it in a way that it would lose money. Meryl deserved more, but at that point it got to be too much. I just started to get sick of the whole thing. I dropped out to do *The Doors*, and then Meryl called me back and wanted to do it at a lower price, but I'd already committed to *The Doors*." (Some newspapers and magazines reported that Streep had not gotten along with Stone, but he says that was hardly the case.)

Within days, Stone moved the Morrison film into preproduction. Working with studio head Mario Kassar (Andy Vajna had split to form his own company, taking out a reported $200 million), Stone had once again thrown his lot in with the independent mogul as opposed to the strict studio deal he had with *Born on the Fourth of July*. Of course, Kassar was richer than John Daly of Hemdale. He was more of the Dino de Laurentiis breed—gutsy individualists, big spenders, and freewheeling dealmakers. By now the film had run up $2 million in development costs alone for the various rights and drafts of the script. All this was picked up by Carolco. There were six producers attached to the project: Sasha Harari, Bill Graham, Nick Clainos (Graham's partner), Mario Kassar of Carolco, Brian Grazer of Imagine, and Stone's producer, Alex Ho.

Stone now threw himself into *The Doors* with a vengeance. He devoured anything and everything to do with Morrison—biographies, poetry, old film clips, videos, tapes, and transcripts of interviews. He listened to the music constantly, visited Morrison's surviving haunts regularly, and met with a steady stream of people who claimed to have known the Lizard King in the flesh. Finally, when he felt ready, Stone wrote his own draft of the Morrison story.

"I read 250 transcripts from people who had known Jim," Stone says. "All kinds of people, including people you never heard of who knew him from various sexual situations. It was like *Citizen Kane* in a way, because every one of these people had a different point of view. Those extracts were priceless, they were like the Egyptian archives. Still, the *Doors* script was always problematic. Even when we shot, but the music helped fuse it together. I wrote it quickly that summer [1989] in Santa Barbara. The script was written more as a tone poem. The concept was that the movie was all in Jim's lyrics. I picked the songs I wanted and wrote each piece of the movie as a mood to fit that song. So it was sort of a new technique. The motivations of the characters were murky to some, clearer to others. I trusted to his lyrics to tell his tale. I tried *not* to put my rationalizations about motivations between us and the songs."

As 1989 drew to a close, Stone's second draft was completed and circulated among the concerned parties. Immediately, there were problems. When Morrison died, he left everything to Pamela Courson, including the rights to his poetry and his share of the rights to the music of The Doors. When Pamela died in 1974, all this went to her parents; after a series of lawsuits, it was now controlled jointly by Morrison's parents and the Coursons. The Coursons weren't at all pleased with Stone's script and tried to slow the production down. The producers had already agreed not to portray Pamela Courson as having anything to do with Morrison's death (some believe Morrison accidentally or intentionally snorted Pamela's heroin stash). Now the family didn't even want Pam to be shown taking drugs in the film. Though she died of an overdose, the family believed it was the trauma of her lover's death that drove her to the drug. Stone disagreed, whereupon the Coursons refused to let him use Morrison's later poetry. Stone flew to San Francisco to talk to them, but they wanted to exchange the poetry for more control over the movie, and he refused.

The Morrisons, on the other hand, didn't even read the script. As far as they were concerned, the sooner the film was over with, the better. They knew better than anyone the power of the Morrison legend and their inability to stop it. Ever diligent, Sasha Harari pleaded with them to go against the Coursons and give Stone permission to use the poetry he wanted. They were adamant throughout filming, but a few months before the movie was released they finally agreed because they became convinced that Stone saw Morrison as a poet more than anything else.

They still wouldn't let Stone portray them in the film. Others essential to the story also hedged on being depicted after reading Stone's screenplay. Former Doors manager Bill Siddons felt the script focused "virtually exclusively on the more sensational side of Jim's personality and not the man I knew—a bright, warm human being who actually gave a shit about some people." Eventually, though, Siddons agreed to be depicted in the movie.

Around this same time Sherry Siddons, ex-wife of The Doors' manager, came to see Stone. Years before Stone had sent *Break*, his somewhat surreal first script laden with Doors imagery, to The Doors' organization in the hope that Jim Morrison would consider playing the lead role. That was in 1970, and he never heard anything back. "So twenty years later, Sherry Siddons walks in and says, 'I thought you'd like to have this,'" Stone recalls. "She pulls out this script and said Bill had found it in Morrison's apartment in Paris after he died. Someone told Bill that Jim had been reading it. It was my script for *Break* . . . it was a strange moment. All those years ago. Now Jim was gone and I was doing a movie about him. It was a sign to me that I should do this project."

By far the loudest objections to the script came from former Doors' keyboardist Ray Manzarek. Though he'd sold his rights, Manzarek vehemently disagreed with Stone's vision, and let everyone know it. "He left out the whole Maharishi thing," Manzarek told Jerry Hopkins in *American Film* (October 1990), "which is how the Doors came together."

"I made repeated overtures to bring Ray into the project," Stone says in reply, "but all he did was rave and shout. He went on for three hours about his point of view, which I think was fairly included in the movie. I didn't want Ray to be dominant, but Ray thought he knew better than anybody else. The more I studied it, the more I realized he and Morrison had less and less of a bond as time wore on. Well, all these factors started to emerge in the script, and Manzarek would say, 'That's not true, that never happened.' Like the story about Pam being in the closet and Jim setting it on fire. Manzarek said that never happened, but Bobby Klein was the neighbor whose house she ran to that night and he swears to the story. Pamela told him. Ray said I was making it up."

Manzarek is equally unenamored of Stone. "Oliver has no sense of the Light in a cosmic, spiritual, or evolutionary sense," Manzarek said in the *American Film*, interview. "He's got the idea of the shaman, man, but doesn't know what the word means. . . . We're dealing with serious darkness, man. This isn't the story of the Doors. . . . It'd be a great movie if it was about the New York Dolls or Aerosmith. It's the evil side of sex and drugs. You want to know what I think, man. Oliver Stone was over there in Vietnam and the hippies were back here smoking dope and practicing free love, and he was jealous. Oliver Stone is using the Doors to get revenge."

It was around this time that Richard Rutowski called Stone after a ten-year absence. "We had a falling out over this book I optioned and this producer I was working with, and were out of touch," Rutowski says. "I liked Oliver and it was uncomfortable. He went on to make other movies and I got strung out on drugs. After I cleaned up, I said, 'Look, I want to work.' I started working on *The Doors* for peanuts, like $350 a week as an assistant to an assistant. I started reading the script, breaking down every scene and writing notes. I suggested the character of Death and ended up playing it. Gradually, Oliver and I connected more and more throughout the project. I'd send him notes every week and he was really receptive. People don't realize, he's very receptive to collaboration."

Casting began and Stone auditioned nearly two hundred actors for the role of Morrison. He had suggested Val Kilmer for the part to Brian Grazer back in 1987, when the actor was cast in Imagine's *Willow*, and now he met with Kilmer to feel him out for the role. "It was the most interesting meeting I've ever been to," Kilmer said. "Oliver was like a reporter, very humble and selfless. He just fired questions at me. I told him if his intention was to glorify Morrison's lifestyle, then I had no interest in the role. That was pretty pretentious for me to say, but Morrison was an alcoholic and that's no way to live."

Stone had always liked Kilmer ever since he'd auditioned for the part of Elias in *Platoon* years before. "He sent me a video of himself doing Elias," Stone recalls. "He was pretty eccentric in those days. His reading of Elias was insane. He sat on a table, took his shirt off, did all kinds of weird stuff. When we got together to talk about *The Doors*, he said, 'You probably think I'm crazy.' He was ashamed of it, but I was interested in him for Morrison from the beginning."

While Stone continued his auditions, Kilmer, now hooked on the idea of playing Morrison, took the offensive. Never a big Doors fan,

Kilmer had speed-read *No One Here Gets Out Alive* (the 1980 Morrison biography by Jerry Hopkins and Danny Sugerman) for his meeting with Stone, but now he immersed himself in the music of The Doors. Fittingly, it was here he found the insights he needed into the Morrison mystique. "The songs, the lyrics are a clear map of Morrison's particular dream states," he says.

Kilmer decided to pull out all the stops and spent several thousand dollars of his own money to produce a video of him impersonating Morrison. A baritone like Morrison, Kilmer believed he could mimic the singer convincingly and set out to prove it. The video was shot in Kilmer's Laurel Canyon home and included four Doors songs—"The End," "Roadhouse Blues," "L.A. Woman," and "Peace Frog." "I had asked Val to do certain things," Stone recalls, "and he went back and did a full video. He really wanted the part. I had doubts about Val because of his age. He was a little too old. But I was already in his camp and he did the tape on his own just to put it over. In fact, I was over there for a while when he was doing the tape."

When Stone showed the video to former Doors producer Paul Rothchild, Rothchild suggested taking Kilmer into the studio and recording his vocals against the music tracks on The Doors' original master tapes. Under Rothchild's direction, Kilmer recorded another demo, and this time, Stone was definitely impressed. The clincher, however, came from The Doors. When they heard Kilmer's recording of "The Wasp (Texas Radio & the Big Beat)" at Digital Magnetics Studio in L.A., one of the band members asked if they were listening to Val or Jim. After nearly two hundred auditions and countless meetings, Stone hired his first choice, Val Kilmer, to play Jim Morrison.

Stone gives a lot of consideration to the right look for a role. "Val's face is very American," Stone says. "The bones are very wide and Slavic. In *Willow*, he was not at all the classic Errol Flynn type, he's more in the anti-hero mold. I liked his implied arrogance."

Physical comparisons always depend on what feature a person tends to notice. Though Kilmer did look amazingly like Morrison in many ways, his eyes were not nearly as piercing and deepset. People generally wouldn't notice this, but those who were most drawn to Morrison's eyes would probably never be convinced. But whereas another actor, Jason Patric for example, might have the right eyes, another feature would invariably be off. It's an unsolvable dilemma. Also, Kilmer's overall look was more cleancut nice guy than rebel bad boy. Sure, he could play the part of a rebel, but would he be convincing as someone who inspired descriptions in the press like "slithering sorcerer" and "demonic vision out of a medieval hellmouth"?

Though not an unknown, Kilmer was far from a bankable star. He was probably best remembered as Tom Cruise's rival, Ice Man, in *Top Gun*, but he had played starring roles in *Top Secret* (1984) in which he did his own singing, and *Real Genius* (1985). "The studio would have preferred a bigger name," Stone admits. "At that price it was risky on a relative unknown. I wasn't worried about that, though. I was more concerned how he was going to approach the part. Before we started, I met with Val and I said, 'The biggest problem we could have with this movie is if you're going to be Morrison as a Method actor. You're going to have to find the Gary Oldman kind of ability to walk out of it and walk into it, and that's going to be hard. Because, if you're going to behave like Morrison in the trailer, or off camera, we're going to have some major problems.' So we had a series of one-to-one meetings, and I think I reiterated this point several times to poor Val. I just wanted to make it real clear that he had an obligation once I accepted him. I said, 'Val, you've got to be very clear, because I'm going to come down on you like bricks if you violate this agreement.'"

The female roles prompted Hollywood's rumor mill. Stone's screenplay contained some particularly outrageous sexual scenes, and there was talk that willingess to do nude scenes was a primary consideration for any actress being hired. Richard Rutowski cites this as another example of Stone's commitment to the artistic process: "He's willing to risk humiliation and attack even though he's very sensitive to it. When he was doing *The Doors*, there was a scene where Jim and Pam were talking about death and Jim says, 'Bend over, your cunt is mine. Tell me your cunt is mine.' And in the scene Pam bends over and spreads her cunt and says, 'Fuck me, Jim, fuck me.'

"Well, Oliver sends this script out to actresses who want to come in to do the lead. Now I had a girlfriend at the time who was an actress and she was home reading that script and preparing for that scene with Oliver. And she would be bent over and saying, 'Fuck me, fuck me,' and it was this kind of psychodrama. Actresses didn't know if they were going to go in there and have to take off their clothes and Oliver was going to fuck them. There was always that fear in their minds. Of course the truth is Oliver has never done anything like that for an audition. I've never seen him abusive of an actress in a casting call. It's always very professional. But he knows that just the idea of it forces them to deal with the character more."

Casting director Risa Bramon García recalls the casting controversy that surrounded *The Doors*: "I don't know why I found it so amusing, but I just couldn't take it seriously when I got phonecalls from managers saying, 'Do you realize that this is pornography? And Oliver is asking girls to give him blowjobs in the auditions? How could you work on a movie like this?' And I'd say, 'Look, I was in the room. All that happened was the girl had to say, "My cunt is yours," and kind of bend over.' I mean, big deal. People were so bent out of shape about that in this town. And not just the actresses. Some of the actors were uncomfortable. I remember Christian Slater was uncomfortable doing that scene. We auditioned about sixty actresses, and the person who we should have kept was Patricia Arquette. She was amazing. She rolled around on the floor. She should have played the part."

Stone talks about the casting couch myth and the folly of having an affair with an actress appearing in one of his films: "Most actresses are really only concerned with getting the job. They're very serious and don't want to have any interference with that process. Besides, to even entertain the idea in this era when sexual harassment charges are everywhere would be a huge mistake. Secondly, I don't need to because I have an ample sex life elsewhere. Thirdly, it's bad for the project. When you go to bed with somebody who is the star of your movie and you have a lousy night, what are you going to do the rest of the shoot? Or maybe you don't like her and she likes you. You have other people coming to see you at the set and she is going insane. All those dynamics are possible. It's just not worth it."

For Stone, the same attitudes carry over into the office. While he's known for teasing the female members of his staff, he never makes advances toward them. "Oliver never hit on me, not once," Kristina Hare, his assistant at the time, says. "Oh, he'd say inappropriate things, like once he called and asked me to handle something and told me to do whatever I could to make it happen, even if I had to perform sexual favors. I turned bright red even though I knew he didn't mean it literally. I'll never forget during the Anita Hill thing, while every boss was paranoid about anything that could be construed as sexual harassment, Oliver was inspired by it. He came up with some real doozies at that time."

As casting for the film was completed, some were shocked when all-American girl Meg Ryan was chosen for the role of Morrison's longtime girlfriend, Pamela Courson. Actually, Courson was an all-American girl at heart. Her dream was that Morrison would one day settle down and they could have a "normal" life. Kyle MacLachlan (*Twin Peaks* Agent Cooper) was cast as Ray Manzarek; Frank Whaley, who played Ron Kovic's friend in *Born on the Fourth of July*, was selected for Robbie Krieger; and Kevin Dillon, who played Bunny in *Platoon*, was chosen for John Densmore. Kathleen Quinlan was cast as Morrison's mistress, Patricia Kennealy; Michael Wincott as the band's producer, Paul Roth-child; and Josh Evans as their manager, Bill Siddons. Michael Madsen and Billy Idol also appeared, as well as cameos by the real Paul Rothchild and John Densmore, Crispin Glover, Paul Williams, Bill Graham, and others.

Stone was ready, but he knew that this was his riskiest project ever. The production would be huge, a logistical monster with eighty locations, including Los Angeles, Paris, New York, and the Mojave Desert, and calling for nearly thirty thousand extras. At one time the film had been envisioned as a low-budget piece that would be shot in six weeks, but it had expanded considerably. "It became a mammoth project," recalls director of photography Bob Richardson. "To our benefit, many of us were set in motion through our work on *Evita* to evaluate what a musical was. We also prepared for extraordinary numbers of extras, so the slide to *The Doors* was not as difficult as if we'd just come straight from *Born*."

For Stone, the project was taking on a greater significance. He was becoming more and more engrossed with the idea that a film about Jim Morrison should have some of the same qualities that dominated Morrison as an artist and a man. That would mean pushing the envelope cinematically, taking risks with the structure and the dialogue; but most of all it meant Stone would have to go more with his gut than his head. If Morrison was anything he was extemporaneous, improvising not only his art but his life. A film about his life should also break tradition.

The driving force of Morrison's art was his poetry and song lyrics, and Stone wanted to play the film around these elements in order to give viewers a deeper sense of Morrison than they would have with the customary linear narrative. Therein lay another problem—Stone wanted to capture Morrison down to the finest layer, not just the physical, but the emotional and the spiritual side as well. Yet this was all based on his vision of Jim Morrison, which he knew might be quite different from the way most people perceived him. "Everybody sees Morrison differently," Stone said to the press at the time. "He's an enigma. No matter what I do, I'm going to get killed on this."

Stone opened the filming with an Indian ceremony held on a hazy morning in March in Malibu. More than a hundred people formed a circle around a crackling campfire on Trancas Beach as an Indian drummer beat out a hypnotic rhythm and Bobby Klein, an old friend of Morrison's and the band's first photographer, recited: "We've come together to form a new tribe. We are all in this together." At this point everyone tossed a handful of herbs onto the fire and began walking around the circle, taking care to step in the footsteps of the person in front of them and wind up at the same spot from which they began.

"Oliver took it seriously," Bob Richardson says. "Everyone took it seriously. I showed up for the ceremony and literally two hours after I'm there, an hour before Oliver shows up, my wife calls and says her water just broke. So here I am at day one about to have a baby, freaking out, and we're having this ceremony all holding hands. They weren't really full Indians, they were Jewish American Indians, and we weren't sure what to make of it. It had the right movement and all, and I guess it was a good idea, but it just didn't quite fit. It was good for the crew in the sense that everybody got tied together instantly. There was a real bonding."

In a further attempt to build the movie around the music, after he heard Kilmer's tape, Stone decided to obtain the rights to The Doors' master tapes minus Morrison's lead vocals, and splice in Kilmer's voice for the scenes of the band in performance. During the concert or club scenes, Kilmer would actually do the singing, thereby avoiding lip-synching, which Stone thinks is almost always noticeable and breaks the reality of the film. When Doors songs are featured on the soundtrack behind other action, Morrison's voice would be heard. This in itself was risky since Morrison's voice is extremely identifiable, especially to his legions of fans. Stone was convinced that no one could tell the difference. While it does take a fine-tuned ear to distinguish between the two, there are people who can. As in several instances, Stone's attempt to make the film more realistic would result in alienating a small segment of his audience. Granted, maybe only a few people in each audience would be bothered by not hearing the original Morrison vocals, just as there would be a few who thought Kilmer didn't look all that much like Jim Morrison, a few who didn't remember the rhetoric of the sixties being quite so naive and free of guile (even though it was), and a few who would be bothered by other efforts at realism. Cumulatively, however, such small segments would eventually add up. Even early on it was apparent that Stone was trying too hard.

Kilmer rehearsed the music day and night. He was amazingly adept at getting Morrison's intonation and exact phrasing down, and even started to develop some of the same musical attitudes. "Sometimes I'd tell Paul [Rothchild], 'I know what I'm supposed to do, but I don't like this song,'" Kilmer recalls. "That's why it sounds so dry. I just don't like it. And nine times out of ten Paul would come onto the headset and say Jim hated the song too."

But before long it became apparent that Kilmer was having problems meeting the physical demands of the shoot. He was good, but he couldn't move at Stone's pace. "I was driving Val nuts in the beginning," Stone admits. "I kept insisting on more music rehearsals. Insisting that he not be late. Insisting he get his energy levels up. I was trying to get vitamins in him, sending over shots, trying to make him a physically strong specimen because Jim was a powerhouse."

Once Kilmer mastered the music, he still had to develop the dramatic characterization. He had plenty of help as numerous Morrison confidants provided him with insights, but since each of them knew a different Morrison, their advice often differed and their evaluations sometimes felt like judgments. "If you talk to 150 people who knew him, you get 150 stories," Kilmer says.

Others withheld their cooperation, most notably Ray Manzarek. Despite Krieger and Densmore's cooperation with the project, Manzarek refused to be involved. "Let me just say this about the film," Manzarek said at the time. "There are two Doors that have absolutely nothing to do with 'The Doors' film: Jim Morrison and Ray Manzarek. I'm basically going to ignore the whole thing."

On the set, Kilmer surrounded himself with books by Morrison's favorite authors—Blake, Rimbaud, Kerouac. He discovered that his favorite Rimbaud poem was also Morrison's favorite Rimbaud poem.

The Doors
319

"I started with the similarities," Kilmer says. "He related strongly to the desert, and I spent a lot of time growing up out there. Morrison considered himself foremost a poet. I understand that part of him. I love writing poetry."

Kilmer wore black contact lenses to simulate Morrison's frequently dilated pupils. "It's like wearing sunglasses with a hole in them," Kilmer said. "It kind of screws up your equilibrium, making it easy to act stoned."

A nonsmoker, Kilmer smoked True Blues during the shoot because it helped to give his voice a rough quality. He found studying videotapes of Morrison helpful in preparing for the role. Volumes have been written trying to decipher Morrison's enigmatic nature, and Kilmer made no claim to having unraveled the mystery. "Morrison is like a religion to some people," he says. "I can't know all the intricacies of what his life represented, but there are things about it I understand—like fame. I know that's what killed Jim Morrison. And I've made a lot of choices in my life, even shying away from opportunities for films sometimes, just because the issues of fame are something I am very conscious of. I think the secret of surviving in this business is not embracing fame. And I think Morrison did embrace it. Very bright guy, Morrison. He understood media, intuitively. And I think in some ways part of what made him a really dynamic character, and his music so dynamic, was that he did go for what he was most afraid of. I related strongly to that about him."

Kilmer also keyed into the parallels between Morrison's art and the way he chose to live his life. "Jim looked at everything as an artistic creation. It's almost like he constructed his life in the same way as he would labor over a piece of poetry or a song. And viewing it that way, I think he looked with utter sincerity for the most poetic time to split. It was that kind of conscious decision. I think Morrison looked at his life as an epic poem, as if it were a long suicide note to those who loved him."

It was the artistic side of Morrison that Kilmer gravitated toward in his portrayal: "That's what enabled me to survive and not go down avenues that I know are deceptive, which was very much part of Morrison's deal. He truly didn't care. If the dragon wasn't staring at him in the morning, he'd *rush* out and try to find it. As loud and as fast and as hard as he could. At the expense of . . . he caused a lot of people a lot of pain. A lot of broken spirits that I've met, who still love him, were tortured—and many destroyed—by him. In a lot of ways he couldn't help it. As many as he affected in a positive way, he hurt plenty."

Stone's excitement grew as he watched Kilmer begin to master the role. "At times I'd see Val's face glint in the sun and I'd say, 'That's Jim.' And he's there for that moment. But it's never quite exactly Jim. A movie is only a reflection, a painting on a cave wall. I know this will sound strange, but I feel the director should not dominate the movie—the idea should. The director should be kind of the Shaman around the stones and the fire, trying to get the idea to spread. And with all the actors so far, it has happened. The great moment is when it comes—there's an electricity when you know the performance is going to work."

Richard Rutowski says Stone's attraction to the idea of the Shaman is very natural. During *The Doors*, he became more involved in Native American culture, but Rutowski says his interest went beyond the film. "He and I have taken a lot of psychedelics together," Rutowski notes. "I took him to South Dakota and we did a couple of Peyote ceremonies there with some very radical, wild medicine men. Real thieves, steal your wife, take your money, and leave you on the highway kind of guys. The Shaman is really a model for Oliver's life. All Shamans talk about facing death, insanity, and disease. They believe that a man cannot have true understanding of other men and compassion without suffering.

"It's through suffering and realization that you gain compassion," Rutowski continues. "If you look at Oliver's life—he came from a very wild mother and a conservative father. He went to a very disciplined military school and developed this powerful work ethic, and then he blew out and went to Vietnam to face death and insanity. He comes out of it in a tremendous fucking rage, which he delivers to every human being that he comes in contact with partly because of his own fear. He's intensely antagonistic and desperate for affection and friendship, which you'd never know unless you get close to him, penetrate the fire of his breath, so to speak. Then, his mind being as perceptive as it is, he begins to direct his energies into a form that allows him to understand what happened to him. The movies are a great vehicle for that, and he catches on through these exposures that there's some kind of higher knowledge, something greater; that nature's laws and God are somehow intertwined. Oliver uses film in a personal way. It's an exploration."

"Confusion is the sound of creation . . . go with it—it's all right."

Jim Morrison in **THE DOORS**

Before taking the role of Pamela Courson, Meg Ryan was not all that familiar with Jim Morrison. "I liked a few songs," she says, "but I had this notion about the sixties that was totally wrong and lopsided. I had to reexamine all my beliefs about it in order to do this movie. And what I realized is, you can't look at that time through the eighties' mentality of right or wrong, good and bad. Even the drugs and sex was not a question of morality. Addiction was a mystery. There was no AIDS. And if you impose this strict point of view on it, you lose the point."

To prepare her for the role, Stone tried to give Ryan a crash course in the culture of the sixties. As Kilmer found with Morrison, Ryan's biggest obstacle was the conflicting accounts she received about Pamela Courson. "It was hell researching her," she says. "One person would say she was a heroin addict, another person would say, no, she was afraid of needles. Some people said she was a monster, mean and awful, and others said, no, she was the sweetest thing that ever came down the pike. The only thing that everyone agreed on was that she was a redhead. I think she was a woman who never got past being a child."

Many have criticized the film for not portraying Pamela Courson with more depth, but Ryan has a different perspective: "The movie really isn't about her. What I did was sort of punctuate Val's character. A lot of what Pamela did was really a reaction to Jim. He was impervious to a lot of things. He left a lot of people in his wake, if you know what I mean. I think she had a personality that was . . . not a victim exactly, but someone who goes with the times and then finds out that the times have failed her. I think she would have been more suited to being a yuppie, given the chance. But she had to . . . not give in to her feelings, put jealousy aside. The notion that passivity was something to value was strong in the sixties. The poor baby didn't have a chance. This was not a woman who gently went over the edge; it was like gravity was the only thing that moved her. She had nowhere else to go but down."

Stone sees Pam and Jim's relationship as a great love story. "She may be basically a figure of innocence, but I see the movie character of Pam as a monster, too. She's very much a sixties child, not too thoughtful, not too intelligent. She decides to ride the snake with Jim, and once having ridden that snake, proves she can hold on and stay with him all the way out—till the point where she's willing to die with him. What I like in their story is that Jim had this loyalty, too. He stuck with her to the end. That's at the center of the movie. He really loved her."

Stone himself played a small role in the film—as a stuffy and pedantic professor complete with goatee who criticizes Morrison's student film as "pretty pretentious and not easy to follow." Considering the direction *The Doors* was already taking, Stone couldn't resist foreshadowing the castigation he anticipated from the critics; but most failed to notice the irony.

One of the scenes that generated the most controversy showed the band taking a mescaline trip in the desert. Bob Richardson describes how he prepared to shoot the scene: "I hadn't tripped in some time and when we scouted locations, I took some mushrooms just to see how things would appear. Later I went back to the same locations when I was straight. And it made a huge difference because the things I saw brought back patterns I emphasized. We talked a lot about how to portray these trips. Oliver was thinking about optical processes, but I kept thinking that every time I see a trip in a film, it's visual effects. I don't want to see visual effects. Just give me reality and get me inside their head with the music and with their dialogue. It's very difficult to convey and can easily become corny with a straight person."

Still, the desert scenes are some of the most unusual in the film. Morrison has a peyote-inspired vision of a naked bald-headed man riding bareback on a white stallion. The man first appears at the roadside crash Morrison witnessed as a child of five, which Morrison claimed resulted in his being possessed by the spirit of an Indian medicine man, and he then shows up at various times in the film. Richard Rutowski, who played the role, describes the character. "It was part of Jim's life, like an alter ego. Jim was smart enough to recognize that death was always present. Once you embrace that, it's liberating. Every one of those scenes when Death appeared had a meaning. Like when Jim did the peyote, and first saw him ride up the hill on the horse. That was from the Morrison poem about the enormous snake with one red eye, one green eye. It was about facing your fears."

Rutowski recounts the Indian myth that is the basis for the scene: "The idea is this giant serpent, this Shaman, his job is to get everybody at the same level through the use of herbal substances, psychedelics.

When you get high, the Shaman introduces you to the snake, the serpent. If you're afraid of it, it will kill you, but if you're not afraid of it, if you kiss it on the tongue, then it turns into the goddess. Then the goddess takes you by the hand and leads you out the gate. The Shaman's job is to get people to the state where they can go into the promised land, if you want to call it that, and be together in Paradise."

The desert sequence was also the cause of a clash with California Park authorities. When Morrison, high on peyote, wanders off following a vision into the cave in the film, he's actually entering Mitchell Caverns. The caverns, a National Landmark, are inaccessible to the public except on guided tours because of the delicacy of the underground coral. At first Stone wanted to release some smoke in the caves to highlight the effect, but park rangers refused. Liquid-based paint was also disallowed because of the damage it could do to the walls, so the crew used a dry powder paint to create the pictographs on the cave walls that Morrison sees in the film. The cave shots were not easy though and took all day. After fourteen hours, a female ranger left to supervise the operation finally said she had to go down to the ranger station and rest for a bit. According to one crew member, who asked to remain anonymous, this is when things really got out of hand.

"Soon as she was gone, Oliver ordered the smoke to be released. But the pictographs weren't coming through. They couldn't see them well enough, so they sprayed the powder down. That was the worst thing they could do. The walls just sucked the paint right into them."

Clayton Townsend, associate producer on the film, disagrees. "That's crazy. I admit ours wasn't the tidiest of crews, but the rangers were very specific about what could or couldn't be used, and they didn't want us to use water or any liquid whatsoever, so we didn't. It wasn't that the smoke would seal the paint on the walls, though, but that it could create discoloration on the ceiling. The ultimate reason the powder adhered was that there'd been heavy rains over the last day or so, and the water seeped through and made liquid of the powder."

At any rate, it was 4:00 A.M. before the scenes were finished. At that point, after working twenty hours, the crew took off, intending to return the next day for their equipment. But when they arrived, they discovered park authorities had bolted the steel door that covers the entrance to the caverns and announced that they were seizing the equipment until their terms on removing the paint from the cavern walls were met. "I think they were pissed off because they were the ones who authorized the powder paint to begin with," Townsend says. "So they took it out on us and said the crew was being irresponsible. After all, they made the decision to let us in there."

Though rumors about the costs ranged as high as half a million, in the end the production had to cough up $20,000 for a special process that cleaned the cavern walls. According to Bob Richardson, Stone held a second Native American ceremony around this time. "Oliver did another one to sort of reverse bad things that were occurring in the film. We'd have breakdowns in camera gear. We'd be going overtime a lot and continually scenes would be going wrong. We had to reshoot some things. Bad weather, all these problems. So we said that whatever occurred on the beach wasn't so good for us, and we decided that maybe we should go back and do it again. So, we had another ceremony with another Native American, and it was very private, just four or five people. It was, I think, a lot more successful. Things seemed to switch when we got to the desert. It sort of reversed the trend."

On March 26, 1990, the Oscars were held. *Born on the Fourth of July* was nominated for eight awards. Stone was given the Best Director Award and David Brenner and Joe Hutshing the Best Editing Oscar, but overall it was a disappointing evening for the film. Stone felt sad that his crew did not win more awards, with *Born* passed over in six categories (Picture, Actor, Cinematography, Score, Sound, and Adapted Screenplay). He was especially disappointed when Tom Cruise didn't win Best Actor, although he is the first to admit that winner Daniel Day Lewis (*My Left Foot*) did an excellent job. It's possible that Cruise's decision to follow *Born* with a more standard commercial effort, *Days of Thunder*, may have influenced Academy voters, but by rights, he should only have been judged for his performance in the film for which he was nominated. At one time Stone had hoped for Best Picture honors for *Born*, but by evening's end he knew this was very unlikely and was not surprised when *Driving Miss Daisy* won the top award. Still he knew that *Born on the Fourth of July* was his best effort to date.

March was also when *Reversal of Fortune* was released. Stone was co-producer of the project, having become involved at the request of his old friend, Ed Pressman. "Oliver did two very important things for that film," Pressman says. "At a certain point the key became getting Glenn Close, because if we got Glenn, then Jeremy Irons would come in as well. Jeremy had turned us down a couple times but it was clear that he was wonderful for the part, as was Glenn for her role. Glenn and Jeremy had worked together before and were friends. Oliver called Glenn Close personally and gave his recommendation and I think that helped her make up her mind. And he also got Terry Semel [president of Warner Brothers] to be more responsive to supporting the film. Those two key things really helped get the movie made."

Jeremy Irons went on to win the Best Actor Academy Award the following year for his role in *Reversal of Fortune*.

As shooting on *The Doors* continued, relations on the set worsened considerably when a memo ascribed to Kilmer was circulated to the cast and crew delineating a list of rules on how the star was to be treated for the duration of the picture. The list reportedly included such morale breakers as it being forbidden to approach Kilmer on the set without good reason, to address him by his own name while he was in character, or to "stare" at him on the set. "I didn't know about it until it came out," Stone says. "I called his agent and I said, how can you do that? Val said it all was a mistake."

Kilmer says the whole thing was a huge misunderstanding. "It really messed me up for a couple of weeks," he admits. "One day Oliver says, 'You know, you've really started off on a shitty foot with this crew with that memo.' I said, 'What memo? I didn't write a memo.' What happened was, I'd hired some people to help me do my job and had them write up some stuff to cover what they were to do. It was for them, not the crew, and it was stuff like I need to have the music track in the left side of the mix so I can reverse the speakers in the car to hear the lyrics and so on. And one part dealt with being called to the set. Sometimes a crew member will call you to the set just to cover their ass in case you're needed, and then you go and they don't really need you. So I said, when I get a call to the set, make sure that it's from Joe Reidy, the assistant director. If it's not, then make sure they really need me. Well, somehow they decided this meant nobody was to talk to me, and they wrote this up and handed it out. I couldn't believe it when I read it. So I tried to apologize to everybody about it, going around to every person and telling the story over and over, but I'm not sure I ever convinced Oliver of what the real deal was. What made it bad is that Oliver's crew is very involved with the process, it's not just a job, and they thought here was a guy who didn't want their input."

There was no question that ill feelings remained. Clayton Townsend claims Kilmer never made an effort to get along with the crew: "I still think he wrote the memo. Val was really concerned about staying in his character, but he could've handled it other ways. He had a massage therapist on the picture that was costing four or five grand a week and that went on for as long as we were shooting. That's like fifty thousand dollars in massages. I didn't talk to him about it, but I remember the question coming up and he said he had to have it. Of course, he is a star and he's working like a dog, but that's going a bit too far. Val was always in his own funk. Other people were friendly—Billy Idol, Meg Ryan—it becomes like a family, but he never wanted that."

Kilmer acknowledges that the role was physically exhausting. "Singing the songs live led to my voice going," he says. "Jim only had to do it once, but fifteen takes in a day is physically hard. I was in shape physically to do it, I just needed that time of just lying there staring at the ceiling, to relax myself. I needed time to recover. It takes an enormous amount of energy to play a character like that all the time."

Meanwhile costs were continuing to mount. The Sunset Boulevard sequence proved to be very expensive. Besides the tremendous design cost involved to restore the Strip to its 1967 heyday, the city of West Hollywood charged $60,000 for allowing the three nights of shooting. Stone insisted on an exact reproduction of the street where The Doors were discovered and where Jim Morrison once stalked from club to club. People who remembered the Strip from the sixties said the look was so perfect that it was "eerie" and made them feel as if they'd stumbled into the Twilight Zone. There were also extensive sequences shot inside some of the Hollywood clubs, including a three-day stint at the Whiskey À Go-Go filming The Doors' famed nightmare epic, "The End." The song required Kilmer to cut loose totally with impassioned rage on a crowded stage for take after take. Kilmer recalls the scene as a brutal test of his endurance that went on for something like twenty-four takes.

As shooting continued, Kilmer's stamina became more and more of a problem and Stone became increasingly frustrated. "It was such a huge role and Val had diminishing energy. He could only go so far; he'd sing two songs or one song for two takes and he'd be tired. That's his nature, he's more catlike. He just doesn't have a very strong physical stamina. Not like Cruise, who was an iron horse. Costner is also strong. Val's also somewhat mischievous. He loves to fuck with your mind, so you have to play mind games with him."

Although he is used to working his actors hard, Stone says Kilmer's endurance problems were far from unique. "Actors, because of the nature of the system, do get indulged," he says. "Their agents get them trailers, they get them handlers, they get them masseurs, they get trainers . . . it becomes their whim."

Things weren't much easier for Meg Ryan: "Oliver told me early on in filming, 'You can't have a pretty movie about rock 'n' roll.' And, as usual, he was right. . . . For me, four months into it, I felt like I was walking under eight feet of water."

Janet Yang, of Stone's Ixtlan Productions, thinks that at least part of Ryan's difficulties came from her inhibitions clashing with the role: "I heard Meg Ryan came home from *The Doors* crying every day, not only because of the confidence factor but also because she wanted consistent direction. Oliver didn't want her to play Pamela Morrison, he wanted her to *become* Pamela Morrison. He wanted her to be passionate, scream, yell, take drugs, get naked and run in the streets, love her man to death . . . whatever it took. Be that, and then it would all come out from becoming that person. Like Tom Cruise was obsessed with playing Ron Kovic, so he took the initiative. Meg wanted the scene that would help bring that out in her. It's a chicken and egg thing. I don't know how it can be resolved."

Risa Bramon García describes the conflict between Ryan and Stone: "Meg wanted a lot of support, but ultimately Meg never bought into the role or the script. She always wanted something different. She wanted a love story. Meg wanted a different movie. We kind of overcast with her. We probably should have cast down, but we wanted her badly in a sense to justify the budget with a name to enhance Val's. We coerced her and seduced her and paid her. And she was overqualified for what Oliver needed for that part. She was too big a star by then, and it was frustrating for her. She never got what she wanted out of the movie. Oliver was never able to give her what she needed, which was a different approach. But, of course, it was a pretty crazy movie and a pretty crazy set. She never could just quite jive with that stuff."

"The American Indian legends say the first shaman invented sex. His name means 'the one who makes you crazy.'"

Jim Morrison in **THE DOORS**

Clayton Townsend remembers Ryan calling herself "the most expensive extra in film history," and she later criticized Stone in the press. Ryan says that she came away from the film relieved that she had missed the sixties. "I kept saying to Oliver, 'This is a cautionary tale, isn't it?'" Stone maintains Ryan developed her own version of Pamela Courson: "Meg had never been through the sixties, of course. She tried to go back, but she was a little frightened. She's a different kind of personality, more conservative, and it was hard for her to reach back and let it all go. But she achieved something else. It's a different kind of take on Pam, not the loose cannon that many of us were in the sixties."

Ryan says Stone tried to help her get into character by perfectly creating the environment: "One thing Oliver does is provide the environment for you as an actor. You just go to work and all of a sudden it's 1969. You've got four thousand extras all dressed and all crazed, and you don't have to pretend you're strung from the tenth floor of a building on heroin. You actually *are* strung from the tenth floor *pretending* you're on heroin."

Kathleen Quinlan seemed to take the opposite approach in playing the free-spirited Kennealy. The Kennealy character is really a composite of three different women who were part of Morrison's life and was originally named Annie O'Riordan, but later changed to Kennealy after the woman who not only had repeated affairs with Morrison but married him in a Wicca wedding ceremony and was carrying his child before agreeing, at Morrison's request, to have an abortion. "Meg was much more about control than Kathleen," Stone says. "Quinlan in dealing with the sixties seemed to understand it immediately and was able to work easily in that framework. She offered her body up. . . . I combined several women from Jim's life and by rights I should have used an alias for the name Kennealy because it's somewhat misleading."

The more passionate love scenes involved Quinlan. She performed in the nude, but Kilmer had a body double for his big lovemaking scene with her. Kilmer and Ryan did a partial nude scene, but according to

Stone, it was more hassle than it was worth. "Meg never took her clothes off until we shot," Stone says. "I never asked her to. When she did take her clothes off, I think she was very self-conscious anyway. It spoiled the scene. It's hard to work creatively with people who are always scared or uptight. It's exhausting. We really did have a lot of nudity in *The Doors*, I guess. I felt it was necessary."

In keeping with its subject matter, *The Doors* was a stormy production, fraught with passionate clashes of will. Not only were there battles between the director and his stars, but major clashes between Stone and the two longest standing and most powerful members of his team— producer Alex Ho and director of photography Robert Richardson. The argument with Richardson almost severed a relationship that had existed since *Salvador*. The problems occurred over the sequence covering Ray Manzarek's wedding ceremony which was shot outdoors on a large estate in Malibu. According to Richardson, the real problem was that the scene was shot too late in the day: "We'd been shooting another sequence, and we had to race in rush-hour traffic on Pacific Coast Highway to this location in Malibu. The idea was always bad. There just wasn't enough time to get there and finish the scene before we lost the light. We had a forty-five-foot track to put down with a crane, and the scene was supposed to intercut with a bright sunny sequence. So we started shooting, but it just wasn't happening. Oliver had flown one of the actors out for the scene and was insistent on continuing. At one point he said, 'Don't worry, I'm not going to use this in the film, but I flew these guys out so just shoot it.' And I started shooting the scene, figuring it's not going to be used, but in the back of my mind I'm thinking the motherfucker's lying to me. He'll say anything to get a shot. But then, the light started dropping out rapidly and it reached a point where I just couldn't make a match any more. And I said, 'I can't shoot it.'"

"Match what light?" Stone exclaims in reaction to Richardson's comments. "It was a one-shot scene. He walked out before we ever shot a single frame. The fog was there and he didn't want to shoot it. He thought it was too dark, he just didn't want that look."

Stone and Richardson got into a heated argument over whether or not to shoot the scene. "I said, 'Listen, I never asked you in all these years to stop shooting a scene for light,'" Richardson maintains. "'I've always washed them. But I cannot make this one work. So let's just stop.' He said, No. We still had a big master to do, and with a wide shot like that there's no chance of matching it. I shut all the lights off and walked away. The gaffer walked away with me. Oliver's last remark was, 'If you leave, that's it.' When I got back to the soundstage, there was Alex Ho. He said, 'You really have to think about this. . . . You have to finish the day's work.' We still had more shots. This was another sixteen-hour day. So Alex asked me to at least finish the day because he couldn't get anybody to do it on that short notice."

A little over two years later—during which Richardson won the Best Cinematographer Oscar for shooting Stone's *JFK*—the wounds have still not completely healed. "The day he walked off, I wanted to kill him," Stone says. "I continued on with the camera operator. I shot the scene and I loved the light."

Stone does not believe that the argument was triggered because he was making unreasonable demands: "The light was very low and he felt I was rushing and I felt like since we were there and a lot of money had been spent, I wanted to shoot the damn thing because I think it'll work. He'd never done anything like that before. In the past if the DP had a protest, he would invert the slate [the clapboard that lists the scene]. I think Bob was really in a phase of his life where he was getting to make demands. That pissed me off. We almost severed our relationship. That evening when we got back we had a big stormy fight in the parking lot of the studio."

Richardson is still somewhat puzzled over the fact that the two men allowed things to go so far: "I've never been caught in that position with Oliver. I shot the rest of the night. I wasn't going to walk away and have someone else take my place on the film. Oliver and I dealt with the issue very briefly. I said, 'I've never gone through this before, Oliver. I've never asked you not to do something' and he said, 'I'm the director. When it really comes down to it, I'm the director and I have to make the decisions.' And he's absolutely right about that."

The two finished out the night, but there was considerable tension between them. "It was pretty icy and it stayed that way for a while," Stone recalls. "I felt like he wanted me to fire him. He was ready to walk, and I think I made the right judgment call by letting some time pass. I tried not to have a fight, or blow it up any more than it was, and not get any more emotional. There was a friendship at stake here and he is a great director of photography, although that night I was thinking of replacements because, as a director, I don't like ultimatums being put to me. I will not bear them from an actor, from anyone, from a studio, from a DP. Ultimatums are a loss of choice, and the director should have that choice."

For Richardson, though he and Stone have sinced patched up and indeed done some of their best work together, the fight is a reminder that any artist who works as close to the edge as Stone does can sometimes go over the precipice. "It was very hard for me," Richardson says. "Part of it is that Oliver is in essence very Machiavellian. He breaks things into very cellular structures and he forms strange allegiances concerning what information can be shared with others. His entire working manner is fractured so one department doesn't know what another department does. And that's his strength, because in his films he creates an energy and a tension that drives the film further forward.

"Sometimes these things miscommunicate," Richardson continues, "then they communicate well. You get breathtaking surges where things work and then they break apart and you have all those people like Alex Ho and Clayton Townsend, trying to fill in the gaps along the way. The result is that you end up sometimes being extremely successful and other times being completely unsuccessful. The wedding scene was a downer for me. That was a time when we lost *complete* sense of what reality was, and I think it probably had ramifications throughout the film in other sequences in terms of the number of extras necessary for a shoot. Part of it was Oliver's madness, but that's part of the choice we make to get his genius, I think."

Richard Rutowski seems to agree: "Oliver's a very smart business-man. He's very clever with choosing stories not only to direct but to produce. His analysis of story is brillant. But in terms of the personal exploration, which he does in his films, he's out there on the trail alone. He doesn't always know what the fuck he's doing. I've watched him rehearse something, prepare it, have a shot list, and then walk out on the set and do it all different. Oliver has the courage and the trust in himself to explore it. He asks a lot of people's opinions. I don't have the business abilities he does, but I have strong instincts. Oliver also has strong instincts, but he's still learning to trust. In *The Doors*, he was dealing with a realm that was not totally historic, it was impressionistic. And he shot from the hip. He tried stuff that a lot of directors would feel foolish trying."

Despite his battle with Richardson, Stone later cut the wedding scene in the editing room. "I liked the light," he still maintains. "I think it was a very bizarre scene, eerie and somnambulant. The only reason I cut it was for length."

The removal of the scene left only a vague mention of Manzarek's wedding, and made what was supposed to be a wedding dinner scene at Pam and Jim's house in Laurel Canyon seem more like a Thanksgiving dinner. That scene, in which Pam and Jim get into a tremendous fight when Patricia Kennealy shows up, is generally regarded as one of the best in the movie. Meg Ryan, playing Courson on acid, has her finest moments in the film when she cuts loose at Kilmer. "We were both picking glass out of our knees between takes," Kilmer says of the scene which has Pam hurling dishes, Jim stomping the turkey, and both of them waving knives around. "How we dealt with it was just with a lot of humor and sensitivity," he continues. "We were very dependent on each other."

But nothing compares to the concert scenes. Even the film's harshest critics agreed that it set a new standard for the way concerts were depicted. Not only did Stone use thirty thousand extras for the scenes in San Francisco, New York, and Los Angeles, but the camera work and sound were some of the best music footage ever shot. In the early part of the film the band performed at the L.A. clubs, the Whiskey A Go-Go and The Central. Later, in San Francisco, Stone not only recreated the legendary Fillmore West at the Warfield Theater, but also held a "Be-In" at the Golden Gate Park Panhandle. The casting call for these scenes drew thirty-five hundred enthusiastic extras in their own hippie apparel. An outdoor concert was also organized and filmed over two nights at the Pulgas Water Temple in San Mateo County.

Some of the real stars of these scenes are the extras, who really cut loose. Bill Graham came offstage during one of the concert scenes and remarked to Kilmer, "These are the best actors I've ever seen in my life." In many cases, the assistant director would have to come onstage early in the day to remind the crowd to save some energy so they could last through the whole day's shooting. But it was more than energy and even more than a supportive attitude. The crowd became involved in the creation of the film. "It was a large beast," Stone says of the scenes. "But the extras were incredible. They came in the right spirit, right clothes. They stood around for ten, twelve hours, and they were juiced. There was a lotta acid going around, a lotta marijuana. They were stripping clothes off, unasked, just to participate. They loved the music and wanted to get back to that time. The concert scenes probably looked better than the real sixties concerts did."

For these scenes, MacLachlan, Whaley, and Dillon were all fitted with molded flesh-colored earpieces through which they were fed The Doors' instrumentals so they could mime their performances while Kilmer sang his. Sometimes Kilmer used the piped-in track for guidance, while other times he sang along to his own prerecorded track, sometimes along with Morrison's vocals and sometimes without. Stone and Richardson wanted to have the freedom to do swooping 360-degree camera moves, and that meant a way had to be devised to allow the extras to keep dancing to the missing beat. The answer was a "thumper track," a low-frequency tone synchronized to the prerecorded track and played for the audience. Later, in postproduction, the thumper track was electronically removed from the recording. "It was like preparing for war—we had to be ready for any contingency," says Budd Carr, who along with Rothchild supervised the music tracks.

The larger concerts were shot with at least five cameras: three cameras on the floor, a Steadicam, and a camera utilizing a new remote control camera crane called the Technocrane. *The Doors* was the first American feature to use the Technocrane, which can telescope in length from 6 to 20 feet and move 14 feet in any direction. The device, which was also used in the film's courtroom sequences, enables the crew not to have to lay as much track.

Stone and Richardson were careful to balance the sixties concert experience with the nineties technology. "I'd watched all the footage that was available on The Doors, as well as other concert material," Richardson says. "The majority of it was very static. We attempted to reproduce the innocence of that coverage without completely forgetting the advances that have become obvious in the nineties with influences such as MTV. The other side of the coin was that so much of what Jim was about was trying to control the masses and take them to a hysterical level. Eventually, the masses ended up controlling Jim. So the audience was more of an integral part of the story than is ordinarily the case in a rock concert."

Stone tries to use as many elements of the film process as possible to convey the story, and Richardson uses his cinematography skills in the same way. "We tried to mirror both the time and the mind of Jim. In the earlier stages of his life, the camera moved very little. We used simple masters, over-the-shoulder shots and closeups. It was motivated by the action of the actor. As the band formed and the music started to flow, the camera again moved in the same way. It progressed that way, until as the music became finer and the band grew into a strong mesh of steel, the camera was rolling even more fluidly, much more gracefully. As Jim started to deteriorate, we deteriorated."

Color and lighting were also used to communicate the Morrison saga. There were long sessions between Richardson, Barbara Ling (production designer), Marlene Stewart (costume designer), and Stone to develop a breakdown of color. "Early on, the film is almost Technicolor, with strong reds, greens, and blues," Richardson says. "The color shifts when the band goes to New York, as both Morrison's life and the film become darker. It moved toward more blacks until at Miami, black is the only tone, with shafts of white and periodic washes of red. The film finishes with a very light tone."

As filming progressed, it became apparent that the project was going to go over budget. The concert scenes were very expensive, and Stone and Alex Ho clashed over them. Ho elaborates: "We went to 32,000 extras on *The Doors* and didn't budget for near that many. When we got ready to shoot one scene, I said, 'Okay, Oliver, I'm going to have a thousand people over here to the left, a thousand in the middle, and a thousand on the right, and we can catch bits of the crowd from the right angles.' He said, 'That's not enough.' He said, 'I want this room filled.' Filled? For several days' shooting? I said, 'Are you crazy?' I mean that was a major improvement on the budget right there. Everything we've done has come in on budget except *The Doors*. It was just totally different. He was on a different trip." Stone says he cut back on the extras after the first day, but felt the additional expense was necessary to get the look he wanted.

It is a well-known fact among Stone's crew that he internalizes the main character of each of his films. The process germinates during the writing of the script, as Stone tries to think like his lead character, and manifests itself when the actual shooting begins. The farther into the shoot, the more Stone resembles the film's protagonist. Frank Whaley, who played Robbie Krieger in *The Doors* and Ron Kovic's best friend Timmy in *Born on the Fourth of July*, comments: "I saw a lot of Ron Kovic in Oliver during *Born* and I saw a lot of Jim Morrison in Oliver during *The Doors*. He kind of plays the roles himself while he's directing."

"Nietzsche said, 'All great things must first wear monstrous and terrifying masks in order to inscribe themselves on the hearts of humanity.'"

Jim Morrison in THE DOORS

"During *The Doors*, he was hanging out with rock-'n'-roll people a lot," says Andrea Jaffe, the publicist for many of Stone's movies. "Morrison's world so absorbed him that it even affected his speech."

Chris Renna, when he first met Stone during *Born on the Fourth of July*, was startled by how much Stone seemed to be like Ron Kovic. But as an avid student of psychology, particularly as it relates to the creative mind, Dr. Renna wondered if what was really happening was that Stone had taken on the persona of the lead character in his project. When *The Doors* began, he had his answer. "Oliver takes on the life of his protagonist," Renna says. "It's not only part of his artistic process, but part of the way he grows as a person."

Elizabeth Stone agrees that her husband is strongly influenced by the lead characters in his films. "Even his wardrobe changes from film to film," she says. "During *Wall Street*, he wore coats and ties. During *The Doors*, he got into jeans with suspenders, so we had to put buttons on all his jeans. So now he's got like fifty pairs of suspenders that he doesn't wear any more. He was also into Indian things during *The Doors*. He was going to peyote ceremonies with the Indian tribes and he got all this Indian art. During *Wall Street*, he was into nightclubs. Nightclubs, booze, he put on weight, out dancing with women late at night. He immerses himself in the work, and it has a lot to do with the actor, too. There's a triangle that happens with Oliver and his actors. He and the actor become one, and the main character is a third person. This triangular effect is like the pivot of every one of his movies. He'll be on the phone at eleven at night in bed talking to his actor. They become like one person. The person they become is the main character."

In the case of *The Doors*, the lead character was wild and excessive, and most of Stone's friends and co-workers agree that it was during the making of this film that he was at his craziest. "He was the craziest I've ever seen him," Kristina Hare says. "The worst incident was the weekend before we started principal photography. He was leaving the office and I asked if I could copy some of the pages he'd been working on for his script supervisor, Susi Mallerstein, and he said, ' NO! NO! NO! I'm going to the house and then to Santa Barbara.' Susi was like on the verge of tears, so I said, 'She just needs the notes for the first three days of shooting so she can do a better job for you—it will take us five minutes. Why don't you leave the script with me, go home, pack, and I'll deliver it in a few minutes.' And he said, 'All right, fine, copy the notes, but if you don't get the script back to me in twenty minutes, you're driving to Santa Barbara with it.'

"I gave the script to Susi and a P.A. to copy, and when we put the originals back in the binder, I noticed the title page was missing. They both insisted there was no title page but I said, 'I know this script intimately. There is a title page and you'd better find it because it's got Oliver's notes all over it.' I started digging around in the trash and found a balled-up copy of the title page. Since we were in such a rush and couldn't find the original, I just Xeroxed the copy and raced off."

The next morning, Saturday, Hare was at home when the phone rang. "I answered it and there was this strange, husky voice on the line saying, 'You're evil. You cursed my project, I'm gonna tear your throat out! I'm gonna rip your head off! You've cursed my project!' I realized it was Oliver, but he sounded like he was out of his mind. It took me a moment to realize it wasn't a joke and to figure out what he was talking about. 'You lost my originals, where are the originals? I need those, it's bad luck!' I explained that it was possible the originals had been thrown out. He said, 'I want you to get Adrienne and Susi and search the dumpsters for them.' Until this point I'd never said no to him, but I wasn't going to search the dumpsters. I'm not superstitious and I knew we'd never find them. Besides, he had all his notes. Susi agreed to look, but couldn't find anything and she was petrified. It turned out they had put the pages in the wrong order and Oliver found them in the script and called back. I didn't even get upset, it was too surreal. I couldn't take it personally; he'd gone a bit mad. The next time I saw him was the first day of shooting, everything was normal, he was fine— and neither of us ever mentioned the incident again."

Stone wasn't much better after filming began. Bob Richardson describes how the subject matter affected Stone's work habits. "I think part of it was his becoming Morrison. He was drinking a lot, doing a lot of peyote, all under what he calls doing research. Oliver was a lunatic on that film. He went as deep and as dark as you can go."

Perhaps Stone is a true Method director. Richardson thinks the internalization process is the flip side of Stone's visionary side: "I think a lot of the problem was that Oliver was making a film about rock 'n' roll," Richardson says. "Instead of thinking as a producer, which he is fully capable of doing, he would make demands as a director: 'I need this many extras. I'm not going to make a rock-'n'-roll film if you don't fill the inside of the auditorium for me.' But I think the result was very authentic. When he thinks as producer, he pulls back. But if he would've pulled back on The Doors he could not have made his vision, because his vision was wild, unleashed.

"One weekend he just disappeared. He finished shooting on a Friday and went on a journey with Richard [Rutowski]. And they did this all-night peyote ceremony. When Oliver finally showed up Monday morning, we were shooting at Barney's Beanery and his mind and his eyes were blank. You could see through him. He was a ghost. Imagine a day and a half of being up on peyote. It took about three hours for him to get it together. We filmed shots which were sort of mindless shots, just to get things moving. Then he was all right. But that's part of his strength as a filmmaker. How far are you willing to go?"

Alex Ho agrees that some of the budget excesses were due to Stone's internalizing of Morrison's character, but he doesn't see it quite as romantically as Richardson: "Yes, that's what causes it. Everything is cathartic . . . he has to go through it. Oliver knows what he wants. And he just wants it. Simple as that. There was no reason for The Doors to go over. We had tons of arguments about it and then all of a sudden, of course, it's my fault. But I kept telling him, I said, 'Listen, we're going over. There's no way this time. We're going over, babe.'"

Stone admits he got a little indulgent during the filming of The Doors. He drank a lot and was more sexually promiscuous than he'd been since his marriage, but stayed away from hard drugs. "I drank tequila, smoked grass here and there, took the peyote trips, but most of this was on the weekends. I was focused during The Doors. I was sexually wild, pretty loose there, but not doing drugs. And certainly not coke. I don't know, I give that impression, I guess. Sometimes I sweat when

I'm straight and when I take drugs, I'm calm. It's like everything else in my life, I'm a heyoka."

Defined by the Eskimos as "one who walks backwards," Stone may indeed be a *heyoka*, but he also admits that he might have gotten too caught up in things Morrison. "We took all of Sunset Strip over one night," he says, "which was fun, but maybe I could have done it some other way, I don't know. We also had a core group of girls around that were sort of like Jim's girls. I kept adding to it, and we kept extending their run instead of paying them off to save money. If you carry them and they say some lines, they become triply expensive. And I ended up carrying a lot of beautiful women throughout the movie . . . because it sort of fit the atmosphere."

Another area that ran up costs was Stone's insistence on exact duplication of scenic elements. This included on a large scale things like staging the Be-In and making over Sunset Boulevard to the minutest detail for other scenes. Patricia Kennealy, who did a cameo in the film as the high priestess who performs the hand-fasting ceremony between Morrison and Kathleen Quinlan, the movie version of Kennealy, reported that her New York apartment had been duplicated so perfectly she found bills bearing her Lower East Side address on the desk.

But Alex Ho doesn't blame Stone for all the budget problems. "It was also the studios," he says. "They just ignored it. The first week I told those guys the picture was going to be a million dollars over before it even started. And they said, 'You can't report that. You don't report things like that.' And I said, 'That's what I've projected right now. It's probably going to be more.' They said, 'You can't do that. You have to give us actuals every week.' Now, that doesn't make sense. I'm telling them what it's going to cost, the first week of shooting. But they don't want to hear it because it's not their policy. So I said, 'Fine, if that's how you want it.' So, that's what I did. And at the end they came in and said, 'How come you didn't tell us?' And I said, 'Well, I'll show you my first cost report—it's a million dollars over.' And they shut up."

Although shooting in Los Angeles is known to be expensive, Stone says transportation and location rentals were even costlier than they expected, and that was part of the reason the film went over budget. In addition, the city is so film-conscious that he felt like he was working in a fishbowl. "We were shooting in the eye of L.A. and I felt very exposed. I felt like everything we did was under scrutiny."

"The camera is whoever you want it to be—a woman you want to seduce, a man you want to kill, a mother you want to upset, a wife you want to lie to or love, whatever you want it to be, it is. . . ."

Gloria (the photographer) in **THE DOORS**

Still, when all is said and done, Stone wouldn't change the way he shot the film. That doesn't mean he doesn't regret going over budget. "I finished close to schedule, but I went about six million over on a film that cost thirty-eight million dollars."

Principal photography lasted sixty days, the longest shooting schedule of any of Stone's film. When it was over, the actors had a heightened perspective on their role in the film, Jim Morrison's life, and even the 1960s. Meg Ryan says, "I think a lot of what Oliver was looking at was here was a guy who was so against the establishment, and then he becomes a rock idol, and that very same establishment starts to embrace him. That creates a sickness in the soul. Oliver took a lot of chances with this movie."

Ryan also gained a deeper understanding into her role: "Pam was a totally defenseless girl. Her whole life was this guy, and she defined herself through his eyes. In many ways it's a very female situation. Love was her justification for everything, which is sweet and nice and wonderful but ultimately lethal."

Kilmer's first reaction seemed to be one of relief that the project was over, but as far as Morrison goes, he too gained a more profound understanding. "He had a sincere search," he says of Morrison. "He may have chosen some of the wrong tools, but I think he tried to keep open an avenue of hope through spirituality. But I also think he was a bit of a cop-out because he was deathly frightened of committing to a practice, a condition, a way to behave, something to live for or live out of. I think *cool* was very important to him, and I've always battled that vanity. I think I've found through playing this character an opportunity to reexperience some of my life, to reevaluate. It seems to have strengthened things I have always believed . . . in God, and a reality that's a foundation for living. To put yourself on the line, to confront that . . . that fear."

Kilmer admitted that he was ready to let go of playing Jim Morrison: "There was a terror raging in him. He was always chasing death. So it was a delight to let him die. It was a terror to be in his head all the time. Look, if you were willing to get into a car with him, you were willing to die that day, because you might. He was really not just willing. He was chasing it."

Kilmer sees the movie as being more about fame and the effect of success than Morrison's life or the sixties. "That's the line that Oliver chose to hang it on," he says. "What do you do when you have everything? Morrison had done it all. And so has Oliver. He's achieved what the business offers. You make the films you want to make, about subjects that contribute to society, you learn some things, make a lot of money and win Oscars. Oliver's done all that. More than once."

Though they often saw eye to eye artistically, the daily drain of the movie-making process on such an exhausting film took its toll on Kilmer and Stone's relationship. By the end of the film, relations were so strained that the actor ended up insulting Stone at the wrap party in New York. "He said I didn't know anything about directing actors. . . . It was a nasty statement and it stayed with me for months," Stone says.

Elizabeth Stone remembers the incident: "It was like slapping Oliver in the face with a wet switch. And it was all because Oliver would goad him to get more energy out of him. Val would be late to the set all the time and he had like six massages a day. And Oliver would make him angry, like, 'Get in there, jump on that fucking stage. Do it, man.' And of course he gave a tremendous performance. But Val, I guess, took it to heart."

Kilmer has strong ideas about how a scene should be shot and feels that sometimes these motivations transcend the requirements of the script or the director's view. "There are times when I think I know what a scene should be about," he says. "But sometimes it doesn't turn out that way, or the director disagrees. . . . You can absolutely fulfill the desires of the director, or the obligations to the camera, or the script, and still be very personal and intimate in a way that, in the editing room, turns out to be what the scene is really about."

After two years to reflect on the experience, Kilmer says that even though he and Stone clashed occasionally about the methods, he was usually pleased with the results. "Sometimes I was foolish in reacting a certain way, but I think we did work together well in terms of the acting, no matter what the emotional side was. If I came up with a good idea, he'd usually shoot it. Sometimes we disagreed, and stuff was always getting moved around, but I knew he was always going to get something that was good. He's an artist."

Though Kilmer is proud of the film and his performance in it, he also thinks that he and Stone could work better together in the future because they understand each other now. "I didn't realize it during the film but there are three different personalities working simultaneously in Oliver," Kilmer goes on. "Well, actually there's about four hundred and eighty-three, but the main ones are the writer, the director, and the producer. The writer is absolutely sympathetic, an extraordinary listener. He's like spongeman. Takes it all in. The director is totally different. He's a tough guy, but that's where I saw him get real personal joy and satisfaction. When he's staring into the monitor or watching the scene, he's a complete, total fantasy-driven kid. He wants to believe. All good directors have a kind of concentration. Oliver would know when anything was wrong. The producer side carries the overall vision. He's reflective and is open to ideas. Sometimes I think Oliver is even better at that than the others. I'm talking about the visionary side of producing. It's a very, hard job and takes a lot of artistic talent and the other sides fit under it. Oliver shifts back and forth between them all."

Despite their differences, Stone is adamant that Kilmer's performance was brilliant and maintains he bears no resentment toward the actor. "I think Val was under enormous pressure. I mean, how can you recreate Jim Morrison? I think Val came as close as any actor could at this point in time. I wish he had been nominated for an Oscar; he deserved it. He's not the strongest human being, staminawise, but he worked himself to the point of exhaustion."

Stone shot over 500,000 feet of film for *The Doors*, and since the final film was to be around 14,000 feet, the editing was a massive job. Bill Brown joined Stone's team on the film and has been his post production supervisor ever since. Brown says that although the average footage shot for a Hollywood feature is around 300,000 feet, the half a million Stone shot was moderate for him. "Generally Oliver's probably shooting about 750,000 feet," Brown says, "and printing somewhere in the neighborhood of a half million feet. But Oliver's scripts are generally quite a bit longer than an average script. And if you take into context what he's doing, it's a very disciplined amount. When you're shooting a film like *The Doors* where the Miami concert scene had eight cameras shooting at once, 500,000 feet of film is not a lot."

Because of the subject matter, Stone worked particularly hard on the sound elements. The film's final cut contains twenty-five Doors songs. Always one to maximize his time, he began holding interviews periodically during the editing. The editing room, with its enormous screen, extra-large leather sofas, and huge neon clock ticking off the frames, provided a suitably formidable high ground on which to meet the press. Throughout the advance promotion for the film, Stone touted the virtues of the sixties, especially the risk-taking mentality. When attacked for belaboring his messages and other cinematic excesses, he snapped back, "Critics say that; audiences don't. I won't ever make boring movies."

Later, Stone was more objective about the issue. "I admit I like excess. I like grandiosity of style. I like characters like Gordon Gekko and Jim Morrison. I believe in the power of excess because through excess I live a larger life. I inflate my life and by inflating my life I live more of the world. I die a more experienced man."

As usual, the interviewers took a mixed attitude toward Stone, criticizing him for "turning the counterculture into a mainstream, bankable product" while also calling him "Hollywood's most successful protester." Hilary De Vries of the *L.A. Times Magazine* summed it up by saying "Stone is Hollywood's most consistent practitioner of point-of-view filmmaking, yet one who just as consistently falls on his own sword."

Though he was tough and confident in the interviews, privately Stone was worried. War had broken out in the Persian Gulf a few months before. With the AIDS crisis and two terms of Republicans in the White House, America seemed more conservative in its views than it had been in a long time. Here was a wild tale of sex, drugs, and rock 'n' roll with a hero who practiced a brand of hedonistic nihilism that was not only outrageous but totally lethal. Far from celebrating freedom, America was wondering if AIDS and crack were the first installment on a bill they had run up during the sixties. Stone confided in one source when asked how he felt about the release of the film at this time: "I think we all feel on the edge of imminent disaster. But then again, one always has that feeling at these times."

In February 1991, Stone tried to persuade CBS to change its decision to postpone airing *Born on the Fourth of July* on network television because of the impending war in the Gulf. Stone wanted to air the film in an effort to help prevent the war, but the network refused. "They basically said that if there's no war, we'll air it, and if there is a war, we'll pull it," says Stone. He would have preferred that the film air unedited on cable, but Universal sold the TV rights to CBS as part of a package deal that was made without consulting Stone or Tom Cruise.

When editing was completed, *The Doors* was as wild and controversial as its subject. With it, Stone took new risks in the cinematic arena. He went for feelings rather than snappy dialogue, sensory perceptions rather than engaging plot, and flowing lyrical movement rather than solid structure. This was not a film to be watched as much as it was a film to be felt.

On March 1, the release of *The Doors* in Morrison's hometown of L.A. added considerable fuel to the sixties revival that was already dawning there. The fashion crowd wore clogs, bellbottoms, and beads, and went to *Doors* parties that climaxed in attending the film. Audiences lined up outside theaters were presented with petitions to legalize marijuana by aged hippies. The word quickly spread amongst the hip crowd that the film was best viewed under the influence of drugs.

Early reviews were sharply divided. It seemed the critics either loved or hated the movie. But as the verdict came in from the smaller cities, more and more reviewers were taking potshots. His philosophy of life regularly displayed on a forty-foot screen and his emotions equally readable on his face, Stone is always an easy target, but with *The Doors* he was especially vulnerable. *The New York Times* review was titled "Oliver Stone and 'The Doors': Obsession Meets the Obsessed," while *The Washington Post* said: "Doors: The Time to Hesitate Is Now," and *Time* magazine's read: "Come On, Baby, Light My Fizzle." Still, the film had its champions. The critic for *Rolling Stone* wrote that "*The Doors* is a thrilling spectacle—the King Kong of rock movies." Gene Siskel termed it a "vibrant tribute to rock cult figure Jim Morrison and to the decade in which he flourished," and the *L.A. Times* called *The Doors* "The 'Raging Bull' of rock movies."

The film *was* flawed, especially when judged by conventional criteria, and Stone knew that. First, it was not done in a strictly linear way, and many critics simply couldn't get into the abstract experimental trip Stone was trying to take them on. Second, there was the Morrison mystique again. Many viewers had their own idea of who Jim Morrison was and resented Stone's impinging on that vision. Then again, a lot of people hate anything to do with Jim Morrison. *L.A. Weekly* film critic

Michael Ventura wrote about a party where "people were putting down Oliver Stone's 'The Doors' before they'd seen it." And this party "had a high head-count of writers who might be assigned by their various publications to review the movie." According to Ventura, "the prospect of a Doors movie brought out the mean in some of us. . . . People use [Morrison's] burnout to justify their compromises, as though burning out and selling out were the only alternatives."

Ventura's review of the film was thought-provoking:

"The Doors" is Stone's best film since "Salvador" because he structures it not like a play but like music. Here is a drama that breaks the rules of structure, doesn't depend on character or dialogue, but moves purely on its rhythm that goes into your eyes the way a tune like "The End" goes into your ears. Music and images move visually around Kilmer like the snake of Morrison's imagery, and the film becomes not a story but an experience. As with the 60's, experiencing "The Doors" is sometimes boring and silly, sometimes thrilling and psychoactive. But after it's over you know you're not going to forget it even if you want to.

Of course, the critic that really matters to Hollywood is the box office. Although *The Doors* opened well, the revenues declined rapidly. The film played strong with the hip segment of the young crowd, but most of the mainstream kids and the older generation stayed away. It seemed a lot of people weren't so keen on the idea of dredging up old memories, especially if that meant they might have to open them up for possible revision. As the negative reviews began piling up, the box office dwindled, and this in turn encouraged more negative reviews that further reduced the crowds. When it was all said and done, the film grossed $37 million domestically and another $25 million in foreign distribution. By the time the video money came in, it was in the black. Though it was by no means the big bomb that Stone's detractors may have hoped for, it was unfortunate that many people only saw *The Doors* on video because it requires a big screen to deliver its full effect.

Stone is convinced the movie would have fared better if it had been released in the summer, as originally planned. "Our first instinct was to bring it out in June, when the kids were out of school," he says. "As it was, it was all kids who came. It would have doubled the money because the kids would have been going anyway. Coming out in midwinter was a mistake, because that's really a good time for *Silence of the Lambs*, not for a celebration of joy and life and death and all that."

The Doors may have faltered at the box office, but those involved feel it succeeded on a number of levels. "Oliver's films can't be judged by box office alone," Richard Rutowski says. "His work is cathartic. It affects people, and that's something Hollywood doesn't measure. You don't leave a fucking Oliver Stone film without feeling something. You're going to walk out with an experience. Something changes in you. That's what makes him special."

Despite their battles during the filming, Bob Richardson bristles at the criticism of the film. "Why do we always want the round peg to fit the square hole?" he asks. "Oliver Stone is Oliver Stone. If you want to get on this ride, get on this ride."

"Hey man it's great, don't listen to 'em, it's non-linear man, it's poetry man, everything Godard stands for."

Ray Manzarek in **THE DOORS**

Recently *The Doors* has been showing signs of becoming a midnight movie favorite among the cultists, but with a few modest exceptions such as *The Buddy Holly Story* and *La Bamba*, movies set within the music industry are notoriously poor box office.

Perhaps more significant was the mood of the nation toward rebellion. After a long standoff, fighting in the Gulf had begun on January 17, 1991. The United States was embroiled in its first real war since Vietnam, and anti-American symbols such as Jim Morrison were not high on the general public's list of favorites.

Of course, Stone never has made films for their boffo box-office potential. His real magic has always been taking noncommercial subjects and making them into hits. But no one likes to fail, least of all Oliver Stone, who reevaluates his self-image on an almost daily basis. There was no question that Stone knew the film was risky. He even knew *why* it was risky. What would drive Stone to take on such a project? Part of it is that Stone sees Morrison's philosophy of life as a key to understanding the sixties. To him, Morrison represents the ultimate rebel.

"Jim talked about experiencing life fully, unlike our parents, who grew up in suits and ties with strict codes," Stone says. "We looked at our parents and what did we see? We saw divorces and addictions, we saw Vietnam and Kennedy being killed. For me, Jim was the first one from my generation who was saying those things. I think his long hair, his dark flashy looks threatened people. He had a Dionysian effect on society, and society tried to maintain their view of culture. When someone like that comes along with his long hair, his good looks, and his ability to fuck, he is a true threat to the civilized man. And scary because he represents lawlessness, like he's the Billy the Kid of the mid-twentieth century. He must be punished, he must be ridiculed, he must be scorned. And part of the scorn is the repetition of the mantra, 'He's a lousy poet,' or, 'He's an adolescent poet.' They think they're safe in that mantra and they can kind of demonize him and exorcise him. But he lived his art. His life became the working out of his lyrics. He didn't put it away into a suitcase when he came off the stage. After a performance, he kept on being Jim."

Some people close to Stone believe he made the film to recapture the period of his life that he lost by going to Vietnam. Others think he was starting to worry that he was becoming the very establishment he had rebelled against. "The scrapper in him needs conflict," Willem Dafoe says. "He's a major player now in Hollywood so he can't be the outsider any more. One of the things he's dealing with is his identity."

Though Stone's films were still radical in their subject matter, their mechanism for getting made was becoming increasingly mainstream. The budgets were larger and larger, and big studios were now the major source of financing. For Stone, success is a double-edged sword, and he struggles to reconcile his renegade past with his present role as Hollywood powerbroker. "Oliver is conflicted about his success," says one industry executive. "He hasn't allowed his political sensibilities to get in the way of taking the money, and he struggles with that."

Stone's friends say *The Doors*, like all Oliver Stone films, is really about himself. There are similarities. Both Stone and Morrison were born into well-off families. Both were avid readers, influenced by the same philosophers and writers, and as youths they dreamed of literary careers. And both were self-exiled prodigal sons who attended college sporadically and wound up graduating from film school. Both had serious anarchist tendencies, a fearless attitude about experimentation, and a passion for discovering and pushing people's emotional buttons. As artists they mixed pinpoint intellectual concepts with outright kamikaze attacks on the emotions. Perhaps most ironic, both were at their best when closest to the edge, and both occasionally crossed the border from gutsy to arrogant or from compelling to pretentious.

If Stone uses his films to search out truths about himself, as many of his associates say, what was he looking for in the Jim Morrison story? Most likely how to deal with death. Or to be more precise, how to live life to the fullest and enjoy it despite the knowledge that all things come to an end, and one day death will be waiting. Richard Rutowski comments: "Morrison had insights, which may or may not have been spiritual teachings, but there was no question that he had a real fascination with death and deathlessness. Oliver is very aware of death and he's afraid of it. I think that's why he did *The Doors*."

Looking back on the work two years later, Stone is philosophical and far less defensive then he'd been in previous interviews. Despite his battles with Kilmer, he still feels he made the right choice. Some Hollywood insiders thought moody heartthrob Jason Patric might have been a better choice because he has a darker, more menacing quality, but according to Risa Bramon García, Patric's reading of the role didn't go well. The fact remains that Kilmer had to be very dark to be believable. The real Morrison had a dark quality no matter what he was doing, even if it was just walking into a room or smiling pleasantly. He was dangerous. Perhaps this is why the film seemed to heavily emphasize Morrison's dark side. Stone says no. "Morrison was even darker than we showed in a lot of ways. Look at the lyrics near his death. From the transcripts I read—and those were the closest I ever came to Jim—what struck me was the sadness and depression. I assumed from the records that he had a lot more fun, but it seemed like he had become this Dionysian figure that was denied fun. He had sexual problems, he was an alcoholic in the severe sense in that he had a cut-off point, so he couldn't really enjoy drinking; it was an all-or-nothing affair. His sensibility to drugs dropped. He couldn't even enjoy most drugs any more, he had to go beyond, into heroin. Everything got jaded. The beautiful women I thought would be all around him were not, on closer inspection, so beautiful after all."

Stone did seem to miss Morrison's humor in the film. The real Morrison could genuinely laugh at himself. Listening to "Roadhouse Blues" or his opening rap in "Break On Through #2" from *Absolutely Live* tells you he had learned to laugh through the pain. Stone agrees. "I believe Morrison had a terrific sense of humor and I'm not so sure that we caught it. Part of it was me, and Val is that way a bit. He's more Norwegian than Irish, heavier water. He gets depressed and moody and so on. But he has that sultriness that Jim had. We tried to show the holy and the fool at the same time. That's the hardest stuff to do. Probably, people might say I didn't get enough holy. I couldn't find the exact Jim. Nobody could play Jim Morrison but Jim Morrison."

Stone's chief regrets about his *Doors* experience center on Ray Manzarek. According to Stone, Manzarek's attitude tarnished the whole project from the beginning: "He took an unnatural dislike to me and he poisoned many people's minds toward the movie. And it just became uglier and uglier and uglier after that. He put out a lot of false information. Like with Bill Graham. I have a long, very sweet letter from Bill that says he was sorry he couldn't be there for input. We called him several times and asked him to do things, but he wouldn't call back for several days. He said that he suffered from narcolepsy and just couldn't be there. His partner, Nick Clainos, was extremely helpful. When Bill was around, he wasn't really there. Then I read that Bill wasn't consulted for input. That's absolute horseshit. He was consulted at every turn. He saw early drafts. He saw the interim draft. I showed him the first cut when I screened the film. Bill Graham told me to my eyes, 'It's great.' He said I could cut ten or fifteen minutes, that it might be too long. That was the only criticism I heard from him. We did cut ten or fifteen minutes. We finished the movie and it came out. He said he loved it, and then I started to hear, from others, Bill Graham's criticism of the movie. He never said a word to me. I know that Manzerek was talking to him, poisoning his ears, which is the way he operates."

In the final analysis, would Stone do anything different if he had another chance? "It's a tough call," he responds, "because you could split hairs and do some scenes differently, but I generally think the structure is correct in that it should have been based on the songs. Actually, the movie follows a chronology pretty close to his life. Very little is out of sequence. The music carries you along. Each song evokes a mood, and I think I put the songs in the correct sequence of moods. From an early carnival innocence to the darker realms of New York and the crystal ships, into the interlude with 'Whiskey Bar,' all the way to 'Love Street,' when they're coming up the hill to the turkey dinner, and then into the madness of Miami, 'Five to One,' ending with 'L.A. Woman' and 'Road-house Blues' over the credits. I think I did the right thing. On the other hand, I'd cut the scene on the ledge between Meg and Val near the end. It was an unnecessary beat."

Late one night, over dinner in a crowded restaurant almost a year later, Stone seems lost in thought. Suddenly, he turns and out of the blue he says, "Maybe I did fail with *The Doors*, but if I did, it's just between Jim and me. I know I tried my best to do something that could live up to him. And I think he would've loved it. But, ultimately, it's just between him and me."

After ten years in development, a year of preparation, shooting, and editing, and $38 million, *The Doors* was not considered a success. But in some ways, *The Doors* was like *Scarface*—it may not have fared that well at the box office, but it made a strong impact on a lot of moviegoers. It was a film that people would remember. And it established Oliver Stone with a whole new generation. Yet as far as the movie industry was concerned, a lot of people were looking for Stone to fail and now they felt justified. Maybe now he would have to play by the rules. Many wondered if he would become a more cautious filmmaker and stay a little closer to the safety of the Hollywood system. Stone's answer was his most outrageous, biggest, and riskiest project ever—*JFK*.

CHAPTER TWELVE

JFK

"The truth is the most important value we have because if the truth does not endure, if the Government murders truth, if you cannot respect the hearts of these people, then this is no longer the country in which we were born and this is not the country I want to die in. . . . Tennyson wrote, 'Authority forgets a dying king.' This was never more true than for John F. Kennedy, whose murder was probably the most terrible moment in the history of our country."

Jim Garrison in JFK

A s soon as *The Doors* opened, Stone left for Dallas to begin filming *JFK*. The project had started back in 1988 when Stone attended the Latin American Film Festival in Havana. There he met Ellen Ray, whose Sheridan Square Press published Jim Garrison's *On the Trail of the Assassins* and the controversial *Covert Action Information Bulletin*, when Ray happened to get on the same elevator at the Nacional Hotel. "It was at this Socialist hotel," Stone says, "where it takes like thirty minutes for the elevator to get to the twelfth floor. We were on this creaky elevator and at first I thought she was another of the three thousand crusaders that go to these things around the world, who would talk my ear off about her pet peeve. But Ellen Ray is an extraordinary person in her own right. Back in 1967 she went down to New Orleans to volunteer her services to work with Garrison. She's one of the most courageous women I've met in my life. She has a small printing press with her husband, Bill, and they publish that bulletin. She's amazingly accurate about some things. And she said, 'Read this book.' I read it from cover to cover and bought the film rights soon afterwards."

The thing that had first impressed Stone about the Garrison book was the *film noir* aspects of the story. "This pistol whipping occurs on the night of November 22, 1963," Stone says, "on a rainy night in which this guy, Jack Martin, gets his skull laid open by his boss, Guy Banister, and out of that little Raymond Chandler kind of incident, Garrison spins this tale of international intrigue—a hell of a trail. As a dramatist, that excited me."

Oliver Stone was seventeen when John Fitzgerald Kennedy was assassinated, and it affected him profoundly. "The Kennedy murder was one of the signal events of the postwar generation, my generation," he says. "Vietnam followed, then the bombing of Cambodia and Laos, the Pentagon Papers, the Chile affair, Watergate, going up to Iran-Contra in the Eighties. We've had a series of major shocks. I think the American public smells a rat that's been chewing on the innards of the government for years."

With Stone, the assassination of JFK goes deeper than politics. His parents' divorce coincided with the event. "It left me feeling that there was a mask on everything, a hidden negative truth. . . . I'm still groping my way, trying to figure it out. I feel you have to keep digging into history to understand what happened to us and our generation."

It was inevitable that Stone's curiosity and penchant for real-life intrigue would have led him to the Kennedy assassination sooner or later. Garrison's book merely provided the trigger. "As an adolescent, I was self-absorbed with other problems, but I still felt like there was something wrong with the official version of the assassination," he says. "I bought the rights to the Garrison book right away out of my own pocket and kept it on ice. I didn't know when I'd want to make it. If I'd brought a studio in, it would have saved me money in the short run, but in the long run it could have been very problematic. Because then, everyone finds out that it's in development. I tend to buy properties for myself and keep them to myself."

Though Stone loved Garrison's book, he felt he needed to meet the man who wrote it before he took the idea of a film much further. Sitting with the sixty-eight-year-old Garrison in the former D.A.'s book-lined chambers, Stone pushed for the truth. He had to know for himself if this man was genuine—a flawed crusader whose great passions may have led to a few bad decisions, but whose zeal was based on a real commitment to solid values—or a flamboyant con man who used the murder of a president as a vehicle for his own gain. Ironically, this was the same question the American people would be asking about Oliver Stone in December 1991.

Stone threw everything he had at the old judge. He brought up all the old accusations: that Garrison had taken bribes while a New Orleans district attorney, that he was nothing but a self-aggrandizer, even that he'd been a front man for Carlos Marcello and the Mob. Garrison, at six foot seven, was a physically imposing man who had been worn down by years of illness. He discussed the issues calmly, but with an increasing attitude of forbearance. He'd been grilled by the best and accused by the worst long before the world heard of Oliver Stone. Finally, after nearly three hours of questions, Stone stopped squinting the way he does when he's listening intently and began staring off and nodding, the way he does when he's processing information. "Are you finished?" Garrison asked.

Surprised at the old man's abruptness, Stone nodded. Garrison bored through him with tired but hard eyes. "Good," he said. "Now, young man, why don't you take your people up north where Carlos Marcello is in jail and go ahead and make your movie about Carlos Marcello?"

Stone was not used to being rebuffed, especially by someone he was thinking of basing a major motion picture on, to say nothing of buying the rights to his book. "Do you mean that?" he asked.

"I certainly do," Garrison said, and with that he got up and walked out of the room.

"Jim never pandered to me," Stone says. "Never played up to me to get the movie made. Jim was twenty-three years in the military, he was second in command of his region for the National Guard, he was a pilot in World War II, three-time district attorney, an ex-FBI agent, an appellate judge, and he'd written two books. He was not the loony tune that had been pictured to me as a kid in the press."

Stone called Garrison the next day to set up a second meeting, but the cross examination was over. Stone had a sense that this man was for real and the idea was worth investigating further. Stone recalls his initial impressions of Garrison: "There was a lone wolf integrity there. He had a lot of weak spots, but the majority of the man was solid as a rock. I thought that from the book, and it was confirmed to me when I met him. When I was shooting *Born on the Fourth of July*, he came to Dallas to see me. It really impressed me that here was a man who twenty some years after the incident went back in his old age and wrote another book about the same event. Though his first book was good, he decided that since he was so obsessed with the event back then he should write it over with a little more understanding of the overall situation. His critics said he did the first book because he wanted to get reelected, but then why do the second book? It was because he cared. He knew that Kennedy had been killed through a conspiracy. Here he was, an older man, and most people would be defeated. But I guess it was a bit like me with *Platoon* or *Born*. He wouldn't give up. Integrity doesn't come cheaply. It cost him his friends, it cost him his marriage, and basically it cost him his job, his situation. He recovered somewhat after a phony stick 'em up trial the government slapped on him for a fraud case that was never proven. He made it back and became a judge again. He couldn't be prosecutor any more, but he could be a good appellate judge. He's a man who gets beaten by the system but never gives up."

To be sure, Garrison, who died in January 1993, a little over a year after *JFK* was released, had his flaws as an investigator, but the more substantiated criticisms impugned his eccentricity rather than his motives. "Jim Garrison made many mistakes," Stone concedes. "He trusted a lot of weirdos and followed a lot of fake leads. But he went out on a limb, way out. And he kept going, even when he knew he was facing long odds."

"Somebody's got to tell the truth around here 'cause it sure ain't the Government that's doing it."

Jean Hill in JFK

There are few qualities that Stone admires more in a person than the willingness to go out on a limb for what they believe and the stubbornness to stay there when it gets scary. But Stone's vision for the film was never the Jim Garrison story—it was the story of the conspiracy to murder John F. Kennedy. He didn't just buy the rights to Garrison's book, he also purchased *Crossfire: The Plot That Killed Kennedy* (1989) by Jim Marrs and hired his own researchers. Stone wanted to write a film which examined the efforts of dozens of investigators into the assassination. Though the plot would center on Garrison's case against Clay Shaw, a New Orleans businessman he tried for conspiracy to assassinate the President, it would also encompass other theories in an effort to discredit the official findings of the Warren Commission.

"I believe the Warren Commission Report is a great myth," says Stone. "And in order to fight a myth, maybe you have to create another one, a countermyth. No one really knows what exactly happened on November 22, 1963, or who did it, but there sure are an abundance of flaws in the official investigation. I wanted to use Garrison as a vehicle for a larger perspective, a metaphoric protagonist who would stand in for about a dozen researchers. Filmmakers make myths. D. W. Griffith did it in *Birth of a Nation*. In *Reds*, Warren Beatty probably made John Reed look better than he was, but remained true to the spiritual truth of Reed's life. I knew this would make Garrison somewhat better than he was and, in that sense, we'd be making him more of a hero. I knew I would catch a lot of flak for that, but I figured it was worth it to communicate, really get across, some truth in an area that had been steeped in lies for nearly thirty years."

Once Stone decided to take on the project, he began collecting everything he could find on the assassination. The Jim Marrs book covered an entire spectrum of Kennedy assassination theories, but still there were more, and Stone knew that he would never be satisfied unless he conducted his own inquiry. He hired Jane Rusconi, a recent Yale graduate, to head up a team of researchers and told her to assemble as much material as she could find on the assassination. He also had her look into a host of intriguing characters that previous investigations had turned up as possible participants in the crime of the century.

This was as he was finishing *Born on the Fourth of July*, a full two years before *JFK* would begin, and Stone insisted on absolute secrecy. He'd learned over the years that the fewer people who knew about a project in development, the fewer roadblocks there would be later. Also, he had reached the stature of a major player, and that meant that there were lots of copycat producers out there who were not above rushing a similar project into production just because they heard Oliver Stone was developing the idea.

But there were other reasons for secrecy, too. So many of the key witnesses in investigations into the assassination had wound up dead that, though Stone continually downplayed it, the possibility of someone attempting to keep him from learning and exposing the truth was a real one. "I had some very hard nights during that time," Elizabeth Stone admits. "I couldn't sleep. I kept worrying that someone might find out and try to stop him. I couldn't put it out of my mind. I'd get up at night and go around and check to see if the doors were latched. Especially in the beginning after I read some of the material and watched the BBC Special on the assassination. Once Warner Brothers got involved, I didn't worry so much. The more people who knew about it, the more suspicious it would be for them to do anything. But those early days . . . he kept saying I was being foolish, but I was afraid for him."

Though Stone wouldn't reveal his fears to Elizabeth, the more he delved into the maelstrom of conspiracy theories, the more convinced he became that some extremely powerful forces had been at work over the years to make sure no one ever found the answers he was now seeking. "When you begin to sift through it, there's no escaping the thread," he says.

By December 1989 it was time to go public and enlist the help of a studio. The topic was so controversial that Stone expected a battle, but that wasn't what was bothering him. He knew once he took this step there would be no turning back. Thus it was with heavy anticipation that he approached three executives from Warner Brothers that December. *Born on the Fourth of July* had just come out and Stone was in the midst of preproduction for *The Doors*, but Warner Brothers had been courting him to make a movie on Howard Hughes. That idea was discarded because Warren Beatty controlled the rights, but Stone had another project they might be interested in.

Stone and his agent, Paula Wagner, went to The Grill restaurant in Beverly Hills where three top Warner Brothers executives were waiting—chairman of the board and CEO Robert Daly, president and chief operating officer Terry Semel, and Bill Gerber, a production executive who had been touting Stone's work for some time over at the corporate offices in Burbank. Stone told the Warner Brothers execs he wanted to write a script about the Kennedy assassination, and had already optioned two books on the subject. "My immediate reaction was 'Wow! What a powerful and great idea for a movie,'" Semel says. "Any time the assassination had come up in the last thirty years, everyone seemed to feel we didn't get the whole story."

Semel already had a reputation for politically controversial films, having made *All the President's Men*, *The Parallax View*, and *The Killing Fields*, among others, while at Warner Brothers. Stone describes the meeting at The Grill: "I told Bob and Terry I wanted *JFK* to be a movie about the problem of covert parallel government in this country and deep political corruption. I laid out the story in fifteen or twenty minutes and they seemed to like it a lot. I told them I wanted to first tell the story as it was initially understood in 1963, and then tell it over and over so it unravels, and by the end you see it in a totally different light."

Semel remembers Stone asking if the company would be concerned politically and what the negatives might be. "My reaction was we should do it," he says. "It was entertaining and intriguing, a great murder mystery, something we cared about and grew up thinking about. It took me two minutes to be totally engrossed in the whole idea."

They made a handshake deal. Warner Brothers would get all rights to the film and put up $20 million. The details would take months of bargaining, but the commitment was there. "The film had a home," Stone says. "I know I could have made a better overall deal by selling off the international market separately, but I wanted to sell the whole thing to Warners because I didn't want the script going all over the world to be bid on and read. I knew the material was dangerous and I wanted one entity to finance the whole thing. Given Terry Semel's record of political films, Warners was my first choice."

A classicist when it comes to storylines, Stone was struck by how Garrison's story related to the classic structure of tragedy: "When I first read Jim Garrison's book on the Kennedy assassination, very clearly imprinted was the soul of a gem. You have a prosecutor, an honest man who had served his country in World War II and in Korea, with a family who believes in the American way. And there's something fishy going on in his backyard in New Orleans, so he does his job, it's his duty. And doing his job takes him into stranger, more bizarre circumstances again and again. And eventually he's accused, pandered, ridiculed and humiliated, then defeated. That is a good story, if you believe what he was after was right."

On the Trail of the Assassins, Garrison's second book, was published in 1988 by Sheridan Square Press. It was an elaboration of the earlier book about the trial. Garrison, now a Louisiana Appellate Court Justice, was addressing the larger issues behind the assassination. The book was edited by Zachary Sklar. Stone now teamed up with Sklar to write a script based on it, as well as the Jim Marrs book, and the massive amount of information gathered by Jane Rusconi. Their goal was not only to reveal the conspiracy theories and challenge the Warren Commission, but also to have the film play like a great detective movie.

For Stone, an unusually long time had passed between concept and script. "I had that one in my head for a long while. I was working out the structure. I made several trips to New Orleans before I wrote the screenplay so I could get the characters down. I met Perry Russo, Jim's legal staff, his wife Liz. I did a lot of reading. The idea marinated a long time, which was really a pleasure in a way."

But, as it marinated, it also grew. Clayton Townsend, co-producer of *JFK*, recalls the research. "We took a trip before Oliver wrote the screenplay in order for him to interview any surviving witnesses or relatives. It was fascinating to listen to his questions. How he would probe and work with these people to get information. He asked some questions that were so point blank I was shocked, while others were just off the wall, funny things. But he got the information out of people, one way or another. And then pretty soon the script started bursting into this monstrosity, this gargantuan thing to even read, much less shoot."

"You never know which one of those people you're interviewing will give you that nugget that leads to the mother lode."

Jim Garrison in **JFK**

With Sklar detailing as much of the Garrison story as possible, Stone began to weave in the other elements: "Zach fleshed that side of the story out because, as Jim's editor, he had the original book, which was much longer. Then I added the Oswald side, the Dealey Plaza story, and the Mr. 'X' side. Put everything in the order it's pretty much in now. It's a complicated screenplay."

Because there were so many complex issues involved, Stone had to make some hard choices in the script. One of them was focusing less on Jim Garrison's life, even though he was the clear protagonist of the film. "I was criticized for it, but it would have taken the better part of the film to show the destruction of his character," Stone says. "He lost it more in real life than I showed. He started drinking more, he was certainly womanizing, but there was not enough time to really deal with that. The film was already going to run over three hours because I was not just dealing with Jim Garrison. It was like four movies. I was doing the Lee Harvey Oswald history, I was doing Dealey Plaza. Garrison was never there, but I was showing it again and again. And I was doing this Mr. 'X' story in Washington. Those four elements were very tricky and they took time. As a result, I couldn't dwell on Jim all the way through, nor was I really interested in doing that. Jim did fuck up several times in his job because he went for something too early or he went for it too late. On the other hand, he was denied a lot of witnesses. Some he couldn't subpoena or get them in the state. And some of them died under very bizarre circumstances."

Despite Garrison's failings, Stone had great admiration for him. "Jim Garrison was one of the first Americans in modern history who really went after the government. He went after the concept of the security state and subpoenaed all these officials, but he couldn't get to fucking first base. In the 1960s when guys like me were worshipping James Bond and the Secret Service, this guy took them on. He said, 'Hey, wait a second, these guys are corrupt.' Think about it. Who's got the power to pull this shit off? People say it was the Mafia, well, the Mafia we now know was working with the CIA hand-in-hand on several affairs. It amazes me to read how tabloids and editorials continue to promote the Mafia as being behind the murder of JFK. There's no way the Mafia could have moved this guy Oswald around the chessboard from Russia to Dallas to New Orleans to Mexico like they did. Who could have got the guns in and got the guns out? Who could have gotten the parade route or the security fixed, or gotten the job for Mr. Oswald at the Book Depository? It takes a lot of power to do all that."

In his effort to encompass as much of the story as possible, Stone also employed the use of composite characters in the script, a technique he would be highly criticized for in the press. The most controversial example was the character called Mr. "X," who meets Garrison on a park bench in Washington, D.C., and spells out the grand theory of the CIA and military intelligence as a secret government. The real Garrison did meet some potential witnesses on park benches, and Stone combined them with a retired Air Force colonel named Fletcher Prouty, a former Pentagon liaison to the CIA, whom he met in Washington while he was writing the script.

"What Fletcher said to me really chilled my bones and I incorporated what he told me into the script. I feel this was in the spirit of the truth because Garrison also met a Deep Throat type named Richard Case Nagell, who claimed to be a CIA agent and made Jim aware of a much larger scenario than the microcosm in New Orleans. The dramatist takes license to put composite events and characters into a condensed space; moving fact around. For example, I took three homosexual characters who spotted Oswald with David Ferrie [a key suspect in Garrison's investigation] and Clay Shaw and made them into one character played by Kevin Bacon. Some people will say this makes it fiction. The thing is, once you put a costume on an actor to play a real person, that puts it into the realm of interpretation already. It's no longer a documentary. It enters the realm of myth."

In truth, Garrison missed a lot of the trial because he had a double hernia and was often helped out by Assistant D.A. James Alcock. He did deliver a summation, though Stone added to it for the film. Of course, Garrison was addressing the here and now, dealing with a trial he was bound to lose, whereas the character of Garrison in the film is speaking to millions for posterity. "I wanted to make it better," Stone says of Garrison's long, impassioned speech in the script. "I wanted to bring the man's whole life into the summation about his feelings and my feelings, which crossed in there."

Stone's critics seized upon his composite characters and elaborated-upon scenes as rewriting history. Zachary Sklar, co-author of the *JFK* screenplay, counters: "Since nobody agrees on anything, nobody is distorting history. The only official history is the Warren Commission Report, and that nobody believes."

After battling his way to completion of a solid draft of the script, Stone was pleased. Not only had he found a way to weave the key elements of the conspiracy into the story, but he had a clearer vision of how the film would be shot. He knew now that it would be an exceptional venture, not only in content but in form—the most technically ambitious project he had ever attempted. There was only one problem. "I had told Warner Brothers that it was going to be a twenty-million-dollar movie,"

Stone says, "but after I wrote that script it turned into a three-hour, actually a four-and-a-half-hour movie at that point, and it went up to forty million bucks. This was my first movie for them. They had been real excited, but I hadn't written the screenplay when I made the deal."

Once Stone had a draft that he felt comfortable with, it was time to move on to casting. The increased budget would look a lot better to Warner if he could line up the right stars. Of course, Stone had been playing with casting ideas for months, but it was now time to make some decisions. Since *JFK* was eventually cast with an abundance of well-known stars and this factor played a key role not only in the film's acceptance but also in the audience's ability to grasp the complex storyline, it is the best example with which to examine in detail Stone's casting methods.

Risa Bramon García describes how the process usually works. "We sit down with a list of the characters and he'll tell us what he wants. Sometimes you have to do it on the fly. He'll give you a type or sometimes he'll refer to a living person like a psychiatrist, a politician, a philosopher, a fictional character, or even an actor who is dead. Then we generate lists and he goes through them and picks people he likes or tells us when we're on the wrong track."

Stone had some extensive casting ideas for *JFK*. He writes a lot of notes to himself as daily reminders, and during the casting process these include his impressions of which actors might be right for various roles. When it comes time to make a decision, he goes over these random thoughts and inspirations before having Bramon García contact the actors and discuss their availability. Because of its large cast, the notes for *JFK* are extensive—over fifty pages of jottings on small colored notepads. Since inspirations vary from day to day, many of these actors were never even contacted for the roles suggested, and in some cases, others were considered as well. But the notes give insight into Stone's thought processes and how he arrives at creative decisions. They are free-form thoughts. Since no one usually sees them, any creative impulse or idea, no matter how outrageous, is fair game. Here are several examples.

One page lists: "Ed Asner—Banister, Harry Dean Stanton—Jack Martin, Goldie Hawn—Mercer." Only one of these ideas, that of Ed Asner for the role of Guy Banister, was actually acted upon, though other notes suggested Brian Dennehy, Gene Hackman, and Glen Ford for that role. John Goodman, Danny DeVito, and Larry Drake are all suggested for Dean Andrews, eventually played by John Candy. One note suggests Gregory Peck for Clay Shaw. Later Peck is suggested for Senator Huey Long. Michael Douglas is mentioned in three separate notes as being right for Clay Shaw, but in a fourth he is targeted as E. Howard Hunt. Other suggestions for Clay Shaw include Paul Newman, Martin Landau, Peter O'Toole, Roy Scheider, and Robert Loggia.

One sheet simply has "Marlon Brando" and the letter "X" underlined. But another reads "Donald Sutherland—XXXX." Sutherland was eventually cast as Mr. "X." There were several possible choices for the role of Lee Harvey Oswald. An early note suggests Charlie Sheen, but on one note dated 6/90, Stone wrote, "C. Sheen—L.A. Oswald," followed by "he's the one," but another dated 10/90 says, "D. B. Sweeney—Oswald." Other choices were Alec Baldwin and Tom Cruise, but Gary Oldman eventually got the role. The role of Willie O'Keefe (played by Kevin Bacon in the film) is earmarked on various pages for James Spader, Matt Dillon, Dennis Quaid, Michael Wincott, and Tom Sizemore.

One page, dated 8/90, suggests "Jimmy Woods as David Ferrie!" Later on the same page is "Willem Dafoe—a David Ferrie as well," and next to this is written "cheekbones." On another page, Gary Oldman is suggested for Ferrie, and in other separate notes Jeff Goldblum, Martin Landau, and Joe Pesci (who wound up in the role) are mentioned.

Most interesting are the other actors Stone was considering for the major roles in the film. Under "Liz," the role of Jim Garrison's wife, Stone has written: "Liz McGovern, Sissy Spacek and Cybil Shepherd." Next to Shepherd's name is a question mark, and next to Sissy Spacek (who was eventually cast in the part) Stone has written "from Texas" in parentheses.

For Jim Garrison, Stone has several notes which change drastically as his thinking progresses. In what appears to be a very early note, the heading reads "Conspiracy Saga," and Harrison Ford, Dennis Quaid, and Jack Nicholson are all suggested for the role of Garrison. Underneath, the following note is written: "go to these people, in a sense endorsing your POV [point of view] not as important a role as it is an endorsement." Another early note says, "Find a *real* person—new Gary Cooper, create him yourself. A James Stewart, like old days." A note marked as "Garrison, 6/90 Finland" lists eight possibilities. Number one is "Billy Dafoe," written in big letters, followed by a short description: "laid back quality, his Wisconsin side—an honesty there." Listed as number two is "Alex B" (Baldwin); number three, Matt Modine, followed by the note, "J. Stewart—see Memphis Belle"; number four, Gene Hackman. On the next page Stone has written: "Bill Hurt—too elaborate," and, "Tom Berenger—straight handsomeness," and, "Kyle MacLachlan—straight, new Jimmy Stewart, tall, from his heart."

In an extensive note dated 7/90, Stone lists his current choices for the role of Jim Garrison. Kevin Costner's name is near the top and the only name starred on either side, but still under consideration were Tom Berenger and Willem Dafoe. Also on the list were Harrison Ford, Nick Nolte, Michael Douglas, Robin Williams, Michael Keaton, Mel Gibson, Gene Hackman, John Malkovitch, Alec Baldwin, Robert De Niro, Dennis Quaid, Jack Nicholson, Robert Redford, and Marlon Brando. Keaton's name is then crossed out and next to "Robin Williams" Stone has written, "not to be denied." Next to De Niro he notes: "interesting gravity here as he gets older."

Another note also dated 7/90 says only, "Robin Williams—Garrison!" while yet another that same month says, "Willem do fine!" Still another 7/90 note reads, "Don't need star as Jim." Both Williams and Dafoe are mentioned on two other notes for Jim Garrison, and Tom Berenger is also mentioned again. On one note Stone wrote of the Garrison role, "destined to go to he who wants it." A final note says, "Kevin Costner—Garrison, all American quality."

In the end, scripts went out simultaneously to Harrison Ford and Kevin Costner. According to inside sources, Ford, who has appeared in two Tom Clancy pro-CIA movies, shied away from the material and later said he never believed there was a conspiracy involved. Initially, Costner also begged off. But, these responses aside, Stone had by now made up his mind on who should play Jim Garrison. Despite his note to himself about the role of Jim Garrison being "destined to go to he who wants it," there is no question that Stone worked hard to get Costner. Alex Ho says Stone has the ability to be single-minded, "like a dog with a bone," and that seemed to be the attitude with which he approached Costner. He wanted him, he was right for the part, and he was going to get him. "Costner was a big break for us," acknowledges Stone. "I chased him and I got him. Mike Ovitz was instrumental in that. It helped that he was a strong fan of the movie and was strongly urging Costner, his client, to be in it. He kept saying, 'He's gonna do it, don't worry. It'll happen. He won't sign on the dotted line tomorrow, but it's gonna happen.'"

Stone went to London to meet with Costner when he was making *Robin Hood*. Costner recalls the meeting: "There's a passion that Oliver carries with him and that's one of his most endearing qualities. He's serious, and I like that. Oliver uses every means available to him. He's resourceful. He's been in the jungle and everything is a war to him. But there's something honorable about a director or anybody who will just come after someone they want and just stay after them. He had to come back twice because I just wasn't sure about it. And he didn't come back twice, like if you tell someone you'll think about something and then they check back. He came back again with full force. Oliver does eventually face reality when he can't get something. Some people don't believe that he does, you know. But until something forces him to quit, he continues like he won't settle for anybody else. I admire that."

Even so, Costner held out, refusing to commit to the role. Meanwhile, there were budgetary concerns. The new budget came in at over $40 million and Stone felt that Warner Brothers was getting a little nervous. And there was increasing concern about the script. Stone knew that a studio talking about doing a controversial movie and actually reading the script were two different things. So far, everything was fine, but he knew the real heat was yet to come. Like any astute tactician, Stone was always careful to protect his backside. He'd been holding an ace for some time and now he decided to play it.

Arnon Milchan is one of the true power players in Hollywood. He's so friendly and unassuming it's hard to believe he's amassed a huge fortune and an even huger power base from foreign arms deals. The owner of Milchan Bros., an Israeli company with interests in half a dozen industries, Milchan has been in the international headlines for making deals to benefit Israel's nuclear arms program, but he claims defense of his homeland, not profit, has been his motive. His Regency International Pictures is a major force in world entertainment, partnering with German conglomerate Scriba & Deyhle and French pay-TV company Le Studio Canal+. Stone had met Milchan years before and got on with him well. Milchan's past and slickness didn't bother him. Stone likes power players from the fringe because they have an independence and a gutsiness that establishment Hollywood lacks. Milchan not only has both, but he's such a nice guy that one tends to trust him immediately.

Therein lies both his strength and his danger. But this kind of thing is not a problem for Stone—he doesn't trust anybody anyway.

"**What do you know, who the hell put things together . . . me! Who do I trust—me, that's who.**"

Tony Montana in **SCARFACE**

When asked about his relationship with Milchan, Stone made references to *The Mask of Dimitrios*, a classic *film noir* starring Peter Lorre as a mystery writer who becomes ensnared by a web of intrigue while tracking an international businessman with shady methods across Europe.

For his part, Arnon Milchan had been eager to work with Stone for some time. "I had met Oliver years before and was impressed with his work because he is a fighter," Milchan says. "An artist and a fighter. Then I saw him a couple of times at Terry Semel's house. And this was when *JFK* started to cook. Now, a few other things were cooking at the same time. I was getting more muscles in the business and Warner Brothers was getting more and more nervous about *JFK*. I liked Oliver and we met for dinner one night, had a couple of beers, at Spago's. We were both drunk at the end, but I remember my last words before I collapsed were, 'Whether you like it or not, I'm going to be your partner.' And he had this manipulative little grin. I call it manipulative because it does magic on you. He could give you a smile and even if you were just about to kill him, you'd change your mind. Oliver can get away with anything."

Stone had let it drop that Warner Brothers might be open to a partner on the film, and that was all Milchan needed. "I'm good at feeling when people are hesitant," Milchan says. "I realized there was discomfort around the project. First of all, Kevin Costner was not committed yet. Warners was a little hesitant. Actually, I practically ignored Oliver and made the deal with Warner Brothers. I said, 'I'll put up all the money, let's go.' My agenda was—I wanted the project. I wanted to start the new company, Regency Films, off with a big bang, whatever happened. And I wanted to nail down the beginning of a relationship with Oliver."

What was it that attracted Milchan to the project? As the producer of the mega-hit *Pretty Woman*, he was clearly someone who knew a good money project when he saw one, yet *JFK* surely wasn't the most commercial project around. But Milchan had also produced the controversial *War of the Roses* because of its message about how easily marital differences can get out of hand. To him, Oliver Stone and *JFK* represented the perfect combination—making big bucks and making a strong statement at the same time. "Doing *JFK* excited my imagination beyond comprehension," Milchan says. "When you live long enough and actively enough, real excitement becomes more and more precious and more and more rare. And my relationship with Oliver has given me a lot of that excitement. The subject matter of *JFK* was exciting. It was my first experience playing the upside of Warner Brothers and Time Warner. It was a very scary subject. And, although Oliver thought he would be the ideal scapegoat, I thought I would be even more ideal because of being Israeli. I had this vision of me being stopped at the airport and the immigration police saying, 'You come here, guy. We want to talk to you.'"

Stone, though he had sown the seeds for the arrangement, reacted customarily. "He was highly suspicious," Milchan recalls. "Nobody like Oliver Stone wants a partner without being asked. I pushed myself right down his throat, y'know? And I sensed that all he wanted really was a relationship with my French partners, Canal⁺. He thought my being so emotional was some kind of Hollywood game. But Oliver is a great whore, in a good sense. He will do what it takes to make the kinds of movies he wants to make. Here is a guy who has chosen for the form of his art moving pictures. His art form is constructed in a way that, unless it reaches a lot of people, it's a waste of time for him. This is not a businessman. He's today's type of artist."

Milchan is the epitome of a long chain of maverick financiers with whom Stone has been associated. Beginning with John Daly, who hustled his way from the streets of London to making movies and promoting Mohammed Ali's boxing match in Africa, to eccentric Ed Pressman, to high rollers Mario Kassar and Andy Vajna of Carolco, Stone has continued to move with independent sources of capital. Most artists, finding the pursuit of funding difficult and even painful, would have stopped with the first comfortable cache; but Stone has always sought more freedom and a larger vision. It's easy to think of Stone as having an extremely calculating nature, but such decisions are made instantaneously. He didn't agonize and scheme for weeks about bringing Arnon Milchan into the *JFK* deal; instead, it was an immediate decision made upon seeing Milchan again. Stone focuses on what he needs to accomplish, and when the solution surfaces, he acts on it instantly. He has cunning and he is calculating, but it's all from his gut. He instinctively knows what to do. This is probably why he's avoided heart attacks, high blood pressure, and the other symptoms of a high-stress power player. He has no time to agonize over things because he sees himself as always fighting a momentous battle in the here and now. He functions like a drowning man playing a chess game for his life: every time he bobs up for air, he makes another move. It might occasionally be wrong, but because his instincts are so focused and attuned, it will be right most of the time.

Of course, these characteristics make him extremely hard to work for, to say nothing of being married to him, but they also make him virtually invulnerable to the shams and scams of Hollywood. The other guys can't figure him out because he's so unpredictable. Stone will never be outfoxed because he's far too caught up in his own world ever to be snared into anyone else's schemes. He fails only because he made a mistake, never because he was conned. He plans, but he doesn't chain himself to those plans. That's one of the reasons why Stone is so secretive. The world doesn't understand intuitive people. If his staff knew all his plans, they might mistake his adaptability for indecisiveness or vacillation. He thinks things through until he feels he has processed the information and then he sets it aside until the right time, at which point he will make an instinctive decision.

By now, Stone had ferreted out another obstacle to Kevin Costner agreeing to do the role—Costner had made a promise to his wife that he would take a year off from work. As soon as Stone discovered this, he sent Garrison's book and the screenplay to Costner's wife, Cindy. It was yet another bold tactic that most directors would never risk. In this case, it worked. "After she read them," Costner says, "she said, 'You have to do it.'"

Costner, thought of by many in Hollywood as a conservative, actually defies such categorizations, preferring to think for himself. He's not one to act on impulse, however, and researched Garrison carefully before agreeing to play him. "This was a man without fear," Costner says of his several meetings with Garrison. "He was a very commanding presence, a man who was made to look foolish by history and given ulterior motives."

Costner also talked to others who knew the man, both friends and enemies. "I met with Garrison's critics as well as the people on the street who still love him," says Costner. "He's got conflicting sides like everybody, and both Oliver and I wanted him played that way."

Stone agrees: "I wanted Kevin to get both sides, to witness the hatred and extremism that Jim engenders, and as an actor to look into the eyes of his enemies and know what he was up against back then. These were tough people, and they'd come in a parade in front of Costner with their New Orleans accents saying that Jim's a snake—that he liked boys and was angry that [Clay] Shaw stole his lover and a lot worse. Kevin read the script several times and saw backup material. It was not easy for him to do. After all, he was a man who was friends with George Bush—and he was at the height of his career. For him to step into this arena, risk his image doing something like this, took courage. I could've been a crackpot, some people think I am. When I got Kevin down to New Orleans and he met Jim Garrison and started to sense that there was integrity and dignity in Jim, he really started to come around. He took the chance—he risked making some enemies with this movie."

Costner signed to play Jim Garrison in January 1991, just two months before his *Dances With Wolves* won seven Academy Awards. His presence greatly enhanced the value of the package, and made Warner Brothers feel a lot better about the increasing commitment. "Kevin was the perfect choice for Jim Garrison," Stone says, "because he reminds me of those Gary Cooper, Jimmy Stewart qualities—a moral simplicity and a quiet understatement. He listens well. He anchors a three-hour eight-minute movie in a very strong way. He guides you through it because you empathize with him and his discoveries become yours. Through Kevin playing Jim you get on the fifty-yard line for the Kennedy assassination."

But Stone wasn't through with casting yet. Not by a long shot. "I also wanted a big cast, because I knew that it was obscure and arcane stuff and I wanted the cast to be like signposts. Darryl Zanuck's *The Longest Day* was one of my favorite films as a kid. It was realistic, but it had a lot of stars. So I said, 'Why can't we do the same thing with *JFK*?' I wanted Jack Lemmon as Jack Martin and Walter Matthau as

Senator Huey Long. The supporting cast provides a map of the American psyche: familiar, comfortable faces that walk you through a winding path in the dark woods."

The presence of Lemmon, Matthau, Sissy Spacek, Ed Asner, Tommy Lee Jones, Donald Sutherland, Kevin Bacon, John Candy, Joe Pesci, Gary Oldman, Bryan Doyle-Murray, Sally Kirkland, and the others was integral to Stone's strategy. Warner Brothers, however, didn't feel this idea was important enough to increase the already sizable budget to pay the huge salaries involved with such a cast. "Once they got Costner, they didn't care about casting other names," Stone says. "They wouldn't give me the money to get these people. We went to all the agents in town, begging everybody to sign on a favored nations [a contract clause where everyone is paid the same]. They'd all ask, 'What's Costner getting?' And I'd say, 'He's getting a full salary.' It was tough, but through the power of the subject matter and the words that were on paper, we got people like Joe Pesci to come down and Donald [Sutherland] to do it. All of them waived their normal fees to help the picture." (Though Costner did take the same salary he had taken for *Dances With Wolves*, the huge success of that film could have justified a substantial increase which he waived for *JFK*.)

This too is an example of Stone's steadfast persistence. Most Hollywood power players would fancy themselves too important to be asking favors from so many actors at once, much less "begging" them to sign on. But Stone is able to submerge his personal ego when it comes to his art. The important thing is getting the project done right, not how he might appear. What most people don't realize is that for every big-name actor who said yes to *JFK*, there was another who turned it down. "Many of them turned me down. They wanted their money or they disagreed with the message of the film. Paul Newman, Gene Hackman, Marlon Brando, lots of people. Of course, Marlon was occupied with his boy. But lots of people turned me down."

Risa Bramon García describes another such turndown: "The David Ferrie role was sent to Jimmie Woods first. But Jimmie thought he should play Garrison, and he couldn't get off that long enough to consider the role of Ferrie, which I think would have been an amazing part for him. We tried Willem Dafoe, but he didn't think it was right for him. We went to John Malkovich, but he just didn't want to do it. We just couldn't find a man that would make Oliver happy. We auditioned a few people for the part and made several lists. Finally, we talked about Pesci and that worked out, but that role was a tough one to find."

The situation with James Woods was an interesting one. Woods saw himself as perfect for the role of Jim Garrison. Though this may seem strange to those so familiar with Costner's excellent performance, it must be understood that Woods was envisioning a different type of film. Had it been a straight biography of Jim Garrison, flaws and all, Woods could have been the ideal choice; but since Stone was opting to focus on the assassination conspiracies and anchor the film with Garrison as a rock-solid centerpiece around which such a mad vortex could swirl, Costner proved the better choice.

Another aspect of Stone's casting methods was revealed in the choice of Tommy Lee Jones. "Sometimes we show him people that we know aren't right for a particular part, but may be right for another one," Bramon García says. "It's like putting a big puzzle together. Like Tommy Lee Jones. I knew he had to be in *JFK* and I suggested him for a part that was ultimately cut. Oliver liked him, but he wound up going with someone else who wound up being cut out of the movie. But we kept thinking that Tommy should be in the film somewhere. Then one day Oliver said, 'What about Tommy for Clay Shaw?' And we said, 'Yeah, if we do his hair white, it's a good idea.' So sometimes an actor will float around in the pool, as we call it, and then we'll be able to find a place for them."

Stone also signed Sissy Spacek for the role of Garrison's wife, and Jay O. Sanders, Michael Rooker, Laurie Metcalf, Wayne Knight, and Gary Grubbs to play his beleaguered staff. All in all, *JFK* had over 220 speaking parts, whereas a normal film has 40 or 50 at most. Consequently, even once the main parts were cast, Bramon García's work was far from over. "For *JFK* we did open calls all over Dallas and New Orleans," she recalls. "Somewhere around ten thousand people showed up. They came because of Oliver and Kevin Costner, but mostly to be a part of the event. We had these mass gatherings of people so we could pick faces and bodies and find the right people for all these smaller roles and crowd scenes."

Once Milchan came in with his German and French money, preproduction moved forward rapidly. Alex Ho and Clayton Townsend began marshaling their forces to secure the almost inconceivable demands that Stone claimed he had to have to make *JFK* all that it could be. This included filming in Dealey Plaza where Kennedy was shot, where no one had ever filmed before. And, of course, Stone wanted to shoot from the Texas School Book Depository where Oswald supposedly fired his rifle. And he had to have the exact window Oswald was supposed to have used. He intended to recreate the assassination down to the last detail.

For the Dallas City Council, this was not the most thrilling of ideas. Ever since that fatal day in November 1963, the city had been trying to live down its reputation as the place where Kennedy was shot. Clayton Townsend, by then a co-producer, describes the involved process the production team went through to secure historic locations: "Initially, we signed a deal with the city for Dealey Plaza. We had to agree to hire thirty-six policemen to reroute traffic in order to close the streets for three weeks. That cost us a fortune. But it wasn't as difficult as getting the Texas School Book Depository. The depository is owned by the county, and it's become the county commissioner's headquarters. Five commissioners had to rule on it. On the sixth floor where Oswald supposedly shot from, the Dallas Historial Society has an assassination museum and they have a board of like twenty-five directors who range from liberal to conservative, from film lovers to diehard Lyndon Johnson supporters. We had to negotiate with them to put a guy in the window so we could film the gun-sight angles the way they would have been.

"We were able to negotiate that for fifty thousand dollars, a huge sum for what we ended up doing, which was basically nothing. It meant we could film from the window from this hour to this hour if only five people went up to the floor—the camera crew, one actor, and Oliver. They had us over a barrel at that point. The authenticity of having the exact window to show the point of view was worth the money and we paid it. It was a nonprofit organization and hopefully they put the money to a good use."

According to Townsend, the hardest part was obtaining permission to restore the outside of the building to its original look. The production wanted to restore the brick facade on the windows, paint the window seals back to their original color, and put the original sign back up. They also wanted to rent the floor above the museum to shoot interior shots. "It took us about five months of negotiations to get the final okay," Townsend says. "First they said yes to changes to the building. Then somebody got to somebody, I think, because one of the commissioners, a judge, then said, no, you can't touch the building. So a whole big political lobbying thing went on with the five county commissioners. So we swayed three members to vote on our behalf. It took forever, with me taking judges and secretaries out to lunch, Oliver coming in and speaking, and lots of other stuff. It was a nightmare. Oliver has trained me from when I was a production assistant not to take no for an answer. It's like, 'Why can't we film in your building?' 'Well, because you'll block the access to our accounting department.' 'Well then, we'll use the back door.' 'Well, the back door won't work because there's no parking.' 'Well, what if we make parking?' You just keep dealing with everything until you hit a final brick wall that won't move. That's when you give up. Sometimes the brick wall is, 'We don't like your script and therefore you can't film on our facilities.' That point is usually where we won't bend."

When does Stone back off? "Well, on a Dealey Plaza you don't back off," he says calmly. "You do what you have to do. You go to Texas. Remember, I had established a very good reputation there with *Born on the Fourth of July*."

How calculating is Stone? When he won his Oscar for *Born*, he thanked the people of Dallas. Asked if perhaps he had mentioned the city with the future filming of *JFK* there in mind, Stone balks. "You're joking, aren't you?" he says. "Of course not. I thanked the Filipinos too. I didn't intend to shoot there."

Most people who know Stone say he never quits. Though he has more persistence than most, what sets him apart in a town full of type-A personalities is that he seems to embrace determination as a sort of faith. "There is a destiny to each film," he says. "At a certain point, it's out of my hands. We had alternatives in other cities that we could have used for Dealey. But it would have never been the same."

Already Stone was being challenged in the entertainment press, just bits and barbs. He knew he should keep quiet at this stage, but having resurrected the issue of Kennedy's murder it was fully alive for him, as if it happened yesterday. "It's the untold story of a murder that occurred at the dawn of our adulthood," he stated in one interview. "It's a bit like 'Hamlet.' The real king was killed, and a fake king was put on the throne."

If the establishment had not been provoked enough by the idea of Stone doing such a film, this statement and others like it threw down the gauntlet. It was becoming clearer that Stone not only thought there was more to the Kennedy assassination than the Warren Report, he actually had the gall to imply that there was some sort of government-aided cover-up. Wait until they found out he was not only talking about government cover-up, but government *participation*. Mainline Hollywood was already saying, and perhaps hoping, that *JFK* would be Stone's *Apocalypse Now*, a monster of a movie, too big for even him to control. Something that would surely serve to take this man down a peg.

Stone was not planning on backing off, but the pressure was building. Around this time he spoke at his old alma mater, the Hill School. While admitting to feeling pain when he thought of his days at The Hill, he also credited the discipline he learned there with getting him through many difficult periods in his life. The following is a brief paraphrase from the conclusion of his speech:

> Some of you arc here as privileged sons, unfettered by the realities of survival, and will follow your path of privilege and do nothing with your lives but feed your own, play golf, and pass on your genes to some lookalike. Others will be the leaders of a new generation. You will know the terror of chaos and have only your own strength of character to pull you out . . . self-pity is not allowable and when you know that, you will be a man. Imagination! Develop it here. *Now!* Before it is too late. Read, dream, see . . . for imagination is power. Oil, business, banking, munitions, the dollar—this is the true world. Greed reigns, greed fights wars, greed kills. The news media for the most part is silenced by that money. You will not get the truth in *Time*, *Newsweek*, or on CBS. You must rely on yourselves for the truth. Cherish it, fight smartly for it, and concede nothing to the bastards who will bedevil you! In the words of Upton Sinclair: "Somehow love has come to be in the world, somehow the dream of justice haunts mankind. . . . I know that Jesus was crucified, and Joan burned and Socrates poisoned. . . . But the dream persists . . . arising from the dust and breaking its way out of its prison and groping its way into the light!"

Stone is hardest to deal with right before and after a shoot. Afterwards, he is detoxing from the high of making the film, while before, he's feeling the pressures of preproduction. Preproduction has been likened to running in front of a freight train. Here comes this $40 million film down the track and you'd better be ready for it. "Oliver gets more insane at a progressive rate as he gets closer and closer to the start of shooting," his assistant at the time, Kristina Hare, says. "Once he starts he's in a sort of Zen state, very methodical. The preproduction for *JFK* was the worst. He had me come to Dallas with no notice. That was normal. He'd keep you in the dark and only give information on 'a need to know' basis. He wanted me to stay for four months, so I had to move out of my apartment before I left and I was already exhausted when I arrived in Dallas. I spent the first week typing script revisions, sometimes until five in the morning. I ate at my desk and didn't even go outside for a week. My eyes were burning, I was exhausted, I was going batty. I'd get frustrated because I'd spend a whole day making changes and the next day he'd want it back the way it was. It's tough to read his writing with scribbles and arrows everywhere, so I'd make educated guesses and usually I was right, but the day before shooting I misread some stuff. He came in screaming at the top of his lungs. I was hurt. I hated him with every bone in my body at that moment. But that's how he is right before shooting. You just have to treat him like he's mad and roll with the punches until the cameras start rolling. During production, he's a dream to work with."

There was no question Stone was taking on more of a physical challenge then he ever had before. The first draft of *JFK* ran to 190 pages. At the standard film formula of one minute per page, that would still have been over three hours, but Stone's people had estimated the actual running time would be over four hours. By the start of shooting he was only down to 156 pages, and cheating on the margins to squeeze in a little extra at that. There was a tremendous amount of dialogue, and much of it was complicated, with things happening in different places at the same time and sometimes several versions of the same instance. As if this wasn't enough, the decision to shoot documentary footage, black and white video, extensive cutaways, and other optical processes basically doubled the amount of shooting necessary. It amounted to making two films instead of one.

As filming approached, Stone knew *JFK* would be his greatest challenge to date and, as much as he was afraid of failing, he was eager for the fight. "I felt like I was about to commit suicide. I thought I might really go down on this one. This could be a movie that totally misses it. Too talky, too difficult, too much information. But I figured, I'm gonna go out in style. I got Kevin Costner, a great cast, and we're gonna spend some money to do it right. Maybe this will be *Heaven's Gate*. But goddamnit, it's worth it. Because this one I believe in. No doubt."

"We'll be lucky to get out of this with our skins."

Bill Broussard in **JFK**

JFK took Dallas by storm. The front line featured a staggering array of big names. The papers wrote about "Oliver's Army," a strong film crew augmented by more than eight hundred locals in an effort to turn the clock back to the day Dallas had always wanted to forget. The production spent $4 million to restore the Plaza to near perfect historical detail, including the $50,000 to the Historical Foundation just so the sight angles on the rifle would be right. The crew removed billboards, pruned trees to the height they were in 1963, repainted storefronts, and rerouted traffic.

"Filming Dealey Plaza was a challenge," Stone recalls of those early weeks. "We had to stage a motorcade through downtown Dallas, close off traffic and shoot the President repeatedly. That was a psychic phenomenon in itself, with thousands of people watching. We did it from every different type angle and position. We did it steadily and we used those doubles. We got some great footage, but it was hard. There were a lot of people who were very sensitive about that issue."

Recreating November 22, 1963, affected the cast and crew deeply. For many, that date stands out like a spark in the night, short-circuiting them to the past. Everybody remembers where they were the day Kennedy was killed. It was the end of America's romance with the presidency and the beginning of a new world order. Watching that motorcade wind through the downtown Dallas streets was eerie. An identical open limousine making the tight turn onto Elm Street, headed for the triple underpass, Governor Connally and his wife in the front seat and the Kennedys in the back, Jackie's pink suit and hat a splash of color as she waves from the left side of the limo, the President's smile as he waves to the crowd, Mrs. Connally's words, "Mr. President, you can't say that Dallas doesn't love you. . . ." Then the shots.

Shooting this scene over and over, coupled with the uneasiness they felt knowing that half of Dallas didn't want them there, gave the cast and crew on that first day a feeling that they were questioning something better left alone, provoking the gods. Kevin Costner describes an accident on that first day which, had fate been unkind, might have altered the entire course of the film:

"I don't think anybody talks about this, but it really could've ended the whole project. It was our first day in Dealey Plaza and thousands of people were watching. There were about fifty or sixty extras sitting on the ground in front of the Book Depository while the crew was working on the sixth floor when suddenly, the window from the sixth floor fell out. This big sheet of glass comes hurtling down. It was terrible. It could've severed heads, severed bodies, it could've easily killed three or four people. Imagine a big plate of glass falling from six floors up, coming straight down like a guillotine. Well, in the last fifteen feet a gust of wind caught the glass and lifted it like a piece of paper, moved it off about twenty-five feet, and then it slammed to the ground where it shattered and didn't hit anybody. I just played the scenario over of the trauma and the controversy of having three or four people killed on the first day of filming. I could just see us being denied Dealey Plaza and the whole film falling apart. We were all shaken. But as the shattered glass was swept up, I just projected that it was the destruction of this dark blemish on American history and the end of everything that didn't want this movie to go forward."

The way Stone responded to the incident is equally telling. "After the glass fell," Costner recalls, "I looked at Oliver and he just nodded and moved on. I felt like saying, 'You don't know how lucky we are,' but Oliver just kept marching. That's what's so great about him. I would've just played the scenario over and over for a while. He just kept on keeping on."

It was at Dealey that the crew fully realized how time-consuming such extensive shooting in different formats could be. Bob Richardson sees Stone's willingness to experiment with the various formats as a tribute to his creative nature: "How many directors do you know to whom you can say, 'Oh, let's shoot the whole first section of the Dealey Plaza in 16mm, mostly in black and white'? Two weeks of shooting on a forty-million-dollar film, and all of the dailies are going to be 16mm. I don't know anyone. He just said, 'Yeah, sure. We'll do it.' He doesn't ever inhibit. In fact, he pushes you a little further."

Of course, the additional shooting costs a lot of money. In most cases, when multiple formats were used they were shot one right after the other. "It depends whether you want to shoot in 35 or 16 or Super 8," Richardson explains. "In many cases the lighting has to be different. For some shots, you could have multiple crews shooting at once, five cameras at the same time in different formats, but that would be even more costly than to just go back over the scene another time."

Contrary to what most people think, even a filmmaker of Stone's caliber has to worry about staying within the budget. "The below-the-line costs are never where you can just afford everything you might want," Richardson points out. "Things just don't work that way. Take something like a crane. Sometimes it's a little difficult to justify getting a crane for a scene because maybe you know you need it in another scene more. Of course, with *JFK*, there weren't really enough days to shoot the script. It comes in at a hundred and fifty-six pages and you're not just shooting one script, you're actually shooting a script and a half because you have to overlap everything. The dialogue has to be covered from beginning to end, even though half of it's going to be in narration format."

After Dealey, it was time to shoot the Rose Cheramie scenes. Cheramie, a hooker who at one time may have been a stripper in one of Jack Ruby's clubs, claimed to have overheard two men plotting to kill Kennedy before being thrown from their car in Louisiana on November 20, 1963. In the film, these scenes are the first to appear after the opening documentary footage. Though she was on the screen for barely a minute, Stone recruited former Oscar nominee Sally Kirkland for the part. It is interesting to note the extensive effort that went into even this short a scene. Kirkland, a Method actor, describes her preparation for the role: "I thought since she was a stripper I'd go to this club and see what it was like to strip on stage. Of course, Oliver loves women. He's thrilled to have a professional excuse to sit there and have all these girls come over to the table, bodies practically falling over him as they brought the drinks. He said, 'Look, you don't have to do this, Sally, but I'm not going to stop you if it's something you think you need to do.' So I tried on the G-string and the what-not. They have some law in Dallas that you have to have the nipples covered with not just costume but a plastic something. They didn't have any to give me and they were worried about legal problems. Then they didn't have any music I could dance to. So I didn't do it. But that night I got excited thinking that, even though it was just a cameo, I'd be playing one of the few people who actually tried to stop the assassination."

Kirkland's scene the next day involved being thrown out of the car. "The makeup people were doing this beauty thing on me and I said I want to look like someone who's on drug withdrawal, who has been lacerated and thrown from a car. Then suddenly a walkie-talkie is put in front of my ear, and it's Oliver wanting to know if I needed anything? When would I be ready? He was miles away on the location. And I thought, Well, I've done sixty-three films, and this is the first film that the director's talked to me on walkie-talkie from the location to the makeup room."

Once on the set, Kirkland says Stone encouraged her to bring what she wanted to the role. "He was very open to my ideas. The stuntwoman took the real hard fall from a distance for the master shot, but I wanted to hit the pavement only half conscious, bloody and teary for my scene. I wanted to stand up and scream, 'You fucking assholes!' That was never in the script. This woman's whole life has been about abandonment, disillusionment. She may be drugged and inebriated, but she knows what's happening and it's like this primal scream. So he said, 'Well, let's shoot it two ways.' And so I had to keep falling from the car and at one point my leg was bloodied a bit. And he said, 'Are you sure you want to do this? We could get a stuntwoman.' But I said no stuntwoman. I felt that we were each challenging the other. How far can we take this small role and give a hundred percent authenticity?"

Kirkland's next scene was a hysterical Rose Cheramie in the hospital trying to warn the doctors about the forthcoming assassination. "I was ready to start the scene and Oliver asked everybody to please be quiet so I could focus and I felt this extraordinary respect that he has for the process," Kirkland says. "Then suddenly I was being wheeled down the hall into the room and lifted into the bed in some footage you didn't see in the movie. Then he sent in some actors pretty much the way [Elia] Kazan works, without me really knowing what they were going to do. He told the actors playing the doctor and the officer what to say, but he didn't do it in front of me. It was all like a theater piece. And so suddenly they were asking me questions and I was in tears and all disoriented. I was purposely fogging up my contacts so that I couldn't quite see and putting sensory things on myself so that I would be disoriented. I answered the questions about how they were going to kill Kennedy and then I remember going into this incredible scream. I thought, somewhere in the back of my head, what will the poor sound people do with this? But it was like from my gut, like back when she was on the road. And in the movie, he had that scream pierce into you so that it sort of set you up for the motorcade that follows."

The mystery element of the film intensifies when, after the motorcade assassination sequence, a drunken Guy Banister—played by veteran television and film actor Edward Asner—loses his temper when his assistant accuses him of running clandestine operations out of their office. Asner, who has long been active in Central American causes, has been a fan of Stone's ever since *Salvador*. "I will be forever grateful to Oliver for what he achieved with *Salvador*," Asner says. "It accomplished an awful lot. And I found him a gentleman to work with. He's open to an actor's ideas. I did discover that *when* I approached him about changing a line seemed to make a difference. If I did it more than five minutes before it was shot, he'd say okay, but then he'd start thinking about it and it was, 'I don't know. Leave it like it was.' But if you did it with less than five minutes, he'd just go with his first instinct, which was usually to let you do what you want. Of course, none of these ideas I had were inventing the atom bomb or anything all that important."

The part of Banister's assistant, Jack Martin, was played by longtime film star and multiple Oscar winner Jack Lemmon. "I had met Oliver, but I had not worked with him and I was dying to," Lemmon says. "I would have done it without even reading the material. It was a pretty great experience. There was enough material so you were really working with the director, not just someone standing in the background."

Lemmon outlines what he feels makes Stone a great director: "Every director who's really good is unique, and yet there are certain characteristics that the great directors all have. The first one is leadership. And God knows Oliver has that. The same quality Patton had or Nimitz or somebody else running an Army or the Navy. You can walk on his set and not even know what the man looks like, but if you look around, *bang*, that's the director. Oliver has that kind of presence. He's the captain of the ship and there's no question about it. Actors love to work for Oliver because, even though he's usually the author and knows what he wants, he does not impose it. Like all the great directors, he gives you the freedom to bring what you have to the role. He is very gracious in his respect for what you might contribute, even though he's written it. Oliver, as a writer, can visualize the scene in his mind, but he still doesn't impose it before allowing you, as an actor, to bring something of your own to it. He might accept what you do or reject it, but he allows you to try it, and that's all an actor can ask. An actor has no right to expect it to be done his way, but he does have a right to say, hey, wait a minute, let me try this.

"Oliver reminds me of [Constantin] Costa-Gavras [*Missing, Z*], whom I respect immensely, in the way he treats actors and also on the level of excitement he brings. Energy. Billy Wilder also has that quality. I have a picture of Billy Wilder sitting down and it's probably worth a million dollars because he only sat down once and that must've been when somebody kicked him. I mean, he had everybody a foot off the floor. Oliver does too. Another thing I love is that he's fearless. The man would shoot in Hell, he really would. And the interesting thing is the crew and the actors would follow him and the cameras would start rolling."

Lemmon was also impressed with the way Stone paced the production: "He makes sure things come in on schedule, but he still will take plenty of takes and he doesn't rush you. I think where he's smart is in setting his original schedule so that you don't feel pressure or panic at any time. With some directors, the actors begin to feel they're late if they're fifteen feet away from the camera. You'll never get that with Oliver. He'll stay until Hell freezes over to get the shot he wants. Just in the brief time I was there, I remember one scene where it was just raining like—I mean, I've seen it rain but oh my God was it raining then! And Oliver had Ed Asner and me walking along drunk and talking. I'll tell you, the difficulty of trying to record the soundtrack while not hearing anything but Niagara Falls was hard enough, but not only that, he had the damn camera on a long tracking shot on top of a crane over the waterfront. But none of this fazed him at all. He was under a poncho and we stayed there until I don't know how long . . . but we got it."

Asner also remembers the scene in the rain. "They were trying to get the right synchronization effect with the rain and sky and everything else," he says. "That was why we had to keep doing it, but Jack and I walked down there so many times that we ran out of things to do, so on one of the takes I stopped and faked taking a piss. You couldn't tell, my back was to the camera and it was raining like a son of a bitch, but they didn't use it anyway."

Despite the problems with the rain, Lemmon saw a different scene as the best example of Stone's determination. "We were shooting in the offices, just quick cuts of me watching people go in and out, and Lee Harvey Oswald comes in at one point. It's just a quick pop of me looking. Well, those pops took a long time setting up, I can tell you. We worked in an ancient building on the sixth flight, a walk-up where the old elevator couldn't carry half the equipment. So they're luggin' this crap up the stairs and it is so hot and muggy. And then when he went into black and white, he used an extremely harsh light to differentiate for the flashback, and the result, of course, was wonderful, but it goddamn near killed everybody.

"I sat for a take that took less than a half a minute, and at the beginning of the take, I put a newspaper in front of me on my desk. By the time he said, 'Cut,' the paper was smoking. That's how much heat there was. I was in hysterics. I said, 'Oliver, I've been in this business for thirty-nine years and I have never seen anything like that.' And he just said, 'Don't worry, we got plenty of papers.' Then he laughed and kept right on going. I love it. The man is devoted to what he has set out to do. And he will not compromise one millionth of an inch. That separates the very good from the great. That's why he ends up with great footage, because he'll just go through anything to get it."

Asner comments, "You knew while he was shooting that the techniques were amazing. The different angles, the cuts, the speed. There was nothing left to chance, nothing left to doubt."

To prepare for the role of former FBI agent Guy Banister, Asner read a couple of books and the notes supplied him by the production company. "The interesting thing to me was that the FBI was all over this thing. Everywhere you looked there was some connection back to the FBI—and they were the ones who eventually investigated everything."

Despite the controversial nature of *JFK*, Asner said he got very little flak for doing the film. "I got a lot of praise. Lot of support. Surprised the hell out of me. I don't know how many people said, 'By God, I didn't know you could do that.' Play a heavy. I think that Oliver deserved the Best Director's Award far and away for *JFK*. Of course, they'll never give it to him. Where he is, everything gets harder and harder, I guess.

The longer you're up there, the more they require of you. But Oliver is an unbelievable giant who has really made an impact on this business."

Lemmon and Asner worked well together, and only experienced a problem during the pistol-whipping scene. "We didn't have a problem except that Ed belted me with the thing," Lemmon says, only half joking. "The first thing I heard was a ringing in my left ear and it lasted for about a week. Of course I told Ed that it was a month. Make him feel guilty. He called me after we got home, called every couple of days to see how I was feeling. But he caught me a pretty good shot. 'Course, that kind of thing can be tough to fake. But we had fun. I did my second Broadway show with Ed as a matter of fact. Thousand years ago."

Asner still claims he didn't do it. "It was a rubber gun and I know how to fake pretty well. Somehow or another, the damn gun . . . I never thought about this before but I think maybe Jack in his reaction threw his face into the gun . . . I just could not believe I ever hit him, but then it kept happening. I just know I did not hit him with the goddamn gun. I'm too fine a craftsman to do that . . . I was flabbergasted the first time it happened. And then the next time we did the damn scene, he came up with more blood coming down his face."

Though he was worried at the time, Stone now laughs at the memory. "Ed felt very bad after it happened the first time," he recalls. "And it scared me because I was worried that Jack was hurt and asked him if he thought we should break. But you know Jack. He said he was okay, so we tried the scene again. Well, now Ed was being so careful, it didn't look good. It looked fake. So Jack kept reassuring him. 'C'mon Ed, make it look good,' he'd say. 'Take a good swing this time.' So finally, Ed got into it again and we started shooting, and *wham*! He hit Jack again. And this time Jack wasn't getting up. I was horrified. I could just see the headlines in tomorrow's paper: 'Madman Stone Sends Nice Guy Jack Lemmon to Hospital.' Then Jack got up and shook it off and damn if he didn't want to do the scene again."

Because *JFK* has so many cutaways and different angles, except for Costner's long monologue at the end of the movie, the actors usually didn't have to do more than a few lines at a time. Jack Lemmon discusses how he and Kevin Costner handled one such scene. "It was when we did the stuff where I'm at the racetrack and Kevin comes up and starts talking to me. Now there's about fifteen cutaways there to other things and you hear my voice over it. So each one was a separate scene. I didn't have to sit down and learn five pages. But I did learn the five pages. I didn't say anything, but I was secretly hoping that Oliver would just continue and let me do the whole thing. Let it all happen and roll. So we got there and Kevin sits down facing me and we're going to rehearse the first little thing. So I finished the first little bit, Kevin answers, and that's supposed to be the end of it. Only I just took a beat and then said the next line. I saw a little blink on Kevin's face, but he just continued on. Kevin had learned the whole scene as well, so we just kept trading lines and we went through all five pages. And Oliver shot it that way too. He didn't bat an eyeball. We kept rolling and just went right on through the whole damn thing, which was just great for us as actors."

Lemmon was also impressed with Stone's crew. "He's got people that worked on every damn film he's done. They kill themselves. I don't know when they sleep. Maybe he's just whittled it down to people who don't sleep. When I left they were going into some frigging swamp and everybody was given these pages of what to bring for snakebites, mosquitoes, and everything else, plus the heat. I thought, 'I'm getting out of here just in time. I'm too old for this crap.' Holy Moly."

For Stone, it was a continual grueling battle, but he was seeing progress. The dailies were looking good. The techniques he and Richardson were experimenting with seemed to be working; the cast and crew were rising to the call. It was a mammoth creature, but he was starting to believe he could tame it. Sure, they'd had tremendous hassles securing permissions and so on, but that was to be expected with this material. But that was all. No unexpected roadblocks. No signs of anyone tampering with anything. No word from Washington, D.C. Stone started to breathe easier.

Then, out of the blue, *Washington Post* national security correspondent George Lardner showed up on the set. "When Lardner showed up at our offices and walked down the fucking hall uninvited, I knew we had a problem," Stone says. "He's an old CIA investigative reporter and has many contacts in the agency. He was snooping around, and we escorted him off the set. And he wrote the worst possible story he could write."

Soon after, on May 19, 1991, *The Washington Post* published an article by Lardner with the headline "On the Set: Dallas in Wonderland," and the subtitle, "How Oliver Stone's Version of the Kennedy Assassination Exploits the Edge of Paranoia." Somehow, Lardner, who had crossed swords with Garrison while covering the original trial, had gotten hold of a first draft of Stone's script for *JFK* and launched an attack on what he called "the absurdities and palpable untruths in Garrison's book and Stone's rendition of it." In the article, Lardner pointed out that Garrison lost his case linking Shaw to a conspiracy, and therefore might be presumed to have defamed an innocent man. He also claimed that Garrison embellished a weak case by picking on the man's homosexual relations to prove guilt by possible association.

Stone says these charges are absurd. He documents Shaw's connection with the CIA, which Shaw denied on the stand, and claims there are photographs and eyewitness reports which link Shaw to the assassination. "He was in the CIA, according to former CIA director Richard Helms, and he was spotted by numerous witnesses with Lee Oswald and David Ferrie [the man Garrison thought was the getaway pilot for the Dallas assassins], whom he denied knowing. So don't give me this jive about Shaw being an innocent man. He was a perjurer at the very least. The judge from the trial, before he died, told me he felt in his heart that Clay Shaw perjured himself on every answer."

Stone also points out that a poll of the Clay Shaw jury in 1969 found that the majority believed there had been a conspiracy but just didn't think Garrison had enough evidence for a conviction. He notes that Garrison only went to trial after a three-judge panel and a grand jury said he had sufficient evidence. He believes Garrison was thwarted at every turn in his investigation by the American legal and political establishment. "His subpoenas against [CIA director] Allen Dulles, Charles Cabel [Dulles's deputy], and Richard Helms [who succeeded Dulles] were all quashed; nor would four governors in four different states honor his extradition requests for different witnesses. His files were copied and passed on to the defense by several traitors on his staff and his office was tapped. He was also offered a federal judgeship as a bribe and his witnesses were bribed, cajoled, threatened, and I believe killed."

When Stone responded to Lardner's 5,000-word attack in the *Post* by hiring a public relations firm that specialized in political issues, he was soundly criticized in *Time* magazine for doing so. *Time* then ran its own criticism of the film-in-process on June 10, and charged that Stone was trying to suppress the making of *Libra*, a fictionalized account of the assassination based on Don DeLillo's 1988 book. Once again, Stone responded with a letter, which *Time* printed July 1.

"The *Libra* script was written way before our script," he says now. "I think it was on the market about ten months before. I gather it was passed on at several financing entities. I had nothing to do with it and I never even read the script until much later. By the time I heard about it, it was supposed to be made for HBO and I was just starting *JFK*. If we tried to stop them from doing anything, it would have only made them want to do it more. It's a competitive town. If a star of any kind calls up and says, 'Hey, I'm doing something similar,' then the person he calls up will want to rush ahead. That's the way it's done here. I've had a lot of projects that didn't get done because other people got them done first. I wanted to do a film on Leonard Pelletier, Native American rights activist, but then *Thunderheart* was made. It's fiction based on fact, but it's as close as you can get to Leonard's story. Another project I wanted to do was knocked out of the box because of *Mississippi Burning*. That's why I'm paranoid about people knowing what I'm interested in doing."

Unlike some rumors, Stone thinks he understands how the *Libra* one got started: "I had a meeting with Phil Joanou, who was going to direct *Libra*, on a completely different project. I wanted him to direct *Contra*. Phil was a young director, and he wanted to do it but he wasn't committed. He came to my office and we talked about it. I asked him if he believed *Libra*—that Oswald really pulled the trigger alone? And he said something like, 'Yeah, kinda, but I'm not wild about this script.' All I said was that I didn't believe Oswald did the firing and explained some of the theories I believed. He later passed on the script, apparently because he had a problem with it. *The New York Times* checked into it and came up with nothing. Joanou confirmed this story to them. The only dissension came from the producer of *Libra*, who had very good press contacts. No filmmaker can stop another film from being made. Look how many times two or three films have come out on the same subject. *Ruby* is another one, where we were supposed to be the bad guys. The *Ruby* people were right behind us photographing our sets and then saying that we squashed them. That was outrageous. When artists bitch about each other to the press it seems despicable to me. There is a brotherhood among us. We struggle too hard for our fellow workers to take jealous potshots. I mean, it's tough enough as it is."

From this time on, Stone would be continually hounded during the filming. He knew the attacks would come, but he had planned on being able to finish and edit the film first. "The Lardner thing was malignant because he was functioning off a first draft and obviously trying to ridicule us from the start," Stone says. "That story was picked up in various forms by *Time* and editorials around the country from the *Chicago Tribune* to *The Washington Post*. I was furious. I called Ben Bradlee [editor of *The Washington Post*] and said I wanted to write a rebuttal. He said, 'Well, let's see what you got.' He was kind of like Mr. Cool, Mr. Condescending. So I sent him a long letter and he wouldn't publish it. He just tried to drop out of the situation. I hounded him. I stayed on top of him. I mean, it was a drag to be trying to make the movie and have to be calling these people to print letters all the time. I kept calling this woman editor at the *Post* and she wouldn't return my calls. Bradlee really plummeted in my mind. I used to respect him for Watergate, but the way he handled this—he didn't care what my side was at all. I think he's an establishment fraud. Anyway, after many phone calls and many revisions, they finally published my letter, but they took out about a third of it. And unbeknownst to me they had Lardner respond to it at the same time. And I had no chance to respond to Lardner. That kind of an attitude was typical of the entire process for me. It was exhausting."

Stone's June 2 reply to Lardner's initial attack ran with the headline "STONE'S JFK: A HIGHER TRUTH" and next to it the Lardner response, headlined "OR JUST A SLOPPY MESS?" It is one thing to attack a film upon release, and quite another to attack it during its creation. No artist should have an early draft of his or her work judged as if it were a completed effort. The fact that a writer/director could have his first draft of a script stolen, judged harshly, and written about in national newspapers is appalling. "To grab his script and leak it borders on being a kind of criminal act," Kevin Costner says. "It's so out of bounds. And it's mean. It was hard for Oliver to work when he was under attack and being turned into a cartoon."

For Stone, a man who almost superstitiously guards his work until its release, the theft of the script was particularly disheartening. "He had the first draft, and I went through probably six or seven drafts," says Stone. "Somebody stole it from Warner Brothers or William Morris, one of those two places."

Even worse than the artistic frustration involved, the theft of the script showed Stone just how vulnerable he was to anyone who really wanted to get at him. "I was paranoid from that moment on. I said, where the fuck is our security? Strange people would come up to the hall and suddenly a lot of strange stuff was going on. I wanted our computers sealed. I wanted security guards. We spent a lot of dough to maintain security for our building in Dealey Plaza. We didn't know where an attack might come from or what might be targeted as an obstruction. Now that the real guts of what the film was about was out, who knew what to expect? Especially if the CIA or the Mafia wanted it stopped."

"This changes everything gentlemen. . . . We either pull out now or we keep going. . . . If we keep going it's going to get hotter than a whorehouse on dollar day."
Jim Garrison in JFK

Nonetheless, the production marched on. It was time to speculate on some other events that happened that fatal November 22. Several of these scenes involved the comings and goings of Lee Harvey Oswald. One sequence dealt with Oswald's activities at the Book Depository that day. Clayton Townsend recalls an incident here that illustrates Stone's passion for technical advisers. "There was a scene in the School Book Depository where Oswald moves some boxes around in the warehouse, and Oliver wanted a warehouse adviser to show how it was done," Townsend says. "Well, I forgot about it until the night before when he reminded me and I said, 'I'll tell you what. I come from Cleveland and I did some work in a warehouse. I'll be your adviser.' We had a little warehouse up there for the set and he made me do it. He insisted I come to the rehearsal and show them how to move the boxes."

Of course, most of Stone's advisers give him valuable information. According to Townsend, not all of it directly affects the look of the film. "Sometimes it just helps the actor. Oliver is pretty good about weeding out bullshit and he gets wonderful snippets of reality in his films that are pretty much absent in most other pictures."

Dale Dye, of course, is in a league of his own as far as Stone's technical advisers are concerned. With all the data on bullet trajectories and weapons capabilities in *JFK*, Stone felt Dye was much needed in Dallas. "I helped him with blackouts, covert operations, the Cuban stuff, the assassination," Dye says. "He had me train some of the actors who would use the weapons and suggest some of the ways covert operations could have been done."

In *JFK*, Dye plays General "Y"—the head of black ops and the man who "X" fingers as having masterminded the assassination.

Much of the film's controversy centered on Stone portraying Oswald as a patsy rather than an assassin. Since he wanted to explore several conspiracy theories, Stone even included second and third Oswalds, loose lookalikes supposedly hired by the CIA to place Oswald at places he may have never been. The role of Oswald was a challenging one because, even though he has little dialogue, he must be played convincingly in a variety of circumstances. Gary Oldman lost a lot of weight right before shooting in order to have the haunted look that Oswald had in his last days alive. "He was a very dark, lonely figure," says Oldman. "He was innocent. . . . He was the patsy, the fall guy. Exactly what he said he was."

Oldman spent time with Oswald's wife, Marina, as well as with his two daughters, and he visited the places Oswald lived. "And where he died, I died," Oldman says. "Right on the spot. The corridor was the real corridor [in the jail]. The elevator was the real elevator. The landlady's house was the real landlady's house [where Oswald stayed]. We even found his furniture, his bed and his wardrobe."

Being cast as the ultimate villain of the last thirty years had its drawbacks. "Gary got into the part, totally immersed," Stone says. "Unfortunately, he had to carry that around with him for a long time because it was such a long production and he had to come back to New Orleans several times. I know it wasn't easy carrying Oswald around for months like that. He was like a prowler on the edge of the set, in his T-shirt with that bruise over his eye. Always unwanted, unloved. He got into a few fights. I think he's had a tough life. He has an inbuilt desire to be loved and watched, and that comes out in his acting like some sort of epiphany."

During filming Oldman stayed in his hotel room at night—watching TV, drinking and thinking. He needed to be alone to stay in Oswald's character. Oldman works from internalizing to the point where he no longer has to think about the role because he has become the character. Like Stone, Oldman is driven. The two understand each other. "Oliver was possessed," Oldman says of the *JFK* set. "He brought a sense of urgency and aggression to it. I likened it to being in the Army. When we were rehearsing it was like, 'Let's synchronize our watches.'"

Playing the role of the man who killed Oswald right before the eyes of millions of startled viewers was Bryan Doyle-Murray, a veteran of countless films. Murray describes how it was to play Jack Ruby under the direction of Oliver Stone: "I love the way he works. He works fast. One of the banes of being an actor is waiting, waiting. It's intrinsic in the process, so it's great when somebody works fast. I remember sitting there watching his crew and they were running! Lighting people were running. People carrying camera cases moving at a full trot. I've never seen that on a film before. Then, all of a sudden, Oliver pops up and goes, 'C'mon, hurry up, step on it!' And they started running faster! I don't know how he pulls it out of them, but he does. Involvement, I guess. He's a leader.'"

Murray said that as he was preparing for the role, he kept remembering how the entire roomful of police jumped on Jack Ruby the moment after he pulled the trigger. "When I got on the set, I saw some of the people who were going to be in the scene," he says. "Some of the stunt guys and extras were thugs. I thought to myself, 'These guys are gonna hurt me. They're going to want to look good for Oliver and they're going to pounce on me with everything they've got.' So I started putting the word out, 'If anybody hurts me, I got a knife in my pocket and I'm going to get you.'

"So, we start the scene, and I shoot him and then I get jumped by all these guys. But they weren't too bad. Of course, they're all on top of me. Well, we did a couple of takes and then Oliver came over, shaking his head. And he goes up to the stunt guys and says, 'I don't know, I don't believe you guys. It don't look real to me.' And I thought, 'Great, now I'm in for it. I'm gonna get hurt.' I knew it was coming and it came. *Wham!* I got hurt. But you know, that's part of it. Oliver lets you know that the stakes are high. You might even get hurt. That's how big a deal it is for him, and he wants you to match his energy and commitment. Which I like. That's part of what makes him great."

Much of *JFK* is set in Garrison's hometown, New Orleans. Indeed, the mysterious New Orleans/Dallas connections are at the heart of many conspiracy theories. Elizabeth Stone came to New Orleans with Sean, who played Jim Garrison's son. Now that Sean was in school, they were unable to come to the set for as long as in the past. "I used to be there and Oliver could lean on me on a daily basis. Of course there's the nightly phonecalls when he's away, but I wanted to physically be there. When I'm there I don't knit or read a book or sit in the hotel, and drop in for lunch or whatever. I like to watch Oliver work and to feel like I'm there for him."

One of the finest performances in the film is given by Tommy Lee Jones as New Orleans businessman Clay Shaw, the only man ever brought to trial for conspiracy to assassinate President John F. Kennedy. Jones was nominated for Best Supporting Actor for his role as Shaw, the gay ex-CIA operative whom Garrison believed plotted Kennedy's murder for higher-ups. What was the most difficult thing about the role? "Dealing with the wig, actually," Jones recalls. "It was hard to get it to fit. We had two wigs—one fit up perfectly and one did not. But it takes a long time to put one of those wigs on and then you have to look good to the camera. We finally got it down to about a forty-five-minute effort, but it took two or three people to do it."

Jones has nothing but praise for Stone's crew. "There is definitely a feeling of camaraderie around the set," he says. "That's the camaraderie of people working hard together. It's especially interesting for me because these are among the best in the world at what they do. I love the motion picture camera. And I love the cinema, the process and the people I work with. I develop relationships with camera crews, lighting people, makeup personnel, costumes. Oliver's company is world class."

Though virtually all of the actors involved with *JFK* said they received much more positive reactions than negative, most also came under the gun a few times as well. Even Jones, though nominated for the Oscar, got a little negative feedback. "There were phonecalls from certain journalists, representing certain special interest groups, wanting to know if our intentions were homophobic, to which I said, 'No. You know better than that.'"

Since so many of the conspirators in the film were homosexual acquaintances of Shaw, there was some antagonism among the gay community, but Stone argues that it was essential to show these elements to link Shaw with his alias in the community, Clay Bertrand. "The homosexual connection in *JFK* was a necessity," Stone maintains. "That was the way it happened and I needed to show the chain of evidence. I got a lot of shit in the press and from the homosexual community for what they call 'gratuitous characterizations in *JFK*.' But it wasn't gratuitous. It was done because it is part of the crucial chain of evidence which establishes that Clay Shaw was really Clay Bertrand, who shows up several places in the story with evidence. And when Shaw was arrested, he signed 'Clay Bertrand' as his alias. That's what all these homosexuals knew him as. That's why we showed the party, because it's the only room where Perry Russo ran into him. The parties were S&M [sadomasochism]. There were several witnesses to this."

Often Stone seems genuinely not to understand why he is attacked, and this is one of those areas. "They said I made all the bad guys gay . . . that's horseshit. That was what I was attacked for when I wanted to do a film about Harvey Milk. Some of that stuff was vicious. One insane, well-known critic wrote as if the only reason I made *JFK* was to degrade homosexuals."

All of the scenes involving Clay Shaw were shot in New Orleans. According to Stone, when he was there the city was still teeming with rumors about Shaw, Jim Garrison, and other players in the real-life drama he was attempting to capture on film. "I heard some absolutely amazing stories. Stories about Clay Shaw, even about Garrison. Some people swore Jim had homosexual tendencies, but I never believed that. In fact, I was stunned when I first heard that idea. But even if such rumors were true, it wouldn't change the nature of the story."

Rumors are still rampant about former New Orleans crime boss Carlos Marcello as well. Some believe it was Marcello who had John Kennedy killed. Others think he had Robert Kennedy killed. Some think he was responsible for both murders. One of the most frequent criticisms against Garrison was that he shied away from Marcello because the man controlled so much of New Orleans; but Stone doesn't buy that either. "Jim explained to me once that New Orleans is divided into two parishes, Jefferson and New Orleans. Jim was over one parish and Marcello operated out of the other. I don't know, it's possible he backed off from Marcello, but not concerning the assassination. He only met the man once in a restaurant in passing. Also, I think that the Mob is overrated in the American media. It's part of the Godfather stuff. The Mob could never have pulled this off alone. In concert with a superior military agency, yes."

Stone pushed harder on this film than he ever had before. The shoot was tremendously complicated, the subject matter dark and disturbing, and the attacks in the press only made it worse. On top of all this he had cast so many big names in the film that he couldn't throw a pebble without hitting a Hollywood ego. When confronted with such overwhelming odds, Stone always resorts to the grunt mentality—he puts his head down and pushes on. Eventually, this attitude works its way through the entire cast and crew. "Oliver works really hard and it's something that is contagious," Kevin Costner says. "When you see that your leader is working really hard, you just tend to try harder yourself. It's inspiring."

Kristina Hare points out that "Oliver has totally subjective perspective, and that's what makes him so forceful and so passionate. Even if he's alone on something, he's very convincing. He gets away with driving everybody so hard because he drives himself so hard. No one works harder than Oliver and no one gets more done; he's a machine."

JFK was so demanding that Stone did little partying compared to other shoots. "He's a warrior when he shoots a movie," Richard Rutowski says. "The only relief he got was when we'd put music on and drive out into the country and never say anything or just laugh about shit. Or go hang with some drunks in a bar somewhere. That's about it. Messing around with women just became less important. Women used to be an obstacle to Oliver's growth. They were floating around in his subconscious, one of those mysteries he could never understand, but he's getting past that."

Rutowski, who is seen briefly in the film as the gunman who shot Kennedy behind the fence on the Grassy Knoll, says Stone works at changing his character when it becomes an obstacle to his goals. "There was a point when cocaine became an obstacle rather than an ally, and he got out of that. I think his drive for consuming women has become different. He has a very turbulent relationship with Elizabeth. She's a strong person and there's been times when he felt like saying, fuck you, I'm getting out of here, but he didn't because there's some deeper connection there that he could not walk away from. So it's like a constant quest for balance and it's not an easy thing."

Stone is both a workaholic and a carouser. He has to focus so intensely for such long periods of time that in order to relax he needs to cut totally loose, almost drive his obsessions away. Exorcise the demons by filling their space with good conversation, loud laughter, and alcohol. As Kevin Costner puts it, "I think, God love him, he'd like it to be easier, but it's just not easy for Oliver to wind down. His mind is active . . . he can't turn the light off. And he doesn't want to be alone then. He wants someone to stay with him a while."

Costner and Stone got along well, which surprised many people who marked them at opposite political poles. "He'd tease me about being conservative," Costner says, "and I'd say he was full of shit. I'd tell him, 'You're more fucking conservative than I'll ever be—that's why you hired me.' But that was just a teasing game. He'll tease you and you have to have the ability to tease back and carve out ground for yourself. I remember one day he'd said something smart to me and I just basically said, 'Why don't you go back by the monitor, 'cause nobody wants to listen to you anyway.' Of course, the whole crew shakes and quakes 'cause I said that to him, but he looked at me and he gave me that really great smile that he has and you know it's all right."

Costner had heard of Stone manipulating, even goading his actors to get a better performance out of them, but says Stone didn't work that way with him. "I've heard that and I don't disbelieve it, but that didn't happen with me. We found a relationship very early on. As a director, he's not that threatened, he's pretty comfortable. He leaves a big window of opportunity for the actor, which is good. My theory behind working for a director is, if it's wrong, I'll say something, but if it's a matter of choice and it's just not my choice, I won't say anything. People are constantly asking me how do I feel about acting since I've directed. Frankly, I don't have a problem with it. I had problems with bad directors long before I became a director. Oliver is similar to the great directors I've worked with because he is clear. He was very careful and considerate with me. No matter what the circumstance was, if I asked him something, his head swiveled around and his eyes got really clear. And when he said, 'What?' it was with a question mark behind it, not like a 'What now?' He was totally for the actor, and that's a situation that many of us don't often find ourselves in. He creates a real environment for you to do the best you can do."

Costner, who obscured his handsomeness in the film behind nerdy glasses and Brylcreemed hair, says he had a real problem with only one scene: "I told him ahead of time that he could not change things on me, or that, if they did have to change something, I needed to know three or four days before. Maybe my pattern is slower than other people. I don't know, but it's the way I like to work. We had one scene, a very little scene that they threw at me, and it wasn't because of rain or because of some technical shit. It was just because somebody did it. He saw me almost implode and I think he was startled because we'd done an eleven-page straight-through scene in a half a day, when he'd scheduled it for two days. This was just like a little itty-bitty scene, but the more I did it, the worse I got, so eventually it becomes embarrassing for me because I pride myself on what I do. So he came over and we sat down in the back and he said, 'God, you're like a self-fulfilling prophecy.' He was doing everything to help me relax, and I was trying to do two things. One, I was trying to relax, and second, I was trying to say, 'You motherfucker, I told you this would happen.' Actually, it was probably somebody else's obligation to remind him, what with the amount of things he's got to think about. I think he was shocked. He looked at me like he couldn't believe it. That wasn't the hardest scene, but it was the hardest one for me."

The eleven-page scene Costner was referring to was his closing trial summary at the end of the film. Even though the scene is intercut several times to illustrate the events Garrison is describing, there are still a good five pages of lines, a huge monologue. "It was great," Costner says. "I think we got that thing done before lunch. It was one of those things that just bubbled up inside as I spoke it. I was surprised at how emotional it was. I'd read it a hundred times, and thought about cutting out the lines 'Ask not what your country can do for you' and to cut out the line 'your dying king,' and yet I refused to do that because it's just the way I was trained. I do the lines. I change things sometimes, but that's such a bold stroke that I felt like I had to give it a chance in my head. I thought, 'What the fuck? Am I gonna say this line or not?' So I'm doing this whole speech and I get to this point and it just has so much gravity and so much weight. Oliver was gonna pull that moment out, quite honestly, he was gonna pull out the Tennyson quote—'Authority forgets a dying king.' I said, 'Don't do it just yet. Let me . . . you know, try it.' Well, when I was doing it, all of a sudden Garrison, the character I was playing, almost couldn't continue. And it worked. But it came naturally."

With that scene, the film wrapped on the last day of July 1991. Unlike *The Doors*, this time there were no nasty surprises at the wrap party, unless you count one of the producers hiring a stripper as extra entertainment, a move not particularly appreciated by Sissy Spacek, who had brought her kids along. Somehow, though shooting had finished, *JFK* did not feel wrapped. First, there was still a massive editing job, which many believed would be impossible to complete before the release date. But, more significantly, everyone sensed that the big battle was yet to come. The film had already received an enormous amount of bad press and no one had even seen it yet. What was going to happen in December?

> "You're a mouse fighting a gorilla. Kennedy's dead. You want to line up with a dead man?"
>
> Dean Andrews in **JFK**

Postproduction is always a very long and laborious job. An average film may take ten or twelve weeks to shoot and spend thirty weeks in postproduction. For *JFK*, the task was enormous: The film was due in the theaters by Christmas, only five months away. It was a three-hour movie, with two hundred speaking parts that required eight weeks to mix, and there were a record two thousand opticals. Virtually no one but Oliver Stone believed the job would be done in time.

As soon as shooting finished and while the work was being prepared, Stone took a few days off and headed up to his Santa Barbara house to join his family. Elizabeth had been suffering from colitis for some time and it had flared up throughout the *JFK* shoot. As a result, she had put on weight and was tired all the time. This dampened Stone's already dim hopes that their relationship might be revitalized.

The outlook improved, however, when the Stones' second child, Michael Jack Stone, was born on October 13, 1991. A blond, blue-eyed little boy, he was an instant delight to his parents. Stone had always thought that having a second child would help heal the family by defusing the disagreements he and Elizabeth were having over how to raise Sean. But shortly after Mikey's birth, he realized that things were now even more complicated. He and Elizabeth were growing further apart, and he didn't know what to do about it. Elizabeth was discovering more and more now that she needed to be her own person, but the family was still her number one priority. She tried to make things better at home for Oliver, but the only way she knew how to do this was by catering to him. This wasn't what he wanted. Stone wanted her to be more of a companion, but wasn't sure how to make this happen or even how to communicate it to her. Their relationship grew worse rather than better.

Chuck Pfeiffer visited the Stones around this time and he describes the change in the family when Oliver came home: "It had been a pretty cheery situation, but when Oliver came in, it was like the whole gestalt of his house changed gears. It was like, 'Oh Oliver, Oliver, what can we do to please you?' It was like the Black Prince arriving at the castle or something."

According to Pfeiffer, things got a little out of hand that night. "I had brought my girlfriend and one of Oliver's assistants [Richard Rutowski] started hitting on her. Of course, we were all drinking tequila, but it kept getting worse. Finally, I just blew my top, right there. I said [to Richard], 'Who do you think you're dealing with here? I'm not some little schmuck you can push around. I'm like the Gambino. Worse, I'm like Mickey Fuckin' Featherstone. I've been a fighter all my life. And you're fucking with me over some dopey girl?' Then, the next day, Elizabeth came down and asked me to leave. Like, I was the one who caused the whole thing. So I left. But I'm still friends with both of them. I found out later Oliver said he was surprised I acted that way, but that's bullshit. He knows me. He once told me I don't have a filter between my brain and my mouth. But that's what he's always liked about me. I used to kid about feeling like a court jester in the court of Louis Quatorze. I do some outrageous thing and he likes it. To this very day I think that's at the heart of our relationship."

Pfeiffer says Stone abhors physical violence, but that both he and Elizabeth are very confrontational in other ways. "Neither one of them is afraid to say anything to anybody. When they get into it with each other, the sparks really fly. They used to go at it and call each other every rotten name in the book. I used to be as horrified at their verbiage as they were at my physicality. But they were under a lot of stress."

Stone has an amazing ability to detach, to block out what he can do nothing about and focus on the issue at hand. As he always does when faced with the abstract, somewhat insoluble problems of his personal life, he threw himself into the work at hand. And this time there was a mountain of it. Bill Brown, Stone's postproduction supervisor, discusses how Stone works in this segment of the production process. "Postproduction is a very long, arduous, repetitive task," Brown says. "It's very hard to stay focused and very hard to stay on top of your game creatively. Especially for the director, because for him, it's a hurry up and wait kind of thing. With most directors, you literally have to kind of drag them through the process. With Oliver, he sets a pace and it's up to everyone else to keep up. And it starts from the very beginning of prep. Because so many of his films are biographical in nature, the research is just incredible and his knowledge of the subject is amazing. In a film like *JFK*, keeping all that stuff in your head is a very complicated narrative. On top of that, just in terms of nuts and bolts postproduction, his films are easily the most complicated being made in Hollywood today. *The Doors* and *JFK* are totally different films, but each of them in their own way—music with respect to *The Doors* and information and opticals with *JFK*—made them very, very complicated. And with *JFK* we had an extremely difficult schedule. It was so difficult that I really think the studio didn't even believe we could make it."

What made *JFK* so difficult? First of all, the number of optical inserts that had to be done in the editing room. An optical is any visual image that has to be inserted into the film apart from the filming process. "The amount of opticals in a normal film is about twenty or thirty," Brown explains. "A show like *Return of the Jedi* would maybe have four or five hundred opticals. For *JFK*, we had two thousand opticals. Of course, the shots in something like *Return of the Jedi* would generally be much more complicated than the opticals used in *JFK*, but the sheer volume of the *JFK* material made it very difficult. We smashed all the records at the optical house. And the number of sources and the man-hours that went into researching and finding some of this footage . . . A line in the script would say, 'A C-130 transport plane flies over the South Pole,' and we would have to find that shot. Now there's a warehouse sitting out in Van Nuys with Air Force footage in it and there's probably hundreds of thousands of feet of C-130s, but the Air Force has to read the script for you to get it. Obviously, we're not going to turn the script of *JFK* over to the U.S. government armed forces, so we have to scrounge it from other places. Or he would ask for a shot of Robert Bissell, who was a CIA agent. Well, these guys are spooks; they're not supposed to have their picture taken. There was film coming from every conceivable source and we were shooting every type of film gauge and it all had to end up looking smooth, like one whole piece of work when it was finished. It took a superhuman effort by a lot of people to make that happen. I really felt we might not make it. People always say that in editing, but I really had doubts this time. It felt like climbing Mount Everest to get that film done right in the time that we had."

In fact, *JFK* won Oscars for its editors, Joe Hutshing and Pietro Scalia, and is recognized within the film industry as a great editing achievement.

Throughout this time, Stone had to maintain a solid position with Warner Brothers. His attitude was a firm, no-doubt-in-his-mind assurance that he would make the deadline. Stone has learned to banish rather than nourish his doubts. He spends careful time evaluating a decision, weighing all the factors and making sure he has all the data he can possibly have to make the best choice. Once he decides, however, he never looks back. Film studios, though traditionally cautious, have learned to take him at his word. So it was that Warner Brothers embarked on their $15 million promotional campaign for *JFK* in the fall of 1991. By mid-October a trailer was running in theaters across the country, and posters featuring a closeup of Kevin Costner were plastered on buses, bus stops, abandoned buildings, subway stations, construction sites, and anywhere else they could be placed without triggering a complaint.

For Stone's editing crew, the posters were inspiring but still a bit foreboding. They were by no means certain that they would be able to deliver the film by the December 20 release date. Though he'd considered a February 1992 opening as a fallback, Stone knew it was in everyone's interest that the picture come out before the end of the year. Necessary in any case for Oscar considerations, the Christmas season has also proved to be the best time to release a heavy drama with regard to box office. But Stone had other motives in pushing for the December release. "At three hours and eight minutes I was beyond the length in my contract, so I was vulnerable," he says. "The contract limited me to two hours and fifty minutes, which was a really good negotiation on Bob Marshall's part. I knew that Warners could pressure me to cut the film down. When their production chief saw the movie, he said it was too complicated and that we should have some test screenings. We had a big fight. I said no to the previews. I felt that by having a short fuse, Warners would be less likely to ask for simplifications. Christmas is a great time to release a film and that makes them want the movie to be ready, so there's no time to futz around with screenings and changes. But if we'd come out in March or April there could've been a protracted discussion with multiple screenings, and to me that's trouble because I don't believe in those kinds of results."

It was now two months before the release date and the press was already gearing up. *Esquire* ran a lengthy, searing criticism of the movie, and Stone took time out again to respond with a long letter detailing the inaccuracies in the account. Back in the editing bays at Skywalker Sound Studios, Stone's work habits were an inspiration to his postproduction crew. "A lot of other directors hire some big-name editor and that's the only person that's cutting or doing anything really creative in the cutting room," Brown says. "Oliver has a tendency to hire two or three people who may be different in their outlook on things, so he can balance their ideas and use them as sounding boards. In *JFK* we had four people cutting, but Oliver worked as a creative force that anchored everyone. He'd literally be bouncing back and forth between different rooms. One editor might reach a certain stage and Oliver might take that scene and give it to another editor who had a slightly different view. It gave him an opportunity to see different approaches and define some of his ideas."

Meanwhile, Warner Brothers was proceeding with their marketing plan. On November 24, a two-page ad ran in both the *L.A. Times* and *The New York Times*. The following day, television spots ran to the top fifty markets. A 30-second spot ran on that week's "Monday Night Football," and a 90-second version which heralded "the movie event of the year" appeared as the first spot on the CBS *M*A*S*H** special, several late night talk shows, and MTV. For the nightly news broadcasts, the studio used an advertising technique known as "roadblocking." Usually only employed the night before a major film is to open, it consists of buying the same time slot on all the networks and their local affiliates in order to reach the largest possible audience. The anticipation for *JFK* was building.

Back in the postproduction studios, the pressure was on. Doing a painstaking task under a great deal of pressure brings out the worst in most people, but Bill Brown says that Stone, despite his intensity, is a reasonable boss. "We had a potentially disastrous situation close to the deadline. I had a meeting with Warner Brothers, and we realized that because the picture was really two movies in length, it would take twice as long to make the release prints. That meant that, even if we made our deadline, there would not be enough time to make all the release prints we needed to make. We figured out that the only way we could do it was if I delivered half of the movie earlier. They would go ahead and make the one thousand two hundred prints of half the reels. Then, when we finished the second half, they would have time to make the rest of the prints and ship them out.

"Now, there were all kinds of different things needed for the different reels, so the half we delivered first turned out to be a chunk right in the middle of the movie. We mixed that first, we finaled it, answerprinted it, and then made one thousand two hundred prints of that part of the picture. Now, I rarely tell Oliver we absolutely can't do something and I think because I do it rarely he believes me when I do say it. I explained it to him and he understood it."

But Stone, though understanding the process and aware of the value of meeting the release date, was still driven by his artistic concerns. Brown continues: "When we finished the two chunks at either end, he said he wanted to play the whole mix back. And I said, 'Well, you know, we've release-printed those reels in the middle, so we don't really need to listen to those' because there are one thousand two hundred prints sitting over at Technicolor waiting for the complement and it's physically impossible to change those and make our dates. He goes, 'No, no, no, I want to see the whole thing.' So we start screening the film, and then we made the changeover to the section that had been printed and I was just freaking out that the lights would come up and he would be adamant about making changes in *those* reels. Though there were a couple of minor things, they were very esoteric and he decided they were okay. If it had been something significant it's not inconceivable that he would've decided to change them, no matter what was affected."

Not only was *JFK* finished on time, but it came in on budget. "I think *JFK* was the only Warner Brothers picture on time and on budget that year," Brown says. "And we had the hardest schedule in terms of the whole thing by a mile of any of those pictures. I'd be willing to bet any other production group that tried to do *JFK* in the same scope would have spent another fifteen to twenty million dollars. If you compare Oliver's budgets with the norm in Hollywood, they're relatively big, but he gets a lot more bang for the buck."

As the prints were being made and shipped, Stone began getting his customary pre-release anxiety. This time there was no new project to immerse himself in—at least none with any impending deadline— because he had cleared the decks in anticipation of a deluge of hard-hitting criticism. He knew this was a film he would have to defend, and he was prepared to go the distance. But now, as he waited for the starting gun, the riskiness of *JFK* became even more apparent to him.

First of all, it was long. At three hours, it would have one or two fewer showings a day in the theaters, compared to most other films. That meant it would be harder pressed to rank well in the Top 10 list of weekly grosses which so many theater owners used as a guideline to schedule films. For every dollar that a typical two-hour film earned, *JFK* would have to earn a dollar and a half. Also, it was talky. In an era where high action was the credo of big box office, *JFK* had an enormous amount of dialogue. Not only was this often a turn-off to American audiences, but it would make it far more difficult for the film to penetrate the world market. Action translates far easier than words.

Then there was the subject matter. The assassination of the thirty-fifth President of the United States was one of the blackest moments in American history, and particularly downbeat for a Christmas release when family films and comedies usually thrive. He had the cast: a huge list of heavies, headed up by the hottest actor in the business. Costner was without doubt a superstar who appealed to the young as well as the old. But this time around he was playing a not-so-sexy sixties D.A., complete with the slicked-back hair and hornrims. And the competition was fierce, with three other adult films out at the same time—Warren Beatty's *Bugsy*, Barbra Streisand's *The Prince of Tides*, and Lawrence Kasdan's *Grand Canyon*.

In the end, Stone banished the marketing problem from his mind. He'd already done everything from oversee the poster to choose the slogan: "To sin by silence makes cowards out of men." He was tired of thinking about it. "I made the best film I could and whatever comes, comes."

In December, the print publicity kicked in with Costner on the cover of *Vanity Fair* and both *Time* and *Newsweek* planning cover stories. Then it began. *The New York Times* ran a story entitled "Does JFK Conspire Against Reason?" and the *Washington Post* ran another entitled "Kennedy Assassination: How About The Truth?" written by ex-President Gerald Ford, who had been a member of the Warren Commission, and David Berlin, the counsel to the Commission. The *San Francisco Weekly*'s article was entitled "JFK: Tragedy Into Farce" and the *Wall Street Journal* ran one under the heading "A Better Conspiracy Theory Than Oliver Stone's."

During the week of the film's release, the cover of *Newsweek* proclaimed: "Why Oliver Stone's new movie can't be trusted," and the article inside completely filled eight pages—three of them blasting the film, two interviewing and analyzing Stone, and a final three arguing that, despite preceding pronouncements, the film just might be true after all. David Ansen became one of the few critics who didn't outright lambast the film when he called Stone "a troublemaker for our times" and advised readers that while they shouldn't accept the movie at face value, they shouldn't "trust anyone who claims this movie is hogwash," either. Though the planned *Time* cover had been dislodged by the disintegration of the Soviet Union, it did mention "JFK: The Movie and the Evidence," and the magazine devoted eight pages to the film, including an interview and pro and con positions. Perhaps the title of an *L.A. Times* article at the time hit upon the real issue: "Oliver Stone: The Most Dangerous Man in America."

There was no turning back now. Oliver Stone had made the transition from Hollywood Rebel to National Rebel. He had challenged the powers that be. He had cast his lot on what he felt was the right side of the truth, but it was also the dark side of power, and he would have to live or die with that choice.

"It has become a dangerous country sir when you can't trust anyone anymore, when you can't tell the truth. I say let justice be done, though the heavens fall."

Jim Garrison in JFK

Beyond the Dream

(1992-1994)

CHAPTER THIRTEEN

Hero or Villain?

"The Official Legend is created and the media takes it from there. . . . We have all become Hamlets in our country—children of a slain father-leader whose killers still possess the throne."

Jim Garrison in **JFK**

The box office started slow. The first week of release *JFK* tied for fifth place with *Beauty and the Beast*, behind the top-grossing *Hook*, *Father of the Bride*, *The Last Boy Scout*, and *Star Trek VI*. Critics of the film began proclaiming it a failure. Warner execs tried to point out that the grosses were deceiving, since *JFK*'s longer running time meant it had several fewer showings a day than these other films and the audience polls were very favorable. But in many publications, this was made to look like a lame excuse. As time wore on, the attacks on the film actually grew more vicious. On Christmas Day the *L.A. Times* ran an article entitled "Suppression of the Facts Grants Stone a Broad Brush." On the 26th, *New York Newsday* ran two articles—

"The Blurred Vision of JFK" and "The Many Theories of a Jolly Green Giant." The next day the *Dallas Morning News* ran one entitled "Oliver's Twist"; the day after that the *Chicago Sun Times* ran "Stone's Film Trashes Facts, Dishonors J.F.K."; and the *Washington Post* continued to lead the charge with "The Paranoid Style." When David Berlin, the Warren Commission attorney who investigated Kennedy's death, labeled Stone an "assassination whore" and compared the film to "the techniques of Adolf Hitler," it made front-page headlines in many newspapers across the country.

For Stone, the real danger was not just from the press and the powers of Hollywood. There were also threats on his life. "I can't even remember all the threats, there were so many of them," Stone admits. "The letters were insane. We had people warn us about many things, but I had no way of checking them out."

As Stone had expected, many of the criticisms of *JFK* centered on the character of Jim Garrison. Political journalists in particular zeroed in on this aspect, and editorial after editorial pointed out the flaws of the "real" Garrison. Few reporters seemed to accept Stone's distinction that the film was about the conspiracy to kill John F. Kennedy, not the life of Jim Garrison.

"If it would've been a biography of Jim Garrison I might not have done the movie," Kevin Costner says. "What we were going for was an emotional truth of what went down, and if we focused all that much on who Garrison was, then we would lose that theme. It's like my film *The Bodyguard* for all its commercial bullshit, never intended to explore a black and white relationship. It was just a get-a-popcorn-and-Coke-and-take-your-girl-to-the-movie kind of film. Well, *JFK* never intended to explore who Garrison was and didn't come close to explaining who that man was. We just used him as the vehicle to communicate what happened. People criticize Garrison, but I think he was like a man who sees a UFO. His life was changed because from that moment on, he could never say that he'd never seen a UFO. His whole life unraveled."

As the lead actor in an extremely controversial film, Costner was also criticized in the press, but often it seemed the media passed over him in favor of indicting Stone as the real culprit. Even so, there was no escaping a little overflow and Costner took his lumps: "I received a lot of strange mail over doing the part and that kind of thing. But I decided long ago that I would never conduct my career out of fear.

When I made my decision about it, I thought that it was right and that it worked. I knew there would be questions answered and new ones raised and debates that I could never really compete in because, when you start slinging thirty years worth of mud, any intellectual in the world can make you seem foolish. What I identified with in the script was the emotional truth."

One of the biggest areas of criticism was what the film's detractors called "rewriting history." This became something of an anti-Stone rallying cry, but the essence of the charge was that Stone, through the use of simulated documentary footage and a script that blended fact and fiction, was not communicating the historical truth.

Stone would later answer his critics by putting out a 593-page book, *JFK—The Book of the Film*, by Oliver Stone and Zachary Sklar (1992), which included the complete annotated screenplay, 97 commentaries by leading proponents and critics of the film, and 340 research notes. Virtually every line of the script is footnoted to indicate where the information came from, with cross-references. Unfortunately, the book received little attention in the press. "It was supposed to be released with the film," Stone says, "but there's just so much information they couldn't get it out in time, so we decided to include the comments of people who attacked or defended the film."

Both Stone and Costner contend that great care was taken to distinguish clearly in the dialogue between what had been proven through investigation by Garrison or others and what was theoretical conjecture based on the investigation. Costner was particularly rankled by this. "I'll tell you something that no one ever talked about," he says. "I saw Oliver take a lot of things out of the script which were kind of sensational. There are lots of other directors who are not as responsible who wouldn't have done that. Also, I busted him over certain things and when he couldn't corroborate it or whatever, he took it out of the script. He never fought me about that. And we were always really, really careful when my character would talk about conjecture or his theories to say, 'Let's suppose.' I was very adamant about that and very clear, and Oliver, to his credit, had already started that process. It wasn't something I goaded him into at all. It was just that when anything seemed improbable to me, we'd say, are we walking on broken glass here or what?"

Ironically, part of what triggered some of the "distortion of history" criticism was Stone's desire to give fair coverage not only to his own personal conspiracy theory but to several others as well. The question of who actually fired the shot that killed the President is answered by Joe Pesci as the deranged David Ferrie, who says, "You just don't get it, do you? Even the shooters don't know." We learn that there may have been riflemen in as many as three locations, but we never learn who was where and who missed and who fired the killing shot. Later, Garrison makes a reference to the President being executed in true firing-squad fashion. The issue is left open-ended and becomes almost Zenlike. Much of *JFK* is in the *Rashomon* style, after the Japanese film classic that juxtaposed different scenarios of the same event. There are several possible scenarios for who killed Officer Tippet (the policeman supposedly killed by Oswald right after the assassination) as well: it could have been Oswald, or another man; Oswald *and* another man; or two completely different men. The viewer decides for him- or herself. Even the all-important question of who was behind Kennedy's murder is left open. Stone suggests the CIA in collusion with the military black ops division, and hints at several possible allies to this coup d'état including both pro- and anti-Castro forces and the Mafia.

He never really says that *all* these people acted in conspiracy together, nor does he say that the media knowingly participated in a cover-up. The film implies President Johnson may have been involved in the cover-up of the crime, but doesn't detail how his influence may have been used. Jim Garrison was certainly denied key evidence in prosecuting Clay Shaw, but Stone never maintains that those who denied it were consciously participating in a cover-up of the crime. Indeed, one of his key points is that people in high places of power can get things done without having to justify their actions or even offering a reason for their requests. Rather than illuminating and endorsing a specific theory, *JFK* focuses more on countering the Warren Commission's Oswald-as-lone-gunman theory. "One of the subthemes of the movie is who owns reality," Stone says. "We used a lot of different film stocks and formats to question the nature of reality. To a large degree, *JFK* is not a political film; it's philosophical. It shows how the truth is fractured until we don't know what the reality is. The Warren Commission Report was accepted at the time of its release for its soothing Olympian conclusion that a lone nut committed this murder. I suppose our movie is a countermyth: that the man was killed by larger political forces, with more nefarious and sinister objectives."

The idea was for the viewer to follow along with Jim Garrison as he uncovers mystery after mystery. We watch him quiz witnesses and gather facts. We also hear him speculate. Sometimes there is a sepia-toned insert shot to dramatically illustrate these speculations and sometimes there is not. Sometimes these speculations come to pass in the film, and other times they are never proven. The question is whether or not such speculations are clearly differentiated from assembled facts. The dialogue seems to indicate that they are. When describing the contents of a missing note Lee Harvey Oswald wrote to an FBI agent in Dallas, Garrison says, "Just speculation, people, but what if the note was describing the assassination attempt on JFK?" Near the end of the film, in Garrison's trial summation, he says, "So what really happened that day? Let's just for a moment speculate, shall we?" He goes on to give his theory on the events of November 22, 1963. The summation is filled with terms that imply speculation, and near its end Garrison says, "There is a very simple way to determine if I am being paranoid here," and he then asks for the release of fifty-one secret CIA documents on Lee Harvey Oswald and Jack Ruby.

As far as passing conjecture off for truth, Stone feels that this is not a valid charge. "Sure, we are showing you our theories and saying that we believe them to be true," he says, "but we clearly differentiate between fact and theory in the film. Any person familiar with film technique knows that when we cut to something like Ruby picking up a bullet in the hospital in black and white, it's a hypothetical image. Or when Garrison's talking about the bullet being placed on a stretcher and we cut to a hand putting the bullet on the stretcher—people realize that is conjecture. And the uses of different film formats are viable techniques which film critics have always recognized. It's the same with the dialogue. The differences between Garrison's conjecture and what was established or proven in his mind is clear, and I stand behind those points."

Kevin Costner sees Stone as a dedicated truthseeker. "Oliver is trying so hard to be true, it's almost an obsession, almost to the point that he's his own experiment. And he's proved himself. As easy as people would like to dismiss him, they just can't because Oliver is just too good. He's too smart and he's too careful. He's got that enthusiasm which can get all of us, but still he's careful. That's why he's smarter than most of these people criticizing him. He's better prepared than they are and he's willing to listen actually much more than they think he is. In fact, the truth is, Oliver is willing to listen and they're not. He may not buy what they say, but he listens to it. Sure, he gets confused sometimes. We all do, but he's talented, and he just keeps trying to go forward and trying to be true. He's true blue."

Stone sees his mission as communicating what he believes is the spiritual truth of a story. He may even slightly distort the factual truth sometimes for the good of this goal. Because of these attitudes, he has never understood why people get offended when he tells what he believes is the truth. To him there's no such thing as an offensive truth. He doesn't factor in that people may get angry because the truth hurts their feelings. And yet this is a man whose feelings are rather easily hurt. When a critic attacks him harshly, he will often say to friends, "Why does this guy hate me so much?" Contrary to his image as a hard-boiled tough guy, Stone is easily hurt by almost any form of criticism. He may be tough, but it's not because he's numb to pain. It's because he refuses to quit *despite* the pain. Stone always leads with his chin artistically and quite often emotionally too. Just as he refuses to calm his passions because that borders too close to indifference, he knows that letting your emotions die in order to kill the pain kills an artist's soul as well. What Oliver Stone lacks in perception, he makes up for in vision.

Costner sees Stone as being very sensitive. "It's a weakness that he should choose to keep," Costner says, "because otherwise he would become a different person, not as vulnerable. I think Oliver wants a world where he knows there's somebody at his back. Like a team playing for the coach, he longs for that camaraderie of pulling together and believing and closing up ranks. But this is a world that kicks a lot at things for no reason. This is a world that does a complete analysis of a football game before it's even half over. This world wants to get at it really quick. It's hard for us to settle anything, and he wants things to be more decisive. So he feels like he needs his friends to close ranks around him, and sometimes, if you don't, I think you risk his wondering if you are with him or against him. That makes him hard to deal with. But he's worth the effort because he's the genuine article. There's nobody like him."

To this day, Stone is still sensitive to the way he came off in the press during *JFK*, saying, "They printed unverifiable material, maligned me, and didn't deal seriously with any of the issues I brought up. It was about criticizing Stone the same way they criticized Garrison instead of dealing with the points that were raised in the movie. Why didn't Oswald shoot when Kennedy was coming straight at him instead of waiting for a worse shot from the rear through a tree? What was Oswald's history? How come he knew these people in New Orleans? What about Ruby's history? Oswald's connections to Cuba? Ferrie's connections to Oswald? Oswald's military history, which seems to border on intelligence work? What about all the dead witnesses? These points were not even raised in the media."

"My guess is he was exactly what he said he was—a patsy."

Jim Garrison in **JFK**

Stone also feels he often had to go to great lengths to get his side of the story told in the press. "When Anthony Lewis [of *The New York Times*] would come out with a strong criticism about the film—and he was so one-sided in some of the statements he made—I would try to correct it and I couldn't get the letter published. I had to go to the mat several times with Warners backing me and say we're gonna take a full-page ad in *The New York Times* denouncing this unfair practice unless you publish this letter. It was that way with several publications. The moment I entered that arena I regretted it in a sense because it's an endless battle—you're attacked, and if you reply, they attack you again. They leave stuff out of your letter to make you look bad. The attacks became a major newspaper event. It was like Tommy Lee Jones said, everybody and their dog got to write an article about it and got paid for it."

One charge that really bothered Stone was that he intentionally made his film controversial because controversy sells. "Just because there's more attention in newspapers doesn't mean more people will go to see the film," he says. "I feel the core of *JFK*'s attendance is because it was exciting and people enjoyed it as a movie. The picture went like a train but the political argument, although interesting, didn't make more people go. If anything, it can be worse, because if it becomes an editorial issue, it turns into an ugly and dry academic thing and turns people off. Actually, I feel that the film may have been able to do a lot more business and all that negativity lost us attendance. I never sought controversy. I tried to make *JFK* as quietly as possible before [George] Lardner took his shot. It was such a demonic article that Warners and Frank Mankiewicz who we hired to help us deal with the attacks from political journalists felt that it had to be responded to. But we hardly sought it out."

Stone claims controversy has hurt a lot of movies, and cites *The Year of the Dragon* and *Mississippi Burning* as examples. "There was a lot of controversy about *Air America*, but it didn't help the film at all," he says. "They were saying the CIA was involved in drug running, which they were, and there were all these editorials debating it. If controversy helps a picture, why didn't it help that one? It's not true that the more press, the better it is for the movie. You want good publicity, positive interviews. If you've made a good film, it's sometimes better to not have any publicity since it can turn negative because some critics think they have to knock it if it gets too much attention."

Part of what angered the media about *JFK* was Stone's regular expounding upon how the press was irresponsible in its initial reporting of the Kennedy assassination. "Most papers just accepted what was told them by the officials," Stone responds. "They did very little investigative reporting. It was in their interest not to rock the boat, I suppose, and I imagine those reporters who tried found they couldn't get anywhere with their editors. There were a few editors who really worked at it, though, and, in general, the Texas reporters did a very good job of picking up stuff. But there seemed to be a blanket on the case, and we still don't know how or why. I'm not saying, like some people have maintained, that the entire American press was in on the cover-up of the assassination. I'm saying a lot of the reporting was shoddy and the vast majority of the press just picked it up, and because of that, whatever conscious cover-up or suppression there was had more influence."

This domino theory of reporting is only made more complicated by the media filter—the fact that only a small section of any story is ever reported, especially in the electronic media where there is less time for in-depth reporting. "Reporters should develop an understanding of all sides of an issue," Stone maintains. "In the same sense, a movie critic or any kind of critic should try to understand and state the author's intention before he or she tears the work apart. Like, 'This is the story, this is what the filmmaker is trying to achieve. But I don't think he achieves it at all. I think it's a piece of shit.' But at least the artist's intention is stated. Most critics tear apart a movie or a play because they don't like the subject matter. They don't even discuss the intention. They attack a film because it's violent or because it's graphic, but never tell you what it was trying to say. A critic, in my opinion, should not be judging the work by whether or not they like the subject. You have to accept one hundred percent the viability of any topic in the world. Live with the subject. Then do your review."

Stone has often been called paranoid for saying the media is against him, because this implies that its many diverse components are working together in some form of conspiracy. "It's not that all of them are gunning for me," Stone acknowledges, "it's that the few who are, influence so many others. People just jump on the bandwagon instead of checking things out for themselves. What scares me most about the media is that so many of them don't realize that by presenting and highlighting certain issues, opinions, and perspectives over others, they can manipulate and control people's beliefs in subtle ways."

Part of the area Stone is really touching on is being judged by his public image rather than by the work he creates. These days even the news is supposed to be entertaining—to say nothing of film reviews. In Stone's case, his public image can make for easy entertaining. With his gap-toothed grin, penchant for somewhat self-righteous seriousness, and passion on his sleeve, he's an easy target. After the lambasting he received in the press for *JFK*, stand-up comics were inserting Oliver Stone jokes into their routines. "Saturday Night Live" had a skit where Stone was looking for a conspiracy behind President Bush's throwing up during his official visit to Japan. Stone plays and replays a video of Bush vomiting and analyzes it over and over, the way Costner/Garrison does the Zapruder film in *JFK*. Paranoid Oliver Stone jokes were showing up everywhere. Ben Stiller even devoted an entire show to "Oliver Stone-land," an amusement park where Stiller, made up to look like a puffed-up, Boris Karloff version of Stone, assures everyone they'll "get to experience reality—my reality." Participants ride in a bathtub through "The Doors" section of the park where a mechanical Indian jumps out at them and repeats: "I'm an Indian, but I also represent death. I'm an Indian, but I also represent death."

Not that Stone doesn't have his defenders. Garry Trudeau, of "Doonesbury" fame, drew an elaborate cartoon for *The New York Times* entitled "Overkill," which depicted Stone cruising down the street, à la the Kennedy motorcade in Dallas, and under fire from a "troubled columnist," a *Washington Post* reporter "with known ties to organized journalism," a drifter who "squeezes off several cheap shots," "a professional character assassin" who launches "a high powered discharge," and even "George Will, a deranged pedant from Bethesda." Many political cartoonists also responded to the overkill in the media by depicting Stone as the victim. One of the best was by Steve Benson in the *Arizona Republic*, showing Stone as Lee Harvey Oswald in the classic execution scene with Jack Ruby, labeled "Media Critics."

A public image is the price of fame. Who can explain why the media chooses to portray one politician, sports figure, or entertainer as positive and another as negative? Since *JFK*, Stone has been portrayed primarily by negative stereotypes. They range from paranoid and tyrannical to arrogant and self-righteous. "They have chosen those images for me and those images keep reappearing," Stone says. "They could do that with anybody, Warren Beatty, Jodie Foster, Barry Diller, Mel Gibson, or anybody. They went negative on Julia Roberts for a while. If they chose to put negative images of Jodie out, they could do so, but they don't. *Everyone* has a positive and negative side. I believe these kinds of decisions are made at the editor level. I know of reporters who have written positive stories about me and then had their stories tampered with. One reporter resigned from the *Washingtonian* magazine after her positive review of *JFK* was spiked by her editor. I'm not saying that there is a coordinated effort for this. It could just come from sheer orneriness because I've been critical of the press, but it's there all the same."

Long a favorite target of film critics, with *JFK*, Stone became fair game for political journalists as well. One highly regarded reporter from *The New York Times* wrote a piece comparing him to revisionists who said the Holocaust never happened. "That was irresponsible journalism," Stone says. "That reporter didn't even know the facts of the case. If someone was at all serious about the Kennedy murder, they would read a little bit and study the case, not just slam me in with the people who dismissed the Holocaust. And this is a supposed cultural critique from one of the leading papers in our country. There's a whole number of reporters who are young and smart, but they haven't been in the field. And they haven't done their homework."

"They never tell the truth on TV . . . that's the trouble with this fuckin' country. . . . They never tell the truth."

Tony Montana in **SCARFACE**

Many of the media attacks were related to Stone's implying that former President Lyndon Johnson may have been a part of the conspiracy or at least the cover-up. Some of the most vicious shots at Stone in the press came from former Johnson administration members. "LBJ was as corrupt a man as I've seen in my lifetime," Stone comments. "Up there with Nixon if not worse. He led the country to war. Destroyed the ethic of the country, destroyed the economics of the country. And still there are people who defend him because he took a civil rights position that Kennedy started and rammed it through. That's like saying Mussolini made the trains run on time. Or Hitler had great architecture."

As the negative press mounted, Stone perceived that he was engaged in a battle for his future, his right to make the kinds of films he wanted, and he pulled out all the stops. He vowed to spend as much time and money as he needed to repudiate what he now considered an all-out assault on his character. He began appearing on television talk shows, especially news and politically oriented programs, and telling his side of the story. The Oliver Stone that people saw on these programs was not the raving lunatic he'd been painted to be. He was calm, spoke in a quiet and reasonable voice, and his comments were well thought out. He seemed unruffled by the pressure, but undeniably passionate in his convictions. He came off not as a Hollywood shyster looking to make a buck off the assassination of a president, but a decorated war hero desperately seeking to unravel the lie at the heart of the American dream.

As Stone took on the role of a passionate crusader trying to convince people he was telling the truth against an avalanche of ridicule from establishment America, he seemed more like the protagonist of his film than the director. Stone, like Garrison, was a man with a mission. And also like the New Orleans D.A., he was a little eccentric—too vehement sometimes, too sensitive others, and known for having a tendency to shoot off his mouth at the wrong moments. Americans have always been attracted to people who are willing to fight for their beliefs, especially if it's against long odds. "People don't see the risks that Oliver takes or the kind of intensity in which he works," Richard Rutowski says. "I mean *JFK* was such a fucking tour de force just to get it done, just to prep it, just to survive it because of all the threats and stuff. People see it for a few hours and they judge it, but they don't see the whole process."

Rutowski maintains that all of Stone's movies are about himself: "Oliver is in a sense a Shamanistic film director. In *JFK*, he was looking at his own soul. He was not only dealing with what happens when men stand by and do nothing, he was also examining his own failures, his own ignorance and his own silence in the face of what he knew should be questioned. Oliver deepens his views by dramatizing them not just for the world to see, but for himself to understand."

Chris Renna believes that Stone's tendency to take on the lead character of his film greatly fortified him for the battles he faced in completing and defending it. Renna, who appears in the autopsy scene in *JFK* and as a man with a spy camera taking pictures of the motorcade at Dealey Plaza, says that "like Jim Garrison, Oliver was unrelenting, dogmatic, and absolutely committed to the telling of that story. Not only that, but doing it in such a way that the common man could understand it."

Perhaps this is what America saw as well. The film, while starting slow, continued to grow in popularity. By the first week in January 1992, *JFK* had grossed over $50 million at the box office worldwide, and polls showed that people attending the film were immensely satisfied and considered it very entertaining.

The tide of public opinion began to turn. Around the country articles started appearing in Stone's defense. Many were halfhearted, more or less taking the view that even if *JFK* was off the wall, maybe Stone had a point about those secret files. Why couldn't the American public see the files? One writer in the *Miami Herald* stated that the media had reduced Stone "to a caricature of his wild genius" and that "the focus on the trivialities of personality conveniently prevents us from having to confront the tough question his film raises." Others commented on the abnormal amount of bad press Stone and his film had received. Roger Ebert wrote an article entitled "Pundits Go Astray" for the Universal Press Syndicate. In it he said, "Never in my years as a newspaperman have I seen one subject pummeled so mercilessly and joylessly as this movie," and later added that "Saddam Hussein did not receive half the vituperation the op-ed crowd has aimed at 'JFK,' and nothing Oliver North did was remotely as shocking to them."

Sensing this change in attitude, Stone pushed even harder. On January 15, he showed up to speak at the National Press Club with a box of buttons that read "Free the Files: JFK." In the later part of January, he appeared on countless television programs, not just national ones, but smaller local interview shows in many major cities. And he no longer confined himself to the "serious" political discussion programs like "Nightline" and "City Desk." Contrary to his image as a rich intellectual, Stone showed up on more down-to-earth popular programs like "Oprah Winfrey." He was convincing. When the heavyweights put on the pressure, Stone turned it back on them. While Dan Rather, who attacked the movie twice on the CBS Evening News, got ruffled when he interviewed Stone, Stone was cool and calm. On the "Oprah Winfrey" show, he was charming; on "Nightline," he was tough.

Even so, the "Nightline" and CBS News interviews were particularly frustrating. "On 'Nightline' they aired something like a six-minute clip and raised all kinds of charges, but then didn't allow me to answer any of them," Stone says. "Because of that kind of prejudice, I was wary about the CBS News interview. When we did it, I was very painstaking about my answers. I left the Q & A session after every question to consult with my research assistants and then I'd come back and lay out the answer. That seemed to upset Dan Rather a bit. In the end, the interview took two hours and must have included twenty questions, but when they aired it they cut all but one question, the most innocuous one. They simply would not allow me to get my point across."

By the end of January, longtime supporters of the Warren Commission were calling for the release of the secret files on the assassination. Because of Stone's incessant questioning of the suppression of those files, even his opponents were saying it was in the best interest for them to be released to the public—if only to silence the doubts that Stone and his film had raised. Even earlier, public opinion polls showed that most Americans did not believe the Warren Commission's finding that Lee Harvey Oswald acted alone. But now, after months of furor over the issue, they were willing to do something about it. More and more people began by sending letters to the editor or writing their congressperson.

Congress responded, first with rhetoric, later with action. On May 12, Robert Gates, director of the CIA, ordered the release of a 110-page secret file on Lee Harvey Oswald. It was a hollow victory to be sure, since much of the material consisted of FBI memos which had already been released through Freedom of Information requests, but at least it signified that the government had taken note of the American public's demands.

"The ghost of John F. Kennedy confronts us with the secret murder at the heart of the American dream."

Jim Garrison in **JFK**

Stone had his diehard critics, but he also had a growing number of supporters and quite a few downright disciples. With *JFK*, Stone clearly established himself as the rebel voice of Hollywood. For many, this made him a hero for the nineties. For others, such as Ben Bradlee, editor of the *Washington Post*, Stone was the ultimate example of hubris—"Who the hell does this young punk think he is anyway?" Bradlee said at a Washington function just after the film's release.

There is no question that Stone is often humiliated in the press, but he has also been accepted in the mind of the public as a provocateur. A lot of the people who admire Stone are plain old "average Americans" who have long sensed that something is wrong. Maybe Stone's real objective with *JFK* was more like what "X" advised Jim Garrison to do; to "stir the shitstorm" in the hope that others will come forward.

"Oliver believes in his country," Kevin Costner says. "He fights for its values. Unlike most of the country, he doesn't let things go by. He writes his letters and he makes his speeches. And don't ever forget he put his life on the line in Vietnam. Oliver believes he has the right to criticize this country and he's earned that right. He pays his taxes and he creates work for people, but even more importantly, he creates vision. He's the best kind of American. He's a dog. He'll fight over a bone but he'll also fight for your right to have it."

Costner believes that there are a lot of people in Hollywood who want to see Oliver Stone fail. "When you have success, it's almost a crime in America in a way," he says. "When you have big success, it's almost like there's no place to go but down. If you endure, then you become almost endearing. Of course, Oliver won't reach that stage for a long time because there's too many people that he's gotten mad at him. Oliver makes a noise when he walks. It's up to his friends to stick by him in these battles so he can keep making his movies, keep creating images and stories that we'll never forget."

Though the tide of public opinion had turned, Stone was kept on the defensive for some months into the new year as *JFK* continued to be a hot issue in the press. Another former Johnson aide, Joseph Califano, Jr., wrote a letter to Representative Louis Stokes (former chairman of the assassinations committee) which appeared in the *Wall Street Journal* under the title "A Concoction of Lies and Distortions." *New York* magazine carried yet another blast from former Warren Commission counsel David Berlin ("The Big Lies of JFK") in February; and in March, Berlin wrote an editorial for *The New York Times*—"Earl Warren's Assassins." Also in March came Alexander Cockburn's "In Defense of the Warren Commission" in *The Nation*. By now, though, the press was much more balanced, and for every attack, there was invariably a counterattack. The issues the film brought up were starting to take precedent in a lot of people's minds. "Why has the burden of awakening this country to the unexplained killing of President John F. Kennedy fallen on the shoulders of a Hollywood film director?" asked one letter to the editor in *The New York Times*. Ellen Goodman in the *Boston Globe* wrote: "Here was a filmmaker with enough guts and egotism to take up the central event of an entire generation—the assassination of President John F. Kennedy. . . . In an era when most people's politics could fit on a bumper sticker, this is a movie that cares."

In Hollywood, the reaction was mixed. Warner Brothers had strongly defended the film right from the start. In fact, their support and refusal to play it safe by watering down their comments was unusual for a major studio. Some resented that stance. Several studio chiefs, who would only speak on the condition of anonymity, told the press they were disturbed by the way Warner Brothers was dealing with the film. Others within the industry spoke out favorably, including Dawn Steel, former president of Columbia Pictures. "An artist paints a picture the way he or she sees it," Steel said. "Filmmakers are artists. But when it comes to historical accuracy, there may be a moral question here. I don't know what the answer to this is. We're making fiction here, we're not making a documentary. A movie can't be judged by the same standards that journalists judge a newspaper story. It's Oliver Stone's vision. It's called freedom of speech."

But others in Hollywood were as shocked and offended by the film as those in Washington, D.C., especially the older generation. Many of the old guard had worked all their lives trying to convince the rest of America that Hollywood could be politically responsible, and they resented Stone for reconfirming the image that they were a bunch of crazy liberals.

In February 1992, the Oscar nominations were announced. *JFK* was nominated eight times, including Best Picture, Director, Cinematography, Adapted Screenplay, Editing, Sound, Score, and Supporting Actor (Tommy Lee Jones). In some ways this was to be expected. *JFK* was a technical masterpiece and it was having a tremendous influence on the nation—it had to be treated seriously. Besides, nominations were one thing, Oscars were another.

From *Gone With the Wind* to *The Alamo* to *Mississippi Burning*, Hollywood has made a habit of distorting history. What singled out *JFK* had to do with the effectiveness of the film and the questions it raised. One of the most important films of 1991 was Warren Beatty's *Bugsy*. There was no question that *Bugsy* was full of falsehoods—the biggest being that Bugsy Siegel invented Las Vegas; but there were many others, including the idea that Siegel never had his family in Hollywood. Nary a review mentioned this, and it certainly didn't inspire public outrage that Siegel was made over in the image of Warren Beatty. *Bugsy*, with its sleek look and snappy dialogue, has a fantasy feel. *JFK* is part documentary, part *cinéma vérité*, and all convincing. There are a lot of people who probably walked out of the theater believing that Bugsy Siegel had the vision for Las Vegas. But so what if they do? And that brings up the real issue. The charges that *JFK* levels are aimed right at the heart of the establishment. It's not just about the murder of a president in 1963. Far more subversive was the idea that the military-industrial complex took over the country through a secret police composed of the CIA, FBI, and covert military groups.

What's worse, if Stone's scenario was plausible in 1963, since nothing has changed, it would most likely still be true today, and the thousands of people who work in these organizations wouldn't even know they were a part of it. Only the people at the very top would know—even the President could be a figurehead. As long as he never went too far against the grain, he would never know the difference. Stone was suggesting that as long as people in power didn't disrupt the usual flow of corruption, graft, and greed, of which war at regular intervals is an essential ingredient, then no one would bother them. But if anyone really tried to splinter or change the system, expose it from within or break apart one of its components, then it would come down upon them with full force no matter who they were—even the President of the United States. This was about as inflammatory a charge as anyone could make. Contrary to what the media and the politicians were saying, the furor wasn't over distorting the facts. Hollywood has distorted the facts before, but it didn't become a national issue. It wasn't about casting aspersions. It was about the direction in which those aspersions were cast.

> "I'm not going to name names, or tell who or what I represent. Except to say— you're close, you're closer than you think."
>
> "X" in **JFK**

As the Oscars approached and critics began listing their favorites, *JFK* was pretty evenly debated. Insiders didn't give it much of a serious chance at the top awards since it had too many enemies, but it was praised for bringing substance to entertainment. Jack Matthews of the *L.A. Times* wrote: "In a year when people actually wondered who touched their genitals in a video most, Madonna or Michael Jackson, and when Liz Taylor's umpteenth marriage was upstaged in society's news only by Warren Beatty's impregnation of Annette Bening, Stone's contribution was no less than heroic."

By the night of the awards, Stone knew that he personally had little chance of winning, but he went anyway to support those who did. *JFK* won two Oscars. Ironically, they were in categories which often go to the winner of the Best Film Award—Cinematography (Bob Richardson) and Editing (Joe Hutshing and Pietro Scalia). These awards signify not only outstanding technical achievement but creative mastery as well. It was no secret that the cinematography and editing of the film were amazing achievements, but considering the absence of other awards it was almost as though the work in these categories was so good that the Oscar was awarded to them in spite of their association with the subject matter. With the Best Editing Award, Stone had now had three different groups of young, sometimes even first-time, editors win the Oscar under his direction, and there is no question he influences the work. He has a gift for editing, and this is another key to the success of his films. If what made *JFK* so brilliant was his vision for the film, one must also acknowledge that his eye for editing is what made that vision a reality.

JFK was the seventh film that Bob Richardson had done with Oliver

Stone. After this long, it's impossible to separate their uncommon bond of inspiration, confrontation, and collaboration. Richardson had been nominated for both *Platoon* and *Born on the Fourth of July*, but had never won before. Though flattered by the acknowledgment from his peers, he doesn't believe in the Oscar process because of the unhealthy comparisons and feeling of competition it generates. "I just don't find it productive to evaluate the work of others in a competitive way," Richardson says." I don't want to think about criticizing these people's work because I respect their work. Who am I to sit here and cast the judgment? Who is anybody to do that? I just don't want to be driven down that line of thinking for a gold statue."

Richardson didn't attend the Academy Awards that year, but claims that the competition mentality wasn't the real reason he stayed home. "Most of the reason I don't go is fear. I have a very difficult time standing in front of that many people and a deathly fear of speaking. I have respect for the Academy even though I don't like the competition thing, and I think it's incredible to be honored. It has nothing to do with that. I watched the awards on television, but I just couldn't take that in person. I'm too nervous."

Like most of the people involved with the film, Richardson expected *JFK* to win more awards. "I thought Oliver would win Best Director," he says. "One thing that I think infuriates him is the level of publicity that surrounds his films and the way so much of it is directed at him. I think it also infuriates certain members of Hollywood to see the amount of publicity he receives. So, no, I didn't think it would win Best Film because of political reasons, but I thought the Academy would nod his way. I really think *JFK* was the best film, though."

Those watching the Academy Awards on television might have thought that Stone didn't even attend. One of the best known directors in the industry, he was rarely shown on camera during the broadcast. Whenever the film was announced, Kevin Costner or one of the other cast members was usually spotlighted. The only time Stone was shown was the moment he lost. What made this even more ironic was that though Stone applauded Jonathan Demme's selection as Best Director for *The Silence of the Lambs*, the next edition of *Entertainment Weekly* showed him in a tux making an unsmiling face with a caption reading: "Oliver Stone took it hard."

The Academy Awards seemed to focus on morbid movies that year. The roles nominated for Best Actor included three mass murderers (Anthony Hopkins in *The Silence of the Lambs*, Warren Beatty in *Bugsy*, and Robert DeNiro in *Cape Fear*); a psychotic street person (Robin Williams in *The Fisher King*); and a neurotic in therapy (Nick Nolte in *Prince of Tides*). The darkest of these films by far, *The Silence of the Lambs*, won the big four awards—Best Actor, Best Actress, Best Director, and Best Picture.

After the Oscar hoopla was over, Stone had thought things might die down in the press. He was wrong. It was now nearly four months since *JFK* had been released, and incredibly, the film continued to be debated in the press. Within days of the awards, Jack Valenti, president and chief executive of the Motion Picture Association of America and a former top aide to President Johnson, denounced *JFK* as a "hoax," a "smear," and "pure fiction" that rivaled the Nazi propaganda films of Leni Riefenstahl. "I waited to speak out because I didn't want to do anything which might affect this picture's theatrical release or the Oscar balloting," Valenti stated. "In much the same way, young German boys and girls in 1941 were mesmerized by Leni Riefenstahl's 'Triumph of the Will,' in which Adolf Hitler was depicted as a newborn god—both 'JFK' and 'Triumph of the Will' are equally a propaganda masterpiece and equally a hoax. Mr. Stone and Leni Riefenstahl have another genetic linkage: neither of them carried a disclaimer on their film that its contents were mostly pure fiction."

Stone was understandably upset by Valenti's comments. "While I respect Jack Valenti's enduring loyalty to President Johnson, I find his emotional diatribe off the mark," he responded. "The overwhelming majority of Americans—and not just the young, whom Mr. Valenti puts down as too impressionable—agree with the central thesis of my film: that President Kennedy was killed by a conspiracy, which included people in the government."

By now Stone had polarized the nation. People either loved or hated *JFK*, and they felt the same way about its creator. The attacks on the film had evolved into outright attacks on Stone, and there seemed to be no limit to how vicious they could become. Peter Collier wrote an article for the *American Spectator* entitled "Oliver Stone, Amerikan" with an illustration of an angry Stone in a commissar's uniform. The article compared Stone to ex-Ku Klux Klan member David Duke *and* Nazi propagandist Leni Riefenstahl and said, "'JFK' is the cinematic equivalent of rape."

Because of his tough exterior and the fact that Stone displays a confidence about his material and a fearlessness about facing the consequences, people assume he is not sensitive to such attacks. Actually, he is acutely sensitive. Elizabeth Stone says that having to defend the film and himself on an almost constant basis was "the most horrible thing he's ever had to go through. It beat him down and took years off his life."

All artists need some insecurity to create, but if it comes down to choosing between popularity and artistic vitality, Stone says he will opt for the latter. "Sometimes it's worth being hated for something that's important. Sometimes you fly in the face of popular fashion when you say something they don't like to hear; but you cannot let your work be influenced by that. A filmmaker must beware of too much flattery and too much praise in his lifetime. That's one of the reasons it's important for me to keep writing. Writing keeps you aware. There's fear and deceit in the paper. It requires a monklike austerity and it keeps you holy, keeps you low to the ground. Also, doing field research. Field research requires you to stay at the level of the subject and interact with real people."

By now, *JFK* was a bona fide hit, having grossed over $70 million. The more box office the film generated, the more Stone was accused of selling through controversy. Elizabeth Stone finds this ludicrous: "Oliver does what they tell you to do in Writing 101—write what you know. He was in the war, he wrote about the war; his dad was on Wall Street, he wrote about Wall Street. The Kennedy assassination had a big impact on him, so he wrote about it. I know it had a big impact on a lot of people, but anybody could have written about it. The point is, they didn't."

The continued press and frequent television interviews made Stone a recognizable national figure. "He's recognized everywhere now," Elizabeth Stone said at the time. "He's very good about stopping for a picture or signing an autograph, and that part hasn't been too bad so far. But it's been hard in other ways. He went from doing one film a year to some sort of event every night, always being asked to speak, getting boxes and boxes of mail from all kinds of people all over the world, having to change our phone number, that kind of thing. And sometimes, if he's had to wait for me somewhere for five minutes or something, he'll be like 'Everyone's recognizing me, this is terrible' and I say, 'Well, you know it's the price of fame, but what are you going to do?' It's a huge transition for any normal person to go through and still maintain an equilibrium, to maintain a placid domestic life—giving your children a balanced life, make good grades, going to Cub Scouts, all that kind of stuff."

Besides the hassles of notoriety and the pressures of success, there is a darker side of fame that the Stones had to deal with after *JFK*. Elizabeth began to worry again for her husband's safety. "I worry about Oliver because he's such an outspoken person and he's in public a lot," she said at the time. "There's a lot of crackpots around and he gets called everything in the press. He gets called a fascist, they talk like he's a threat to the country. He gets attacked from the left and he gets attacked from the right. I'm afraid that somebody will take all that seriously. We've gotten some strange phone calls and weird mail sometimes."

In April 1992, Stone went to Washington, D.C., to address Congress on the importance of releasing the sealed files related to the Kennedy assassination. He also met in closed-door sessions with leaders of the Senate Intelligence Committee, including its chairman, Senator David Boren, who assured Stone that he saw no legislative or administrative obstacles to the release of the tens of thousands of CIA, FBI, and military documents. At the last minute, however, the Justice Department issued an objection to the congressional resolution to release the documents. The Justice Department's nine-page letter, which was criticized by both Republicans and Democrats in the House legislation and National Security Subcommittee, said that the President, not the federal courts, should have the power to appoint and oversee members of any documents review board, and cited the need to protect intelligence sources and methods and the prerogative of the executive branch to protect its secrets. Stone was incensed over the ruling and also over the sparse coverage it received in the media. By this time 15 million Americans had seen *JFK*, and the film was ranked number one in ten other countries. On May 13, the CIA released a token 34 documents from its 33,000-page classified file on Lee Harvey Oswald.

Stone also met with Congressman Lee Hamilton, Democrat of

Indiana, at this time. This came about through Hamilton's aide, Eric Hamburg. Hamburg had met Stone back in 1987 at the National Convention of Vietnam Veterans when he worked for Senator John Kerry of Massachusetts. Stone was receiving an award for *Platoon*, and Kerry was honored as Legislator of the Year. When Hamburg heard Stone was going to make *JFK*, he wrote him a letter and began a behind-the-scenes effort in Congress with Representative Hamilton to introduce a bill that called for releasing the sealed JFK assassination files. Hamburg then hooked Stone and Frank Mankiewicz up with Hamilton, and the four met together and mapped out a strategy for getting the files released. After months of struggle on Capitol Hill (and a deluge of mail supporting the effort from the public), the bill was passed. President Bush signed it one week before the November 1992 election.

Kristina Hare said the Washington trip was a classic example of Stone's paradoxical nature, as he'd be meeting with congressmen by day and immersing himself in the party scene by night. "I always felt like a proud mother whenever I watched him speak," Hare says. "He always wanted to know afterwards, 'Was it all right? How did I do?' He always needed that reassurance. He's a tough boss, but then he's like a child and you want to mother him. Then he'd hang out at night with a bunch of dilettante kids with bad reputations. But that's Oliver for you, he goes from one extreme to the other and doesn't care what people think. He's full of contradictions; he's the most complicated man I know."

There is a quality in Stone that almost compels him to play the bad boy, especially after doing something as dignified and upstanding as addressing Congress. It's as if he might lose himself if he begins to take it all too seriously, or as if part of him is still afraid he's going to turn into his father. Meanwhile, his increased visibility on a nationwide scale was greatly adding to his staff's workload. "You can't imagine how many letters we got at that time," Hare says. "It just kept building, and he would insist that we respond to every single letter. He's incredibly open-minded. He really gives the little guy a chance. He often meets with people who write him and sometimes he even gives them jobs."

Azita Zendel, Hare's assistant, describes the huge volume of mail that poured into Stone's offices then. "We used to respond personally to every letter," she says, "but after *JFK* we were getting six or seven big boxes of mail every day. I was staying at the office till 3:00 or 4:00 A.M. even on Saturdays and Sundays, because Oliver wanted each reply to be personalized. Finally when we had about six hundred letters still unanswered, we decided to send out form letters thanking people for taking the time out to write us, regardless of what their stance was. We encouraged them to write to their senator to open the JFK files. Oliver feels this is at least a step toward having more aware citizens who hold the government accountable."

By now though, after over three years of working as Stone's assistant, the pressure was starting to get to Kristina Hare, and she decided she wanted to resign. "He was totally sweet about it. I think we both knew I'd grown out of it and there wasn't anywhere for me to go in the company at the time. There were a couple of times he made me cry over the years, but I never cried in front of him until the day we parted. That day, everything rushed to the surface—I cried like a baby. He gave me a big hug and was completely understanding and encouraging. It was very emotional."

Azita Zendel was asked to replace Kristina. "I got caught up in the whirlwind of it all and I found myself putting in a lot of overtime," Zendel says. "It's very difficult to work for Oliver for a long time and take the long hours, the fast pace, and the sheer magnitude of the workload. Oliver doesn't care how many things you're getting done at the same time and how long you've been there; he expects perfection with everything. He tries to hire people who have the stamina and energy to keep up with him."

As Stone's new assistant, Zendel soon found that her boss's unusual methods often added to this workload by making things more complicated. "His schedule is so busy that we have to bring people in back to back, but often he doesn't want the people who are waiting for him to see each other, so sometimes we've had to play musical chairs, hiding them in different offices and finding ways of keeping them apart when they wanted to make phonecalls or go to the bathroom."

Later that month, Stone spoke at the "Salute to Excellence Weekend" sponsored by the American Academy of Achievement, held that year at the Mirage Hotel in Las Vegas. He was among a distinguished group who were addressing the four hundred high school students from around the country who had achieved the highest scores on the SAT. The list of dignitaries was extraordinary. It included not only such leading figures in the entertainment industry as Stone, George Lucas, Barry Diller, Kevin Costner, Dolly Parton, Tom Selleck, and Barbra

Streisand, but also military leaders Norman Schwartzkopf and Colin Powell; Robert Gates, director of the CIA, Richard Sessions, director of the FBI; authors Tom Clancy and Michael Crichton; scientists Edwin Teller and Arthur Kornberg; Olympic skater Bonnie Blair; William Gates, the founder of Microsoft and inventor of DOS; Surgeon General Antonia C. Novello; Secretary of Health and Human Services Louis W. Sullivan; and many others.

Early on in the festivities, Tom Clancy made a speech which, among other things, indicated that the students should be grateful for the world they'd been given because the previous generation had conquered communism. This bothered Stone, and after joining a small group for a swim in Barbra Streisand's suite, he told Streisand, "I don't think we should let such a right-wing attitude go by. I think we need to address this, Barbra." To which Streisand replied, "I think *you* need to address it, Oliver. I'll have a hard enough time just giving the speech I've been planning."

And address it Stone did. That and more. Stone's speech gave several examples of what he called "official history" as opposed to what actually happened. He encouraged the students to seek out the truth for themselves and noted several books he felt would help them. He concluded with the following points:

> I think I've reached a point, cynical as it may sound, where I think that history is written by those who win. They killed Kennedy, and they rewrote American history to justify the killing of Kennedy. And I think if Hitler had won World War II you'd be reading a hell of a lot different about the United States right now. Think about George Orwell; you are the future. He who controls the past controls the future. Think for yourselves. Think freely, and do not ever believe at face value what somebody in power tells you to think.

Stone also made references to the CIA's involvement in "covering up or possibly even participating" in the assassination of President John F. Kennedy. In the audience for his speech were Robert Gates of the CIA and Richard Sessions of the FBI, both of whom seemed visibly upset. That night, when Gates accepted the Golden Plate Award given to the honorees, he criticized Stone, but also promised to release the assassination files. When Stone received his award, he thanked Gates and added, "Remember Mr. Gates, *all* the files."

"You're no better 'n me. You just know how to hide—and how to lie. Me, I don't have that problem. I always tell the truth—even when I lie."

Tony Montana in **SCARFACE**

It was around this time that Stone went to Brazil with Richard Rutowski on another of their self-discovery adventures. These trips, which seemed to be part getaway, part loosely based research for one project or another, and part spiritual quest, were becoming more frequent. "We went to Brazil to explore the idea of the doors of perception," Rutowski says. "The American Indian and the Shamanistic path seemed most available to me and also very functional, so we went to Brazil and tried something called ayahuasca. It's a herbal medicine that the Indians give in South America for healing. It's a tea you drink that's made from the tallest vine in the jungle: when you drink it, you get a vision of your weakest point. For me, because I had so much death of loved ones and a feeling of abandonment in my past, I wound up being afraid that anyone I loved would leave me or die. You can have very powerful visions on it: you could be thinking about sex or your car or God or whatever and it will lead you to the realization of the inner connectedness of everything. The thing that keeps you from getting to the light are your fears and your pain, and the ayahuasca takes you through the fear and pain to their source, their seeds. It demystifies these problems. They no longer have the same power over you. As corny as it sounds, the vehicle to the light is love."

Both Stone and Rutowski tried the ayahuasca in the jungles outside Rio with a *Paz e Luz* (Peace and Light) cult called the *Oniao Do Vegetal*. Rutowski believes it helped them better understand not only themselves but each other as well. "I've always said truth without compassion is brutality, and I think that Oliver has always focused on truth, but it used to be more brutal and wouldn't help anyone because they were too affected by the pain it caused. He lacked compassion."

Stone's second in-depth experience with ayahuasca came back in America in July at his newly completed house in Colorado. "He saw himself laying in a crib," Rutowski says. "His mother was standing over him, and it was very loving and it was very secure. Then he began falling, dropping down and down underwater. His mother was reaching for him as he was drawn down into this darkness, but she couldn't get him. He was underwater and down there were the most ghoulish demons, and wrathful creatures. Then he saw the light. He saw an exit, or he saw safety or sanctuary, and he was fighting to get to it. For me, that's Oliver in a nutshell. If you look at his life, this guy's gone and taken this journey and now he's trying to get back to the light."

Stone describes the effects of the ayahuasca: "It gives you visions. Not necessarily the Wagnerian kind—sweeping clouds and red dawns and sunsets. They can be subtle. I often make major sojourns to my childhood, and work my way through into evil caves, dark caves. Sun, light, water and snow, flowers and music. It's like being reborn, but then I come back to what I know and think about the things I don't know. It doesn't answer the questions, it only enhances the mystery for me. It does give me a certain faith in the spiritual mechanism called the mind. And it becomes increasingly spiritual the more you do it. I don't see it as a drug; I see it as a healing medicine. I consider LSD a chemically synthesized drug with very powerful spiritual overtones, but nothing compared to the purity and the innocence of peyote and ayahuasca."

The house near Telluride, Colorado, was begun in 1989 and finished in July 1991. Stone had spent far more than he planned on it, but there was no question it was magnificent. Located on 1,000 acres, the finished house is 15,000 square feet. For some time now, as the mammoth project was drawing to a close, Elizabeth Stone had begun to wonder if her husband would really be able to be comfortable there: "Oliver has never liked big open rooms to live in. He likes things cozy, sort of a cluttered feel because it makes him feel safer. He has an aversion to being alone and to too much space around him, which implies to me a real loneliness. I think it goes back to when he was a kid living in those big rooms in his parents' town house."

Even with regards to money, Stone is a paradox. Azita Zendel comments: "One of the things I find most interesting about Oliver is his relationship to wealth. He's very frugal in some ways. He's still driving the Ford Mustang convertible he got six years ago, when most people of his caliber have Porsches or Mercedes. He doesn't care about status or style that much and almost always buys American-made goods. He's also actively involved with at least twenty different charities and social or political organizations, and tries to help over a hundred others in various ways."

Not surprisingly, the Colorado house was a problem for Stone. He was uneasy with such an obvious display of wealth. He tended to see himself as an underdog, the outsider even now, and didn't want people to think of him as being rich before they thought of him as being an artist or someone who's politically concerned. But though he couldn't be considered among the wealthiest group in Hollywood—many executives, producers, and even a few actors and directors have amassed more— he was well off by any standards, with houses in Santa Monica, Santa Barbara, and a condo in Palm Springs. And now a veritable mansion in Colorado. "Colorado's not necessarily a haven for me," Stone says. "I think a person's demons come out when they're alone in a big space like that. That's when you've got to wrestle with the biggest fucking enemy of all—yourself. That was a flaw I think Morrison had. He seemed rarely to be alone. He was always surrounded by people, always a perpetual party. That tends to corrupt you easier. Sometimes you should be alone."

In any event, the Stones spent most of their time at their Santa Monica house, with occasional weekend excursions to Santa Barbara or Palm Springs. They only got up to Colorado for a rare extended vacation. What was it like to live with Oliver Stone? "He's a passionate man," Elizabeth said in the summer of 1992. "He's an extremely passionate man . . . about everything. We've been together thirteen years, married for eleven now and he's passionate about his work, about how his son should be raised, but also about where his red shirt is that went to the dry cleaners. Once you really get to know him, you realize that a lot of it is hot air. I think he's saving himself an ulcer basically. He rants and raves, but he assumes no one's going to take him seriously, and if you do take him seriously and your feelings get hurt, that's when he really gets mad. He wants you to hear what he says, but not crumble and cry or be crushed because of the manner in which he says it. He's just a loud person. His mother was loud. His mother had tantrums until she had menopause. His child has tantrums on a daily basis. There's just something very volatile in them. It's like *wham!*—and then it's over with. So when people—especially me or people that work with him— crumble and get our feelings hurt, he gets really furious. It's like, 'Don't take me serious, just listen to what I say and then get on with it.' It's been hard, but actually he's mellowed a lot. He used to be very abusive verbally. He's a very sort of four-letter-word person, and sometimes that hurts."

There are other key differences between Oliver and Elizabeth. "I'm home on the range," she says. "That's part of the reason he married me. I like home and family life. I went to parties a lot with him when we were single, but even if I went now, by ten or eleven I'd be ready to go home and he'll want to stay until two or three in the morning. So that's a problem sometimes, it's like, 'Oh, she's dragging me home,' this kind of thing. I like to get up early in the morning and it's not just because I have kids. I'm a morning person. I'm very domestic. I'm like the harbor that he comes back to. He knows I would never play around. I don't even leave the kids except maybe to go to a spa for two days or something. He knows I'm boringly consistent or whatever. I'm the rock. And yet he can't take more than two or three days at home without going stir crazy. So he'll go out, which is why it's to the point now where he'll take meetings at night. He'll go to business dinners. It's like his every moment has to be filled with something constructive.

"Like yesterday, Father's Day, we socialized with friends, but there was still business talked because they were people in the industry. But to just go out and have dinner with friends is not something he would do. There's always got to be some purpose. Traveling on airplanes to him is relaxing. To have no one telephoning him and to have his books and all his work projects to catch up on. He also likes to see other cities and hear other accents. He picks up a lot of his writing on the street. That's why he can't stay at home too much. He's got to go out and actually hear dialogues walking past him and see people interacting."

Another difference between the Stones was their energy levels. Oliver was constantly on the go. Elizabeth, especially since her bouts with colitis which began around the time of *Platoon*, required a lot more rest. "Oliver's energy level not only astounds me," she says. "It astounds his doctor. Chris [Renna] says he's checked Oliver and his ticker is like an eighteen-year-old. How does he do it? He's leading this wild life, burning the candle at both ends, but he's got this energy that fortifies him. He works out, but not like he should. He still runs sometimes. I'm trying to talk him into doing walks now. He lifts weights. He used to do it every day religiously. But that was pre-*JFK*. Now he's traveling a lot more. It was busy before, but it's gotten mad now. His diet is getting better, but he's a hard liver."

Elizabeth found that she had to schedule their family life in order to keep the near-constant barrage of high-priority demands on Stone's life from overwhelming them. "I set up the family's schedule which I give to Oliver's assistant, and she fits it into Oliver's schedule," Elizabeth says. "I'll set up things that I know I'm going to do with the kids. Some of it's compromisable, but there's not really that much at this point— it's baseball games, school functions, that kind of thing. Oliver will choose one of Sean's three minor league All-Star games to come to. I've learned over the years that it's much better to arrange things through his assistant. The office staff always assumes we talk about what's coming up and so on, but we don't. By the time Oliver gets home, he's talked out and doesn't remember if he's supposed to tell me something. So then, all of a sudden, I'll find out I've got eight people coming to dinner tomorrow night, and I'll say, 'How come nobody told me?' and they'll say, 'Oliver knew about it for a long time.' So I say, 'He doesn't tell me anything. *Please* tell me, especially if it's at my house.'"

According to Elizabeth, Stone pursues fatherhood the same way he pursues anything else, with sudden intense bursts of time and energy. "He kind of wants to set the same standards for his kids that he had to deal with as a child. It's like, 'I took Latin in fourth grade,' or, 'I went to summer camp early,' or, 'I let the nanny take care of me—they should too.' He has this Victorian attitude on child rearing that says, 'I was a better person for having been alone.' He sees that it made him into a writer, made him have to invent imaginary characters or whatever. Sean has Oliver's metabolism and sometimes I'm just exhausted from trying to keep up with them. There's been a lot of working compromises. For example, Oliver brings work home with him and he's not really ready to eat dinner until nine or ten at night. I can do that now and then, but not every night. I put Sean to bed at nine and frankly, I'm usually asleep by ten. Because by six I'm up again because of the baby. Oliver wants company while he's sitting up, but he's watching casting tapes. I can't get into that and I have to be up early."

That brings up another question. What kind of a home life do the Stones have when there's nobody around? Is it ever just the family sitting around the TV like in most American homes? "Well, sometimes. Oliver's a channel-changer. He even does that at the movies. When he goes to the theater, he'll see part of one movie and then he'll go check in on another one. He asks me to go with him, and I'll go, 'No, I'm going to sit here and watch this whole movie; you go visit the other movies if you want to.' We disagree on almost every movie we see, anyway. Sometimes he likes really silly things. Like he loved *Wayne's World*, which I hated. I'm too serious for that movie. Now I liked *Bill & Ted*, and so did he. At home he loves the junky kung-fu Hong Kong movies. He sits and watches these things and I get bored right away. To him, it's like a release. There's nothing to think about. I think we have the record at our local Blockbuster store. They said we've rented something like 504 tapes. Whenever we rent movies it's like catchup time for us because we can't go to the theater that much. He watches movies for his work to see the style or for research or something, so he'll get his nine or so and Sean gets his Nintendo tapes and I get my movies. We always rent tapes. We don't watch commercial TV. I find it insulting. It's like they're playing to the lowest common denominator."

Talking about their frequent trips to the video store reminds Elizabeth of a revealing story. "We were in the video store checking out the *JFK* racks and there was a couple standing there looking over a copy. It's in two boxes because they found that when they put the long movies like *Dances With Wolves* on one video, the tape can break easily. So this couple is trying to decide if they're going to rent it. The man wanted to see it, but the woman didn't. Oliver goes over by them and listens intently. And she says, 'I really can't sit for three-hour movies.' Well, I think the guy might have recognized Oliver, but she didn't. She says, 'That's too long of a movie for me.' And I said, 'Why don't you watch it over two nights? You don't have to sit and watch the whole thing at once.' But they didn't look like they were going to get it. So when we left, Oliver was real discouraged. He said, 'They're not going to get it just because it's three hours. She must be a moron if she doesn't care about her own history. . . .'" And he goes on and on about it. But that's how he is. He cares."

Elizabeth is well aware that her husband is a mass of contradictions. "He has the best heart. He's a good, fine man. Yet he can turn around and have people in tears. He's very honest and he says everything that comes into his mind. Someone will walk in and he'll say, 'Put on a little weight, haven't you?' Often, he doesn't even realize he's hurting the person's feelings. To him it's just a statement of fact. He even thinks that he owes it to that person to let them know that there's something they should work on. He sees that as one of his jobs in life. He thinks most people settle for less. He really does strive for perfection and he thinks everyone should. 'Now, insults or criticism don't motivate me. Praise works for me. It inspires me.' But after all these years, he still doesn't get it. He says, 'Well, it worked for me, people criticized me and it made me a better person.'

"Also, he likes to rattle people's cages," Elizabeth goes on. "He loves to get reactions out of people, whether it's in his work or on a more social level like at a party. He likes to dramatize life, to see what he *can* say. Oliver can be a monster, just terrible, say the evilest and meanest things. He likes to find out what someone's weakness is and push the button to see if they respond. They may wind up screaming back at him. Sometimes, he'll say something totally insulting and think he's being funny. When I'm with him, I'll try to laugh it off, like, 'Oh, isn't he being funny?' as people are standing there with their mouths open. He'll say something like, 'God isn't there any good food around here?' when there's a big buffet laid out. Or, 'Why is this party so dead, where is everyone?', or, 'Where did you get that dress, the Salvation Army?' Then he can turn right around and be the nicest guy in the world."

On a nearby table is a picture of Oliver and Sean mounted on a plaque that reads "Father of the Year," an award from a local organization. Elizabeth's response to this is, "Yeah, he gets a lot of awards. I always thought that one was funny. The funniest award that he got was when they asked him to be the keynote speaker at the American Psychiatric Association. We were saying that this is really the inmate addressing the asylum because most people that know him and work with him think that he's just the craziest person they've ever seen. He's a great speaker and I understand it was very well received. I can just see all these learned doctors sitting around listening to this guy who's practically certifiable. I mean, I love Oliver, but he's really out there. He's like Beethoven. He's mad, but he's brilliant. It's that frenetic energy, that passion and self-consumptive energy. Oliver has like twelve channels going in his mind all the time, which is why, when I really want to get through to him, I'll write him a note. Because if I talk to him, even if he appears to be listening it may not be registering."

Different in so many ways, Oliver and Elizabeth seem to balance each other. But it has not been easy. "There have been a lot of rocky roads," Elizabeth said in July of 1992. "A lot of shocks for me to try and figure out somebody who's not figure-outable. I've had to learn what to accept and what to reject or actually put my foot down about. For a while Oliver tried to have it both ways. He tried to have his father and mother's life and my life. But I won't go along with any of that. I don't mind him going out and having a good time, but I'm not going to have any playing around going on. I can't deal with that."

Stone was still keeping his affairs hidden from Elizabeth. He hated lying to her, but he hated hurting her more. Since they had clashed over this issue during the making of *Wall Street* in 1987, Stone had come to accept the deceit as an ongoing way of life. For a while it seemed that he and Elizabeth could go on this way forever. By the time of Mikey's birth, though, he knew there had to be some changes. He hoped having another child would balance the family somewhat, and reignite things between the two of them, but it had been eight months and he still felt distant from his wife. Sometimes he enjoyed his home and his family more than anything else. At other times, he couldn't stand to be there. He thought of leaving, but couldn't. He was in a no-win situation that he knew would someday have to change.

"We are tired and worn out with Ourselves."

Monk in **HEAVEN AND EARTH**

Richard Rutowski recalls when Oliver and Elizabeth first started going out together back in 1979. "I remember I went over to his apartment and Oliver was sitting at his desk writing as he always did and he said, 'Oh, I want you to meet Elizabeth, my fiancée.' And I remember turning around and Elizabeth was just coming out of the bedroom. She was this sort of clean-cut blonde, very attractive, and what went through my mind was, 'This girl's never going to be able to handle somebody like Oliver. She'll never last.' Well, she's had a rough time, but she's hung in there and she supports him. She accepts him for who he is. They may argue and be critical of each other, but there's something deeper. They do love each other and there's an acceptance and understanding."

Those who have been around the Stones know that they also have their share of loud fights. "They argue a lot over how to raise the children," Rutowski said in 1992. "Mikey is still pretty small, but Sean is a very smart, precocious child. Oliver is away so much that Liz is very protective of Sean. Oliver feels Sean should experience life more directly without so many cautions and fears fostered on him by his mother. She's a good mother, they just have different views."

But the issues in the Stones' marriage went deeper than that. Elizabeth may have suspected he was seeing other women, but she didn't know. And she didn't want to know. "The real issue in their relationship is that they've been together for thirteen years and some of the mystery has gone," Rutowski said at the time. "Oliver is absolutely fascinated with mystery and constantly trying to enter the mystery deeper, and that means the trail gets narrower. Then he's pulled between wanting to be reckless just to discover what will come out of it or stay in a situation that is safe but less interesting. He wants the security of a family and dinner at home, but he wants it to be exciting. So, with one hand he's reaching for madness, and with the other hand he's reaching for tranquility. Actually he wants both, but he's got a more powerful fascination with the destructive forces of disorder and chaos than he does with tranquility and harmony. He wants to be able to step out into darkness and still come home to clean sheets."

Yet Oliver and Elizabeth had lasted far longer than most Hollywood relationships. Part of it was because their differences and their passions had kept it interesting. Rutowski describes one of the Stones' arguments. "I was there one day when they had a series of fights about a year, year and a half ago. They were raving at each other—'Fine! Fuck you! We're getting a divorce!' And Oliver and I went out that night. He was so distraught about the idea of divorcing her. Then it just so happened that his business manager was there and he was talking about the money thing. But, for Oliver, it isn't about money. Oliver's materialistic in the sense that he likes to have things around him, he's like a kid with a bunch of toys. But that's not really what's important to him. He's much more interested in the internal conflicts. I saw how distraught he was about losing her and we talked about it. I remember the day when my wife and kids left the house and I was alone and there was that horrifying hole inside myself. We went through all the scenarios in his mind, like, 'Oh well, maybe it will be cool to be free. I'll get an apartment and she can have the house.' And I could tell that he didn't want that. When we went home that night, we thought the door was going to be locked, but it wasn't and Elizabeth was at the door waiting. It was like he couldn't wait to get his arms around her. They were so happy to see each other. You can see when something real is going on between two people, you can even see it when it's conflicted and insane."

Oliver Stone was now a symbol not only of controversy but of conspiracy. He was asked to play a cameo in the movie *Dave*, which featured Kevin Kline as a presidential lookalike thrust into the White House after the real President has a heart attack. Stone plays himself appearing on a television talk show to point out the inconsistencies between photos of the real President and his double. "It's a conspiracy," Stone insists. Although he was a bit reluctant at first, Stone decided to do the role. "At first, we argued about it," says Mike Menchel, Stone's agent at Creative Artists Agency. "I said, 'Give yourself a break and give the public a break. Let them laugh at you a little and let them know that you can laugh at yourself a little bit.'"

Stone's Ixtlan Productions was in full swing with Janet Yang at the helm. Altogether there are about a dozen employees and interns working at the office, including Stone's executive assistant Azita Zendel and her staff of four interns. Generally, people join the staff as interns, donating as much time as they have available in return for learning about the area they would like to specialize in. As they are ready and openings become available, the interns are converted into paid employees. Of the last twelve people hired at Ixtlan, ten had interned for anywhere between three months to a year. The hours are demanding and the pay is only average, but the employees do advance. Suzi Czerner was a receptionist, now she is Janet Yang's assistant. Alan Chu started as an intern and now works in development. Edwin Zane assists Azita Zendel in the same way that Azita used to assist Kristina Hare. Stone tends to be demanding of the staff and is often manipulative, but as he is also inspiring and the work is interesting, they hang in there. Most of all it is because they feel they are a part of something that matters. Stone doesn't make movies just to entertain and make money, and the people who work for him feel they are helping to change things that need to be changed.

As someone who deals with Stone in both business and creative matters on an almost daily basis, Janet Yang has considerable insight into his complexities. "Oliver is an artist first," Yang says, "and that's the best way to deal with him—by understanding his emotional undercurrents. He's usually too caught up in his ideas to play games. He's more spontaneous than strategic, and what rubs him the wrong way are the typical Hollywood games and insecurities. A friend of mine once commented that Hollywood is like one huge dysfunctional family, all of us enabling one another in our worst behavior. Oliver's one of the most straightforward players around. He can be incredibly vulnerable and open, but he makes little effort to be nice just for the sake of it, and that unnerves people. He has a huge agenda, so he's always in a hurry. He isn't into being in control for his ego. He just needs to have certain things done in a certain way."

Yet Stone is a gifted businessman who is very conscious of budgets and schedules. "He's extremely disciplined, self-motivated and organized, yet structure and bureaucracy set off alarms in him. What a paradox—he's focused and intense one minute and utterly indulgent the next."

In the fall of '92 Ixtlan had several projects in development, including three films that would be released later (*South Central*, October '92, *Zebrahead*, October '92, and *Joy Luck Club*, September '93) and several other ideas in various stages. Among these was a biography of former Black Panther and San Quentin Six member Johnny Spain (written by Anne Hamilton Phelan of *Mask* and *Gorillas in the Mist*), and a feature based on the life of Harvey Milk, the gay San Francisco city supervisor who was assassinated in 1978. Even with all this on the fire, Stone signed on with Alex Ho and writer Bruce Wagner to begin producing a television mini-series to air in May 1993 (*Wild Palms*).

All this activity kept Ixtlan employees in constant overdrive, yet regular visitors to their Venice offices claimed they could tell if Stone was in town the moment the elevator doors opened just by the prevailing atmosphere. "Yes, there's a distinct difference," Yang admits. "I feel like I have to be extra sharp when he's here. I try to be very conscious of what he's doing when he's here, does he want to be disturbed, what's a good time to discuss this, and so on. But it's in bursts. Like when he's shooting, I may not talk to him for a week or two, and then, when he's in town, I might hear from him five times in one morning—because that's the way he focuses his energy—and that's fine. To work with him you have to be able to stay very flexible. I love the serendipity in his life. We don't have planned meetings, where I report to him. I grab him on the run. Mood and timing play an important factor. It's all ad hoc."

Stone's offices at this time were next to Arnold Schwarzenegger's above Schwarzenegger's Schatzi's restaurant. Azita Zendel tells a funny story about the time Stone, always one to place functionality above formality, went to Schwarzenegger to complain about the building. "Oliver always deals with everything in the most efficient way possible, so when he was told that the dirty windows in our office wouldn't be cleaned for another week, he went over to Arnold's office and complained to him. Of course, Arnold merely owned the building and didn't preoccupy himself with these kinds of tasks—but sure enough, the windows were cleaned the next day! Oliver is very good at getting what he wants. In general, he doesn't like to go through in-betweens and tries to have as few people in the loop as possible."

A common concern around Stone's offices is confidentiality. Though most of the employees are friendly and seem to enjoy their demanding jobs, they are often reluctant to discuss their work even with each other. The truth is none of them is sure what the others know, and as a result, everyone is uneasy whenever talk turns to upcoming projects. "Oliver told me to be totally candid for this book, and I was pleased but somewhat surprised," Yang tells me, "because he tends to be extremely protective of information and our goings-on. He doesn't even like us to share information with other departments. He needs a dark place to germinate ideas, to create. The harsh light of public scrutiny makes him wince. But his attitude's changed a lot about the company.

"When I first started," she goes on, "he shuddered at the idea of lists. He couldn't stand having our projects actually enumerated on a piece of paper. As our repertoire grew to over a dozen, I had to make secret lists for myself, hiding them in my desk. Every now and then they would slip out and he'd have a fit. He wanted to make sure nobody else in the company ever saw one, not to mention our agents or lawyers. Then one day, before we went to a meeting at CAA [Creative Artists Agency], he matter of factly said, 'Bring your list.' I guess he finally realized there was a limit to how much I could keep in my head."

Like its president, Ixtlan began often to find itself at the center of controversy and rumor. Part of Yang's role is to deal with the rest of Hollywood and coordinate with Stone's method of operation. Frequently this means Yang must play the Hollywood game, which she doesn't enjoy, and still interface with Stone, who practically refuses to play the game at all. "It's about finding a balance between doing what's most expeditious at the moment and doing what's most effective in the long term," she explains. "I can't alienate people. If Oliver had his way, I'd be able to get anyone on the phone instantly and simply command them to direct or act in our projects. Also, the script would be perfect so there would be no need to 'develop.' That's a dirty word for Oliver. As a filmmaker, developing is just an excuse for a committee of people to waylay your project. Oliver's so unusual in that he sees the big picture, the essence of things. He's terribly strong and direct, and he forces you to contend with him. In the process you learn so much about yourself. Where you stand, what you're willing to put up with, what's important and what's not. You wind up feeling like—thank God there's somebody around who can cut through all the bullshit out there. There are very few individuals like Oliver. He gets just as heated about traffic problems as assassination conspiracies. He generates so much that I think is really noble. He's like this bullet train—high speed and unstoppable, and those of us who jump on do so with excitement and trepidation."

As Ixtlan grew, it began to develop a reputation for taking on projects that had a powerful message, especially about minorities. Janet Yang had long been a driving force in bringing Amy Tan's best-selling novel *Joy Luck Club* to the screen. She had seen the book long before publication when Putnam sent her a few chapters while she was working for Universal Studios. "Reading Amy's book was the first time I'd seen the experiences of growing up Chinese American written about in such a personal way. I identified with it very deeply and realized that it had never been represented in entertainment. Because I was Universal's liaison with Amblin [Steven Spielberg's production company], I tried to get them to do it, but they had just made *Empire of the Sun* which I worked with them on, so they had sort of done their China project. Then, shortly after I came here, I talked to Oliver and he was receptive. Most people are really scared to tread the same territory more than once. Oliver is one of the few directors who doesn't mind going back deeper and looking at things from a different angle."

Stone's involvement as a producer fluctuates from just helping put the deal together to overseeing every aspect of the filmmaking process. He describes producing as being "like directing, but from a distance. You try to line up people that will work well together and get the best out of them, you put the right elements together and let them interact. Janet's my partner, she's really been helpful. We haven't locked in on a commercially successful film yet. That seems to have eluded us [*Joy*

Luck Club would change this the following year]. The more overtly commercial projects that have been presented to me are just not that interesting. I like doing things a little different."

How has running Ixtlan affected Stone's other projects? "To some degree it's helped, because it's given me more awareness of what's being written, what's being done. It also gives me a broader field of play. But it saps your energy in that sometimes you have to deal with producing problems. It takes meetings, it takes time, it takes calls. Calls which I hate to take. So all that process becomes difficult. There is not often satisfaction in producing because all the credit generally goes to the actor or director or writer. I sympathize with the legions of Hollywood producers who nurture, baby-sit, and sell movies, and in the end are ignored. But it's a chance to help people who need help. There were times I needed help."

Yang says that Stone continues to surprise her not only by his unpredictable way of working, but also by the many sides to his character: "One time I accompanied him up to U.C. Davis where he spoke in front of hundreds of students and I saw him in a completely different light. Wearing his glasses on the edge of his nose and a wool vest, he looked like a distinguished college professor, but his message was a youthful one. 'Follow your heart. Don't be afraid to speak your mind, always challenge, question. Don't be complacent.' He's a role model to many college kids. They really revere him for taking the stand he did with *JFK*. He's not the extreme liberal people think. Complacent liberalism really bothers him. He has his own brand of radical conservatism. Even though lots of people see him as sort of an icon, he still questions. He's a learned, well-read rebel with a cause."

The year 1992 was one of honors and awards. After agreeing to present the America's Best Screenplay awards for the Writers' Foundation in Syracuse, New York, Stone was told the group wanted to present him with a special award. Stone asked not to be given the award because he feared it might take attention away from the winning screenwriters. In July, he was awarded the Torch of Liberty Award, presented annually by the American Civil Liberties Union of Southern California. Later that month he attended the Democratic National Convention at Madison Square Garden in New York as a delegate pledged to Jerry Brown. He had supported Brown in some of the primary campaigns until it became apparent there wasn't enough momentum to make an impact on the presidential race. On July 15, Stone addressed the convention. His speech emphasized cleaning up the environment, eliminating government corruption, reducing federal spending, and opening all files on the Kennedy assassination—"We want to know what we did, who we are, and what we're coming from," he told the crowd. He also called for the dismantling of the CIA. "We must behave not as global tyrants, but as global citizens. The CIA *must* be broken. And its history must be revealed as the Nazi party was in Germany."

Such statements do not go unnoticed. With enemies not only in the press but the CIA and the FBI, Stone must consider himself a target. If even a very small part of the theories advanced by *JFK* were true, then Stone would have to be in danger for exposing it. Asked if he thought "X's" remark in the film about being safe "as long as there's a lot of light on you" applied to him, Stone replies, "Yes, to a certain degree. Of course, if they really want to get rid of someone, they can. They'd make it look like an accident. A plane could go down. They would kill other people to make it look good if I was enough of a problem. You can't underestimate their power."

Stone admits that not knowing how long he might be around was one of the reasons he agreed to cooperate with this book. "I don't care who else is interviewed or quoted. They can say I'm a madman or full of shit as long as I'm sure my side of the story is told as well."

As he moved on to new projects, Stone was haunted by the long-range effects of *JFK*. He couldn't help but wonder if the enemies he had made during such a lengthy and heated battle would hinder his future efforts. Perhaps he had gone too far.

"The potential for the disastrous rise of misplaced power exists and will persist . . . we must never let the weight of this combination endanger our liberties or democratic processes. We should take nothing for granted."

Dwight D. Eisenhower in **JFK**

CHAPTER FOURTEEN

Heaven and Earth

"If the monks were right and nothing happens without cause, then the gift of suffering is to bring us closer to God, to teach us to be strong when we are weak, to be brave when we afraid, to be wise in the midst of confusion and to let go of that which we can no longer hold. Lasting victories are won in the heart, not on this soil or that."

Le Ly Hayslip in **HEAVEN AND EARTH**

S tone now chose to embark upon his third Vietnam-related film. In many ways, *Heaven and Earth* was a risky choice as the film to follow *JFK*. Based on two volumes of autobiography, *When Heaven and Earth Changed Places* and *Child of War, Woman of Peace*, it is the story of a Vietnamese peasant woman named Le Ly Hayslip. "This is a moral thing for me," Stone says. "It's like *Platoon* and *Born* were, a bit of a duty. I really see it that way—as my form of public service. It'll be a hard movie to make, especially with a mostly Oriental cast, many of them unknowns. It's a tough one. Very far-ranging, with makeup, hair, and the emotions involved. But I made a promise I would do it one day, and now is the time."

Born in a small Vietnamese village, Hayslip saw her land, which she calls "the most beautiful place on earth," ravaged by war. Fed the propaganda of a corrupt South Vietnamese regime by day and hearing of the liberation promised by the Viet Cong by night, Hayslip's family only wanted to be left in peace. Gradually, though, as she saw her family and neighbors victimized by both sides, Hayslip's mother became convinced that they had to do something to resist the American invaders, and sent her sons to fight for the North. Hayslip, though still a young girl, decided to take action as well, spying for the Viet Cong until arrested and tortured by the South Vietnamese. Her brother-in-law's influence with the government saved her, but Hayslip was released only to find herself considered a traitor by the Viet Cong. She feared for her life, and when two Viet Cong soldiers took matters into their own hands and raped her, she left her idyllic childhood home. Fleeing to the city, she and her mother began a new life as servants. Before long Le Ly was impregnated by the master of the house. His angry wife turned her out on the streets and Le Ly struggled to raise her child by working odd jobs and hustling black market goods. Eventually, she met a fifty-five-year-old American contractor who fell in love with her and asked her to marry him. As the city fell, Hayslip agreed to marry the man and was evacuated along with her child.

In America, she faced a new battle as she tried to integrate two very distinct cultures and lifestyles. After the death of her husband and another marriage that ended in divorce, she finally returned to Vietnam in 1986 at great risk and found the few relatives she still had left alive. From that point on, Hayslip devoted her life to building a bridge between the two cultures that have made up her world. In 1987, she started the East Meets West Foundation to care for people left crippled and homeless by the war. The foundation built a clinic called the Peace Village Medical Center just outside Danang on China Beach, where twenty-five years earlier U.S. forces staged their first offensive of the Vietnam War. Much of the clinic's support comes from ex-GIs, including Oliver Stone, who also funded a second clinic, Mother's Love Clinic, built in 1989 near Ky La, the village where Le Ly grew up in Vietnam. Le Ly Hayslip sees the organization's mission as "healing the wounds of war and breaking the circle of vengeance that perpetuates suffering in the name of justice around the world."

This concept has long been an issue for Stone as well. Back when he was filming *Talk Radio* in Dallas in 1988, he attended a showing of *Dear America*, a film based on letters that GIs wrote home from Vietnam, and was quoted as saying, "Now there's one job left for Hollywood to do. We've got to tell the Vietnamese people's story. We need a movie that's more than just American losses. We need both sides. We need to explain the whole ideology of the war."

Hayslip's first book came out the following year, and Stone optioned it not long after finishing *Born on the Fourth of July*. He said nothing about this to the press, however, preferring as always to play it close to the vest. "I first met Le Ly at Bob Kline's house," Stone says. "Bob was in the process of optioning the book and had a dinner for Le Ly and her agent. We chatted and got along very well."

Robert Kline, one of the producers of *Heaven and Earth*, had read the review of *When Heaven and Earth Changed Places* in the *Los Angeles Times*. At that time Kline, president/CEO of Todd-Ao and Translantic Enterprises, was also teaching a course on the Vietnam experience at the University of Southern California. He contacted Hayslip's agent and began negotiations. A few months later Kline was directing Christina Rodgers's documentary series, *Profiles of Excellence*, which included as one of its subjects Oliver Stone. When Rodgers asked Stone if he was going to do any more stories on Vietnam, Stone replied that he would be interested in something that showed the Vietnamese side of the war. "I told him we had a project that would be of interest to him," Kline says. "I loaned him Le Ly's book to read on his flight down to Argentina where he was scouting for *Evita*. I knew Oliver would get the movie made and that it would be faithful to Le Ly's vision. Later, he called and said he loved the book, and I set up the dinner for him to meet Le Ly."

Le Ly Hayslip describes that first meeting. "I knew Oliver's name, but not really who he was," she says. "But it's so funny that when *Platoon* came out, I had gone to see NGO, the Non-Government Organization, which raised money to help Vietnamese. They gave me this stack of flyers to hand out in front of the theaters down in San Diego. So I went to see *Platoon*, and I was scared because I didn't know what the movie was about. Afterwards I had the same questions as the flyer. 'Now you've heard the side of the American GI, how about the Vietnamese side? Yes, 58,000 Americans died, but how many Vietnamese died?'

And so on. I stood three nights in three different theaters to pass out the flyers, and I still didn't know who Oliver Stone was."

Hayslip, though now a successful American author and business-woman, still retains a humble charm from her days as Phung Thi Le Ly, a rice farmer's daughter. "We met and I had that feeling like I'm so small to meet Oliver Stone," she says, "but he's really an enjoyable person. He plays and jokes with me and says, 'I'm going to torture you,' and I said, 'You would, but you don't know how.' And we just got along very well. We still do."

Stone was about to embark on preproduction, something he hadn't done for a while and he was looking forward to it. "It's like playing with new toys every day. It could be plot points, feelings, or actors, but I've found each movie since *Salvador* has been thoroughly a process of discovery."

Richard Rutowski envisioned the film as the vehicle by which Stone would learn to develop more compassion in his character: "I think this movie is going to be a lot about the compassion a person must have. It's also about love and ancestral connections. It's a spiritual movie about Buddha's principles, the Buddhist path, a way of seeing."

Janet Yang was also looking forward to the effect the film would have on Stone. "It will allow Oliver to tap into his feminine side, which I think will be good for him," Yang says. "He made a promise to Le Ly that he would do *Heaven and Earth*, and for years he's gone to her fundraising events. He'd sit through these painfully long evenings just to demonstrate his commitment to the project and to the issue."

By August 1992 preproduction was under way. For some reason Stone was less tense during this period than usual; perhaps it was the desire to get back on a film again and away from the *JFK* controversy. Perhaps he was mellowing a bit with experience. "I don't get as upset," he admits. "The anxiety for me always came over the idea that, are they really going to let me make this movie? Now I feel I've reached a position where I'm confident the picture is going to be made. I see it more now as a playground for choices. You have to be very specific and exact, like a scientist doing an experiment. I enjoy picking locations, balancing one against the other and getting input from my associates—the production designer, the cameraman, the producer. Anyone, actually. I value the input of the gaffer, the grip, the set dressers, art directors, location scouts.

They're very bright. I enjoy the collaborative effort of the movie where, while I may have a very significant feeling, it can be modified into a sort of Zeitgeist."

Refining the script and the business of casting are also key elements of the preproduction process. For a long time Stone had struggled with a structural problem in telling Le Ly's story. He always loved her first book, but it ended with her leaving Vietnam in triumph, and Stone didn't feel right about ending the movie there when he knew Le Ly had experienced so much difficulty adjusting to life in America. He was still wrestling with this on a location scouting trip to Hanoi and Bangkok. "I noticed Le Ly proofing a manuscript on the plane," Stone recalls. "I said, 'What's that?' She said, 'It's just this thing I'm writing about the rest of my life.' I said, 'What? Let me see that.' I took it and read the first few chapters, and by the time the plane landed I knew I had it. I had a movie!"

Stone combined both books in his script. He took three men who were significant in Hayslip's life, including two of her husbands, and made them into one character, Steve Butler, which helped bridge the gap between her Vietnamese and American experiences.

Known for constant revisions of his scripts even as he's shooting, Stone also seeks the input of many people. Of course, he doesn't always use the suggestions he receives. Sometimes, in fact, he gets offended by them. Arnon Milchan, producer of *Heaven and Earth* (along with Stone, Kline, and Alex Ho), elaborates. "For example, if you said, 'Oliver, this movie's too violent,' he would say, 'Okay, tell me exactly where. Give me a point-by-point breakdown,' knowing of course that you're totally unprepared for that. He'll say, 'Explain to me at which point in the movie it becomes too violent.' Or if you said, 'It's too long,' he would say, 'Tell me where it's too long.' And if you don't know exactly, which you probably won't, he'll say, 'You see? You don't know.' And then he goes off and makes you end up apologizing."

Milchan describes how this dynamic worked in Stone's latest film. "On *Heaven and Earth*, he said, 'Arnon, tell me what you think.' I read the script once and I loved it. I was crying on the plane when I read it, but I had some notes. I came to his house in Santa Monica and I tried telling him, 'Oliver, I didn't take any notes, really. Here's what I think from memory. I think a little more tenderness. Don't be afraid to show emotion. It's about a woman, get a little more humor.' I'm telling him this came from memory. All of a sudden he went, 'What are you doing? Trying to destroy the structure of my movie!' I said, 'Oliver, I like the movie. You asked what I think, here's what I think, and you can do whatever you want.' And I said, 'I'm leaving now.' A few weeks later he hands me this next draft and says, 'I'm curious to see what you think. Actually, a lot of what we talked about you might find in the new draft.' Not that I was right or he was wrong. What happens is, if you don't push him, he can get heavy-handed. He's a very sensitive guy."

Others, such as Stone's assistant, Azita Zendel, feel that he was very open to their suggestions. "He listened to me and even changed certain scenes because of my comments, adding my lines here and there. How many directors would give that opportunity to someone right out of school?"

Stone's favorite part of preproduction is the casting process. "This is the longest casting process for a film we've had," he said during preproduction for *Heaven and Earth*. "And we're still casting children because we have so many age changes in this movie—three different children growing throughout the movie. We had a bigger cast in *JFK* but we did it more like a bang. It was pure madness—chaos-driven insanity. This is a more elegant and refined kind of film. And it requires more detachment, more of a classic style. I've never taken so long on preparation, but I value the time I've had. I was so exhausted from *JFK* and I wanted a bit of a rest. So I took a longer summer, I spent more time with my family at our new place in Colorado, which was wonderful."

Casting had indeed been difficult. Risa Bramon García had begun in September 1991, a full year before production, with open calls held in several areas—San Francisco, Houston, Dallas, New Orleans, Washington, D.C., and Vancouver. "We infiltrated Vietnamese communities all over the country," Bramon García says. "We saw ten thousand Vietnamese people. We needed several Vietnamese actors, but primarily it was to find the girl to play Le Ly. When you work with Oliver, you're on a mission with him. So our mission was to find this girl. We'd first promote the search and then we'd process maybe two thousand people within the course of a day. We have a system where people fill out cards and then I go through the lines and meet as many people as are there. Also, I'll go through and pick out people to send to my next team, who will then audition them. And then the ones who are selected will be called back at some point to do improvisations. That way you'd see it right there. There were occasions where everybody in the auditorium would burst into applause. If they could cut it I'd send them upstairs, and if they couldn't they would get processed out. Then we'd videotape the ones who were selected to show to Oliver. And this went on in every city."

Eventually cast as Le Ly was Hiep Thi Le, a twenty-two-year-old physiology major at the University of California, was one of thousands who answered the casting call for the Northern California area. "I've never thought about becoming an actress before," she says. "My sister and a friend were going to the audition in Oakland. I wanted to go with them to town and when we got there, obviously, I couldn't sit in the car and wait all those hours, so I went in. They asked my sister to do an improv while I watched and she's really good and convinced them. So they brought us in to be videotaped and I didn't understand why I was brought in . . . I thought maybe they wanted me to improv with her, so my sister and I did an improv and I slapped her and she slapped me. It was like when you have an argument and you don't have anything to say, but you're so mad. In reality, I'd never slap her though."

Tommy Lee Jones was then cast as Le Ly's husband, Steve Butler, and Joan Chen as her mother. For Chen, the role of a Vietnamese peasant was a significant departure from the beautiful Chinese actress's best known roles as Empress Wang Jung in Bernardo Bertolucci's *The Last Emperor* and as the mysterious Josie Packard in David Lynch's cult TV series *Twin Peaks*. Dr. Haing S. Ngor, an Academy Award winner for his performance as journalist Dith Pran in *The Killing Fields*, was cast as Le Ly's father. Veteran star Debbie Reynolds was chosen for the role of Abigail Butler, Le Ly's American mother-in-law. Other key roles were to be played by Dustin Nguyen of *21 Jump Street* fame as Sau, Le Ly's brother; Conchata Ferrell of *L.A. Law* as Bernice; Vivian Wu as Madame Lien and Dale Dye as Larry.

Now that casting was nearly completed, preproduction moved swiftly ahead. There began to be speculation in Hollywood that one of the reasons Stone was doing *Heaven and Earth*, a woman's story, was to silence these critics who said he had problems directing women. "I really don't have to do something like that because I've already done pretty well without it," he responds. "I'm genuinely interested in Le Ly's story. It moves me. She went through heaven and hell to get to America and then back to Vietnam. Also, it's about the Vietnamese culture. She was a peasant in the rice fields. She had a real relationship with the land. She went to the city, became a maid, a hooker, a housewife, a Buddhist. She got involved with the Viet Cong and she became an American. It's a story of so much of that country. She touched all the bases. And she's had three husbands, three children. She's a fascinating character. It's not about whether she's a man or a woman; that's boring and it oversimplifies it."

Still, many of his friends anticipated that doing a film with a female protagonist would prompt new changes in Stone. Sergio Premoli, the Italian painter who has known Stone for over a decade, was one of them. Premoli has watched Stone go through many changes, including those brought on by success, but maintains that Stone still has the inner qualities that he first admired. "Oliver is still a very giving person. And he has a tremendous sense of loyalty. He never forgets his friend, he never forgets his enemy. If he says he will do something, he will do it. And it doesn't matter how 'important' you are, everybody's important."

Along with character qualities, there are other things that Premoli says have remained inside Stone. "One night, years ago when he used to do cocaine, it was after midnight and I was stoned like him and I went back into the bedroom and I saw the picture of the platoon hanging in his closet so you see it when you open the door. I said, 'Oliver, you look like a young Marlon Brando in *On the Waterfront*, you know, with the hair hanging down.' And Oliver looked at the picture and I still remember his eyes. He was very quiet. And it was not because of the drug, not because he was high. It was something connecting with the moment in that picture . . . I don't know. It's still important for him to tell every young American and young people around the world that this big dream broke in his mind when he was so young. Vietnam. The people who went to the Second World War, they see it as the past. The people who went to Vietnam, it is never past. It's like a permanent torture, lots of emotion . . . like they were cheated. Oliver went through the dream, and the broken dream made him stronger spiritually and gave him an incredible sense as a director, but with one empty dark space."

"We look into the face of God and forget the past."

Monk in **HEAVEN AND EARTH**

Perhaps filling that dark space is part of what drives Stone so relentlessly to higher and higher plateaus of achievement. "To me, a flying eagle represents Oliver perfectly," Premoli adds. "It is the essence of his personality and his feeling about life. Because an eagle is always alone and Oliver is always alone. And, at the same time, no mountain is too high. It's very important for Oliver to feel that people love him, but he is only afraid of one thing. Death. He's fascinated with death, but at the same time, it's his only fear—to die before he can accomplish all that he thinks he can accomplish."

And yet Stone continues to take risks, even with his life. On an August afternoon in the Ixtlan offices, he and a well-known actress were trying a "smart drug," amino acid. Instead of taking two teaspoons as advised, Stone took two tablespoons on the assumption that his threshold would be higher, as it is with most other drugs. It was a nearly fatal overdose. Azita Zendel describes what happened: "About five minutes after he took it, Chris Renna called and I tried to put him through, but Oliver wasn't picking up. I went in and found him asleep in his chair [the actress had left]. I told Chris what was happening and he advised me to let Oliver sleep it off, but check his pulse every fifteen minutes [Renna, being unaware of the dosage Stone had taken, naturally assumed he would respond normally to the drug]. We were concerned about undue publicity, and since Oliver always says I'm too protective, I didn't want to overreact."

Zendel then canceled Stone's five o'clock meeting and checked on him periodically. After about an hour she became concerned when his breathing became irregular and called 911. "His breathing became slower," she continues. "I thought perhaps we should start mouth-to-mouth respiration. Then his pulse rate started dropping, and as I heard the ambulance's siren, I prayed, 'Dear God, please don't let him die.'"

The paramedics administered an epinephrine shot to shock Stone's system into working again, and when there was no reaction, employed the defibrillator to revive him. Though he was now breathing normally, Stone still didn't wake up, so they took him to the hospital and pumped his stomach. A few hours later he became conscious. Richard Rutowski was in the emergency room. "He was half out of it and kept saying he had to go to the bathroom," Rutowski recalls. "The nurse was trying to help him. Then he became fully conscious and the first thing he noticed was that this nurse had his dick in her hands, trying to get him to pee in a cup. He's naked on the table screaming, 'I gotta pee, I gotta pee,' and then he's looking around, like, 'Where the fuck am I?' It was so weird because it was similar to another time I'd been with him, when he'd taken a fall from his horse at a full gallop at his place in Colorado and was totally out of it for about an hour. He didn't even know what movie he had finished making. He had just finished *JFK* and he thought he was still working on *The Doors*. But this time, the overdose, was even stranger, like that scene in *Seconds* with Rock Hudson."

Rutowski also saw a deeper meaning to the time in the hospital: "When he started coming out of it, he couldn't control his body, but his mind was starting to wake up. It was a like a soldier who's been shot, their body has been blown away, but their mind is still working. They're trying to gather themselves together, saying, 'I'm okay, I'm going to get up now,' but they can't get up. They can't make their body work. That's how Oliver was. To me it was symbolic. Oliver has the technical ability to make movies and he has this incredible intellect to write them, but inside it's not something that he can control. So he spends his whole life in this kind of exploration, trying to find some peace of mind and some understanding of what is happening inside him."

After another shot was administered, Stone went back to sleep. During this time Zendel and Rutowski called Elizabeth Stone in Santa Barbara and told her what had happened. A few hours later Stone woke up in a more normal state and asked to speak to Rutowski, who filled him in on the events of the past six hours. Rarely does Stone let his wild side hinder his work. He views this as an important line not to cross so it's not surprising that once he fully grasped the situation, the first thing he wanted to know was what calls or meetings he'd missed. "He paused long enough to admit that what he had done was stupid," Zendel recalls, "but when he found out he couldn't leave the hospital until morning, he wanted some books to read."

"Reading helps me relax," Stone says. "It's not like my other work, and that was all I had the strength to do. I was really out of it. It was frightening. One minute I was in my office talking to a beautiful woman and the next I was naked in the hospital with another women in white whom I'd never seen before, holding my penis and yelling at me to pee in her hand. It was strange."

Rutowski says Stone is driven to self-discovery. "When the media comment on who Oliver Stone is, they're just rehashing the myth. That's not who he is. Oliver created his own myth, like we all do. But he really knows very little about himself on one level. That's what he's trying to discover and understand. I see it in his movies as clear as a bell. One of the most powerful scenes in any of his films was in *Born* when Tom Cruise has come home drunk and he pulls his catheter out and his father's trying to console him and say, 'Look, you've got to cool out,' and Tom says, 'But Father, who's gonna ever love me? Who will ever love me?' In a way I feel that really sums up Oliver. Oliver's a loner and feels like he doesn't have a lot of friends. He has a lot of people that are around him and want something from him, but not true friends that completely accept him as he is. It's really about that 'Who will ever love me for who I really am?'"

As the October date for *Heaven and Earth* to begin filming neared, problems began to develop. Stone expects his actors to do work on their own to get into their characters long before filming or even rehearsals start. In fact, he prefers the actor to initiate the process. Sometimes this can be a problem, as it was with Joan Chen in the months before filming began on *Heaven and Earth*. Stone wanted Chen to go to Vietnam and live the peasant's life for a week in order to prepare for the role of Le Ly's mother. According to Janet Yang, a longtime friend of Chen, the problem wasn't that Chen refused, but how the issue was communicated.

"It really boiled down to Oliver wanting to hear from Joan," Yang says. "I was surprised he was being shy with her because he really likes her as a person and his reservations are from the technical side as a director. I think what he would like is for her to come and say, 'Oliver, I want this part. I'll do anything you want. I'll go to Vietnam, I'll be a peasant, I'll get calluses, I'll do whatever it takes to work with you.' And Joan actually feels that way and is willing to do all that, but first she needs Oliver to say, 'I really have confidence in you.' Some actors or actresses can start from a basis of insecurity and then rise to the challenge. Others need to work from a basis of confidence. Oliver keeps everybody disarmed, on edge and uncomfortable so they can rise to a level of confidence, but some people need to feel really good about themselves in order to do their best."

Stone says the issue with Chen was more than that. "She didn't want to blacken her teeth and it was absolutely necessary to the piece," he pointed out at the time. "There is not even a doubt that it has to be done. She has to be uglier. If anything, Joan is very aristocratic. She has to become a peasant, so I'm sending her to Vietnam to be a peasant. She'll get up at dawn, sleep on the floor and work in the ditches until she gets her feet wet and muddy. By feeling what it is to do backbreaking work all day long, she'll respect the peasants and be able to play one. I don't want her to be one of those phoney actors going out there with a hoe and pretending she's digging rice. That just won't work. I'm putting it into her contract that she has to complete the test course. The same thing for the guys. They have to complete the two-week training course to be in the movie. Unions hate those clauses and I'm criticized for being too tough, but *Platoon* wouldn't have been any good if it hadn't had a military feeling. Now practically every film like that automatically installs a training course. It's important because the military life is as far from somebody's normal experience as peasant life is to Joan or Hiep."

In the end, Joan Chen not only worked in the fields in Vietnam, but acknowledged that it helped her performance. "Oliver took us to Vietnam two months before shooting started and put us in the fields," Chen says. "And we worked like peasants. It was very good for me, for all of us, because it toughened us up. I was able to see all these people and know who I'm playing. Then right before shooting we came to Thailand to work for a week in the fields there. Believe me, it was a good workout."

Ironically, Chen was one of the first people in Hollywood to try to option Hayslip's book. Chen's agent and attorney met with Hayslip's agent, and negotiations were under way when Bob Kline came in with his link to Stone. Hayslip's agent knew the project would have a much better chance of getting made if Stone was involved, and that was the deciding factor. Now, four years later, Chen is brought in to play the mother of the character she originally wanted to portray. "So many years passed, I'd almost forgotten about it," Chen says, "but I was very happy when they asked me to be in it. When Oliver asked me if I wanted to play Le Ly's mother, I said, 'I'll play her father, I don't care, I just want to be in it.'"

Like so many of Stone's films, *Heaven and Earth* was a mission, a film he had to get made, and everyone involved felt strongly about being a part of it. "The film tells the story of the Vietnamese people," Chen goes on. "The story of the war has been told many times, but it's never about the people who were caught in between and who suffered the most. They have always been dehumanized as faceless, nameless creatures. That's why this story is an important one."

As he continued rewriting and mentally preparing for the shoot, Stone's lifestyle began reflecting the inner changes as well. "He's eating a lot of rice now and papaya," Elizabeth Stone said at the time. "And wearing a lot of khaki, light colors. It's subtle, but I can tell he's gearing up for Thailand."

Stone was also exploring the spiritual aspects of his character—getting more and more into Buddhism. Though the religion's passive nature is somewhat in conflict with Stone's natural assertiveness, he began meditating on a regular basis and even converted his backyard treehouse into a Buddhist shrine with pictures of his relatives inside. Part of it was an effort to better understand his character's mentality, but part of it was genuine exploration. At this point one could speculate that the god Stone serves is art; that appears to be what he is most committed to and the arena in which he is most conscientious. Yet he seems to be seeking more.

South Central was released in September 1992. A cautionary tale about an ex-con who tries to save the son he hardly knows from repeating his mistake of becoming part of a street gang, the Ixtlan film received some excellent reviews but did little box office.

By the middle of the month, Stone's crew was preparing for Thailand. Vietnam had been ruled out as a location because there were so many restrictions, Stone felt it wasn't worth it. He would build Le Ly's peasant village in Thailand. His vision was growing. As it had on the last several films, the more he worked on the project, the more elaborate it became. *Heaven and Earth*, with virtually no big-name salaries except Stone's, was budgeted at $33 million. "The studios set the budget as tight as they can," Stone says. "They want every film to be twenty million or less. If Arnon comes in, then he gets fifty percent. It's always a battle. The studios go over every line in the budget. My problem is I get enthused over each project and tell them I don't think it will cost a lot. And sometimes that's unrealistic."

Bob Richardson felt that the epic scope of the film would tax Stone's powers. "It seems to me that each film is becoming progressively more difficult," Richardson said in September 1992. Unlike some, Richardson wasn't worried whether Stone, who's often criticized for the predominantly male viewpoint of his films, could tell the story of *Heaven and Earth*. "It's not just a story about a woman," Richardson says. "It's also a story of war. It's a woman caught between two forces. To me, what will be interesting is to see how Oliver handles the attachment to fathers, sisters, and mothers. And then later there is this search for an understanding of good within her. And Oliver, more and more in his life, has been trying to understand what it is that truly matters."

As the start of filming neared, there were increasing rumors of a rift between Stone and his longtime producer, Alex Kitman Ho. Ho had known Stone since *Year of the Dragon* and under Stone's direction had produced every one of his films since 1986, beginning with *Platoon*. Though Stone and Ho had clashed repeatedly over the years, this time the rumors seemed stronger than before. Both men were involved in projects apart from each other; and though they joked like old friends when they were in public, but spent little time alone with each other any more. The office staff and film crew would not find out for a few months, but in fact Stone and Ho had already decided that this would be their last picture together. "People change and grow," Ho says, "and Oliver is not really the kind of person who shares well. He likes to be the only one. In the beginning, we shared in a lot of things, but more and more that's not been the way he wants to do it. He's got his own production company which Janet [Yang] is involved in, and whenever they've run into any trouble they've called me up. If he had five projects and one they couldn't sell, he'd give me the one they couldn't sell. But if I suggested for them to do this or that, then Janet would get upset. Obviously, she doesn't want anybody interfering, which I understand, but then I'm not able to be involved in other things so I'm not growing. Everything I want to do has to be done in his timing and on his terms. It isn't that I'm negating his projects or the projects we've done together. We did very, very well, and productionwise they worked very well. I got to have some creative input which I really like to do, and Oliver listened, and when he listens it's really cool. But it has come to the point where that relationship doesn't exist any more."

"There's no question that Alex was a significant part of my life for several years and several important movies," Stone responds. "I enjoyed his company. We had a ball. But he was developing projects under my banner that I had nothing to do with. While he was ostensibly working for me, he was doing his own thing without even telling me about it. I never took Miracle Pictures [Ho's own company] seriously. I just thought it was an ego thing. He had a name for a company and gave business cards out, but for him to be making separate deals while being funded by us is a violation of the code. It's just wrong."

Stone's Ixtlan offices were in Venice, while the production team under Ho's direction was housed in Santa Monica and paid for by Stone's company. Keeping two offices is unusual and costly, and Stone says he suggested combining them, but didn't because Ho liked keeping them separate. Ho maintains it was Stone's idea. "All I know is that Alex used to say he didn't want Oliver in with us," Clayton Townsend says. "We'd talk about combining the offices and he'd say, 'Don't bring him over here, he'll drive us nuts.'"

Ho maintains Stone wanted to have complete control, and that eroded their relationship over the years. "All of us who have worked with him a long time realize that we had more input in the beginning, but as Oliver has gotten stronger, his vision has gotten clearer and larger," Ho says. "You can't be a lone sailor in business and Oliver's desire to keep everything separate hurts him a lot. That's not the way I like to operate. I like everybody knowing everything, but he doesn't feel he's in control that way. I helped put a lot of this crew together. The people doing this picture and the ones who will be doing his next picture. I've known Victor Kempster for a long time. I hired him as a decorator and encouraged him to become a designer because I saw he was talented. And Clayton Townsend and I go way back, ever since he was seventeen years old. I got him his first job as a location manager, then he became production manager. It's the same with a lot of those guys. I do know how to put a team together. That's what I do well. In the old days, those were the things Oliver didn't care about or even want to know about. He just wanted to direct the movies. Now, he wants to know about everything. His use of this separating technique to keep everybody dependent on him has become more masterful, so the teamwork aspect of everything has dissipated into more of a singular effort."

"I've heard Alex has criticized Clayton's work, implying that nobody can handle me but him," Stone says. "That doesn't make sense. Alex just told me my options. He never had the power to tell me no. Clayton does the same thing. He gives me options, but at least he gives me the truth. He gives me information correctly and doesn't try to hide anything. I introduced Alex to the top levels of this business and I believe he became jealous of people like Arnon Milchan and Arnold Kopelson, Mario Kassar, Ed Pressman. He'd always say, 'Get rid of them. I could do the same thing for you,' but the fact is he couldn't. He never put any money together. He's not any sort of mogul."

Most people on one staff or the other believed that the ongoing disagreement between the two men was over credit—Ho felt he should get more and Stone didn't want to give it. "What more credit do you get?" Stone asks. "I mean, he was the producer. What else could I do? I always decided where I was going to make the movies, be it 20th Century Fox [*Wall Street*], Universal [*Born on the Fourth of July*], Carolco [*The Doors*], or Warner/Milchan [*JFK*]. I always made the deals via Bob Marshall and CAA."

Steve Pines, Stone's business manager since 1977, points out that Stone also paid the commissions on these deals. "Oliver pays the ten percent agency commission to CAA," Pines says. "Alex not only rode along on those deals, but Oliver also always gave him an additional six percent of his end as a bonus, which is probably unheard of in this business."

Ho was credited as either producer or co-producer on the seven films he did with Stone, depending upon how many other producers were involved. The issue may be less about the credits and more a result of Ho being overshadowed by Stone's notoriety. Even if he was an equal partner with Stone instead of an employee, Ho's mild-mannered persona would still tend to be overshadowed by Stone's more outrageous nature. This is not to negate Ho's formidable skills. His work on *Platoon* is often cited as an outstanding example of getting the most out of a budget. Many in the industry believe that Alex Ho has amazing talents when it comes to prepping a film and saving production money, although Stone's fast-paced, no-frills method of working also contributed in this area.

Realizing they were at an impasse, Stone told Ho he could finish out the film or not, it was up to him, but this was their last project. Ho elected to stay on through *Heaven and Earth*, but many of the remaining production chores were assigned to Clayton Townsend.

Stone was getting excited. *Heaven and Earth* would span forty years and three wars, and would be shot in multiple locations on two continents. He had made big overseas epics before, but never on an epic budget. Even *Born* had been made for less than $18 million, a shoestring when you consider all it entailed. The big budgets came later, and much of the money had been spent on special circumstances like shooting in L.A. and the emphasis on music in *The Doors* or an expensive cast and special opticals for *JFK*. This time, more of the money would go on the screen in the form of the classic Hollywood epic. The subject matter might be provocative, but the style would be lush, big old-fashioned Hollywood epic lush—a great story and magnificent panorama on the screen. Stone was ready.

On his forty-sixth birthday, September 15, 1992, Stone was reflective as he anticipated the shoot. He believes that making the Vietnam movies has been good for his psyche. "I've examined it from four different points of view," he says. "The real action and three reflections of it. And even *JFK* was a political aspect of Vietnam that was overlooked— NSAM 263 and 273." He smiles, mocking his own tendency to harp on the two memoranda that were such an important part of the case he argued in *JFK*. (National Security Action Memo 263 discusses President Kennedy's intention to pull out of Vietnam, while NSAM 273, issued four days after Kennedy's assassination, concerns President Johnson's intention to escalate the war.) Stone is well able to laugh at himself. Indeed, his sense of humor surprises people who only know him from his public image. Stone not only has a sense of humor, he even has a frivolous side, but the public rarely sees it. A person has to be pretty serious when appearing on a national television show to discuss the murder of a president, especially if they're pointing the accusing finger at the government.

Stone takes the day of his birthday off, but downplays any celebration at the office the day before or day after. One senses that, like most people his age, he doesn't really like birthdays all that much. Presents come in from all over the world: Tom Cruise sends a case of Chinaco, Stone's favorite brand of tequila, and there are countless calls from well-wishers. Stone doesn't have many close friends because he doesn't allow many people to get close. Success brings out people whose eagerness for friendship may include ulterior motives. "There's always that suspicion underneath my relationships," he admits. "But I don't think we can limit this to success because people always form relationships on a basis of need to some degree. Even when we were nobodies, we had something to offer. It might be charm, intellect, a sense of humor. All relationships have a need in them, either to love or be loved, or to be the slave or the master or something. Philosophically, money is another separation, but it isn't the only separation. I weigh the money issue and if it's obvious, I will back out. On the other hand, if I know what the person wants to use me for, I'm fine with that. To be a human being in this world you must learn to be used but accept that you also are using. I get twenty-five letters a day asking me for money. I constantly get calls from people who want money. That's not to say love is not blind, because it is, but whether you can love a friend is a significant question. Because how do you prove your friendships? There's always a test point. And long ago I banged up against that wall and found that I was wanting in many ways in my friendships because I could not deliver and I did not care to deliver. So I accepted the fact that I would probably not be the most friendship-oriented human being. I think that I have a lone wolfism very deep in me. I have close friends and I've always had a series of friends, a circle, that's floated through time, and I felt very fond of these people, very close to them at the time. But very few of them carried on, stayed with me through levels of time, out of loss of interest—them in me and me in them and/or a change in place or circumstance. Curiosity moves us on."

Stone is subdued, even mellow as he anticipates Thailand, now only a few weeks away. This is a man who lives to work, only happy when accomplishing something and happiest when accomplishing something extremely difficult. There is no question that Stone has a fear of death, as his friends have indicated, but he may have an even greater fear of getting stale. Elizabeth Stone confirms this.

"He's very sensitive to the idea of losing his edge. He talks about directors who made a great film or two early in their career and then made a lot of schlock because they've gotten spoiled by the yes men around them and lost their touch. They became formula. He's very sensitive about becoming mediocre. That's why he wants to develop an original piece after *Heaven and Earth*, something that's not a true story. He could've done Harvey Milk's story this time, which would've been easier because it didn't require going to Asia and trying to convince a studio to make a movie about a Vietnamese woman. But then he said, 'I'd be going from one assassination movie to another, and what I need is to stretch my brain. I need to get into a romance, I need to get into Asia.' Over the last few years he's noticed that he is getting his own formula down. Directing's actually become easier for him. During *JFK*, he said, 'I've got it down . . . now I have to be careful.' His biggest fear is all of a sudden sitting down at the paper and having nothing to say."

Usually, worrying about making such a mistake is enough to prevent it, and Elizabeth, like most who know Stone well, doesn't think he could make a formula picture if he tried. "Oliver is a message director. I don't see him ever doing a film for the heck of it. He's written comedies, he's written science fiction, but he's never been that interested in making them. He wrote something based on a book that came out in the sixties called *The Demolished Man*. It's a great story, but it sits on the shelf at Universal or somewhere and I said to him, why don't you make that? Or he wrote *Tom Mix & Pancho Villa*. He's got all these projects sitting on shelves that are wonderful scripts, but just aren't dear to his heart. They don't communicate a message he feels strongly about. He says, 'Maybe I'll do them when I'm older and bored and just want to work for the exercise.'"

In October, as Stone prepared to leave for Thailand, Elizabeth admitted that she did not share his enthusiasm. "People think it's easy once you've succeeded, but the films are always hard. It's hard to get the studios to give you the money. They always give you some kind of hassle. The conditions are hard. There's always sickness, long hours, hassles with personalities, and lots of pressure to get it done under budget and on time. All those things are very straining. But on top of all this is the mental strain that goes into how can I make this scene interesting? Oliver tends to be a rather broadstroke painter when he writes and when he shoots. He'll shoot an extra hour, and then comes the painful process of editing it down. It's not easy. And this time I just can't go with him. I do as much as I can. My plate is full between the kids and the houses and keeping up with him when he's around, and that's it. My family is more important to me than anything."

Filming began in and around Phang-Nga on the relatively less populated Malay Peninsula in Southern Thailand. A spectacular bay forty-seven miles north of the city of Phuket, Phang-Nga features towering limestone formations that rise dramatically out of the Andaman Sea. There, production designer Victor Kempster and supervising art director Alan Tomkins (*Lawrence of Arabia*) created the village of Ky La. After scouting the Philippines, Malaysia, and the Chiang Mai and Chiang Rai areas in Northern Thailand, Phang-Nga was selected because it bore a remarkable resemblance to the Marble Mountains which loom over Ky

La. The film company then irrigated and planted 150 acres of rice paddies. Kempster and Tomkins and their crews constructed the village from the ground up, making the buildings out of concrete with brick and tile roofs, rather than the thatched huts usually seen in Vietnam films. "There are regional architectural differences in Vietnam," producer Alex Ho says. "In Central Vietnam, those familiar thatched bamboo huts just don't exist."

Filming began with the village as it was when Phung Thi Le Ly was born in 1949. In many ways, the simple life of the village is the heart of *Heaven and Earth*. When Le Ly Hayslip first saw the set, she was shocked at how similar it was to the village she remembered. "People ask me what Vietnam was like before the war. It was this. Lots of rice paddies, water buffalo with a little boy or little girl riding on them, and farmers working in the field. That is Vietnam. Not the image of Saigon or Danang."

Americans tend to dehumanize Vietnam because of the pain they associate with it and because of its alien culture, but one of the clear messages of Stone's film and Hayslip's first book is that people everywhere are the same. Vietnamese fathers laugh and joke and play with their children the way American fathers do. *Heaven and Earth* breaks down the symbols that we have chosen for Vietnam and replaces them with the reality of a simple people whose first love was for family and the land.

The first three weeks of shooting were very difficult due to sudden weather changes, especially the second week, which the crew labeled "Hell Week." "We had a lot of rain, a lot of heat, and a lot of problems in the crew," Stone recalls. "We lost several key people just to weather and injury, including Chris Centrella, our key grip, to a broken collarbone in a motorcycle accident. Part of the village we built was washed out by the rains. For me there was also the pressure of getting thirty-two million bucks and making a film with nobody in it. Tommy Lee was considered a supporting actor at that point in time. There's a lot of pressure that way. Was I being indulgent? All those questions come to mind. Did I have the story worth telling? Did I have the goods to deliver?"

Although he wanted to begin earlier, Stone had delayed shooting until October in the hopes of missing the tail end of the monsoon season, but apparently he hadn't delayed it long enough, as torrential rains pounded cast and crew on a daily basis the first week. Consequently, Stone set an even faster tempo than usual and by the end of the second week the crew was clicking in and things were rolling.

An important crew addition was editor David Brenner; Stone set him up in his own cutting room at his hotel so they could edit each evening. Brenner, long a part of the Stone fold, had left after *The Doors*. "David's wife was having their first child and he decided to take a bit of time off and then cut another picture, *Night in the City*," post production supervisor Bill Brown says. "It was interesting for me to talk to him about his non-Oliver experience. Sometimes, we take for granted how special Oliver's films are. And then, when you work on something that's more mainstream Hollywood . . . I remember him calling and saying, 'Gosh, I miss it.' It's not just the subject matter. That has a lot to do with it, but it's also the challenge of it. The hardest thing you can do is an Oliver Stone film, so when you go away and do something else, you're not working nearly as hard, but there's something missing, like this magic spark that just isn't there. People come back and work for Oliver because they get a sense of purpose, like they're accomplishing something."

Stone had been concerned about the loss of another key crew member, assistant director Joe Reidy, who had been with him through four films but had opted for staying home with his new baby instead of signing on for Thailand. But new AD Herb Gains was proving to be an able replacement. "He relies on his assistant director for the organization," Gains says, "and he's so unique in his style and unpredictable it makes being an AD for him a tremendous challenge. He approaches things strictly from the story level, so it's important for him to keep the shooting schedule in story order, which isn't always efficient. But whatever time you lose by shooting in sequence, he makes up for by working so hard and fast. It causes chaos at times but he seems to thrive on it. He demands staying on schedule. It never lets up. It's a three-ring circus."

Heaven and Earth, like every film, had its own unique logistical problems, some of which centered on the recreation of Le Ly's village. "The Vietnamese village set was huge," Gains goes on. "It felt like it was about the size of Central Park. The good news was that we didn't have a lot of locations. The bad news was that the location was so big that it was hard just to keep track of people and difficult to move people around in that environment. We were feeding between five hundred and seven hundred people a day, and that was without extras. It wasn't just that the set was so immense, it was because we had to maintain its look. We had to make sure that people didn't walk through the rice paddies because we wanted it to look beautiful for some later shots."

Just as the rice crop was tremendously important to the Vietnamese farmers, Stone tried to make it a significant part of the film. "Everything was the rice," Le Ly says. "The rice was our food. When the troops walked into the village, we could see right away that they didn't know anything. They couldn't tell the difference between the rice and the grass. When the Americans came with the helicopter landings, they destroyed everything that we worked so hard for. It was very painful for me the way they wasted things . . . especially the rice. The rice is God's thing. He gave it to us to eat."

The most difficult scene was shot on the last night of the village schedule. It depicts Le Ly being taken away and raped by two Viet Cong who had previously been her friends. "It was the hardest scene for me emotionally," Hiep Thi Le says. "It took me a whole week to recover. I had nightmares."

Since this was early in the filming, some thought it might have been better to wait until Hiep Thi Le had grown more comfortable with her role. Stone disagreed. "Each movie is a journey and each scene is a step along the way," he says. "The characters change as the movie goes on. Le Ly was raped early, so Hiep had to be. It would have been rough no matter when we did it, so it was better to get it over with. We discussed it a lot before, I told her we're going to build prosthetic breasts, etc., and she understood. But after the scene she was in some sort of shock for a couple of days and her work was impaired. But in some ways whatever she did in subsequent scenes was better for having gone through this one."

After the first village segment was filmed, the crew moved on to the island of Phuket, where some of the more urban scenes were shot representing Le Ly's time in Saigon and Danang. Stone's relationship with his crew is generally one of authority and distance, but he's not above joking and kidding around with them when the mood strikes him. During the first of the Phuket scenes he grabbed camera assistant Elizabeth Carr and dunked the end of her ponytail in a fishpond. Nowhere is this working closeness more prevalent than in Stone's relationship with Bob Richardson. There is an ongoing banter which seems to consistently revitalize both men during the strain of a shoot. Stone will suddenly question Richardson as to why he has to re-light so often and Richardson will needle back that the cost of the film is getting out of control. It's almost a running joke. Both are kidding and yet both are serious.

Working with so many newcomers was tough. Stone tried desperately to maintain the mood, starting with rehearsals each day and closing the set whenever he felt he needed to, for example during the scene where Anh, the master of the house (played by Long Ngu-yen), makes love to Le Ly, his servant girl. The scene was hard, and at one point Stone enclosed himself in black cloth screens (scrims) positioned around his monitor to seal him off from everything but what was being seen through the camera. "I was trying to recapture the vision I originally had for the scene," he explains. "There's something important about even the small connecting scenes, and the focus still has to be there. Every scene, you push until finally you can't stand it any more. Like Godard said, 'Finish, no matter what. Finish.'"

For Joan Chen, the film was becoming more rewarding all the time. Chen says she feels Stone has been unfairly labeled as having problems handling actresses: "It's because he's very straightforward. He can say things that might hurt some people's feelings. Some of that comes from there being so many amateur actors. One time I told one of them, 'If you have a mark, stay on that mark.' And then Oliver shouted at me, 'Don't direct her.' He was very frustrated because we never hit any marks right and I was just trying to help. So I was a little bit scared and hurt, but it didn't matter. I have learned from Oliver that a person can be forgiven many times for his shortcomings because of his other unique qualities. He's an artist with a greater capacity for feelings than most. He's fearless and straightforward and he makes you do better than you have ever done before. That's what counts for me."

Chen, who starred in Bertolucci's *The Last Emperor*, compares the two directors: "Oliver is very energetic. He'll run ahead with things. Bernardo kind of finds what he wants along the way. But both of them share a sense of poetry. That's what's nice about Oliver. Though he can be very strong and you feel like he's hitting you over the head with what he wants to convey, he doesn't lose his sense of poetry. In all his movies, and especially in this script, he has a sense of poetry."

Chen says playing the role of a Vietnam peasant woman was difficult, but also a good experience. "It was very challenging. And difficult, because I have never been this old and ugly in any other project. It's actually a life lesson for me. I never knew how I communicated without being flirtatious or without knowing the fact that I'm pretty. When that was taken away, I felt very handicapped. That was very challenging."

Her only criticism is almost a backward compliment: "Oliver's crew is very dedicated, almost too dedicated. It's almost a dictatorship in that nobody dares to ask questions. Sometimes they bring actors in unnecessarily early because they don't dare not have them there for him. The crew is afraid of him in a way."

Stone leads his crew the way a general would an army and unequivocal following of orders is something he insists upon, although he does frequently ask for input. Similiarly, while he is known for pushing actors to the limit, Stone can be very gentle when he needs to be. A great director is a master manipulator, and that means learning to deal with each individual slightly differently. Ultimately, Stone's style is push—push with business partners, push with crew, push with actors—but there's an infinite variety of ways he pushes. Sometimes he even pushes by backing off. Mike Menchel, Stone's agent, who visited the set in Thailand, agrees: "Oliver is very shrewd, very calculated, and a wonderful negotiator. He knows all the different sides of getting what he wants. And he knows how to finesse it. He knows how to compliment you and how to insult you. He knows when it's time to invite you over to his house and when it's time for him to come over to your house. He knows the difference between the two. He knows all of it and he uses all of it."

Menchel, now even more active in Stone's career since Paula Wagner left CAA to form a production company with Tom Cruise, admits that working with Stone is a challenge. "He does not like to be around passive people," Menchel says. "If you're not challenged or if you're not thinking, if you're not excited or if you're not asking why, then you're not in Oliver's world. He'll only work you as hard as he works himself. He figures if you're gonna get on his train, you've gotta stoke the coal. You've gotta be able to keep up with him. If not, go ride somebody else's train. It's a challenge. There's no doubt about it, but it's exciting."

Also visiting Stone in Phuket was Clive Ng, a young Malaysian entrepreneur with whom Stone had formed a partnership to invest in media companies with special emphasis on cable and satellite opportunities in Europe and the Asian market. "Oliver's the only white man I know who really is at ease in Asia," Ng says. "He fits in here. I think it's because he allows the culture to be what it is without trying to decide what is right or wrong. He has an incredible ability to assimilate another culture. The first time we went to Hong Kong together, he wanted to meet the bankers, and all day we ran around the city meeting with different bankers. He would ask them questions about how they did things and rather than judging it, like most people, he'd just take it all in. By the end of the day he really understood that element of the culture and how it applied to business. It was amazing."

Meanwhile, back in the States, the November 1992 issue of *Elle* magazine featured an interview with Stone entitled "When Elle meets Ollie." The idea, which came from Stone's former assistant Kristina Hare, now the West Coast editor at the magazine, was for supermodel Elle Macpherson to have lunch with Stone and write about the meeting. The article had a full-page picture of Stone laughing his famous grin and some small shots of Stone and Macpherson together, including two where he seemed to be nuzzling her neck. The subtitle read: "Or How Elle Macpherson and Oliver Stone Had a Heart-to-Heart Date."

Though the obvious thrust of the piece was all in fun, sexual innuendo was heavily applied. The caption on the second page read, "Oliver Stone makes sexy small talk with Elle." After the first interview, Macpherson said Stone looked "yummy and vulnerable." And though the article concluded that Stone "was not so much a troublemaker as someone whom trouble seeks out," and Macpherson said he was "a charming man with a little boy's desire to please and overall he was a perfect gentleman," it also included some heavily loaded questions. When Macpherson asked Stone if he thought men were more promiscuous than women, he answered: "Not all men, but I think most men. It's a classical approach. It's the way God made it. It's a spirit thing that drives men towards curiosity, towards excitement, towards adventure. It's in Homer's *Odyssey*. And I find that it is a recurring cycle in my life. One is always venturing out to new islands. Every woman, in a sense, is an island, has her own mystery. There is a raging desire to know."

Elizabeth Stone was greatly bothered by the article. She had long been telling herself that she had nothing to worry about. She told herself that when, at the wrap party for *The Doors*, a beautiful young girl suddenly grabbed Oliver and kissed him long and passionately and he didn't make a move to pull away. She told herself that last April, when Oliver was quoted as telling someone from *US* magazine, "Why are you wearing that—I can't see your breasts." She'd tried to shrug it all away and told herself that since the *Wall Street* incidents, there had been no problem. But something about the *Elle* article pushed her over the edge of doubt.

"It just really bothered me," Elizabeth says. "So, I went into his office and found his diary. Then I knew. He'd been lying to me for years. And I think that finally made him a little crazy. I think that a lot of his anger toward me came out of that. That was the big monkey on his back. I think he wanted to be caught."

By now, the journal Oliver Stone had been keeping since he returned from Vietnam ran to some twenty-five volumes. He had written in it almost daily with the exception of a few years in the late seventies and early eighties when his drug use was at its peak, and it provides an extensive and detailed account of his life. It includes insights on the artistic process, philosophical theorizing, hopes, fears, and dreams. The journals also catalogue Stone's thoughts during the writing and directing of his films, and his daily experiences, including business meetings and personal relationships. Most of the volumes are stored away, but a few remained in his office at home.

Stone says the journals were kept in a private place and that he never anticipated that his wife would read them without his permission, as she had never done so in twelve years of marriage. Elizabeth maintains that the diary was left where she could find it and that this is an indication that Stone wanted to be found out. What is not disputed by either party is that the journals describe scores of affairs in explicit detail. According to Elizabeth, the affairs began when Stone was out of town for long periods of time because he couldn't stand being alone.

After reading the journal, Elizabeth sent a blistering letter to Thailand, telling Stone what she had discovered and that she was filing for divorce. The next week she called him. "He was cold and distant," Elizabeth remembers. "He said, 'I'm not a man who should ever be married.'"

"I was faithful with Elizabeth for several years," Stone says. "I was monogamous with her for quite a period of time. I felt very strongly in love with Elizabeth, very much in love. I thought she was my mate for life. I tried to be faithful, but then we drifted apart. In the beginning I was pretty mad, crazy in a lot of ways, and Liz would help me. She would listen to me and tell me I was okay. Then after Sean was born I thought she was being too soft on him, too easy, I thought. But then I realized that she was doing the same thing with him that she'd done with me."

Stone is quick to add that he doesn't condone his dishonesty. "I'm not saying it's right because it often necessitated lies," he says. "Much pain was prevented, much happiness was kept, and many good years were had. But then you have to live with your lie. My mother was fond of the white lie in her life. She was a great prevaricator. She always told me the white lie was acceptable, and my father had the same attitude. He thought that if you told the truth, you could get into trouble. I used to say pretty outrageous things when I was little, and he would say, 'You know, you're going to get into trouble some day if you keep trying to tell the truth.' It's too bad he didn't live to see *JFK*. But I lied to keep Elizabeth from being hurt and I'm glad that's over."

"It wasn't a lie exactly. . . . It was a white lie . . . a good kind of lie."
Steve Butler in **HEAVEN AND EARTH**

Though Stone feels most of the problems between him and Elizabeth had to do with them growing in different directions, he also recognizes that they failed to cope well with the changes their marriage went through. "There were a lot of upheavals. Elizabeth was felled by colitis, which was a problem off and on from *Platoon*. She went in and out several times. Then there were the miscarriages . . . several of them, one of them at six months. That was very hard. On her and on me. I felt by having a second child it would take the pressure off all of us—the family knot was tight. But we kept losing the babies. And she gained weight. And she wasn't interested in anything I was interested in. We had no life together any more. I felt she cared about the family, but not about me."

For the next few weeks in Thailand, Stone proceeded as if nothing had happened, and did not tell anyone about the breakup except for Richard Rutowski and Steve Pines, his close friend and business manager for over a decade. He had kept his rigid six-day-a-week shooting schedule, preparing for the following week in detail on Sundays, his day off.

They were still filming in Phuket, concentrating on scenes that took place in a small downtown apartment, representing Le Ly's sister Kim's place in Danang. Preparations were elaborate even down to the last-minute touches—as Stone assumed his position, wedged behind the monitor in a cramped corner of the room, Victor Kempster straightened pictures on the wall, Bob Richardson draped a towel over a chair, and stand-by painter Bill Darrow sprayed soapy water on the curtains to give them a worn, older look.

"Oliver is incredibly hands-on," says co-producer Clayton Townsend. "And he really is more understanding of what people do on a movie and what the various departments are up to than most directors. When there's a problem, he doesn't just take a break like most directors would. He'll call me over and ask what the problem is, and when I explain it to him, he'll want to get into it and talk to the specific person who has to deal with it. Then he'll stand there and watch while they fix it, like if a problem with a light takes too long, he'll stand there and watch it. He's very hands-on—sometimes more than I would necessarily like, but he's not changing."

Dr. Haing S. Ngor's role was pivotal in *Heaven and Earth*, for it was through his loss that many would understand the real tragedy of the people of Vietnam. To play Le Ly's father, he had to sit in makeup for two hours and forty-five minutes each morning. The makeup job was amazing, but became hot and sticky in the afternoon heat, causing him to get irritable over retakes. Haing Ngor is an outspoken critic of the Communist regimes in Southeast Asia, having been forced to work as a slave laborer, imprisoned and tortured under the Khmer Rouge. He lost much of his family, including his wife and child, during that period. Consequently, he was glad to be a part of the film because he felt it had an important message. "This movie has a lot of opportunities," Ngor says. "It tells more about the war in Southeast Asia than we usually see. When I was living under the Communist regime, it was a similar experience."

After the scenes at the apartment were completed, Stone moved on to film a large scene of Le Ly selling contraband to soldiers on the streets of Saigon—a logistical monster involving troop trucks, jeeps, motorcycles, rickshaws, countless extras, and a flock of geese. Though Stone shoots a lot of film, he actually shoots less takes than most directors. "Most conventional directors will do a master shot and coverage,"

Herb Gains explains. "Oliver often combines a sequence into one fluid, liquid shot. It's almost as if every shot is a master. Now, he does shoot more scenes. Oliver comes strictly from an artist's mentality. He will not only shoot everything in the script, but throughout the process of shooting he is always adding and changing scenes, adding characters to places you wouldn't think they would be."

The following week's schedule included just such a scene. "For example," Gains continues, "there's a scene where Le Ly is being tortured and a CIA guy, a State Department type, is standing there observing. We shot the scene, and then, about a week later, Oliver comes up to me and says, 'In the shot where Le Ly's sister comes out of the bar because her father's arrived, I want the CIA guy that was in the torture scene in that bar. I want to further establish him there.' Now, this is a detail that was never in the script and it's so subtle, I never would have put it together. My initial reaction was, it doesn't make sense to have that here. But he likes to bookend things, in very subtle ways. I've never seen any other director approach it that way."

This kind of skill is related to Stone's ability to envision his films. He sees them so clearly in his mind that they become much more literary and detailed during the shooting process than the original script. In this example, we're talking about a character who never has any lines and appears only briefly in the background of one scene, and yet Stone wants to establish him further. Few people who see the film will even catch this detail, much less connect it; but for Stone, it's important.

Stone describes how a script evolves for him during the filming: "In the beginning, it's a bit nervous and I want to get the basics down, but as the film goes along, if things are going well, I relax and allow for more experimentation. The script is crucial to me, but there's a texture of flesh that comes in on the actors with a production. It's like having a baby. The fetus is the script. But it comes out and grows. The baby changes shape. It's very much yours, but the look is a little bit different than you originally imagined."

Many directors, especially writer/directors, stick much closer to the script. "Crew members have told me about directors that come in and know exactly what they want," Stone says. "They build a house and they won't deviate. I'm amazed by that. It seems all human beings are control freaks of some kind or another."

The torture scenes in the Vietnamese prison are only one of many aspects of the war that are shown. Since the film spans so much time in Vietnamese history, it reflects the country's occupation by several different armies, a nightmare for technical adviser Dale Dye. "This was a genuine challenge," he admits. "I had to dress, train, and stage the French Foreign Legion, Arbon Rangers, Arbon Airborne, American Marines, American Army, and God knows what else. The fascinating thing was to train the other side. We got a super bunch of youngsters and made a guerrilla unit out of them. After we had them for four or five days, they were really becoming sharp. When we shot, we had mist and rain and the scene called for the VC to melt out of the bush. You see them as specters literally just melting out of the background. When we did it, I was standing next to Oliver. Seeing those guys come through the mist, wearing the turtle baskets with the camouflage all over them so they can bend over and hide from air patrols, was spooky. The hair stood up on the back of our arms."

After the prison and bar scenes, the crew headed back to the village. It was around this time that Stone called Elizabeth and told her he wanted a reconciliation. He asked her and Sean to come to Thailand so they could work it out. "He called and said he wanted to keep our marriage together," Elizabeth recalls. "That we'd put too much time in to let it fall apart now. He said he'd stop screwing around and we could both go see a therapist. That he'd do whatever we had to do to make it work. I was so glad he called. After I got over the initial shock of finding out he'd been playing around, I just couldn't accept that our marriage was at an end. I love this man, I know this man, and I care."

Elizabeth and Sean arrived in Thailand three days later, and the Stones had a joyous family reunion. They agreed to try to work things out. "I wasn't sure we could make things work because we've changed so much, but separation is not an easy thing," Stone says. "I didn't want to lose my family, but I didn't want things to go on as they were, either. I didn't want to lie to Elizabeth any more."

For the rest of the week, filming took place on the village set. The production would spend only two more weeks in the Phang-Nga/Phuket region and then move on to film more city scenes in Bangkok. Obviously, the transportation requirements were extensive. Moving a large cast and crew back and forth from half a dozen hotels and to several locations required detailed organization and many man-hours. Transportation coordinator Joel Marrow and transportation captain Randy Cantor both worked with Stone on *The Doors* and the Washington, D.C., segment of *JFK* before *Heaven and Earth*. They say Stone is significantly different to work for compared to other directors. In one sense, he is the most demanding of them all. "As far as the work goes, he wants you to be totally committed to the film," Marrow says. "And not just in your job, in your attitude as well."

"Yeah," Cantor agrees. "During *The Doors*, he kept asking if we thought people were treating it like just another film. He was leery that L.A. crews would have a different kind of attitude, a doing-it-for-the-job attitude, and not really be committed. But actually, people were into it. He *makes* you get into it. You can't work on an Oliver Stone film and not wind up being enthusiastic for the project."

According to Marrow, Stone also stands out because his demands are always about the film and not his own personal comfort. "I had one guy, a director whose name I won't mention, who I must have had a half dozen meetings with just on what he wanted in his trailer. Just on his personal comforts. Oliver doesn't care about that stuff. He wants the money to go on the screen. As long as he's got a place to go to get away and relax, that's fine. His trailer is a basic one-room job. He's the most demanding all right, but it's all about the project, not about personal luxury."

The following week, Tommy Lee Jones arrived for his scenes as Steve Butler, the compassionate but tormented soldier who marries Le Ly and takes her to America. This was Jones's second film for Stone, whom he heartily endorses. "There are four things that I really like about working with Oliver," Jones says. "First, he's always thoroughly prepared. That's the most important thing. Second, he inspires people to do their best work. The people that you are lucky enough to work with when you work for Oliver have been chosen very well. And you get the feeling that they're just desperately afraid that they're going to be merely good. Everybody goes for the home run or the TD on every single play. So, one, he's prepared; and two, you work with good people. Three, the screenplays are always wonderful. They get better and better. I think the screenplay for *Heaven and Earth* can stand on its own as epic poetry. That's the third plus. The fourth thing—well, I'm not going to tell you what the fourth thing is."

The somewhat cryptic answer is not unusual for Jones, whose off-stage persona often reflects his powerful but slightly eccentric screen characterizations. Stone had been concerned about the chemistry between Tommy Lee Jones and Hiep Thi Le. Would her natural shyness show too much on the screen, or could he turn it into an interesting and alluring quality, making the scenes more believable rather than less? Not only did Hiep rise to the occasion, but she was actually better in the scenes with Jones, drawing well off his considerable skills.

On a break, Rob Carlson, the assistant cameraman, took photos of the Thai children clustered around one of the stand-by Panavision cameras, as the crew set up for the scene when Steve Butler comes to the apartment with gifts for Le Ly and then proposes to her. Jones is especially impressed with Stone's film crew. "People are not only committed to what the movie's saying but also to being at the top of their profession. So, you find that things stay in focus. Lenses show up and get installed without a problem. Lights go up and are focused beautifully and with no undue delays. You don't have a lot of backbiting. I like Oliver's crew. I was glad just to have a part in *JFK*. It was really an honor that he would think of me as being able to play that part. I felt the same way about the role I play in *Heaven and Earth*."

The standard answer given by crew members whenever someone mentions how fast they are is always along these lines: "Well, you got to be that way with Oliver to keep up the pace." This really becomes clear when you watch them work. With Stone, it's never a job, it's a passion, a need to do the film, and he expects it to be a need for grip Dean Eilertson, camera assistant Keith Smith, electrician Kim Kono, or anyone else in the crew. And it is. Stone only uses people who are good at what they do because they care about what they do.

The crew finished out November with city scenes shot in Phuket of Steve and Le Ly, and Stone worked his son into a scene as an American schoolboy being led through the streets of Saigon by a priest (Chris Renna). It was Sean's sixth film appearance.

On December 5, the production broke for the Thai holiday honoring the king's birthday, but worked on Sunday to make up for it. That evening the trucks were loaded and traveled to Bangkok, where more city sequences were shot, including one that was the largest and most complicated scene in the film, panic during an attack on Saigon. Herb Gains describes the scouting process for this scene: "We were talking about how many people we should have, four or five thousand, or could we get away with a thousand, talking about the shot, etc. In the middle of all this, Oliver says, 'Let's do this, this, and this—and get me a tiger.' And everybody just stops dead in their tracks. A tiger? Most of us think he's just kidding, but I've learned that every time Oliver has an idea, you'll see him write it down in his script. I know when I see him write something down in his script that it's going to come up again. The tiger goes down in my notes, and everyone's kind of laughing about it, figuring that's the last we'll hear of it. So after we've been shooting for eight or nine weeks, we start preparing Bangkok, and now it's almost four months since we scouted for the scene. On Monday morning, Oliver comes to the set with the notes for the upcoming week, and he says, 'Who's getting the tiger?' And we all looked at each other, like, 'Uh-oh.' Sure enough, he wanted a tiger, and he staged a whole little scene involving the tiger and troops in the middle of this evacuation scene. It was amazing, and it worked."

The eventual scene was so involved that the crew had to close down the palace streets in Bangkok; not an easy task, and one that caused international headlines when it was falsely assumed by locals that so many military vehicles in the streets on a Sunday meant that a coup was taking place. The U.S. press reported that "Oliver Stone Stages Coup d'Etat in Bangkok."

A week later the production was finished in Thailand and the crew was ready to return to America. The schedule called for the crew to prep the L.A. scenes from December 15 to 24, then break for Christmas and the New Year, with shooting in Los Angeles to commence on January 6. Despite the grueling schedule of their eight weeks in Thailand, Stone actually seemed reluctant to go. Herb Gains remembers: "We got the last shot in the village and there was a real sense of relief, but Oliver seemed very emotional. I walked to the car with him and he started reminiscing about how a year ago he was walking through these fields and there was nothing here and how it all materialized into a village and now into a film. And now we were walking away. I was very moved by it. Suddenly, he was this person who was sad with almost a sense of loss because he put so much effort and so much of his heart and life into it. It was like there was a chapter coming to a close. I think it hit all of us, but it emanates from the top and it hit him the hardest. He may not like people knowing that, but it was very touching to me."

For Stone, the filming of *Heaven and Earth* included a significant process of self-discovery. "I think part of my motivation for making the film was getting back in touch with the land," he admits. "When people ask me why I did the movie, I say because it's from the victim's point of view. But it's also my interest in the land of Vietnam. When I was in the Army, we controlled it, we shot it up. I got to know the land, but I still didn't understand it. When I went back with Le Ly, she enabled me to understand the agricultural cycle. I shot the whole sequence of rice harvesting and transplantation. I had to cut it out of the film because it was just like a documentary, but it didn't matter that I cut it out. I got to shoot it. And by shooting it, I began to understand the power of the land. It's something that's been an undercurrent in my life. When I was a kid in France, we worked on farms and picked potatoes. Later, in Long Island, I owned an old potato barn. And now in Colorado, I'm making an effort again to get back in touch with the land. I feel it's something going on in me that is beyond me. I keep coming back to these situations, and *Heaven and Earth* triggered another appreciation of an agricultural cycle in my life."

During the break, the Stones spent a week in Chiang Rai (Thailand) before returning to the States. Oliver and Elizabeth agreed to start seeing a marriage counselor when the film was over in February. On January 6, 1993, shooting renewed, with L.A. locations substituting for San Diego in the scenes depicting Le Ly's arrival in America and meeting her in-laws. As Le Ly tries to cope with supermarkets, modern appliances, and prejudice in America, she starts to realize that freedom is a relative thing. Though the film begins with Le Ly's birth, the story actually picks up with Hiep Thi Le in the role when she is thirteen years old and continues until she is nearly forty. These later scenes had always been the ones Hiep was most concerned about playing. "The hardest part for me is playing Le Ly when it's the eighties," she said. "The makeup makes me look older, but it's speaking correctly, talking as if I'm wise, with confidence and wisdom. I want to deliver my lines and not sound phony or preachy."

Filming in L.A. continued throughout January. The heart of these scenes depicted how, though "free" in America, Le Ly still had to deal with discrimination from the world around her and abuse from her husband, the tormented Steve Butler. Once again, Le Ly's love of family and the spiritual attitudes that her father taught her in Vietnam enable her to survive the ordeal. She learns new skills to help her function in this new society and again achieves independence. Eventually, she triumphs in

America. But Le Ly's real victory is a spiritual one, which occurs when she is able to reconcile the great suffering she has endured with the good things life has to offer. The film ends with her returning to Vietnam, reunited not only with her family but "returning to the spirit of her father"—reaffirming the truths and the bonds of the heart she learned so long ago in Ky La.

In the press there was already talk of "yet another Oliver Stone Vietnam film" and many references to "Stone's Vietnam Trilogy." The truth was that Stone didn't look at it that way. Arnon Milchan agrees. "People say, why does he keep doing Vietnam movies? We are all impacted by something. He has a lot of aborted growths from Vietnam. That's as good as drawing your growths from Kansas or anywhere else. Nothing wrong with it. After all, he did not do the same movie three times. *Platoon, Born on the Fourth of July*, and *Heaven and Earth* are all different movies. They just happen to take place in a similar, interesting background."

At his house in Telluride in August 1993, Stone looked back on making the film: "It was a great experience for me. It got me out of the country to Asia to do scouting at a key time when the *JFK* furor was first becoming insane. And it put me on a whole other journey. It was very detached and calm, and with Le Ly's help I was able to step outside some of the angers that I felt. . . . *JFK* could've dragged me into a pit of bitterness. You can defend and defend and defend and then you start to go down. I pulled away deliberately."

As filming wrapped, Dr. Haing Ngor expressed the truth at the heart of *Heaven and Earth*. "What is the difference between American people and Vietnamese or Cambodians? Maybe my language is different, my culture, my skin is different than yours, but if you cut your hand and you see the blood, it is the same color as my blood. We are the same world! So this movie is very good because it will show the world, especially those too lazy to read, here is a picture of the real life during that time."

And in some respects, that is what Oliver Stone does best: he takes the things that people don't want to know about and tells them in a way that is entertaining, in a way they can accept. He makes films for the common people.

Le Ly Hayslip hopes that her story will change the way the American people think about Vietnam. "They don't see that the people who live in the land know nothing but the land and their ancestors. We talk about freedom in the United States. The freedom of speech, freedom to vote, freedom of religion. In Vietnam before the war, the Vietnamese had freedom. Freedom to us was to live on the land with one little house. To be born in the house and die in the house. Freedom for us was not the freedom to vote because we didn't know how to read or write or what the issues were about. Freedom was to walk from city to city and only have to be scared of the dogs. To move from one village to another and cut down a bamboo tree and build a hut. Everything you want right there. Make a living from the rice paddy and have drinking water from a spring and a well. And nobody to hurt you or make you fight. That is freedom."

When one looks at this gentle woman, it is hard to conceive of her surviving such incredible trials, but Hayslip dismisses her courageousness. "I didn't know any other way is all," she says. "It was my only choice. I don't think it's easy to die. Sometimes people say it's easy, but I don't think it is. All things happen for a reason. People look at me and say, 'Oh, you went through so much pain,' because that's what we tend to talk about. We don't talk about my water buffalo that had two babies, we don't talk about my chicken that laid an egg which I stole to sell and buy candy. Or all the fish I caught in a pond. Those were good things. I had to write about rape and torture, the bad things that happened, so people would understand. But there were many good things. Life is heaven and earth."

Making the film helped Oliver Stone better understand what really happened in Vietnam. "A few years ago I visited the site of Dau Tieng in Vietnam," he recalls. "It's where I was stationed for a while in 1967. I was looking for our old airstrip, and then I realized I was standing on it and I couldn't even see it. It was all covered with weeds. I walked down the road and I found a helmet with a bullet hole in it. How could that be there after all these years? As I walked around the village that was now hiding all the remains of our military past, I realized that we were never part of that land. No matter what Johnson or Westmoreland or anybody said, we were always ghosts in that landscape."

"To forgive our brother is to forgive ourselves. We abandon our revenge. Our lives have seen suffering enough."

Monk in **HEAVEN AND EARTH**

Heaven and Earth

CHAPTER FIFTEEN

Natural Born Killers

"I see angels, Mickey . . . comin' down for us from heaven. I feel their feathered wings . . . I see you ridin' a red horse, drivin' the horses, whipping 'em—they're spitting frothin' all over the mouth—comin' right at us. . . . I see the future . . . and there's no death, Mickey . . . 'cause you and I are angels. . . ."

Mallory Knox in **NATURAL BORN KILLERS**

"God created me . . . if what I did was so bad why didn't he stop me . . . why didn't he protect me when I was a kid . . . ? If he's not doing it he's allowing it."

Mickey Knox in **NATURAL BORN KILLERS**

Through the end of filming for *Heaven and Earth*, Stone lived at home with his family in Santa Monica. Of course, for six days a week all that meant was that he was there to sleep, since by the time he was through shooting, took a break for dinner, and did preliminary edits, it was usually past midnight. In February 1993, after the film ended, the Stones went into marriage counseling. According to Elizabeth, the sessions focused on how they could better communicate and resolve their differences. "For Oliver this was absolutely grueling," she says. "You would have thought his chair was wired, he was so uncomfortable being there."

"It was helpful to air our differences," Stone says of the sessions, "but I don't think it was ultimately dealing with the problem. I feel that both Elizabeth and I need to have a reconciliation with our past, including our relationships with our parents. I wanted to work things out, but I'm not going to not accept the assumption that I'm wrong just because I'm different. People have told me that all my life and I'm not going to start believing it now."

Over the next few months, the relationship began to deteriorate again. "We'd be out somewhere and I'd look over at him and he'd go, 'What? What are you looking at?'" Elizabeth recalls. "It just kept getting worse. January was fine, but then February was testy, and by March he was like, 'Leave me alone. You're driving me crazy.' I began to worry that he was going to leave."

Stone admits that he was growing more and more uneasy. "It got to the point where I couldn't even talk to women without exciting her antipathies. I felt like she was judging me . . . I can't stand that. I like being able to communicate freely. I couldn't go to a party and have a conversation with a woman without her being upset."

By April, the situation was becoming intolerable. Stone went on a whirlwind tour of college speaking engagements. "Before he left, he was pacing the house like a caged animal," Elizabeth says. "One night I said, 'I suppose if you want an open marriage, I guess I should be loving enough to let you do it,' and I think that's what he wants, but I just knew I couldn't do that. I can't be that tolerant, that accepting."

Though he sensed it was doomed, Stone tried again to constrain his wild and excessive nature. Each day was crammed with intense, high-pressure situations, but at night now, he tried to stay home. There, with his wife and children, he tried to make himself embrace peace, accept harmony, enjoy the things others sought: but inside the tiger gnawed. It wasn't that he didn't love his family. He enjoyed their company, but the simple fact was they did not provide enough of an escape. In the calm, the loud voice of memory reigns supreme. In the quiet, the pain shrieks. Mirroring the turbulence in his personal life at the time, Stone now embarked on the most violent and turbulent film of his career—*Natural Born Killers*. It was a fictional story of a modern-day Bonnie and Clyde who are turned into living legends by the tabloid press and "reality" TV shows. Though it contained elements of black comedy, it was a dark and disturbing project. Part of Stone's attraction to the theme was no doubt his natural bad-boy tendency. It seemed that every time he did something the world might accept as fine and noble, he felt an almost compulsive need to do something it would disapprove of. Now, after the spiritually uplifting *Heaven and Earth*, he was clearly drawn in the opposite direction.

"I felt attracted to it out of instinct, but I never know exactly why," Stone says. "I know that starting to work on it has brought some turbulence up to the surface. Elizabeth said, 'Why are you making this movie? It's immoral. I don't want my son to be in it.' It's true that . . . there's a demon in *Natural Born Killers*. There's a demon that drives it. I can't understand it exactly . . . but it captivates me."

The project came about when Stone had dinner with longtime producer Thom Mount and actor/director Sean Penn. "Thom told me about the script at the table, but he didn't tell me that Sean Penn was supposed to direct it," Stone says. "Sean Penn's my dinner guest. Days later I read it and told Thom it was a great idea, but I wanted to rewrite some things. Then I went back and I found that there was a whole devil's nest involved with this thing."

Don Murphy, who along with his partner in J. D. Productions, Jane Hamsher, controlled the rights to the screenplay, tells how the deal came about. "We knew [screenwriter] Quentin Tarantino from well before he was successful and had the script a long time. We decided we'd rather see the film made on a low budget, even a million dollars, and still be involved than just sell it off. To be quite honest, there were many people who just felt 'Don and Jane, they'll take anything that's offered to them,' because we don't have an enormous track record and all, but when push came down to shove they found out that wasn't the case."

Mount had approached Stone with the idea of running the film through Ixtlan, Stone's production company. Part of Stone's deal with Arnon Milchan stipulates that, for every film Stone directs for Milchan's company, Milchan agrees to finance a movie with Stone's company for up to $20 million. According to Don Murphy, after Stone read the script, he called Mount. "He wanted to know if Sean Penn was really interested in directing the film," Murphy says. "Of course Mount, who like most producers has a reputation for creating fantasy situations and then making them real, says, 'Well, why?' And Oliver says, 'Well, I might want to direct it,' and in a blink of the eye, Sean's out and Oliver can do it."

Stone says the script had major litigation possibilities. Though negotiations began before his success, Quentin Tarantino was by now being hailed as Hollywood's next big thing based on the critics' response to *Reservoir Dogs*, which he wrote and directed, and he was claiming some control. "So I got an angry Tarantino, an angry Sean Penn. . . ." Stone says. "I don't want any hassles, but on the other hand a voice in my head is muttering, 'You know, every great American fortune is built on a theft.' There were a lot of legal hassles that we had to pay off to settle out people who might want to sue."

For Don Murphy and Jane Hamsher, a Hollywood fairy tale was about to happen. Murphy describes how it came about: "We get this phone call from Thom Mount saying we have to do a deal immediately because Oliver Stone wants to direct it. I'm thinking, 'Yeah, right.' So I say, 'I'll tell you what, why don't we meet him. Let's see where his head is at.' I figured that would be the end of that, but Mount called back an hour later and said, 'Monday at six.' I still thought it wasn't going to happen. Even sitting in the lobby watching Stone come in, I'm still waiting for the April Fool to come. So we met with Oliver and, to our great surprise, he seemed like he was on our wavelength with the movie."

Since Stone is at the level where he doesn't need people to get him deals, his agents and attorneys tend to work harder in other areas, often going above and beyond the call of duty to protect their client. Jane Hamsher elaborates. "After Don had thought everyone agreed to all of his points, he suddenly gets the contracts and none of them are included. So he types up this blistering fax and I freaked. I'm going, 'Oh my God, Don, you can't send this to Oliver Stone. This is our chance, our breakthrough deal!' And he goes, 'No, no, we have to stand firm.' I figured if they didn't respond favorably, maybe I could go back in and say, 'Ha ha, that Don's just a little crazy. Don't take him too seriously.' So he sends out the fax and the next day everything is worked out. Our people are patting themselves on the back for being such shrewd negotiators, but it was Don's fax. Oliver had gotten it and called his attorney and told him to stop being so efficient. I think that was also the beginning of Oliver's affection for Don. He really responded to his take-no-prisoners, kamikaze style."

Still to deal with was the problem of Quentin Tarantino wanting control over his script. Deeply immersed in these battles was Stone's attorney, Bob Marshall. After nearly ten years and negotiations of nine film deals, Marshall—like business manager Steve Pines, Bob Richardson, Mike Menchel, Clayton Townsend, Arthur Manson, and a handful of others—was a key player in Oliver Stone's organization. Why do some last while others fall by the wayside or simply decide they can no longer take the wild ride? Marshall can only speak for himself, but his explanation is interesting. "I can relate to Oliver's intensity. Early in my career I did a lot of trial work, and trying a case is the same kind of battleground as directing a film. Before you walk into that courtroom to conduct a trial, you try to anticipate everything that's going to happen. You try to predict every word that is going to come out of every witness's mouth. But you also have to be prepared for the unexpected, think on your feet. When Oliver directs a movie, he has a vision of what's going to happen. He's got it charted out and he's thorough to the extreme degree in making that happen, but he also knows when to go with his instinct and adapt to any spontaneous situation. It's like fighting a battle. You have to be tremendously disciplined. There's a lot of time in preparation and then, during the trial, you work all day and you prepare all night, just like directing. Oliver is strategic. He does things in a very analytical way. He's emotional, but he rarely loses sight of the big picture."

After shooting was completed on *Heaven and Earth*, Stone pushed ahead into preproduction on *Natural Born Killers*, scheduling shooting for May 1993. This meant he would literally be shooting one movie while editing another. Even for less hands-on directors this was pushing it. But for someone like Stone, who is intensely involved at every level of the project, it was ludicrous. "I couldn't believe it," Murphy says. "The wrap party for *Heaven and Earth* was January 30 and on February 1 we were working on *Natural Born Killers*. Even while he was shooting *Heaven and Earth*, Jane and I were busy. Despite our deal, I fully expected that our function in the film would be, 'Coffee, extra sweet and low?', and all of a sudden we are bringing in actors and helping him with writers as he did some new drafts of the script."

It was also in February that Stone met with Eric Hamburg, who had helped so much on the congressional effort to get the JFK files released. Hamburg, an attorney, had contacted Stone and expressed an interest in working for him. "We discussed politics, foreign policy, and a variety of issues," Hamburg recalls. "I remember my mind racing and feeling that I had not been so intellectually stimulated in a long time.

Oliver doesn't fit into any of the stereotypes created for him by the media. His mind is much more interesting and complex than that."

Hamburg was later named vice president for business affairs at Ixtlan, but was also active on the creative side, frequently contributing ideas on various projects. "The main reason I wanted to work for Oliver is that he is such a political filmmaker in a broad sense of the word and his films affect how people think. The thing that's most surprised me since I've been here is that he's also a very astute businessman. That was something I didn't expect."

Stone had been working with writing partners for some time. In fact, *Heaven and Earth* had been his only solo script venture since *Platoon*. Of course neither Ron Kovic (*Born*) nor Zachary Sklar (*JFK*) were screenwriters. Stone had chosen to partner with them because of their knowledge about the subject matter and book writing/editing abilities. *Wall Street* was written for the screen by Stone and Stanley Weiser together, but this was more like *The Doors* (J. Randal Johnson) in that Stone was working from an existing script. There were a lot of changes he wanted to make to the Tarantino script, but he knew he wasn't going to have much time to do it. When he's pressed for time, Stone likes to develop a good first draft with another writer and then come in and do the rewrites himself.

Jane Hamsher describes how this step took place on *Natural Born Killers*: "Oliver wanted to do some rewriting on the script, so he called and said, 'Jane, I want you to get one of your wild and crazy friends to work with Richard [Rutowski] and me on the rewrite.' I really had to scratch my head because he wasn't offering that much money. There was one guy, David Veloz, who was just out of film school but had written a couple of good screenplays and had the sensibilities to write extreme material that still retained its humanity. It turned out to be a very long and arduous process for Dave. He'd get these weird calls from Oliver in Thailand at all hours of the night—he was now on what we refer to as the 'Oliver Stone roller-coaster ride.' Oliver would goad him, punch his buttons, rake him over the coals about what they'd written, barely listen to anything Dave had to say in his own defense, and then they'd do it again. Dave would call me and I'd do my best to help him draw some sense out of the contradictory things Oliver would tell him, and all the time I'd be thinking, 'Shit, I'm glad this isn't me.' Little did

I know, my time would come. In spite of this, or perhaps because of it, Dave wound up contributing some very good stuff, and Oliver rewarded him by giving him some other projects so he could make some decent money. It established his career."

"We changed significant things," Stone says of the rewriting process. "In the original, the film was essentially an homage, tongue in cheek. You really didn't know who Mickey and Mallory were—they were mythic characters. We tried to get to know them, to put some story in there and give them some hope of redemption."

For Stone, it was the first time he had done a totally fictional film since *Wall Street*. "I didn't want to make a realistic movie about serial killers. That was well done in *Henry, Portrait of a Serial Killer*. I'm really onto something else. It's a larger portion of American life that's enamored of violence, enamored of crime, promotes it on television, and essentially lives and dies by it. It's a reversal of movies like *Bonnie and Clyde*. The chase is over early. They've been caught by the end of Act One. It's about how their careers are revived by the media in Act Two. They become a national phenomenon."

For Oliver and Elizabeth, this was a time of great turmoil. Though he'd genuinely attempted to participate in marriage counseling, Stone had a difficult time not taking things personally and often felt Elizabeth and her therapist were ganging up on him. "I had never gone to a psychiatrist in my life before," he admits, "and I went back for at least a dozen sessions, but I didn't feel it was working. I think you have to go into a deeper level, to work through that kind of thing. I think you do it through meditation, not through talking about it. I'm seeing someone separately where I work in a trance state. I'm living through my feelings toward my mother and my father. I believe in meditation. I believe in prayer; you should go to deeper levels."

Part of the problem was the huge amount of pressure Stone had put himself under. With two major films in the process of being made and the corresponding marketing and scheduling concerns, several large projects under his production arm, and increased financial demands from purchasing the Colorado house and expanding his staff, Stone was under more pressure than ever before. "Even he admits that he overdid it this time," Elizabeth said at the time. "He's overworked, he needs to rest for a month up in Colorado or somewhere and just get away from it all. *Heaven and Earth* took a lot out of him and now he's trying to do this new movie and rush it out. And still produce other ones. He's pushing himself."

Though he may rant and rave about it, Stone loves the pressures that go into his work. It is the best escape there is, and so it was quite natural that as his personal life became more and more uncomfortable, he took on more and more work. Once most artists succeed, the output and intensity of their work drops severely. The will that pushes them declines because they no longer feel the need to prove themselves. In Stone's case, however, the work output seems to continually increase. He's mellowed a bit, most of those close to him agree, but the work continues. "One of the things that drives Oliver is he has a tremendous fear of failure," Chris Renna says. "But he pushes right into the heart of it and uses the energy from the fear to fuel the drive. He has a way to transform fear as well as pain and loss into will. There have been times when I felt his physical being might just disintegrate into a mass of willpower, sort of a locomotive of determination."

It's no secret that Stone has a few vices, be they women, booze, or drugs, but whereas most artists find their work hindered by such things, Stone seems to have found a way to use these as yet another motivating factor. "I believe Oliver not only pushes himself with his fears, but also pulls himself with desire," Chris Renna maintains. "He's a man of tremendous appetites, tremendous desires, and these things often pull him as much if not more than his ambitions and his fears push him forward. He loves to work, and as soon as work lapses, his appetites and the desire to satisfy them are there waiting, like an immediate reward system ready to kick in at any time. That's not to say that all his desires are smoothly integrated. It's the size and dimension of his appetites that causes him to feel unfulfilled and pulls him into new problems as well as new ventures."

As Stone moved closer to filming *Natural Born Killers*, he was gone more and more from home. His feelings about his marriage were mixed. He wasn't sure if he could hold to his promise of fidelity, but he had resolved that he was no longer going to lie about it. He didn't have much confidence in counseling and wasn't sure what else he could do. In the past he had overcome great obstacles by sheer will. He'd conquered loneliness at Hill, vanquished fear in Vietnam, overcome rejection in New York, defeated failure in Hollywood, and purged himself of cocaine in Paris. Perhaps he could beat this as well. But the only way he knew to overcome something was by facing it. Thus, already he began to approach the new film in a cathartic light. He would find the demon that drove *Natural Born Killers* and face it head on, exorcise his madness by exploring it through his film.

"I saw this demon in my dream . . . twenty years ago."

Indian in **NATURAL BORN KILLERS**

Although Stone initially envisioned *Natural Born Killers* as a medium-budget project, like his previous three films, it soon grew. These increases had more to do with the expansion of his creative vision of the project than anything else. Stone works in layers. At the outset of the project, he views the overall focus and thrust of a film; but as he concentrates on how to execute those ideas, his creative juices start to really kick in. The result is often an increased budget. Arnon Milchan elaborates: "Every movie he wants to do now, he says at first is going to cost twelve to sixteen million dollars because he really believes he can do it for that. Then all of a sudden it's a lot more. He means well. With *Natural Born Killers*, he says, 'Arnon, I'm gonna do this cheap.'"

This was Milchan's third movie with Stone, and he had agreed to do three more. "This is not a guy who cares that much about money," Milchan goes on. "If I said, 'Oliver, make this movie and you'll make two billion dollars,' he'd say, 'Aw, c'mon, that's not a movie, it's a business deal.' And then if I said, 'Just produce it, just put your name on it,' he'll say, 'Yeah, okay,' at first, but then he'll think about it and go, 'No, no. I can't even put my name on it.' It wouldn't matter what his money situation was. I could say, 'You have debts, you're bankrupt.' Whatever. It wouldn't matter. Believe me, there are easier ways to make a living than by being in business with Oliver Stone. He has taken upon himself a serious responsibility to reach out without compromising. He'd rather have to work hard to sell it than compromise in his work."

Stone dutifully stumps for his movies. Because he tends to choose noncommercial topics, he figures he has to work that much harder to ensure that the films find their audience. As a result he often gets taken to task for what is erroneously labeled self-promotion. In actuality, while Stone may occasionally enjoy a moment in the limelight, he's not comfortable with it unless he has a concept to communicate, "a reason to be there."

Though he views Stone as sometimes being difficult to work with, Milchan has immense respect for Stone and a great deal of affection. Among other things, the two have a friendly banter going about who is the worst dressed. Stone says Milchan is the originator of the "laidback rich look." Milchan shakes his head. "He comes in wearing violet shirts, green ties and red socks, and thinks he's being classy. He looks at me with that condescending look, Mr. Ralph Lauren to begin with, right. He's like one of the greatest artists we have and he worries about losing some hair, like all of us. I mean, nobody wants to lose their hair, but tough luck, you know? With all the incredible things he's done and doing, who cares about his hair? It's sweet in a way. He wants to be loved and he doesn't want to admit it. He's tormented because he's so unique. And that's not going to change."

Though Stone's budgets are larger than they used to be, many people feel that they are reasonable. Mike Menchel is one of them. "You've got to understand where he came from," Menchel says. "He's a low-budget filmmaker. That's where he started. He's a guy who has come up through the trenches on a shoestring and he knows how to put films together that way. And sure, his budgets are growing. Oliver's desire to have a little more money in the budget is only natural given the times and what's going on in the business. But he's never excessive. Everything is on the screen. There's no waste, no bullshit to it at all. What you see is what you get."

Bill Brown, Stone's post production supervisor, believes that Stone has a firm grasp on the relationship between responsibility and freedom. "In the big scope of things, that's what every person making films in Hollywood is aspiring to—creative freedom and control. To get enough money to make the movies you want to make and be left alone to make them the way you want. By being so responsible in financial areas, Oliver's created an environment for himself which is extremely free and creative. People respect him creatively, but they feel very comfortable about him from a sensible scheduling and money point of view. Ultimately it gives him more creative freedom."

Though he was once more in the midst of extensive editing demands, this time for *Heaven and Earth*, Brown stressed that Stone can be tough and even explosive occasionally, but he calms down just as quickly. "One thing I really like about Oliver is that he can get very upset about something, even furious, and be adamant about how it's really bothering him, but as soon you address it and fix the problem, it's fine. He doesn't hold a grudge about little things and grind a person down about it. He's very confrontational and if there's a problem, he says right to your face exactly what's bothering him. A lot of people will hold it back, which sometimes makes things more difficult."

Casting *Natural Born Killers*—or *NBK*, as the production company had already nicknamed it—presented some unique problems. Risa Bramon García was again a key partner in Stone's decision-making process here. This was her seventh film with Stone, and she talks about how he has changed over the years. "I think he's mellowed, and I feel like he's gotten more collaborative. He has grown tremendously as a filmmaker in that there are more levels to his work. I believe a filmmaker, especially Oliver, takes on the nature of his movies. As to how he's changed over the years, just look at the movies. He was very heartful during *Born on the Fourth of July*, very whacked during *The Doors*, very cerebral and analytical and intense during *JFK*; he was a lot more sensitive and sort of soulful during *Heaven and Earth*. He has been wild and funny and crazy during *Natural Born Killers*. There's absolutely no question that he takes on the personality of each film. I mean, the films came from him, and then each one went right back into him. I think that's true for every director to a degree, but more so for him than anyone I've seen."

Once again Bramon García was credited not only as casting director but as an associate producer on the film. "I guess that's because my work has gotten more and more involved as the movies went on," Bramon García says. "I really do enjoy the production elements in the film. Also, my assistants, Heidi Levitt and Mary Vernieu, and I give him a woman's point of view. He gives us a hard time, sometimes he calls us the three witches from *Macbeth* ["because they're tiny and cackle"], but I don't take it personally any more.

"It's kind of funny. I think I've been able to really fight for a woman's point of view in his movies. His movies were very male and it's been important to me to get him to be open to the female point of view. He's listened about the scripts, he's listened about the actresses. Sometimes, I'll write a critique of his script and he'll yell at me because I don't agree with him, but I don't care. I know he likes to be challenged. He gets rude sometimes, but I don't take it personally any more. I know he doesn't mean it. He gets very involved in his work and the message that he's bringing to the people, and it becomes such an enormous thing that he loses himself, and sometimes he loses his grace. But for the most part, he really lets people do what they want to do. I've never had that kind of freedom. He rarely has to answer to a producer or studio. He has only to answer to his vision and we have to answer to his vision."

From the moment he read the Tarantino version of the script, Stone decided he wanted Michael Madsen for the role of Mickey Knox. He had worked with Madsen in *The Doors* when Madsen played the role of Tom Baker, a wild Irishman who acted in a couple of Andy Warhol films and later became Jim Morrison's drinking buddy. The female component of the infamous Mickey and Mallory couple-on-a-crime-spree was given to Juliette Lewis. The role of Wayne Gale, the glib and often irritating host of *American Maniacs*, a popular television show that focuses on serial killers, is also a key element to the film. Robert Downey, Jr., was someone Stone had always wanted to work with, and Bramon García was convinced he was the right choice.

It was around this time that Stone and Arnon Milchan went to Warner Brothers to discuss the project in depth. There was some concern that Warner Brothers might balk at the increased budget. "Oliver knows that I'd do anything to make the movie happen," Milchan says, "but he's smart enough to know that if he doesn't get this movie institutionalized, backed by a big conglomerate, he might not get the support he needs in marketing it. There's a big difference between a studio just doing the distribution and actually investing in the movie as well. Well, Warner Brothers was nervous. They said, this is violent, this is dangerous, why don't you just pick up all the money and we'll distribute it. I said, 'Fine, no problem.' Then Oliver got nervous because he knew that meant they were afraid of the movie. He had decided to cast a certain actor who was not a name [Michael Madsen]. So when we're meeting with Warners, Terry Semel was talking names like Mel Gibson, Kevin Costner . . . big names. And Oliver says, 'Why would we even listen to you guys since you're not even involved?' I'm sitting there saying, 'I don't care, whatever Oliver wants.' I'll put up the dollars. But I'm praying inside that Oliver realizes that, even though we don't need the money, this means Warners would not be publicly committed to the movie. The movie could become history tomorrow and they could say, 'Oh, we just distributed it.' But Oliver knows that he needs a full-time corporate machinery behind us defending that movie. Like *JFK*, it needed a lot of people helping, not only us.

"Okay, so here's a guy who's smart and cool who makes a mistake in bargaining. To himself, he says, 'Fine, I'll give up my position.' To them, he says, 'What's your suggestions?' Then, he takes the riskiest one on their list, Woody Harrelson. Now, this is before *Indecent Proposal* and everything. He says. 'The last guy you mentioned, Woody Harrelson, I like him. Now I listened to you, so I guess you're my partners, right? You're in.' He turned what was a mistake into a great thing."

But where is the line drawn? What if Woody Harrelson hadn't been on that list? "Oh, we wouldn't have done it," Milchan says. "Oliver wouldn't have done the movie. He would not do it if it meant changing his vision too much. He knew that Woody would work for what he had in mind. Otherwise, he'd have just said no. Also, when you're smart, you also get luckier somehow. So then the chairman of Warner Brothers [Bob Daley] called and said, 'I know you and Terry like this project, but I'm very concerned that the cumulative effect of this movie is going to be dangerous.' I said, 'You know what, I fully agree with you. I think you should tell it to Oliver.' I wanted to add, 'And frankly, I don't think you should be involved in a movie, if you don't believe in it,' but I started to realize that Oliver was right. We need the institution with us on this one. Then Oliver called me up and said, 'Oh, it was a great meeting. Bob loves the project. They're in.' I said, 'What do you mean, they're in?' He said, 'They loved it. They're our partners.' I don't know what he did in the meeting. He just made it happen."

Don Murphy was one of many shocked by the decision. "When I heard he was casting Woody Harrelson, I thought, 'Is he nuts?' I went to see him while he was working on *Heaven and Earth* in L.A., and I just looked at him and said, 'Woody Harrelson?' He said, 'Look, I can see it in his eyes, it's his relationship with his father. He visits his father regularly in prison and look, I think I can get a great performance out of Woody.' I said, '*Touché*. I will never bring it up again and you have my entire support.' And he was so right. Woody is fantastic in this movie. When he shaves his head on camera, he is the scariest thing in the world."

Indeed, it is possible that Harrelson's past is part of what influenced Stone to hire him for the role. Harrelson's father vanished from his life in 1968. Charles Voyde Harrelson is currently serving a double life sentence for the hired-gun murder of a federal judge and is frequently rumored to be one of the "three tramps" arrested in Dallas on the day of Kennedy's assassination. Woody Harrelson, quite understandably, rarely talks about his father other than to say that he believes he is innocent and "one of the most articulate, well-read, charming people I've ever known."

For Risa Bramon García, the casting of Harrelson meant the unpleasant task of uncasting Michael Madsen. "We've had to, quote, 'uncast' people a few times," Bramon García says. "Oliver does a lot of writing after casting has started, and sometimes he changes a particular character and then wants to change the cast, or he'll be in rehearsal and it just doesn't work. Sometimes we have to pay them off and sometimes we don't. Sometimes I fight with him to hold on to the people and they stay. Rehearsals are the most uncomfortable times for us on his movies 'cause we always dread his phonecall saying that he wants to uncast so-and-so. Usually it's not a very big part."

In Madsen's case, it didn't work out so smoothly. "That was a very difficult time," Bramon García admits. "It was very hard to do that. In the end it helped Michael's career much more than it hurt it. As soon as everybody knew, they wanted to know what Michael was about and he's been working nonstop. This was the way it had to be. Oliver had to compromise to get the money to make the film. He knows that to get people in the seats, he needs stars in his movies sometimes. He has to have certain star power, but he also likes to get great cameos and he also likes unknowns. He does it different all the time depending on the project."

"I did ask him not to take anything for the spring because I wanted him in the movie," Stone admits concerning Madsen. "Warners was adamant about it, but I also happened to like Woody a lot. The budget had gone up considerably because I wanted to put more things into it and I jumped the gun by telling Michael he had the role. I fucked up, but after I got back from Thailand in December and made my final decision, I told Michael he didn't have the role so I don't really think that he lost a lot of roles because May was a long way away. Michael was not harmed, but I wronged him by promising him the role and not being able to deliver. It happens. I made a promise I couldn't keep."

Natural Born Killers was a return to a small ensemble of lead actors rather than the big casts of *Heaven and Earth* and *JFK*. Besides Mickey, Mallory, and Wayne Gale, there were two other key roles—Prison Warden Dwight McClusky and detective Jack Scagnetti. The role of Scagnetti was given to Tom Sizemore (*Heartbeats*), who had worked with Stone briefly in *Born on the Fourth of July*. Ironically, the role of Warden McClusky wound up being recast as well. It was initially offered to veteran powerhouse actor Jack Palance, who had expressed interest until he read the script. According to Stone, Palance said he was shocked and horrified by the script and that he would never be involved in something so violent. "I said, 'But Jack, you did *Shane*. You played Attila the Hun.' And he said, 'Well, I go around the country talking against violence all the time and I symbolize peace.' And I thought, 'Gee, Jack, I must've missed that one.'"

Tommy Lee Jones stepped in on relatively short notice to play the role, which meant he had appeared in three consecutive Oliver Stone films.

Another role, that of a prison guard, had to be recast because of the actor's temperament. Risa Bramon García elaborates: "There is an actor whose name I will not mention because we were sued by him. Anyway, Oliver was obsessed with the guy, and we tried to warn him that this guy was going to be a nightmare, but Oliver just wouldn't listen because he thought he was right for it. The guy was a drunk and he was crazy, and in the end he got into a fistfight with Woody during a rehearsal. It was awful. He had to be taken out of the building and of course because he was taken off the movie he was going to sue us. Oliver just kept saying he was right for the part. He *was* right for it, but he was also too difficult to work with. Oliver can get obsessive about actors sometimes and we have to just roll our eyes and say, 'We'll try him, we'll try him.' Sometimes that's difficult."

Rehearsals were far from smooth and there was almost another major replacement—Juliette Lewis. Once again, the issue was preparation for the role. Stone wanted her to train, but she kept missing kick-boxing lessons, shooting practice, and weight-training and workout sessions. "Oliver goes through sort of a dance with each person in a major role," Bramon García says. "Juliette had a hard time at first. He wanted a warrior, and she wasn't a warrior. You have to be committed and passionate and driven with him. I know he was angry because she came into rehearsal once at a hotel and ordered room service, and she was sitting there eating greasy eggs and smoking cigarettes while he was trying to rehearse, and it made him crazy. Understandably so. She is an incredibly talented girl, but he wanted a young Linda Hamilton from *Terminator*. He wanted a warrior, and she had to understand that. It was a fight. A fight to keep her in the movie and a fight to get her in shape and in line to do it."

Even so, Lewis wanted the role and wanted it precisely for those reasons. "It was a whole extreme that I hadn't done before," Lewis says. "I specifically wanted to get something with these colors. Because even though I did [*Kalifornia* and *That Night*], they're like my other films in that they have in common being young and naive. Mallory, the character I am here, is naive too, but it's played a different way. I'm a real calm person and I wanted to play something like an angry wildcat. The innocence and naïveté gets really dull after a while. This part is made up of pain, rage, and not a lot of respect for yourself. It was a challenge."

When Stone returned home from his speaking tour of colleges (that ironically included a major address at the Yale Political Union, his old school) in April 1993, his private life was in turmoil. He and Elizabeth quarreled frequently. In the end they decided to have a trial separation, and Stone moved out of the house and into a small apartment in Santa Monica. "It was a wonderful marriage," Stone says. "I think we had many good things, but things started getting tougher after six of the twelve years. We grew in separate directions. To me a soft person I had known became angrier and tougher. Her very nature changed. At the same time I wanted more freedom for myself. It became clear it was over. The separation has been generally positive. Elizabeth is going through a lot of pain. It's not about me and women. It's about being someone else. It's about her changing and me changing. I feel like my experimental side is being choked off."

Like any father in this situation, Stone was concerned about the effect of the separation on his children: "It was heartbreaking for the kids, Mikey two, and Sean eight, but Sean is taking it really well so far. A lot of people tell me they wish their parents had gotten a divorce because of all the tension that was in their house. For the first month, Sean was very upset, but lately he's been behaving like he's enjoying my company more and he's been communicating to me more. Sean's had the risk of being pampered a little too much and being spoiled. The divorce is one of the first real struggles in his life that's really hit him in the face. I don't think that it's all bad for a kid to experience struggle and a change in his life. Though it caused me much pain, it wasn't a wholly bad thing when my parents got divorced. The winters seemed much colder. I had to figure out how to compete. But nobody told me anything. It was like my parents were ashamed to tell me. I think Liz and I handled it much more maturely—as badly as we were fighting, I think we both knew that the kids would be damaged unless we dealt with it."

"Indians say you're either stronger than the poison or you die. You're strong. . . ."
Mickey Knox in **NATURAL BORN KILLERS**

Wanting more freedom and going through a separation is not uncommon for men in their mid-forties, but Stone doesn't see this as a reaction to midlife crisis. It is his second divorce, and he seems prone to periodic eruptions in his life. "We used to have a very sane and healthy married life. I lived in a picture postcard of a neighborhood and it was a role that I played and I enjoyed. The suburban life was a life that I never had as a kid and I wanted to have that, but I don't think it was meant for the rest of my life. I can't explore within the confines of that marriage any more. Elizabeth was tougher on me and was demanding more, and I couldn't provide it. Twelve years is a long time. Elizabeth and I are different in many ways. My argument with her was always, 'Elizabeth, the people you work with and create with are not always the people you choose as friends. We're not looking for a comfort zone in making a movie here. You often work with a devil to make something good.' She doesn't understand me. She judged my behavior as a disease, laying guilt on me like there's something's wrong with me . . . the way you need to travel, you need to work, you need to see women. I'm not a monogamous man. I never was . . . never could be."

That May, Elizabeth Stone still hoped that the marriage could be saved. "I think we're in midlife and both working out whatever you work out in midlife and we're doing it separately. But that's why I don't think our marriage is at an end. I pray it's not. I think in his wisdom and inner goodness, Oliver's going to realize that there can be more of a moderation in his life. I think that's the reason why he built this big house in Telluride and bought that land up there. And I think it's the reason he married me, frankly. I think it's the reason he invested so much in me who is a real bare bones, down-to-earth, no-fakeness person."

Many of Stone's friends hated to see the marriage break apart, including Chuck Pfeiffer. "Oliver is never going to get it any better than the household that Elizabeth created for him," Pfeiffer says. "It's probably going to be a lot worse. She's a good mother, too. But Sean needs a man around. He's seen Oliver react—he has tantrums, gets moody, but he's a good kid. Oliver's a great human being, but he's not a great father. He's extremely selfish. His vested interest is in his career, but you know something? Practically all the great men in history have been shitty fucking fathers. You're probably either going to be a bureaucrat and work in the fucking post office and be a good father or be somebody and be a shitty father. I've seen it with CEOs' sons, with generals' sons. It's almost impossible to be a great father and make pictures."

On May 24, 1993, after an argument, Elizabeth Stone suddenly filed for divorce. The news appeared in papers and magazines across the country. Two days later she withdrew her petition. "I got upset with him and filed," Elizabeth said at the time, "but later we talked and sort of came up with a plan to work things out and I unfiled. I'm hoping things are going to work." Coverage of the filing was publicized coast to coast, but few publications carried news of the withdrawal of the petition.

That May, filming began on *Natural Born Killers* in New Mexico. The cast by now also included Rodney Dangerfield, Russell Means, and a host of cameos. The New Mexico schedule included several different locations and required a blistering pace even from the outset. "Oliver doesn't make simple movies," Herb Gains says. "His movies require a lot of detail and a lot of complexities, so there's always a logistical problem of some kind to deal with. On *NBK* we had to shoot in several different cities within a very short period of time. So it was check into a motel, go to sleep, wake up, shoot, and at the end of the day travel to another hotel."

Don Murphy describes the hectic schedule that began filming: "Jane [Hamsher] and I were the new kids on the block, everybody else had worked with Oliver before. We sort of hit the ground running. We shot in Albuquerque, Sante Fe, Winslow, the Shoshone and Navajo reservations, Redrock, Taos. We started with footage that was going to be on the monitors for Wayne Gale's TV show. For some reason, Oliver wanted to finish this film by August 1, and that meant an incredible pace. We were literally having six-and sometimes seven-day weeks with a lot of overtime—sixteen-, seventeen-hour days, pushing twenty hours a few times. After the first week it became really clear that this was not going to be an easy show."

Though Stone's life was complicated by the pressures of working on two films, producing several others, and an impending divorce, Herb Gains reports he was sharp as ever: "The man is brilliant and very intense. When I work with Oliver, I know that I have to be sharp. I have to be on from the moment he arrives until the moment he leaves. Because if I tune out ten seconds, I'm fucked. If I just tune out a moment, I'll miss a beat, and each beat is so important that I'll be lost and I'll never catch up. He's a very quick thinker and he's a very quick doer. And he expects the people around him to keep up with him. He relies on that. He sees weakness very quickly and he doesn't stand for it."

A film crew has to work long hours often in close proximity, and sometimes personality conflicts are as much of a problem as incompetence. People seem to either love or hate working with Stone. "I've had to fire a few people," Gains admits. "Sometimes that happens. You have to have a sense of humor to work with Oliver. That's very important. If you don't have a sense of humor, you're fucked. He's the first one to want to have a good laugh. And at the end of a hard day, there's no one who is more fun to go out to dinner with and laugh and unwind. Because the work is so intense, the relaxation is just as intense."

The cast and crew of *Natural Born Killers* recall the film as a wild, mad ride from Day One. Stone geared them up early and then kept pushing. The New Mexico filming was as wild off camera as on. Chris Renna was again the doctor on the set and he describes some of the action: "One night I heard a bunch of noise coming out of Juliette Lewis's room at about four in the morning and I went to investigate. She and Tom Sizemore were bouncing up and down on the bed. I tried to get them to calm down, but they weren't listening. Then a Rolling Stones song off of *Beggar's Banquet* came on the radio and I thought maybe I could settle them down by drawing their attention to it, so I said, 'Listen you guys, this is what it's all about. This song is for the common man. The workers should hear this.' I held the cassette player up to the window and shouted, 'You guys down at that stoplight need to hear this.' Sizemore is shouting, 'They can't hear you, but you're right . . . they need to hear that.' I turned just in time to see the desk chair flying through the air headed for the window to smash it in order to allow the message to be heard, but it hit me instead. Actually, I was glad it hit me instead of the window."

But the night wasn't over yet. "Juliette then suggested ordering some cornflakes from room service," Renna goes on. "But Tom claimed he couldn't eat cornflakes. Juliette argued that they would be just the thing, so she ordered up eight boxes. When the cornflakes came, she fixed a bowl and fed Sizemore a bite, which he then spit out all over her and the bed. 'See what you made me do!' Sizemore shouted. Instead of being mad about it, Juliette said, 'I'm sorry, Tom. It was my fault. You told me how much you hated cornflakes and I didn't believe you. I see that I was wrong now.' And with that they settled down. They had reached their own repartee and I wasn't sure whether I'd helped them or not. *NBK* was crazy like that a lot."

Also in May, *Wild Palms*, the six-hour mini-series that Stone produced, aired over four nights on ABC television. The series was based on Bruce Wagner's weirdly futuristic "Wild Palms" cartoon series which appears in *Details* magazine, and starred James Belushi, Dana Delany, Kim Cattrall, Robert Loggia, and Angie Dickinson.

With a complex plotline centered on holograms, microchips, and other technologies of the future, and how they affect religious cults and media empires, *Wild Palms* was too bizarre for many television viewers, but those who held on for a while were treated to some of the most original programming ever aired on mainstream television. The story concerns a young television executive (Belushi) whose world spins out of control when, after his network introduces Virtual Reality programming to America in the year 2007, he realizes nothing in his life is really as it seems. "It's Jimmy Stewart meets Franz Kafka," says Belushi. "Oliver came down on the set one day and encouraged us to take the characters as far as we could. He said things like, 'Maybe in the year 2007 people talk differently, maybe in a different rhythm. Go for it. What the fuck do we have to lose?' He instilled a confidence in me to risk more. He gave off this energy. I ended up just doing the stupidest things in the next couple takes, but it was good because he gave me the freedom to look bad. And as an actor when you have the freedom to look bad is often when you do your best."

Stone also did a cameo in *Wild Palms*. Older and grayer, he appears in the background of one scene on television where he is being interviewed on a talk show in the future. The moment gave Stone an excellent opportunity to spoof those who had ridiculed him. When he's asked on the show if he feels bitter now that the JFK files have been released after all these years and he's been proven right, Stone answers, "No. I'm not bitter . . . If Jack Valenti were alive, I'd be the first to extend an olive branch to this guy." The sound fades as the interviewer remarks that the actual conspiracy turned out to be so much larger than was depicted in *JFK*.

Meanwhile, Stone was engaged in a battle to extend some of the same frontiers in feature films. According to Arnon Milchan, he had promised Warner Brothers that *Natural Born Killers* would not be rated NC-17. "He reassured everybody," Milchan says. "But at the same time he keeps calling me every two days and saying, 'Why can't we go NC-17?' I said that's okay with me, but we wouldn't be able to advertise the movie in a lot of places and some theaters won't show it. What he was doing was testing how far he can go. He's as smooth as they come. Probably based on the experience of being screwed and manipulated and lied to, Oliver will test whatever you tell him. He'll ask someone else and see if the stories match. He'll talk to two or three people he trusts, and ask the same questions. And when he gets the same answer, then he'll accept it as being for real. If he found a hole in the story, he would push.

"The guy's brilliant in a way," Milchan continues. "He has a real sweet and sincere way that really encourages you to tell him the truth. Now what will he do after all this? My guess is that he will go for the most extreme version possible. He'll test it. Push it as far as he can. And this is even though the worst thing that can happen to him is for his movie not to sell tickets—he'd be a nervous wreck. Still, he will push it." (After five passes at the ratings board, the film was eventually rated "R," as Milchan predicted.)

Filming moved to the Midwest where Stateville, a large prison in Joliet, Illinois, became the primary location. The prison scenes were a nightmare. "I hated it there," Bob Richardson says. "Besides the difficult conditions, there is a real racial attitude in the prison because you've got thousands of mostly black men being incarcerated and ruled over by mostly white guards. A lot of them resent us being here. We shot a scene where a black guard was thrown off the third-story tower and they went crazy. They would've liked it better if it had been a white guard. Most of the prisoners are totally uneducated and some of the people in the crew make more in a week than most of these guys have ever made in a year. And everybody is angry."

"Just the idea of making a film in a place like that presents all kinds of problems," Herb Gains says. "A lot of them were anticipated, but we knew there would be some that no one could anticipate and we'd just have to respond accordingly. So we went into the cell blocks and got to know the temperament of the prisoners in the different areas. When you're in a prison, you're in the prisoners' world and it's like going into a neighborhood in New York, you gotta find out who runs the neighborhood. It's the same thing in the prison. You've got to find out who runs what."

From the moment they entered Stateville, the crew faced a steady stream of problems. "Even the simplest things became more difficult. Normally, when you're making a movie and someone says, 'Go put a light on a roof,' you just do it," Gains says, "but it's not like that in a prison. We say, 'Can we put a light on the roof?' and they say, 'You can, but you're going to have to wait a few minutes. We've got to call the guys on the tower, because they're trained to shoot anybody they see on the roof.' So, while they're radioing the tower saying don't shoot this guy on the roof, twenty minutes has gone by and Oliver's like asking, 'What are we waiting for?' It can be tough."

Of course, when it comes to making a film, quite often more problems means more money. Clayton Townsend, who after Alex Ho's departure became Stone's producer, acknowledged that the film was costing more than they had originally expected. "The budget has increased, but for the most part, Oliver's budgets are lower than other 'A-list' directors, and all the bucks go on the screen. Besides, you can't make a wildly free-spirited, out-of-control story without getting into some of that. We're doing stuff that is very cutting edge. Some of the things have totally not been done before—especially the projections and different film formats all over the place."

How does Townsend as a producer deal with Stone as a director? "It's a barter kind of thing. Oliver started as a writer, and a big part of it is putting what he's written onto the screen. And he really doesn't like to deviate from the scope of the movie laid out in the script, he's not a big fan of that. I'll say, 'Gee, do you really need a thousand extras here?' and he'll say, 'Well, let's check the script. Let's see. It says a teeming crowd of people, maybe a thousand people. Yeah, guess we do.' It's like it was written by God or somebody and he has to follow it. I try to whittle away at my case. Oliver's perception of what it takes to get certain things done differs from what it really takes sometimes, like when he says he wants a thousand extras, that means a thousand tuxes, a thousand haircuts, a thousand everything that goes with that. When that case was presented by me or Alex in the past, he's been pretty reasonable. He might come back and say, I think I can get by with eight hundred or something. He takes those things seriously. But he questions everything. Part of it is his natural curiosity. Like last night, we were talking. I'm expecting my first baby in a couple of weeks and I said, 'I always wanted a girl,' and he said, 'Why?' It seemed like an innocent question, but I didn't know the answer to it. I had to search my soul to come up with an answer and Oliver seemed to like that. He likes it when he can make people think."

The decision to use rear-screen projection and other optical processes in *Natural Born Killers* not only raised the budget, it also increased the amount of time needed to shoot. Don Murphy felt that this would be the difference between a good film and a great one. "Oliver's directorial touches made it brilliant. For example, in the opening after this great scene in the diner, Mickey and Mallory pile into a car and start driving, but it's real obvious it's on the sound stage and in the background there's this whole montage scene. It's all cut to music with them driving to a black and white movie, driving down a winding road in Monaco, a giant bunny appears in back of the screen, newspapers with clippings that came out go by, it's this weird surrealistic thing. Very tripped out. In another scene, Scagnetti [Tom Sizemore] looks out the window and instead of it being the sky, you see like a giant flower opening and fire burning in the background. Oliver took this thing to another insane level."

Later Stone added a brilliantly vicious spoof of a TV family sitcom centering on Mickey and Mallory's first meeting amidst the bizarre world of Mallory's abusive home life. In it Sean Stone, in his seventh film role, played Mallory's brother. As more layers of surrealism were added, the feeling on the set was that *Natural Born Killers* was an existential movie. It was what it was and there was no point in looking for a deeper meaning. Despite the frequent speculation, Stone avoided discussing this aspect of the film. Because of the way he creates, he can't really seriously discuss a work in progress with any sense of finality. To him it is still a changing, evolving thing. Only when he has finished creating can he step back from the process and try to understand it.

Since special optical processes are added in postproduction, the cast and crew must allow for them during the shoot, working around where they will later be inserted and sometimes pretending they are already there. This adds time and of course increases the tension level and all-around chaos on the set. Don Murphy is one of many who believes that Stone thrives on chaos. "The man functions with chaos like nobody I've ever seen. I don't think he's very comfortable with calm day-to-day life, but in the midst of chaos, he's in his element. You would think the most peaceful time of the shoot would've been the week and a half we had on the soundstage in Chicago because it's the most controlled. But the reality is that everybody's mood on the set is reflected by Oliver's mood. If you're in a good mood and Oliver starts in on you, you're out of the mood pretty quickly. And Oliver was the most miserable during our time on the soundstage, while in the prison where it was crazy, psycho prisoners everywhere, depressing circumstances, little control, Oliver loved it. When we went to the stage, he hated it and made everybody else miserable. I think he was bored, like, 'Oh, fine, great, this is so easy my dog could do it.' Then, when we went back to the prison, he loved it again.

"I realized the chaos was the variable," Murphy goes on. "He was thriving on it. Being in a maximum-security prison with a bunch of murderers running around. He used to love the stories like when the crew had some cables stolen or the prison guards were shaking someone down because a camera was missing, or the prisoners wouldn't shut up in their cells and we'd have to negotiate with one of the big gang leaders to get peace. In between times, they're throwing milk down on Tommy Lee and there's all this craziness. The women are worried and we're all wondering if we're safe. He was eating that up. He loved it."

"Got my whole prison worked up. Like sharks to chum bait. Smell of blood drives 'em nuts. . . . This ain't a prison anymore—it's a timebomb."

Warden McClusky in **NATURAL BORN KILLERS**

Tommy Lee Jones, as always, was nearly flawless. Always prepared, always on time, and always bringing his best to the scene. The only exception was his first day of shooting at the prison, when Stone had a full set waiting because Jones failed to show up on time due to a faulty alarm clock. Chris Renna tells the story of how he and Richard Rutowski went to pick up Jones at his hotel that morning. "We raced over to the hotel to try and rouse Tommy. There was a lot of traffic and Richard, as usual, drove like a madman. When we got there, we hurried up to Tommy's room and banged on the door. A moment later the door sprang open and there was Tommy Lee, fully dressed and ready to go except that he was wearing only one shoe. 'Gentlemen, I know why you're here,' Tommy said. 'Now, the problem was that clock radio over there. The alarm did go off, but when I hit it, it stopped and it didn't go off again. However, I am now ready to go and we can leave as soon as we find the one missing shoe.' With that we set off through the apartment looking for the shoe. Richard then noticed another similar pair of shoes on top of a suitcase and said, 'Hey, Tommy, there's another pair of shoes.' Without a beat, Tommy said, "All right. You put those on and then you help me look for the shoe that I need.' Richard just looked at me and I shrugged. We kept looking for the shoe and a few minutes later we found it behind the commode."

For his part, Tommy Lee Jones once again enjoyed working with Oliver Stone. "Part of Oliver's education was in the military," Jones says, "and he is a good leader out in the field no matter what he encounters. He's a very cool head under any kind of fire. The more pressure you put on him, the more grace he's able to find. I like that just fine. That's my kinda guy. That's what I want to be and that's what I strive for."

Jones claims he sees no need to look further than the films themselves to understand Stone. "Oliver's work speaks deeply for himself," Jones says. "What you see on the screen, all those feelings are really there in the man's mind. That's the real guy and those are real movies. Real movies for real people."

In his own way, Tommy Lee adds to the chaos on the set. Though he's a consummate actor, his friendly but slightly quirky personality fits in well with Juliette Lewis's pouty rebellion, Robert Downey's hyperintensity, Tom Sizemore's smoldering anger, and Woody's oddball contentedness. Stone loves this cast. Though he's intent on getting the job done, part of him seems to love their craziness, as if the madder they are, the happier he is. Juliette Lewis seems to agree. "He wants you to totally lose your mind and be chaotic," she says.

This same love of chaos carries over into Stone's office. He promotes a conflicted atmosphere, believing that this often produces better work. "He's got an assistant from heaven who takes care of him like I've never seen," says Don Murphy, "but sometimes he'll come in when everything is calm and just start yelling about anything, provoking the atmosphere. It seems that he's happy in a situation where everybody is off balance, where chaos is ruling, because ultimately, it gives him more control."

Mike Menchel believes that a lot of what others perceive as Stone's love of chaos is a misunderstanding of his extensive mental capabilities. "What looks crazy to the average person is not really crazy, it's just fast. Oliver is not only thinking about what he's doing at the moment, but how he's gonna accomplish what he wants to do in ten minutes or the next day or next week. He's thinking about all that stuff at once. It's the same with his films. When he goes to direct a movie, I believe that the whole movie is shot in Oliver's mind before he even sets foot on the stage or location. He experiments, but that's only because he's got a fallback position if it doesn't work. He's that calculated."

This is counteracted by Stone's extensive loyalty to his people. "If someone had a problem with Jane or me," Don Murphy adds, "Oliver might later come over and take a pound of flesh out of us just because he feels he needs to, but he'll defend us to the death to anyone that has a problem with us. If I thought less of one of his people, I'd think long and hard before telling him about it because he would spend twenty minutes chewing me out for even thinking that. That kind of loyalty is admirable, and quite frankly, it's astonishing. I have never seen anything like it in Hollywood."

Jane Hamsher, Murphy's partner, believes that one of the qualities that makes Stone such a great director is his ability to bring the best out of people. "Oliver has a way of keeping the energy level up on the set, and that's one of the reasons he gets such good performances out of actors—everyone is constantly being pressed by this great directorial fist, from the lowliest PA to the loftiest star. Nobody on the set ever feels like they have enough time to do their job—the makeup people, the hair people, whoever, you take as much time as you can and hope that's enough—and that creates a level of intensity on the set that comes across on the screen, but it also wears out everyone involved in the process."

Hamsher believes that setting up enormous challenges is an important part of Stone's working method. "My theory is that he's someone who never wants himself to be limited by his own successes. He has the courage to push himself the way he pushes other people. He keeps expanding his horizons, takes on new things, confounds his critics and anyone who thinks they know what to expect from him next. I think that Oliver took on this project to give himself a difficult new obstacle to overcome, and I can't think of another filmmaker of his stature who constantly tests himself to that extent. Almost all of them carve out their niche and stay safely there. This is a funny over-the-top movie that completely veers away from everything he's ever done. It gives Oliver the broadest dimension of any major filmmaker. Nobody has taken on such a wide range of material.

"I think everyone," Hamsher goes on," when they encounter difficulty, defaults to what's been successful for them in the past. It's just the way people operate. The only way you can get past that to do any better is to get shaken up very hard. Somebody really has to worm their way into your psyche and push your buttons and disturb you in order to make you start looking at the world in a different way. That's what Oliver does, and he's very gifted at it. He's like a Zen master, full of apparent contradictions, who will never let you rest on firm ground. As a result, you're always going for something deeper. You're prying into your instincts, traveling into places you don't normally go for answers. The reason this myth has developed about his being such a difficult person to work with is because of this method that he uses to motivate people. I'm not sure it's even conscious, but it's very successful. He never lets you feel safe. He'll rattle your cage just for the sake of rattling it and nothing else. It may not be over what you deserve it for, it may be for something totally different, but it's a marvelous way to keep you constantly striving for something much better."

Hamsher believes this process works wonders. "I know Oliver's got some of the best work out of me that I've ever done. I look back on the way I was doing things before I started going to the Oliver Stone film school and I'm ten times better now. And that's why I submit to the process every day. If it was just the glory of being next to Oliver Stone, it's not worth it. It's a very hard process to go through. Actually, you have to be very confident to withstand him, and that's why it takes a Bob Richardson or a Victor Kempster or a Michael Douglas to submit to it, because at the end of the day you've got to be able to regroup. You have to be able to say, 'I'm okay, I'm fine,' despite the fact that I've just had every insecurity in my being dragged to the surface. But the media doesn't generally analyze anything with that kind of depth, so all they see is the shaking-up part."

Richard Rutowski, co-writer and associate producer of *Natural Born Killers*, points out that by creating a persona that triggers vulnerability in others, Stone shields part of himself. "A lot of the people never see the true Oliver. They see what he gives them in his display—his aggressive behavior, his cutting sense of humor, his disarming kind of pushing people. Sometimes he shows people the other side, but they're so taken aback by these other things that they can't get to it. That's what's interesting to me, because that's where you find the real Oliver. Oliver is in all of the image he creates, but the interesting person is this complex being who is both wrathful and terrified and sits behind all of the stuff that most people see."

Rutowski, like most who are close to Stone, claims that behind all the blustering is an alarming vulnerability. "Oliver's incredibly vulnerable in one sense," he says. "He's like a kid. He's insecure about a lot of little things that many less talented or powerful people never even think about. He keeps his insecurities close to the surface and he's not afraid to let them out once in a while. That's what's great about it, that's what's healthy. On one level he's a five-hundred-pound gorilla and on another level he's a kitten on the freeway."

As the Stones' separation became more of a reality, their friends began to accept the disintegration of the marriage. For Elizabeth Stone, it has been a painful time. This is the first of her husband's films she is not a part of. There will be no Naijo No Ko credit on this one. "I talked to Oliver recently and I started crying on the phone," she said at the time. "I told him I don't want to end the marriage, ruin the family. But he's still mad at me. I would think he would want someone who knew him and still loved him. Someone who knew his secrets and still accepted him for who he is. My therapist said that Oliver must have learned to harden his heart at a very early age, probably when his mother left him at camp when he was four—he was abandoned for nearly two months and had to harden his heart to survive."

Stone says this is the kind of attitude that drove him from counseling: "My wife and her shrink. They saw me as a decadent, self-destroying animal. It's all based on some narrow, dualistic point of view. Elizabeth has a very condemning attitude, but she certainly drove the stake into the heart of the marriage by insisting on being right and trying to fix blame to the indiscretions that came out. That was not the solution to the problem. That only exacerbated the problem. The problem was Liz and Oliver. Two people. Two different value systems. Neither is right or wrong. Just human."

Filming heated up. The previous day there were five injuries on the set, and the next day was not off to a good start. The scene was a difficult one in which Tom Sizemore, as sadistic cop Jack Scagnetti, attempts to rape Mallory in her cell. At first, the problem was Juliette's lack of energy. She was so tired that she could hardly keep her eyes open. On one take, Sizemore burst into the cell and shouted his line, "Okay, rise and shine Mallory," only to discover that she was really asleep—Juliette had passed out between takes. Stone called out, "Cut!" and sighed deeply. "Somebody wake her up." He walked away from his post and muttered, "I heard she was out until five in the morning. This is like walking through pea soup. It's so hard to get through, to get things accomplished."

A few takes later, Lewis came to life but miscalculated a move and smashed Sizemore in the nose. Blood began spurting out and Chris Renna was called to the set. He didn't think the nose was broken, and they decided to wait to treat it until the scene was finished so they could use it for the shot.

Lewis claimed these episodes were the exception to the rule. "I really never hang out," she said back in her trailer on a break. "I'm usually alone so I kind of went out . . . anyways I didn't get any sleep, but that's not how I usually am. That's the most irresponsible I've been, but I knew what I had to do the next day. Had it been another scene I might've had problems, but because it was a scene where I had been in jail for a year and hadn't spoken in five months, I knew I'd be able to pull it off."

Were these actions the result of internalizing Mallory's wild and crazy character? Lewis said not. "No, it's because of where I'm at in my life and because I'm working on this movie and everyone's kind of a little bit wacky. I don't internalize the characters. If anything, I get bored with them. I get that way actually with all my characters. I like to know what I'm doing and not be too schizophrenic. Acting is a joke, in a way. It's 'Do your southern accent really heavy. Dress up, more lipstick.' When I'm in costume with all that exterior, it helps me project a certain character. For me, the emotions are what sum up a character— what they're predominantly made up of. And with Mallory, that's rage or hostility. Pain. I make sure I show some pain in there because that's real. Multilayered. It's not just an ego. I make sure to make it human."

Later Stone admitted he lost his temper with Lewis when she showed up at the prison somewhat out of it. "I was screaming at her. I couldn't help it. We've been having all these problems, and she wasn't responding. I had a bunch of squibs [special effect devices which release screen blood] going off, and she was missing her cues, her lines, her marks, and I said, 'Look, people can get hurt. It's a real serious thing, you can't take it that easy. You have to do it right.'"

Overall, though, Stone was very happy with Lewis. "It's not an easy role and she's getting it," he says. "She's making Mallory come alive. She *is* Mallory. A great instinctive actress. And very sweet. I'm very attracted to her actually, but I don't want to be a dirty old man so I act like her father."

The most expensive and difficult scenes to shoot were the prison riot scenes. "You're talking about doing a riot scene in a real prison, with real prisoners around and real weapons," Herb Gains points out. "Put all of those elements together and it's a huge problem. We had many meetings with the prison administrators and then we designed the schedule so that we went into the prison twice. The first time we were there for about eight days and we did a lot of dialogue and story set-up, stuff like that. Then we decided that on the last three days there we'd get our feet wet with some riot stuff. It was done basically as a test, an experiment to see what the problems were going to be. We did some of the smaller riot scenes without the shooting stuff, and that gave both us and the prison a tremendous education. We wound up making a considerable amount of changes because of the problems that surfaced. For example, when we used prisoners as extras, it was good because it gave them a chance to do something and got their cooperation, but it also gave us more limitations on the equipment we could use and the hours we could be in certain places. When we went back to the prison, we took this into account and were able to move much more efficiently and had more time to shoot."

Most of the cast dreaded returning to the prison because it was such a dismal and depressing environment. Juliette Lewis had mixed emotions about it. Though she disliked the environment, she also admitted that it gave her a lot of energy from which to draw on for the more physical scenes. "The scenes we've been shooting have been rough. There's a lot of physical stuff, but the prison is really weird. It gets the adrenaline going. I remember when we first walked through it, I didn't get sad and think about the human condition and all. I know what these people have done. I have an imagination. But the hardest thing for me is working hard physically. I'm really not into that. When I was in P.E. I'd bunt the ball. I'd do the least amount of effort possible and still try to play the game. But because of Oliver keeping on me, I decided to work physically harder. The emotional part, rage and all that stuff, it was all there. I just wanted to put it out on the canvas, so to speak."

Lewis and Stone clashed most over the physical requirements of the role. "Oliver wanted me to keep up with the physical workouts, pull-ups and stuff," she said, "which near the middle of the movie I didn't do any more. So he kept on me in that aspect, making me work out. I'm a person who only does what I absolutely need. I'm just that way. He wants you to just do it all."

In spite of this, Lewis and Stone got on pretty well. "What I really like about Oliver is that we work very fast. He also brings out your feelings a lot. We had one scene where he told Woody to ask me how I felt. It was like, 'You guys get into how you felt about the killing.' He'll just throw stuff like that out there to help you improvise a scene.

"He's antagonistic sometimes," she continued. "It's not like he just picks on a female entity. It's not like you're alone. He picks on the cameraman, the sound guy, the hair guy, the makeup woman. Everybody gets their share. Oliver and I have a good rapport because he doesn't relate to me like a woman, it's as an artist. I don't get easily offended. I told Oliver in rehearsal that if he tries to relate to me as a woman, he'll only confuse himself. This isn't about that. This is about making good and interesting scenes."

This attitude is also prevalent in Stone's relations with the crew.

Stone may be a dictator, but he's a dictator with a sense of humor. His crew accepts his quirks as a small price to pay for working with such a giant talent. They are a crack outfit, but not beyond taking an occasional potshot at their leader. When a crew member is told that he must take down and store part of a set today instead of tomorrow, he haughtily asks the production person why it must be done today. "Because the Creative One wants it that way, that's why." The crew member nods. No further explanation is needed.

"Contrary to the Oliver Stone myth, Oliver is not a real tyrant on the set," Jane Hamsher says. "He's so comfortable in his role as a director that he doesn't get that angry or upset. From watching him, I think his process is very much one of having confidence about his instincts so that whatever is thrown at him on the set he just merges with it."

Hamsher, who along with Don Murphy has become part of Stone's production team with several projects in the works, including a revival of *The Planet of the Apes*, also worked extensively on the music for the film. She was surprised at Stone's openness here. "When we first started working with him, I was worried because I thought he was going to be so firmly tied to using sixties music. He'd never had much exposure to any experimental or alternative music, and that's what I was really passionate about using in the film. So I put together a tape for him, at his request, of all the music I'd like to use. It was a dream tape, really, because I couldn't imagine any major film studio incorporating this kind of music. There was a real temptation to pull my punches, and that was the first time I learned you should never try to second-guess Oliver. It was very edgy stuff. Everything from L7 to Jane's Addiction, Captain Beefheart and the Velvet Underground, Diamanda Galas, and even the murder scene from Alban Berg's *Wozzeck*. I threw in stuff that was unlistenable, even to me, just to challenge him, and I figured if he hated it, I would have at least made my mark way over to the extreme side, so if we agreed on something in the middle, it would be a little closer to what I wanted.

"After I gave him the tapes I didn't hear anything until we left on a trip to scout locations in the Southwest. It was just me and Clayton and Victor and Bob in the back of a very small van and Oliver was in the front. All of a sudden Oliver pops in these tapes as we're barreling down the road at ninety and starts screaming the lyrics to 'Shit List' by

L7 at top volume, much to the annoyance of everyone in the van. I was stunned. This was one of my first experiences in the ways of Oliver Stone, because nobody wants to hear that shit at eight o'clock in the morning, not even me, and I like it."

Stone's appreciation of the music carried over into the shooting of the film. "When a scene was going to be shot, Oliver would frequently have a song already in mind that he wanted to use as playback on the set to create a strong ambience," Hamsher goes on. "Almost all of his choices came from those early tapes I'd done for him. Sometimes, I would think, 'That song doesn't make any sense for this scene,' and then I would see how it was all coming together and how he had comprehended the song in a way that I clearly hadn't. He had an idea of the energy of the scenes even when they weren't altogether there yet; the actors would improvise around that energy and he would bring his own experiences to it. It would all sort of merge then and there, and the method was incredibly successful. For scenes where he hadn't decided on music beforehand, he would come in and ask what I had. I would pull some stuff out and say, what about this or what about that? He would pick something really unlikely in my book, but I just stopped worrying because it would always work beautifully when we were ready to shoot. It was unnerving, however, when he didn't want to select it until that very last moment. I would tear my hair out trying to anticipate him, pissed off that we hadn't done this two weeks before. But it was futile. If he wanted to go with how he felt at that moment, then that's exactly what he would do."

The biggest clash with the prison authorities came over using guns in the riot scenes. "The prison was giving us a hard time about using the guns," Herb Gains says. "Oliver isn't the kind of guy to go down without a fight. It's not an option with him to quit. Over a period of weeks of constant pushing, if one approach didn't work, he'd try another. Compromise is the last solution with him."

Stone wanted to use prop guns in the riot scenes, but the prison was concerned about security since prop guns contain a mechanism that could be disassembled and used to make real weapons. Stone turned to Phil Krone, a friend of his with some influence in Illinois politics. After a few calls to the right people, the administration changed their mind so long as real prisoners were not allowed near the filming area.

As the riot scenes were shot, Stone added more and more outrageous sequences. The longer shooting had gone on, the more radical the picture became. It almost seemed as if there was a theme to *Natural Born Killers* after all. All this excess was a statement of its own. Here was a film which dealt with America's schizophrenic fascination with crime, fueled by the proliferation of tabloid and "reality" TV shows. And by making the violence in the film so extensive, Stone seemed to be saying, 'Yes, the media has an effect on crime, and if you don't believe me, look at *this*." A longtime foe of any form of censorship, Stone seemed now to be presenting a viable argument in its favor. With all the controversy over violence in film and on television, Stone was once again tapping into a controversial issue just as it reached the apex of public interest.

> "You're a parasite, Wayne, you feed on misery."
>
> Mallory Knox in **NATURAL BORN KILLERS**

"Oliver has his ear to the ground," Mike Menchel confirms. "It doesn't matter what echelon of the social strata he's at, doesn't matter whether you're talking about truckers or politicians. He can foresee the proper times to make films about issues. Political hotspots, social hotspots, things that should be questioned and brought to the attention of the public. Sometimes he'd say, 'Make a note about this,' and six months later you remember you made a note about something that is now in all the papers, on all the news stations, a world event. And Oliver's already making a film about it. He just knows this stuff. That's not luck. It's because he's bright."

As the filming wrapped at the end of July, the crew was excited. It had been a grueling project, but a startlingly original one. For Harrelson, Lewis, and Sizemore, it had been easily the most demanding film of their careers, and Robert Downey, Jr., had shown yet another side to his strong acting ability. Tommy Lee Jones had now completed his third Oliver Stone film. (John C. McGinley has been in four, but his appearance in *Born on the Fourth of July* was only for one scene.)

Once again the editing process was a formidable task. As he had done in *JFK* and to a much lesser degree in *Heaven and Earth*, Stone had again used several film formats. And *Natural Born Killers*, like *JFK*, included an abundance of special opticals, over a thousand, in fact. Yet

Bill Brown says editors don't mind going the extra mile with Stone because of his commitment: "He works with you. A lot of guys will say, 'I've got reservations at Spago's at seven. You guys work on it all night and I'll look at it in the morning.' But if they would stay the extra three hours it would be finished, instead of us having to come in so he can look at everything we did which takes another three hours. Oliver's the kind of guy who will just hang with you until you get it right, and that makes a big difference. It also makes people work harder for him."

Stone is exhilarated about the project. "There's a savagery and a voracity in there," he says, "but it's filtered now by a more satiric point of view. There's an element of humor in the tragedy. It's about excess, but only partly about insensitivity. What is the act of killing? The movie delves into that question. It asks the taboo questions. Do people deserve to be killed? For those who see it, there is a wisdom in *Natural Born Killers*. It may not be easy to see and it may be controversial, but there's a deeper meaning to it. It's not so direct. It's like the French puppet players. It has meaning but it's shadow meaning."

Richard Rutowski believes that *Natural Born Killers*, like all of Stone's films, helps him better understand himself. "It's an exploration of what's going on inside him. It's analytical to a point, but he doesn't have control of it. I think that's what he's looking for—how to control it. He has control of the medium, but I don't think he has control of his mind. He can control his mind in a working structure but not how he feels about himself. He's constantly trying to explain that and put those demons on celluloid—writing and filmmaking are his psychotherapy."

Chris Renna agrees. "I think that at times, when he sees faults and flaws in himself or in those very close to him, he deals with it by projecting it onto someone or something else. 'I didn't do that, you did,' or, 'That's not the way it was, this is how it was.' That's projection. In a very obscure way, I think that may be what his films are. A giant projection of some of these conflicts. He directs so that he can get those images into a visual form that he can send off on a beam of light, out of the projector, onto an enormous screen for him to see, and for him and the entire world to interpret."

In August 1993, after the film was completed, Stone returned to his ranch in Colorado to spend time with his kids, ride horses, and think about his next step. "Here in Colorado I've made an effort again to get back in touch with the land. The need for that has stayed with me. There's something going on and it's beyond me. This is an austere and rugged land. It's a strange place for me to end. Do you think I'll end here? Is this me? Is this austerity me? Or do you think it's just me looking for another me? I wonder sometimes how I might end my life. What is the third act?"

Epilogue:
Searching
Within

"The past is prologue. . . ."
Jim Garrison quoting Shakespeare in JFK

In October 1993, Stone went to China with Janet Yang to investigate film production possibilities there. This trip was followed by one to Tibet with Richard Rutowski to visit the Rinpoche monks. This excursion in particular was part of Stone's increasing spiritual quest. As a young man he sought to find the meaning of life at "the bottom of the barrel" in Vietnam, and for the last decade he experienced the best the world has to offer at the top in Hollywood. Neither has been enough.

In December, *Heaven and Earth* was released, with disastrous results. For the most part, the critics lambasted it as yet another Vietnam diatribe from Oliver Stone. Many of the reviewers seemed to be concerned with attacking Stone instead of the film. A few prominent writers

516

trashed his entire career in their articles as if he had never done anything worthwhile. Perhaps he had gone too far in defending *JFK* and had made too many enemies. The idea of the film being among the first to explore the viewpoint of the Vietnamese people seemed to elude or bore most critics. One couldn't help but wonder how *Heaven and Earth* would have been perceived had it come from someone else. Audience exit polls were very high—people who saw the movie liked it, but very few actually saw it. In the wake of bad reviews and poor attendance, *Heaven and Earth* was pulled rather quickly from theaters and shelved.

In late August 1994, *Natural Born Killers* was released and shot to Number One immediately. It was the biggest opening of any Oliver Stone film. Critics seemed overwhelmed. Roger Ebert called it "a masterpiece." Richard Corliss of *Time* said it was "the work of a virtuoso" and called Stone "Hollywood's most audacious auteur." While some claimed the film was "incomprehensible" and "reveled in violence," most of the top critics agreed that it reestablished Stone at the forefront of today's filmmakers. The box office success didn't last long, however, and after three weeks in the Top Five "Killers" began to sink. In the end it was a hit (grossing fifty million in the U.S. alone before year's end), but not a blockbuster.

In October, *Natural Born Killers* was overshadowed by Quentin Tarantino's *Pulp Fiction* which had won the Palme d'Or at Cannes and became an instant critical and popular favorite. Both movies had a dark appeal, but *Pulp Fiction* was much easier to digest with its funny banter and entertaining glimpse-through-the-peephole approach. *Natural Born Killers* supplied an almost science fiction kind of escape, but its startling glimpse inside the mind of a mass murderer, rampant with horror and confusion, is simply too much for most people. It's as if Stone, by expanding upon the somewhat limited vision of the original script with new layers had left his audience behind.

Now forty-eight, Stone stays for the most part in a small apartment only a few miles from the Santa Monica home where his wife and children still live. He and Elizabeth have been divorced since August 1994. Stone agreed to give up the California properties but retained the Telluride, Colorado, house. Keeping the Colorado house was not a wise financial move according to his business people, but Stone refused to sell it. Colorado represents a retreat to him, a place of introspection. The large rooms which used to make him uneasy now signify his determination to overcome such anxiety. In fact, the entire house is perhaps a symbol of his new direction—the voyage inward, the search to understand and come to terms with himself. "It's been a year of tremendous change," Stone acknowledges. "But I feel like a big weight has been removed from my shoulders. They were vast changes, but good ones. Ultimately, Elizabeth will understand that. I think in many ways she probably is in a stronger place now than she ever was. She is coming to terms with things not only to do with our marriage but in herself, which are important for her to deal with. We experience pain when we look at ourselves, but pain is part of life too, and through the pain comes growth. It's possible Elizabeth and I will become partners in parenting the children in a way we never have before. And, as time passes, I hope that we will become friends again and that our friendship will last."

It is more than ironic that it was during the making of *Heaven and Earth*, which deals with the struggle for freedom, that Stone first seriously entertained the idea of divorce, and it was during *Natural Born Killers*, in which the protagonists refuse to be confined by any limits or laws, that he went through with it. His relationships with his co-workers and employees, such as Alex Ho, changed as well. Like his protagonists, he loosed himself from the things he felt were binding him. In some ways, it seems as if the increased freedom has left him a more relaxed and gentle man.

Stone has been seeing different women, but is not yet seriously involved with anyone. "I still have a family," he says. "There are some days where I'll sit here and feel a tremendous loss for my children. Sean's a strong kid; Mikey doesn't understand. Elizabeth, on her better days, has been great. I've had much anger toward her inside me on certain days. I look at it as a state of mind to be overcome, but it's going to take time. I don't think I necessarily have to be married. For the last twenty-five years of my father's life, people would say, 'Why don't you remarry?' and he'd say, 'Why?' I might do that. I see who I want to see and I'm happy. I don't know what is going to happen by Tuesday of this week, but I like having the freedom to do that."

Too unconventional for organized religion, Stone has been seeking spiritual answers on his own and has found comfort in Buddhism. Though he considers himself a student, he has been investigating the discipline for some time through his association with Le Ly Hayslip and Richard Rutowski. Filming *Heaven and Earth* was an important turning point. "I saw the temples when I was nineteen in Vietnam, but I didn't relate to them as deeply as I do now," Stone says. "Seeing the monks with their begging bowls on the sides of the roads at dawn and how the people of the villages feed them, make them a part of their life, made a strong impression on me. And how every house has a shrine, both exterior and interior, to their ancestors. The people are surrounded with the spiritual because they live it on a daily basis. It's in the rice growing, it's in their respect for nature and their respect for each other. That's not to say that there is no crime or no problems. There are many corrupt 'Buddhists' as well. But still, I saw a sense of harmony and gentility in their society. It's not just a Sunday thing like it is in America. We live our lives in layers, I think, and the most important layer is the spiritual layer, but we lose sight of that when we're under a lot of stress."

Stone has learned to take the feelings of others more into consideration, and this has made the breakup with Elizabeth more difficult for him. "We're both trying to deal with the things we took for granted, like success, life, happiness, idealization, etc. I send her books and she sends me books. Ultimately, though, we're different people. We don't have the same values and we don't see the world in the same way. There is no right or wrong in this situation. We're just different. I do know that by severing the cord with her I ceased lying and that was positive. Light came in, a more honest light."

When the Writers Guild of America Foundation honored Stone with its Lifetime Achievement award shortly before the release of *Heaven and Earth* he said: "I hope I never lose my need to write. Tennessee Williams once wrote a piece about his later years in which he said that the greatest danger facing any writer is not privation but luxury. Luxury is the wolf at the door and the fangs of the wolf are all the little vanities and conceits that success is heir to. I hope and pray that I will be writing when I am old . . . that I will be able to feel the sufferings and pleasures of this life, or if not, that the serenity of wisdom may allow me to express myself in fewer and fewer words."

In many ways Stone is now facing the greatest battle of his life—mastering his own mind. As of January 1995, he has been living alone for over a year and a half and many of his perceptions have changed. Those around him agree that he gets less upset than he used to and recovers from a setback much more quickly. He still has dark moods and bouts with depression, but seems better able to see these things for what they are—old enemies rising up from his past as projections of his mind, rather than signs of impending doom. "Buddhism teaches the world and its desires to be illusory—samsara, a whirlpool—and in accepting them as such you teach yourself to step outside it, the world, and become detached," he says. "I've been able to step back from the abyss of pain. I've had luck, misfortune, success, and failure, and I think that now I can accept them equally as impostors. Being able to spot that early enables me to be less drawn in and less tossed and turned by the winds of fate. I often see desire as elusive. Eros is the most underrated force in the universe. It carries us through the darkest hours and hides in the deepest tunnels of the mind. It's been a consistent, driving thread in my life. Simone de Beauvoir wrote of sex as 'the sixth continent.' It's the place everyone can go for free. But it's also part of the illusion. I'm aware of that, but sometimes I'm pulled in because I don't mind being pulled in. I'm not sure if I'm ready yet to step outside the cycle of life. In some ways I am, but in some ways I'm not able to. Or don't want to."

The key for Stone has been an increased awareness. Long known as a person who never stops pressing ahead, he has learned the value of introspection and self-examination. Rather than agonize over the negative, his focus now is more on finding the positive aspect of every experience. "I know if I can be forgiving of myself, then I can be forgiving of others," he says now. "If I can genuinely appreciate and love myself more, then I know I can better love others. I had black periods in my teens, my mid-twenties, and probably this period has been one of the most painful of my life. The suffering overwhelmed me when I was younger, it made me a creature of my moods. Now I am more of a warrior. I am able to use pain and to see through suffering. And I'm trying to plant the seeds of joy.

"I understand now more fully the power of karma—karma *not* as fate, but as your responsibility, your character, the result of your actions. The final law of cause and effect. Not looking outside yourself, but looking inside to yourself."

For years, Stone has functioned by taking the pain he has experienced in life, using it as a springboard for creativity and drive. "It's crucial to turn our negatives into positives," he says. "I've had feelings of inferiority which have often turned into self-loathing and depression. But I've sometimes been able to turn that depression into melancholy and the melancholy into good work. I've also tried to turn excess into a productive thing and use it in my work. Either you use something or you don't. It is worse to be ignorant of it. Ignorance is one of the six negative emotions that Buddhism describes—pride, jealousy, desire, ignorance, greed, and anger."

These days Stone is attempting to transcend his pain by examining it instead of running from it. He meditates daily on this and on cultivating more joy and happiness in his life. One of his great strengths as a dramatist has always been his ability to get in touch with suffering, but now he seeks to develop compassion on a more personal level. "The work has been compassionate, but I don't feel I've been a particularly compassionate human being. That is the greatest lesson I have to learn. I was always willing to expose myself to discomfort and uncertainty, but now I'm trying to expose myself more to love and compassion. I no longer have the feeling that I have to justify my life by my work. My focus has to be more spiritual and less materialistic. Otherwise I'll always be at the mercy of others and there's no peace in that. In fact, for the first time in a long time I feel I could handle life without ever making another movie. I want to make movies, but I don't feel so compulsive about it any more. I hope the films I do make reflect honestly the things I experience in life and continue to grow with me, become more refined, more soulful."

For most of his working life, Stone has been an intensely private person whose personal life seemed to burst out compulsively despite his desire to conceal it. He has only recently begun to see the value of sharing difficult experiences as a way in which to reduce their power over his life. "Being interviewed for this book, looking back over my life, has made me more sentient," he says. "What we think is secret is really seen anyway. It's a lesson in life. Nothing is really hidden. Even when you're fucking in your bedroom, your ancestors are watching. There are no secrets. It's not that I haven't known that, but at the age of forty-eight, maybe I'm more aware of it and am taking some active steps, especially in telling the truth. I've had a lot of work to do on my craft and on myself, and I've had periods of doubt and lack of confidence that sent me astray for months or even years sometimes. Like everyone, I have my complaining side, my whining side, my self-pitying side, my angry side. I see through it sometimes and sometimes I don't. But I've learned that, just as I can affect things in the world around me, I can change things about myself. I've been getting in touch with memories and working through things in my past. Also, taking stock of where I am at this point in my life and becoming more at peace with the idea of death."

Much of Stone's work has a recurring theme of facing death and surviving. "I was always fascinated with it," he says. "The fact that I wrote a book about suicide that was thirteen hundred pages long at the age of nineteen certainly illustrates a very strong propensity toward it. Death is really not talked about. Death and women are two unknowns to males. Because of that, women assume this mysterious power over our psyche, and death is the same way, it's the other unknown, and it terrifies us. And I think death and sex are intertwined, death and love, death and women. And that intertwining is partly the demon that motivates me. I think that sometimes you want to locate that demon and purify it, and at other times you should never expose that demon. To exorcise that demon may be to lose the better part of yourself. Originally, I wanted to push that part of me down; now I don't feel that it should be exposed. I don't think it is something I should be ashamed of, but I don't think it should be discussed. We all have certain fantasies, we all have secrets. A filmmaker prostitutes himself already by making his fantasies public, but it is at least in his power, the limited power he has, to cut the length of the revelation. And why not? At least we have something we can control. We can't control our compulsions, our desires, our obsessions. I still question the cosmos regularly. I still have suicidal mentalities, the attitude 'Why go on, why not put a gun to your head?' But I have a choice. Every morning when the alarm goes off and I get out of bed, I'm aware of that choice. On a good day when I wake up, I breathe, and I decide to put my left foot down, then my right foot, and I get up. There is a decision in that, and on a good day I am aware of it each morning. You can wake up with your cup half full or half empty. That's a choice we have—how we accept our karma or start changing it."

As a child, Stone learned more about how to achieve than he did about how to be happy. After the many traumas that grew out of his parents' divorce, he reinvented himself. He didn't like who he was becoming, so he broke away to Asia and created a new Oliver Stone. But while this new person lived life with great gusto, his joy was more about experiencing pleasure than real happiness. Only in his work did Stone seem to really find peace. Writing and directing became his escape. They not only allowed him to immerse himself in another world where the pressures of his private life were neutralized, but they also gave him a vehicle to express the pain he was concealing. Without realizing it, Stone has long been practicing his own form of prayer and meditation. In his work he sought what the Tibetan Buddhists call *rigpa*—awareness, pure Mind. Christians call it "God," Muslims define it as Allah, Hindus as the "Self." More than anything, it means attaining peace within yourself and with the world around you by acknowledging a greater and purer power. When an artist creates, he or she is in touch with this pureness. Stone now seems to have rediscovered something he long sensed, an exteriorization of an inner state that has existed within him since he was a child.

Stone no longer sees himself as a lone wolf. He has met many on a spiritual quest like himself—wild Indian medicine men in peyote ceremonies, Brazilian Shamans on ayahuasca, Tibetan monks, Vietnamese villagers, artists and just simple people—all of them looking for the truth. And ironically, for a child who thought the only way to be satisfied was to be the very best, he has found a peace in being like so many others. "Suddenly, I am good enough because I'm like everybody else," Stone says. "I feel like all these years I've been battling my mind. And now instead of my mind controlling me, I'm controlling my mind. But that brings up the idea of who's the 'I'? I feel the only way to make peace with my mind is by experiencing the absolute Mind, the pure consciousness of life."

More than anything else, what has enabled Stone to succeed is his stubborn refusal to give up. His attempts to reconcile the inner strife that powers him have been successful in enabling him to live more contentedly with his private conflicts, but not to overcome them. He remains driven and searching. This is part of what makes him such a powerful artist and unique human being. Which is as it should be.

For that fine madness still he did retain
which rightly should possess a poet's brain.
—Michael Drayton
(1563–1631)

Great wits are sure
to madness near allied
And thin partitions do
their bounds divide.
 —John Dryden
 (1631–1700)

After marshalling his forces around *Noriega* (with Al Pacino) *Hoover* (with Robert DeNiro as J. Edgar), and *Evita* (with Michelle Pfeiffer), Stone settles on *Nixon* (with Anthony Hopkins) for his next project. He then splits with Arnon Milchan and Warners and looks into new deals with Andy Vajna and Disney. Seven weeks before shooting a first draft of the *Nixon* script is stolen from 20th Century-Fox and given to the press. Almost immediately the old *JFK* struggles begin again in the press. Stone's script is attacked before it is filmed. The last act continues.

Stone

The Early Screenplays

BREAK

Break centers on Anthony Darnell, who in Stone's first draft of the script has a brother, a poet named Alexander. They seem to represent two sides of Stone: Anthony, the restless adventurer, who searches for the meaning of life by smashing into it, and Alexander, the reflective poet/philosopher, who stands back and comments on the madness. Early on, Anthony tells Alexander his poems are anarchy and his pen could be used to move men if he wanted to. Alexander points out that he at least has a definite point of view while Anthony is still searching, trying to make sense out of chaos. By the end of the screenplay Anthony is speaking more and more in poetry, but his experience in the Eastern wars has led him to a better understanding of life. Alexander, meanwhile, has been overcome by nihilism, throwing himself into a fire made by burning his books and papers. This may well reflect Stone's belief that by living life to the hilt, the classic Dionysian view, he is more likely to attain some modicum of peace than by analyzing it in an attempt to make the right decision, the Apollonian view.

Taking another step toward what would ultimately become *Platoon*, in his final draft of *Break* Stone combined Anthony and Alexander into one person, a poet and truthseeker willing to take his quest to the ends of the earth. This version also featured the music of The Doors, employing lyrics and even some of the more complex interpretations of the songs to enhance scenes. It is loaded with Morrison-like imagery, including Shamanic symbols such as the Great Snake and allusions to Rimbaud, the poet Morrison idolized.

Break contains many revealing biographical touches, most of which reflect Stone's attempt to assimilate his conflicted view of his parents. Early in the script, Anthony enters his father's apartment and encounters his father's mistress wearing only bra and panties and toting a gun. A portrait of his father on the wall is described as "a psychic abstraction of a man with seven faces blending into a mask of chaos." On the elevator down, Anthony runs into his mother on her way to a party. As she enters the blue bus (à la "The End" and "meet me in the back of the blue bus"), he hops on the back and peeks into the window, to see his mother lying naked with a headband around her head and smoking hashish from a hookah. At the party, Anthony observes various stages of sexual activity and even more innuendo. A man wearing a skintight plastic mask says he'd like to hear one of his poems. Anthony recites the following passage:

> The day Mommy ate Daddy, that was the day the cannibals came in to play. . . . One cannibal was as big as day. . . . Another . . . was as red as clay. One asked me . . . where the weed was. . . . Another asked what happened to the wine. And the biggest cannibal of all said . . . Mmmmm, your hind is divine.

Later in the party Anthony has sex with one of his mother's friends whom the narrative explains could, in her relationship to Anthony, be the same as his mother. Afterwards, to the music of "Not to Touch the Earth," he races down a hallway, encountering a bizarre image behind each door, including his mother "crucified on a cross, wearing rags and on the verge of death. Above her, painted in crude lettering is the word WITCH." In another room Anthony sees himself sleeping naked while a long green snake writhes over him. After more curious images, he makes his way outside, where he again sees his mother through the window. This time he perceives her as young, "in a long dress reaching to her ankles. She looks sweet and virginal, of simple allure, a woman much different from what she is now."

Anthony then goes off to the Eastern wars where he meets Lee and Isaac, who are based on Barnes and Elias. As in *Platoon*, Barnes (Lee) kills Elias (Isaac), but in this more surrealistic encounter it is a resurrected Elias who exacts his revenge. In the jungles, Anthony falls in love with a native girl and deserts her to join her cause until he is killed. He then finds himself in the underworld held captive by longhaired barbarians and a Pharoah god who tells him he is condemned to live "in a prison of your own devise." In the end, however, the Lizard King appears and leads Anthony to resurrection.

DOMINIQUE: THE LOVES OF A WOMAN

Dominique is a middle-aged but attractive widow, and living with Gilberto, a man ten years younger than herself, much as Stone's mother did after her divorce and was in fact doing at the time of writing. Like Jacqueline, Dominique grew up in France and met her husband during the war when he was stationed there. On her dresser is a picture of him in a captain's uniform—"a strong, clean, American looking man, out of another age." In the screenplay, Dominique is a widow; her husband has been killed in a car accident and it is clear that she still loves and misses him. In an earlier draft of the script, Dominique revealed in the last act that she had been lying to herself all these years about her husband's death. The truth was he left her after he caught her having an affair. The fact that he had been seeing prostitutes for years, often flaunting them in front of her, made no difference to him. The marriage was over. In later drafts, Stone cut this scene, preferring Dominique to be a woman abandoned by fate instead of her own sins and those of her husband.

Although she appears well off, Dominique's life is not to be envied. She is getting older and "tries to remember when she was young, but the memory is bad." At one point she describes herself as "a lovely antique and nobody wants to buy." She has a little money, but not vast amounts, especially when you consider that she is accustomed to high living. Her butler complains constantly, her live-in boyfriend is charming but too lazy even to pursue his painting or poetry with much zeal, and everywhere she goes she encounters the poor who expect her to take care of them simply because she appears to be rich. Dominique is bothered by all these concerns, but seems to have no idea how to solve problems, only avoid them. Unfortunately, all her skills are social.

Her greatest affection is for her eighteen-year-old son, Claude, whom she also supports. Claude, a personification of Stone before he went to Vietnam, has no desire to go to college or for that matter to do anything else except observe life. He is constantly watching the world around him, prodding it, testing it, wondering what is really going on. Claude—as Stone must have been then—seems to be in an incubation stage, examining, digesting, evolving, waiting to change. Early in the script, his mother denounces him for looking out the window at life, but never doing anything about it: "Last week you wanted to go to Brazil and work in a silver mine. The week before you wanted to be a movie director . . . it never stops." When Dominique accuses him of sleeping with anything that comes his way, Claude answers, "It's true. It's a problem I have. If I'm not sleeping with someone, I'm not consuming, and when I'm not consuming I'm not happy because I don't feel I exist . . . sometimes I wish somebody would stick a knife in me and wake me up."

When at one point Gilberto defends Claude to Dominique, saying the boy will "be a genius someday. Not just New York, the whole world is going to kiss his feet," Dominique counters, "Genius at what? At living in the desert and staring at the sun?" It is clear that she loves the boy, but doesn't understand him. The screenplay presents Dominique as someone who is basically very kind, but naively wants everyone to be happy all the time. Given unlimited funds, one gets the impression she wouldn't mind supporting the world. Just as long as she could still have her parties.

The story ends after a huge orgy in which Dominique participates enthusiastically. Tired now and feeling old, she walks home alone, having left Gilberto engaged in still more passionate sex with one of her closest friends on top of a large dining-room table. She pauses briefly at a bridge and looks into the river, seeing various stages of her life in the reflections on the water. For an instant she considers jumping in and ending it all, but instead moves on and a moment later is stopped by a man in a sportscar who claims to have been at the party. Lost in her spiraling world of pleasure for pleasure's sake, she hesitates only a moment before getting in. The car drives off into the distance, Dominique in yet another sportscar with yet another exotic stranger.

THE WOLVES

The script is loosely based on the Oresteian myth in which a banished prince returns home in disguise to avenge the murder of his father, the king, by slaying his mother and her lover. In *The Wolves*, the exiled son, Christopher, has plastic surgery, then returns to take a job on his wealthy family's Greek island and murder the father who cast him out. The plot is complicated when a younger brother, Anthony, shows up just in time for the murder and vows to find the killer. The story further deviates from the Greek myth in that Christopher's mother knows of his presence on the island, but does nothing to prevent him from murdering her husband.

While riveting at times, *The Wolves* loses momentum because it is written as an "open mystery," where the audience sees everything, instead of the more popular film form, a "closed mystery" which the audience unravels right along with the hero. Stone acknowledged this in notes he wrote at the time to introduce the screenplay: "In writing this draft I didn't try to conceal anything from the audience, letting them in early on all the secrets so that, like in Greek tragedy, they could watch with detachment and superiority the foolish mistakes of the characters." Detachment, as Stone would later learn, does not make for compelling film watching; the open mystery form, when used, must be surrounded with exciting sequences and surprise twists. For example, in *Platoon* we see Barnes kill Elias, but we don't know if Chris Taylor will avenge his friend's death until the moment he does it. Even in *JFK*, which is based on one of the most well known murder and conspiracy theories of modern time, Stone chooses to unravel the events and open the mystery gradually as New Orleans District Attorney Jim Garrison uncovers more and more evidence.

The Wolves has other flaws. Often characters' motives are described in the written text but not shown through action or dialogue. One of the first rules of good screenwriting is "to show and not tell," and Stone, now recognized as one of today's most visual screenwriters, has learned this well over the years. In *The Wolves*, Stone compensates for such errors with some very interesting characterizations. These are not simple, one-dimensional characters; they have complex motives and conflicting emotions like real human beings.

ONCE TOO MUCH

After being swindled by a hooker and her pimp in Mexico, college student Eric Welles (named for Orson Welles) is busted at the border with a small amount of marijuana. A San Diego judge gives him a choice between joining the Marines or going to jail, and Welles is soon shipped off to Vietnam. There, he loses his left arm and his innocence, but falls in love with a hooker he meets in a Saigon bar. When he returns to the United States he sets out for his parents' home near Santa Cruz, but never makes it. Instead, he falls into an almost hypnotic scenario of returning to Mexico where he encounters the same Tijuana hooker and sleazy street pimp who stole his money the first time around. This time he fights rather than be tricked and winds up killing the pimp. Arrested and jailed, he escapes, but is gunned down at the border, the same place his life was irrevocably altered before.

Once Too Much seems to be about destiny. Eric Welles lives his life as if he has little say in it, and indeed this may be the point. Between the corrupt Mexican police and the ironfisted courts at home, the savage Viet Cong and heartless fellow Marines he encounters in Vietnam and the contemptuous protesters and unscrupulous politicians who await his return, Eric is a pawn in his own life. He dreams about what might have been, reminisces about the hooker he never returned to, and fantasizes about having a normal life at home. But nearly every action he takes seems designed to set him up to fail again. This was the tragedy of so many of the Vietnam vets, who could not let go of what had been lost to the past long enough to find something worth having in the present. No doubt it was one route that Oliver Stone could have chosen when he came back from Vietnam. *Once Too Much*, as *Born on the Fourth of July* would later be, was a homage to the walking wounded.

THE UNGODLY

The film opens with a series of frighteningly up-close images that convey death, decadence, and decay—huge horseflies buzzing, fleabitten dogs shredding raggedy cow bones, a group of cavalry soldiers bathing in greasy water, the squirming corpse of a snake shot by a sharpshooter from a hundred yards away, a doctor opening a boil on a soldier's backside, a priest leading a hymn while nearby soldiers line up for five minutes with a painted and toothless Mexican whore.

Whereas previous Stone screenplays contained violence, here for the first time is the coolly detached attitude toward it that makes his characters so dangerous. The way in which Cogan, the Charles Bronson character, is introduced is a good example. A couple of rough-looking Mexicans are trying to outdo each other with a knife. The first man severs a beetle crawling on the bar, then the second man tosses a lime peel into the air and pins it to the far wall. Not to be outdone, the first notices a man about to inhale a newly rolled cigarette across the room and, before the second Mexican can warn him, he throws the knife and cuts the cigarette in two. Bad move. The stranger, who turns out to be Cogan, slowly walks over to the Mexican and grabs him by the throat, choking him with one powerful hand. When the Mexican pulls another knife, Cogan locks on his wrist with his other hand and wrenches the knife loose. Then, still strangling the Mexican, he takes the whiskey bottle, pours himself a drink, and swallows it down. Finally, after the Mexican turns blue, Cogan sticks his cigarette stub into the man's gasping mouth and drops him to the floor. He walks out with his back to the Mexicans. When one starts to go after him, their leader restrains him, knowing better.

What makes Cogan such a fascinating western hero is the other aspects of his character. He reads books, smokes marijuana (Mexican loco weed), and has been to China, Paris, and Africa. The plot, with Cogan serving as a guide for a wagon train going deep into Indian territory in order to gain access to the gold he believes is buried there, follows the basic Leone form, but Stone's images and main character are more compelling. In fact, many aspects of his writing come together in this screenplay. His previous tendency to describe a character's motivation rather than provide action to show it has evolved into an ability to dramatize inner emotion while still providing room for the actor to flesh out the scene. Though used here as a writing technique, this attitude would later develop into an integral part of Stone's directing style—giving the actor a specific way to go and then allowing him or her to expand on it.

THE COVER-UP

The Cover-Up is a story of intrigue and double cross, a strong character piece in which the protagonist, in this case a virtually unredeemable thug named Charles Baker, undergoes a major transformation. In the beginning, Baker is helped to escape from prison by a secret, high-powered organization in return for heading up their next operation. Using a hefty wad of cash fronted to him by the organization, he assembles a crew of lowlifes, some of whom consider themselves radicals for a new world order and others who are just plain killers for hire. The only thing that holds them together is that Baker is stronger and more vicious than the rest, with an innate, animal-like cunning that has long been his key to survival. The gang kidnaps the ten-year-old daughter of a powerful businessman, but instead of pocketing the $3 million ransom, the money is given away to charity to help the poor of New York City. Naturally, this generates major headlines across the country. It is then that we learn that the secret organization is composed of some key officials from the intelligence community, especially the FBI, and that the plan is to publicly discredit all such politically radical organizations.

Baker is ordered to kill the young girl. Faced with true innocence for the first time in a life of pain at the bottom of the barrel, Baker finds he is unable to destroy her. By refusing to carry out the plan, Baker knows he is signing his own death warrant. From this point on, the plot centers on his efforts to protect the little girl from the organization out to kill her. As the noose grows tight around the odd pair and several of Baker's compatriots are murdered, he devises a desperate plan.

Unfortunately, the plan only succeeds after the girl's parents are murdered, and finally even Baker and the girl themselves are killed. This unhappy ending reduced the commercial appeal of the piece, but it was still a compelling story. The secret organization is exposed and brought to justice, but this is little consolation. At the heart of *The Cover-Up* is the revelation of an essential goodness in even the worst of men, as a lifetime criminal tries to become gentle and understanding enough to relate to a little girl. But its ending suggests the opposite: that an inherent evil in all men overcomes such goodness. This reflected Stone's world view at the time: good may triumph, but only at the cost of great sacrifice. When the man at the top of the conspiracy is asked by a reporter how he could have such a convoluted picture of the world, he replies, "Oh no, you gentlemen make pictures of the world. I take the world—as it is."

THE RASCALS

The notes that open the 54-page treatment indicate that instead of the "despair of so many realistic New York films like *Midnight Cowboy* [1975 Oscar winner for Best Picture]" Stone wanted to show "a younger, more carefree attitude towards living—using New York '76 as our Henry Miller Paris of the 1920s." The notes even quote Miller and George Orwell. "Poverty," Orwell wrote, "annihilates the future." The notes add that it "forces you to live in the Here and Now—which, ironically, is one of the philosophical benefits of being poor. The only thing money can't buy *is* poverty."

Like so many of Stone's scripts, much of *The Rascals* is autobiographical. Chris, the writer, is described as "a Dostoyevsky kind of figure—he can't write until he's miserable," but inside he is "very much The Worker, wanting to perform only through his work." One of the best moments in the script comes when Chris goes to see his stockbroker father to borrow $200 on his twenty-ninth birthday (Stone's age at the time). As a hooker moves from room to room in the background, Chris's father tells him that "the last thing he believes in are birthdays and Christmas. That's for the suckers and the rest of the people. Besides, Chris is a bum, masturbating at this writing that never gets sold." But, the treatment notes, there is a gruff sense of humor in the old man, who smiles at his son with his eyes. A moment later he launches into another tirade: "Jesus, one fucking night of pleasure with your mother has sure taken its toll. I'm still being fucked for the fucking I had." He then runs down the list of crimes Chris has committed. It cost him $2,500 to bail Chris out of a San Diego jail on a dope charge. "And whoever told you to leave college and end up in Vietnam?" He didn't even call when he got back, Chris's father says. Instead, he went to jail. Then he busted up his marriage to a woman the father "never approved of in the first place. She wasn't even rich. And he's been soaking the Unemployment Bureau for more than a year. What kind of a son is that?"

Some of the best lines in the entire treatment come shortly afterward when the father says: "I once had a real nightmare when I was young—I dreamt I was alive. The only thing I can hope, for you, Chris, is an early death. Don't forget, I want you to give my body to science as long as they don't use any part of it for somebody else. I mean I don't want my eyeballs to be in somebody else's head." The treatment ends with a summary of what happened to each of the characters. Chris eventually finishes and sells his novel and then becomes miserable again until, with a sense of relief, he starts writing something new. He concludes by saying that "One day I think I'll start to take life a little more easily—as I get older." For Oliver Stone, this has yet to come to pass.

Major Influences Studied at NYU Film School

ORSON WELLES (1915-1985)

Orson Welles achieved some of the most significant cinematic breakthroughs of the century. His films of the forties foreshadowed contemporary film, even to the point of widescreen photography and stereophonic sound. *Citizen Kane* (1941) was radically experimental and its impact was enormous. Welles pioneered startling camera techniques, low-key lighting, wide-angle lenses, and flashback narrative, all of which were then imitated in countless films. Oliver Stone not only has built upon Welles's technical approach to narrative but also on his themes, which correspond to classical Western literature—the destructive nature of self-delusion and obsession, the tendency of power to corrupt, the distinction between social and psychological reality, and the value of learning from the past.

But in studying Welles, Stone was also studying many of the greats who came before him. Although Welles once claimed his preparation for *Citizen Kane* was watching John Ford's *Stagecoach* (1939) forty times, he was strongly influenced by the major European directors. The visual texture of *Citizen Kane* can be traced to Fritz Lang, the moving cameras to F. W. Murnau, the look to Joseph von Sternberg, and the deep focus realism to Jean Renoir.

FRENCH NEW WAVE

Stone studied many approaches to film theory, but the one that made the greatest impression on him was the French New Wave. The New Wave developed when a group of critics who wrote for *Cahiers du cinéma*, the French film magazine, decided to make their own films. Having studied film at Langlois Cinémathèque Française and written about it for nearly a decade, they were the first film-educated directors in history. But while they knew more about the medium as an art form, they probably knew less about the practical aspects of film production than anyone who had ever made films before. They made many mistakes which their low budgets would not allow them to correct and used editing to conceal the flaws. Instead of considering this a drawback, these directors saw it as an opportunity to break away from traditional filmmaking. They couldn't create a seamless flow that enabled audiences to forget they were watching a film, so they took the opposite approach and reveled in the fact that the audience was aware of the filming process. New Wave films constantly remind an audience that it is watching a film. Their techniques reflect the documentary style—hand-held cameras, natural lighting, location settings, direct sound recording, and improvised plot and dialogue.

JEAN-LUC GODARD (1930–)

Jean-Luc Godard was probably the most prolific and radical of the New Wave group. His most famous film was *Breathless* (1959), which Stone cites as the single work that most influenced his own. Modeled after a low-budget American gangster film, with a loose plot about a man on the run who is finally betrayed to police by his American girlfriend, *Breathless* contains the New Wave techniques mentioned above and others, such as beginning a scene with a huge disorienting closeup, then cutting or pulling back to reveal the context, a complete reversal of the standard practice.

The most characteristic New Wave technique was the editing style, which, instead of being seamless, was irregular and frequently broke the continuity. In *Breathless*, Godard eliminated transitional scenes or establishing shots, as Hollywood calls them, and used the jump cut, where a portion of a shot is edited out and the two ends are spliced together to create an unnatural progression and a sense of disorientation.

The jump cut is an essential element in Oliver Stone's style today and it works because the viewer's mind makes the necessary connection. Though it was used effectively as far back as 1925 in Sergei Eisenstein's *Battleship Potemkin*, with its famous scene on the Odessa steps, Hollywood felt orderly transitions were crucial as late as 1957, when Universal forced Orson Welles to shoot additional "establishing" scenes for *Touch of Evil*. The jump cut did not become acceptable to Hollywood until the success of the New Wave directors in the early sixties.

ALAIN RESNAIS (1922-)

Alain Resnais is considered part of the New Wave because his two greatest successes, *Hiroshima mon amour* (1959) and *L'Année dernière à Marienbad* (1961), came during the peak of the movement. But Resnais was older and began his career as an editor and director of short films, not as a critic for *Cahiers* like classic New Wavers Godard or François Truffaut, and it was his editing techniques that made an impact on Oliver Stone, especially in *La Guerre est finie* (1966).

LUIS BUÑUEL (1900-1983)

Luis Buñuel was one of the most experimental and anarchistic filmmakers in history. Though Spanish, he was part of the Renaissance in film which occurred at the time of the French New Wave. Buñuel is a vicious social critic who tries to advance humanity by exposing its flaws. He often uses sexual pathology to discredit what he sees as the bourgeois Christian culture, and considers such extremes as sadomasochism, fetishism, necrophilia, cannibalism, and bestiality all part of the mass psychosis of Western civilization. *Los Olvidados* (1950) appears to be about juvenile delinquency in Mexico City, but is actually a disturbing voyage into the dark side of man. Buñuel's Spanish-language *Wuthering Heights* (1952) ends with Heathcliff tearing open the recently interred coffin of his beloved and attempting to make love to her corpse. *The Discreet Charm of the Bourgeoisie* (1972) made a real impression on Stone's editing style, as did *Simon of the Desert* (1965) and *Viridiana* (1961). Buñuel was often criticized for a lack of style, but this may have been intended to be ironic. It was Buñuel himself who, when asked if he had ever been religious, replied, "I have always been an atheist, thank God."

Filmography

SEIZURE. 1974.
DIRECTOR/CO-WRITER OF SCREENPLAY

Seizure is scary, even when viewed today. The idea of crazed maniacs breaking into the home of a family is so close to the real fears most people have that it does indeed play, as Stone intended, like a nightmare come to life. The film is also odd. The low-budget and on-set chaos coupled with Stone's experimental approach results in a twisted cross between a New Wave foreign film and a grade-B horror movie. The rapidly moving camera, weird angles, strange lighting, sharp jump cuts, and other techniques must have made distributors uncomfortable, but they work to the film's advantage. Though the acting and production flaws are evident, they often add to the eerie anxiety. Instead of laughing and making jokes about "da plane, here comes da plane," when Herve Villechaize leaps through a window as a crazed, blood-stained midget wielding a huge knife, the viewer reacts with terror. It's only after the film is over that the comedy of the situation becomes apparent.

The story centers on the recurring nightmares of a horror novelist and his increasing fears that they will one day come to life. When the dreams do begin to happen in reality, one of the crazed invaders says to him, "Our hate was born inside of you. We breed inside of you." The entire film is dreamlike—the three maniacs are a horrifying but curious and outlandish combination, and the guests are an equally strange lot. Only the Blackstone family, the father, a forty-seven-year-old somewhat neurotic writer, his proper, family-oriented, still-pretty-but-getting-older blond wife, and their precocious ten-year-old son seem real and worth caring about, and that tension is what propels us to the ensuing madness. In the end, after the family and their guests are killed off, the entire film turns out to be yet another bad dream. But then, in a final twist, just as it seems the nightmare is destined to be played out yet again, we discover that the dream was so real this time that the novelist has died of a heart seizure.

MIDNIGHT EXPRESS. 1978. WRITER OF SCREENPLAY

(Discussed in detail in Chapter Four)

THE HAND. 1981. DIRECTOR AND WRITER OF SCREENPLAY

(Discussed in detail in Chapter Five)

CONAN THE BARBARIAN. 1982. CO-WRITER OF SCREENPLAY

(Discussed in detail in Chapter Four)

SCARFACE. 1983. WRITER OF SCREENPLAY

(Discussed in detail in Chapter Five)

YEAR OF THE DRAGON. 1985. CO-WRITER OF SCREENPLAY

(Discussed in detail in Chapter Five)

8 MILLION WAYS TO DIE. 1985.
CO-WRITER OF SCREENPLAY
(Discussed in detail in Chapter Five)

SALVADOR. 1985. DIRECTOR/
CO-PRODUCER/CO-WRITER OF SCREENPLAY
(Discussed in detail in Chapter Six).

PLATOON. 1986.
DIRECTOR/WRITER OF SCREENPLAY
The many parallels between the film and Stone's life go far beyond a loosely based character and display a startling candidness. Up to a point the storyline follows Stone's experience near perfectly. The film begins with a symbol of birth: the young soldier, Chris Taylor (Sheen), is "delivered" from the womb of a large transport plane into the harsh light of Vietnam. One of the first images he sees are those of bodybags, presumably the bodies of men whose place he has come to take. Through narration (letters written to his grandmother, as Stone had done) and his encounters with other GIs, we learn that Chris is a twenty-one-year-old child of privilege who volunteered for Vietnam because he was convinced that young men who had grown up with less than him could teach him something about life. Like Oliver Stone, the war was to be his metamorphosis, his passage to manhood.

Following his script, Stone staged versions of the battles and incidents he remembered from the war, and created the same tensions that had been within his original platoons—the division between the redneck "juicers," many of whom were gung-ho, and the "heads," pot smokers just trying to get out of the war alive. As much as they battle the enemy, the film shows these groups on a collision course. In Vietnam, *Platoon* suggests, American GIs recreated the world back home, with its strife over lifestyles, race, region, and class. Since the nature of the war left no clear and honorable path to victory, some of the soldiers focused their resentments and their guns on their comrades.

The acknowledged leader of the "heads" is good-guy Sergeant Elias (Dafoe), a survivor with a sleepy grin who wears two dice and a crucifix around his neck. He feeds recruit Taylor a hit of marijuana down the barrel of a shotgun. Elias is the platoon's conscience, its Shaman of compassion, guts, and racial harmony. As the merciless Sergeant Barnes, Tom Berenger represents the leader of the juicers and a man for whom combat and killing has become the only world. In *Platoon*, the North Vietnamese Army (NVA) and the Viet Cong are background figures in a more startling family tragedy—a sibling rivalry between a good brother, an evil brother, and the youngest brother forced to choose between them. Caught between Dafoe's philosophical Elias and Berenger's ruthless Barnes is Sheen's Chris Taylor, an Everyman (a young and not-so-romanticized Oliver Stone) whose purity of soul becomes the stake in an allegorical battle of good and evil. As the film develops in almost classic Shakespearean fashion, Chris hangs suspended between these two factions with his life and ideals in the balance.

Platoon is a lean and terrifyingly real vision of war. After finding one of their men ruthlessly butchered, the platoon enters a Vietnamese village that they suspect might be an enemy stronghold and, under Barnes's direction, a My Lai-type massacre is about to ensue when Elias comes upon the scene and forcibly restores order and sanity. Though his action saves the innocent villagers, Elias has finally crossed the point of no return with Barnes.

When the platoon is ambushed a few days later, Barnes takes the opportunity to catch Elias unawares in the bush. As he locks in his sights, Elias looks at him and smiles ingenuously. Barnes fires and leaves him for dead. When the platoon is evacuated by helicopter a short time later, Chris Taylor is shocked to see Elias, whom Barnes has reported as dead, racing desperately across a field as the enemy guns him down.

Though Taylor is sure that Sergeant Barnes is responsible, he is loath to confront him. He doesn't have to wait long, however, because it is Barnes who does the confronting when he bursts in on the potheads in their bunker and virtually dares them to attack him. Berenger gives Barnes an odd vulnerability as he almost pleads with the men to have the courage to kill him. But when Taylor takes him on, he turns the tables and nearly stabs the younger soldier until they talk him out of it.

When the camp is attacked by a large force, Barnes tries to kill Taylor again, but an air strike wounds him severely. Taylor, also wounded in the strike, finds him and at Barnes's request finishes him off. As the wounded Chris is airlifted from the bloody scene, his voice-over, speaking from the present, says: "Those of us who did make it have an obligation to build again, to teach others what we know and to try with what's left of our lives to find a goodness and a meaning to this life."

In the end, Chris Taylor is a true son of both "fathers," Elias and Barnes. Like Stone in Vietnam, he feels a kinship to both good and evil, and the fact that *Platoon* can support such a paradox without ambiguity echoes back not only to its classical structure but also to Stone's contradictory nature.

(Also discussed in detail in Chapter Seven)

WALL STREET. 1987.
DIRECTOR/CO-WRITER OF SCREENPLAY

Stone's story is not so much a Hollywood version of the Boesky-Levine scandal as a story about ethics and fathers and sons. As in *Platoon*, two father figures vie for Charlie Sheen's soul. Bud Fox (Sheen) must choose between the fast-buck schemes of the beguilingly corrupt Gordon Gekko (Michael Douglas) and the old-fashioned work ethic of his father (Martin Sheen), a blue-collar union man who refuses to "measure success by the size of a man's wallet."

The film opens with aerial shots of New York and the Frank Sinatra/Count Basie version of "Fly Me to the Moon." Stone and Bob Richardson shot the city as if it was a battle zone, with a camera that Vincent Canby of *The New York Times* described as "so restless and edgy that it defines Bud Fox's ambition better than the screenplay does." As the film opens, Bud wants what he thinks are the best things in life, and knows that the fastest way to get them is to hitch up to the current star of the Street, Gordon Gekko, an unscrupulous but devilishly charming multimillionaire corporate raider whose snaked-back hair gives off just a hint of Cobra. Though Sheen as Bud Fox is clearly the protagonist, the heartbeat of the film is the charismatic performance of Michael Douglas as Gordon Gekko. The character was named for the gecko, a tropical lizard with a large head that preys on small animals and never blinks its eyes. Looking as ferocious as a miniature crocodile, the gecko hides during the day and comes out at night to feed on insects. It sheds its tail when trapped, but its suction-cup feet enable it to walk fearlessly across ceilings and the slickest surfaces. And, as Sheila Benson said in the *Los Angeles Times*, "Wall Street is about the slickest surface possible."

Perhaps the best photographic sequence is Gekko's entrance—wheeling and dealing on the phone and monitoring his own blood pressure at the same time. The window behind him reveals his domain, New York's financial district, and in front of him is yet another loyal subject, quaking stockbroker Bud Fox. It's a rare view of life at the top, so perfect in its illusion that one desires not to look too closely, for fear of spoiling an ideal vision. After calling Gekko every day for thirty-nine days, Bud finally gets an appointment and spouts out a tip about Blue Star Airlines he chanced upon in conversation with his union rep father. Once Gekko bites, Bud finds he must keep the information coming; so he weasels secrets from one of his lawyer friends (James Spader), spies on Gekko arch rival Larry Wildman (Terence Stamp), and even partners in an office-cleaning service to provide the continued inside info it takes to keep the master happy. Lou Mannheim (Hal Holbrook in the role based on Stone's father) is a fellow broker who refuses to gain from inside trading info even as his livelihood begins to fail. He tries to persuade Bud that anything gained through obtaining inside, illegal information is not worth the price. But Bud ignores him, falsely assuming that honesty is just another has-been practice of the old guard.

As David Denby noted in *New York* magazine, one of the real strengths of the film is that Stone never falls into minimizing the lure of money. He gives the devil his due and never pretends that proper conduct is easy. Virtue may be its own reward, but Lou Mannheim's rumpled suits and Carl Fox's worn coveralls look pretty paltry next to Gordon Gekko's $1,500 suits. As Mannheim says, "That's the problem with money—it makes you do things you don't want to do." The choice between noble failure and victorious cad is not an easy one, and *Wall Street* is a fervent meditation on the real value of ethics. As in Woody Allen's *Manhattan*, long shots of the city at dusk and sunrise create a romantic mood, but the romance here is one of money and power. The characters may have a special love for the beauty of nature, but it's as if big success has endowed them with a swelling new appreciation of anything they can't own—sunsets, oceans, the stars and the moon.

While it makes all the financial maneuvering seem complicated and convincing, *Wall Street* is always easy to follow. The intricacies of the business are filtered through the characters' motives. Consequently, the audience usually knows what is going on and it always knows why. This is why *Wall Street* succeeds where other high-finance films failed. When Bud prospers, he rents a posh Upper East Side apartment and furnishes it with the best, including money-hungry interior designer Darien Taylor (Daryl Hannah). It's obvious he's going overboard. For those who might miss it, Stone cleverly drops in "Stopped Making Sense" by the Talking Heads as background music for the scene. Eventually, Bud sees the error of his ways when Gekko double-crosses him, choosing to trash the company Bud's father works for rather than run it as a business the way he promised. To top things off, Bud's father has a heart attack. In desperation, Bud seeks out Gekko's nemesis, Larry Wildman, to help him turn the tables on his former mentor and save the company for the men.

Of course he loses his material girl and the posh digs in the process, but Bud seems to think the truth is worth the price. Crime doesn't pay in Stone's version of *Wall Street*, however, and Bud is not allowed to get off that easy. His insider trading crimes catch up with him, and he is arrested at the investment firm where he works, humiliated in front of those he sought to impress, and taken away in cuffs. Once he realizes that Gekko orchestrated things so that he took all the risks, Bud decides to take his ex-idol down with him, and tricks Gekko into confessing on tape. The film ends with Bud having a chance at a reduced sentence, but it offers no gurantees. As the last shot pans slowly from the courthouse where the inside traders are standing trial to the gigantic World Trade Center, the tower from which the mighty have fallen, the message is clear: Despite Gekko's brilliant speech before the shareholders of a company he was about to trash, in the end, greed is bad.

(Also discussed in detail in Chapter Eight)

TALK RADIO. 1988.
DIRECTOR/CO-WRITER OF SCREENPLAY

Talk Radio may have been a better stage play than a movie because the kind of energy and excitement created in a live performance offsets the depressive feelings that rise up when an audience is confronted with such grim voyages into a part of reality most choose to ignore. The world of radio is made fascinating with colorful high-tech sets and stimulating photography, but this only sustains us for the first hour or so. Film is a medium that makes up for its impersonal nature by easily enabling an audience to get inside a character's head, but Barry Champlain's (Eric Bogosian) head is not a very comfortable place to be. What on stage might be a provocative mind-set comes across on film as a brutal assault that we want to look away from rather than embrace. Stone's skills as a director add intensity to a script and lead actor who are already overflowing with it. Consequently, the verbal abuse and psychological games that Barry Champlain plays with his listeners and himself become almost unbearable. *USA Today* critic Mike Clark commented that the film was "directed like a panther on steroids," and the truth is that *Talk Radio* was far too intense for most moviegoers to handle. It would have been easier to digest if Barry was fighting a real war in the jungle somewhere; easier if there was an explosion now and then, or a bit of mindless pillaging to take our minds off the inner turmoil. Anything to escape the pain in Barry's mind. This is both the real strength and the real weakness of the film. It is a alarming portrait of mental anguish—an in-depth look at something that none of us wants to see.

As Barry's show is about to go national, the tension finally explodes in his own gut-wrenching confession. Thrown off his routine by a caller who suggests that he must not think much of himself since he spends so much energy hurting other people, Barry begins to lose it on the air, finally dropping his charade and admitting, "I'm a hypocrite. I ask for sincerity and I lie. I denounce the system as I make love to it. I want power and money and prestige. I want ratings and success and I don't care about you or the world."

As the show ends and Barry stumbles out of the control room, his disgust with life is reconfirmed when he discovers that his co-workers have all taken his soul-baring tirade as just another clever shtick. Moments later in the parking lot when he says good-bye to his producer/girlfriend by telling her he's too old for her, it seems as if Barry is about to turn over a new leaf. Then, out of the darkness comes a middle-aged man asking for an autograph, and as Barry takes his pen to sign, he is gunned down.

The cast is particularly good—Bogosian is outstanding, but Alec Baldwin and John C. McGinley do fine jobs as his station manager and engineer, and Leslie Hope is convincing as his frustrated producer and girlfriend. Next to Bogosian, Ellen Green is the most interesting. She plays Barry's ex-wife with a mixture of frustration, love, and pity. When she looks at this successful man who has nothing but abuse for even his closest friends (as his ex-wife, she has obviously had more than her share), it's as if she is staring at a crippled boy in a wheelchair. She knows Barry is so insecure that he is walking a continual psychological tightrope. But even as she watches him get himself in deeper and deeper, she can't help but feel it's not his fault. Like the vast majority of his callers, Barry really isn't equipped to deal with a world as cruel as this one.

Bob Richardson's photography is captivating throughout and, along with Bruno Rubeo's sets, provides some of the more uplifting moments. Not that Bogosian isn't fun to watch. Through most of the movie he is pure magic, and never predictable. It's only at the end, when his personal pain is so apparent, that it becomes hard to hang on. Champlain's lengthy and often compelling monologues enabled Stone and Bogosian to communicate their views on all sorts of relevant topics, and to their credit, they maintained the right balance for the character and subject matter here. For people with such strong opinions it must have been difficult to resist the temptation to seize this aspect of the film as the ultimate soapbox.

Talk Radio would be worth inclusion in a time capsule as a startling portrait of its era. It makes a strong political statement, critical not only of sarcastic talk-show hosts who ridicule their callers and the world at large, but also of the people who have made such shows popular and the evils of a society that breeds them.

(Also discussed in detail in Chapter Nine)

BORN ON THE FOURTH OF JULY. 1989. DIRECTOR/PRODUCER/CO-WRITER OF SCREENPLAY

(Discussed in detail in Chapter Ten)

THE DOORS. 1991.
DIRECTOR/CO-WRITER OF SCREENPLAY

Loaded with sixties-type symbolism, even the title sequence has deeper meaning. After Morrison recites the "Enough to base a movie on?" poem, "Riders on the Storm" begins and the camera soars over desert cliffs as huge transparent letters form: "THE DOORS." Naturally, we must pass through these open letters, the "doors of perception," to "see things as they are." It is fitting that Stone follows this with the episode Morrison called the most significant of his life, when five-year-old Jim and his family came upon the scene of a horrible automobile accident—an overturned truck loaded with Native American workers now dying in the sand. For the rest of his life Morrison would believe that the spirit of one of these dying Indians, a Shaman, somehow entered his soul. And throughout the film, another of these Indians, a bald-headed man, appears often in the background to signify Morrison's obsession with death, which never left him from this moment on.

In L.A., Morrison meets Pamela Courson and attends film school, where only Ray Manzarek seems to understand his artistic visions. Later, Morrison and Manzarek agree to form a band and as they walk on the beach talking of a planet "screaming for change" and "making the myths," the dialogue seems beyond idealism; through the scarred and cynical eyes of 1991, it even borders on absurdity. The funny thing is people *did* talk that way in the sixties—without a trace of guile. On Sunset Boulevard, as his star is about to rise, Morrison climbs on top of a parked car and shouts: "Let's take a poll here. How many of you know you're really alive?" But as he shouts it, the acid kicks in and his voice becomes a possessed gutteral sound, and for just a brief instant, the stars in the background above him start to revolve. It is a true sixties moment, a time when the magic, the mystery, the music, and the madness all crystalized into the indescribable joy of coming of age.

In the desert on peyote Morrison follows Death, the bald man, naked this time and riding a white stallion, into a cave, and there sees a vision of the Shaman. We smashcut through the Shaman's eye onto the stage at the Whiskey during The Doors' performance of "The End." "Kill the father, fuck the mother"—those were the words that crossed the line. Morrison's incestual madness and repressed anger were on overload. And briefly, there in the balcony, just as he began, Death was watching.

The group's appearance on the Ed Sullivan Show provides one of the few touches of humor when one of the producers tries to get Morrison to change the "Girl, we couldn't get much higher" line in "Light My Fire." The producer suggests "Girl, we couldn't get much better," and Morrison counters with, "How 'bout, 'Girl, you couldn't bite my wire'?" much to the producer's chagrin.

Appendix III: Filmography

Eventually, the rest of the band agrees to change the line; but Morrison balks and of course, when they perform the song on live TV, he shouts the forbidden line with full force.

Later, a female photographer takes sexy Morrison shots, including the famous "Young Lion" photo, actually taken by Joel Brodsky. This bit of Doors trivia brings up another enigma Stone encountered with the film. How faithful should he remain to the original Morrison lore? He was going for a poetic feel, more musical than drama. Pleasing The Doors' serious fans meant treating it like the Bible, and that was something he could never do. The bottom line and the biggest problem with *The Doors* is that Stone tried to be both faithful and fanciful at the same time.

At a New York jet-set party, the bald man's face is on a giant video screen as The Doors enter. Stone plays off the comedic aspects of the jet set but they are believable even in their outrageousness. The other Doors members are soon ready to go, but Morrison, enraptured with the sensory overload, pleads with them to stay. They miss the moment—one of the few times he is really vulnerable with them—and leave. As Jim moves toward jet-set idol Andy Warhol, the Shaman appears. Whether it is to warn him off or push him on, we don't know, but on Jim thrusts. Fate casts him one more warning when, just as he passes Death (this time dressed as a woman with diamond earrings), he encounters a man dressed like himself—the first lookalike of the new superstar. Jim shrugs that off too. He has long ago stopped heeding warnings of any kind.

Warhol is in the center of a group of admirers, including his own lookalike. He acknowledges Jim enthusiastically, then ignores him. One of Warhol's fans says that it is Andy, and not his painting, that is now the art, and tries to quote his most famous line, "In the future everyone will be famous for fifteen minutes," but botches it, saying, "everyone will be famous for fifteen days," instead. These people worship Warhol, but don't understand his art. Morrison leans over and takes Warhol's glasses off, breaking his spell. Andy is no fool, however, and gives Morrison a golden phone, saying, "Someone gave me this. They said you can talk to God on it, but I don't have anything to say. You take it."

From this point in the film, Morrison rapidly descends. He meets music critic/witch Patricia Kennealy at a press conference and moves quickly to having wild orgies with her. There is a Gothic quality to these scenes, and when Kennealy entices him to drink blood, it's as if another barrier has been crossed.

In one of the best scenes in the film, Morrison is at his most vulnerable when, while having sex with Kennealy in a shower stall backstage at Yale, she tells him she tracked down and phoned his parents. It is one of Kilmer's finest moments as he literally reels for an instant under the pressure of suddenly snapping back into a reality he's been trying to escape for the past few years. He had told everyone his parents were dead for so long that he was actually starting to believe it. Then Kennealy, instead of asking, "Why don't you want to talk about your parents?" says the more apropos, "What did he do?" This is something Morrison can't verbalize, so Kennealy says, "Did he love you?" Like a child, Morrison raises his hand, holding two fingers an inch apart. When she asks, "Your mama?" he opens them another quarter inch and says, "Hatred's a very underestimated emotion." Unfortunately, this scene never really happened. It might have been good for Morrison if it had. The girl in the shower at Yale wasn't Patricia Kennealy either (the New Haven concert took place in 1967 and Morrison didn't meet Kennealy until 1970). Of course, these kinds of facts can be found in a book. A movie should show the essence of the man, and you get that from this scene—an especially poetic beat that most Doors fans, because of their obsession with trivia, missed. The scream of "When the Music's Over" leads us onstage where, from Morrison's viewpoint, a catapult of joints floats eerily toward him, a gift from adoring fans.

More than anything, this film is driven by the music: a two-hour poem with matching visuals. Of course, a two-hour Jim Morrison poem is pretty hard for most people to take. Morrison's poetry is best read one or two at a time, with a breather in between. It's heavy, swimming in imagry, dark and disturbing. So is the film. As much as Stone tries to add a poetic lightness, Morrison's music, his words, and his life are just too dark.

Older, heavier, bearded and wearing football jersey #66 (accurate to the number), Morrison raps about his life between takes during his poetry recordings: "Let's just say I was testing the bounds of reality. . . . In me they see exactly what they want to see. Some say, Lizard King, whatever that means? . . . But, really I think of myself as a sensitive, intelligent human being . . . but with the soul of a clown that always forces me to blow it at the most crucial moments. A fake hero. A joke the gods played on me."

The softer, more humble side of Morrison is best evident when, after walking Pam home from the store, he sings to her. Though the concert scenes are more spectacular, Kilmer is as good here. When he sings a cappella and tries to soothe Pam in a benign, gentle way, Kilmer conveys a bit of the genuine Morrison mystique. He may or may not look and sound like Morrison, depending on one's perspective, but overall, Kilmer gives a strong performance.

The Doors are at their peak in the concert sequence in San Francisco. As bonfires burn in the crowd and Morrison dances wildly in a trance onstage, Death appears behind him spinning for just an instant. The crowd, entranced, revels in Dionysian ecstasy as the concert ends and Morrison shouts, "I am the

Lizard King, I can do anything!" And they believe it. Here is Morrison at his greatest—howling his most pretentious aphorism. As the crowd chants his name, we believe it too.

Then there's Miami—the concert from Hell. It took place in an overstuffed hall that far exceeded its legal capacity on a night when Florida broiled in a heatwave, and Morrison was drunk out of his mind and on acid to boot—and the devil was dying to come out. He arrives at the hall long past late, but when John Densmore complains, Jim responds by offering him acid. Angry, Densmore says, "We took drugs to expand our mind, not to escape." It is a moment we've longed for. The confrontation. But Morrison chooses to shock and offend Densmore rather than answer him. Of course, by this point, it's doubtful Jim had any answers. Up on stage, wearing a cowboy hat with a skull and crossbones on it and black shades, Morrison is at his most evil. Manzarek sees the ghost of the Shaman appear, look despairingly at his once great host, and then vanish, reminiscent of the keyboardist's real-life description of how Morrison's spirit seemed to drain out of him at The Doors' last concert in New Orleans.

With the Miami insanity swirling about him and his own madness swelling inside, Morrison sings "Touch Me," but stops the song in the middle and shouts drunkenly, "This is all bullshit." Then, as it actually did in the weird Miami diatribe, his voice seems to change drastically, rumbling, "I'm coming out, I'm coming out," with hideous overtones. Part slobbering lush and part demoniac, he could be talking about whatever inhibitions were left (including exposing himself) or something deeper, something more terrifying—the source of his madness. Later, a riot ensues and Morrison is thrown offstage, only to surface amid the crowd and lead a frenzied conga line to the opening of "Break On Through #2." He's lost. He's over the edge and doesn't care if he never gets back. And there, dancing wildly behind him, with one hand on his shoulder, is Death. As "Break On Through" begins, the irony is overwhelming. After years of seeking, Morrison has broken on through . . . but to where?

At Morrison's trial for lewd and lascivious behavior, famed radical attorney William Kunstler does a cameo as Morrison's lawyer Max Fink. He gives a moving speech, but to no avail. Morrison is sentenced to six months of hard labor in the Dade County Jail. In Miami, more hard reality hits home. Patricia Kennealy is pregnant. Morrison wants her to have an abortion. When she says the child would be "a fucking genius . . . a goddess or a god," Morrison looks at her with a sincere acknowledgment of what his life has become, saying, "It'd be a monster." Though he promises Kennealy he'll be there for her every step of the way during the abortion, she already knows he'll never show. In the end it is her fault for believing him. "You never pretended," she says. "I did."

After being banned across America and enduring press ridicule, Morrison abandons rock to go to Paris and concentrate on his poetry. In the film he visits Ray's house, where a children's birthday party is going on, to say good-bye. As The Doors listen to "Riders on the Storm" from their new album, they seem closer than in a long while. The scene is awkward, probably because it never happened. People like Jim Morrison don't make nice, tidy good-byes. When Robbie says, "As far as I'm concerned we made music with Dionysus," it really starts to stretch, but the scene is saved by an excellent sequence at the backyard party. There Morrison, in a goofy party hat, watches as a child opens a present— a Jim Morrison doll. "It's you!" the child exclaims. Morrison nods, but says only, "Forever young." He then looks off in the distance and adds, "This is the strangest life I've ever known." As he does so, he sees himself—young Jim Morrison (played by Sean Stone) as he looked in the back of his parents' car the day the Shaman found him. The boy walks hesitantly through the crowded party as Jim strains to see him. But then he finds a friend. Death, complete in white-faced clown makeup and top hat, takes young Jim on his lap. It's macabre but fitting in a way. After all, this is Jim's oldest friend and he has never been very far from his grasp. Morrison watches this, but then loses focus and passes out right on top of the doll of his younger self.

We view the poetry sessions one more time with Morrison asking, "Did you get all that?" And there, looking at him, is the Indian Shaman. We hear the voice of John Densmore, who plays the recording engineer, saying, "Yeah, I got it, Jim," with a strange knowing smile. Perhaps, after all these years, he did.

Cut to Paris, to the inevitable. As Pam sleeps, the shadow of Jim passes by and we hear his voice, "Death, it's not so bad. I love my girl." Moments later, she wakes up to see the bald-headed man walking silently down the hall. She finds Jim in the tub with a strange smile on his face. At first she thinks he's joking, but then realizes the truth and says, "Was it all right, Jim? Did you enjoy it when it came? Just like you said you would."

At Père Lachaise cemetery the camera pans across the graves of Chopin, Georges Bizet, Oscar Wilde, Sarah Bernhardt, Honoré de Balzac, Marcel Proust, Rossini, Molière—and Jim Morrison.

The film closes, fittingly, with scenes of L.A. which end with a closeup of Morrison walking on the beach, young, wearing shades, cocky, his whole life before him—as he was.

"There's no way I'm not going to get killed on this," Oliver Stone said during the making of *The Doors*. "No matter what I do, a lot of people are going to hate it." He was right. *The Doors* may justifiably be called Stone's best and worst effort as a filmmaker. There is no question that it is a courageous film. It is flawed, to be sure, but the vast majority of these flaws are the result of risk taking. Stone could have played it safe or pandered to the legions of Morrison fans and likely had a hit. Instead, he tried to make the kind of film he felt that Jim Morrison's life as a risk-taking artist demanded—one that tested the boundaries. In that, he apparently succeeded.

(Also discussed in detail in Chapter Eleven)

JFK. 1991. DIRECTOR/PRODUCER/ CO-WRITER OF SCREENPLAY

(Discussed in detail in Chapter Twelve)

HEAVEN AND EARTH. 1993. DIRECTOR/PRODUCER/ WRITER OF SCREENPLAY

(Discussed in detail in Chapter Fourteen)

NATURAL BORN KILLERS. 1994. DIRECTOR/ PRODUCER/CO-WRITER OF SCREENPLAY

(Discussed in detail in Chapter Fifteen)

PRODUCER OR EXECUTIVE PRODUCER ONLY

Blue Steel. 1990. Producer
Reversal of Fortune. 1990. Producer
Iron Maze. 1991. Executive Producer
South Central. 1992. Executive Producer
Zebrahead. 1992. Executive Producer
The Joy Luck Club. 1993. Executive Producer
The New Age. 1993. Executive Producer
Wild Palms (television miniseries). 1993. Executive Producer

Bibliography

"Acoustic Evidence in Kennedy Shooting Fails." Editorials/Letters, *The New York Times*, March 28, 1992.

Adams, Cindy. "Out of Towners." *New York Post*, August 10, 1992.

"An Oscar Argument Gets Hotter." *The Los Angeles Times*, January 12, 1987.

Ansen, David. "What Does Oliver Stone Owe History?" *Newsweek*, December 23, 1991.

———. "A Troublemaker for Our Times." *Newsweek*, December 23, 1991.

———. "Your Not-So-Basic Showbiz Movie Bio." *Newsweek*, March 18, 1991.

Auchincloss, Kenneth, Ginny Carroll, and Maggie Malone. "Twisted History." *Newsweek*, December 23, 1991.

Auletta, Ken. "*Wall Street* Review." *Vanity Fair*, December 1987.

———. "Stone's Brokers." Movies, *Vanity Fair*, January 1988.

———. "What Won't They Do?" Annals of Communications, *The New Yorker*, May 17, 1993.

Avins, Mimi. "Oliver Stone Molds His Vietnam Nightmare Into A Masterpiece." *US*, February 9, 1987.

Bailey, Elaine. "Reel Men." *Movieline*, July 1992.

Baltake, Joe. "These Are the Big Ones." *Sacramento Bee*, December 11, 1987.

Barra, Allen and Ty Burr. "*JFK*: The Film and The Furor." *Entertainment Weekly*, January 17, 1992.

Beale, Lewis. "'Platoon's' reality vs. vets' reality." Arts and Entertainment, *Daily News*, December 24, 1986.

———. "The Vietnam War According to Stone." LA Life, *Daily News*, December 24, 1986.

Beck, Marilyn. "Latest 'Death Wish' just needs a script." People, LA Life, *Daily News*, December 9, 1986.

———, and Stacy Jenel Smith. "Morse is Heart of Palms." *New York Daily News*, June 7, 1992.

Belin, David. "Earl Warren's Assassins." *The New York Times*, March 7, 1992.

———. "The Big 'Lies' of 'JFK.'" *New York*, February 17, 1992.

Benson, Sheila. "'Wall Street' Lays an Egg." *The Los Angeles Times*, December 11, 1987.

Bernstein, Fred. "Good-time Charlie Sheen Puts the Pow in 'Platoon.'" *People Magazine*, February 1987.

Bernstein, Richard. "Yale, Class of '68: Time to Take Stock." *The New York Times*, June 1, 1993.

Berry, Pat. "Two Weeks of Hell." *Splice*, January 1987.

"Beverly Hills 213." *The Los Angeles Times*, October 11, 1989.

"Biggest Eavesdropper of Them All." The National Security Agency, *Covert Action Bulletin*, No. 11, December 1980.

Biskind, Peter. "Stone Raids Wall Street." *Premiere*, December 1987.

Blauner, Peter. "Coming Home." *New York*, December 8, 1986.

Bradley, Bill. "Piercing the Veil." *Sacramento News & Review*, July 2, 1992.

Breskin, David. *Inner Views*. Boston: Faber and Faber, 1992.

———. "Oliver Stone." The Rolling Stone Interview, *Rolling Stone*, April 4, 1991.

Bryant, Helen. "Star Search." *Dallas Tribune*, November 22, 1988.

Bush, Anita M. "Cruise, Wagner Partnering In Prod'n Company." *The Hollywood Reporter*, July 13, 1992.

Byrge, Duane. *Wall Street* Film Review, *The Hollywood Reporter*, December 7, 1987.

Caine, Michael. *What's It All About?* New York: Turtle Bay Books, 1992.

Califano, Joseph A., Jr. "A Concoction of Lies and Distortions." *The Wall Street Journal*, January 28, 1992.

Canby, Vincent. "From Oliver Stone, Greed on 'Wall Street'." Film, *The New York Times*, December 11, 1987.

———. "*Wall Street* Review." *The New York Times*, December 1987.

Caraco, Andre. "*The Doors.*" *Phoenix Gazette*, February 28, 1985.

Carlson, Timothy. "Stone Promises Wild Miniseries." *TV Guide*, April 25, 1992.

Carr, Jay. "*Wall Street* Review." *Boston Globe*, December 1987.

Carroll, Kathleen. "Remember the Greedy." *New York Daily News*, December 11, 1987.

———. "*Wall Street* Review." *New York Daily News*, December 1987.

Carter, Bill. "Movie Director Oliver Stone Planning to Produce Series for ABC." *The New York Times News Service*, April 26, 1992.

Carter, Graydon. "Talk Man." *Connoisseur*, November 1987.

Champlin, Charles. "Spotlight on a State-of-the-Art Film Producer." *The Los Angeles Times*, January 7, 1988.

Christy, George. "The Great Life." *The Hollywood Reporter*, September 5, 1991.

Chutkow, Paul. "The Private War of Tom Cruise." *The New York Times*, December 17, 1989.

———. "Oliver Stone and 'The Doors': Obsession Meets the Obsessed." *The New York Times*, February 24, 1991.

"CIA Relations with Media." *Covert Action Bulletin*, No. 7, December 1979.

Clark, Mike. "Stone's Stock Soars." Movies, *USA Today*, December 11, 1987.

———. "*Wall Street* Review." *USA Today*, December 1987.

Cockburn, Alexander. "In Defense of the Warren Commission." *The Nation*, March 9, 1992.

———. "Oliver Stone Takes Stock." *American Film*, December 1987.

Collier, Peter. "Ollie uber Alles." *The American Spectator*, April 1992.

Collins, Monica. "Collins Report: *JFK*: The too-much-TV-airtime theory." *TV Guide*, February 23, 1992.

———. "Collins Report: Bringing *Born on the Fourth of July* to TV." *TV Guide*, December 29, 1991.

Collins, Pat. "*Wall Street* Review." WOR-TV, December 1987.

"Committee Approves Legislation." Sen. John Glenn News Release, June 25, 1992.

Considine, J.D. "Reopening the Doors." Entertainment, *Baltimore Sun*, March 3, 1991.

Cook, David. *A History of Narrative Film*. New York Norton, 1981.

Cooper, Mark. "*Wall Street*: An Interview on Jungle Warfare with Oliver Stone." *Playboy*, February 1988.

Corliss, Richard. "A Season of Flash and Greed." Cinema, *Time*, December 14, 1987.

———. "Come on, Baby, Light My Fizzle." Cinema, *Time*, March 1991.

———. "*Platoon* Vietnam As It Really Was." *Time*, January 26, 1987.

———. "*Wall Street* Review." *Time*, December 1986.

———. "Who Killed J.F.K.?" Cinema, *Time*, December 23, 1991.

Cosford, Bill. "The box office outlook: bullish on 'Wall Street'." Movie Review: *Wall Street*, *Miami Herald*, December 11, 1987.

Cremer, Janet. "Stateville Jail to be Scene of Stone Film." *The Daily Journal*, May 28, 1993.

Curtright, Bob. "Pushing all the buttons is what makes Stone happy." *Wichita Eagle*, March 21, 1992.

———."Stone doesn't hold the key to *The Doors*." *Wichita Eagle*, March 8, 1991.

———."Stone, Wagner had fun with 'Wild Palms'." Broadcasting, *Wichita Eagle*, May 16, 1993.

Daly, Steve. "Camera Obscura." *Entertainment Weekly*, January 17, 1992.

Davidson, Casey. "Door Trippers." *Entertainment Weekly*, April 23, 1993.

"Days of 'Heaven'." *Premiere*, December 1993.

Denby, David. "*Wall Street* Review." *New York*, December 14, 1987.

Dershowitz, Alan M. "Suppression of the Facts Grants Stone a Broad Brush." *The Los Angeles Times*, December 25, 1991.

DeVries, Hilary. "Rider On The Storm," *The Los Angeles Times Magazine*, February 24, 1991.

Dieckmann, Katherine. "Willem Dafoe: Against Type," *The Village Voice*, December 17, 1986.

"Discourse on Oliver Stone." *Congressional Record*, June 25, 1992.

"Distinguished Company." *Billboard*, July 18, 1992.

"Distortion rap riles Stone." *Associated Press*, January 15, 1992.

"Doc breaks silence on JFK wound." *Kankakee Sunday Journal*, April 5, 1992.

"Doctor who saw JFK breaks 29-year silence." *Associated Press*, April 5, 1992.

Dolce, Joe. "The Year of Acting Dangerously: Willem Dafoe." *Elle*, December 1986.

Dooley, Kirk. "Oliver Stone-Directed Movie to be Filmed Here in May." *Los Colinas Weekly*, March 24, 1988.

Dorman, Michael. "The Many Theories of a Jolly Green Giant." *New York Newsday*, December 26, 1991.

DuBrow, Rick. "Carson Signs Deal." *The Los Angeles Times*, July 13, 1992.

Dutka, Elaine. "Marketing JFK's Murder," Calendar, *The Los Angeles Times*, December 15, 1991.

Easton, Nina J. "Sydney Pollack: Consummate Insider's Views on the Industry, MPAA and Movies."

Ebert, Roger. "'Doors' Wallows in Hero's Mire." *Chicago Sun Times*, March 1, 1991.

———. *Wall Street* Movie Review, *New York Post*, December 11, 1987.

———. Movies, *Chicago Sun Times*, March 1, 1991.

———. "Pundits Go Astray Taking Aim at JFK." *Universal Press Syndicate*, January 15, 1992.

Edelstein, David. "Brains Over Budget." *Rolling Stone*, January 1987.

———. "*Wall Street* Review." *Village Voice*, December 1987.

"Eerie TV From Oliver Stone." Newsmakers, *Newsweek*, February 8, 1993.

Elder, Sharon. "*Wall Street* via Vietnam." Yale, November 1987.

Elliot, David. "*Wall Street* Review." *San Diego Union*, December 1987.

Emerson, Jim. "Taking Stock." *The Orange County Register*, December 11, 1987.

Erickson, Steve. "The Doors, Seduction and Sedition at the Beach." *L.A.* Weekly, March 1–7, 1991.

Fabrikant, Geraldine. "Wall Street Reviews 'Wall Street'." *The New York Times*, December 10, 1987.

"Fans to Flock to Jim Morrison's Grave on Birthday." *Chicago Sun Times*, December 8, 1993.

"Fatal Bullet, The." Editorials/Letters, *The New York Times*, March 28, 1992.

Fernandez, Enrique. "Damned Yankees." *The Village Voice*, December 2, 1986.

Ford, Gerald R. and David W. Belin. "Kennedy Assassination: How About the Truth?" *The Washington Post*, December 17, 1991.

Fischoff, Stuart. "Oliver Stone." *Psychology Today*, September/October 1993.

"*Fourth of July* is a New Kind of Role for Tom Cruise." *Dallas News*, November 1988.

Frankel, Martha. "Ryan's Hope." *One on One*, Movies March 1991.

Franklin, Gary. "*Wall Street* Review." KABC-TV, December 1987.

Freedman, Richard. "Moralizing Dampens Interesting 'Wall Street.'" Films in Focus, *The Star Ledger*, December 11, 1987.

F.Y.I. Boxoffice, *Premiere*, September 1992.

Gabel, Peter. "The Spiritual Truth of JFK." *Tikkun*, February 1992.

Galbraith, Jane. "*Wall Street*." *Daily Variety*, December 4, 1987.

Gardella, Kay. "Stone is casting his lot with Showtime." *Knight-Ridder*, January 1992.

Garner, Jack. "*Wall Street* Review." *Gannett Newspapers*, December 1987.

———. "With 'The Doors' Director Oliver Stone." *Gannett News Service*, February 26, 1991.

Garrison, Jim. *On the Trail of the Assassins*. Sheridan Square Press, 1988.

"Garrison, theorist on JFK, dies at 70." *The New York Times News Service*, January 1993.

Gates, David, and Howard Manly. "Bottom Line: How Crazy Is It?" *Newsweek*, December 23, 1991.

Gelb, Leslie. "JFK and NSAM 263." *The New York Times*, January 8, 1992.

Giammarco, David. "Oliver Stone shoots back." *Movie Eye*, May 21, 1992.

Gilmore, Mikal. "The Legacy of Jim Morrison and The Doors." *Rolling Stone*, April 4, 1991.

Gindick, Tia, and Mary Rourke. "Will the Power Look Work in Laid-Back Los Angeles?" Fashion, *The Los Angeles Times*, January 8, 1988.

Gitlin, Todd. "The Stoning of Oliver and the Fascination of JFK." *Tikkun*, February 1992.

Gleiserman, Owen. "Wild Child." *Entertainment Weekly*, February 27, 1991.

Goldman, Aril. "Ron Kovic Today: Warrior at Peace." December 12, 1989.

Goodman, Ellen. "Shooting JFK." *Boston Globe*, January 8, 1992.

Goodwin, Betty. "Retailers bracing to take stockbroker look to the bank." *The Los Angeles Times*, January 1988.

Gordon, George. "The Ghost Platoon." *Associated Press*, June 1987.

Granger, Susan. "*Wall Street* Review." WMCA, December 1987.

Green, Tom. "Sheen earns his stripes: 'Platoon' promotes a star." *USA Today*, January 13, 1987.

Greene, Ray. "Fighting Words." *Boxoffice*, November 1993.

Grove, Martin A. "Hollywood Report." *The Hollywood Reporter*, November 26, 1986.

Guthmann, Edward. "Oliver Stone Lights a Fire: Oscar-winning director brings Doors' Jim Morrison to life." Film, *Datebook*, March 3, 1991.

Haig, Alexander M. "Eric Bogosian." *Current Biography*, September 1987.

Halstead, Richard. "High-stakes money culture draws Hollywood interest." Review, *Marin Independent Journal*, December 11, 1987.

Hamilton, Edith. *Mythology*. New York: The New American Library, 1940, 1942.

Hammer, Joshua. "Total Free Fall." *Newsweek*, March 9, 1992.

Handelman, David. "A Man Under the Influence." *Rolling Stone*, June 19, 1986.

Harmetz, Aljean. "Film Directors Start Strike Vote Today." *The New York Times*, June 30, 1987.

————. "Unwanted 'Platoon' Finds Success As U.S. Examines the Vietnam War." *The New York Times*, February 9, 1987.

Harti, John. "The Other Side." *Seattle Times*, March 1, 1991.

Harvey, Pat. "The New Movie 'The Doors.'" *Audio Video Reporting Services*, March 6, 1991.

Hawkins, Robert J. "Stone's Soulful 'Doors' Brilliant." *San Diego Tribune*, March 1, 1991.

"Headlines." *People Magazine*, June 14, 1993.

Healy, Michael. "'Wall Street': Greedy Diary of the American Dream." *L.A. Daily News*, December 1987.

————. "*Wall Street* Review." *L.A. Daily News*, December 1987.

Heath, Chris. "Killer Instincts." *Details*, January 1992.

"Hemdale aglow after success of Platoon." News, *Screen International*, February 21, 1987.

Hensley, Dennis E. "With His Eyes Wide Open." *Writer's Digest*, February 1994.

Hayslip, Le Ly, with Jay Wurts. *When Heaven and Earth Changed Places*, New York: A Plume Book, 1989.

Herbst, Peter. "Young at Heart." *New York Fast Track*, June 1987.

Hillegass, C. K. *Mythology*. Lincoln, Nebraska: Cliffs Notes, Inc., 1973.

Hinson, Hal. "'Doors': The Time To Hesitate is Now." *The Washington Post*, March 1, 1991.

Hirsch, Neil. "*Wall Street* Review." *N.Y. Law Journal*, December 1987.

Hoberman, J. "The Lizard King's New Clothes." *The Village Voice*, March 12, 1991.

Holden, Stephan. "Bogosian's Voices." *The New York Times Magazine*, May 24, 1987.

————. "New Face: Kevin Dillon Baby-Faced Soldier of 'Platoon.'" *The New York Times*, January 9, 1987.

"Hollywood Freeway." LA Life, *Daily News*, October 23, 1986.

Hopkins, Jerry. "Mr. MOJO Rises." *American Film*, October 1990.

Huffhines, Kathy. "'Wall Street' is Energetic, Morally Solid." *Detroit Free Press*, December 11, 1987.

Hughley, Marty. "Morrison Larger Than Death." *L'Estrange Association*, March 1, 1991.

————. "A Window on the Doors." *L'Estrange Association*, March 1, 1991.

"If There's a Boring Moment In the Suave *Wall Street*, I Didn't Notice It." *New York*, December 14, 1987.

Jarvis, Jeff. "Oliver Stone: Inside Out." First Looks, *TV Guide*, March 21, 1992.

Jerome, Deborah. "'Wall Street' Trades in Hollow Characters." *The Bergen Record*, December 11, 1987.

Jerome, Jim. "The Men of 'Platoon.'" *US*, April 6, 1987.

———. "Travels With Charlie." *US*, January 25, 1988.

"*JFK* Director Praises Congress For Opening Files." "Newsmakers," *USA Today* May 1992.

"*JFK*: The Assassination." Letters, *Book World*, February 2, 1992.

"*JFK* May Elicit Action On Files." The New York Times, January 10, 1992.

Johnson, Bonnie. "Boom or Bust." *People Magazine*, January 1987.

Johnston, James. "Questions Linger on *JFK*." *Wichita Eagle*, December 20, 1991.

Jones, Bill. "Hit by Rebel Fire." *Phoenix Gazette*, March 1, 1991.

"Kato Unites Stone and Die Hard Writer." *Kansas City Star*, January 3, 1992.

Kehr, Dave. *The Doors* movie review, *Chicago Tribune*, March 1, 1991.

———. "Stoned 'Doors.'" *Chicago Tribune*, March 1, 1991.

"Kennedy Backs Release of Papers on JFK Killing." *Associated Press*, January 11, 1992.

Kilday, Gregg. "Love Me Two Times." *Entertainment Weekly*, March 1, 1991.

Klein, Stewart. "*Wall Street* Review." WMYW-TV, December 1987.

Klien, Andy. "Opening 'Doors' for a Hero." *San Francisco Examiner*, February 28, 1991.

Kmetko, Steve. "*Wall Street* Review." KCBS-TV, December 1987.

Kogan, Rick. "'Wild Palms' No Day at the Beach." Tempo, *Chicago Tribune*, May 16, 1993.

Kroninger, Stephen. "Oliver Stone." Power 101, *Entertainment Weekly*, October 22, 1993.

Kwitny, Jonathan. "A Better Conspiracy Theory Than Oliver Stone's." *The Wall Street Journal*, December 19, 1991.

LaBrecque, Ron. "Tom Berenger: Satanic Sergeant Barnes." *People Magazine*, February, 1987.

Lambert, Bruce. "Jim Garrison, 70, Theorist on Kennedy Death, Dies." Obituaries, *The New York Times*, October 22, 1992.

Lane, Anthony. "The Current Cinema." *The New Yorker*, January 17, 1994.

Lardner, George, Jr. "On the Set: Dallas in Wonderland." *The Washington Post*, May 19, 1991.

Lemann, Nicholas. "The Case Against Jim Garrison." *GQ*, January 1992.

Lerner, Michael. "JFK and the Possibility of Possibility." *Tikkun*, February 1992.

"Letters Column." *Premiere*, August 1993.

Levine, Bettijane. "Men Are Bullish on Power Styles Seen in 'Wall Street.'" Fashion, *The Los Angeles Times*, January 8, 1988.

Lewis, Anthony. "*JFK*, Abroad At Home." *The New York Times*, January 11, 1992.

Lindstrom, Pia. "*Wall Street* Review." NBC-TV, December 1986.

"Line of Cheap Guns, A." Editorials/Letters, *The New York Times*, March 28, 1992.

Loud, Lance. "Out Loud." *The Advocate*, June 2, 1992.

Luft, Herbert G. "The Obsessive Screen." *Critics Corner*, November 21, 1986.

Lyons, Jeffrey. "*Wall Street* Review." WPIX-TV, December 1987.

Machiavelli, Niccolo. *The Prince*. New York: New American Library, 1952.

MacKenzie, John P. "Oliver Stone's Patsy." *The New York Times*, December, 1992.

"Made Students Think." Editorials/Letters, *The New York Times*, March 28, 1992.

Mahar, Ted. "Love Me Two Times." *L'Estrange Association*, March 1, 1991.

Mahler, Richard. "The Great TV Movie War of 1990." *The Los Angeles Times*, September 9, 1990.

Maltin, Leonard. *TV Movies and Video Guide*. New York: New American Library, 1990.

Mann, Roderick. "'Platoon' Just Part of Sheen's Basic Training." *The Los Angeles Times*, December 28, 1986.

Margolis, Jon. "JFK Movie and Book Attempt to Rewrite History." *Dallas Morning News*, May 14, 1991.

Marrs, Jim. "Crossfire—The Plot That Killed Kennedy." New York: Carroll and Graf, 1989.

Martin, Mick. "'Wall Street' Trades on Good Yarn." *Sacramento Union*, December 11, 1987.

Marvel, Bill. "Oliver's Twist." *Dallas Morning News*, December 27, 1991.

Marvin, Mary. "Inside the 'Doors.' *Producers Quarterly*, Spring 1991.

Maslin, Janet. "*Wall Street* Review." *The New York Times*, December 1986.

———. "Flying and Falling Through the 60s: A Life of the Doors." *The New York Times*, March 1991.

———. "Unlikely Casting Can Reward Actor and Audience." *The New York Times*, January 4, 1987.

Mathews, Jack. "The Vietnam War's Other Side." Calendar, *The Los Angeles Times*, January 17, 1993.

———. "Who Issues Historical Licenses Anyway?" Calendar, *The Los Angeles Times*, January 5, 1992.

McBride, Joseph. "Film Review: South Central." *Daily Variety*, September 18, 1992.

McCarthy, Todd. "Stone to Lens Hemdale's 'Platoon,' Recounting Vietnam Experiences." Pictures, *Variety*, February 26, 1986.

McGilligan, Pat. "Point Man." *Film Comment*, February 1987.

McGrady, Mike. "Behind-the-Scenes Treachery on Wall Street." *Newsday*, December 11, 1987.

———."Oliver Stone and a Grunt's-Eye View of War." *Newsday*, December 14, 1986.

McGuigan, Cathleen. "Back from the Other Side." Movies, *Newsweek*, March 18, 1991.

———. "A Bull Market in Sin." Movies, *Newsweek*, December 14, 1987.

———. "From Fringe to Uptown." Entertainment, *Newsweek*, March 24, 1986.

McGuire, Michael. "Top Salvador Command Blamed For Killing of 1,000 Civilians." *Chicago Tribune*, March 15, 1993.

McNamara, Sean, and Steve Marshall. "Inspiration for 'JFK' Dies." Newsmakers, *USA Today*, October 22, 1992.

Mills, Bart. " 'Wild Palms': Futuristic Yarn With Hitchcockian Plot." On the Cover, TV Week, *Chicago Tribune*, May 16–22, 1993.

Minsky, Terri. "Friend Dafoe: SoHo Avant-Gardist or Hollywood Hard Guy?" *LA Style*, November 1986.

Mitchell, Sean. "Oliver Stone." *USA Weekend*, February 22–24, 1991.

———. "A soldier leaves the trenches: 'Platoon' marks 'end of a cycle' for Oliver Stone." Style, *Los Angeles Herald Examiner*, December 21, 1986.

Molloy, Philip. "*Platoon*: Oliver Stone's Emotional Rescue." Director in Focus, *Movieline*, December 19, 1986.

Mooney, Joshua. "Talk Radio." Video, New Releases, June 1989.

Moynihan, Daniel Patrick. "The Paranoid Style." *The Washington Post*, December 29, 1991.

Natale, Richard. "Solid as a Stone." *Box Office*, January 1987.

Norman, Michael. " 'Platoon' Grapples With Vietnam." Film, *The New York Times*, December 21, 1986.

Novak, Ralph. Picks & Pans. *People*, March 11, 1991.

O'Hehir, Andrew. "JFK: Tragedy Into Farce." *San Francisco Weekly*, December 18, 1991.

"Olé!" *The Los Angles Times*, August 27, 1989.

"Oliver Stone Divorcing." *Chicago Tribune*, May 25, 1993.

"Oliver Stone Takes On New Film Projects as Longer 'JFK' and Script Are Released." Arts & Entertainment, *The Suns*, June 14, 1992.

"Oliver Twist." *Entertainment Weekly*, June 1992.

Osborne, Robert. "It's True: 'Falsettos' Coming To Big Screen." *The Hollywood Reporter*, September 1992.

Osborne, Robert. "Ramblin Reporter." *The Hollywood Reporter*, November 1986.

O'Shea, Stephen. "When Elle Met Ollie." *Elle*, November 1992.

Pacheco, Patrick. *"Wall Street." New York City Lights*, January 1987.

Pally, Marcia. *"Wall Street* Review." *Penthouse*, December 1987.

Parks, Steve. "The Blurred Vision of JFK." *New York Newsday*, December 26, 1991.

Powers, John. "The 'US' Directors Series." *US*, March 21, 1991.

———. *"Wall Street,"* LA Weekly, December 1987.

Pristin, Terry. "The Filmmakers vs. the Crusaders." *The Los Angeles Times*, December 29, 1991.

Prouty, L. Fletcher. *JFK: The CIA, Vietnam and the Plot To Assassinate John F. Kennedy.* New York: Carol Publishing Group, 1992.

Queenan, Joe. "The Stone Age." *Movieline*, August 1992.

Rafferty, Terrence. "The Current Cinema." *The New Yorker,* March 1991.

"Raiders of the Lost Market." Film Reviews, *The Village Voice*, December 15, 1987.

Rainer, Peter. "Bully Loose on 'Wall Street.'" Movies, *Los Angeles Herald Examiner*, December 11, 1987.

———. *"Wall Street* Review." *Los Angeles Herald Examiner*, December 1987.

Ratliff, Larry. "Oscar's Mired Winner." *San Antonio Light*, December 13, 1987.

Rattner, Steven. "A View From the Trenches." *Newsweek*, December 14, 1987.

Richardson, John H. and Judson Klinger. "'The Doors' Jim Morrison is a Natural Subject." *Premiere*, March 1991.

Richman, Alan. "For his look back in anger at Vietnam, Platoon's Oliver Stone is bombarded with Oscar nominations." *People Magazine*, March 1987.

Rickey, Carrie. *"Wall Street* Review." *Philadelphia Enquirer*, December 1986.

Riding, Alan. "Jim Morrison's Fans Keep His Fire Alight." *The New York Times*, December 9, 1993.

Riordan, James, and Jerry Prochnicky. *Break on Through: The Life and Death of Jim Morrison.* New York: William Morrow & Co, Inc., 1991.

Roberts, Jerry. "Review: 'The Doors' Kilmer and Crew Winningly Stoned." *The Outdoor*, March 1, 1991.

Robotham, Rosemarie. "Michael Douglas." Life Visits, *Life Magazine*, February 1988.

"Rock, as Such, Seemed Too Simple For the Doors." Arts & Entertainment, *The Sun*, March 3, 1991.

Rose, Frank. "Swords Into Blockbusters." *Premiere*, June 1993.

Rosenbaum, Jonathan. Movie Review of *The Doors*, *Chicago Reader*, March 1, 1991.

Rosenbaus, Ron. "Primal Stone." *Vanity Fair*, January 1989.

Rosenthal, Jack. "Get the Rest of the JFK Story." Editorials, *The New York Times*, January 16, 1992.

Rubin, Saul. "The Players Behind 'The Doors' Movie." *Players*, March 1991.

Ryan, Desmond. "Stone Offers Grunt's View of Vietnam." *Long Beach Press Telegram*, January 6, 1986.

Sager, Mike. *Interview*, March 1991.

Salamon, Julie. "Film: Absurdity, Alienation, Papal High Jinks." *The Wall Street Journal*, September 5, 1991.

———. "On Film: Success of 'Platoon' Surprises All." *The Wall Street Journal*, January 15, 1987.

———. "On Film: Oliver Stone Takes On The Street." *The Wall Street Journal*, December 10, 1987.

Sarris, Andrew. "Oscar and Oliver." Films in Focus, *The New York Times*, February 1987.

Saul, Jamie M. "Willem Dafoe: Saintly Sergeant Elias." *People Magazine*, February 1987.

Saunders, Debra J. "JFK: The ends don't justify this movie." *L.A. Daily News*, January 7, 1992.

Scanion, Tom. "'Wall Street': Its Stock is High." *Tacoma Times Tribune*, December 10, 1987.

Scheer, Robert. "Oliver Stone Builds His Own Myths." Calendar, *The Los Angeles Times*, December 15, 1991.

———. "Pssst: Give Stone an Oscar." Reporter's Notebook, *Playboy*, April 1992.

———. "Who Killed JFK?" *Wichita Eagle*, December 20, 1992.

———. "The Most Dangerous Man In America." Calendar, *The Los Angeles Times*, December 15, 1991.

Schiff, Stephen. "*Wall Street* Review." Vanity Fair, December 1987.

Schmidt, William E. "6 Years Later Olof Palme Street Keeps Its Secret." *The New York Times*, February 20, 1992.

Schruers, Fred. "Michael Douglas." *Rolling Stone*, January 14, 1988.

———. "Soldier's Story." *Rolling Stone*, January 29, 1987.

Scott, Peter Dale. "The Assassination and the Cover-up: What Really Happened." *Tikkun*, February 1992.

Segell, Michael. "Tom Berenger, The Tender Tough." *Red Hot Right Now*, January 1987.

Seidenberg, Robert. "To Hell." *American Film*, January 1990.

Sharbutt, Jay. "The Grunts' War, Take 1." Calendar, *The Los Angeles Times*, May 25, 1986.

———. "New Film Brings the Old War Home." Movies, *The Los Angeles Times*, January 22, 1987.

———. "Reunion: Men of a Real Platoon." Calendar, *The Los Angeles Times*, February 7, 1987.

———. "Vietnam through the eyes of a grunt." Movies, *Newsday*, May 25, 1986.

———. "Vietnam Vets Launch Film Assault." *The Los Angeles Times*, May 26, 1986.

"Showbiz and Local Politics." *Variety*, July 10, 1992.

Siegel, Joel. "*Wall Street* Review." *ABC*, New York, December 1987.

Silverman, Kendra. "Charlie Sheen: Following Big Brother's Lead." *'Teen*, November 1986.

Simels, Steve. "Unhinged." *Entertainment Weekly*, September 27, 1991.

Siskel, Gene, and Roger Ebert. "*Wall Street* Review." *Chicago Tribune,* December 1987.

Siskel, Gene. "Oliver Stone's 'The Doors' an exciting trip to the '60s." Siskel's Flicks Picks, *Chicago Tribune*, March 1, 1991.

Small, Michael. "By Turns Hilarious and Bizarre, Talk Radio's Eric Bogosian Finds The Real Voice of America." *Stage*, August 17, 1987.

Smith, Laurie Halpern. "Darryl Hannah, Dazzler with a Difference." *Movieline*, June 19, 1987.

Staples, Brent. "'The Doors' Distorts the 60s." Editorial Notebook, *The New York Times*, March 11, 1991.

———. "Hollywood: History by Default." *The New York Times*, January 1992.

Stein, Ben. "Romancing the Military." *Elle*, October 1986.

Sterritt, David. "The Grime Beneath the Glitter." *Christian Science Monitor*, December 11, 1987.

———. "Oliver Stone: Why 'Platoon' was made so harsh." *Christian Science Monitor,* January, 1987.

———. "*Wall Street* Review." *Christian Science Monitor*, December 1986.

Stivers, Cyndi. "Fifth Anniversary Section." *Premiere*, September 1992.

———. "Souvenirs of a Career: Oliver's Treasures." *Premiere*, September 1992.

Stolley, Richard B. "Shots Seen Around the World." *Entertainment Weekly*, January 17, 1992.

"Stone Again." *Entertainment Weekly*, July 6, 1992.

Stone, Andrea. "Stone on Convention: 'It's a circus.'" *USA Today*, July, 1992.

Stone, Oliver, and Zachary Sklar. *JFK: The Book of the Film*. New York: Applause Books, 1992.

Stone, Oliver. "One From the Heart." Behind the Scenes, *American Film*, January/February, 1987.

———. "Stone's JFK: A Higher Truth?" Outlook, *The Washington Post*, June 2, 1991.

———. "Where I Find My Heroes." *McCall's*, November 1992.

———. "Who Is Rewriting History?" *The New York Times*, December 20, 1991.

"Stone's Film Trashes Facts, Dishonors J.F.K." *Chicago Sun-Times*, December 29, 1991.

"Stone Urges Filmmakers to Stay Independent." *Variety*, March 27, 1989.

"Stone's New War." *Hollywood Reporter*, July 31, 1992.

"Stone Unturned." *Herald Examiner*, December 23, 1986.

Summer, Jane. "Filming of 'Lonesome Dove' and 'Hugh Hudson' fills Texas coffers." Texas Press Clipping Bureau, Dallas, March 27, 1988.

Sun Tzu. *The Art of War*, trans. by Samuel B. Griffith. London: Oxford University Press, 1963.

Swertlow, Frank. "Actors' actual suffering makes 'Platoon' realistic." LA Life, Hollywood Freeway, *Daily News*, December 23, 1986.

———. "A 'Wild' Time is Had by Stone." L.A. Beat, *L.A. Life*, July 29, 1992.

———, "It was about time for Oliver Stone's 'Platoon.'" Hollywood Freeway, *Daily News*, December 29, 1986.

———. "Vietnam is refought on big and small screen." Hollywood Freeway, LA Life, *Daily News*, January 15, 1987.

Talbot, Stephen. "60s something." *Mother Jones*, March/April, 1991.

Taylor, John. "Lip Stix Stox Fax In Biz Pix." *Chronicle*, December 1987.

Terry, Wallace. "In His Own Words." *People Magazine*, April 1987.

Toumarkine, Doris. "Van Zant set for Milk Biopic." *The Hollywood Reporter*, July 15, 1992.

———. "Cowgirls' Rights Are Hitched to New Line Units." *The Hollywood Reporter*, August 1992.

"Theories in no shortage." *Knight-Ridder*, December 20, 1991.

"The Tet Offensive: How They Did It." *Newsweek*, March 11, 1968.

Thomas, Karen. "JFK theories etched in Stone." *USA Today*, January 16, 1992.

Trager, James. *The People's Chronology*, Rev. Ed., New York: Henry Holt & Co., 1992.

Travers, Peter. "Rider on a Sixties Storm." *Rolling Stone*, March 21, 1991.

"Tremors in the MIA Story." *The Los Angeles Times*, June 19, 1992.

"Truth Unearthed, The." *Time*, November 2, 1992.

"Unorthodox Behaviour." Books and Arts, *The Economist*, March 18, 1991.

"Untold Story of the Warren Commission." *U.S. News & World Report*, August 1992.

"The 'US' Directors Series.'" Oliver Stone, March 21, 1991.

Ventura, Michael. "The Strange Days of: Notes on a Ceremony Half Begun." *L.A. Weekly*, March 1, 1991.

"*Wall Street.*" Film Reviews, *Variety*, December 4, 1987.

"*Wall Street* Review." *Newsweek*, December 1987.

"*Wall Street.*" *New York*, December 14, 1987.

"Wall Street corruption stars in films." *U.S.A. Today*, May 18, 1987.

"Wall Street is morally solid." *Detroit Free Press*, December 11, 1987.

Walters, Barry. "'Doors' Won't Light Your Fire." *San Francisco Examiner*, March 1, 1991.

"The War In Vietnam." *Newsweek*, February 26, 1968.

"Week in Review." *The Hollywood Reporter*, July 28, 1992.

Weinraub, Bernard. "Valenti Calls JFK Hoax and Smear." *The New York Times*, April 2, 1992.

———. "JFK: How Hollywood Tells The Truth." *Kansas City Star*, January 3, 1992.

Welles, Chris. "The Platoon of Pros Who Helped Out On Wall Street." *Business Week*, December 2, 1987.

"Why Did It Have To Take *JFK* to Wake Us?" Editorials/Letters, *The New York Times*, January 3, 1992.

Wicker, Tom. "Does *JFK* Conspire Against Reason?" *The New York Times*, December 15, 1991.

"Who Shot JFK?" Letters, *The New York Times*, January 12, 1992.

Wiley, Mason, and Damien Bona. *Inside Oscar*. New York: Ballantine Books, 1986, 1987.

Williams, Scott. "48 Hours looks at JFK killing, life of Oswald." *Wichita Eagle*, January 1992.

Winsett, Stella. "Denton to Star in New Film by Oliver Stone." *Denton Record-Chronicle*, November 1988.

———. "Director has big news for Big D." *Denton Record-Chronicle*, March 25, 1988.

"What We've Heard." *The Washingtonian*, July 1992.

Wuntch, Phillip. "The war on 'Wall Street': Oliver Stone gets brutally bullish on Wall Street scene." *Marin Independent Journal*, December 11, 1987.

Zahradnik, Rich. "N.Y. box office: 'Platoon' leads pack." *The Hollywood Reporter*, December 23, 1986.

Index